VINT

PRICE OF THE MODI YEARS

Aakar Patel is a syndicated columnist who has edited English and Gujarati newspapers. His translation of Saadat Hasan Manto's Urdu non-fiction, *Why I Write*, was published in 2014. His study of majoritarianism in India, *Our Hindu Rashtra: What It Is. How We Got Here*, was published in 2020. And his analysis of India's performance under Prime Minister Narendra Modi, *Price of the Modi Years*, was published in 2021. *After Messiah*, his first book of fiction, was published in 2023. He is chair of Amnesty International India.

Celebrating 35 Years of
Penguin Random House India

PRICE OF THE
MODI
YEARS

AAKAR PATEL

VINTAGE
An imprint of Penguin Random House

VINTAGE

USA | Canada | UK | Ireland | Australia
New Zealand | India | South Africa | China | Singapore

Vintage is part of the Penguin Random House group of companies
whose addresses can be found at global.penguinrandomhouse.com

Published by Penguin Random House India Pvt. Ltd
4th Floor, Capital Tower 1, MG Road,
Gurugram 122 002, Haryana, India

Penguin
Random House
India

First published by Westland Non-Fiction, an imprint of Westland Publications Private Limited,
in 2021
Published in Vintage by Penguin Random House India 2022
This edition published in 2023

ISBN 9780143463764

Typeset by SÜRYA, New Delhi
Printed at Replika Press Pvt. Ltd, India

www.penguin.co.in

MIX
Paper from
responsible sources
FSC® C016779

Dedicated to the victims and survivors of demonetization, the lockdown, the second wave, and the events in Manipur and Kashmir, who were brutalized by incompetence, apathy and solipsism

CONTENTS

PREFACE TO THE 2023 EDITION

This is the third edition of this book, first published in 2021. Each edition has required adding to the chapters that record the performance of the Modi government. This has not been difficult because the data is available to all who seek, but it has been painful to see it. The *Spectator* magazine in the UK used to publish a wonderful column by Jeffrey Bernard called Low Life. It chronicled Bernard's days spent drinking and betting recklessly (some might say joyously). A reviewer in the *Evening Standard* once referred to the column as a 'suicide note in instalments'. That has been the experience also of updating this book: observing a nation eat itself, joyously (though some might say recklessly).

We are now in the tenth year of the Modi era, and we have more than sufficient evidence at hand to judge him and his record. The writing of history usually requires chronological distance from events because at times consequences may not be clear. That is not so here. It was evident early on in Narendra Modi's prime ministership that the power he had acquired, his style of functioning—which has been examined in the first chapter at length—and his Manichaean view of society would leave an impact on India. It has, as it was expected to. And that was why this book was written and published two years ago.

Though there has been increasing clarity with each passing year and each edition, that first draft of history was not especially different from this third one. The writing has been on the wall for some time.

Bangalore   Aakar Patel

PREFACE

This book seeks to explain the data and facts on India's performance under Narendra Modi through character flaws in its transformational leader.

These defects are Modi's intellectual indifference, his inability to change perspective and his impatience with detail and nuance. This should have been obvious much earlier: his bigotry admitted no shades either. But as prime minister and a figure of mass adoration the flaws ran alongside his power to bring about rapid and momentous change.

The results became apparent quickly enough. His predecessor as prime minister, Manmohan Singh, had once said that Modi would be a disaster as prime minister. This book shows how. It concedes Modi's popularity; this is an accounting of the damage he has wrought.

Our memories are not long, news cycles are transient and incidents are forgotten or misclassified as being only episodic unless documented, unified and placed together as a record.

And therefore this book—a history of these present times.

I'd like to thank Elizabeth, Vineet and Gunjan at Penguin Random House and Tushita at home.

Thanks also to Ajaz, Anusua, Alex, Deepthi, Ghazala, Hartosh, Karthik, Kiran, Mahmood, Mihir, Naresh, Rahul, Reetika, Samar, Shailesh, Somesh, Suhasini, Sushant, Usman, Venu and Vivek.

Aakar Patel

INTRODUCTION

On 23 May 2019, Narendra Modi returned to power winning a magnificent victory in the world's most populous democracy. He did this by widening the base and bringing more voters into his Bharatiya Janata Party (BJP) than its leaders before him. The BJP's vote share under Modi in the 2019 election was 38 per cent nationally. This is twice what it was under L.K. Advani in the election of 2009, and considerably higher also than what the party had secured before that under Atal Bihari Vajpayee. The BJP (and its earlier form, the Jana Sangh) was not originally a particularly popular national party. Even at the regional level, it did not win a single state on its own from 1951 till 1990. It was Advani's mobilisation of Hindus around India against Muslims using the totem of the Babri Masjid that made the party nationally popular. The mass mobilisation around violence took the BJP's national vote share to double digits for the first time in 1989 (11.3 per cent), and it continued to climb before pausing at around 25 per cent in 1999.

Vajpayee had inherited a Jana Sangh that was a cadre-based party with a frame provided by the Rashtriya Swayamsevak Sangh (RSS), whose ranks staffed the organisation's bureaucracy and leadership. He then announced the transition of the Jana Sangh to a mass-based party with a renaming in 1980, but the BJP under him was not really mass-based or popular because Vajpayee didn't know what issue to mobilise the masses on. Discovering it was an efficient tool for mass mobilisation, Advani aggressively pushed the Babri campaign, bringing in crores of new voters enthusiastic about the BJP's anti-Muslim image.

Modi's contribution has been to align the party to its original RSS roots while retaining and increasing mass support and bringing crores more to the ideology of Hindutva. He has legitimised and normalised the RSS and made its values promoting an exclusionary nationalism acceptable to Indians. What was once communal is now legitimate and what was secular has been made inauthentic. It is a remarkable achievement and must be acknowledged.

Modi has done this through his person, not through the BJP, which has been almost incidental to Modi's popularity. The RSS is today a sub-set of the Modi BJP, rather than the other way around, as it was before. The head of the RSS, Mohan Bhagwat, is actually junior to Modi in that sense.

The two go back a long way and have likely known each other since 1967 when both of them were boys of seventeen. Modi was familiar with Bhagwat through Bhagwat's father Madhukarrao, who was Modi's mentor in the RSS, and Modi stayed with the Bhagwat family during his essential training when he was around twenty.

Madhukarrao was one of the many Marathi Brahmins dispatched by the RSS from Nagpur in 1941 to infect Gujarat with Hindutva. He was a competent organiser and set up shakhas or neighbourhood branches in 115 cities and towns, including Surat, Baroda and Ahmedabad.[1]

He learned, according to Modi's biographical sketch of him, 'to speak a beautiful and fluent Gujarati' and, in the Baroda shakha, which had a large number of Marathi speakers, 'forbade the speaking of Marathi'.

Under Modi, the RSS cadre owes its loyalty first to Modi and then to Bhagwat. There is no way that the RSS can order Modi around, and it would amuse its storm troopers to think that it was possible even if the RSS desired it, which it of course doesn't.

Modi has no internal challenge in the party, either, of course. Those who built it, like Advani, he has brushed aside and made irrelevant. There is no 'leader' in the BJP except at Modi's sanction, and no other power centre. It is not easy to think of the last time—perhaps it was never—that an Indian leader with a majority had such absolute authority and control over party, government and people. Modi is unfettered also by the political opposition, which he has in fact bent to his will.

On that triumphal night in May 2019, he said: 'Brothers and sisters, in our country no election has happened like this. You have seen that for thirty years especially—although the drama has been going on for years—it had become fashionable to wear a tag called "secularism". And there used to be chants for the secular to unite. You would have seen from 2014–19, that entire section has stopped talking.

'In this election, not even one political party has the guts to wear the mask of secularism to fool the country. They have been unmasked.'[2]

---

[1] 'Narendra Modi's mentor: Madhukarrao Bhagwat', (the author's translation of *Jyotipunj*, Narendra Modi's biographical essays on his RSS mentors), 9 January 2014, *firstpost.com*
[2] PM Modi's Victory Speech | Lok Sabha Election Results 2019, Rajya Sabha TV YouTube Channel

This is quite true. Modi has taken India to a place where political parties dare not speak of secularism and pluralism though it is the basic structure of our Constitution. The pushing of constitutional secularism has also disappeared from the mainstream media today, as had happened earlier in Gujarat after 2002. We can legitimately call it the 'Modi effect'.

Modi's victories and unchallenged position have given us an opportunity to observe a rare phenomenon in democratic politics: a leader of strong character traits that find expression in his manner of functioning and no restraint. Modi has been able to craft and mould the entire polity with his talents and present us with the finished product.

Seen over the years of his two terms, the man in full is revealed, and so is his effect on the nation. We have the data and the evidence to see what and where he has led India to, and plot his achievements against his character traits. We have results.

Modi's character traits are that he is decisive, full of certitude, transparent, unlearned, energetic and charismatic. Both his devoted following (they are called and often call themselves 'bhakt', meaning devotee) and his opponents will likely agree that he has these traits. Certainly, Modi himself would not only likely agree with this but pride himself on it, as we shall see presently.

There are some other qualities that were hidden because they did not have the opportunity to present themselves earlier but have revealed themselves since, and we shall look at them as well. In particular, a bravado that on occasion transforms into a reluctance to acknowledge facts. A backing away from a threat, and the refusal to acknowledge retreat, accompanied with a refusal to fight.

Other than his character, his actions can be said to be shaped by his ideology. So far as that goes, Modi is sought to be placed on the right by commentators, especially those writing in English and those abroad. But he is not a conservative at all, he is a radical. Not only has he no concerns about preservation of political tradition, he is openly contemptuous of it and eager to break continuity. He is, in the jargon of our time, a disruptor.[3] In a place of stasis or inertia, disruption may have its uses. India is chaotic. It does not require further disruption. It needs order and predictability in governance; however, this is not for Modi.

What does a disruptor with the character traits Modi has, deliver when in possession of absolute power? That is what this book seeks to examine.

[3] One of Modi's hagiographies, written by R. Balashankar, once editor of RSS weekly *Organiser* and national convenor of the 'BJP Intellectual Cell', is titled: *Narendra Modi: Creative Disruptor.*

Before we begin, it is necessary to clarify some of the terms used to describe Modi.

What, for instance, do 'decisive' and 'charismatic' mean?

Charisma is the ability to attract attention and admiration. Humility, modesty and self-effacement are attractive to only a few. It is bravado and bombast that attracts the many. Modi sees himself in a heroic way and tells us about it through claiming a chest size of '56 inches', through many references to himself in the third person and through presenting himself before the president of the US wearing a suit with his name woven in gold stripes. This is the charisma of Modi. It is transparent in the sense that he is not reticent about publicly communicating his self-image.

On the night of his second victory, in 2019, Modi said: 'This is the twenty-first century and this is new India. Our victory in today's election is followed by chants of "Modi! Modi! Modi!". This is not a victory for Modi. Today's victory is not a victory for Modi. This is a victory for the aspirations of every citizen of this country craving for honesty.'[4] This false modesty coupled with an inability to stop referring to himself is typical.[5]

The dictionary defines decisiveness as 'the ability to make decisions quickly and confidently'. This confidence is what certitude is: the conviction that the self is right. It springs from intuition rather than from knowledge and external input.

What is meant by calling him unlearned and why do I say he would agree with the definition? I do so because this is something Modi has himself revealed in an extraordinary interview he gave to the journalist and activist Madhu Kishwar just before the 2014 election. It was shot on video, is quite long, and is available on YouTube.[6] In it, Modi tells Kishwar about his style of functioning. He had at that point been chief minister of Gujarat for a dozen years and so this style was something he himself was comfortable with. In Modi's words:

'Three or four days after I had taken office as chief minister, the chief secretary (CS) came to me. He brought a heap of files this tall [gesturing

[4] PM Modi's Victory Speech | Lok Sabha Election Results 2019, Rajya Sabha TV YouTube Channel

[5] A British journalist who was paid to write a hagiography of Modi said it was strange to interview Modi and hear him speaking of himself in the third person even in personal conversation: 'He talks about "Modi this, Modi that, The Modi".' 'Lance Price had unique access to PM Modi, these are his insights', 21 March 2015, *The Quint*

[6] 'Narendra Modi biggest interview: Modi's historic revelations', 30 March 2014, NewsX, https://www.youtube.com/watch?v=VRODGLMtAgM

about three feet high]. They must have weighed 15 or 20 kilos. The peon left them on my table. The chief secretary sat and said to me: "This is the file for Narmada"—I can remember Narmada but there were three other files also. The CS said: "These are on Gujarat's vital and sensitive issues. Take the time out to read them. You may need to speak on, and take a position on, at any time and address all these issues."

'I kept looking up and down the height of the stack three or four times. I said to him: "You leave these here and we shall meet in a few days."

'I did not even open those files. They stayed where they were. A voice came to me that I could not work through academics study (sic). I can't do that. That voice came from within. I said to the three officers who were working with me that "The CS has given these to me. I will not be able to read so much. First, you people make me understand what masala (sic) the files contain. If I begin reading all this material, there's no end to it. It is not in my nature (prakruti) to read files."

'Three or four days after that the CS returned. I said to him: "Tell me what the important things are in these files." He did so and I said: "This much is sufficient for me, you can take the files back."

'After that I have never had to be briefed on these issues, and it's been thirteen years since.

'I had such ability that I was able to grasp the granularity of the issues. Such things left an impact on the officers. I don't argue. I am a good listener. Don't go by my reputation outside: I listen a lot. I can say today that if in my development, reading played a 30 per cent role then listening had a 70 per cent role. What I hear, I analyse, and classify the "maal"' (sic) in different boxes in my mind. This takes me no time and when needed I can retrieve it. This extra method I have been able to develop.

'Even today if my officers show me some paper, I say: "Tell me what's in it in two minutes." For me two minutes is sufficient for a ten-page document. This skill is something I have developed.'[7]

---

[7] The other aspect to this style of working was that Modi only knew what he was told. Gatekeepers determined what was to be fed to the prime minister. Even individuals on the Economic Advisory Council to the Prime Minister—an elite group of just six people (and actually only four advisors plus the chairman and secretary) dedicated to advising Modi—could not communicate with the prime minister directly. If they sent a paper containing material of the highest importance, such as the fact that the economy was in structural trouble and India was headed for disaster, it did not reach Modi because he did not himself read and a bureaucrat determined it was not necessary to summarise it for him. The prime minister was 'ring-fenced'. Modi sometimes discovered the views of these advisors only when he saw them on television to say what they had sent to him previously

This exchange Modi described was typical. Weeks after he gave this interview and took office as prime minister, Modi received input on the country in similar fashion.[8] A news report said that dozens of secretaries—the bureaucrats heading various departments—would be clubbed into nine groups and each group would get ten minutes to present the state of the nation to Modi. The order of the grouping was apparently random. Another report of the same meeting said that 'while the PM had earlier restructured the ministries, clubbing some together, the departments that had been called together for presentations did not follow the same pattern. For instance, one group had the secretaries of Textiles, Steel, Chemicals and Food Processing; another clubbed the Commerce, Information Technology, Tourism, Housing and Culture secretaries; and the Railways, Telecommunications, Road Transport and Highways, and Civil Aviation secretaries had been grouped together.'[9]

What a ten-minute briefing from any one of these groups would have been like can only be imagined.

This 'skill' that Modi possessed is what he has brought to the office of prime minister. It was decisiveness without the need to understand in depth the issues that were to be decided. It was said of French president Valéry Giscard d'Estaing that he was fascinated by the idea of a European Union but bored by its details. Modi is similar.

Former Cabinet ministers I spoke to and asked about what this style of functioning meant said that it was an impatience with the facts. One said that 'You lose the nuances and the shades of grey. This reduction is I think what CEOs typically demand.'

Government, of course, is different because it does not function on the profit motive, because its constituency is so diverse and on a scale so vast that it cannot directly be compared to the CEO's focus on quarterly profits and instinct for sharper trade-offs.

Decisiveness is the ability to arrive at conclusions quickly and order decisions firmly. This is often seen as a virtue. Being indecisive is seen as

---

in writing. One former advisor said: 'Nobody in the government at the political level had read a word of what I had given them. Otherwise they wouldn't have got mad (on seeing him express the same views on television).' 'We are no longer a functioning, growing and aspirational India.'—Dr Rathin Roy, https://www.youtube.com/watch?v=oE48XvvJlrM (21'30" and 43'51")

[8] 'Top bureaucrats to meet PM Narendra Modi today, they will get 10 minutes to give 10-slide presentations', 3 June 2014, *The Times of India*

[9] 'As part of his larger political vision, PM Modi calls all Secys for meeting today', 3 June 2014, *The Indian Express*

a weakness though, often, indecision is only another name for thinking something through carefully. And, if on occasion there is uncertainty or potential turbulence beyond tolerable limits, one does not conclude or decide on a course of action.

The quality of being decisive can also be seen as being sure one is right through conviction rather than through knowledge and after accommodating differing views and doubts. India has a history of such people in authority. Sanjay Gandhi was also 'decisive'. He was a barely literate man (Class X dropout) given great power. He wielded it casually and Indians suffered because of this confidence that he knew what was right.

Modi says his development of this style is his own. He is at the height of his powers, with a full majority, unencumbered and unrestrained, within his party and without. Since 2014 we have witnessed the full effects of his unique style.

'India can no longer wait for problems to remain unsolved,' Modi told the Lok Sabha on 6 February 2020, 'and rightfully so. That is why our aim is: speed and scale. Determination and decisiveness. Sensitivity and solutions.'[10] This quality in him was recognised early. At the moment of his first victory, the *Bloomberg* editorial board, which apparently has the ability to divine our minds, wrote that 'Modi's victory testifies to Indians' hunger for decisiveness'.[11]

Those who have worked with him agree and have said this over the years: 'Modi govt very decisive, will change system: Sukhbir Badal' was a headline just after Modi won his first national election.[12] 'Rafale acquisition possible due to Modi's decisiveness: Rajnath Singh' was another just after he won his second.[13] Modi 'is known not just for his decisiveness but also a strong political will emerging from his courage of conviction', wrote BJP Rajya Sabha member Vinay Sahasrabuddhe in 2020.[14] 'PM Modi to global business leaders: decisiveness makes India unique' was the headline to a report from New York in which Modi said India's advantage over the world was its demography, democracy, demand and his decisiveness.[15] Yet another

---

[10] 'India can no longer wait for problems to be solved, says PM Modi', 6 February 2020, PTI

[11] 'What India should expect from Modi's big win', 16 May 2014, *Bloomberg.com*

[12] 21 September 2014, *Free Press Journal*

[13] 8 October 2019, *Outlook*

[14] 'PM Narendra Modi has changed the discourse and connected with the people', 18 September 2020, *The Indian Express*

[15] 25 September 2019, *Republic*

from 2020 was: 'PM Modi decisive, strong-willed, says Scindia, refrains from commenting on Manmohan Singh.'[16]

Some on the other side have observed that Modi is in thrall of his self-created image of decisiveness. 'It was a useful electoral gimmick against an often divided and perennially indecisive UPA,' wrote Harish Khare, an editor who served as Manmohan Singh's media advisor, 'but it is not able to recognise that after seven years in the saddle this infatuation with decisiveness has become a definite enemy of good governance, even plain common political sense.'[17] The 'decisiveness' has caused damage, as this work will demonstrate.

Modi has an intense desire to do something, the sociologist Ashis Nandy said after demonetisation was announced, 'but he does not have the imagination or wherewithal to do it. No doubt he is energetic, hardworking and driven to do something positive, as everyone wants to leave a mark on history.'[18]

This yearning of Modi's to do something but not knowing what and not having an interest in depth or detail has resulted in his style of running India. A glimpse of it can be seen in a speech he gave to the Indian Merchants Chamber and the All India Business Council in 2013:

'If we think small we will get nowhere. We have to think big, on a massive canvas.

'What do Indian governments do? They say we will move ahead 0.1 per cent or 0.2 per cent or 0.001 per cent. This will not do. I once told Manmohan Singh: "Look, nobody is talking of all of China. They only show the world Shanghai, not the rest. I said we should also show our strength. Like the 26 January parade, where we display our missiles to impress the rest of the world. Just like that, the business world also needs a show of strength. You (Singh) should do one small thing: begin a Bullet train from Ahmedabad to Mumbai. It will introduce India to the world. Nobody will come to sit on it, but that was fine because it was symbolic."'[19]

Such genius operates from instinct and a folksy wisdom. The style manifests as a fascination with the branding and the nomenclature—what a thing is called and what it signals—but a lack of real interest in the actual

---

[16] 28 October 2020, ANI

[17] 'Is Narendra Modi's demagoguery finally losing its bite?', 31 December 2020, TheWire.in

[18] '"Modi has intense desire to do something, but lacks imagination," says Ashis Nandy', 10 December 2016, TheWire.in

[19] 'Narendra Modi 2013 speech on bullet train', www.youtube.com/watch?v=T3 p6rxesx-w

process or product, whether it is writing a law, executing a policy or thinking of and building an institution. There is an absence of any proper knowledge and no ability to learn how it works. But there is a strong desire to engage with its brand and in particular its coinage. The Modi years are littered with the corpses of projects thus taken up and discarded once a new toy had been identified.

'Make in India', 'Demonetisation', 'Surgical Strike', 'Amritkaal', 'Smart Cities', 'Namami Gange', 'Lockdown', 'Vocal for Local'… It is governance by catchphrase. A clever name, often a dazzling event with little follow-up and not much thinking.

Years before Modi became chief minister, Nandy, along with the writer Achyut Yagnik, met and interviewed him. Nandy wrote: 'It was a long, rambling interview, but it left me in no doubt that here was a classic, clinical case of a fascist. I never use the term "fascist" as a term of abuse; to me it is a diagnostic category comprising not only one's ideological posture but also the personality traits and motivational patterns contextualising the ideology.

'Modi, it gives me no pleasure to tell the readers, met virtually all the criteria that psychiatrists, psycho-analysts and psychologists had set up after years of empirical work on the authoritarian personality. He had the same mix of puritanical rigidity, narrowing of emotional life, massive use of the ego defence of projection, denial and fear of his own passions combined with fantasies of violence—all set within the matrix of clear paranoid and obsessive personality traits. I still remember the cool, measured tone in which he elaborated a theory of cosmic conspiracy against India that painted every Muslim as a suspected traitor and a potential terrorist. I came out of the interview shaken and told Yagnik that, for the first time, I had met a textbook case of a fascist.'[20]

Unlike Nandy, the rest of us use that word too loosely and too often and it has lost meaning. And name-calling leads us nowhere. We can safely refer to Modi's style as being authoritarian and his rule as that of developmental authoritarianism. Equal emphasis with authoritarianism here is on the word development, which is to be achieved overcoming all obstacles. And if achieving it requires the leader to be forceful, then he will be.

Modi claims his special ability is 'good governance' in a part of the world which is anarchic and difficult to discipline.[21] He can bring the State to heel and get it to function.

[20] 'Obituary of a culture', May 2002, Issue 513, *Seminar*
[21] 'PM's message to the nation on good governance', 25 December 2014, pmindia.gov.in

Such governance as Modi speaks of can be described by another word, used by military historians. That word is 'grip'. It refers to the ability of a general to be in total charge of his command. Being aware of the situation, being knowledgeable about what resources are at hand and what may be required in the future and being conscious of what events to anticipate. Knowing what his side is capable of and being prepared. Julius Caesar had grip and he had control over his armies in a time when communications were poor and supply lines very long. He could predict the consequences of his actions because he could not only think them through, but anticipate what they would cause.

We have the opportunity to see in detail what the results and consequences of good governance under Modi have been.

Manmohan Singh said just before demitting office that Modi would not make a good prime minister. His exact words were: 'I do believe, that having Mr. Modi, whatever his merit, as the Prime Minister, will be a disaster for India.'[22]

Singh would have had opportunity to meet Modi many times in the decade he was prime minister and Modi, the lord of Gujarat. Enough one-on-one meetings, enough observations of Modi in a group of his peers, to have judged and understood the man and his quality. Singh is famously reticent and understated and so such a firm and direct opinion on Modi and the future was unusual and surprising. A disaster for India in what way? This Singh did not say. Perhaps he thought he didn't need to because it would become apparent. If so, he was right.

This book tells the story of how what Singh predicted came to be. It shows across the spectrum of governance. It showed in obvious and unambiguous fashion, on the issues that Modi was convinced he would transform through his energy, freshness, genius and strength of will. On the economy, national security, on institutions and ultimately on India's standing in the world on several parameters.

In the first chapter, we will begin by looking at this data.

---

[22] '"It will be a disaster if Modi becomes PM of India," says Manmohan Singh', 3 January 2014, ANI

1

BRAND VERSUS PRODUCT

The Modi brand was built on the promise of delivery. The 2014 campaign was promoted under the theme '*Achche din aane wale hain*' (good days are on the way). It assumed that Modi would bring change. It was not an empty promise: it came from his certitude and his reductive understanding of the problems that India and its government grapple with.

The Modi view of the world is also the view of the middle classes, generally speaking. It can be understood thus: the system is bad, but it cannot be fixed because politicians are corrupt. India's poverty and inefficiency was the product, therefore, of bad politicians.

The view also is that India's potential has been kept suppressed and the people, especially the middle class, have suffered for this. The nation had not become developed though it was full of people who were talented. The politicians had let the rest of us down.

The system had failed because of the party which had created it and run it. The Congress stood for corruption and socialism and dynasty (this last bit is less damaging than is assumed, in a society where such things as a 'good family', meaning virtue spread through genes, are believed to be true). The Gandhis were nepotistic, and people like Rahul Gandhi are not equipped or qualified in any way to lead India to its deserved greatness.

A good man, an honest man, a strong man who means well is the thing needed to fix this system because the system is the problem and needs to be fixed. Once that is done, this great society will be able to take its destined place in the world.

The person who would take it there is Modi because he had seen through the problem and created a template for this transformation. India was suffering, but Gujarat was very different because of its years under Modi. It had the silver bullet which would solve the things plaguing India, and this cure was the 'Gujarat Model'. Enough has been written about this since Modi was elected for it not to be repeated here in detail.

But briefly, two claims were made most strongly. Firstly, that Modi had the vision to deliver transformative economic growth. Secondly, that he was tough on terrorism as no other leader could be. The first has been examined in great detail by scholars since the idea of the 'Gujarat Model' was proposed.

Let us look at their findings.

In annual growth rate, Gujarat was slower than Maharashtra, Tamil Nadu and Bihar in the Modi years.[1] Gujarat had in fact grown faster between 1992 and 1997 than under Modi.

The state had been in third position nationally before Modi and remained third during his years in office. There was no change in that sense. We can accept that Modi continued the work of his predecessors, and accept that he even improved upon it. But it is not only a stretch but a fabrication to claim that he was the author of a new form and some new model that produced a revolutionary shift.

All the evidence shows this to be the case. For instance, except for fewer than 200 villages in the state, all had been electrified before Modi.

Writing in the *Economic and Political Weekly*, economists Maitreesh Ghatak and Sanchari Roy also made the case that there was no special sauce Modi possessed. To the question: was there a difference between Gujarat's growth rate and that of the whole country during Modi's years as opposed to before him, the answer was, 'No'. Gujarat had been 1.1 per cent ahead of the national average in the 1990s and 1.3 per cent in the 2000s. If there was such a thing as a Gujarat Model under Modi, it could at best make the claim to have improved Gross Domestic Product (GDP) growth by 0.2 per cent.[2]

Meanwhile, unemployment rates were lower in Chhattisgarh and Karnataka than in Gujarat, and foreign direct investment (FDI) was higher in Maharashtra, Tamil Nadu, Karnataka and Delhi.[3]

Human Development Indicators (HDI) fell under Modi, and Gujarat dropped five places from sixth to eleventh among states on this measure which looks at life expectancy, income and education. Gujarat stood 21st in child malnutrition. Asked by the *Wall Street Journal* why half of Gujarat's children under five suffered from stunting (low height for their age), Modi

[1] 'Did Narendra Modi make Gujarat vibrant?', 16 May 2019, *Business Standard*

[2] 'Did Gujarat's growth rate accelerate under Modi?', 12 April 2014, *Economic and Political Weekly*

[3] 'Narendra Modi's track record in Gujarat is not the runaway success he claims', 7 April 2014, *Quartz*

replied that the problem of malnutrition was due to Gujarati girls being 'more beauty conscious than health conscious' and refusing to drink their milk.[4]

Economist Indira Hirway examined Gujarat's economy in terms of policy. It appeared to consist primarily of subsidies, mainly through sales tax waivers to corporates to encourage industrialisation.[5] But even so, the state had 93 per cent of its workforce in the informal sector. After incentives to corporate units, the Gujarat government was left with limited funds for education, health, environment and employment for its citizens, and this showed in the fall in its HDI rankings. The number of girls attending secondary school in rural Gujarat was only 29 per cent versus 93 per cent in Kerala. The number of boys was 45 per cent versus 90 per cent. This was the worst record of all states surveyed.[6] The Gujarat Model was a term coined and promoted by Modi (or on his behalf) without expanding on what it meant and without an explanation of how it was distinct or new in what the state was doing or had achieved. It existed because it did.

No Karnataka leader is given the credit for the rise and presence of Infosys, Wipro, TCS or Cognizant and the sudden emergence of Bengaluru as an outsourcing and information technology powerhouse, producing lakhs of white-collar jobs. Similarly, despite Mumbai's domination of the entertainment and media industry and of the finance sector, there is no talk of a 'Maharashtra Model'. There is no 'Tamil Nadu Model' and there is no political credit associated with the recent rise of Gurugram or Hyderabad. All these were organic; only Gujarat apparently had a model. This was, of course, more a claim than it was fact.

The claim would come undone when the model moved to Delhi.

In 2020, the Modi government decided to improve India's standing on various indices that showed a deterioration in governance. These indices that were upsetting Delhi spanned from those produced by non-profits working in specialised areas, multilateral bodies like the United Nations, institutions traditionally seen as being on the right, like the World Economic Forum and *The Economist*, and also the government's own data.

The government was clearly concerned about its drop. We know this because first the NITI Aayog ordered a 'single, informative dashboard' be prepared 'for all the twenty-nine (later 32) global indices'. This doodad

---

[4] 'In slowing India, a fast-growing star', 29 August 2012, *Wall Street Journal*

[5] 'The truth behind the Gujarat Model', 8 December 2017, *TheWire.in*

[6] 'Data | Only 29% rural girls attended higher secondary school in Gujarat in 2019-20', 17 June 2021, *The Hindu*

would 'allow for monitoring of the parameters as per official data as well as the data source used by the publishing agencies'.

This monitoring exercise was 'not just to improve rankings but to improve systems and drive reforms to attract investments and to shape India's perception globally'.[7]

Presumably after it had done this exercise, the government appeared to believe that the issue was one related to image rather than reality.[8] The following month, a report said the government was 'working to improve India's ranking on twenty-nine global indices, and it wants the message to reach everyone loud and clear'. The way it would do this was 'a massive publicity campaign' that would 'shape India's perception' through advertising and 'micro-sites of ministries' and it would also 'publicise the problems, parameters and data sources of global indices'.

How this would address the problem at hand was not apparent. The issue was not one of perception or bias, but of fact. The world was not conspiring to show India in a bad light. The solution lay in acknowledging that India had been declining in several areas since 2014 and working on trying to improve things. Spending money on a media campaign would not change the numbers. India discrediting the data of all these agencies and institutions was unlikely to reverse the views of those who had looked at and understood the facts.

To see what the problem was, let us examine what global indices were revealing, comparing both the Modi years with the period before him and some which shifted during the Modi terms itself.

Index: The Economist Intelligence Unit's Democracy Index[9]

Monitors: Civil liberties, pluralism, political culture and participation, electoral process

Method: Global ranking

India 2014 ranking: 27

India 2022 ranking: 46

Result: India fell 19 places.

Reasons cited: Classifying India as a 'flawed democracy' in 2020, the report says 'democratic norms have been under pressure since 2015'. This was the 'result of democratic backsliding under the leadership of Narendra Modi' and the 'increasing influence of religion under Modi, whose policies

---

[7] 'NITI Aayog organises a virtual workshop to monitor performance of 29 select global indices', 10 July 2020, Press Information Bureau

[8] 'Modi govt plans media blitz for 'image correction' to boost India rank on global lists', 20 August 2020, *ThePrint.in*

[9] 'Frontline democracy and the battle for Ukraine', The Economist Intelligence Unit 2022, eiu.com

have fomented anti-Muslim feeling and religious strife, has damaged the political fabric of the country'. Modi had 'introduced a religious element to the conceptualisation of Indian citizenship, a step that many critics see as undermining the secular basis of the Indian state'. In 2019, India was ranked 51st in the Democracy Index, when the report said, 'The primary cause of the democratic regression was an erosion of civil liberties in the country.'

Index: United Nations Development Programme Human Development Index[10]

Monitors: Life expectancy at birth, education, national income

Method: Global ranking

India 2014 rank: 130

India 2022 rank: 132

Result: India fell by two positions.

Reasons cited: Fall in average income, disinvestment in girls' health and education.

Index: CIVICUS Monitor's National Civic Space Ratings[11]

Monitors: Freedoms of association, peaceful assembly, expression

Method: Rating—Open, Narrowed, Obstructed, Repressed, Closed

India 2017 rating: 'Obstructed'

India 2023 rating: 'Repressed'

Result: India fell one grade.

Reasons cited: 'The deterioration of India's civic space is alarming—particularly its assault on freedom of expression using an array of restrictive laws—and its attempts to impede human rights groups.' In March 2022, Civicus said: "India has been added to a watchlist of countries that have seen a rapid decline in civic freedoms" and that Modi "continues to resort to drastic measures to silence critics."

Index: Pew Religious Restrictions[12]

Monitors: Levels of social hostility and religious restrictions

Method: Rating

India 2014 rating

    Social hostility: 9.0

    Religious restrictions: 5.0

---

[10] '2022 Human Development Report HDI ranking', hdr.undp.org

[11] Tracking civic space, monitor.civicus.org

[12] 'How COVID-19 Restrictions Affected Religious Groups Around the World in 2020', Pew Research Center, pewforum.org

India 2022 rating
  Social hostility: 9.4
  Religious restrictions: 5.8
  Result: India fell by 0.4 in social hostility and by 0.8 points in religious restrictions.
  Reasons cited: In 2019, India was in the top 10 in each of the following categories:

- Countries with high levels of social hostilities related to religious norms
- Countries with high levels of inter-religious tension and violence
- Countries with high levels of religious violence by organised groups
- Countries with high levels of individual and social group harassment

'Among twenty-five most populous countries, Egypt, India, Russia, Pakistan and Indonesia had the highest overall levels of both government restrictions and social hostilities involving religion.'

Index: Lowy Institute Asia Power Index[13]

Monitors: National power and influence based on economy, diplomacy, military capacity, resilience, trade, future trends, cultural influence
  Method: Ranking and score
India 2018 score: 41.5
India 2023 score: 36.3
  Result: India lost its 'Major Power' status by falling below the 40-point threshold in 2020 and then falling further in 2021 and 2022.
  Reasons cited: China's growing influence in South Asia, economy hit by Covid, India's withdrawal from the Regional Comprehensive Economic Partnership. The 2022 report said, 'India dropped one place for both economic relationships and defence networks to ninth and eighth, respectively' and that India's 'overall score has declined every year since 2018'.

Index: Brand Finance Global Soft Power Index[14]

Monitors: Perception of nation brands through surveying 75,000 individuals in 102 nations and 778 experts
  Method: Global ranking
India 2020 ranking: 27
India 2023 ranking: 28
  Result: India fell one place.
  Reasons cited: India lacked 'consistency and stability in policy making and governance' and it needed more 'tolerance to help create a sense of trust' (2021).

---

[13] Asia Power Index 2023 Edition, Lowy Institute, power.lowyinstitute.org
[14] Global Soft Power Index 2023, brandirectory.com

India was high on brand familiarity, low on reputation (which declined to 65th from 47th) and on influence (2023).

Index: IMD World Competitiveness Ranking[15]

Monitors: Competitiveness of nations in economic performance and government efficiency

Method: Global ranking

India 2014 ranking: 44

India 2023 ranking: 37

Result: India rose seven places. India was once ranked as high as 27 in 2007 but has never gone back there, going to 45 in 2017 and then remaining at 43 since 2019.

Reasons cited: 'India improved its score in 2022 compared with previous years on economic performance, government efficiency, business efficiency and infrastructure.'

Index: Freedom House's Freedom in the World[16]

Monitors: Rule of law, political pluralism and elections, functioning of government, civil liberties, freedom of expression, association and organisation, individual rights

Method: Ratings/100

India 2014 rating: 77 (free)

India 2023 rating: 66 (partly free)

Jammu and Kashmir 2014 rating: 49 (partly free)

Jammu and Kashmir 2023 rating: 27 (not free)

Result: India fell by 11 points and its status changed from 'free' to 'partly free'. Jammu and Kashmir fell 22 points to become 'not free'. India scored poorly on political and civil rights and on internet freedom.

Reasons cited: 'Political rights and civil liberties deteriorated after 2014; increased pressure on human rights organisations; pattern of pro-government decisions by the Supreme Court; rising intimidation of academics and journalists; spate of bigoted attacks, including lynchings, aimed at Muslims; decline accelerated after Modi's reelection in 2019; a ham-fisted lockdown that resulted in the dangerous and unplanned displacement of millions of internal migrant workers; encouraged scapegoating of Muslims, who were disproportionately blamed for spread of virus and faced attacks by vigilante mobs. Rather than serving as a champion of democratic practice

---

[15] IMD World Competitiveness Ranking 2022, imd.org

[16] 'Freedom in the World 2023: Marking 50 Years in the Struggle for Democracy', freedomhouse.org

and a counterweight to authoritarian influence from countries such as China, Modi and his party are tragically driving India itself toward authoritarianism; the fall of India from the upper ranks of free nations could have a particularly damaging impact on global democratic standards.' The 2023 report referred to the extra-judicial demolition of Muslim homes in Gujarat, Madhya Pradesh and Uttar Pradesh.

Index: World Justice Project's Rule of Law Index[17]

Monitors: Criminal and civil justice system, fundamental rights, constraints on government powers, absence of corruption, transparent government, order and security, regulatory enforcement

Method: Global ranking through 130,000 household surveys and 4,000 expert surveys

India 2014 ranking: 66

India 2022 ranking: 77

Result: India fell 11 places.

Reasons cited: India fared poorly on absence of corruption (93rd), order and security (105th), fundamental rights (94th) and the criminal justice system (89th)

Index: UN Sustainable Development Solutions Network World Happiness Report[18]

Monitors: GDP per capita, social support, healthy life expectancy, freedom to make life choices, generosity, perceptions of corruption and dystopia

Method: Global ranking

India 2014 ranking: 111

India 2023 ranking: 126

Result: India fell by 15 places.

Reasons cited: 'Large and steady decline in life evaluation', low optimistic outlook of inhabitants (2020), 'longer-term slide in Indian life evaluations' (2021).

Index: Legatum Institute Prosperity Index[19]

Monitors: Access to education, healthcare, protection from violence, transparency

Method: Global ranking

---

[17] WJP Rule of Law Index 2022, worldjusticeproject.org

[18] Happiness Report 2023, worldhappiness.report

[19] Legatum Prosperity Index 2023, prosperity.com

India 2014 ranking: 102
India 2023 ranking: 103

Result: India fell by one place.

Reasons cited: India rated poorly on safety and security, personal freedom, living conditions, health, education and the natural environment.

Index: Reporters Without Borders' World Press Freedom Index[20]

Monitors: Media independence, pluralism, self-censorship, abuses, transparency

Method: Global ranking

India 2014 global ranking: 140
India 2023 global ranking: 161

Result: India fell 21 places.

Reasons cited: 'The violence against journalists, the politically partisan media and the concentration of media ownership all demonstrate that press freedom is in crisis in "the world's largest democracy"' (2023). 'Pro-government media pump out a form of propaganda, journalists who dare to criticise the government are branded as "anti-state," "anti-national" or even "pro-terrorist" by supporters of the ruling Bharatiya Janata Party (BJP). This exposes them to public condemnation in the form of extremely violent social media hate campaigns that include calls for them to be killed, especially if they are women. When out reporting in the field, they are physically attacked by BJP activists, often with the complicity of the police. And finally, they are also subjected to criminal prosecutions.'

Index: Georgetown Institute Women, Peace and Security Index[21]

Monitors: Justice and security for women, inclusion

Method: Global ranking

India 2017 ranking: 131
India 2022 ranking: 148

Result: India fell by 17 places.

Reasons cited: India fares poorly on education, financial exclusion, employment, political representation and son bias.

Index: Fraser Institute Global Economic Freedom Index[22]

Monitors: Size of government, legal structure, freedom to trade internationally, regulation of credit, labour, business

Method: Global ranking

---

[20] 2022 World Press Freedom Index, rsf.org

[21] Women, Peace and Security Index 2021–22, giwps.georgetown.org

[22] 'Economic Freedom of the World: 2022', fraserinstitute.org

India 2014 ranking: 112
India 2022 ranking: 89

Result: India rose by 23 places.

Reasons cited: India was ranked 32nd in size of government, 66th in legal system and property rights and 121st on regulation. The data had a two year lag and the 2022 report reflected 2020 data and the 2016 report reflected 2014 data.

Index: Cato Human Freedom Index[23]

Monitors: Rule of law, religious freedom, civil liberties, freedom of speech, association and assembly, legal system and property rights, freedom to trade internationally, regulation of credit, labour and business

India 2016 ranking: 87
India 2022 ranking: 112

Result: India fell by 25 places.

Reasons cited: India's scores were lower on personal freedom and economic freedom. The data came with a lag of two years: the 2022 report reflected 2020 data and 2016 report reflected the 2014 data.

Index: World Economic Forum Global Gender Gap Index[24]

Monitors: National progress on gender parity

Method: Global ranking benchmarking economic, political, health, survival, educational gaps

India 2014 ranking: 114
India 2022 ranking: 127

Result: India fell by 13 places.

Reasons cited: India performed poorly on economic participation and opportunity (143rd in world); health and survival (146th); female mortality rates; on gender gap 'Afghanistan, Pakistan and India are among the worst-performing countries globally'.

Index: World Bank Women, Business and the Law Index[25]

Monitors: Laws and regulations that limit women's economic opportunities on indicators like mobility, workplace, pay, marriage, parenthood, entrepreneurship, assets and pension

Method: Global ranking

India 2014 ranking: 111
India 2023 ranking: 126

Result: India fell by 15 places.

---

[23] Human Freedom Index 2022, cato.org
[24] Global Gender Gap Report 2022, weforum.org
[25] Women, Business and the Law 2023, openknowledge.worldbank.org

Reasons cited: India rated poorly on equal pay, parenthood and entrepreneurship.

Index: Foundation for the Advancement of Liberty World Index of Moral Freedom[26]

Monitors: Religious, family and gender, sexual, drugs, bioethical freedoms

Method: Global ranking

India 2016 ranking: 41

India 2020 ranking: 70

Result: India fell 29 places.

Reasons cited: India scored poorly on gender and religious indicators. 2016 was the first year India was ranked.

Index: US Chamber of Commerce Global Innovation Policy Center International Intellectual Property Index[27]

Monitors: IP protection

Method: Global ranking

India 2014 ranking: 25

India 2023 ranking: 42

Result: India fell by 15 places, being last placed of 25 nations in 2014 and 42nd of 55 nations in 2023.

Reasons cited: While India had made improvements, 'rights-holders in India continue to face substantive challenges, particularly regarding the patenting environment, in which India's policy framework continues to deny patent eligibility to a broad range of innovations (2020)'; 'barriers and requirements have intensified in the past few years as part of the "Make in India" campaign'.

Index: Transparency International Global Corruption Perceptions Index[28]

Monitors: Corruption in public sector of nations

Method: Global ranking

India 2014 ranking: 85

India 2022 ranking: 85

Result: India remained in the same position.

Reasons cited: India's score on the perceived level of public sector corruption was unchanged in the last three years.

---

[26] World Index of Moral Freedom 2020, fundalib.org

[27] International IP Index, 2023 Eleventh Edition, uschamber.com

[28] Corruption Perceptions Index 2022, transparency.org

Index: Heritage Foundation Global Economic Freedom Index[29]

Monitors: Rule of law, government size, regulatory efficiency, open markets

Method: Global ranking

India 2014 ranking: 120

India 2023 ranking: 131

Result: India fell 11 places, behind Bangladesh, and was rated 'mostly unfree'.

Reasons cited: India had 'large scale political corruption'; 'little evidence that anti-corruption laws are effective' (2021). 'The foundations for long-term economic development remain fragile without an efficiently functioning legal framework', 'The overall rule of law is weak in India'. In contrast to Singapore, 'the process for obtaining a business license can take much longer and involve endless trips to government offices and repeated encounters with officious and sometimes corrupt bureaucrats' (2023).

Index: Bertelsmann Stiftung BTI Transformation Index[30]

Monitors: Transformation processes towards democracy and market economy

Method: Global ranking

India 2014 ranking: 26

India 2023 ranking: 57

Result: India fell by 31 places and was seen as a 'defective democracy' with 'limited economic transformation'.

Reasons cited: 'Reforms such as hastily conceptualised and inefficiently implemented Demonetization of 2016 have been entirely unsuccessful and even harmed economic growth. New schemes and programs often amounting to little more than renaming existing ones ... the most problematic development is the growing influence of hardline Hindu-nationalist groups (which) aim to undermine the secular credentials of the Indian state... The government will have to withstand such pressures from hardliners if it wants to keep intact the fragile equilibrium that characterises Indian society.'

Index: World Intellectual Property Organisation Global Innovation Index[31]

Monitors: Innovation in nations through quality of universities, availability of microfinance and venture capital infrastructure, business sophistication

Method: Global ranking

---

[29] 2023 Index of Economic Freedom, heritage.org

[30] BTI Transformation Index, bti-project.org

[31] 'Global Innovation Index 2022: What Is the Future of Innovation-Driven Growth?', wipo.int

India 2014 ranking: 76
India 2022 ranking: 40
 Result: India rose by 36 places.
 Reasons cited: Number of start-ups, 'Bengaluru occupies 11th position in most entrepreneurial cities in the world'.

Index: World Economic Forum Global Economic Competitiveness[32]
 Monitors: Progress against a full set of factors that determine productivity, organised into 12 pillars: institutions; infrastructure; IT adoption; macroeconomic stability; health; skills; product market; labour market; financial system; market size; business dynamism; and innovation capability
 Method: Global ranking
India 2017 ranking: 40
India 2020 ranking: 68
 Result: India fell by 28 places.
 Reasons cited: 'Faster improvements of several countries previously ranked lower', India's economy experiencing 'slowdown or stagnation'. In 2020 the ranking was paused amid the pandemic but India was the worst performer on 'percentage change in the skill sets of graduates' and Indian business leaders had the least confidence that the future would be more globalised. The 2017 ranking was the first with a new methodology. The report appears to have been discontinued after 2020.

Index: IMD Smart City Index[33]
 Monitors: Health and safety, mobility, activities, opportunities, governance
 Method: Global ranking
India 2019 rankings
 Bengaluru: 79
 Delhi: 68
 Hyderabad: 67
 Mumbai: 78
India 2023 rankings
 Bengaluru: 110
 Delhi: 105
 Hyderabad: 116
 Mumbai: 109

---

[32] Global Competitiveness Report 2019, weforum.org
[33] Smart City Index 2020, imd.org

Result: Bengaluru fell by 31 places, Delhi fell by 37 places, Hyderabad fell by 49 places and Mumbai fell by 31 places.

Index: Economist Intelligence Unit Global Liveability Index[34]

Monitors: Living conditions through stability, healthcare, education, infrastructure, culture, environment in cities

Method: Global ranking

India 2015 rankings

Delhi: 110

Mumbai: 115

India 2022 rankings

Delhi: 112

Mumbai: 117

Result: Delhi fell by two places and Mumbai also fell by two places.

Index: EIU Inclusive Internet Index[35]

Monitors: Internet availability, affordability, relevance and the readiness of people to use it

Method: Global ranking

India 2015 ranking: 36

India 2022 ranking: 50

Result: India fell by 14 places.

Reasons cited: 'Deficiencies are rife, such as availability (63rd globally) in ensuring female access to the Internet. Only a few countries in the world fare worse than India.'

Index: Access Now Keep It On Internet Shutdown Tracker[36]

Monitors: Internet blockades and shutdowns by governments on its citizens

India 2014 shutdowns: 6

India 2022 shutdowns: 84

Result: India led the world in internet shutdowns.

Reasons cited: India imposed 17 months of internet blockade on Kashmiris, 'India leveraged blackouts to crush the nationwide farmer's protests, the world was outraged, but we were not surprised'.

India had 6 shutdowns in 2014, 14 in 2015, 31 in 2016, 79 in 2017, 134 in 2018, 121 in 2019, 109 in 2020 and 106 times in 2021.

---

[34] Global Liveability Index 2022, eiu.com

[35] Inclusive Internet Index 2022, impact.economist.com

[36] 'Weapons of Control, Shields of Impunity: Internet Shutdowns in 2022', accessnow.org

Of 213 total global shutdowns in 2019, India accounted for 56 per cent (12 times more than the next nation, Venezuela). Of 155 global shutdowns in 2020, India accounted for 70 per cent, denying people—patients, students—even during a pandemic.

Index: World Bank International Logistics Performance Index

Monitors: Performance on trade logistics through weighted average of six dimensions—efficiency of the clearance process (speed, simplicity and predictability of formalities) by border control agencies, including customs; quality of ports, railroads, roads, information technology; ease of arranging competitively priced shipments; competence and quality of transport operators, customs brokers; ability to track and trace consignments; timeliness of shipments in reaching destination within the scheduled or expected delivery time

Method: Biennial survey

India 2014 ranking: 54

India 2023 ranking: 38

Result: India rose by 16 places.

Reasons cited: India improved its performance on international shipments and logistics competence and fell on its customs score and infrastructure score (compared to 2016). Its rank of 38 was one position above its rank in 2007 of 39 and its overall score of 3.5 was slightly below that of 2016 (3.42).

Index: Numbeo Quality of Life Index[37]

Monitors: Purchasing power, pollution, house price to income ratio, cost of living, safety, health care, traffic commute time, climate index

Method: Global ranking

India 2014 ranking: 48

India 2023 ranking: 54

Result: India fell six places.

Reasons cited: India performed poorly on the cost of living, commute and purchasing power.

Index: Fund for Peace Fragile States (formerly Failed States) Index[38]

Monitors: Social cohesion, economy, polity

Method: Global ranking (lower better)

India 2014 ranking: 81

India 2023 ranking: 73

---

[37] Quality of Life Index by Country 2023, numbeo.com

[38] Fragile States Index, fragilestatesindex.org

Result: India fell by eight places moving away from Finland (179) and Norway (178) towards Yemen (1) and Somalia (2).

Reasons cited: India declined across a range of indicators including its security apparatus, factionalisation, group grievance, economic decline, uneven development, brain drain, state legitimacy and human rights and rule of law. India was listed among the states on 'Elevated Warning'.

Index: Access Info and Centre for Law and Democracy Global RTI Rating[39]

Monitors: Quality of access to information laws

Method: Global ranking using 61 indicators measuring seven categories: right of access, scope, requesting procedure, exceptions and refusals, appeals, sanctions and protections, and promotional measures

India 2013 ranking: 2
India 2023 ranking: 8

Result: India fell by six places.

Reasons cited: India's RTI law was hampered by 'blanket exceptions for various security, intelligence, research and economic bodies'; 'Indian legal framework also does not allow access to information held by private entities which perform a public function'; 'exceptions, including for information received in confidence from a foreign government, cabinet papers and parliamentary privilege, are also problematic'.

Index: International Food Policy Research Institute's Global Hunger Index[40]

Monitors: Hunger, stunting in children, undernourishment

Method: Global ranking

India 2014 ranking (of 76 nations): 55
India 2022 ranking (of 121 nations): 107

Result: India fell 52 places, falling behind Pakistan, Bangladesh and Nepal.

Reasons cited: Prevalence of child wasting in 2014–19 increased to 17.3 per cent from 15.1 per cent in 2010–14

Index: Knight Frank Global House Price Index[41]

Monitors: Performance of national housing markets around the world using official data from Central Banks or National Statistic Offices

---

[39] Global Right To Information, rti-rating.org
[40] Global Hunger Index, globalhungerindex.org
[41] Global House Price Index, knightfrank.com

Method: Global ranking of 56 nations
India 2015 ranking: 17
India 2022 ranking: 32

Result: India lost 15 places and in some quarters taking the lowest rank of the 56 nations surveyed in 2020 and the second-lowest by Q2 of 2021. In 2020, residential property in India depreciated by 3.2 per cent, making it the world's weakest-performing market.

Index: Save The Children End of Childhood Index[42]

Monitors: Under-5 infant mortality rate, child stunting, out of school children, child labour, adolescent marriage, adolescent birth rate, forcible displacement through conflict, child homicide rate

Method: Global ranking
India 2017 ranking: 116
India 2021 ranking: 118

Result: India fell by two places.

Reasons cited: India had high rates of infant mortality, stunting and out of school children.

Index: Institute for Economics and Peace Global Terrorism Index[43]

Monitors: Incidents, fatalities, injuries, damage to property from terrorism
India 2014 ranking: 6
India 2023 ranking: 13

Result: India rose by seven places.

Reasons cited: India became less violent than Yemen, Nigeria, Niger and Somalia. Impact of terrorism high, fatalities have come down but incidents remain high.

Index: Henley Passport Index[44]

Monitors: Global access of national passports
Method: Global ranking
India 2014 ranking: 76
India 2023 ranking: 81

Result: India fell by five places.

Reasons cited: Few nations give Indian nationals visa-free access. In another passport index, India was ranked 144th, falling below its pre-

---

[42] 'The toughest places to be a child', Global Childhood Report 2021, savethechildren.org

[43] Global Terrorism Index 2023, visionofhumanity.org and economicsandpeace.org

[44] Henley & Partners Passport Index, henleypassportindex.com

pandemic score, being one of the countries that 'have not capitalised on the global uptick in mobility'.[45]

Index: *University of Gothenburg Varieties of Democracy (V-Dem) Index*[46]

Monitors: Levels of institutional democracy and autocratisation
Method: 3,500 scholars and country experts looking at over 400 indicators
India 2013 rating: 0.57
India 2023 rating: 0.39
Result: India fell by 0.18 points, 'one of the most dramatic shifts among all countries in the world over the past 10 years'.

India lost its status as a democracy and was classified as an 'electoral autocracy', joining nations like Hungary and Turkey. On freedom of expression, media and civil society, India was 'as autocratic as is Pakistan, and worse than both Bangladesh and Nepal'. India had introduced 'discrimination by religion' through its citizenship laws.

On V-Dem's Alternative Sources of Information Index, which tracked the media's ability to report without fear of reprisal, India fell from 0.89 (out of a possible score of 1) before 2014 to .70 in 2019. India used 'legal means and extralegal force against journalists who do not toe the line'.

Index: *World Bank Human Capital Index*[47]

Monitors: Ability of nations to mobilise citizens' economic and professional potential
Method: Global ranking
India 2018 ranking: 115
India 2022 ranking: 116
Result: India fell by one place.

Index: *AT Kearney Foreign Direct Investment Confidence Index*[48]

Monitors: Impact of likely political, economic, and regulatory changes on the foreign direct investment intentions and preferences of CEOs, CFOs and other top executives of Global 1000 companies
Method: Global ranking of top 25 countries

---

[45] 'Passport Index points: India ranks at 144th spot in 2023, sees the largest global drop', 29 March 2023, *Economic Times*
[46] 'Defiance in the Face of Autocratization: Democracy Report 2023', v-dem.net
[47] The Human Capital Index, worldbank.org
[48] 'Optimism Dashed: The 2022 FDI Confidence Index', kearney.com

India 2014 ranking: 7
India 2022 ranking: Did not make it to the top 25

Result: India fell more than 18 places

Reasons cited: 'Uncertainty surrounding the long-term impact of some new foreign investment policies. These include regulations on foreign investment into the fast-moving e-commerce space and on global payments processors'. India consistently fell in the Modi years: India was 11th in 2018, 16th in 2019 and, in both 2020 and 2021, failed to make the list of the top 25.

Index: TomTom Traffic Index[49]

Monitors: Most congested cities in the world through real traffic data measuring extra travel time

Method: Global ranking of 416 cities

India 2015: No cities in top 10
India 2022: India had two cities in the top 10

Bengaluru was the second most congested city in the world (after London), and Pune was sixth worst in the world. In 2020, Mumbaikars lost 172 extra hours (more than 7 days), and Delhi residents 156 extra hours (6 days) in commuting. In 2022 Bengalureans spent an average of 260 hours per year in rush hour traffic while Punekars spent 249 hours.

Index: IQAir World Air Quality Index[50]

Monitors: Air pollution in cities around the world through tracking particulate matter (PM2.5) through ground stations

Method: Global ranking

India 2017 (number of cities in global top 30): 11
India 2022 (number of cities in global top 30): 22

Result: India added 11 more cities—Bulandshahr, Jalalpur, Bhiwadi, Greater Noida, Meerut, Hisar, Muzaffarnagar, Fatehbad, Bandhwari, Yamunanagar and Dharuhera—to Gurugram, Agra, Jind, Faridabad, Delhi, Noida, Lucknow, Kanpur, Ghaziabad, Muzaffarpur and Rohtak as the ones with the world's worst air pollution.

Index: Yale Environmental Performance Index[51]

Monitors: Protection of human health and protection of ecosystems

Method: Global ranking

---

[49] TomTom Traffic Index 2022, tomtom.com

[50] 'World's Most Polluted Cities (Historical Data 2017–2022)', iqair.com

[51] Environmental Performance Index, epi.yale.edu

India 2014 ranking: 155
India 2022 ranking: 180

Result: India fell by 25 places to be last in the world and behind Pakistan (176), Nepal (162), Sri Lanka (132) and Bangladesh (177).

Reasons cited: India ranked 178 in health and 165 in climate policy. In 2020, India was ranked 139 in sanitation and 150 in ecosystem vitality.

Index: Germanwatch Global Climate Risk Index[52]

Monitors: Which nations suffer most from climate change, exposure and vulnerability to extreme events

Method: Global ranking (lower rank better)

India 2014 ranking: 18
India 2021 ranking: 7

Result: India fell 11 places, behind Sri Lanka (30), Pakistan (15) and Bangladesh (13).

Reasons cited: India led the world in human lives lost due to climate change. It also led the world in economic losses suffered due to climate change.

Index: Sustainable Development Index[53]

Monitors: National progress made on 17 indicators—poverty, zero hunger, health, education, gender equality, clean water, clean energy, decent work and economic growth, infrastructure, reduced inequality, sustainable cities, responsible production, climate action, conservation of marine resources, conservation of ecosystems, justice system, government spending

Method: Global ranking

India 2016 ranking: 110
India 2022 ranking: 121

Result: India fell by 11 places behind Bangladesh (104), Nepal (98), Sri Lanka (76) and Bhutan (70).

Reasons cited: India was stagnating or declining on seven indicators.

Index: Coursera Global Skills Report[54]

Monitors: State of skills of national populations across Business, Technology and Data Science

Method: Global ranking measured through 77 million learners, 4,000 campuses, 2,000 businesses and over 100 governments

India 2019 ranking

---

[52] Global Climate Risk Index 2021, germanwatch.org
[53] Sustainable Development Report, sdgindex.org
[54] Global Skills Report 2022, coursera.org

Business: 50
Technology: 44
Data Science: 51

India 2022 ranking
Business: 62
Technology: 56
Data Science: 76

Result: India fell by 12 places on Business, 12 places on Technology and 10 places on Data Science.

Reasons cited: India lagged behind global counterparts in technology skillsets in sectors as varied as telecom, healthcare, manufacturing and automotive (2019); women received lower pay and spent more time in unpaid care work; four out of five Indian women did not work; in absence of policies that improve access to education and employment for women, output by mid 2020s could be 5 per cent lower than before the pandemic. 'With a data science proficiency level of 26%, India's companies may struggle to find the talent to fill those roles without more training' (2022).

Index: Oxfam Commitment to Reducing Inequality Index[55]

Monitors: What governments are doing to tackle the gap between rich and poor by comparing spending on health, education and social protection; labour market policies; and progressive structure and incidence of taxation

Method: Global ranking

India 2020 ranking: 129
India 2022 ranking: 123

Result: India rose six places

Reasons cited: India was fifth lowest in the world in health spending and fell 19 places on labour policy. However, some nations fell faster. In 2020 India ranked below Pakistan, Sri Lanka, Bangladesh, Nepal and Afghanistan to be the most unequal place in South Asia. In 2022 it went ahead of Pakistan.

Under Modi, across 48 indices, India's ranking rose on 6 but fell on 41.[56] The decline was broad and pronounced enough for organisations to have captured similar results through different methodologies. India under Modi did poorly on 6 indices that tracked civil liberties and pluralism, 5 that tracked health and literacy, 2 tracking religious freedom and minorities, 2 tracking internet denial, 9 tracking national capacity of various types, 5 tracking rule of law, corruption and transparency and remained the same

---

[55] 'The Commitment to Reducing Inequality Index 2022', oxfam.org

[56] In the 2021 edition of this book, India fared worse: falling on 49 indices and rising on four. Indices discontinued or not updated since 2018 have been taken off in this edition.

on one, 4 tracking sustainability and the environment, 3 tracking gender issues and women's safety, 3 tracking the economic freedoms of Indians and 4 tracking urban spaces.

On 4 other new indices India under Modi was placed at the bottom or near the bottom.

Index: Migrant Integration Policy Index[57]

Monitors: Policies to integrate migrants in countries across five continents

Method: Assessing eight policy areas: Labour Market Mobility, Family Reunion, Education, Political Participation, Long-term Residence, Access to Nationality, Anti-discrimination and Health

India 2020 rank: 52

Result: India was last of the 52 nations monitored

Reasons cited: India had unfavourable ratings on access to nationality, anti-discrimination, health, political participation, education and labour market mobility. 'While most countries, including China and Indonesia, have improved their integration policies over the past five years, India has not yet developed immigrant integration policies. India did not follow the international reform trends'. India was added to the index in 2020.

Index: World Economic Forum Global Social Mobility Index[58]

Monitors: Equality and opportunity through 10 'pillars': Health, Education Access, Education Quality and Equity, Lifelong Learning, Technology Access, Work Opportunities, Fair Wage Distribution, Working Conditions, Social Protection and Inclusive Institutions

India 2020 rank: 76

Result: India was sixth from the bottom, behind Saudi Arabia, Indonesia, Sri Lanka and Vietnam.

Reasons cited: 'Second highest level of workers in vulnerable employment, low female labour force participation, poor performance on fair wage and social protection expenditure (2.6 per cent of GDP) and coverage.' This was an index that began in 2020.

Index: Bloomberg Covid Resilience Ranking[59]

Monitors: Normalisation in nations as they exit the pandemic

Method: Global ranking of 54 nations measuring Reopening Progress,

---

[57] Migrant integration policy index 2020, mipex.eu

[58] 'Global Social Mobility index 2020: Why economies benefit from fixing inequality', weforum.org

[59] 'The Best And Worst Places To Be As The World Finally Reopens: Covid Resilience Ranking', bloomberg.com

Covid Status and Quality of Life through data on mobility, vaccine coverage, 2021 GDP growth forecast, universal healthcare, human development index, Covid cases and fatality rates

India 2021 rank: 50

Result: India was fourth from bottom, behind Pakistan and Bangladesh

Reasons cited: India scored poorly across the board, 'amid a perfect storm of variant-driven outbreaks, slow vaccination and global isolation'.

Index: Economics and Peace Positive Peace Index[60]

Monitors: Socio-economic resilience, capacity to protect citizens and institutions from adverse impact of a shock and the ability to rebuild its socio-economic system after the shock

Method: Ranking of 51 high-income plus BRICS nations

India 2021 ranking: Last out of 51 nations

The record leaves little room for debate or dispute. The scale and rapidity of decline in governance after 2014 is manifest. India was struggling to keep up with the world and sinking on several fronts. It may appear strange that anyone should have thought that reversing this performance required 'a massive publicity campaign' which would 'shape India's perception' through advertising and more websites, but that is what Modi thought and how he oriented his government to act.

As the second wave of the Covid-19 pandemic exposed India's healthcare system, left thousands dead and dying without medical attention or oxygen, the government held a meeting with 300 officials on how to improve its image.[61] When the world's media showed mass cremations because incompetence was killing people by the thousand daily, the government again assumed that the problem lay in perception.[62]

The solution was not image correction but improving performance through governance and more grip.

After the publicity strategy referred to earlier (which appears to have fallen through for whatever reason), the government decided around the end of 2020 that if it asked ministries to 'ensure swift and updated data'

---

[60] 'Business and Peace Report 2021', Institute for Economics and Peace, economicsandpeace. org

[61] 'Top Central government officials attend session on boosting image, perception', 5 May 2021, *Hindustan Times*

[62] 'Counter "one-sided" world media narrative on govt's pandemic "failure", Jaishankar tells Indian diplomats', 30 April 2021, *The Indian Express*

it would help on the indices.[63] This was based on the assumption that the
government's work was excellent; it was data lag that had caused indices to
plummet. This was also, of course, wrong, and the indices that came out after
that showed continued decline.

A more credible response might have been to say that the decline was not
the Modi government's doing entirely, or that many issues did not concern
the Union fully or that the states were also responsible; to deny the decline
in toto was to run away from the problem. The government's response to
the Freedom House finding that India was not free but only partly free was
to trot out a press release which said: 'Many states in India under its federal
structure are ruled by parties other than the one at the national level, through
an election process which is free and fair and which is conducted by an
independent election body. This reflects the working of a vibrant democracy,
which gives space to those who hold varying views.'[64]

This was dishonest. The Freedom House report had two parts. The
first, given 40 per cent weightage, was on political rights. Here India got a
score of 34/40 (falling to 33/40 in 2023), including full marks for free and
fair elections, election commission impartiality, freedom to start political
parties and opportunities for the Opposition to increase their power. In this
part, India did not get full marks on whether voting was unhampered by
violence and unaffected by communal tension. This is hardly arguable. In
fact, the government even got 3/4 on transparency, which was probably over-
generous. The government response was therefore merely repeating what
Freedom House had anyway said.

Where India's rating was hurt was in the other 60 per cent, for civil
liberties, which are also a part of freedom. Here it performed poorly
(33/60). On the issues of freedom of expression, freedom of religion,
academic freedom, freedom of assembly, freedom for NGOs to work (the
report named the government's attack on Amnesty International India
specifically), rule of law, independence of judiciary and due process by
police, India's rating was poor. But the scores merely reflected the reality.
The government appeared baffled by the results. It sought details from
ministries of the parameters used by the Economist Intelligence Unit in
its downgrading of India to a 'flawed democracy' though the report itself

---

[63] 'Government's fresh push to boost rankings in global indices', 26 November 2020, *The Times of India*

[64] 'Rebuttal to Freedom House report on India's declining status as a free country', 5 March 2021, Press Information Bureau

clearly says that the 'primary cause was an erosion of civil liberties' and introduction of religion into citizenship.[65]

When India plummeted in the Hunger Index, the government said in Parliament it was not possible that Indians were hungry because 'whenever a street dog gives birth in our village, even though it bites, our women provide them with sheer (sweet dish). So…we should not be sensitive to such reports. As far as these surveys are concerned, even healthy and strong children are counted…there should be awareness in society, our dynamic minister Smriti (Irani) ji has started a Jan Andolan, and 13 crore events have been done'.[66]

What these different indices listed above revealed was also borne out by groups and individuals in India working on the issues of rights, the environment, health, law and the economy, and also in other indicators generated elsewhere. The data tells us that India deteriorated under Modi across the spectrum of governance in ways that are noticeable and objectively measurable.

The Indian government's own indicators also reported a decline in governance. With regard to the economy, the performance was revealed by the government's data on GDP growth and employment and consumption, as we will see in a later chapter.

Spending on food by the poorest Indians had declined before the pandemic. Consumer expenditure of Indians was lower in 2017-18 than in 2011-12.[67]

Joblessness rose consistently under Modi. The total numbers of Indians with work shrank under Modi from 44 crore in 2013 to 41 crore in 2016 to 40 crore in 2017 then to 38 crore in 2021, though the workforce grew from 79 crore to 106 crore.[68] In February 2023, 40.9 crore Indians were working, fewer than had been in 2014.[69]

Consequently the Indian middle class stopped growing under Modi. Residential sales in eight major cities (Ahmedabad, Bangalore, Chennai,

---

[65] 'Govt seeks details of parameters to improve India's ranking on global Democracy Index', 17 April 2021, *The Hindustan Times*

[66] 'Modi government questions methodology and data accuracy of Global Hunger Index', 20 March 2021, *The New Indian Express*

[67] 'Consumer spend sees first fall in 4 decades on weak rural demand: NSO data', 15 November 2019, *Business Standard*

[68] 'Revealing the Real Picture Behind India's Unemployment Problem', 8 March 2021, vivekkaul.com

[69] 'Employment Inches up in Urban India', 6 March 2023, cmie.com

Delhi, Hyderabad, Kolkata, Mumbai and Pune) remained stagnant[70] from 3.3 lakh units in 2012 to 3.2 lakh in 2019.[71]

In 2020 they fell to 1.5 lakh units.[72] In 2021, they were 2.6 lakh units.

Passenger vehicle sales remained stagnant for a decade, with sales of 27 lakh in 2012, 27 lakh in 2019 and 27 lakh in 2020.[73] In 2021 they were 30 lakh, a number achieved in 2016. Much was made of the record passenger vehicle sales in 2022–23 (39 lakh) but average sales of the three pandemic years from 2020–21 to 2022–23 were lower than the numbers in 2017–18.

Two wheeler sales were stagnant at 1.6 crore in 2014, 1.7 crore in 2019 and 1.5 crore in 2020. In 2021, they fell to 1.3 crore, the worst in 10 years.[74] Three wheeler sales were 5 lakh in 2012, 5 lakh in 2015, 5 lakh in 2016, 6 lakh in 2019 and 2 lakh in 2020. In 2021 they were 2 lakh. Commercial vehicles sales were stagnant at 7.9 lakh in 2012, 6 lakh in 2015, 7 lakh in 2016, 7 lakh in 2019 and 5.6 lakh in 2020. In 2021 they were 7 lakh.

The total Indian market for consumer durables (air conditioners, washing machines, television sets etc) was estimated in 2014 to be worth Rs 150,000 crore by 2020. It was Rs 76,400 crore in 2019 and Rs 50,000 crore in 2020.[75]

Total passengers (rail plus air) fell from 840 crore in 2012 to 826 crore in 2019, and this is before the pandemic.

China's Li Keqiang index measures real GDP growth through three indicators: railway cargo volume, electricity consumption and loans disbursed. Total tonnes ferried by railways was 1.1 billion tonnes in 2014, 2015, 2016, 2017 and 2018. It was 1.2 billion tonnes in 2019, 1.2 billion in 2020, 1.4 billion tonnes in 2021 and 1.4 billion tonnes in 2022, growing since 2014 at a rate of 3 per cent a year.[76]

Electricity generation remained at 1.3 trillion units for four years in 2017, 2018, 2019 and 2020 while India's population grew by 7 crore people.[77] It was 1.4 trillion units in 2021 and 1.6 trillion units in 2022, growing annually at 5 per cent.

[70] 'Sale of ready homes rise in FY20, overall housing sales fall: Report', 15 May 2020, *Outlook*

[71] 'Housing sales down 40 per cent in 2017 from 2013/14 levels', 18 March 2018, PTI

[72] 'Housing sales plunge 50% in National Capital Region during 2020', 6 January 2021, PTI

[73] Automobile Domestic Sales Trends, siam.in

[74] 'Two-wheeler sales in 2022, worst in a decade', 28 February 2022, *Hindu BusinessLine*

[75] 'Consumer Durables Industry—Review & Outlook', Care Ratings

[76] *Indian Railways Year Book 2019-20*, indianrailways.gov.in

[77] 'Power sector at a glance All India', powermin.gov.in

The growth of bank credit to industry fell from 15 per cent in 2013 to 12 per cent in March 2014, 5 per cent in 2015, 2.7 per cent in 2016, minus 1.7 per cent in 2017, 0.7 per cent in 2018 and 6.9 per cent in 2019. Growth of credit to medium sized industries was minus 0.5 per cent in March 2014, 0.4 per cent in 2015, minus 7.8 per cent in 2016, minus 8.7 per cent in 2017, minus 1.1 per cent in 2018 and 2.6 per cent in 2019. All this was before the pandemic. Credit to micro and small industries grew minus 2.3 per cent in March 2016, minus 0.5 per cent in 2017, 0.9 per cent in 2018 and 0.7 per cent in 2019.[78]

Before Modi, between 2009 and 2013, loans disbursed (non-food credit) had grown at an average of 17 per cent. This then was the performance. The National Crime Records Bureau and National Human Rights Commission said that crime in India rose in 2019, the year before the pandemic, over 2018. Overall, the number of crimes registered went up from 26 lakh in 2013 to 32 lakh in 2019, then 42 lakh in 2020 and 36 lakh in 2021. Kidnappings were up 10.3 per cent and crimes against women were up 7.3 per cent (4.05 lakh versus 3.78 lakh). In 2021, the number of crimes against women rose to 4.28 lakh. The crime rate (incidence per 1 lakh population) went up from 229 in 2014 to 268 in 2021. The number of women murdered after being raped increased, apparently because of new laws in BJP states that punished rape with the death penalty, because the rapist was given an incentive to murder his victim.[79]

Crimes against children rose 4.5 per cent. Crimes against children were up 16 per cent in 2021 over 2020. Cases of sexual violence against children increased from 31,668 in 2017 to 38,802 in 2018 and then 46,005 in 2019.[80] Crimes against senior citizens rose 13.7 per cent between 2018 and 2019, and 5.3 per cent between 2020 and 2021. Sedition cases rose from 30 in 2015 to 70 in 2018 to 93 in 2019. Only one person was convicted between 2016 and 2019.[81]

UAPA cases rose 72 per cent between 2015 and 2019 though the conviction rate was 2 per cent.[82]

Cybercrimes rose 63 per cent after having risen 77 per cent the previous year. They rose 5.9 per cent in 2021, for a total of 52,974 cases. Custodial

[78] Economic Survey 2018–19, Volume 2, indiabudget.gov.in
[79] 'Explained: In crimes against women, rise in cases of rape with murder', 10 January 2020, *The Indian Express*
[80] 'Decoding the proposed changes in the POCSO Act', 23 March 2021, *Hindustan Times*
[81] 'Sedition cases jump 160 per cent between 2016–19: Rights lawyer', 15 July 2021, PTI
[82] 'Parliament proceedings | Over 72% rise in number of UAPA cases registered in 2019', 9 March 2021, *The Hindu*

deaths were recorded between 2009 and 2015 as being around 600 by the National Crime Records Bureau,[83] but custodial deaths apparently shot to 17,146 between 2010 and 2020.[84] Crimes against Dalits rose 7 per cent, having risen 5.5 per cent the year before, and crimes against Adivasis rose 26 per cent. Crime against Dalits rose again in 2021 (1.2 per cent) over 2020, for a total of 50,900 registered cases. Against Adivasis, they rose 6.4 per cent in 2021. And this rise in crime before the pandemic came despite the fact that the latest numbers did not include any 2019 data from West Bengal.[85]

The quality of law enforcement agencies directly under the Union has deteriorated, being misused against opponents and critics. The Enforcement Directorate (ED) conducted 62 'raids' (the official term is 'search and seizure') in 2013 but more than ten times as many—670 raids—in 2019. Between March 2011 and January 2020, it conducted 1,700 raids in connection with 1,569 investigations. In that same period, it managed only nine convictions, mostly in low-profile cases.[86] The ED conducted 27 times more raids (3010) between 2014 and 2022 than in the period between 2004 and 2014 (112).[87]

The ED was extraordinarily focused on targeting Opposition parties and leaders.[88]

In 2019, the Income Tax department, another favourite instrument for 'raids', could not deliver convictions in 82 per cent of the cases it chose to prosecute.[89]

Further, some of the indicators released externally were using data sourced from India that had a lag. The numbers were worse on things like labour force participation rate, which, according to the World Bank (using the International Labor Organisation's data), had fallen in India from 51.4 per cent in 2014 to 46.2 per cent in 2020.[90] However, as studies showed, the actual number of people in the workforce in 2020 was even lower at 40.7 per

[83] Crime in India, ncrb.gov.in

[84] 'Five deaths in police custody every day over 10 years, but few convictions', 6 August 2020, Business Standard

[85] 'Data of West Bengal not included in NCRB report', 1 October 2020, Asianet News

[86] 'IT dept and ED raids are at an all-time high, but convictions remain elusive', 3 March 2020, TheWire.in

[87] 'ED raids up 27x in 2014-2022 compared to 2004-14: Govt', 27 July 2022, Times of India

[88] '95% Of Political Leaders Investigated By CBI & ED Are Opposition Leaders: Non-BJP Parties Tell Supreme Court', 23 March 2023, livelaw.in

[89] Ibid

[90] 'Labor force participation rate, total (% of total population ages 15+) (modeled ILO estimate)—India', data.worldbank.org

cent.[91] This was more than 20 per cent lower than that in the US.[92] Modi was talking about India exploiting its demographic dividend at the same time that his governance of the economy had taken crores of Indians out of the workforce.

Similarly, the participation of women in the workforce had fallen from 36 per cent to 23 per cent by 2018, according to a United Nations Development Programme report.[93] But it fell further to 18 per cent in 2019, and this was before the lockdown.[94] In February 2021, it was only 9.42 per cent.[95] In April 2022, it was at 9 per cent.[96] In recent years, India has had two strong preconditions—falling fertility and rising female education levels—for women's participation in employment. Women want to work but are 'hampered by a combination of factors. One, they need work commensurate with their rising educational qualifications; two, they need conducive conditions (transportation, toilets, regularity); and three, they have to balance the pressures of domestic chores'.[97]

India had lagged behind large parts of the world on most of the meaningful indicators for several decades, but it had also made improvements, even if these may have been slow. Under Modi, this has actually been reversed in several areas, including in the HDI indicators, where improvement first plateaued and then deteriorated as the effect of executive strokes like demonetisation and the 2020 national lockdown hit the poor. The full impact of the actions from above was visible on the population.

The Record on Terrorism

The other issue for which Modi was lionised is his toughness, especially on Islamist terrorism. His claim to have a chest '56 inches' around is not based on any particular act of personal bravery. Presumably, it is based on his actions in office. Here, the record will surprise those who assume this toughness against terrorism to be fact.

[91] 'Labour force shrinks in September', 2 October 2020, CMIE

[92] 'Civilian labor force participation rate', bls.gov

[93] 'Corporate engagement in women's economic empowerment', in.undp.org

[94] 'Women's participation in Indian workforce plummets from 37% to 18% in 13 years: Report', 9 March 2020, PTI

[95] 'Women are bearing the brunt of India's unemployment problem', 17 March 2021, vivekkaul.com

[96] 'Retreat of female labour participation', 18 July 2022, cmie.com

[97] 'India's budget needs to address gender inequality in employment', 29 December 2020, *Mint*

Toughness here must show in management of the criminal justice system. Much has been written about the abuse of law and process by his associates and ministers, some of whom have spent time in jail. Let us look carefully at an emblematic case that will show how incompetent the Modi enterprise is when it comes to the very subject that he is meant to be a champion in. This was the most important case of terrorism in all the years that Modi headed Gujarat.

Briefly, on 24 September 2002, six months after the Godhra riots, two men with assault rifles murdered over thirty Gujaratis and security personnel in Ahmedabad's Akshardham temple. The two killers, apparently Pakistanis, though we are not sure, were also shot dead. The act was said to be in revenge for the pogrom in the state against Muslims earlier that year.

It took 11 months for the Gujarat police to act. The investigation was given to the anti-terror squad on 3 October 2002 but it got nowhere, and on 28 August 2003 it was handed over to the crime branch. That same day, after receiving 'verbal instruction' from a policeman named D.G. Vanzara (later jailed for faking encounters), the crime branch said that it had solved the thing. It arrested five people the following day and a sixth a day later. But despite contributing this case-cracking material, Vanzara was not produced as a witness in the case by the state.

The six Muslims were tried and convicted by the Prevention of Terrorism Act (POTA) court in Ahmedabad that heard the trial *in camera* (meaning in private rather than in open court). The Gujarat High Court, which for some reason also heard their appeal *in camera*, agreed with the trial court and the prosecution, with three men getting death sentences and the others, imprisonment. The men were in jail for a long time, with one of them actually completing his sentence before the Supreme Court heard the appeal.

When the Supreme Court judgement arrived, even Modi's fiercest critics would have been taken aback by the performance of his government in investigating and prosecuting the case. The judgement came, conveniently for Modi, on 16 May 2014, the day he won the general election and moved to Delhi.

Acquitting all the men, the Supreme Court said: 'Before parting with the judgement, we intend to express our anguish about the incompetence with which the investigating agencies conducted the investigation of the case of such a grievous nature, involving the integrity and security of the nation. Instead of booking the real culprits responsible for taking so many precious lives, the police caught innocent people and got imposed the grievous charges against them which resulted in their conviction and subsequent sentencing.' (Page 280 of the judgement.)[98]

[98] Adambhai Sulemanbhai Ajmeri vs State Of Gujarat on 16 May 2014, Indiakanoon.org.

Of Modi's own role as home minister (he held the Cabinet post) in approving the POTA charges, the court said he had 'simply signed the proposed note as a mark of approval' (page 107). The court added, 'This would go to show clear non-application of mind by the Home Minister in granting sanction.' (Page 109)

The bumbling goes on and on. The Gujarat police had a handwriting expert—J.J. Patel—who verified the Urdu handwriting of the accused, while admitting he knew no Urdu and could not tell it from Arabic or Persian.

The court said that 'the story of the prosecution crumbles down at every juncture'. Because it arrived on the day Modi won his famous victory, the news was buried and the issue hasn't received much attention. A newspaper report analysed some of the details.[99]

The trial court and the Gujarat High Court had relied on confessions, but the Supreme Court found that those confessions were not voluntary because of the way they had been extracted.

The chief judicial magistrate, who had a critical role in verifying the confessional statements (the main evidence used to convict), went on to confess during cross-examination that: 'I did not make inquiry with any police officers with regard to the said confessions. I had not asked the two accused produced before me as to whether they need any lawyer or not. I had not taken the said accused persons in my custody. It is true that I did not issue any warrant for them to be sent to judicial custody. It is true that I did not inquire with the accused about where and at what time and who recorded their statements.' And also: 'It is true that I have not kept any rojkam (daily register) or record in my court about the accused persons produced before me.' (Page 127)

The Supreme Court said: 'The statements by the CJM show how casually the mandates under Sections 32(4) and 32(5) were followed, rendering the said requirement a hollow and empty exercise. (Page 128).

Of the magistrate's role, the court observed that he had been able to 'record the statement of the accused persons, read it over to them and enquire about any coercion and torture, all in a period of half-an-hour.'

This was not possible for a statement that was more than 15 pages long. And even this cooked-up story was done incompetently by the Modi government. The confessional statements gave 'different versions of the same story, each of which contradicted the other and was actually fatal to the case of the prosecution'.

[99] 'Akshardham attack case: Decoding the other verdict of May 16', 2 June 2014, *The Times of India*

The Modi government said it had recovered letters from the trouser pockets of the killed attackers. The statement of the man who actually recovered them, a brigadier of the National Security Guards ('the most important witness for proving the recovery of the alleged letters', according to the Supreme Court), was not even recorded.

Though there were bullet holes even in the trouser pockets, the Supreme Court observed, the letters apparently recovered from them were clean, without any tear or crease, soiling or stains of blood. The court said that 'With regard to the letters being in a perfect condition, the High Court merely observed that "Truth is stranger than fiction".' And it then added: 'We cannot accept the recording of the High Court that the secret behind the crease-free unsoiled and unstained letter lies in the divine philosophy of "Truth is stranger than fiction" for this renowned epithet by the author Mark Twain comes with a caveat that says, "Truth is stranger than fiction. Fiction must make sense".'

The Times of India analysis said that 'The case would not have gone to trial with such infirmities had Gujarat's home department—a portfolio then held by Narendra Modi—denied the necessary sanction for prosecution under POTA. KC Kapoor, who was principal secretary, home, admitted that that (sic) in the material placed before him for sanction, he had not seen any papers suggesting compliance of the statutory conditions. As a corollary, the SC said that the sanction was neither "an informed decision" nor was it on the basis of "an independent analysis of fact in consultation with the investigating officer".'[100]

Even in terror cases, Modi's Gujarat followed no governance process. What does it say about the state administration that its police and the judiciary can act in this fashion? The Supreme Court judgement is sobering reading for those who equate clever slogans with substance. For those who assumed Gujarat was some ideally governed state. And for those who assumed there would be instant transformation in the way Delhi functioned now that the genius had moved. The Supreme Court said that there was 'perversity in conducting this case at various stages, right from the investigation level to the granting of sanction by the state government'.

Perversity. A word the dictionary says means 'a deliberate desire to behave in an unreasonable or unacceptable way', 'contrary to the evidence' and 'aberrant'. This, then, is the record in Gujarat. To be fair, this is also more or less the record of all Indian governments.

---

[100] 'Akshardham attack case: Decoding the other verdict of May 16', 2 June 2014

And yet the claim was made and the belief existed that Modi's win would enable him to change the mess he was himself a part of. *Achche din aane wale hain!* This Indian version of the Great Man theory (which posits that history is largely explainable through the impact of great individuals) didn't look at the societies and economies of developed nations and what they had done to reach where they had. It didn't look at why India was sailing in the same boat as its neighbours when it came to key indicators and indeed trailing in some of them. The problem was not that of India alone in South Asia, and the solution did not appear to reside in the idea of a missing messiah.

The myth was spread aggressively in the campaign leading up to the 2014 general election, and it was believed because of a successful campaign. Modi became one with the messaging. His actual performance and delivery in the past was not important enough to have been considered seriously. The focus was on the promise and the image. The media analysed this in articles, columns and slide-shows.

One concluded that Modi's 2014 run was 'an example of how to prepare and successfully implement a marketing and branding campaign'.[101] Another ('PM Modi is proving to be the world's best marketing professional. Here's why')[102] explored why Modi was so brilliant and decided that it was his saying things like 'I dream of making India a $20 trillion economy' and 'I thought of my government as a start-up'.

A third 'How "Brand Modi" came to be: A masterclass in PR & Marketing'[103] claimed 'following Modi's campaigns and political messaging is akin to studying a full public relations course at university'.

And another—'India matlab Narendra Modi: How the PM learnt branding from Coca-Cola'—referred to his 'permanent election mode'.[104] Meaning that he was always promoting himself, which was true. Yet another—'How Modi is a success with marketing in politics'[105] concluded that Modi's assets were: 'thinking out of the box' and 'disruptive positioning'.

Clearly, the brand was a hit. But at some point the product had to reflect this quality promised by the brand. The problem was that, as the experience in Gujarat over 12 years showed, the packaging was not quite the product. And the dissonance between performance and delivery began to reveal itself in the numbers. At home, the indicators of bad news could be finessed or

[101] 'Just the right image', 8 June 2014, *Business Today*

[102] 12 August 2016, *Business Insider*

[103] 29 May 2019, *TheQuint.com*

[104] 23 May 2019, *ThePrint.in*

[105] 20 December 2017, *The Economic Times*

tweaked and data could be cooked or simply hidden, as it was indeed under Modi as we will see. It is less easy to do that abroad. Here the problem has shown itself across several indicators.

And yet, it is also clear that Modi remained not only popular but also adored. Through the entire part of his first term in office, he retained the aura he brought to it in 2014. When he inflicted deliberate hardship on hundreds of millions through his eccentric economic decisions, the voters did not rebel. His charisma was intact. And though admittedly this is a less tangible and less measurable metric, it appears to be the case that certainly his popularity did not dip. The BJP took Uttar Pradesh in a landslide victory months after demonetisation and gave the party its largest vote share and seat share in that state ever.

While the BJP did lose some local elections in Modi's first term, he returned to power in 2019 by adding more votes and more seats to what had already been, in 2014, a record by a non-Congress party. We have to come to terms with this and be able in some measure to explain the paradox. The record is not that of success: the indicators we have seen and the rest of the material we will examine makes that clear. Put together, the numbers on the economy, the loss of access to territory on the border and the data of the various indices seem to confirm failure of a fairly large magnitude. This is certainly not the record of a performer or reformer. It is not even the record of an average leader. It is difficult to defend against the charge that it is a disaster. But not only did Modi defend it, he was able to get popular endorsement of his record.

Having accepted this, we must also explore why this was the case. For that we must leave the numbers and the data for now and try to form a thesis that might conflate all the things that we have put up on our board. A highly charismatic leader promises great change through two facets that he projects strongly. The first, as a catalyst of economic growth. Add him into the mixture and there will be produced a spontaneous combustion which will power India out of its historic stasis and take it to the developed world.

The second is his toughness on the internal enemy, the minority and, especially, the Muslim. He did not project this side to him overtly in the campaign—indeed, the slogan in the first term was 'sabka saath, sabka vikas' (inclusion and development of all)—but it would be wrong to say that he concealed it. He had already established his credentials through his presiding over—whether the charge is incompetence at stopping it or complicity—the massacre of 1,000 Gujaratis, mostly Muslim, in 2002. This is what made him the Hindutva hero with the chest 56 inches around. And, only weeks later, it was his aggressive owning of his government's actions and inactions during the riots that blocked Atal Bihar Vajpayee from trying to replace him as chief minister.

He won the full-throated backing of those gathered at that conclave in Goa on 12 April 2002,[106] and became at that point the acknowledged favourite of both the BJP's cadre and also that of the RSS. They received from Modi an unapologetic endorsement of their own worldview, which may be considered their prejudice and their bigotry. Did they care at all about the aspects that were linked to Gujarat's economic growth? We cannot say. But it is clear that even Modi's failure and incompetence on the issue of prosecuting terrorism did not appear to affect his popularity. His action or inaction in the violence of 2002 had validated him and this validation was to stay with him forever. The national and international notoriety that he earned would remain on both the credit side and debit side of his aura and his brand.

From here on, Modi had only to signal his connection to that Modi of the past and the bond with the follower would be re-established. This might explain why the lack of overt communal signalling during the 2014 campaign did not affect in any way his core vote.

This might also be why, to take our point further, his popularity with a large part of the population and the voter base remained and, if anything, grew. Even if they acknowledged arguable failure on the side of governance, Modi was delivering to them what they wanted on the side of identity and passion. And he was also continuing to keep the vision of dramatic change alive, amid the ruins of his performance, through the power of his rhetoric.

The charisma of leadership and the power of speech appears to be for many an actual and real reason to vote for someone. The candidate's performance in office is incidental and perhaps even irrelevant.

To look at it in another way, many Indian voters, especially the urban upper classes, appear to engage with politics in the same manner as they do to Bollywood. The appeal of the politician is similar to and perhaps the same as the appeal of the film star. The depth of engagement from the audience is also the same. No delivery in the real world is actually expected of either; the performance on screen is all there is. It is entertainment, and the performer appeals to our emotions, what we like, hate, love and are prejudiced about, more than they do our actual, lived reality.

Modi has not brought much real positive change to the majority of those who adored him. But neither has the Bollywood star, and that isn't expected

---

[106] For a fuller discussion on this, see the chapter 'And then came Advani' in the author's earlier work, *Our Hindu Rashtra*, 2020, Westland Publications

of him either. It is entertainment. The hero's charisma remains intact at the end.

Others have also speculated on this idea that the appeal of Modi is divorced from his performance. Academic Neelanjan Sircar has written that Modi's 2019 win was on the basis of the trust people reposed in him.[107] Modi expanded his 2014 slogan to 'Sabka saath, sabka vikaas, sabka vishwas' (inclusion, development and trust of all).

Sircar explains that this comes from a personal politics in which voters prefer to centralise political power in a strong leader. They trust him to decide on issues and have faith that whatever he does is for the best. This is different from the traditional way in which politics functions—through accountability and a demonstration by politicians that they have performed on the economy and elsewhere.

Two things made this possible. The pushing of a Hindu nationalist identity for India, as opposed to the traditional multicultural identity. This religious nationalism supported centralised politics (because India's messy regional politics involves a federalism that must negotiate across language, region, caste and religion). What Sircar describes as 'vishwas' is easier explained as tribalism—support empty of all content other than visceral identity. It is hollow and with no real expectation of delivery or performance.

And secondly, Sircar argues, the BJP's control over media and communication gave it structural advantages in mobilising the voters around Modi.

This is a convincing explanation for why Modi's popularity is disconnected from his performance. Pratap Bhanu Mehta explores the idea further, writing that three things follow from the politics of this 'vishwas' or 'bhakti' (as noted, Modi's supporters are sneeringly referred to as bhakts or mindless devotees on social media). First, that there is an immunity to any accountability: 'You can preside over poor economic performance, suffer a military setback, inflict suffering through failed schemes like demonetisation, and yet the trust does not decline.'[108]

The second is that this form of politics required continued pushing of religious majoritarianism. And the third is that it has to be continually sustained through control of the media.

The reason that bhakti has taken such strong hold on the polity, Mehta

---

[107] 'Not vikas, Modi's 2019 election was built on politics of vishwas', 30 May 2020, ThePrint.in

[108] 'The greatest allure of vishwas is that you maintain it by simply believing', 26 August 2020, The Indian Express

wrote, is a deep pessimism. Faith was necessary only when there was no confidence in one's own ability to influence the economic and political world. Handing one's agency over to the great leader was easier and liberating because one didn't have to do anything. The leader would take care of it all.

In this framework, competence is not as important as intent. Criticism of Modi was then criticism of his intent and not of his competence. Because his intent was impassioned and sacred, it must remain unquestioned.

Failure was not the result of deficiency but of fortune. It was not the defeat of strategy or execution but merely the inability to attain success at the present time. The demonstrable bumbling on the economy and on governance could carry on, because the intent was 'good'. Thus was Modi able to divorce his brand from what he actually delivered. And he was not held to account either by the political opposition or, as we will see in the next chapter, by India's media.

2

THE GODI MEDIA

To understand the shift towards majoritarianism in the media in India (obvious to anyone who has watched its news channels become deranged, a process which has accelerated after 2014), it may be instructive to look first at the background.

If there is such a thing as a national media in India, it is the English newspapers and English news television channels ecosystem. The so-called regional language media, even if large by readership, is restricted mostly to a single state, such as the newspapers of Kerala, Gujarat, Tamil Nadu, Odisha, Bengal, Punjab, Karnataka and Andhra Pradesh. Hindi has a much bigger audience than English in terms of numbers, but it is geographically narrower. English alone can claim to reach all states, especially all the urban spaces.

The paradox is that English media is less expressive of its audience's sentiments than the regional language media for the following reasons. Firstly, English newspapers address a more disparate audience than, say, a Gujarati or Tamil newspaper does. The geographical spread, the levels of exposure, the varieties of educational background and professions, the levels of cultural and political interests are much wider in the all-India readership of the English newspaper than any other medium. And, naturally, English communicates in a highly globalised vocabulary. This makes it difficult for the English newspaper to be as eloquent idiomatically as a regional language paper.

Secondly, English newspapers come from a longer tradition than most regional newspapers in India, with only very few exceptions like *Bombay Samachar*, a Gujarati newspaper which is 200 years old. English newspapers had a precedent in British-run media in India, and for decades after independence continued or tried to continue this tradition. This made our English newspapers less Indian in tone. Meaning they were more reserved and more formal.

Assistant editors, inexperienced individuals often from elite institutions and sometimes even from Oxbridge, were put in charge of or wrote on these organs' opinion pages.

Thirdly, because English newspapers attracted a disproportionately large part of advertising revenue, the content had to be such that it did not put off the elite and, in fact, catered to them. This elite had global exposure and did not see themselves as identifying purely with nativism.

For these reasons, English newspapers have always been edited socially to the left of the reader, meaning that on many issues the English newspaper editor in India was more liberal than her reader. Certainly, on social issues, this was the case.

There were exceptions to this but they were so few that they could be singled out as being very different. Girilal Jain, editor of *The Times of India*, who supported the campaign against Babri Masjid, was the most striking of these. In our time, it is the columnist Swapan Dasgupta. These individuals ploughed lonely furrows in the English press, till the arrival of Modi. The acceptability and legitimacy of Hindutva, meaning an explicitly anti-Muslim majoritarianism, is recent in English media.

This is a different position from what has historically been the case in the regional media. The local language had idiomatic connect with the reader and was more expressive. These papers, and particularly ones in the north, were also edited closer to the reader, meaning they were less liberal and more aligned to the conservatism of the broad readership. To illustrate this, let us look at a study done on the media in 2002 after the riots in Gujarat. After the violence, the Editors Guild of India sent three of its members to do a fact-finding mission report on the role of the media in the violence. I was one of the three along with Dileep Padgaonkar and B.G. Verghese, both senior newspaper editors. Our findings were published and released on 3 May 2002.[1]

This was perhaps the first time that many who read and viewed their news mainly in English saw what all of India began to see later with respect to reporting on Muslims. We interviewed Modi, all the major owner-editors of newspapers, bureaucrats, Vishwa Hindu Parishad (VHP) and RSS leaders, businessmen and members of civil society between 31 March and 6 April.

The report concluded that 'the role of sections of the Gujarati media, especially the *Gujarat Samachar* and more notably, *Sandesh* (the state's largest

---

[1] 'Rights and wrongs: Ordeal by fire in the killing fields of Gujarat', Aakar Patel, Dileep Padgaonkar, B.G. Verghese, 2002, Editors Guild of India

and second largest newspapers), was provocative, irresponsible and blatantly violative of all accepted norms of media ethics. This cannot be lightly passed over.'

Here is some of what the fact-finding report found:

Falgun Patel, owner-editor of *Sandesh*, said the English media had sided 'out and out' with the Muslims, but the Gujarat papers were 'pro-Hindu'. He said Hindus were not temperamentally prone to starting riots, but this time Hindu anger, irrespective of class, was inflamed by the incident at Godhra. Even Hindu women felt *'Theek hai, salon ko maaro'* (Good, kill the scoundrels). He asked of Muslims: 'Can a 20 per cent minority take the majority for a ride? There has to be a limit.'[2] He said that Muslims had thought that they could get away with anything, but when Modi took office a clear message had gone out to them.

When the Guild members asked Patel how collective punishment was justified, he said the idea was 'to pressurise ordinary Muslims to put pressure on Muslim goons to behave'. After the way 'these Muslims' had behaved, *'Hinduism ke naam per hum kuch bhi karenge'* (We can also do anything in the name of Hinduism).

The Guild report said: 'An article in *Gujarat Samachar* had implied that former Congress MP Ehsan Jafri, who was brutally slain, "got what he deserved". Queried on this, the owner-editor Bahubali Shah said he stood by what the paper had written.' *Sandesh's* Patel dismissed Jafri's murder saying that he had a 'bad record'.

The Guild report said that the Gujarat government press notes reflected similar language: 'The phraseology most often used for the Godhra incident was "inhuman genocide", "inhuman carnage" or "massacre" while the subsequent riots were invariably described as "disturbances", and occasionally as "violent disturbances/incidents".'

One paper, *Madhyantar,* carried an eight-column commentary on its front page headlined: 'Muslims will have to prove that they are full Indians!' (*Mussalmanon-e puravo aapvo padshe ke te kharekhar Hindustani che!*).

This may appear shocking to the reader even today, but it is not recent or new. This was how large parts of the regional media had always operated. What Modi has done is to align almost all national media with the sentiment that the media in Gujarat had shown against Muslims. Modi has legitimised and given credibility to Hindutva, which expresses itself essentially in anti-minority terms. This has made it easier for the media to broadcast their material through its filter.

---

[2] Ibid.

Even the English media, which for the reasons we have seen above, was structurally not prone to being extreme, succumbed. The decline of print and the dominance of television news made this easier: it is easier to communicate emotion and anger through visuals and sound rather than through the written word. The regional media has shifted farther away from inclusion and is comfortable with its coverage of a Hindutva-minded Union and what it is doing to Indian society. The interesting thing is to examine the ease with which this has happened.

One reason is economic. The media space in India is funded primarily by advertising. The reader or viewer pays very little by way of subscription and our newspapers are the cheapest in the world. *The New York Times* and the *Guardian* cost the equivalent of Rs 100 or more per copy for about the same amount of newsprint material that goes into a copy of *The Times of India* or *Hindustan Times*, which charge their readers only Rs 5 or less (of which one-third goes to the distributor and vendor). Even in Pakistan, Sri Lanka and Bangladesh, newspapers cost three or four times more than papers in India.

How is it then possible for Indian newspapers to exist and be profitable? Advertising, of course, which is by far the largest source of revenue for media companies. And the largest advertiser in India is the Union government through its Directorate of Audio Visual Publicity (DAVP). In the year ending March 2017, the Modi government spent nearly Rs 1,300 crore on advertising and publicity, of which Rs 468 crore went to newspapers. This was down from Rs 508 crore the year before, though DAVP's budget went up by 8 per cent.[3]

Television and digital had got the rest. To put the sum in context, it is more than what is spent on advertising by all of India's telecom companies put together. When you see Swachh Bharat and PM Garib Kalyan Yojana ads on TV and in newspapers, this is paid for by taxpayer money, but it gives the government extraordinary leverage and control over the media.

When the Covid crisis broke and it was apparent that government revenues would be squeezed, Sonia Gandhi wrote to Modi suggesting that government advertising be put on hold. She was saying this both for economic and political reasons. She knows a lot about what that spending on media means to Modi. She pointed out that the government currently spends an average of Rs 1,250 crore per year (not including an equal or greater amount spent by PSUs and government companies), and that this amount could instead be used to alleviate the social and economic impact of Covid-19.

---

[3] 'DAVP spent nearly Rs 1300 crore on advertising and publicity', 20 July 2017, *Mint*

There is, therefore, a total of Rs 2,500 crore a year that Modi can give at his discretion to the media. It should not surprise us, therefore, that India's media has been unable to perform its essential function in the Modi years.

Severely hit by demonetisation[4] and the national lockdown,[5] the media not only stopped short of criticising Modi, it was in fact obliged to turn to him to save it. The government slashed media spending after Covid, but this was due to a shift away from mainstream media to more efficient digital. The share of print went from Rs 636 crore in 2018 to Rs 179 crore in 2022. Television's share fell from Rs 468 crore in 2018 to Rs 101 crore in 2022.[6]

The soft consumer economy meant advertising generally was low and the dependence on government money continued.

The share of print (newspapers and magazines) in the overall advertising pie across sectors is shrinking. In 2019, for the first time in history, digital advertising overtook print in India, and by a lot.[7] Digital got 27 per cent of advertising money spent in India, while print got 22 per cent.

Television remained number one at 43 per cent, but both TV and print shrank further in 2020 and conceded share to digital. The Covid crisis accelerated this process and newspapers are now going bust. They cannot afford, therefore, to antagonise their largest advertiser—the Modi government. This is why readers may have noticed that many newspapers have attempted to bring in 'balance' on their opinion pages by adding writers who promote the government or the Hindutva perspective.

After the lockdown had cut circulation and advertising numbers in half, the Indian Newspaper Society wrote to Modi asking for a 'stimulus package' to save India's print media. The proprietors wanted the government to: increase the spend on newspapers by 200 per cent, pay its old dues, increase the rate DAVP paid them by 50 per cent, remove the customs duty on newsprint and give them a two-year tax holiday.[8]

The industry had lost around Rs 12,500 crore in the eight months after the lockdown. The same newspapers which had to report on the Modi

---

[4] 'How demonetisation and GST impacted Indian media and entertainment industry', 20 December 2017, *The Financial Express*

[5] 'Entertainment and media to lose 20% in revenue: KPMG report', 1 October 2020, *The Economic Times*

[6] 'Govt spending less on ads every year', 2 August 2022, *Hindu BusinessLine*

[7] 'Digital surpasses print to become 2nd largest advertising medium after TV', 6 February 2020, *The Financial Express*

[8] 'Newspaper society seeks government stimulus package for sector', 12 December 2020, *The Economic Times*

government and were expected to be critical of it were going to Modi, cap in hand, asking to be saved. It should not surprise us that the media is called 'Godi' (a word meaning to be in the lap of, and of course, rhyming with Modi), because he is their patron and can do them damage.

It is true that this power has been in the hands of all governments of the recent past as Union advertising spends have gone up. But under Modi, the Union has used the advertising carrot also as a stick. Advertising money was denied to those publications which fell foul of the government for a variety of reasons including being 'disrespectful' and for reasons of 'inaccurate news reports'.[9] The Modi government actually brought the newspapers to heel.

India has more cable news channels than any other nation. In 2021, India had 178 functioning news channels. Tata Sky lists 143 of them (51 Hindi, 12 English, 8 Kannada, 7 Bengali, 8 Marathi, 15 Telugu, 14 Tamil, 9 Gujarati, 6 Odiya, 8 Malayalam, 5 Punjabi). All of these must kowtow or face punishment. Even the granting of a licence to broadcast depends on the approval of the government. It is withheld for those who are seen as not being pliant. Raghav Bahl, who set up Network 18 and is one of the most respected names in television news globally, for years did not receive a licence to set up a TV channel. It was kept pending by the Modi government till Bahl folded up his TV operation in April 2020.[10] This may help explain why media has shifted so effortlessly in television to become overtly majoritarian with no internal resistance.

There is another reason why media has become more majoritarian and this is a result of technology and the understanding of what the consumer wants and is comfortable with. The newspaper is a product created afresh every day, but its feedback loop is quite slow. Meaning that it is not easy for the editor to tell what the sentiment or mood of the reader is. One objective way is through the sale of copies. Say, a particular banner headline on Tuesday results in an increase over the number of copies sold on Monday. That would indicate that the reader is more interested in the content of that Tuesday story. However, the majority of newspaper sales is through subscription (home delivery). The sample size of retail sales through stands or vendors, where the headline actually matters because it is on display before the purchase is made, is low.

---

[9] 'DAVP penalised 51 newspapers for two months in Sept: Govt', 8 March 2018, *The Economic Times*

[10] 'I&B ministry had cited security report to reject Raghav Bahl's application for TV channel', 12 October 2018, *The Economic Times*

A longer-term way in which an editor can judge the mood and sentiment is through skewing the newspaper towards a particular ideology. Meaning, load the stories with opinion passing off as reportage (like TV news does). This may show results over the course of a few months or so. The growth in readership (usually measured annually by an industry body in a sort of census) or circulation will then indicate what the public mood is. Naturally, such an experiment could also backfire and readers might leave, because they prefer their papers non-ideological. Also, keep in mind the earlier point made about English newspapers being structurally less able to shed their centrism.

For these reasons, the feedback loop received by the newspaper editor is slow and it is not easy for her to change. This is not however the same for television news. TV news is measured through something called television rating points, commonly called TRPs. The measuring agency sets up a few thousand devices connected to set-top boxes in homes across the country. These record what was watched and when. The aggregated data is then extrapolated for the country and there is a rating that shows how many people are likely to have watched something.

This rating is made public weekly and so the feedback loop is much shorter. The TV news producer will have a good idea of whether story A, which was broadcast on Monday, was viewed more than story B on Tuesday. The content can then be sharpened and focused. Material that doesn't appear to interest the viewer can be discarded and only that which 'sells' retained. The danger, from the journalistic point of view, is that the content becomes skewed away from material that might be important but is serious and not entertaining. However, the benefit of more viewers is material from the revenue point of view—higher TRPs result in more advertising. For this reason, TV journalists are better judges of mood and sentiment than newspaper journalists, on the issues that they choose to cover. We can also conclude from this, with some dismay, that the bilious anti-Muslim material that is regularly produced and often concocted by Indian television is broadcast because it meets with viewer approval.

A third reason why TV has shifted—less important than the previous two, but as visible—is the success of its most shrill voices in the important time band of 8–11 p.m., which is when most advertising revenue comes in. The rest of the day doesn't really matter. In this space, *Republic*'s Arnab Goswami is the main figure in 'national' (i.e., English) news. He has imitators, but they are not as good as he is at what he does, and what he does is to run down the Opposition and attack Muslims and Pakistan. With this basic formula and plenty of theatrics, he has the highest ratings along with *Times Now*.

Let us see how these channels function to understand why it is that their content appears to many as so removed from reality. On 19 June 2020, *NDTV* correspondent Arvind Gunasekar tweeted the text of a note the government had given to journalists as 'talking points' after an all-party meeting on the Chinese intrusion. This was the meeting in which Modi claimed that there had been no intrusion by China.

Gunasekar said: 'This was circulated to media from PMO as "Govt Sources" even when the meeting was underway. Whoever has drafted this, didn't know that Naveen Patnaik didn't attend the all party meeting convened by PM Modi while Pinaki Misra represented BJD.'[11]

The talking points that the Modi government wanted the media to focus on in their headlines included:

- India stands solidly behind PM. Most leaders express their confidence in way Modi Government has handled the situation.
- Congress efforts to create wedges trashed by KCR, Naveen, Sikkim Kranti Morcha.

The channels obeyed the instructions. The primetime debate for *Times Now* a few hours later was headlined: 'All parties unite behind India but Sonia Gandhi won't slam China?'. The next night it was: 'Congress disarmed our braves first and now supports "tukde" ethos?' and 'PM Modi's strong message over India–China LAC standoff decoded'.

Republic TV's main debates by Goswami on 19 June were headlined: 'Unarmed with fact, Congress insults army'; 'Is there a "special relation" between Congress and China?' and 'People's movement against China gets bigger'.

The next day's debates were: 'PM sends a powerful message to the nation on LAC' and 'Cong traitor caught: "Break India" forces reveal their agenda'.

Not all channels followed the prime minister's office's (PMO's) line. *NDTV India*'s Ravish Kumar's debate was headlined, *'Desh ke liye jaan dene wale jawanon ko shhradhanjali* ('Tribute to India's martyrs). The next day it was, *'Pulwama ke samay jaisi parampara jari reh sakti thi'* (Pulwama's tradition could have been continued)—a reference to how differently the State had treated the 20 men killed by China against the 40 killed by a bomb in Pulwama in February 2019, whose coffins were received by Modi personally.

---

[11] 'For your eyes only: The 15-point note senior journos received on WhatsApp on how to interpret the India-China "mutual disengagement" for their audience', 7 July 2020, *Indian Journalism Review*

A few days later, the *Indian Journalism Review* published another note that the PMO had circulated to channels, instructing them on what to focus on. The note read:

Modi Effect loud and clear.

Taming expansionist China is a herculean task but the right strategies and actions can yield to (sic) outstanding results.

China hasn't pulled back. China has been pushed back, by a united nation led by a leader who led from the front.

Chinese had come to expect that India would be soft going by past precedent. However, within days, they got to know they're dealing with New India of Narendra Modi.

PM has made it clear that this is an India that knows to embrace friends as well as to embargo adversaries.

By taking decisive military, economic and strategic moves, PM Modi has pushed back China.

On China, PM Modi was clear since day 1—India's sovereignty will not be negotiable.

All options on the table were exercised.

PM Modi's visit to Leh seems to be the final nail in the coffin.

It showed the world India will fight and overcome any challenge to its strategic interests.

His speech to the army personnel has boosted the morale of the forces, who are more than ready to deliver a severe blow to any expansionist eyes.

In the past, people have seen how in Doklam also PM Modi showed remarkable patience and strength.

Even in case of the talks on One Belt, One Road initiative, PM Modi stood his ground and did not even send any representation worth talking about. This when other nations send high ranking representatives for the talks.

The notion of economic infallibility of China has received a tight slap with the PM's clarion call of Aatmanirbhar Bharat.

Etcetera.[12]

Times Now responded with debates headlined:

—'PM Modi punishes "Expansionist" China, doubters put to shame?'
—'China admits it was "pushed back", will army doubters surrender?'
—'China admits push back but Lobby continues to lie?'

---

[12] Ibid.

And Republic with:
—'Prime Minister leads from the front'
—'PM Modi's strong leadership pushes back China'
—'Ladakh reality check: Galwan victory a slap in Lobby's face'.

Note the alignment, including the specific use of phrases the government wants promoted—'expansionist' China, China 'pushed back', PM 'led from the front', and even 'slap'. In essence, the two largest English news channels in India speak in Modi's voice. They are told what to carry by the government, and they do so, with enthusiasm. It is instructive to examine what this is. What follows is the full list of the subjects on which the two channels had primetime debates over three months, from the beginning of May 2020 to the end of July. This was a period in which between 7 June and 27 June, the price of petrol/diesel was hiked every single day for 21 days.

On 16 June India announced that it had lost 20 soldiers, who were bludgeoned to death in hand to hand combat with the Chinese in Ladakh.

On 14 June, Bollywood actor Sushant Singh Rajput killed himself.

Daily Covid infections rose from 2,300 cases on May 1 to over 57,000 daily cases on July 31.

It was also a period in which it was announced that India would have its first economic recession in forty years. In such a period what were these channels were broadcasting every night?

Headlines on *Times Now* like:
—'Congress accuses NDA of exploiting migrants for train fares. Is Party faking fear?'
—'Rahul Gandhi lauds pictures of "Azad"'. Sacrifice of braves insulted?'
—'Handwara martyrs avenged. Dreaded terrorist killed but backers attack our braves?'
—'PoK on India weather map. Safest in PM Modi's hands?'
—'India united to fight pandemic but Lutyens spreads "Communal virus?'
—'PM-CMs crucial meet to put lifeline back on track but why Opposition red flags?'
—'PM Modi's motto to power self-reliance but Congress sees "No real relief"?'

and on *Republic* like:
—'Congress and Lobby politicise Aurangabad tragedy'
—'Rahul Gandhi aide to Nirav Modi's rescue?'
—'Congress in trillion-dollar controversy'
—'Are states blocking migrant movement?'
—'Mystery over Congress' China strategy'

—'Congress plays petty namecalling over 20 lakh crore package'

—'India leads global fight to expose China'

—'Migrants need trains, not lies and propaganda—Congress dumps migrants'

—'Proof demolishes Congress' '"1000 buses"' claim'

—'Priyanka Gandhi's bus sham falls apart, Congress loses plot'

(For the full list of *TimesNow* and *Republic*'s primetime headlines from May, June and July of 2020, see the Appendix.)

Total number of *Times Now* prime time debates in May, June and July which:

Criticised Opposition's actions: 33

Criticised Modi government's actions: 0

Were on economic recession: 0

Were on petrol and diesel prices: 0

Were on Sushant Singh Rajput's death: 4

In August, *Times Now* and the rest of the Godi media was instructed to focus on the actor's suicide and especially to spin stories about him being murdered. Apparently, this would serve several purposes: it would distract from the problems on the economic and national security front; it would put Bollywood's liberal establishment under pressure; and it would in some way help in the election in Bihar, where the dead actor Rajput was from. This directive led to a skew away from reality which is hard to wrap one's head around. *Times Now*'s headlines that month:

On Sushant Singh Rajput's death: 35

On economic recession: 0

On unemployment: 0

On Ladakh intrusion: 0

On petrol and diesel prices: 0

On Congress: 2

On 'Lobby': 1

On Muslims: 2

Total number of *Republic* primetime debates in May, June and July which:

Criticised Opposition's actions: 47

Criticised Modi government's actions: 0

Were on economic recession: 0

Were on petrol and diesel prices: 0

Were on Sushant Singh Rajput's death: 11

Republic also swivelled its debates in August towards the actor's suicide. The total number of *Republic* debates and specials that month was 45. Of these:

On Sushant Singh Rajput's death: 38
On economic recession: 0
On unemployment: 0
On Ladakh intrusion: 0
On petrol and diesel prices: 0
On Congress: 1
On 'Lobby': 1
On Muslims: 1
The number of *Republic* primetime headlines in August:
Criticising Modi government's actions: 0
Criticising Opposition's actions: 10

The word 'lobby' here is left undefined by the channels who use it, but it is used to attack 'liberals' (again undefined). 'Lobby' is used as a synonym for 'anti-national', 'tukde-tukde gang', 'Khan Market gang', 'urban naxal' and 'Lutyens mafia'. These terms are again all undefined but are generally understood to mean a group of elitists who from their 'air conditioned rooms' are conspiring against the nation.

Anything is sufficient to trigger an attack on the perfidy of this 'Lobby'. Two of the one-hour debates listed in the appendix from this period on *Republic* were over two of my tweets.

In a study published at the end of 2020, political scientist Christophe Jaffrelot and data analyst Vihang Jumle examined *Republic*'s content. They wrote: 'We studied all prime-time debates held since the channel was launched in May 2017, until April 2020, when we began the study—1,779 in all. Our conclusion was clear: *Republic TV*'s debates have been consistently biased in favour of the Modi government and its policies, as well as the ideology of the BJP. What's worse, these debates have rarely featured some of the most pressing issues that impact Indians, such as the state of the economy, education or health. Instead, they have consisted mostly of attacks against the Opposition as well as any groups or persons that oppose the ruling government's ideology.

'Some figures are staggering, if unsurprising. Nearly fifty per cent of Republic TV's political debates criticised the Opposition, but it has not conducted even one debate that we could classify as being in the Opposition's favour.'[13]

In January 2021, the Mumbai Police chargesheet in a fraud involving fixing the television ratings system included WhatsApp messages from

---

[13] 'One-man show', 15 December 2020, *The Caravan*

Arnab Goswami in which he appeared to know what the national security establishment was about to do.

On 23 February 2019, he told Partho Dasgupta, of the Broadcast Audience Research Council, which measures television ratings, that 'on another note something big will happen'.

Dasgupta asks, 'Dawood?' The conversation continued:

Arnab Goswami: 'No sir Pakistan. Something major will be done this time.'

Partho Dasgupta: 'Good.'

Partho Dasgupta: 'It's good for big man in this season.'

Partho Dasgupta: 'He will sweep polls then.'

Partho Dasgupta: 'Strike? Or bigger'

Arnab Goswami: 'Bigger than a normal strike. And also on the same time something major on Kashmir. On Pakistan the government is confident of striking in a way that people will be elated. Exact words used.'[14]

Three days later, on 26 February 2019, the Indian Air Force struck what it said was a Jaish-e-Mohammad training camp in the Pakistani town of Balakot.

This breach of national security will not surprise those who are themselves in journalism and have had the opportunity to observe what has happened to media in India under Modi. Most of it has joined the State and can be seen as a part of the government propaganda machinery. The purpose of the Godi media is to distract, attack Modi's opponents, laud him, and to divide society and discredit and vilify those who resist the division.

On the morning of 25 October 2018, four men from the Intelligence Bureau were caught spying on the CBI director, whom the Modi government was trying to get rid of.[15] The CBI was going through a period of turmoil caused by government meddling in the agency. Later the same day, the offices of Amnesty International India (where I was working) in Bengaluru were raided. The primetime debates that night were about the raid and not the fact that the Union government had been caught spying on the CBI chief.

The next morning I got a call from an anchor who said that, the previous night, the PMO had sent channels talking points on the Amnesty India raid and asked them to focus on it rather than the CBI. During the 'raid', I was

[14] 'Three days before Balakot strike, Arnab Goswami said "something big will happen" on WhatsApp chat', 16 January 2021, *Scroll.in*
[15] 'CBI feud: 4 men caught outside Alok Verma's house, handed over to police', 25 October 2018, *Business Standard*

questioned and my statement was recorded. When I asked for a copy of it after I'd signed it, I was told that it was confidential and would be given to me only if and when the case was formally prosecuted.

A few days later, my statement was read out during a two-hour debate on *Times Now*. When I asked the ED officers why they were playing these games, they were apologetic and said Arun Jaitley's office had given it to *Times Now*.

It used to be the case that the government mouthpieces in India were the State-run channels. Whichever party was in power, one remembers the Opposition of a few decades ago complaining that it was not given enough representation on Doordarshan. During the tenure of Hamid Ansari as vice president, *Rajya Sabha TV* (which was under the control of the vice-president, as chairperson of the Rajya Sabha) used to have open debates. In fact, it was more open than the privately owned channels, many of which had become shills for the government and more particularly for Modi personally. That freedom for *Rajya Sabha TV* has now, of course, gone. But State-run media is not required in India any longer when it is the free press that is doing the propaganda and the disinformation.

The feedback loop referred to earlier is even shorter for social media, and is close to instantaneous. What is popular, what is 'trending' and what tends to be circulated and 'go viral' is public information. This has advantages and the most obvious of these are the democratisation of media, with every individual having the ability to reach the world. There is also transparency, in the sense that everyone knows what is popular and therefore, at least to some extent, relevant. Social media is one of the great developments of our society in that respect.

The danger is also manifest. It is that as a society we discard what is boring and serious in favour of what is entertaining or emotive. The boring and serious material might be more important in the longer term and, in fact, even vital, but it gets discounted because we have 'voted' in some fashion for what is currently popular and 'viral'.

In societies where the basics are sorted, meaning that everyone has access to food, shelter, education, healthcare and rule of law, it may be less important for the serious material to be thus demoted. There is no need to discuss food, shelter, education, healthcare and rule of law if it is already available for the most part.

In societies where these conditions are not prevalent, such as India and our neighbourhood, it becomes dangerous for us to be distracted endlessly. The question is what can be done about this. The answer is nothing. The democratisation of social media carries with it the understanding that its users will be responsible. For this reason it is less regulated than print or television media, if indeed it has any regulation at all.

On Twitter, the government has aggressively sought to silence dissent. Of the total global legal demands on Twitter, 96 per cent came from only five countries: Japan, Russia, South Korea, Turkey and India.

Between July 2013 and July 2014, the Manmohan Singh government sent Twitter 13 legal demands for removal of content.

In the first six months of 2020, the Modi government sent Twitter 2,772 legal demands for removal of content or blocking accounts.[16]

On 11 June 2020, I got an email from Twitter saying my account had been 'withheld' because of a legal notice from the government. The offence was my retweeting a 31 May video from the *Colorado Times Recorder*. Their tweet described the video in these words: 'Incredible scene at Colorado's Capitol right now. Thousands of protesters are lying face down with their hands behind their backs chanting "I can't breathe." They're doing this for 9 mins. #copolitics #denverprotest #GeorgeFloyd'.

My retweet carried this text: 'We need protests like these. From Dalits and Muslims and Adivasis. And the poor. And women. World will notice. Protest is a craft.'

My neighbourhood police inspector registered a case accusing me of inciting violence.[17] The case was filed *suo motu*, which in India's quaint legalese means the State was itself the complainant. Of all the police stations in India, it was my neighbourhood one that took offence. Asked by the *BBC* why the case had been filed, Bengaluru's police commissioner said my tweet was dangerous because it instigated people to gather at a time when Covid protocols were in place. I wrote to Twitter asking for a copy of the legal order from the government so I could challenge it in court, but they did not reply.

After online protests, Twitter reinstated my account, partially at first, making it fully accessible to those outside India but preventing those in the country from accessing my homepage, and then, a few days later, completely. Three weeks later, on 2 July, a BJP legislator in Surat filed another case against me, this time a non-bailable offence, for a tweet recording the official history of the community Modi is from.[18]

---

[16] India Transparency Report, transparency.twitter.com
[17] 'Bengaluru cop files FIR against journalist Aakar Patel for "trying to incite" US-like protests', 5 June 2020, *ThePrint.in*
[18] 'FIR against Aakar Patel for tweets on Ghanchi community', 4 July 2020, *The Indian Express*

The suppression of voices is all one-sided: the attack on free speech in the Modi years is accompanied by hate speech flowing freely from the ruling party on Facebook, which lets the government get away with inciting murder in India.[19]

On various Facebook posts, BJP MLA T. Raja Singh has said, 'Rohingya Muslim immigrants should be shot', has called Muslims traitors and threatened to raze mosques. Facebook monitored his account and, in March 2020, concluded that Singh had not only violated the company's hate-speech rules but qualified as dangerous, a designation that takes into account a person's off-platform activities.

'Given India's history of communal violence and recent religious tensions his rhetoric could lead to real-world violence, and he should be permanently banned from the company's platforms world-wide,' according to Facebook employees that the *Wall Street Journal* spoke to.[20]

However, Singh remained active because Facebook management did not act after its India head for public policy, Ankhi Das, refused to apply its hate speech rules to BJP and RSS leaders.[21] Das was Facebook's lobbyist in India and, according to the current and former employees the *Wall Street Journal* interviewed, she told her company that acting against the BJP 'would damage the company's business prospects in the country, Facebook's biggest global market by number of users'.

Singh's Facebook page said Muslims who killed cows should be slaughtered. He posted a photo of himself with a drawn sword alongside text declaring that Hindus' existence depends on taking vigilante action against Muslims. Facebook looked away from this because if it acted against the BJP, it feared the Modi government would punish it.[22]

The Modi government had significant leverage over Facebook which it did not hesitate to use. Being banned in China, Facebook felt it had to succeed in India and chose it as the market in which to introduce payments, encryption and initiatives that Mark Zuckerberg has said will keep the company occupied for the next decade, the report said. In June 2020, Facebook announced it would invest $5.7 billion in Jio, the Ambani-owned telecom company. This agreement had come after the government put hurdles in Facebook's path.

---

[19] 'Facebook's Hate-Speech Rules Collide With Indian Politics', 14 August 2020, *Wall Street Journal*

[20] Ibid

[21] Ibid

[22] Ibid

Facebook's proposal to provide a free telecommunications service called 'Free Basics' was blocked by the Modi government in 2016 and its plan to launch WhatsApp payments nationwide had been stalled for two years as it awaited government approvals, the *Wall Street Journal* report said.

Current and former Facebook employees told the US daily that Das's intervention on behalf of Singh was part of a 'broader pattern of favoritism by Facebook toward the Bharatiya Janata Party and Hindu hard-liners'.

Whether social media or mainstream media, the control of Modi and the BJP over opinion and information is overwhelming. And this is unlikely to be reversed in the near future due to a particular phenomenon unfolding in the print media.

A long-term media trend has become sharper and more pronounced in the Modi era, and that is the death of the newspaper. The withering away of its revenues both through the erosion of marketshare as well as the contraction in advertising and marketing budgets in India's recession has begun killing off papers. They would, of course, have died in any case over time because there is no longer any sustainable print model in the medium term, but the Modi economy has accelerated the pace.

When the pandemic unfolded in March 2020, and as it began to become clear that the economy would not revive but get worse after Covid, media businesses began shutting down permanently.

Publications that suspended print operations included *Outlook, Hamara Mahanagar, Forbes* and *Andhra Bhoomi* in March, *Star of Mysore* and *Nai Duniya Urdu* in April, *The Times of India* editions in Malabar and Kochi up-country and the *Telegraph*'s Northeast and Jharkhand editions in May, *Sakal Times* and *Gomantak Times* in June, *The Economic Times* (Gujarati) in July, *Mail Today* in August, and *Mumbai Mirror* and *Pune Mirror* in December.[23]

It may seem that there is nothing really special about these closures. Usually other companies come up where previous ones have failed and that is the law of a healthy business environment. That is not the case here, because there are no longer any investments in print, which is a sunset business globally. The other thing that could mitigate this is that other forms of media can take their stead, for instance, television news or online publications.

Actually, they cannot. Print media, especially newspapers, have an asset that only they possess, and that is the beat reporter—the individual whose job it is to daily track one subject, whether it is the municipal corporation, the magistrate's court, the secretariat, health, education, crime and so on. There

---

[23] Compiled at medium.com/@Cyril_Sam

are thousands of these individuals around the country (the last newspaper I worked at had 300 in Gujarat alone).

These reporters are a newspaper phenomenon and do not exist in television because their material is not visual. Television is a medium of 'debate', and not reportage. It doesn't make economic sense for TV channels to deploy large numbers of reporters who cannot produce visual material or who produce visual material that is mundane, such as an interview with the education secretary, municipal officer or the public prosecutor. This is why TV has few of these reporters and these beats, and mostly only print does. Their output is the mainstay of news in the country. It is what keeps scrutiny of the government going.

Most television 'breaking news' is secondary and taken either from material already published in newspapers or by wire agencies like the Press Trust of India. The death of newspapers will end both the information stream currently available to citizens and it will end scrutiny of the government. Websites cannot fill the gap because they do not have the economics that print has. There is not a single digital publication anywhere in the world with the number of reporters that a large Indian newspaper of any language has.

As newspapers go under, we will lose the largest, most widespread, most valuable and most reliable source of our information. We will be left with a social media that is controlled by corporations like Facebook that have no compunction in contributing to the damage caused by majoritarianism, and we will of course continue to have the TV 'debates'.

The last part of this sorry story is the conduct of the media's own institutions. The Editors Guild, as we have seen earlier, was interested deeply in the functioning of the media, especially during episodes like the Gujarat riots. It was eager to engage with the State to protect the interests of a free media. The Editors Guild was founded in 1978, its website says, with the 'twin objectives of protecting press freedom and for raising the standards of editorial leadership of newspapers and magazines'. It does neither today. Unlike the Guild in 2002, the current Guild's membership is unwilling to antagonise the Modi government and it openly advertises the case that this is so. Its Twitter handle says that the Guild is 'not a watchdog, but a conscience keeper'. It is not clear what a conscience is and how it is kept.

The reality is that India's media needs a watchdog to ensure that the government does not abuse press freedom. India has one of the worst records of any democratic nation on this front. Journalists are regularly killed (six in 2018 alone), assaulted and arrested and jailed without charge, often in preventive detention.

Reporters Sans Frontiers (RSF) says that 'ever since the general elections of 2019, won overwhelmingly by Modi's BJP, pressure on the media to toe the Hindu nationalist government's line has increased'.[24] The RSF says that 'those who espouse Hindutva, the ideology that gave rise to Hindu nationalism, are trying to purge all manifestations of "anti-national" thought from the national debate. The coordinated hate campaigns waged on social networks against journalists who dare to speak or write about subjects that annoy Hindutva followers are alarming and include calls for the journalists concerned to be murdered. The campaigns are particularly virulent when the targets are women. Criminal prosecutions are meanwhile often used to gag journalists critical of the authorities, with some prosecutors invoking Section 124a of the penal code, under which "sedition" is punishable by life imprisonment.'

Media outlets that want to cover India freely faced shutdown and harassment under Modi. *The New York Times* reported[25] what happened in one such case—the Malalayam channel *Media One* was taken off air for its coverage of the Delhi riots.

The Ministry of Information and Broadcasting order said that the channel 'questions RSS and alleges Delhi Police inaction', 'seems to be critical towards Delhi Police and RSS' and focusses on the 'vandalism of CAA supporters'—meaning those who were supporting the government on the Citizenship (Amendment) Act.[26]

The *New York Times* report said that Modi 'has tried to control the country's news media, especially the airwaves, like no other prime minister in decades' and that 'Modi has shrewdly cultivated the media to build a cult of personality that portrays him as the nation's selfless saviour'.

The report added: 'At the same time, senior government officials have pressed news outlets—berating editors, cutting off advertising, ordering tax investigations—to ignore the uglier side of his party's campaign to transform India from a tolerant, religiously diverse country into an assertively Hindu one. With the coronavirus pandemic, the Modi government has gotten more blatant in its attempt to control coverage and, as with other difficult stories, some Indian news executives seem willing to go along.'

The Modi government and the BJP filed criminal cases to intimidate those voices in the media who did not succumb to the lure of his godi. Attacks

---

[24] 'Modi tightens his grip on the media', *RSF*, https://rsf.org/en/india
[25] 'Under Modi, India's press is not so free anymore', 2 April 2020, *The New York Times*
[26] 'In Backing Kapil Mishra, RSS Shows Riot Hand', 8 March 2020, *TheWire.in*

on *The Wire*'s Siddharth Varadarajan,[27] *Scroll*,[28] *The Caravan*, the anchor and columnist Rajdeep Sardesai[29] and a 100-hour ED 'raid' against *NewsClick*[30] were in keeping with the pattern. Many of India's best journalists gave up. Harassed by the government for years, Prannoy Roy sold his stake in NDTV to Gautam Adani and resigned from the board of the company he founded, in December 2022.[31]

Raghav Bahl also sold his company to Adani in March 2023.[32] His company and home had been raided and under attack for years by the Union government's agencies.[33]

We looked at three reasons—the feedback loop, the economic and regulatory stranglehold the Modi government holds over proprietors and the decay and the success of the angry primetime format—why the national media has shifted from being or at least attempting to being balanced to becoming fully deranged. There is a fourth reason, and it is Modi's dominance of national politics.

Modi's popularity, his open bigotry and his willingness to communicate his prejudice made it easy for the media to make the transition. What was acceptable to voters must surely be good and fit for print and broadcast.

Thus the most dominant forms of media in India became those that were the most bigoted. Journalists and anchors were willing to ascribe almost anything to Muslims and their perfidy. The later finding that the reckless accusations, as in the case of the spread of Covid, were, in fact, totally false and based on falsehood did not produce correction or apology. More demonisation was always required and was always delivered.

The damage that has been done to Indian society and its polity is permanent. And Modi's performance on major issues remains mostly unexamined.

---

[27] 'Yogi Adityanath vs Siddharth Varadarajan: Why were two FIRs filed against The Wire by UP police?', 13 April 2020, *Free Press Journal*

[28] 'Scroll FIR latest in cases against Indian journalists', 18 June 2020, *Article-14.com*

[29] 'Indian journalists accused of sedition for farmer protest reports', 1 February 2021, *Al Jazeera*

[30] 'Enforcement Directorate conducts raids on NewsClick office, officials' residences', 9 February 2021, *TheWire.in*

[31] 'NDTV founders, Prannoy and Radhika Roy, resign from board after Gautam Adani takes control', 30 December 2022, *Business Today*

[32] 'Gautam Adani acquires 49% in Quintillion Business Media for Rs 48 crore', 28 March 2023, *Indian Express*

[33] 'Tax raids on Quint founder Raghav Bahl's Noida home, office', 11 October 2018, *Hindustan Times*

3

MODINOMICS

In 2020–21, India managed to go into its first recession in four decades.[1] The per capita GDP of India in dollar terms went below Bangladesh for the first time. Two years, in fact most likely three years of economic growth, was wiped out by the weakness of the economy and an 'external' shock supplied by the Modi government. This was the lockdown, the harshest in the world,[2] that knocked off, according to official data, a quarter of GDP from the April–June 2020 period and hobbled an economy already limping at 3 per cent growth.

This is the story of how India got there.

Let us go back to the beginning to understand the inanity that was the root cause.

Part 1: Moditva

A book called *Moditva* was released by the BJP president Rajnath Singh during the closing days of the campaign for the 2014 election. Opinion polls had shown that the BJP would win and this work introduced India to Modi, the thinker and administrator.

The book's full name is *Moditva: The Idea Behind the Man*, and it lists the fourteen things that apparently underpin Modi's worldview and economics. In it, Modi's economic advisor Bibek Debroy says: 'What does Moditva or Modinomics mean? Straddling fourteen themes, this compilation seeks to pin down a term Modi has used, explains what NaMo intends and extrapolates this into meaningful solutions. People are hasty in criticising and

---

[1] 'India in recession after 41 years', 21 January 2021, *Business Today*
[2] 'India implements strictest lockdown in the world, lags in testing: Expert', 10 April 2020, *India Today*

labelling Moditva, without bothering to find out. Unless one suffers from pre-conceived biases, here is one means of finding out.'[3]

Given this endorsement, it is perhaps fair to assume that this work can give us the insights we need to understand whatever Modinomics is. The fourteen themes are laid out and defined, and then what are called 'Modi's solutions' are given. They are:

Moditva 1: Secularism means India first.

Definition: Appeasement of any community at the cost of another endangers the very social fabric of India.

Modi's solution: For every citizen their primary identity must be their nationality.

Moditva 2: Minimum government, maximum governance.

Definition: Citizens should also be a part of governance.

Modi's solution: Government should not downsize but be of right size.

Moditva 3: Government has no business to be in business.

Definition: Government should be an enabler for businesses to flourish.

Modi's solution: Government should not engage in those activities that the private sector can perform more efficiently.

Moditva 4: Co-operative, not coercive federalism for a strong republic.

Definition: Decentralisation of power but not equal sharing of responsibility.

Modi's solution: Centre–State relation should not be one of subjugation but collaboration.

Moditva 5: Development politics over vote-bank politics.

Definition: Division of electorate on caste and religion makes them vote on sectarian considerations.

Modi's solution: Politics of development over divisiveness.

Moditva 6: *Aatma gaanv ki, suvidha sheher ki* (The soul of a village and the conveniences of a city).

Definition: Develop villages but preserve and nurture their essence.

Modi's solution: Build Rurban centres and Rurban clusters.

Moditva 7: Tourism unites, terrorism divides.

Definition: A majority of people gravitate towards terrorism due to compulsion rather than choice; on the other hand, tourism ushers in prosperity.

---

[3] *Moditva: The Idea Behind the Man*, 2014, Navbharat Sahitya Mandir

Modi's solution: If more people go to Kashmir than Switzerland, it would weaken the impact of militant forces.

Moditva 8: Per drop more crop.

Definition: Higher agricultural productivity with less water.

Modi's solution: Increase research in agricultural activity and promote 'smart farming' techniques.

Moditva 9: Farm to fibre, fibre to factory, factory to fashion, fashion to foreign.

Definition: Capture global markets by integrating agriculture, industry and services.

Modi's solution: Stable and favourable policy regime.

Moditva 10: From a nation of snake charmers to mouse charmers.

Definition: Change India's stereotyped image of snake charmers, rich maharajas and very poor people.

Modi's solution: Use information technology to enhance India's standing.

Moditva 11: Take the university outside the campus.

Definition: India's focus has only been on a few institutions of higher learning.

Modi's solution: Use information technology to link villages to universities.

Moditva 12: *Pehle sauchalaya, phir devalaya.*

Definition: Toilets first, temples later.

Modi's solution: While lakhs are spent on building temples, a majority of people have no money to build toilets.

Moditva 13: Economy with mass production by the masses.

Definition: Thrust on mass production creates several skilled jobs.

Modi's solution: Government must expand industrial workforce.

Moditva 14: People public private partnership.

Definition: Add a fourth P to Public Private Partnerships.

Modi's solution: NGOs and local communities must do a social audit of development projects.

What connected these fourteen and emerged as some sort of unified theory worthy of the name Moditva or, as Debroy says, Modinomics? What was 'the idea behind the man'?

This is not easy to say because there is no clear thrust and many of these are bland statements and truisms that nobody could object to. Some, like number 7 ('tourism unites, terrorism divides'), make less sense than others. Though this booklet, and its list in particular, purported to be a sort of unification of what Modi intended, the list did not make clear what the redefined role of the State was. Where was the thought or idea powerful enough to merit the coinage of 'Moditva' or 'Modinomics'?

Perhaps the work was incomplete (half the booklet comprises full-page pictures of Modi striking poses) and, at the function to release it, Debroy added some other things he felt missing, such as decentralisation, rule of law and empowering the bureaucracy. Again, all unobjectionable. BJP MP Subramanian Swamy also spoke at the book's release and said Moditva was the practical realisation of the message in four speeches made by BJP/Jana Sangh leader Deendayal Upadhyaya, collectively called 'Integral Humanism'. And this message was that 'material progress must harmonise with spiritual development'.[4] This sounds more interesting but again does not give us much insight into Modi's economic outlook.

The Moditva work was originally written in Gujarati and Hindi and its title in Gujarati is *Moditva: Vikas Ane Aashavadno Mulmantra*, meaning the mantra for development and optimism. This is a more accurate representation of the book's contents.

The fact is that Moditva and Modinomics has never been defined by Modi himself through any written work. We are left with a series of mantras offered as acronyms and alliterations (like Moditvas 9 and 14), through which he has on several occasions pronounced his ideas.

He does appear to spend a lot of time thinking up and polishing acronyms and alliterations. Here are some examples of things Modi has said.

5 Ts—Talent, Tradition, Tourism, Trade, Technology

3 Ss—Speed, Skill, Scale

3 Ss—Speed, Simplicity, Service

5 Is—Intent, Inclusion, Investment, Infrastructure, Innovation

3 Ps—People, Planet, Profits

3 Is—Incentives, Imagination and Institution-building

4 Ps—People Private Public Partnership

3 Ds—Democracy, Demography, Demand

3 Ds—Democracy, Discipline, Decisiveness

4 Ds—Democracy, Demography, Decisiveness, Demand

3 Es—Enterprises, Earning, Empowerment

4 Rs—Recognition, Recapitalisation, Resolution and Reform

3 Ns—Nav Arjan (new revenues), Nav Manak (new norms), Nav Sanrachna (new structures)

---

[4] 'Moditva—The Idea Behind the Man', 25 February 2014, BJP YouTube channel

EPI: Every Person is Important

ART: Accountability, Responsibility, Transparency

SMART: Strict and Sensitive, Modern and Mobile, Alert and Accountable, Reliable and Responsive, Techno-savvy and Trained police force

FUTURE: Farmer, Underprivileged, Transparency, Technology upgradation, Urban rejuvenation, Rural development, Employment, Entrepreneurship

FDI: First Develop India (mantra of 'Make in India')

FDI: Foreign Destructive Ideology (on singer Rihanna and activist Greta Thunberg's tweets during the farmers' agitation in late 2020)

ABCD: Avoid, Bypass, Confuse, Delay (on the bureaucracy)

ROAD: Responsibility, Ownership, Accountablity, Discipline

GST: Good and Simple Tax

IT + IT = IT: Indian Talent + Information Technology = India Tomorrow

FAST: Fisheries and Fertilisers; Agriculture and Ayurveda; Skill development and Social justice; Tourism and Technology (on 'fast' development of Kerala during the state election campaign of 2021)

BEST: Business hub, Education hub, Spiritual hub, Tourism hub (on 'best' development of Puducherry during the election campaign of 2021)

Then there is Modi's need to craft the names of various schemes to make their short forms acronyms. Such as:

USTTAD: Upgrading Skills and Training in Traditional Arts/Crafts for Development (for artisans from minority communities)

AMRUT: Atal Mission for Rejuvenation and Urban Transformation

AMRIT: Affordable Medicines and Reliable Implants for Treatment

HRIDAY: Heritage Development and Augmentation Yojana

PRAGATI: Pro-Active Governance and Timely Implementation

PM CARES: Prime Minister's Citizen Assistance and Relief in Emergency Situations

PM AASHA: Pradhan Mantri Annadaata Aay SanraksHan Abhiyan (subsidies to farmers for pulses)

PM KISAN: Pradhan Mantri KIsan Samman Nidhi

PM-DevINE: Prime Minister's Development Initiative for North East Region

PM-SHRI: Pradhan Mantri Schools For Rising India

PM-PRANAM: PM Promotion of Alternate Nutrients for Agriculture Management Yojana

PM VIKAS: Pradhan Mantri Vishwakarma Kaushal Samman
CHAMAN: Co-ordinated Horticultural Assessment and Management using geoinformatics
UDAY: Ujjwal DISCOM Assurance Yojana
UDAY: Utkrisht Double-Decker Air-conditioned Yatri express
URJA: Urban Jyoti Abhiyaan
UDAN: Ude Desh ka Aam Naagrik (regional airports)
NITI: National Institution for Transforming India (replacement for Planning Commission)
NIDHI: National Initiative for Developing and Harnessing Innovations
NARI: Nutri-sensitive Agricultural Resources and Innovations (on better nutrition for women)
VAIBHAV: Vaishvik Bhartiya Vaigyanik (a summit for Indian scientists)
GOBAR: Galvanising Organic Bio Resources
SUTRA-PIC: Scientific Utilisation Through Research Augmentation Prime Products from Indigenous Cows
SVAROP: Scientific Validation And Research On Panchgavya (mix of milk, cow faeces, urine, curd and ghee)
ASPIRE: A Scheme for Promotion of Innovation, Rural industry and Entrepreneurship
TOP: Tomato Onion Potato
CO-WIN: Winning Over COVID-19
VATICA: Value Addition and Technology Incubation Centres in Agriculture
RISE: Revitalising Infrastructure and Systems in Education
LaQshya: Labour room Quality improvement initiative guideline
MUDRA: Micro Units Development and Refinance Agency
MITRA: Mega Integrated Textile Region and Apparel Park
DARPAN: Digital Advancement of Rural Post Office for a New India
DIPAM: Department of Investment and Public Asset Management
DEEP: Discovery of Efficient Electricity Price (portal for e-bidding on electricity)
MERIT: Merit order despatch of Electricity for Rejuvenation of Income and Transparency (portal for electricity generation by states)
MANAS: Maulana Azad National Academy for Skills
DISHA: Digital Saksharta Abhiyan (literacy mission)

DIKSHA: Digital Infrastructure for Knowledge Sharing (teacher-training)

eNAM: Electronic National Agricultural Market

PACE: Project Appraisals and Continuing Enhancements (monitoring highway construction)

AIM: Atal Innovation Mission

SMART: Specially Modified Aesthetic Refreshing Travel (railway coaches)

SOLVE: System for Online Vigilance clearance Enquiries (appointments in central public sector enterprises)

SAUBHAGYA: Sahaj Bijli Har Ghar Yojana

SUPREMO: Single User Platform Related to Employees Online

ARYA: Attracting and Retaining Rural Youths in Agriculture

BHIM: Bharat Interface for Money

MAA: Mothers' Absolute Affection (promoting breast-feeding)

SHAKTI: Scheme for Harnessing and Allocating Koyla Transparently in India (coal allocation)

PRASAD: Pilgrimage Rejuvenation and Spirituality Augmentation Drive

PAHAL: Pratyaksha Hastaantarit Laabh (direct benefit transfer for LPG subsidy)

SWAYAM: Study Webs of Active-Learning for Young Aspiring Minds (free online courses)

SAMAVAY: Skill Assessment Matrix for Vocational Advancement of Youth

SWIFT: Single Window Interface for Facilitating Trade

BAPU: Biometrically Authenticated Physical Update

SWADES: Skilled Workers Arrival Database for Employment Support

SETU: Self-Employment and Talent Utilisation (support to start-ups)

SRESTHA: Special Railway Establishment for Strategic Technology & Holistic Advancement

PM SHRI: PM Schools for Rising India

NIPUN Bharat: National Initiative for Proficiency in Reading with Understanding and Numeracy

NAVIC: Navigation with Indian Constellation (GPS system)

IMPRINT: Impacting Research Innovation and Technology

SVAMITVA: Survey of Villages And Mapping with Improvised Technology in Village Areas (ID cards for property)

KSHAMTA: Knowledge Systems and Homestead Agriculture Management in Tribal Areas

MUSK: Madhyamik and Uchchtar Shiksha Kosh (education corpus)

SPREE: Scheme for Promoting Registration of Employers and Employees

GIAN: Global Initiative of Academic Networks

GARV: Grameen Vidyutikaran (rural electrification)

HOPE: Harmony, Opportunity, People's participation, Equality (aim of Indian Constitution)

TIES: Trade Infrastructure for Export Scheme

TARANG: Transmission App for Real time monitoring and Growth

SEVA: Saral Eindhan Vitaran Application (coal dispatch)

SAMPADA: Supplement Agriculture Modernise Processing And Decrease Agriwaste

SAUNI: Saurashtra Narmada Avtaran Irrigation Yojana (Sauni means 'belonging to all' in Gujarati)

SANKALP: Skill Acquisition and Knowledge Awareness for Livelihood Promotion programme

UJALA: Unnat Jyoti by Affordable LEDs for All

SHAGUN: Shala Gunvatta (monitoring Sarva Shiksha Abhiyan)

STRIVE: Skill strengthening for Industrial Value Enhancement

SATH: Sustainable Action for Transforming Human capital

SPICE: Simplified Proforma for Incorporating Company Electronically

SAMADHAN: Smart leadership, Aggressive strategy, Motivation and training, Actionable intelligence, Dashboard-based KPIs and KRAs, Harnessing technology, Action plan for each theatre, No access to financing (strategy to counter Maoists)

HELP: Hydrocarbon Exploration and Licensing Policy

Also Modi often communicates foreign policy initiatives through his coinages:

B2B: Bharat to Bhutan

INCH to MILES: India–China towards a Millennium of Exceptional Synergy

HIT: Highways, Informationways, Transmissionways (on Nepal relations)

HEALTH: Healthcare cooperation, Economic cooperation, Alternative energy, Literature and culture, Terrorism-free society and Humanitarian cooperation (Modi's mantra for Shanghai Cooperation Organisation)

JAI: Japan–America–India relationship
SAGAR: Security and Growth for All in the Region
STRENGTH: Spirituality, Tradition, trade and technology, Relationship, Entertainment, Nature conservation, Games, Tourism and Health and healing (on people-to-people contact with China)
He also spends time coming up with coinages on his political opponents:
RSVP: Rahul, Sonia, Vadra, Priyanka
ABCD: Adarsh, Bofors, Coal, Damaad (son-in-law)
3 AKs: AK 47, A.K. Antony and AK-49 Arvind Kejriwal ('Admired in Pakistan')
SABKA: Samajwadi Party, Bahujan Samaj Party, Congress
SCAM: Samajwadi Party, Congress, Akhilesh, Mayawati

It goes on, but this is perhaps sufficient to get an insight into the mindset at work. External affairs, domestic politics, grand strategy and major and minor projects of all sorts are sought to be pigeonholed and communicated through words and bite-sized phrases. They appear to be mantras, which will make a difference to the world they are set in. Like all magic incantations, they exist independently; no action other than uttering them is required to activate their powers.

There is an obsession with reduction and a fascination with the trivial. The names of pet schemes are phrased to fit some preconceived word and this is done in earnest across all ministries in the Union government. It appears that, at times, a word is thought up first and then the scheme named around it. Perhaps even the scheme itself and what it is meant to do is cobbled together after some name or word has struck Modi's fancy. What a scheme is called appears as important and perhaps more important that what is hoped to be achieved through it. This was not new, and Chief Minister Modi delayed the release of a project because a suitable name had not been coined.[5]

So why do this 'A for Apple' form of governance? It is difficult to say, but clearly the wordplay seems to be important to Modi. To please him, the BJP coined and gifted him an acronym of his own on the third anniversary of the 2014 victory—MODI: Making of Developed India. Leaving aside the fact that this approach is juvenile and embarrassing, it is also not representative of anything coherent. This naming existed for its own sake. There was no Modinomics and there was no written strategy for how to get India to grow faster.

But post the 2014 election, Modi launched straight into action with schemes and names and dramatic interventions.

[5] 'Catchwords wrap Modi's plan in smart packages', 18 February 2004, *The Times of India*

Part 2: Abolishing India's Currency

'India remains a bright spot in the global economy,' the International Monetary Fund's (IMF) chief Christine Lagarde said in April 2016.[6] This would all change in a few months as Modi executed his first stroke, one that would gut the Indian economy and push millions into distress.

Demonetisation was the idea of a man with a diploma in mechanical engineering from Latur, a town in Maharashtra.[7] Anil Bokil runs an institution called ArthaKranti (economic revolution), and describes himself as an economic theorist. His thinking was: in a country like India where 70 per cent of the population survives on just Rs 150 per day, why do we need currency notes of more than Rs 100?

He revealed in an interview days after Modi abolished 86 per cent of India's currency how the prime minister had got the idea.[8] In July 2013, soon after Modi was declared the BJP's prime ministerial candidate, Bokil went to Ahmedabad with his colleagues and sought to make a presentation about an ArthaKranti proposal.

Modi gave Bokil ten minutes. 'By the time I was done, I realised that he had listened to me for ninety minutes. He said nothing after I had made my presentation,' Bokil said. This is not surprising. The idea that a simple, magical and transformational action could be executed by him would have transfixed Modi.

On the ArthaKranti website, the benefits of demonetisation which were conveyed to Modi at that meeting are listed, including: 'Terrorist and anti-national activities would be controlled', 'the motive for tax avoidance would be reduced', 'corruption would be minimised' and there would be a 'significant growth in employment'.[9] What's not to like?

But there are no details about any of this nor how demonetisation would be executed and its benefits achieved. There is no reference to or analysis of what the fallout could be. ArthaKranti also proposed withdrawing the entire taxation system in favour of a transaction tax, accompanied by a Rs 2,000 limit on cash transactions. Its ideas were reductive, simplistic and, apparently,

---

[6] 'Decisive action to secure durable growth; lecture by Christine Lagarde', 5 April 2016, imf.org

[7] 'Who is Anil Bokil? The man who suggested note ban to Modi', 8 November 2017, *The Financial Express*

[8] 'Meet Anil Bokil, the man who gave Narendra Modi the idea of demonetisation', 22 November 2016, *Mint*

[9] 'Proposal benefits', arthakranti.org

easy to implement. It was perfect for Modi, who picked out the single most dramatic element from this—demonetisation—and pushed it through.

In his speech announcing it on 8 November 2016, Modi said the problems of India were corruption, black money and terrorism. And strong steps would need to be taken against these and he would take them.[10]

He was doing this for the poor of the country and to empower them, he said, peppering his talk with anecdotal material. The common people of India were honest. An auto driver had recently returned a passenger's gold ornaments. Taxi drivers at their own expense drove to return items left behind. Shopkeepers called out to customers to ask them to return to take the extra money they had left behind. Indians were honest and yet India was corrupt, and so a powerful and decisive step was needed against corruption, black money and terrorism.

Had people ever thought about where the money for terrorism came from, Modi asked. It came from Pakistan's counterfeiting operations in India, which was proved by the frequent arrests.

He said the circulation of cash was linked to corruption and this was why Rs 500 and Rs 1,000 notes were between 80 per cent and 90 per cent of the total currency. He was cancelling them as legal tender in four hours, at midnight. That would mean that 'such notes currently in the hands of anti-national people would become worthless'.

Modi acknowledged that there would be some discomfort through this policy, but it would not be a problem. This was because, he said, ordinary citizens were enthusiastic about sacrifice and hardship for the country. He spoke of a poor widow giving up her LPG subsidy, a retired schoolteacher who gave some money from his pension to Swachh Bharat, an Adivasi woman who sold her goat to make a toilet and a soldier who contributed money to make his village clean.

In the war against corruption, black money, counterfeit notes and terrorism, people would be fine with 'a little difficulty and only for a few days', he said.

To ensure minimal distress, Modi said that people could deposit their Rs 500 and Rs 1,000 notes in the bank till 31 December. He asked those who could not do so to not worry because they had till 31 March 2017 to deposit their notes with the Reserve Bank of India's (RBI) offices. People could withdraw Rs 10,000 a day and Rs 20,000 a week for a limited period of time.

---

[10] 'Full text: PM Modi's 2016 demonetisation speech that shocked India', 8 November 2017, *Business Standard*

Strangely, he also announced the introduction of a Rs 2,000 note and a new Rs 500 note. Effectively, India replaced its Rs 1,000 note with a Rs 2,000 one. Any black money held in four Rs 500 notes could now be held as one note of Rs 2,000.[11] Modi's demonetisation exercise had all the eccentricity of the Bokil plan without any real change in high value currency notes as Bokil had envisaged.

No nation has fought corruption by abolishing its currency. It didn't work in India either. On Transparency International's Corruption Perceptions Index of 2015, India was ranked 76. In 2016, India fell to 79. In 2019, it fell further to 80. In 2021, it fell again to 86. Even the perception of corruption had not improved.

The total currency in circulation only a few months after demonetisation was already higher than it was in 2016. There was more cash in the system and at higher denomination.[12] 'Less cash', one of the post facto justifications, did not materialise. The other arguments also fell apart quickly, as the data showed.

Terrorism is not a problem of counterfeit notes. It is incredible that someone should think that about such a complex phenomenon. Modi referred to Pakistan's role, but fatalities in Kashmir rose after demonetisation—from 267 in 2016 to 357 the next year to 452 in 2018 and 283 in 2019. In 2020, they were 321. The lockdowns and resumption of internet lowered violence levels in 2021 (274) and 2022 (253), but they remained above the levels of 2011 to 2015. The most peaceful years in Kashmir in recent times before this were 2012 (121 fatalities) and 2013 (172 fatalities), both before demonetisation.[13] And the people being killed there are almost to a man locals. Counterfeit money has made no difference.

The prevalence and wide acceptance of black money is a problem of society and the fault doesn't lie in the size of the denomination. But this is how it was sold. The important point here is that Modi was naive enough to believe what he said on television to the country. That corruption, black money and terrorism resided in paper and could be combatted and ended with a strike of firmness.

---

[11] This Rs 2000 note was 'withdrawn' by the RBI in 2023, again without clarity on whether it would remain legal tender and leading to similar chaotic problems. See 'Shopkeepers in Dakshina Kannada refuse to accept ₹2,000 notes' 26 May 2023, *Times of India*

[12] 'Currency in circulation rises 22% in May over pre-demonetisation level', 26 June 2019, *The Economic Times*

[13] Datasheet—Jammu & Kashmir, satp.org

Modi had been specifically warned by the RBI—the body that actually had to demonetise the notes of currency its governor had guaranteed with his signature and was arm-twisted into doing so—that demonetisation was a mistake. Raghuram Rajan resigned as governor after having discussed and disapproved of this move. The new governor Urjit Patel was forced to accept it by Modi within weeks of taking office. He then refused to release the minutes of the meeting the RBI urgently held on 5.30 p.m. on 8 November (just before Modi's speech) to approve the unhinged move, citing national security and a 'threat to life'.[14]

When the minutes were finally leaked to the press two years later in November 2018, Patel quit and left the following month. The RBI minutes said it had been told by the government that:

- The economy had grown 30 per cent between 2011 and 2016 but the currency notes of higher denomination had grown at a much higher rate.
- That cash was the facilitator for black money.
- That counterfeit money of an estimated Rs 400 crore was present in the system.
- And, therefore, the Rs 500 and Rs 1,000 notes should be made invalid.

The RBI's response to the government was:

- That the economic growth referred to by the government was real while the rise in currency was nominal and not adjusted for inflation and 'hence this argument does not adequately support the recommendation' for demonetisation.
- That most black money was held as land or gold and not cash, and abolishing currency would have no effect on curbing black money.
- That demonetisation would have a negative impact on GDP.
- That Rs 400 crore in counterfeit currency was insignificant (only 0.02 per cent) compared to the total cash in circulation, which was Rs 18 lakh crore.

Having said all this, the RBI board nonetheless put its rubber stamp on Modi's idea. The reason why it fought to keep this capitulation secret is clear. It had done its job in pushing back and pointing out the flaws; it was now protecting Modi. That is why Urjit Patel shamefully claimed there was a national security reason why he could not reveal the minutes, when Right to Information (RTI) activists sought to access them.

---

[14] 'RBI cites threat to life, national security as Modi's note-ban mystery deepens', 12 January 2017, *Mint*

Of course, events proved that on every count the RBI had accurately predicted both the damage and the lack of benefit. What the RBI was hiding was the fact that Modi had ignored its concerns—all of which turned out to be true—and gone ahead anyway.

In India, the unorganised or informal sector (including agriculture) is about half the total economy and it operates almost entirely on cash. The scale and depth of the trauma inflicted on this sector and on India's poor can only be imagined. There was no preparation for it from Modi because that was mere detail and, therefore, not interesting or attention-worthy. The Cabinet itself did not know about the decision till a few minutes before the announcement, meaning that the departments run by the ministers did not know and did not prepare.[15]

Immediately, the shoddiness of the enterprise revealed itself, even in the metro cities. The sizes of the new currency notes were different from the old ones and no thought had been given to the problem this would create. ATMs had to be re-calibrated, delaying a return to normalcy, in some cases for many weeks, as technicians struggled to fix the problem machine by machine. Stories also emerged almost immediately about how the new notes had begun to be both counterfeited and hoarded as black money.[16]

On the first anniversary of demonetisation, the media reported a timeline of what had happened after Modi's announcement.

November 2016 saw long queues, a cash crunch and protests across the country. The RBI issued constantly changing guidelines on deposits, withdrawals and exchange of cash post demonetisation as it struggled to manage the chaos. The daily limit on cash withdrawals kept changing from Rs 4,000 a day to Rs 2,500 to Rs 2,000. Reports began to emerge of 'round-tripping'. Basically, bank employees would collect old notes, issue new ones, and then take the old ones out and bring them back to get more new notes.[17] Manmohan Singh said demonetisation was 'organised loot and legalised plunder' and that 'monumental mismanagement has taken place'.[18]

---

[15] 'Don't bring your phones: Modi's cabinet meet that took everyone by surprise', 10 November 2016, *Hindustan Times*

[16] 'Two arrested for printing, circulating fake ₹500 and ₹2000 notes in Delhi', 10 January 2017, PTI

[17] 'Rs 1.15 crore in demonetised notes stolen from Odisha bank', 21 November 2016, *Scroll.in*

[18] 'Demonetisation anniversary: A timeline of how note ban unfolded in the country', 8 November 2017, *The Indian Express*

By December 2016, incidents of starvation and deaths were reported from across India.[19] There were also reports of people dying while in queues in front of banks, waiting to get cash. The Supreme Court asked the Modi government why, even after a month of demonetisation, it had failed to provide the allowed limit of Rs 24,000 for bank withdrawals. Unusually for the court, it questioned Modi's competence, asking: 'Can you put what you had estimated when you took the decision to scrap Rs 500 and Rs 1,000 notes? Did you make any estimation at all? Was there a plan? Or, did you take the decision just like that? If you had thought notes worth Rs 10 lakh crore would come back to the banks, did you take steps to urgently put in that much of new currency back in circulation? Can you produce the Cabinet note before the decision was taken?'[20]

Chief Justice T.S. Thakur asked why most people were unable to receive their rationed amount of cash while others were getting lakhs in new currency.[21] This is when the role of bank managers involved in illegal activity emerged (rather than curbing it, demonetisation had provided another opportunity for corruption). The Supreme Court asked the Modi government whether demonetisation was constitutional, though it kicked the can down the road on deciding this and shamefully never got down to it.[22]

On 31 January 2017, the Economic Survey for 2016–17 said that demonetisation would reduce GDP growth by up to 0.5 per cent.[23] Modi's economic advisor Bibek Debroy had claimed that the exercise would not affect GDP growth.[24]

In February 2017, there were strikes across India. Banking operations came to a halt as employees demanded that the government bring more cash into the system, and also sought relief in their workload. GDP growth was found to have slowed during the October–December 2016 quarter.

---

[19] 'Demonetisation-induced unemployment is pushing some in Bundelkhand to the brink of starvation', 13 December 2016, *Scroll.in*

[20] 'Did you have a plan at all, Supreme Court asks govt about demonetisation move', 10 December 2016, *The Times of India*

[21] 'Supreme Court raps Modi govt over demonetisation, asks why hospitals not accepting old notes', 15 December 2016, *India.com*

[22] 'With no Constitution bench set up yet, challenges to demonetisation now an "academic exercise"', 5 January 2021, *ThePrint.in*

[23] 'Economic Survey 2016–17: Demonetisation's top 5 short term and long term effects', 31 January 2017, *The Financial Express*

[24] 'Bibek Debroy to *India Today*: Manmohan Singh has lot of experience in loot and plunder', 25 November 2016, *India Today*

In April 2017, after repeated appeals from the Opposition, the RBI agreed to submit the minutes of its meeting on demonetisation before a parliamentary panel, in a 'sealed cover'.

In June 2017, finance minister Arun Jaitley refused to accept that the sharp drop in GDP growth rate during the fourth quarter (it fell from 10.4 per cent in the first quarter to 6.1 per cent[25]) of 2016–17 was because of demonetisation.[26] The next month, Urjit Patel said the RBI was still counting demonetised notes and didn't know how much had been returned. Despite its best efforts to keep people from exchanging currency, it ultimately turned out that over 99 per cent of the cash came back.[27] This ended another myth about demonetisation. The government had spoken of how plenty of black money would not be returned to the RBI, which would then be struck off its books as a liability, producing a profit and a big dividend for the government (which owns the RBI).[28] This turned out to be entirely bogus as, despite creating hurdles for citizens returning money, almost all the cash came back.[29]

Three years after demonetisation, a report assessed the medium-term effects on the economy.[30]

Real Estate

The total number of developers in the top nine Indian cities shrunk by over 50 per cent by 2017–18. Three-quarters of Gurugram's builders were wiped out: from 82 firms in 2012, the number fell to 19 in 2018. In Noida, it fell from 41 firms to 11.

Small developers faced financial distress. Also, the lack of execution capability and over-supply of inventory played a key role in the downturn.

All major cities with significant potential for real estate development— Mumbai, Pune, Thane, Kolkata, Bengaluru and Hyderabad—saw a decline

---

[25] 'Demonetisation pulls down India GDP growth rate to 6.1% in Q4 2016–17', 1 June 2017, *Mint*

[26] 'The great GDP-demonetisation fight: NITI Aayog backs Arun Jaitley after Chidambaram raises doubts', 2 June 2017, *India Today*

[27] '99% of demonetised notes returned, says RBI report', 31 August 2017, *The Hindu*

[28] 'What about cash that doesn't return?', 23 November 2016, *The Hindu*

[29] '99.30% of demonetised money back in the system, says RBI report', 30 August 2017, PTI

[30] 'Demonetisation, 3 years on: A look at impact on key sectors of the economy', 8 November 2019, *Business Standard*

in the number of developers. Three years later, sales were still flat as demonetisation's long-term effects ate through the economy.[31]

Farm income and wages

Both farmers' incomes from crop cultivation as well as wages of farm labourers contracted in 2016–17 despite the above-normal monsoon season.

In a period of low supply of cash, input suppliers demanded higher prices. Demonetisation was carried out after the harvest of the kharif season entered the markets and when the entire rabi output was yet in the fields.

Factory investment

Investment in the country's factories contracted 10.3 per cent over 2016–17, showing their worst performance since 2002–03.

An unusual rise in imports in the quarters after demonetisation led to speculation that India's supply chains had been 'disrupted'—meaning firms had gone bankrupt and shut down. And so India was importing things it could no longer produce enough of.[32] No national poll captured the full effect of Modi's strike on Indians. But the Reserve Bank of India's Current Situations Index asks people if they were better off than a year ago. In December 2016, weeks after demonetisation, it began to decline. It remained negative after that, except for one month, April 2019, for four and a half years. For fifty-three months, Indians felt they were worse off than twelve months ago. In June 2021, the index fell to its all time low.[33] Even in March 2023, the majority of Indians said their general economic situation was worse off than a year before.

For a while, Modi could hide behind the lack of data. India's economy is monitored mainly through looking at the organised sector, and the damage to the unorganised half would not be seen except through long-term indicators in consumption.

These would come in time.

Part 3: Things Fall Apart

Modi's 2019 manifesto said he would 'work towards improving GDP share from manufacturing sector'. To that end, Modi launched the 'Make in

[31] 'Realty market sentiment falls to demonetisation levels, residential sales may dip further: Survey', 18 October 2019, *The Financial Express*

[32] 'Is a strong import surge behind Indian economy's slowdown?', 29 September 2017, *Mint*

[33] 'Consumer confidence hits all-time low: RBI report', 4 June 2021, *The Times of India*

India' scheme in September 2014; it was one of his first big launches, with a striking logo of a lion striding forward. An American firm was asked to make the logo, for which it charged Rs 11 crore.[34] The Make in India website says it 'aims to raise the contribution of the manufacturing sector to 25 per cent of the Gross Domestic Product by the year 2025 from its current 16%'. This was a classic Modi scheme: mostly logo and name and little actual strategy, detail or follow-up. The results were visible soon.

In 2019, according to the World Bank's data, instead of growing, the share of manufacturing in GDP fell to 13.6 per cent from 16 per cent.[35] It fell further in 2020. In the same period, Bangladesh's share of manufacturing[36] rose from 16 per cent to 19 per cent, and Vietnam's rose from 13 per cent to 16 per cent. So increase was possible, but it required thinking and application rather than mere announcement and spectacle, which made it difficult to be achieved under Modi.

Six years after Make in India was launched, data showed that industry's share of GDP in India was at a two-decade low, falling behind Sri Lanka.[37] The Modi government had managed to reduce manufacturing's share by 2.5 per cent over what it had been under Manmohan Singh.[38] Outside of its share of GDP, the manufacturing sector itself actually began to contract in the second quarter of 2018–19, having steadily fallen since demonetisation.[39] This was not acknowledged by Modi or the government. A study in May 2021 revealed that jobs in manufacturing had halved in the five years since 2016, down to 2.7 crore from 5.1 crore, and that more people were being employed in agriculture, the least productive part of the economy.[40]

Under Modi, the share of central-sector projects stalled/delayed stood at an average of 100 per cent for the atomic energy sector, 50 per cent for civil aviation and 45 per cent for coal. The UPA, maligned for being 'policy

[34] '"Make In India" logo designed by foreign firm, says RTI', 14 January 2016, *The Times of India*

[35] 'Manufacturing, value added (% of GDP)—India', data.worldbank.org

[36] 'Manufacturing, value added (% of GDP)—Bangladesh', data.worldbank.org

[37] 'Despite "Make-in-India" push, industry share in GDP hit 20-year low in 2019', 19 November 2020, *Business Standard*

[38] Ibid.

[39] 'Manufacturing contracts for first time in 2 yrs, pulls down GDP to 6-yr low', 29 November 2019, *Business Standard*

[40] 'CEDA-CMIE Bulletin: Manufacturing employment halves in 5 years', May 2021, Centre for Economic Data and Analysis, Ashoka University

paralysed', had lower figures of 71 per cent, 45 per cent and 44 per cent in comparison.[41]

The Modi government's manifestos, rhetoric and even intent diverged from reality after it became clear that the initiative had failed. Though the writing for Make in India was on the wall by 2018, a NITI Aayog document from that year says that the Modi government would double manufacturing's growth rate by 2022.[42] To understand this in its entirety, it is important to remember that 50 per cent of all manufacturing in India is part of the automobile sector, and both the Make in India strategy and this NITI document said growth here would be a special focus.

Let us examine what happened to the automobile industry in India under Modi.

The domestic sales of passenger automobiles in India fell from 30 lakh units in 2016–17 to 27 lakh units in 2019–20. This was before the Covid pandemic. The finance minister said that this was not a reflection on the economy or the Modi government, but consumer behaviour and the rise of ride-hailing apps.[43] The auto industry, unusually, pushed back to say this was not true.[44] In fact, ride-hailing apps have not affected other nations, including ones which have much higher sales per capita of automobiles. For instance, sales even in the world's most mature auto market, the US, have grown in the same period from 1.6 crore in 2016 to 1.7 crore in 2019. When Uber was launched in 2009, US automobile sales were only 1 crore a year.

The Uber/Ola explanation also does not account for the fall in the sales of commercial vehicles (down from 8 lakh units in 2017 to 7 lakh in 2019 to 5 lakh in 2021) or the decline in sales of two-wheelers (down from 2 crore in 2017 to 1.7 crore in 2019 and 1.5 crore in 2021). Across the automobile sector, domestic sales in 2019 were more or less the same as they were in 2014–15. 2020–21 was even worse.[45] Though much was made of the recovery in car sales, the average sales of the period from 2020–21 to 2022–23 was the same as it had been in 2016–17. The Society of Indian

[41] 'Why the Modi government's "Make in India" scheme failed to deliver what it promised', 26 March 2019, *Scroll.in*. Excerpt from *A Quantum Leap in the Wrong Direction?*, Rohit Azad, Shouvik Chakraborty, Srinivasan Ramani, Dipa Sinha (eds), Orient BlackSwan, 2019

[42] 'Strategy for New India@75', niti.gov.in

[43] 'On declining automobile sales, FM Nirmala Sitharaman says Ola, Uber one of the factors', 10 September 2019, *Outlook*

[44] 'Maruti differs with Nirmala Sitharaman, says Ola, Uber not big factor in auto crisis', 28 June 2020, *Hindustan Times*

[45] 'Automobile domestic sales trends', Society of Indian Automobile Manufacturers, siam.in

Automobile Manufacturers, assessing the period just before Covid, said the industry was in structural and long-term trouble.[46] Six years of growth in this sector, dominated by middle-class consumption, was wiped out during the Modi era. This was the result of the special focus brought to manufacturing.

The other area where high ambition, grand announcement and executive failure came together was in exports. Modi said his government would 'work towards doubling the total exports'.[47] The NITI document from 2018 says, 'Exports of goods and services combined should be increased from USD 478 billion in 2017–18 to USD 800 billion by 2022–23.' The focus will be, the document said, 'particularly in the production and exports of manufactured goods'.

Exports of goods in the financial year ending March 2014, two months before Modi took over, was $312 billion. The following year, exports fell to $310 billion. They fell again in 2015–16 to $260 billion. In 2019–20, they returned to where they were when Modi took over, to $314 billion. In 2020–21, they fell to $290 billion.[48] When the world opened up after Covid and global trade boomed, India's exports went up as well, hitting $419 billion in 2021–22. Immediately, victory was declared by the government,[49] even though exports would begin to deflate naturally as global trade cooled.[50]

There had been no growth for years when the announcement, again without a plan and lacking any real pathway for execution, was made about doubling exports.

In the decade under Manmohan Singh, exports had risen about 500 per cent from under $60 billion to over $300 billion. Elsewhere, Bangladesh had also grown its exports since 2014, powered by its garment exports, which were at $40 billion.[51] In the same period, India's garments exports fell from $18 billion to $16 billion and then to $15 billion in 2021. Garment or apparel manufacturing is important because large numbers of semi-skilled workers

---

[46] 'Auto sector facing long term, structural and deep slowdown, says automotive industry body', 28 January 2021, siam.in

[47] 'Modi wants to double India's share in world exports to 3.4%', 22 June 2018, *The Hindu BusinessLine*

[48] 'India's merchandise trade: Preliminary data for March 2021 released', 1 April 2021, Press Information Bureau

[49] 'India will achieve $2 trillion export target by 2030: Piyush Goyal', 16 October 2022, PTI

[50] 'India's exports decline by 8.8% to $33.88 billion in February 2023, trade deficit narrows', 23 March 2023, cnbctv18.com

[51] 'Indian Textile and Apparel Industry 2021', Annual Report, Apparel Export Promotion Council, aepcindia.com

are employed, especially women, who are comfortable in a workplace that is dominated by women. In the approximately 5,000 garment-manufacturing units in Bangladesh, 85 per cent of the employees are women. Even Vietnam exports more garments in dollar terms than India, which used to have a lead in this industry but has ceded it in recent years.

'The total export of textiles and apparel are expected to touch US$ 82 billion by 2021,' the Ministry of Commerce and Industry forecast through its think-tank.[52] In 2018–19, exports were a total of $36 billion ($20 billion in textiles and $16 billion in garments). They would remain at this level five years later.[53] In 2019–20, they fell to $34 billion and then fell again in 2020–21 to $29 billion. The drop in garment exports was 20 per cent.[54] Part of this was due to the Covid pandemic and the problem of migrant labour in India, given the mismanagement of the crisis. The business lost by India was immediately picked up by Bangladesh and Vietnam.[55] India's share of global garment exports halved from 6 per cent in 2013 to 3 per cent under Modi.[56]

This divergence between what was sought to be achieved and what is actually achieved comes from the lack of an integrated economic strategy. There is no real thing called Modinomics. It can be understood as a series of one-liners and hashtags and often conflicting statements—'Government has no business to be in business', 'Make in India', 'Make for World' and 'Atmanirbharta'. 'Interconnected and interdependent world' was mentioned in the same speech by Modi, on 15 August 2020, as 'go vocal for local'. But how does globalism fit with economic parochialism? That was neither understood nor explained.

Modi's desire to make a quick difference and create a project with little work and no thinking came together magnificently in India's ranking on the World Bank's Doing Business index. His 2014 manifesto made no mention of it, but the one in 2019 did after it was discovered that this ranking could be gamed officially.

Since Modi took office, India climbed to 63 in 2020 from 142 in 2014. On 27 August 2020, the World Bank, which conducted the exercise,

---

[52] 'Apparel And Garment Industry And Exports', ibef.org

[53] 'India's RMG exports up 3.28% to $14.74 bn in Apr-Feb FY23', 16 March 2023, fibre2fashion.com

[54] 'Textile exports fell 13% in FY21 on COVID-19 impact', 5 May 2021, *The Hindu*

[55] 'Why Noida textile exporters are losing biz to Bangladesh and Vietnam', 25 May 2021, *The Times of India*

[56] 'What explains India's poor performance in garment exports?', 28 August 2019, *Ideas for India*

announced that it was suspending the ratings because of countries committing irregularities to game the system. In 2021, the ratings were permanently discontinued, but it is instructive to see how India improved its ranking. Akshay Deshmane, reporting for *Huffington Post*, wrote of how the Modi government 'prioritised minor institutional and procedural tweaks to game the ranking system'.[57] India rose in the rankings because of a 'methodological weaknesses' that put disproportionate emphasis on insignificant changes.[58] For instance, 'eliminating the need for a company seal or rubber stamp to open a bank account, dropping the need to submit a cancelled cheque with employee provident fund applications, removing the need for traders to submit hard copies of documents, and increasing the capacity of an online customs payment gateway'.

What did the rating actually mean? The World Bank said in its methodology that the data collected refers to businesses only in two cities (Mumbai and Delhi, in the case of India) and did not represent regulations in other locations of the economy. Also, the data referred to regulation of a particular kind of company, a limited company of a specified size. It didn't reflect conditions outside those two cities or for firms that were smaller or different.

The World Bank also cautioned that 'data before 2013 are not comparable with data from 2013 onward due to methodological changes'.

Deshmane writes that 'the 2019 ranking for instance, put China—arguably the one place where the world has done the most business in the past decade—at 46 (31 in 2020), while Rwanda is ranked 29th (38th in 2020)'.

Instead of actual reform legislation, the obsession with the Doing Business ranking 'hijacked' the agenda during the first four years of the Modi term, Deshmane's investigation found.

India's ranking shot up to 63 from 142, but India's investment rate fell from 38 per cent of GDP in 2011 to 28 per cent in 2020, its lowest ever.[59] Private 'projects under implementation' have been in decline since 2011, and at the end of 2020, were lower in value than in 2019. The Doing

---

[57] 'How Modi and Jaitley gamed the World Bank's Doing Business rankings', 20 November 2018, *HuffingtonPost.in*

[58] 'Much ado about nothing: What India's ease of biz ranking won't tell you', 31 August 2020, *Business Standard*

[59] 'Share of investment in GDP to hit all-time low in FY20: Advance estimates', 10 January 2020, *Business Standard*

Business rating was the ideal toy for Modi. Unfortunately, it made little or no difference to the economy.

Part 4: Good & Simple Tax

Seven months after demonetisation, the Modi government sent down another disruptive move, the Goods and Services Tax (GST). The intent to implement GST was surprising because Modi had doggedly opposed it, along with his opposition to MGNREGA (the rural scheme guaranteeing 100 days of work) and Aadhaar. He had said that GST would never succeed.[60]

This system replaced most central and state taxes with a country-wide framework and common rates across the entire country. Losses made by the individual states in giving up their local taxes would be compensated with a share which the Union would transfer to them.

Ideally, the system should have only one rate of taxation. But in India, several GST rates were introduced (which continued to be tweaked to try and keep up with the fall in overall tax revenue).

The system required compliance by applying strong data reporting requirements electronically and cross-matching of reported data. This was beyond the capacity of many small traders who would now either have to modernise, which many did not even know how to do, or go out of business.

GST was meant to be revenue-neutral, meaning it would give the government back as much tax as all the other taxes it was replacing.

However, this did not happen because there was political interest in keeping the tax rates low and economic growth under Modi began to implode.[61] 'Slippage' is normal in India. What looks achievable on paper becomes difficult on the ground. This should have been understood and accommodated when GST was being framed and implemented. It wasn't. This was precisely the sort of thing—hard to implement, requiring much thinking, deliberation and calibration—that Modi would have difficulty with, but he dived headlong into it anyway.

Modi made a midnight speech in Parliament to launch GST on 1 July 2017. He called it historic and said it was not just an economic policy—it was an example of cooperative federalism. It would also benefit small traders, he said.

GST was implemented in a very brief period of time, possibly to ensure that states didn't back out after consensus had been arrived at. There was also

[60] 'Congress tweets old clips of Modi saying "GST can never be successful", 30 June 2017, *Business Standard*

[61] 'GST may not have been revenue-neutral', 15 January 2020, *The Indian Express*

insufficient time to create the system and to test it, because it was a gigantic and complex network.

In many ways, GST unified India as a market. But it also cleaved the marketplace. Because input credit could not be received by or from those not registered under GST, the small producer, who could earlier directly work with the organised sector, now had to either stop producing for them or deal with them through an intermediary. One of the objectives of GST, at least according to those pushing for it, was formalising the economy in favour of larger firms. But it also put at risk the Micro Small and Medium Scale Industry (MSME) sector, which does most of the hiring in India.

This is how the sector is described by the Confederation of Indian Industry: 'Indian MSME sector is the backbone of the national economic structure and has unremittingly acted as the bulwark for the Indian economy, providing it resilience to ward off global economic shocks and adversities. With around 63.4 million units throughout the geographical expanse of the country, MSMEs contribute around 6.11% of the manufacturing GDP and 24.63% of the GDP from service activities as well as 33.4% of India's manufacturing output. They have been able to provide employment to around 120 million persons and contribute around 45% of the overall exports from India. The sector has consistently maintained a growth rate of over 10%. About 20% of the MSMEs are based out of rural areas, which indicates the deployment of significant rural workforce in the MSME sector and is an exhibit to the importance of these enterprises in promoting sustainable and inclusive development as well as generating large scale employment, especially in the rural areas.'[62]

Half the sector was both too large to come under the GST exemptions (businesses with turnover of more than Rs 40 lakh per year had to be GST-compliant) and too small to be able to fit into the patterns of filing and compliance that GST demanded. It is this set that began protesting vocally against GST. Because they were not organised in the form of a unified voice, there was little data on the damage done to their businesses and trades other than the anecdotal and what could be learnt through inference.

One estimate said that 230,000 small businesses had shut down since they were unable to comply with GST requirements.[63] Another said that a third of India's small businesses had shut down by 2020 or were in danger

---

[62] 'Micro, Medium & Small Scale Industry', cii.in

[63] 'India after Goods and Services Tax: Hundreds of thousands lose jobs, small businesses shut down', 6 September 2018, *Reuters*

of shutting down.[64] This was based on a survey report by the All India Manufacturers' Association, which reached out to 46,525 MSMEs, self-employed, corporate CEOs and employees. Of them, it was largely the corporate CEOs and employees who foresaw a quick recovery. Many of the rest were despondent and had debts piled up, which overwhelmed them during the lockdown after their already weak position of the last few years. A survey during the second Covid wave of 2021 found that more than half of all MSMEs saw themselves either scaling down or shutting shop.[65] The backbone had been broken.

India's rate of growth under Modi had been falling consistently since January 2018 according to the government's own data. It dropped in a countdown across the quarters from 8 per cent to 7 per cent to 6 per cent to 5 per cent to 4 per cent to 3 per cent to, in 2020-21, an annual contraction for the first time in more than four decades.

By the time Covid and the lockdown had arrived, several other indicators had already been trending down in tandem and some were even in the negative zone. The Index of Industrial Production and the output of eight core sectors went negative in August, September and October of 2019. Gross tax revenues were negative in May, August, September, October, November and December 2019. In December, they were minus 19.8 per cent year-on-year. Electricity demand fell 13.2 per cent in October that year.

The Modi government made much of Covid's effect but did not acknowledge that the economy had slowed much before Covid. It soldiered on, ignoring bad news and trying to hide it even when it came from government sources.

Part 5: Fudging The Numbers

The numbers for the fourth quarter of 2019–20 put out by the National Statistical Office (NSO) 'raised doubts on data quality'.[66]

The official figure said growth for the January–March quarter of 2020 was 3.1 per cent. Former chief statistician Pronab Sen said this number was overstated by about 1 per cent. The State Bank of India's chief economic

---

[64] 'One in three small businesses stares at shut down; but, coronavirus is not sole culprit', 2 June 2020, *The Financial Express*

[65] 'Nearly 60% Covid-hit startups, MSMEs may scale down, shut down, or sell themselves in 6 months: Survey', 26 May 2021, *The Financial Express*

[66] 'Q4 GDP figures overstated? Economists raise doubts over quality of data' on 24 June 2020, *Business Standard*

advisor, S.K. Ghosh, said that while it was 'customary to change the quarterly numbers in May, the extent of such revision reveals possibly the loss in Q4 because the impact of the lockdown may have been evenly distributed across quarters'.[67]

What was meant was that the Modi government had reduced the growth figure for all three previous quarters to distribute the much sharper fall in the fourth quarter, which was either flat or negative in growth.

Former RBI governor Y.V. Reddy has said of India's GDP data that 'everywhere in the world the future is uncertain. But in India even the past is uncertain'.[68] This was always the case with the Modi government.

In 2015, India changed the way GDP growth was calculated. It changed the base year (the starting point, when the index is set to 100) from the financial year ending 2005 to the one ending 2012. Changes of base year are a normal occurrence and done to keep up with the times and the composition of the economy.

Another change was that growth in the organised sector would now be measured through the data of companies registered with the Ministry of Corporate Affairs. Previously, actual output had been measured; now, the balance sheet data would be considered. Data from the unorganised sector, which accounted for about 45 per cent of GDP and employed over 90 per cent of all workers, was collected only once every five years in India. And it was collected through surveys. In between these years, a proxy was used, meaning that it was assumed that the unorganised sector was also growing at about the same pace as the organised sector. Such a linkage was inevitable given that the 'unorganised sector' by definition could not be accurately measured by the government because it referred to unregistered and unincorporated units and household businesses. But should this sector begin to markedly depart in growth from the organised, then the overall data would not just be off by a bit, it would be totally wrong.

For example, if the 55 per cent of the organised sector was growing and the 45 per cent of the unorganised one was flat or in contraction, calculations based on the linkage would throw up incorrect numbers.

The new series was then used to back-calculate or recalculate the growth of the previous years. The recalculation decreased growth for the Manmohan Singh years, while increasing the rate, which had already begun weakening, of the initial Modi years.

---

[67] 'Sharp GDP data revision triggers row', 31 May 2020, *The Times of India*
[68] 'Making sense of India's GDP data amid its many revisions', 28 February 2020, *Bloomberg Quint*

The growth during the UPA era was in this manner shown as lower than the growth during the Modi years. A report produced under the Modi government that showed that growth was definitely higher under the UPA was removed from the Statistics and Programme Implementation Ministry's website.[69] The problem was that from exports to automobiles, and bank credit growth to corporate profits, the numbers were strong during the UPA period and weak or even negative during the Modi years, and so the data did not seem to hold. There appeared to be something amiss with the new numbers, which many noticed.

The Modi government's former chief economic advisor, Arvind Subramanian, published a paper saying India's GDP growth since 2011 was overestimated by 2.5 per cent a year.[70] The overestimation came from a key change in measuring the formal manufacturing sector.

The change in methodology began before the Modi government but the new numbers made no sense. Manufacturing data had moved plausibly with other indicators like the Index of Industrial Production till 2011 but then inexplicably diverged. There was also positive correlation between GDP growth and manufacture and exports till 2011, after which they again diverged with the latter falling but the former still claiming growth.

The new series revised growth in the UPA period downwards, but for two disruptive years (2016–17, which saw demonetisation, and 2017–18, which saw the introduction of GST), growth was revised upwards. Also, official data that showed unemployment had shot up was not released.

In 2015–17, India claimed to have posted average real GDP growth of 7.5 per cent, though the government's other figures showed that investment growth was only 4.5 per cent, exports growth 2 per cent, and the credit to GDP ratio fell by 2 per cent. Subramanian looked at how many emerging market nations between 1991 and 2015 had hit 7.5 per cent growth with India's combination of investment, export and credit growth. The answer was zero. Countries with performance on those indicators similar to India's had not even managed average real GDP growth of 5 per cent.

To check his hypothesis of India overestimating its GDP growth, Subramanian compiled 17 indicators that were strongly correlated with GDP growth. They included two-wheeler, commercial vehicle and tractor sales, airline passenger traffic and foreign tourist arrivals, railway freight traffic,

[69] 'Report showing higher GDP growth during Manmohan era removed from govt website', 21 August 2018, *India Today*
[70] 'India's GDP Mis-estimation: Likelihood, Magnitudes, Mechanisms, and Implications', June 2019, Centre for International Development, Harvard University

total exports and imports, electricity and petrol consumption, petroleum consumption, cement and steel production, and growth in credit. Of the 17 indicators, 16 had positively correlated with GDP growth before 2011. However, post-2011, out of 17 indicators, 11 negatively correlated with GDP.

For example, production of commercial vehicles grew at 19 per cent before 2011 and –0.1 per cent after 2011. Exports grew at 14 per cent till 2011 and only 3 per cent after. Imports grew at 15 per cent till 2011 and 2 per cent after. This was compelling evidence that the GDP growth data was wrong because 'such staggering declines are simply incompatible with stable underlying GDP growth'.

The government's response (delivered informally through a paper by Modi's economic advisors) to Subramanian's paper was to accept the data he presented on good faith but to reject the conclusion since, according to the advisors, it did not point out any specific problem with the way in which GDP was calculated in terms of its coverage or methodology. And because Subramanian didn't show that the drivers of growth had not changed in the period he was mapping—i.e., there could have been other things other than his 17 indicators that may have risen.

A July 2019 paper by the National Council of Applied Economic Research (NCAER) doubted that India achieved a 'staggering 8.2 per cent growth rate in the year of demonetisation when more than 80 per cent of the cash in the economy was removed from circulation overnight dealing a severe blow to the unorganised segment of the population'.[71]

Economics is not part of the political debate in India to any large extent and the government could afford to ignore the accusation that its numbers on GDP growth were off and the economy was stagnant.

In December 2019, Subramanian published a second paper that showed India had been in a long economic decline, followed by a 'sharp collapse' in 2019. India was heading for the Intensive Care Unit, the paper concluded, and this was before anyone had heard the word coronavirus.[72]

The data was revealing. Production of consumer goods was growing at only 1 per cent. The manufacture of capital goods (the machines used for production) was in negative territory at -4 per cent. Non-oil exports were shrinking at -5 per cent, while non-oil imports were also negative.

---

[71] 'Four Years after the Base-Year Revision: Taking Stock of the Debate Surrounding India's National Income Estimates', India Policy Forum, ncaer.org
[72] 'India's Great Slowdown', December 2019, Centre for International Development, Harvard University

The overall numbers were close to those India had in 1991 (with the exception of inflation and foreign exchange reserves), a period when India's GDP had grown by only 1 per cent.

Electricity generation, a critical and reliable indicator of economic activity, showed that growth was in fact even worse than in 1991. It had fallen from about 6 per cent growth to under 2 per cent in 2019–20. After the paper was published, electricity generation fell into the negative territory, falling 25 per cent in April 2020, 15 per cent in May, 9 per cent in June, and 1 per cent in July. After this, it grew, but not at the same pace to go back to what it was. It grew 1.9 per cent in November 2020, 6.1 per cent in December and 5.3 per cent in January 2021. It fell 10 per cent again in May 2021.[73]

The report pointed out what journalist Harish Damodaran has noted— that the slowdown was not accompanied by the three standard triggers: food harvests, fuel prices and a high fiscal deficit. The answers to the slowdown lay elsewhere, but were not easy to locate.

Subramanian speculated that the slowdown was both structural and cyclical and had been exacerbated by the crisis in non-banking financial companies, particularly after the collapse of the infrastructure finance firm IL&FS on Modi's watch, and the subsequent weakening of the financial position of real estate companies.

Previously, the slowdown had been attributed to structural issues like inequality, governance, and land and labour laws. Or cyclical ones, such as demonetisation, the haphazard implementation of GST and other such policies. The sagging of GDP growth began officially in January 2018, but Subramanian says that the decline had already begun before that. He said India had never really recovered from the global financial crisis in 2008. Compared to the period since 2002, a series of indicators showed that growth in the 2012–18 period was anaemic. These included investments (12 per cent versus 2 per cent), credit growth to industry (16 per cent versus -1 per cent), corporate profits (22 per cent versus 1 per cent), direct taxes (14 per cent versus 4 per cent), total credit (11 per cent versus 4 per cent) and exports (15 per cent versus 5 per cent).

India's growth in the 2002–08 period was boosted by global factors such as a boom in trade, making India's exports and investments, especially in infrastructure, the drivers of growth. GDP growth almost touched 10 per cent before beginning to soften long term. And so it was global growth and

---

[73] 'India's May electricity use down 10.4% from April', 1 June 2021, *Reuters*

de-growth that in large measure is to account for India's story over the last two decades. But while this explains why global trade fell in the first term of the Modi years, there was no reason for India's export growth to have ended. Vietnam and Bangladesh grew exports in this period that Subramanian speaks of. The opportunity was there; it was not taken by Modi.

Elsewhere, gross non-performing assets of banks went from 4.5 per cent in 2015 to around 10 per cent in the Modi era and the RBI warned they would rise to over 13 per cent.[74] The problem was 'addressed' by writing off over Rs 10 lakh crore in loans.[75]

The material signaling alarm came from the outside: the Modi government did not even acknowledge a slowdown in the economy, much less discuss its causes. Perhaps, as we noted in the introduction, Modi did not even know about it because he hadn't been told. The rosy optimism of 2018 continued till the first quarter of 2019 and then the economy ceased to be a topic discussed, especially after the resignation in May and then passing away of Arun Jaitley in August that year.

The Modi government had also been fudging its budget figures, especially the fiscal deficit, by burying spending in the so-called 'off-budget' spaces, i.e., shifting government spending to government-owned entities like the Food Corporation of India and the National Highways Authority of India.[76] If these numbers were taken into account, the fiscal deficit, meaning government borrowing, was considerably larger and more threatening than it was being made out to be. This was not acknowledged till 2021,[77] resulting in further erosion of global credibility in India's numbers. The deficit in the Modi era was higher than at any time since the global financial crisis.

India's housing market in its top eight cities consistently recorded unsold inventory of 8 lakh units versus sales of 2 lakh units from 2016 onwards, with the real estate sector having Rs 5 lakh crore in oustanding loans. The assumption of a fast-growing and bullish middle class has to be seen in this light. The unsold inventory was under 3 lakh units in 2011. The inability to pay these back on time has led to what is called the 'four balance sheet

[74] 'Banks' gross NPAs may rise to 13.5% by Sept: Financial stability report', 12 January 2021, *Business Standard*
[75] 'In last 5 years, Rs 10 lakh crore in write-offs help banks halve NPAs', 21 November 2022, *Indian Express*
[76] 'FCI borrowings to be more than Centre's food subsidy bill', 2 February 2020, *The Indian Express*
[77] 'Going easy on loans: FM brings transparency in off-budget borrowings', 2 February 2021, *Business Standard*

problem' (the weak finances of infrastructure companies, banks, non-banking finance companies and real estate companies).

What was already an issue of corporate and bank debt was now aggravated by the weakening finances of non-banking finance companies and real estate firms.

Subramanian had a list of suggestions to begin fixing the problem, including reforms in banking, laws and regulation. Assuming his analysis was correct, the fix was deep and required a lot of thinking and work. But again, this was Subramanian's thesis. In hundreds of speeches in this period, Modi had not acknowledged anything approaching a problem in his management of the economy, leave alone accept that there was a crisis. When the going got tough, he simply changed the subject. If you do not think there is a problem at all, it is unlikely you will bother with finding a solution. And so it has been with Modinomics. But ignoring the issue did not mean that long-term and structural effects had not been introduced into the economy by Modi's actions.

In June 2017, the Centre for Monitoring the Indian Economy (CMIE) reported unemployment was 4 per cent. In June 2018 it said unemployment had reached 5.5 per cent. The CMIE is the only body that looks at real-time data, but because it is a private firm, its data is not available for scrutiny except to subscribers.

The first government data on employment that showed things were bad came when it was reported that millions had lost their jobs because of demonetisation and unemployment was at a four-year high.[78] This report was 'withheld' and not revealed even to parliament.[79] It was released only after the 2019 elections were over. A more comprehensive survey by the government's National Sample Survey's Office (NSSO) found that from 2.2 per cent unemployment in 2012, unemployment in India had shot up to 6.1 per cent in 2018.[80] This was the highest in four decades.

The paper reporting it said that the 'findings of the report hold significance as this is the first survey on employment conducted by a government agency after Modi announced demonetisation of high-valued currency notes in November 2016'.

---

[78] Unemployment rose to a 4-year high during demonetisation: Govt survey', 11 January 2019, *Business Standard*

[79] 'Polls done, Modi govt releases jobs data that showed unemployment at 45-year high', 31 May 2019, *ThePrint.in*

[80] 'Unemployment rate at four-decade high of 6.1% in 2017–18: NSSO survey', 6 February 2019, *Business Standard*

A few days later, it was reported that for the first time more than half of India's working-age population was out of the labour force and not contributing to any economic activity, according to the same survey that the government was now refusing to release.[81] Labour force participation had gone from 55 per cent in 2012 to 49 per cent in 2018 for the first time in India. At this time, 65 per cent of India was in the working age group, but only 49 per cent working or available for work. A smaller labour force and higher unemployment were disastrous. How would India be able to harness its demographic dividend—when most of its population was of working age and working—if most were in fact not working or looking for work? It in fact wouldn't.

Two members of the National Statistical Commission (NSC), including its interim chairman, resigned, saying that the government had withheld the report's release despite the NSC's approval.[82]

The report leaked out only days before the general election of 2019 and Rajiv Kumar, the NITI head, was sent out to explain why the report had not been released. He said that the methodology had changed and that it could not be compared to previous surveys (though the survey report had itself drawn comparison with previous data), and its numbers were incorrect in some manner. Kumar said the report needed to be 'approved' but was stumped when asked who would approve it given that this was the job of the NSC, which had already approved it. The cabinet, Kumar speculated, before saying he didn't know. Asked why the NITI head was sent out to defend a report instead of the NSSO, Kumar said it was because 'the chief statistician is today not in Delhi'.

The proceedings were shambolic. Kumar's deputy Amitabh Kant said that unemployment couldn't be high because there were lots of Uber and Ola drivers. When told that the numbers were duplicated and many drivers were registered with both Uber and Ola, Kant said: 'Maybe… that's exactly what I'm saying… like the nature of jobs across the world is changing.'[83]

The NSSO survey was finally released but only days after the election results came in, and, contrary to the NITI bluster, retained all the findings. Presumably it was released because, having won, Modi didn't see the point to

[81] 'More than half of India's working-age population out of labour force: NSSO', 6 February 2019, *Business Standard*

[82] 'Was sidelined, govt not releasing job figures, says National Statistics Commission chief P.C. Mohanan on why he quit', 30 January 2019, *India Today*

[83] 'NITI Aayog officials in knots trying to explain report on skyrocketing unemployment', 1 February 2019, *Scroll.in*

misleading people any longer (assuming he knew about the report in the first place). The report revealed that a drop in farm jobs was a key reason for the rising unemployment. In February 2019, the CMIE said the unemployment rate was now 7.2 per cent. It would hover around there or higher from here on. The same month, it was reported that government data showed unemployment was 8.9 per cent in 2018.[84]

Between 2016 and 2018, five million people lost their jobs and the labour force participation started declining suddenly between September and December 2016 for both urban and rural men. The rate of decline slowed down by the second half of 2017, but the general trend had continued and there had been no recovery.

The CMIE said that 1.89 crore salaried jobs had been lost between the previous year and July 2020.[85] This was 22 per cent of the total number of salaried jobs in India. On the other hand, 80 lakh jobs had been gained in the non-salaried (i.e., casual labour) market. It was likely that many who had lost salaried jobs had taken up whatever work they could find. The management of the pandemic meant that, in the first wave alone, 23 crore Indians, one out of every seven in the population, fell into poverty, a catastrophe of global scale (23 crore is 3 per cent of the world's population).[86]

Some of this was due to the Covid disruption, but the data shows that there has been a sharp trend of rise in unemployment in the Modi era, and especially after demonetisation. This had been revealed by the government's own data but neither Modi nor his ministers acknowledged it, spoke about it or its causes and have shown no intent of owning responsibility for it, not even for jobs that the government itself refused to add.[87]

The lack of work meant that India was at disastrously low labour force participation rates. Women, who are disproportionately hit when there is lack of work, were participating in the economy at a rate of under 10 per cent, according to the CMIE, and urban women only at 6.9 per cent.[88] Even

[84] 'Demonetisation, GST impacted jobs more than NSSO's headline numbers suggest', 4 February 2019, *Business Standard*

[85] '18.9 mn salaried people lost jobs since April, 5 mn in July, says CMIE', 19 August 2020, IANS

[86] 'Additional 230 million Indians fell below poverty line due to the pandemic: Study', 5 May 2021, *TheWire.in*

[87] 'UPSC, SSC, Railways, Banking—recruitment for govt jobs shows massive dip in last 5 years', 8 March 2021, *ThePrint.in*

[88] 'Urban female labour participation rate falls to its lowest in November since 2016: CMIE', 17 December 2020, *The Economic Times*

older government data says it was at 25 per cent, down from 33 per cent a couple of decades ago. Overall, labour participation, including men, had fallen from 50 per cent before Modi to 40 per cent by the end of 2020.[89]

A McKinsey Global Institute report says that at least nine crore additional Indians would be in search of non-farm jobs during the eight years from 2022–23 to 2029–30, and India needs to grow over 8 per cent annually to employ them.[90] The figures do not include 5.5 crore women who may come back to the labour force to 'partially correct the historical underrepresentation'. Neither the growth rhetoric ('world's fastest growing economy') nor the promises of job creation is realistic given the history and economic trajectory and record of the Modi era.[91]

The household debt of Indians has risen in the Modi years to record levels.[92] It almost doubled from Rs 3.7 lakh crore in 2017 to 6.7 lakh crore in 2018. It kept climbing from 30.1 per cent of GDP in 2018 to 31.7 per cent in 2019 to 32.5 per cent in 2020 and then 37.3 per cent in 2021.[93] The anecdotal evidence suggested that things were getting worse. A single gold loan company sold Rs 404 crore of jewellery after defaults in the first three months of 2021. In nine months of the previous year, the amount in default had been only Rs 8 crore.[94] This problem became amplified as the lockdown threw millions more into distress.[95] But it became clear that, as economic growth and hope fell away after 2016, Indians began to spend less as they had less confidence in the future.

A survey by the government conducted between July 2017 and June 2018 showed something astonishing: the average amount spent by Indians in a month had fallen in 2018 compared to 2012.[96] Adjusted for inflation,

[89] 'ExplainSpeaking: Why rising unemployment, not GDP growth, is the biggest challenge for India', 24 February 2021, *The Indian Express*

[90] 'India will need to find jobs for additional 90 mn, says McKinsey report', 26 August 2020, *Business Standard*

[91] 'Budget 2019: Did Modi govt create as many jobs as it promised?', 1 February 2019, *Business Today*

[92] 'Indian households' debt doubles in FY17–18: What are we borrowing for and how much?, 28 January 2019, *The Economic Times*

[93] 'Household debt jumps to 37.3% of GDP in fiscal 2021, says report', 6 July 2021, *Business Standard*

[94] 'Amid Covid, surge in pawned jewellery sale', 6 July 2021, *The Tribune*

[95] 'Covid-19: At Rs 43.5 trn by March, Indian households' debt at record high', 18 April 2020, *Business Standard*

[96] 'Consumer spend sees first fall in 4 decades on weak rural demand: NSO data', 12 November 2019, *Business Standard*

the average fell from Rs 1,501 to Rs 1,446. In 2012, it had risen 13 per cent over two years.

The report revealing this said that in the last 50 years there had never been a time that consumption had decreased, and that such a fall indicated an increase in poverty in the country by at least 10 per cent. The most worrying trend in the report was a dip in food consumption. The amount spent on food by urban Indians remained flat at Rs 946 per person per month in 2018 compared to Rs 943 in 2012. But rural Indians were spending less on food in 2018 (Rs 580) compared to 2012 (Rs 643).

India usually recorded an average increase in consumption of around 3 per cent a year, and a fall over six years suggested a fall in consumption of around 20 per cent, wiping out years of progress. This data set corroborated with a shortage of demand in the economy, especially in the rural market, seen in falling growth rates even in the organised sector.

The report was approved for release by a committee on 19 June 2019. But, like the unemployment data, it had been withheld by the Modi government because it had such negative news.[97]

The government said the report had not been released because of 'data quality issues' and that the findings were 'draft in nature'. Experts,[98] including those backing the government, said that the government should have released it anyway so that the flaws, if any, could be examined in the interests of transparency.[99] This it chose not to do. The government said its own survey did not align with its estimation of GDP growth, and so junked its findings entirely, saying it would 'examine the feasibility' of redoing the survey in 2022. Even this was false, as other government data also revealed that consumption was plummeting.[100] Modi refused to release it even after the government's chief economic advisor himself asked for it to be made public.[101]

This unreleased report, the Consumer Expenditure Survey, incidentally, was the quinquennial or five-year survey used to measure GDP growth in the unorganised sector. The data it gathered revealed the average expenditure

---

[97] 'NSO will not release report showing first decline in consumer expenditure in 40 years', 18 February 2020, *TheWire.in*

[98] 'Not in favour of scrapping consumer survey report: NSC's Bimal Kumar Roy', 6 December 2019, *Business Standard*

[99] 'Is the NSO's consumption data for 2017–18 beyond salvation?', 28 November 2019, *Mint*

[100] 'GDP data confirms demand slowdown; consumption expenditure at 17-qtr low', 30 August 2019, *Business Standard*

[101] 'CEA Subramanian asks NSC to make junked consumer spending report public', 7 December 2020, *Business Standard*

on goods (food and non-food) and services. It actually aligned both with the dramatic rise in unemployment as well as the fall in consumption that had led to a decline in GDP growth according to the government's own estimates.

India's chief statistician had twice in 2019 assured the country that this Consumer Expenditure Survey would be released on time.[102] And no data or methodology issues had been flagged before the report's findings were leaked. If there was any documentation flagging it after the leak, that was not released by the government either. No evidence had been provided by the Modi government to back its claim that the survey was in any way incorrect or even off. The excuses the government had given for not releasing the survey were 'spurious' and 'hurriedly invented'. Even if there were technical reasons for not approving it, the report should have been put in the public domain, because this was the first time in India's history that an NSSO survey had been completed, approved but then not released.[103]

The government's decision to push the new survey to 2022 meant that, instead of a five-year interval, data on consumption and growth (and in effect numbers on actual GDP) would now not be released earlier than ten years after the 2012 survey. This survey was, in fact, not conducted even in 2022, though the government said it was being undertaken.[104] India would not have a poverty estimate for ten years. This action violates India's obligations to the IMF, which has already previously expressed concern about India's delay in releasing economic data.[105] The scrapping of the survey also hampers India's policy-makers, who are flying blind in the absence of essential data.

Other government data showing that the number of self-employed people had fallen corroborated the findings in the NSSO survey. The number of self-employed people declined in rural India from 52.2 per cent in 2018 to 51.7 per cent in 2019. In urban India, it declined from 32.4 per cent to 31.8 per cent during the same period.[106] This suggested that small businesses had wound up because of stress and people were turning to labour. Entrepreneurs and businesses are very valuable because they have organisational capital that cannot be easily replaced.

The Modi government's insistence on pursuing the National Register of Citizens (NRC) after the experience had traumatised millions in Assam and

---

[102] 'NSO will not release report showing first decline in consumer expenditure in 40 years', 18 February 2020, *TheWire.in*

[103] 'Why the picture on poverty is incomplete', 20 November 2019, *Mint*

[104] 'Govt. initiates work on consumer spending survey', 27 July 2022, *The Hindu*

[105] 'IMF report flags several delays in India's data reporting', 26 August 2019, *The Hindu*

[106] 'India sees a dip in number of self-employed households in FY19', 9 June 2020, *Mint*

also jeopardised data collection. The NRC process (see the chapter 'The Devil's Workshop' for details) required those individuals identified as foreigners to prove their citizenship through documentation linking them definitively to ancestors in Assam at a particular time. This was not easy to do for many people, and the threat from the BJP that this would be done nationwide before 2024 produced great fear and uncertainty in neighbourhoods which began to refuse cooperation with surveyors of all types.[107]

Somesh Jha, who had reported on the scrapped consumer survey, also found that, after the protests against the Citizenship Amendment Act (CAA), the government would defer another key survey.[108] This would reveal information about food insecurity, migration, household facilities, residences, documents like birth certificates and so on. It was deferred because of a 'lack of cooperation by households, as they are either being shown the door or attacked during their work, putting their lives at risk. People fear that survey officers are collecting data that can be used for determining their citizenship'.

Modi has consistently turned his face away from bad news. When the problem of unemployment shooting up after demonetisation began to be reported, Modi said this was wrong. In an interview, Modi dismissed the findings of his own surveys.[109] He ignores the issue either by not releasing the data or discarding it when it shows him the mirror. Two other employment reports—the Annual Employment-Unemployment Survey and Quarterly Employment Survey—were also thus discarded. Parliament was told that no survey on jobs data had been conducted since 2016, i.e., before demonetisation.[110] The government's explanation that survey data revealed 'significant divergence and direction in the consumption patterns when compared with other administrative data sources' was a knee-jerk reaction, and the main reason for it was embarrassment.[111]

The Modi government then made public a draft bill for the National Statistical Commission. But it did not give this supposedly independent body the authority to approve and release its own survey reports.[112]

---

[107] 'Will panic over NRC put census in danger for the first time in India's history?', 4 February 2020, *Scroll.in*

[108] 'CAA protest fallout: Govt likely to defer key socio-economic survey', 21 February 2020, *Business Standard*

[109] 'Jobs not lacking, data on jobs lacking: Modi', 2 July 2018, IANS

[110] 'Survey discontinued, Centre clueless about unemployment', 6 March 2018, *DNA*

[111] 'Govt shouldn't junk unpleasant data', 17 March 2020, *The Hindu BusinessLine*

[112] 'Who will approve and release official surveys? Draft NSC bill stays silent', 24 December 2019, *Business Standard*

As the bad news started coming in, the Modi government began covering up at scale, the data journalism website *IndiaSpend* reported.[113] It said that other than the jobs data, the government was not releasing reports on the caste census, on children, crime, prison records and agricultural wages. The data was being collected regularly; it was merely not being released. Another report revealed in 2021 that the Survey of the Services Sector (2016-17) had been abandoned, Survey of Debt and Investment (2019) and Survey of Multiple Indicators (2020) had been completed but not released and the Survey on Domestic Tourism Sector (2020) was suspended.[114]

Part 6: Locking Down The Poor

With no desire to examine the damage he is doing and no restraint on him internally, Modi has continued in the style he is comfortable with. Dramatic disruption continues to be prioritised. What it seeks to achieve and what it ultimately achieves is less important. On 24 March 2020, Modi appeared at 8 p.m. to speak to the nation. He announced what was measured later to be the harshest lockdown in the world (in Modi's words 'complete lockdown, complete nation') for three weeks. No movement in public would be allowed. Everybody had to stay home for three weeks and not cross their doorstep.

No time was given for people to prepare for a siege of 21 days in a nation where the majority do not have savings and hundreds of millions are 'daily-wage earners', a phrase used so casually in India as to lose its meaning, which is that they eat only if they work.

No time was given even for the government itself to prepare. Before the announcement was made, no ministry was consulted on what the impact on the country would be.[115]

And this lockdown was enforced through a police force always enthusiastic about using violence. Modi used the word 'curfew' in his speech, which gave the police the cue. They began to assault people on the road. In the rest of the world, lockdowns were voluntary restrictions on movement. Exceptions were carved out. In India there were none: the population was treated as if by an occupying power. Even the poorest were humiliated and brutalised as hundreds of videos showed.

---

[113] 'Jobs, caste, farm suicides, crime, nutrition: Some subjects on which government is withholding data', 30 January 2019, *IndiaSpend.com*
[114] 'Govt's data apathy harming pandemic response: Experts', 21 June 2021, *Mint*
[115] 'कोरोना लॉकडाउन का फ़ैसला मोदी सरकार ने आख़िरि किसकी सलाह पर लिया? –बीबीसी पड़ताल', 22 March 2021, *BBC*

Modi spoke of an economic cost to the lockdown but made no reference to migrant workers. His speech had the expected theatrical flourishes ('I beg you with folded hands to remain where you are for three weeks'; 'I am speaking not as prime minister but as a member of your family'; 'Come what may, do not cross the Lakshman Rekha of your door') but little of how alert and aware the State was to what was coming.

To break the cycle of Covid's spread, he said, 21 days were necessary. The Mahabharat had been won in 18 days, but this war against Covid would be fought over 21 days and, under him, India would try and win it in that period.[116] All else would have to come after the lives of people were secured from Covid infections, he said. '*Jaan hai to jahan hai*' (When there is life, there is hope), he said before signing off.

He made a couple of remarks in his speech regarding what the State had done and would do in preparation. These had no details but expressed a breezy confidence: all solutions were already in place and what needed to be done in future would be done; the State was making relentless efforts to ensure there would be no problem during the lockdown.

In Sri Lanka, about a week before their lockdown, construction activity was asked to wind down so migrant workers could head home. The State also took on the responsibility of ensuring essential supplies.[117] The announcement was separated from the execution. In India, on the night of 24 March, a part of the population found itself stranded with no work, few resources and no means of reaching safety. The total lockdown made no exceptions and all public transport was shut down.

Millions of workers and their families began walking to their villages. Many starved, many died. Many who walked on the highways were harassed and bullied by the police. Some walked on the railway tracks to avoid harassment and were run over.

The State had shown zero responsibility towards these millions. Avoiding accountability, the Modi government lied to the Supreme Court, saying there were no migrant workers on the road even while media reports daily showed images of the masses walking home.[118] The court in turn let Indians down by denying these workers their wages (see the chapter 'Their Lordships' for details).

---

[116] 'Mahabharata war lasted 18 days, war against Coronavirus will take 21 days: PM Modi', 25 March 2020, PTI

[117] 'Ethical responses to the COVID-19 pandemic—lessons from Sri Lanka', 3 November 2020, *Asian Bioethics Review*

[118] 'Coronavirus: "No migrant workers on roads as of 11 am," Centre tells Supreme Court', 31 March 2020, *Scroll.in*

Such people were now being expected to show exemplary behaviour towards a higher cause. Any examination of India's failure to control the spread of the pandemic must begin with understanding this fact. Modi's unprepared lockdown busted the social contract.

On 24 March, only three dozen new cases and a total of 536 positive cases had been detected in India. On 14 April, when the lockdown was meant to end, there were still only a total of 11,487 cases across the country. Was the Mahabharat won? Apparently not. On the night of 14 April, Modi again spoke to the nation and extended the lockdown till 3 May. There was no apology for the incompetence and no explanation for why the lockdown had been announced without preparation, as events had exposed. He merely asked people to help the poor and not fire their workers.

He said it wasn't appropriate to compare the position of nations, but some truths could not be denied. European nations had been equal to India in terms of the number of cases only a few weeks ago, but they now had 25 to 30 times more cases and thousands had died.

If India had not applied, in Modi's words, a 'holistic and integrated' approach and not shown 'decisiveness', he shuddered to think of what would have happened.[119] The road taken through his no-notice total lockdown, Modi said, was the right one.

The spread of Covid has shown how meaningless it all had been. India showed the most perfect representation of an exponential curve, with unrelenting growth in the spread of Covid. Even the US and Brazil, the other two nations with the most infected, had an episodic spread; India alone in the world kept going only up and further up for six full months from the lockdown till the middle of September when the first wave peaked.

In March 2021, the second wave began (see details of that in the chapter titled 'Mahabharat').

For four months after the national lockdown was announced, there were still shutdown conditions and chaos. The Indian economy's reliance on migrant labour showed through economic destruction and enormous loss of productivity.[120] Two crore workers are estimated to have left, mostly from the south and west of India, and returned to their villages in the north and east. This migration gutted the economy and production. The fear of what would happen if these two crore women and men again submitted themselves to

[119] 'Holistic & integrated approach controlled the spread of Covid-19 in country: PM', 14 April 2020, All India Radio, newsonair.nic.in

[120] '10,113 companies voluntarily shuttered operations during Apr 2020–Feb 2021 period: Govt data', 8 March 2021, PTI

Modi's whims, the absence of public transport (the railways remained shut though inexplicably airlines were allowed to operate at full capacity with middle seats occupied) and the lack of work kept them in their villages for an extended period. This artificial migrant crisis was predictable and a peculiarly Indian issue. And yet Modi and his advisors had not anticipated it when going ahead with the instant lockdown, as Modi's speech showed.

What was the purpose of the lockdown? Was it to buy time, and if so, for what? The logic of a lockdown was that it would allow the State to build capacity in healthcare. This was not what Modi articulated nor indeed was it what India did. Its testing rates were among the lowest in the world. Why was the lockdown extended and why was it lifted when it was? This was not explained.

There was no sense to any of it. Two weeks after it was clear that the second wave had begun, the famous Narendra Modi Stadium was filled with crowds for matches,[121] Modi was holding election rallies in Bengal with lakhs in attendance,[122] and 32 lakh people had gathered for the Kumbh Mela.[123] At the same time, the Centre was also telling states to control the pandemic by taking 'necessary measures' and ensuring 'appropriate behaviour'.[124] It should not surprise anyone that this randomness exacted a toll on India.

To illustrate the economic fallout, let us consider one industrial city. Surat's Rs 50,000-crore powerloom sector, which accounted for 80 per cent of the country's man-made fibre production and almost 100 per cent of the production of synthetic sarees and dress materials, had been able to resume just 10 per cent of its usual capacity even after the lifting of lockdown curbs.[125] The reason, of course, was shortage of manpower caused by the exodus of workers. Some 35 lakh people left Surat and its surrounding industrial zones in April and May of 2020. As the lockdown kept getting extended, and employers stopped paying wages, the situation deteriorated. Even in the initial weeks of the lockdown, Surat saw thousands of workers wandering in the streets without food or shelter, the *Frontline* report said.

---

[121] 'India vs England: Record crowd post Covid-19 in 1st T20 International', 14 March 2021, IANS

[122] 'Assembly election 2021: PM Modi to address rally in Kharagpur today, four rallies scheduled in 10 days', 20 March 2021, *DNA*

[123] 'Explained: Why new Uttarakhand CM wants no "rok-tok" on Kumbh crowds', 21 March 2021, *The Indian Express*

[124] '"Strictly enforce Covid norms": MHA writes to states amid rising cases', 19 March 2021, *The Times of India*

[125] 'Surat: Silence of the looms', 31 July 2020, *Frontline*

In Bengaluru, one of India's main garment manufacturing hubs, a report by the Garment and Textile Workers' Union and Alternative Law Forum found that nine out of 25 garment factories surveyed had closed down and the others had downsized, resulting in 16,600 workers, mostly women, losing their jobs during the pandemic.[126]

By the time the first wave of Covid had ended, India's middle class was smaller by 3.2 crore people, shrinking the pre-pandemic 10 crore middle class by a third. Those pushed into poverty were individuals who had been earning between Rs 21,000 and Rs 42,000 per month but had lost their source of income or were now making much less.[127] Indians making between Rs 50,000 and Rs 1 lakh per month fell by 70 lakh. The number of poor Indians (making $2 or less per day) went up by 7.5 crore in 2020.[128] Another, more detailed, study by the Azim Premji University showed that this number may actually be 230 million or 23 crore people reduced to poverty.[129] Thus did Modi undo the entire work of the previous government on social welfare and put crores of Indians through trauma. What Indians generally refer to as the middle class (and is actually elite) was being hammered under Modi as well. The numbers of those earning more than Rs 50 lakh a year contracted by a fifth, those earning between Rs 8 lakh and Rs 50 lakh fell 8 per cent. Those earning more than Rs 5 lakh a month shrank 5 per cent. And all this was before Covid.[130]

The really rich fled India. Between 2014 and 2018, a total of 23,000 dollar millionaires (meaning Indians worth Rs 7 crore or more) left India, the highest number of millionaire migrations out of a nation in the world.[131] Seven thousand left in 2017 alone. Another 5,000 departed in 2020.[132]

The poor had nowhere to go. In July 2020, the demand for MGNREGA work around India was 70 per cent higher than in the previous year even after

[126] 'Thousands of Bengaluru garment workers forced to resign amid pandemic: Report', 21 March 2021, *The News Minute*

[127] 'Indian middle class shrinks by 32 million due to Covid-19 pandemic: Pew', 19 March 2021, *Business Standard*

[128] 'In the pandemic, India's middle class shrinks and poverty spreads while China sees smaller changes', 18 March 2021, pewresearch.org

[129] 'State of working in India: One year of Covid', Azim Premji University

[130] 'Incomes of Indians were shrinking even before Covid, pandemic will only make it worse', 5 June 2021, *ThePrint.in*

[131] '23,000 dollar-millionaires have left India since 2014', 19 March 2018, *The Economic Times*

[132] 'Covid accelerates India's millionaire exodus', 12 April 2021, *BBC*

migrant workers went back to their farms.[133] From 1.84 crore households asking for MGNREGA work in 2019, the number rose to 3.15 crore in 2020. A staggering 4.3 crore households sought MGNREGA work in June 2020. Across north India, skilled workers—weavers, diamond polishers, masons, carpenters, cooks, mechanics, garment stitchers, plumbers, waiters, drivers—were without employment—a manmade crisis that could have been mitigated if not entirely avoided.

As the second wave of Covid-19 smashed into an already distressed rural India, Jan Dhan accounts began to shrink as the poor ate into whatever savings they had.[134] For the first time in eight years rural fixed deposits shrank in 2021.[135] Between January and March 2021, before the second wave, four times as many districts of India had negative fixed deposits compared to the quarter before and the normal average.[136]

The Budget estimate for MGNREGA till March 2021 was Rs 61,500 crore. What was spent instead was Rs 1.11 lakh crore, more than Rs 40,000 crore over what was estimated. It helped blow the fiscal deficit, but the crisis could no longer be hidden even if it could not be spoken about. And even with this increase, about a quarter of the demand from those wanting MGNREGA work went unmet. For FY 2022, only Rs 73,000 crore was allocated, 34 per cent lower than the previous year. Though the distress and unemployment has remained, the government has no money to allot. It could only hope that employment would spontaneously rise and MGNREGA demand would fall.

Part 7: Advisors and Advice

While business as usual carried on in the economy, the Modi government saw the departure of people, and indeed, its most reputable names, from its institutions and advisory groups. RBI governor Raghuram Rajan, who opposed demonetisation, was left in the dark regarding his position and departed in September 2016, the first governor of the RBI to not get a five-year term in three decades. Urjit Patel, who took over as RBI governor from

---

[133] 'MGNREGA work demand drops in July 2020 as labourers get jobs in farms', 1 August 2020, *Business Standard*

[134] 'Total balance in Jan Dhan accounts goes down by Rs 2,787 crore in April', 10 May 2021, *The Hindu Businessline*

[135] 'Rural term deposits fall for first time in eight years', 21 June 2021, *Mint*

[136] 'Push for cash amid Covid: 159 districts in 25 states see decline in fixed deposits', 21 June 2021, *The Indian Express*

Rajan, was in office only two years. He oversaw the period of demonetisation, and left after differences with the government.

Arvind Panagariya, economist and professor at Columbia University, championed Modi on the assumption that Modi, like Panagariya, was a free-market man. He resigned as deputy head of the NITI Aayog (the head is Modi) in September 2017 to return to the US. Since then, he has been a critic of the Indian government's protectionism. He believes that India's new tariffs on tyres and television sets,[137] which came in 2020 will reverse the thinking of demonetisation and encourage the creation of micro and small enterprises.[138] He said he was worried that the 'wrong turn' taken in 2017 by Modi, towards protectionism, had not yet been reversed.'

After the Atmanirbhar Bharat plan was made public in August 2020, Panagariya said that 'policy mistakes' by Modi on international trade were undoing the good work done in 1991.[139]

'What has this policy achieved in six years?' he asked of Atmanirbhar Bharat. 'Imports of electronics goods have gone up from $32.4 billion in 2013–14 to $55.6 billion in 2018–19, while exports inched up from $7.6 billion to $8.9 billion over the same period. Predictably, protected and subsidised, several mobile phone assembly firms have come up during these years but they have not added up to a vibrant electronics industry. Nearly all locally owned firms are small by global standards with none that is about to turn into an export powerhouse.'[140]

Panagariya was talking of the 'Make in India' initiative and the Atmanirbhar Bharat when he spoke of the six-year time period. Regardless of that, the problem here is the assumption that Modi had some strategic direction in the first instance. It is hardly Modi's fault that Panagariya saw himself and his free-market ideology in the person of Modi.

Panagariya flitted between adoration[141] and deification of Modi one day[142] and the next day producing a paper the key thesis of which was that India's best growth years were actually from 2003–14.[143]

---

[137] 'Thailand, European Union question India's import restrictions on tyres, ACs and TV sets', 1 November 2020, *The Economic Times*

[138] 'Arvind Panagariya cautions govt: Import licences will be a complete violation of WTO', 8 August 2020, *The Economic Times*

[139] 'Giving up on the world?', 17 August 2020, *The Economic Times*

[140] 'Arvind Panagariya says despite protection Indian electronics sector is not world class', 21 March 2021, *CNBC*

[141] '"Modinomics" gets thumbs up from Arvind Panagariya', 4 January 2019, *Mint*

[142] 'Arvind Panagariya calls Budget 2021 "mind-blowing", says hopes from PM Modi now coming true', 3 February 2021, *Times Now News*

[143] 'Arvind Panagariya says despite protection Indian electronics sector is not world class', 21 March 2021, *CNBC*

Such people could not be relied on to guide someone as mercurial as Modi.

Other respected economists to leave after problems with the government were Viral Acharya, deputy governor of the Reserve Bank, who left in June 2019, and Rathin Roy from Modi's economic advisory council, who left in September 2019. Debroy has been the only economist who has remained with Modi, defending his policies in public no matter how bad the news has been.

The Ministry of Finance is now more or less run by Modi's office, and the finance minister is an individual of low importance. First Arun Jaitley, then Piyush Goyal and then Nirmala Sitharaman, none of whom has ever won an election, offered themselves to serve in that position. This ministry and the external affairs ministry, which is run by someone who also has not won an election, S. Jaishankar, are the ones that Modi has a keen interest in and regularly engages with personally.

The role of the ministry, the NITI Aayog think-tank and the PM's Economic Council led by Bibek Debroy is to supply Modi with advice. Think-tank members on leaving have said the prime minister was receptive to ideas that were in conformity with what he wanted but uninterested in the rest. Knowing this, his bureaucracy also stopped passing along material from his advisors which was in contrast to what they thought he preferred.[144]

The finance ministry and the foreign ministry are managed at the top by individuals who find it difficult to say no to Modi, whether it is because they have no authority of their own (which they do not) or because they are opportunists who don't care about the consequences. Or both. The results in the Ministry of Finance can be seen, even from the data that the government itself has presented—an economy in free fall since January 2018 and finishing up in a recession. However, the ministry has not acknowledged this long-term decline and perhaps rightly. Why should the minister carry the can for Modi in failure when she can have no claim when there is success? India's record under Modi, from unemployment to exports, remains unspoken about by the government because accountability doesn't exist at the ministerial level. The damage can be disowned merely by not speaking of it at all.

Under Modi, tax revenues have fallen but the fiscal deficit was being shown at the same level. Tax to GDP had fallen but the Budget maintained the fiscal deficit levels—right up till the time when the recession made fudging

---

[144] 'We are no longer a functioning, growing and aspirational India: Dr Rathin Roy', https://youtu.be/oE48XvvJlrM

the numbers impossible. The fall was primarily due to an overestimation of indirect tax collections.

After Modi was re-elected in May 2019, the first budget of the new administration was presented on 5 July 2019 and the real numbers were hidden in the Economic Survey. This was spotted by Rathin Roy, part of the PM's Economic Council but still not privy to the data.[145] It was speculated that Modi was unaware of what was going on. The budget speech made by Sitharaman did not even contain the words 'fiscal deficit'.

Modi's response to a shortfall in indirect tax revenues was to slash direct taxes. The government announced corporate tax cuts on 20 September 2019. The announcement could have been made without actually effecting the cuts immediately, so that the government could have benefited from the existing rate till the new financial year when the cuts would kick in. But this was not apparently thought through or not important enough. Or perhaps revenues, even in the middle of a crisis, took second place to publicity as the headlines revealed.[146] The day after the cuts were announced—21 September—Modi flew to Houston for the 'Howdy Modi' event with Donald Trump and to meet American business executives to invite investment.

The cuts cost India Rs 1.45 lakh crore in lost revenue.[147] Only the top 1 per cent of corporate India's companies benefited from the cuts (including many public sector units whose profits would come back to the Union, their owner).

An analysis showed no increase in FDI after the cut was announced.[148] Also, most of the FDI coming in was for services, which had not received any tangible benefits, unlike manufacturing firms.[149] And FDI in manufacturing had actually decelerated, in keeping with the trend we have seen earlier. In effect, India gave up a large proportion of its tax revenues for no real return.

It is true and fair to say that such policies pay off only in the medium and long term. It is not fair to expect them to bear fruit immediately. That is precisely why the key point was that the cuts could have been announced without being immediately implemented, saving some of the now lost revenues. But that may not have been dramatic enough for Modi.

---

[145] 'A silent fiscal crisis', 6 July 2019, *Business Standard*

[146] 'Tax cut gives PM Narendra Modi perfect pitch to win American investments', 21 September 2019, *The Economic Times*

[147] 'Corporate tax cut to cost govt Rs 1.45 lakh crore', 20 September 2019, *Business Today*

[148] 'Why India needs to rethink its corporate tax cut', 14 May 2020, *Scroll.in*

[149] 'Greenfield FDI may contract for second straight year: UNCTAD', 22 June 2021, *Mint*.

Modi's eccentric and arbitrary functioning mixed with his keen interest to meddle and put a PR spin to everything has affected the economy in profound ways. A key indicator of economic activity is the flow of bank credit to productive sectors. It was growing at 14 per cent when Modi took office in 2014 but has remained in the single digits for most of his time in office. It began to plummet in 2019. It stood at 5.8 per cent in July 2020, the same figure that it was in 2017 just after demonetisation. It fell to 4.9 per cent in mid-2021.[150]

Loans to micro and small industries in June 2020 actually shrank 7.6 per cent, and for medium-sized industries they shrank by 9.4 per cent.[151] Even growth in lending to large industries was flat at 0.4 per cent. Chetan Ghate, external member of the RBI, expressed his worry that a negative credit supply shock to the MSME sector may lead to small businesses shifting towards higher-cost providers of credit, affecting growth and wages long-term.

Prasenjit Bose and Zico Dasgupta came to the same conclusion in their contributing chapter in a book on Modi's first term.[152] They wrote that, 'Our calculations, based on RBI data on bank credit to the MSMEs in the industrial sector, show that aggregate credit flow to them in the past three years has actually been negative, in keeping with the general trend in the industrial sector. For the MSMEs in the services sector, the aggregate net credit flow in the past three years has increased in comparison to the two years before the introduction of the MUDRA scheme. Being unable to revive bank credit to the MSME industrial sector, bank credit growth seems to have been channelled into the MSME services sector. Yet, even if we combine the two, the net aggregate bank credit flow to the total MSME sector in the post-MUDRA period is actually lower than the previous two years.' Credit to MSMEs in 2022–23 was expanding at a slower pace than it had contracted the previous year.[153]

Total new investments announced fell by 70.5 per cent in 2020–21.[154] But even before Covid, investment had ended in India. New investments

[150] 'Bank credit grows slowest in 4 years', 1 May 2021, *The Times of India*
[151] 'Credit growth to MSME sector falls sharply despite government's relief measures', 21 August 2020, *The New Indian Express*
[152] 'Breaking Bad—India's banking stress', in *A Quantum Leap In the Wrong Direction?*, Rohit Azad, Shouvik Chakraborty, Srinivasan Ramani, Dipa Sinha (eds), Orient BlackSwan, 2019
[153] 'Credit growth to MSME sector firm in 2022-23: SBI research report', 31 July 2022, PTI
[154] 'The copywriting skills of RBI governor Shaktikanta Das', 11 April 2021, *Deccan Herald*

announced in 2019–20 were lower than in each of the years between even 2006–07 and 2011–12. Total lending to industry by banks was Rs 27.86 lakh crore as of February 2021; it was Rs 27.45 lakh crore as of February 2016. There had been no growth.

Credit was falling not because of the higher cost of funds but lack of genuine demand on the ground.[155] The 'worsening economic slowdown has hit consumer confidence prompting customers to postpone purchases'. And the RBI's Consumer Confidence Survey confirmed this trend. A full 70 per cent of those surveyed by the RBI in 2021 expected their non-essential spending to be flat or in decline into 2022.[156] A CMIE survey asked people to compare their incomes in May 2021 to a year ago. Fifty-five per cent said it was worse than in 2020 and 42 per cent said it was the same. Meaning that, accounting for inflation, 97 per cent of Indians were poorer in 2021 than they were in 2020.[157]

Modi put a one-year freeze on one of his key economic reforms in 2020 and through the beginning of 2021. This was the Insolvency and Bankruptcy Code. It shifted the balance of power from borrower to lender, allowing banks to recover defaults and restructure debt. Banks could do this with a fairly potent tool: they could throw the promoter out. As the economic crisis accelerated with the spread of Covid, the government excluded Covid-related debt from being resolved in this fashion, meaning all future cases of default.

This meant that India's debt problem was bigger than was accepted (because banks were under no obligation to show their real debt, since the default was not a default but merely a rollover or a moratorium).

The suspension was lifted and the law watered down to make it easier for smaller firms to restructure but even after it was lifted, 'sentiments surrounding distressed assets was discouraging creditors from dragging debtors to tribunals'.[158]

It was true that Covid brought stress into two specific parts of bank credit where it may not have existed in large measure before.

The first was the services side, which now began to show an inability to pay back, especially sectors like hospitality, entertainment, travel and transport, including aviation. And the other was on the personal loan side,

[155] 'Why is bank credit growth plummeting?', 2 March 2020, *moneycontrol.com*
[156] 'RBI Consumer Confidence Survey: Consumers see current economic situation as significantly worse than a year ago', 10 February 2021, *moneycontrol.com*
[157] '97% Indians poorer post-Covid; steady fall in salaried jobs: Mahesh Vyas', 29 May 2021, *Business Standard*
[158] 'No surge in fresh bankruptcy filings post lifting of one-year IBC ban', 19 May 2021, *Mint*

where individuals out of work were skipping EMIs on homes, appliances and vehicles. Auto-debit failures (payments for EMIs, utilities and insurance) rose from 21 per cent in April 2017 to 34 per cent in April 2021, showing real stress in the system.[159] This real red ink on the balance sheets of banks would reveal itself only with time.

What used to be India's growth drivers have fallen off in the last few years. Before Modi, exports were growing at 16 per cent and investment at 10 per cent a year. After 2014, exports flatlined as we have seen and investments began to slow to a stop, and contracted in 2019–20. Even before Covid, investments were already at a two-decade low.[160] The third driver, private consumption, grew at 7 per cent on average but slowed to 5.3 per cent in 2019–20, before Covid. It then crashed to -9 per cent in 2020–21, the lowest since 1951.[161] It was government spending that had been holding up an economy whose 'animal spirits' were threatened to be unleashed by Modi, but this did not happen. With the fiscal deficit blown, the space available for the State also contracted. In 2019–20, government spending rose 7.8 per cent, but in 2020–21, only by 2.9 per cent. There is no dispute that the economy is shattered. The defence that this is entirely externally induced is false.

Modi's time in office came with some advantages and some disadvantages. Global trade fell before he took office and so, again with the caveat that this did not apply to nations like Bangladesh, Vietnam and China which executed a strategy to grow, exports suffered. On the other hand, petroleum prices fell so Modi was able to shore up the Union's revenues by not passing on the benefit to citizens. Having said that, all these things are not material in the larger sense. The fact is that Modi did not enter office by saying he would carry on business as usual. His promise was great change for the better, particularly with the economy. Here he has failed to deliver and failed also to imagine.

Part 8: Leading India Into The Trap

Rathin Roy, who spent a term on Modi's Economic Council, has a thesis about the economy which was also articulated in a 2002 article (which later

---

[159] 'Auto-debit defaults rise amid COVID second wave', 14 May 2021, *CNBCTV18.com*
[160] 'Investment rate in India at two-decade low in FY 20, says CARE Ratings', 30 March 2020, *The Hindu BusinessLine*
[161] 'India FY21 GDP data: Major decline in private consumption even as government spending grows', 31 May 2021, *moneycontrol.com*

became a book) by C.K. Prahalad and Stuart Hart—'The fortune at the bottom of the pyramid'. The thesis is that if corporates engaged with the poor as consumers instead of engaging just the middle class, everyone would benefit.

Roy says that for three decades since liberalisation, growth has come from and been focussed on the consumption of the top 15 crore Indians. The high frequency indicators of the economy reflected this. The month-on-month and year-on-year increase of sales of automobiles, two-wheelers and air conditioners were tracked as the leading indicators of growth. But how many Indians consumed these things? Only the top 15 crore, not the remaining 120 crore.

In Roy's telling, GDP growth has structurally tapered off in India because the consumption of this privileged set has now plateaued. Most of them have already bought their house (urban housing had more supply than demand) and their car (sales of cars and two-wheelers in 2020–21 were lower than they were six years before) and also their appliances. Replacement of these were not frequent. Their next spends, Roy says, were made abroad, in terms of holidays, education and often even health. Their contribution to GDP growth is now flat.

Roy has written that, relative to the incomes of this segment, the prices of the things they consumed—cars, fast-moving consumer goods, air travel—fell after liberalisation, and this segment also enjoyed the benefit of being able to more easily access credit.[162]

If India must have high growth again, the demand would need to come from the remaining 1.2 billion Indians. They consume those things that all Indians do: food, clothing, healthcare, education and housing.

However, the Indian market is unable to provide these to them without a subsidy. Where market forces has products or services for them, say in education or health, these are of inferior quality. The Indian who makes a median income has never been able to purchase with her living wage the sort of quality that she deserves and is her right.

Arvind Subramanian has countered this by pointing to the fact that the consumption of fast-moving consumer goods, such as cosmetics, soaps and detergents, had risen at the same rate since 1991 as nominal GDP. Meaning that people being lifted out of poverty were consuming and contributing to economic growth. So there may be, according to Subramanian, some issue with this inequality thesis. But let us stay with what Roy is positing. He

---

[162] 'Demand, supply and growth slowdowns', 6 December 2019, *Business Standard*

says, 'Structural barriers continue to limit aggregate demand for the things consumed by the next 300 million.' The example he gives is textile imports from Bangladesh and Vietnam, which flooded the Indian market for shirts. If you bought a shirt made in India, it would be more expensive than the one imported from these places because they had wage advantages over those parts of India where manufacturing facilities existed. This was primarily in western and southern India, where wages were high because demand for labour and the cost of living were also higher than the rest of India. Wages in Bangladesh were about Rs 5,000 to Rs 6,000 per month, half of what they were in India (Rs 10,000 a month), and the productivity of the workers was double.[163]

Even those Indian workers who lived in cities did not get the sort of facilities that they should be able to afford on a living wage because of the cost of housing. Many lived in hovels, despite the fact that the government is the largest landowner in the country, especially in urban spaces.

Minimum-wage earners in urban India could not access decent healthcare and education. This was because there was no provider of these necessities to them at the cost that they could afford. The market was not focussed on the needs of these next 30 crore consumers and the drivers of economic growth had not been those producing for their consumption. These things that all Indians consume—food, healthcare, housing, clothing—were not seen as economic indicators, and there was no high frequency data on them. If there had been, Roy argues, it would have been noticed that India could produce and export garments for the wealthy but didn't produce them for its own people. In the Modi years, India's textile and garments exports sputtered while imports grew.[164]

There were constraints to supplying these essentials to India's minimum-wage earners, and these were the costs of logistics and energy, a lack of investment in human capital and research, and poor productivity. Combined, these struck at India's ability to produce essential services and goods at scale and quality.

One reason and perhaps the main one for this was that those parts of India that might be able to produce goods and services more cheaply because of a labour cost advantage, like Uttar Pradesh, Bihar, Chhattisgarh, Jharkhand, Odisha and Bengal, had little industry. It wasn't as if the people

---

[163] 'Why India is losing out to neighbouring Bangladesh in textile exports', 16 January 2019, *Business Standard*

[164] 'Unusual trend: Textile imports zoom as exports falter', 10 January 2020, *The Financial Express*

there didn't have the ability to produce. It was actually the individuals from these very parts who migrated and lived in pitiable conditions in the west and south of India where they worked and produced the goods and services that they themselves could not afford. They had the skills but no opportunity where they lived, and so were forced to migrate.

India needed to take production, especially manufacturing, to where the large part of its population was—in the north and east. This would not be easy and needed a lot of thinking, planning and execution capacity. But unless it happened, India would continue to chug along at the current pace at best, and in the current skewed manner of growth. This, in turn, was taking it inevitably to what is called a middle-income trap.

The middle-income trap is where a country finds itself when wages rise to the point that growth in export-driven, labour-intensive, low-skill manufacturing is exhausted before the country attains the innovative capability to boost productivity and compete with developed countries in higher value-chain industries. This closes off the avenues for further growth and wages stagnate.

Middle-income nations are those where the per capita income is between $1,000 and $12,000.

South Korea, Taiwan and Singapore spent about twenty-seven years each as middle-income economies before moving up to upper-income level, above $12,000. Today, South Korea is at over $30,000 and Singapore over $60,000. There's no specific number of years in which a nation must make the jump, since this is only a theory, but around thirty years is seen as a sort of cut-off.

Nations that enter the 'trap' have never been able to leave it. They are Russia, Argentina, Brazil, South Africa and Mexico. India became a lower middle income nation in 2007 when its per capita income crossed $1,000. Today, the figure is just under $2,000. China was at $1,000 only eight years before India, but its per capita income today is $10,000.

India has until 2025, perhaps 2027, to turn this around because we are already off the pace and lagging.

No such theory of change such as expressed by Roy is visible in Modinomics, which is a series of scattershot pronouncements with no coherent centre.

The assumption made thus far has been that Modi has no real economic framework and no depth of strategy. The failure of demonetisation, the unravelling of federalism through GST, the lack of preparation before the national lockdown and the surprise return to 1970s-style import substitution (Atmanirbhar Bharat) seem to suggest that.

We must also look at what Modi has succeeded in doing—wiping out a substantial part of India's informal and unorganised sector—and ask if this was deliberate.

In December 2020, NITI Aayog's chief Amitabh Kant was attacked for saying that India had 'too much democracy'. However, another part of his speech went relatively unnoticed. Kant said: 'In India we are too much of a democracy so we keep supporting everybody.' He went on to elaborate, 'For the first time in India a government has thought big in terms of size and scale and said we want to produce global champions. Nobody had the political will and the courage to say that we want to support five companies who want to be global champions. Everyone used to say I want to support everyone in India, I want to get votes from everyone.'[165]

What he was saying in essence was that the government of India would back a very small set of elite firms. This was being done in two ways. One called 'formalisation' and the second through blocking foreign competition in crucial sectors ('import substitution').

The formalisation theory was that India had too many small companies and this was inefficient. It should instead have only a handful of very large players running its economy, and these giants would then compete with large firms around the world. So what could the government do to make this possible? It would try and make it difficult for the small- and medium-sized industrialists to exist. This is also called formalisation because it assumes that the small- and medium-sized entities in business are generally inefficient and tax thieves. They cheat the government by operating in cash. To make their existence difficult, if not impossible, the first step was to remove cash from the economy. This was done on Tuesday, 8 November 2016. Businesses that depended on cash transactions, even if they were legitimate ones, were not able to operate for weeks and were hampered for months. The large businesses were not affected because they could use electronic transfers, just as the upper class in the metropolitan areas managed with their credit and debit cards.

The second stroke against the small and medium sector was GST, which was designed in a way as to require significant expertise in-house or on contract for compliance. The repeated and frequent filing of returns and the managing of the digital system meant that once again a large number of people exited from businesses that became unviable because of the added cost

---

[165] '"Too much democracy": NITI Aayog CEO Amitabh Kant denies what he stated twice', 9 December 2020, *altnews.in*

or simply because people could not cope with the new complications and chose to do something else. Who benefited from the exit of the small and medium businesses? Again, the large ones.

The third stroke was the lockdown of 2020, which broke the back of the small and medium sector, which had neither the cash reserves to be able to deal with such a blow nor the ability to get their staff to 'work from home'.

Everything that appeared to be puzzling to many about the Modi government's economic policy appears to make sense after we consider what it is deliberately doing to this nation. Modi's former advisor and enthusiast Arvind Panagariya had complained about the Atmanirbhar Bharat programme, saying that it was merely import substitution and had failed before. But what if it was deliberate to ensure that some industrialists could sell their goods at a higher price to Indians than the cheaper imported products from the competition?[166]

Panagariya wrote a book, a review of which laid out the case: 'How can a 20-person firm from India compete with a 200-person firm from China in the global marketplace? Why are we surprised the apparel opportunity passed us by? Going forward, a renewed focus on exports should endogenously put pressure on firm size to grow, with implications for productivity and wages.'[167] Again, make firms larger by wiping out the small ones.

Atmanirbhar Bharat privileges the industrialist over the consumer, but that is not the way that it is advertised. Who does the policy seek to make atmanirbhar? It is not the consumer or the citizen, who must pay more. It is those selected favourites of the government who have been tasked with winning, while the rest are left deliberately to fail.

Let us take this a step further and see if what Kant says the Modi government is intent on doing has worked.

An analysis of 3,220 listed non-finance companies revealed that in the last quarter of the calendar year 2020, the companies in the bottom 70 per cent showed a fall in sales which they surrendered to the top tiers.[168] Sales had been down by 6.7 per cent in the September 2019 quarter, down 5 per cent in the December 2019 quarter, down 9.8 per cent in the March 2020 quarter (just before the lockdown). In the first quarter post lockdown ending June 2020, net sales were down 39 per cent. In the September 2020 quarter, down 10 per cent, and in the December 2020 quarter, down about 1 per

---

[166] 'TV prices have soared 300% in the last eight months', 5 March 2021, IANS

[167] 'Arvind Panagariya's book points out that export remain key to economic growth', 19 November 2020, *The Indian Express*

[168] 'Firm size matters in recovery', 4 March 2021, *cmie.com*

cent. In a declining market, the large fish were taking a bigger share.[169] And they were profiting. The share of corporate taxes in government revenue fell to its lowest in a decade after the tax cuts on corporates and the tax rise on petrol and diesel.[170] The ratio of corporate profits to GDP also hit a ten-year high.[171]

The Economist reported that Gautam Adani's net worth went up by 750 per cent in 2020. Mukesh Ambani's went up by 350 per cent in that year—the year in which India's GDP shrank and crores became destitute.[172] In the first five months of 2021, Adani's wealth grew by $32 billion (over Rs 2 lakh crore) and he became Asia's second-richest man, behind Ambani.[173] The money was flocking to where it was felt to be winning in the long term under Modi.

Amid the pandemic, in 2020, India added 55 new dollar billionaires (individuals worth more than Rs 7,000 crore), more than one every week.[174] This was a 45 per cent jump compared to the year before and took the total number of Indian billionaires to 177.

The Economist stated that 'most alarmingly, in India some of the rich have become super-rich by using their heft to crush smaller competitors and thus corner multiple chunks of the economy. The tilt in fortunes has rewarded not so much technical innovation or productivity growth or the opening of new markets as the wielding of political influence and privileged access to capital to capture and protect existing markets'.

This is, of course, deliberate.

Oxfam reported at the beginning of 2019 that the top 1 per cent of India had 73 per cent of the nation's wealth. In the next two years, this would change even more in favour of the wealthy.

The Economist said that the share of wealth and income going to the top 1 per cent has accelerated in recent years in India, quoting Credit Suisse to say that the richest 1 per cent of Indians controlled more wealth than the richest 1 per cent of Americans or Chinese.

---

[169] Ibid.

[170] 'India's tax burden shifted from boardrooms to petrol pumps during Covid-19', 1 June 2021, *Hindustan Times*

[171] 'Corporate profit to GDP ratio hits 10-year high of 2.63% in FY21', 31 May 2021, *Business Standard*

[172] 'Compounding inequality: India's super-rich are getting much richer, even as economy shrinks by a tenth', 3 December 2020, *The Economist*

[173] 'Gautam Adani beats China's Zong Shanshan to become Asia's second richest man', 20 May 2021, *The Economic Times*

[174] 'In 2020, world added 3 billionaires every two days, India added one every week', 2 March 2021, *The Hindu*

Even if Atmanirbhar and formalisation and the rest of it was designed as some secret strategy to pump up five companies, the thinking is still shallow. India has low levels of consumption. There is not a large enough market within India to develop a world champion that is not exposed to global competition simply through being protected by tariffs. On the other hand, India also has a large pool of talent that could be more productive when engaged with the global economy.

The foreign policy of Manmohan Singh made Indian access and openness towards furthering economic opportunity the focal point of engaging the world. This was likely one reason why a quarter billion Indians (27 crore) were pulled out of poverty in his two terms, according to a study by the Oxford Poverty and Human Development Initiative.[175] Atmanirbhar Bharat suggests something of the opposite in terms of engaging the world while also being intangible and vague. Foreign minister Jaishankar says it means self-reliance but also that it means not shutting out the world.[176] In practice, it takes on the form of import substitution and tariffs, making India uncompetitive and closing off access, as nations retaliate. How would it help India grow economically? Modi has not been pressed to answer this just as he hasn't on why the numbers are so weak under him. All in all, Atmanirbhar Bharat is as thought-through as the rest of Modinomics.

Indeed, it is evident that even the scattershot pronouncements we looked at in the beginning of this chapter have been just that, words without meaning. Many of them have resulted in actions that have set India back or done the opposite of what their stated intention was.

The Union has steadily denied revenue to states by raising it not as taxes but as cess, which it is not obliged to share with states. In 2021-22, the Centre halved the amount of excise duty on petrol it would share with state governments.[177] What part of this sounds like Moditva 4 ('Co-operative, not coercive federalism')? In August 2020, Modi refused to honour the Centre's solemn commitment made to states on GST revenues, claiming Covid was an act of god and asking them to fend for themselves. This is not co-operative federalism.

---

[175] 'India lifted 271 million people out of poverty in 10 years: UN', 12 July 2019, *The Hindu*

[176] 'Nationalism will be a dominating feature in post-Covid world, says Jaishankar', 9 September 2020, *The Indian Express*

[177] 'Only 1.7% of Central Govt Petrol Taxes Shared with States—Where Has Cooperative Federalism Gone?', 6 April 2021, vivekkaul.com

Terrorism in Kashmir measured by fatalities is up, and tourism is on the ventilator. Where does that leave Moditva 7—'Tourism unites, terrorism divides'.

In Moditva 14 ('People public private partnership'), Modi's 'solution' is 'NGOs and local communities must do a social audit of development projects'. The Modi government's Environment Impact Assessment 2020 does the opposite. Far from a social audit, it exempts projects from any public consultation.

'Economy with mass production by the masses' (Moditva 13) is not the line to describe a contracting manufacturing sector. And whatever 'Development politics over vote-bank politics' (Moditva 5) might mean, what it has delivered is a weakened economy, more poverty, an oligarchy and a divided society through aggressive majoritarianism. Releasing the book on Moditva when he was BJP president, Rajnath Singh said, 'Moditva is an idea and a phenomenon.'[178] No, it is not.

Modi's one-liners have not shown any evidence or result of being rooted in strategy or a vision. He has a record, often ignored, of making statements detached from reality. When I interviewed him as chief minister of Gujarat, he said he would make the state's GDP grow at 15 per cent a year and that would take India's growth to 10 per cent. Neither happened, of course. Aspiring to something while acting incompetently was good enough. Often, what was running, even if not perfectly, was destroyed.

The Planning Commission was replaced with the NITI Aayog, which is meant to be a think-tank but has no independent voice and usually jumps in to act as a cheerleader for whatever acronym Modi announces.

What Modinomics has achieved in office is apparent and visible. It has put under stress, if not entirely wiped out, large parts of the unorganised sector through deliberate action. It has put hurdles in the way of and made it more difficult for the proprietor, the micro-sized unit and the household firm to operate and compete. It has not been able to recognise the exhaustion of the engine that drives the economy. And it has cut at the root of the part that was already being ignored.

Even before Covid and the lockdown, analysts observed that the Budget of 2020 was 'an admission of defeat' because it contained no ideas about how to get out of the problem the government had put itself into.[179] Before the

---

[178] 'Moditva—The Idea Behind the Man', 25 February 2014, BJP YouTube channel
[179] 'Budget 2020 reads like a five-year plan with lots of targets but no road map', 3 February 2020, *The Indian Express*

Covid crisis and the recession, the problems of demand, declining savings rate and the banking crisis were already peaking.

The prospects for the economy even after Modi has gone are grim. The price that Modinomics has extracted shows unambiguously in the data, whether it is the numbers on the economy, employment or the data on the health and well-being of Indians.

The percentage of daily-wage earners in those who die by suicide has been steadily rising under Modi, doubling to 23.4 per cent in 2019 as compared to six years before. This is per the government's own data.[180]

At nearly a quarter of the suicides, or 32,563 of the total 1,39,123, daily-wage earners comprised the largest chunk of such deaths recorded by the National Crime Records Bureau, the report said. The data for daily-wage earners excluded agricultural labourers, who would add another 4,324 suicides to the total.[181] A doubling of suicides in such a short period is unprecedented.

India's efforts at reducing infant mortality faltered after demonetisation. The annual rate of decline in the infant mortality rate, which was 4.8 per cent per year between 2005 and 2016, fell to 2.9 per cent in 2017 and 3.1 per cent in 2018.[182] Several states had inexplicably reversed course and recorded worsening levels of child malnutrition, undoing decades of progress.[183] This data was captured before the Covid pandemic and the future numbers will be worse. The report said that reversals had also happened in child stunting, which reflects chronic undernutrition, and refers to the percentage of children who have low height for their age.

Stunting, more than any other factor, was likely to have long-lasting adverse effects on the cognitive and physical development of a child. This data had come from the government's own National Family Health Survey of 2019–20.

What had the government been doing about this during the year Covid hit? It had not even met on this issue despite having three 'high-level' bodies

---

[180] 'Steady rise in share of daily-wagers in suicides, 23% in 2019', 6 September 2020, *The Indian Express*

[181] 'NCRB data shows 42,480 farmers and daily wagers committed suicide in 2019', 1 September 2020, *The Economic Times*

[182] 'Infant mortality rose after DeMo, Covid may cause another setback: Study', 13 November 2020, *Business Standard*

[183] 'Malnutrition in kids worsens in key states 2015–19', 14 December 2020, *The Indian Express*

that were required to meet every quarter.[184] The three bodies included NITI Aayog's Rajiv Kumar-headed National Nutrition Council (NNC), which comprises 12 Union ministers and five chief ministers on a rotational basis. This body had not met since October 2019. The National Technical Board of Nutrition headed by NITI Aayog member V.K. Paul[185] had not met since August 2018. It appears to have been disbanded and its page on the NITI site has been taken down in 2021.[186]

In October 2020, the Global Hunger Index (GHI) placed India 94th among 107 countries, much behind Bangladesh, Pakistan and Nepal. India was now battling widespread hunger, in their view.

GHI is based on four indicators: the proportion of undernourished; the proportion of children under the age of five suffering from wasting (less weight in proportion to their height); the proportion of children under five suffering from stunting (low height in proportion to their age); and the mortality rate of children under five. India is harming its next generation.

The government had no response to this finding, just as it had none when India fell in GDP per capita behind Bangladesh. In 2014, India's per capita GDP ($1573) was about 50 per cent ahead of Bangladesh's ($1118).[187] At the end of the financial year 2020–21, Bangladesh was at $2227 and India at $1947.[188] In the Modi years, Bangladesh has quietly doubled its income while India has produced much bluster without performance.

---

[184] 'Three top panels on nutrition, but zero meetings in pandemic year', 7 January 2021, *The Hindu*

[185] At a press conference Paul put up a slide saying India would be over the pandemic by 16 May 2020: 'Coronavirus | Surge disproves NITI Aayog's "zero cases by May 16" prediction', 17 May 2020, *The Hindu*

[186] http://niti.gov.in/national-technical-board-nutrition-ntbn

[187] 'GDP per capita (current US$)—India', data.worldbank.org

[188] 'Bangladesh beats India in per capita income', 20 May 2021, *The New Indian Express*

4

A POLICY OF NO NAME

Question: Which of these statements was a part of the Modi government's official Pakistan policy?
1) India will talk to Pakistan.[1]
2) India will not talk to Pakistan.[2]
3) India will not talk to Pakistan so long as it keeps firing across the LoC.[3]
4) India will talk to Pakistan only after it stops exporting terror.[4]
5) India will not talk to Pakistan if it talks to Kashmiris.[5]
6) India will talk to Pakistan but only about terrorism.[6]
7) India will talk to Pakistan about Kashmir.[7]
8) India will talk to Pakistan but only about PoK not about Kashmir.[8]
9) India will talk to Pakistan but only about terror, not Kashmir.[9]

---

[1] 'Narendra Modi holds impromptu talks with Nawaz Sharif in Lahore', 25 December 2015, *Scroll.in*

[2] 'No message for talks sent to Pakistan, says MEA', 15 October 2020, *The Hindu*

[3] 'Sushma Swaraj squarely blames Pakistan for spoiling foreign secretary-level talks with India', 26 September 2016, *Business Standard*

[4] 'India can talk to Pakistan but not to "Terroristan": S Jaishankar', 25 September 2019, PTI

[5] 'No talks with Pakistan if it meets Hurriyat: Sushma', 22 August 2015, *Rajya Sabha TV*, *rstv.nic.in*

[6] 'India will talk to Pakistan only on cross-border terrorism, not Kashmir', 18 August 2016, *India Today*

[7] 'Ready to talk with Pakistan on J&K within bilateral framework: India', 28 August 2014, PTI

[8] 'Any future talks with Pakistan will be on PoK, not on J&K: Rajnath Singh', 22 September 2019, *Mint*

[9] 'Ready to talk on terror but not Kashmir: India to Pakistan', 17 August 2016, PTI

10) India will talk to Pakistan because it had already lectured it on terror.[10]

11) India will exchange sweets with Pakistan on Independence Day.[11]

12) India will not exchange sweets with Pakistan on Independence Day.[12]

13) India will exchange sweets with Pakistan on Republic Day.[13]

14) India will not exchange sweets with Pakistan on Republic Day.[14]

15) India will exchange sweets with Pakistan on Diwali.[15]

16 India will not exchange sweets with Pakistan on Diwali.[16]

17) India will exchange sweets with Pakistan on Eid.[17]

18) India will not exchange sweets with Pakistan on Eid.[18]

19) India will do cricket diplomacy with Pakistan.[19]

20) India will not do cricket diplomacy with Pakistan.[20]

21) India will not talk to Pakistan but will reply to each bullet with a bomb at LoC.[21]

22) India will talk to Pakistan because war was not an option.[22]

23) India can defeat Pakistan in war in a week.[23]

---

[10] 'After tough talk on terror, India ready to restart talks with Pakistan', 28 May 2014, *The Economic Times*

[11] 'Independence Day: India-Pak security forces exchange sweets at border', 15 August 2018, *NDTV*

[12] '73rd Independence Day: No exchange of sweets at Attari-Wagah border post', 15 August 2019, *The Hindu*

[13] 'On Republic Day, Indian, Pakistan troops exchange sweets on LoC', 26 January 2017, *Zee News*

[14] 'BSF, Pak Rangers not to exchange sweets on R-Day', 25 January 2020, *Hindustan Times*

[15] 'On Diwali, India, Pakistan troops exchange sweets at Wagah Border', 7 November 2018, *Outlook*

[16] 'No exchange of sweets at Attari border this Diwali', 30 October 2016, *Deccan Herald*

[17] 'Indian and Pakistani armies exchange sweets on the occasion of Eid-ul-Fitr', 5 June 2019, *The Indian Express*

[18] 'No exchange of sweets between BSF, Pakistan Rangers at Wagah Border on Eid', 25 March 2020, ANI

[19] 'Modi's cricket diplomacy: Renewing political contact with Pakistan', 13 February 2015, *The Indian Express*

[20] 'Amit Shah rules out Indo-Pak "bilateral" cricket series; BJP backs him', 18 June 2017, *Business Standard*

[21] 'Will reply to Pakistan's bullets with bombs: Amit Shah', 29 March 2019, IANS

[22] 'War with Pakistan not an option, India will continue talks: Swaraj', 16 December 2015, PTI

[23] 'India can now defeat Pakistan "in 7-10 days", says Narendra Modi', 29 January 2020, AFP

24) India would not give in to pressure on LoC firing.[24]

25) India will agree to LoC ceasefire because violations have increased.[25]

26) India will trade with Pakistan.[26]

27) India will not trade with Pakistan.[27]

The right answer is, of course, all of them were part of the official policy.

The truth of it is that the Modi government has no actual Pakistan policy, if, by policy, we mean a deliberate system of principles to guide decisions and achieve rational outcomes. He has no real Pakistan strategy, if, by strategy, we mean a plan of action designed to achieve a long-term aim.

Magnanimity, pettiness, confusion, disinterest, passion, bipolarity. That is the sum and substance of it. It is a hot mess.

Pakistan is the enemy. Talking to it is distasteful. The Modi government is most comfortable with hostility. But it hasn't thought through what hostility is intended to achieve. Instinctively, it wants to hurt Pakistan because it had maliciously undone Bharat Mata. Pakistan's behaviour is assumed to be pathological and not based on self-interest, and that means India's response also has to be demented. The government is reluctant to engage at all but doesn't know what to do when engagement becomes inevitable, except to reverse course.

On a matter of strategic importance, the Modi government's behaviour resembles that of a child. Either it will do 'katti' or give a hug. The response to Pakistan is driven by instinct and to apparently blurt out whatever comes to mind at that moment.

It likely did not occur to Modi that by choosing to be mercurial, India was giving Pakistan or agencies inside it a veto over engagement with India. They could determine, direct and even calibrate what Modi was likely to do. It did not occur to him either that permanent disengagement was not possible and some framework was required to be thought up and pursued. This was difficult for Modi because it required subtlety and negotiating uncertainty.

India was able to exercise none of the agency a larger power should have over a smaller one because of this surrendering of the veto by Modi.

Cooperation that was mutually beneficial with Pakistan required suppression of emotion and dispassionate analysis. This was hard for Modi.

---

[24] 'Everything will be fine soon: Narendra Modi on LoC firing', 9 October 2014, *Mint*

[25] 'The surprise India–Pakistan ceasefire call and what it means, explained', 26 February 2021, *moneycontrol.com*

[26] 'Modi seeks full trade normalisation with Pakistan', 24 November 2017, *The Hindu BusinessLine*

[27] 'India suspends cross-LoC trade with Pakistan', 18 April 2018, PTI

It was easier instead to carry on by instinct, resulting in the absurdity of the statements listed above.

In 2019, India did a chest-thumping demonstration to warn Pakistan (the Balakot air-strike post the Pulwama attack in February); in April, India threatened Pakistan with a bomb for every bullet;[28] in 2021, India immediately agreed to a ceasefire on the Pakistan front (the firing had begun in November 2020 along the Line of Control (LoC) in Kashmir and continued till end February when the ceasefire was agreed upon).

Why did this reversal happen? We do not know because the Modi strategy was never explained and each headline existed for its own sake. It is easy for rational actors to engage with irrational ones. Particularly if the irrational power is the weaker one. In this instance, China's likely strategy included peace between India and Pakistan to ensure that its interests in Pakistan—especially the Belt and Road Initiative—were not threatened. Modi was compelled in the end into doing something that was the opposite of what he was boasting about only a few months earlier.

This inconsistency and mindlessness separate Modi's external outreach with what came before him. Let us understand what Modi inherited.

Vishwaguru

On 4 November 2013, Prime Minister Manmohan Singh spoke to over 120 heads of Indian missions and outlined the five principles that defined his foreign policy. These were:

First, recognition that India's relations with the world—the major powers and Asian neighbours—were shaped by its developmental priorities. Singh said that 'the single most important objective of Indian foreign policy has to be to create a global environment conducive to the well-being of our great country'.[29]

Second, that greater integration with the world economy would benefit India and enable Indians to realise their creative potential.

Third, to seek stable, long term and mutually beneficial relations with all major powers. And to work with the international community to create a global economic and security environment beneficial to all nations.

Fourth, to recognise that the Indian subcontinent's shared destiny required greater regional cooperation and connectivity.

---

[28] 'Under Narendra Modi, India would reply to every bullet with bombs: Amit Shah', 7 April 2019, *The Hindu*

[29] 'A free and prosperous India: Five principles of foreign policy', 5 November 2013, mea.gov.in

Fifth, a foreign policy defined not merely by interests, but also by the values dear to Indians: 'India's experiment of pursuing economic development within the framework of a plural, secular and liberal democracy has inspired people around the world and should continue to do so.'

This was a clear exposition of what was sought to be achieved. India would use foreign policy to advance its economic development; it would be friendly with global great powers and its neighbours; and it would be helped in doing this by continuing to be a pluralist and secular democracy.

Whether this policy succeeded and to what extent and what its failures, if any, were can be debated, but there is clarity about what the foreign policy is meant to do. The following year, Narendra Modi released his manifesto for the 2014 elections. Its foreign policy section was headlined 'Nation First, Universal Brotherhood'. It made the following points:

- The BJP believes India must get its rightful place in the world and in international institutions.
- Political stability, progress and peace are essential for South Asia's growth and development, however the UPA 'failed to establish enduring friendly and cooperative relations with India's neighbours' and 'India and its neighbours have drifted apart'.
- In the UPA's policy, 'instead of clarity, we have seen confusion' and because of 'absence of statecraft', India 'is seen to be floundering, whereas it should have been engaging with the world with confidence'. One reason for this floundering was 'the collapse of the Indian economy' which 'has contributed to the sorry state of foreign affairs in no small measure'.

Having set up the problem, the manifesto looked at solutions:

- The BJP would be 'firstly guided by our centuries old tradition of "Vasudhaiva kutumbakam"', however, 'at the same time, our foreign policy will be based on best national interests'.
- It would 'integrate our soft power avenues into our external interchange, particularly, harnessing and focusing on the spiritual, cultural and philosophical dimensions of it'.
- It would 'revive Brand India with the help of our strengths of 5 Ts: Tradition, Talent, Tourism, Trade and Technology'.

These 'solutions' would be achieved through a set of guiding principles, and these were:

- To 'champion uniform international opinion on issues like Terrorism and Global Warming'.
- To not be led by big power interests.

- With its neighbours, India would be friendly, but 'where required we will not hesitate from taking strong stand and steps'.
- It would strengthen SAARC and the Association of South-East Asian Nations (ASEAN).
- It would engage with BRICS, G20 and other global institutions.
- India's states 'will be encouraged to play a greater role in diplomacy'.
- NRIs, PIOs and professionals settled abroad would be mobilised to 'strengthen Brand India'.

The text was accompanied by some NITI Aayog-type jargon. For instance, this sentence that the BJP's 'vision is to fundamentally reboot and reorient the foreign policy goals, content and process, in a manner that locates India's global strategic engagement in a new paradigm and on a wider canvas, that is not just limited to political diplomacy, but also includes our economic, scientific, cultural, political and security interests, both regional and global, on the principles of equality and mutuality, so that it leads to an economically stronger India, and its voice is heard in the international fora'. And 'we will leverage all our resources and people to play a greater role on the international high table'.

It is not easy to narrow down the deliverables and outcomes of Modi's 2014 foreign policy as it was Singh's. What is apparent in it is the idea that India has a 'rightful place', which was being denied it (the text refers to India as being 'Vishwaguru' or the world's teacher). Also, India's primacy would be restored through leadership on global warming and terrorism and through the revival of 'Brand India'.

Modi spoke on 17 January 2017 at the second Raisina Dialogue in Delhi. He said the following about his foreign policy:

- He was here to change mindsets from a state of drift to one of purposeful action. This would come through bold decisions.
- India's economic growth, the welfare of its farmers, employment opportunities, access to capital, technology, markets, resources and security were impacted by external developments. But the world also needed India to rise and so the two were linked.
- Sluggish economic growth and trade volatility were now a fact. Gains from globalisation were not as easy to come by.
- Political and military power were more diffused. The world and Asia had become increasingly multi-polar.
- India's strategic intent was rooted in its civilisational ethos and consisted of realism ('Yatharthvad'), coexistence ('Sah-astitva'), cooperation ('Sahyog') and partnership ('Sahbhagita'). Self-interest

alone was not in Indian culture or behaviour. India would be an anchor for regional and global progress.

- It would help reconfigure global institutions and organisations. It would spread yoga and ayurveda to the world.
- India would take a 'Neighbourhood First' approach. It would shed the burdens of the past and connect the region. With Afghanistan, Bangladesh, Nepal, Bhutan, Sri Lanka and Maldives, India would engage robustly, but Pakistan would have to first give up terror.
- Farther along, India would partner Iran on Chabahar. And it would have strategic maritime interests in the Indian Ocean region.[30]

We can observe that some of the more interesting facets of the 2014 manifesto—for instance, the idea that India's states play a bigger role in diplomacy—appear to have fallen away or been demoted.

Similarly, South Asia drops out entirely of the 2019 manifesto for some reason and there is no mention of SAARC either. It repeats the point about vasudhaiva kutumbakam, a phrase that means all the world is one family. How does that sentiment translate into actual policy in the realm of diplomacy, which is about pursuing self-interest? Something was missing here, and from broad platitudes, the manifesto text goes directly into programmatic detail. It adds a deliverable at the end: India would seek permanent membership of the United Nations Security Council.

How would this be secured? This was not elaborated on. Other than the idea that India was entitled to more than it had and should be given it by the world, there appears to be no direct and specific aim of the Modi foreign policy such as those articulated by Singh.

A link was required to connect Modi's helter-skelter manner with something resembling a doctrine. This came from S. Jaishankar, who served as foreign secretary to Modi and, after the passing away of Sushma Swaraj, as foreign minister in Modi's second administration.

Jaishankar produced a book, which is a compilation of the speeches he gave as foreign minister on things as diverse as China's rise to power, India's lost decades, the Mahabharata, maritime power and the Covid pandemic.[31] This muddle shows in the book.

As a professional, Jaishankar makes much of the word 'outcomes' (used six times in one lecture delivered in November 2019) and says that, in the past, Indian diplomacy has had an obsession with words. Form and process

---

[30] 'Inaugural address by prime minister at second Raisina Dialogue', 17 January 2017, mea.gov.in

[31] *The India Way: Strategies for an Uncertain World*, HarperCollins India, 2020

had become more important than outcomes, but this has now changed and outcomes, meaning the end result, would now be the target of the Modi government's foreign policy.

Jaishankar assumes that the US and Europe will continue to look inward (his book was published just before Trump lost), while China would continue to rise. This would open the space for countries like India to be opportunistic in their engagements with the world and they did not need consistency. What India wanted was a 'multi-polar Asia'—meaning one in which India could claim parity with China. Many balls would need to be kept in the air (Jaishankar has a fondness for stock phrases) and India would handle them with dexterity. This was opportunism but that was all right because opportunism was India's culture. The Mahabharata's lessons, Jaishankar says, are that deceit and immorality are merely to 'not play by the rules'.[32] Drona's despicable demanding of Eklavya's thumb, Indra's duplicitous appropriation of Karna's armour, Arjuna using Shikhandi as a human shield, these were but 'practices and traditions'.[33]

Inconsistency in policy was not only fine but required because 'obsessing about consistency' made little sense in changing circumstances.[34]

Here was a man who could put into words the inane approach Modi displayed, such as we have observed in his Pakistan policy, and make it sound reasonable. But what was such a doctrine to be called?

In a speech he made where he first laid out this doctrine of opportunism and inconsistency, Jaishankar said it is hard to give it a name. He takes up and discards the phrases—'multi-alignment' ('sounds too opportunistic') and 'India first' ('sounds self centred'). He settles at 'advancing prosperity and influence', which he says is accurate but admits is not catchy. He believes some name for it will eventually come if it is pursued long enough, because part of the challenge is that we are still in the early phase of a major transition.[35]

Perhaps that is so.

Another reason could be that this was no real foreign policy at all.

What interested Modi, and what made for pageant and ceremony, was being passed off as something meaningful.

It is not easy to escape the conclusion that Jaishankar provided the sophistry to cover what was essentially random and directionless Modi behaviour passing off as foreign policy strategy.

---

[32] Ibid., p. 52

[33] Ibid., p. 53

[34] Ibid., p. 68

[35] 'External affairs minister's speech at the 4th Ramnath Goenka Lecture', 14 November 2019, mea.gov.in

There is no role for India the civilisational entity, which nationalists from Nehru to the BJP have made much of. There is no vasudhaiva kutumbakam-type romanticism or Vishwaguru-type nonsense here, and Jaishankar's nameless doctrine is stripped of all forms of morality and ethic. This is not India engaging with the world on the strength of Indian pluralism. The world is a transactional place and India must be dexterous enough to be able to take advantage of it. The centrepiece of this line of thinking was to take advantage of the war in Ukraine and buy cheap Russian oil. Europe, dependent on Russian gas for energy could hardly press other nations for buying from Russia. India did so, along with China. How much cheaper was it? The average landed price of imported crude for April–December 2022 was $99.2 per barrel. If oil from Russia was excluded, the average price was $101.2, meaning a saving of $2 per barrel.[36] And this money did not come back to the taxpayer, instead it enriched private refiners like Reliance.[37] Jaishankar does not appear to have anticipated that this theory of his worked both ways. In such a world as he imagined, others would also seek to take advantage of India. Jaishankar also appeared to have assumed that the BJP's 'nationalism', aimed inwards at its own minorities, would not be a problem for it. If it did become a problem externally, his ministry would manage it. There is no reference to Hindutva or what it was doing to India's citizens or what its fallout has been, in Jaishankar's book. But it was this issue—his government's internal misbehaviour with minorities—which would keep him busy. In a series of engagements at think-tanks around the US in late 2019, Jaishankar spoke about some of the issues he was dealing with. The situation in Kashmir—its leaders locked up indefinitely without charge, its people denied internet in an act of collective punishment—'took centre-stage in almost all of Jaishankar's interactions in Washington'.[38]

Two months after Jaishankar's tour, India passed its citizenship law which discriminates against Muslims. This came amid the jailing in detention camps of hundreds of people, mostly Muslim, in Assam, who were unable to prove their nationality to a prejudiced state run by the BJP. And it was accompanied by the language used by Amit Shah, alluding to Muslim refugees as termites and promising a nationwide NRC and the setting up of detention camps around India.

---

[36] 'Little gains: India saved just $2 per barrel even after Russia's "deep discounts"', 7 March 2023, *Indian Express*

[37] 'Indian private refiners profit from cheap Russian crude as state refiners suffer', 1 June 2022, Reuters

[38] '5 key highlights of India's foreign policy that Jaishankar amplified in the US', 8 October 2019, *ThePrint.in*

These actions by India were not something that its diplomats could explain away with soothing words. The diplomatic fallout was real, instant and harsh.

A Country Of Particular Concern

On 22 January 2020, a motion was tabled in the European Parliament against India's citizenship laws. The motion in full detail laid out what the laws were, what they were leading up to and where India was headed.[39] It said that the 'CAA is explicitly discriminatory in nature as it specifically excludes Muslims from access to the same provisions as other religious groups'. And this was offensive because 'according to the Indian Constitution, India is a sovereign secular democratic republic and including religion as a criterion for citizenship is therefore fundamentally unconstitutional'.

Paragraph A of the motion reads: 'Whereas since the BJP won the general election in May 2019 and Prime Minister Narendra Modi returned for a second term, the Government of India has reinforced its nationalistic orientation, discriminating against, harassing and prosecuting national and religious minorities and silencing any opposition, human rights groups, human rights defenders, and journalists critical of the government.'

It was reported that the motion had the support of a majority of the EU's members of parliament. India headed this off by using its diplomatic outreach to get the EU Members of the European Parliament (MEPs) to delay the vote on the motion, though it could not stop the text from being tabled. Jaishankar himself had to visit Brussels to meet a group of MEPs to try and stem the damage.[40] The motion remained on the table, awaiting a vote, and awaiting also India's next move. Modi decided discretion was the better part of valour, and held off on framing the rules for CAA, effectively putting the law in cold storage.[41]

On 28 April 2020, the United States Commission on International Religious Freedom (USCIRF), an independent and bipartisan federal US government entity, recommended that India be designated as a 'Country of Particular Concern'. The report reads: 'India took a sharp downward turn in 2019. The national government used its strengthened parliamentary majority

---

[39] European Parliament resolution on India's Citizenship (Amendment) Act, 2019, europarl.europa.eu
[40] 'S. Jaishankar discusses CAA with EU MPs', 19 February 2020, *The Economic Times*
[41] 'A year on and two extensions later, Modi govt is "yet to frame CAA rules",' 11 December 2020, *ThePrint.in*

to institute national-level policies violating religious freedom across India, especially for Muslims.'[42] It said the Modi government's prejudice against India's Muslims was showing through India's actions on citizenship laws, cow slaughter, Kashmir and conversions. The report notes the Ayodhya ruling and the conduct of the Uttar Pradesh chief minister Yogi Adityanath. It recommended to US president Donald Trump that he designate India as a Country of Particular Concern 'for engaging in and tolerating systematic, ongoing, and egregious religious freedom violations, as defined by the International Religious Freedom Act'. It sought sanctions against India.

Jaishankar's response to the report was churlish: 'We reject the observations on India in the USCIRF Annual Report. Its biased and tendentious comments against India are not new. But on this occasion, its misrepresentation has reached new levels. It has not been able to carry its own Commissioners in its endeavour. We regard it as an organisation of particular concern and will treat it accordingly.'[43] India did not respond to a single accusation or deny any of the facts.

On 21 April 2021, USCIRF again recommended that India be named as a Country of Particular Concern on a list which read: 'Burma, China, Eritrea, India, Iran, Nigeria, North Korea, Pakistan, Russia, Saudi Arabia, Syria, Tajikistan, Turkmenistan and Vietnam'. This time, the Modi government did not respond.[44] In 2022 and then in 2023, for the fourth year running

---

[42] 'India: USCIRF-recommended for countries of particular concern (CPC)', uscirf.gov

[43] 'Official spokesperson's response to media queries on the observations on India in the USCIRF Annual Report', 28 April 2020, mea.gov.in

[44] To understand the motives of those on the USCIRF, consider this text at the end of the chapter on India: Individual Views of Commissioner Johnnie Moore:

I love India. I have floated early in the morning down the Ganges in Varanasi, walked every alley in Old Delhi, stood in awe of the architecture in Agra, sipped tea next to the Dalai Lama's temple in Dharamsala, circled the shrine in Ajmer, and looked in awe at the Golden Temple. All along the way, I have met Christian brothers and sisters who serve the poor selflessly, often in difficult circumstances.

Of all the countries in the world, India should not be a 'country of particular concern,' or CPC. It is the world's largest democracy and it is governed by a pristine constitution. It is diversity personified and its religious life has been its greatest historic blessing.

Yet, India does seem to be at a crossroads. Its democracy—still young and freewheeling—is creating through the ballot box difficult challenges for itself. The answer, of course, is for India's institutions to draw upon their rich history to protect their values. India must always resist allowing political and intercommunal conflict to be exacerbated by religious tensions. India's government and people have everything to gain and absolutely nothing to lose from preserving social harmony and protecting the rights of everyone. India can. India must.

India made it to the list. The Indian government said the report was 'biased and inaccurate' and reflected a 'severe lack of understanding' of India and its constitutional framework, its plurality and its democratic ethos.

The USCIRF sought sanctions from the Biden administration against individuals and entities and asked the US Congress to 'continue to raise religious freedom concerns in the US–India bilateral relationship and highlight concerns through hearings, briefings, letters, and congressional delegations'.

In late 2019, US Congresswoman from Washington Pramila Jayapal introduced a resolution 'urging the Republic of India to end the restrictions on communications and mass detentions in Jammu and Kashmir as swiftly as possible and preserve religious freedom for all residents'.[45] It had 66 co-sponsors, including Republicans, and was referred to the House Committee on Foreign Affairs. India used its leverage with the Republicans to block it from moving further.

It was reported that the 'Indian government deployed an arsenal of lobbying tactics to hinder the House resolution's momentum since its introduction in early December—expending a disproportionate amount of resources and manpower to prevent the House from taking an official stance on Kashmir'.[46]

Jaishankar was rattled. In Washington and scheduled to meet the chairman of the House Foreign Affairs Committee, India's foreign minister ducked from the meeting after discovering that Jayapal would be there officially and then trying, and failing, to get her dropped.[47] Of his reasons for running away from confrontation, Jaishankar only said, 'I have no interest in meeting her.' The foreign minister had said his policy would need him be dexterous, he had not revealed he was required also to be fleet-footed.

The Americans closed ranks behind Jayapal. Bernie Sanders tweeted: 'Shutting out US lawmakers who are standing up for human rights is what we expect from authoritarian regimes—not the government of India. Jayapal is right. She must not be excluded for being outspoken about the unacceptable crackdown on Kashmiris and Muslims.'

---

[45] 'H.Res.745—Urging the Republic of India to end the restrictions on communications and mass detentions in Jammu and Kashmir as swiftly as possible and preserve religious freedom for all residents', 6 December 2019, congress.gov

[46] 'India lobbies to stifle criticism, control messaging in US Congress amid rising anti-Muslim violence', 16 March 2020, *The Intercept*

[47] 'Top Indian official abruptly cancels meeting with congressional leaders over Kashmir criticisms', 20 December 2019, *The Washington Post*

Elizabeth Warren said: 'The US and India have an important partnership—but our partnership can only succeed if it is rooted in honest dialogue and shared respect for religious pluralism, democracy, and human rights' and that 'efforts to silence Jayapal are deeply troubling'.

Kamala Harris tweeted: 'It's wrong for any foreign government to tell Congress what members are allowed in meetings on Capitol Hill. I stand with @RepJayapal, and I'm glad her colleagues in the House did too.'

Jayapal herself tweeted: 'The cancellation of this meeting was deeply disturbing. It only furthers the idea that the Indian government isn't willing to listen to any dissent at all.'

Jaishankar's and the rest of the Modi government's task became more difficult after the Biden win. This was because the Democrats now controlled the House and the Senate and resolutions like the one on Kashmir would be more difficult to block or evade. Another development was that Jayapal became Chair of the Congressional Progressive Caucus, which had such liberal stars as Ro Khanna, Ilhan Omar and Alexandria Ocasio-Cortez. These were individuals who were activism-minded, knowledgeable and willing to act.

This is the difficulty of the Modi foreign policy when it comes to engaging the great powers in the West. It is lacking in terms of internal substance when it comes to the broad values that India claims to share with the civilised world. It is enthusiastic about the official and legal brutalisation of its minorities, but it had deployed a foreign policy and a diplomatic corps that are meant to pretend that the persecution is not happening. Running away, as Jaishankar did from honest debate, was the only way out for the diplomat. There is no real defence, and India's principal asset abroad—secularism and pluralism—has been squandered. Where there is real confrontation about what was going on in India under Modi, as with the US Congress, with the USCIRF and the EU MEPs, there is no defence from India's foreign policy leaders.

This was mainly because the Indian Foreign Service (IFS) had no stake in what they were defending—raw Hindutva unleashed on India's own. Historically, and even under Modi, Indian diplomacy operated under a Nehruvian and secular carapace and claimed that India was pluralist and liberal. Not all of India's diplomats were personally invested in Hindutva; if anything, it represented the antithesis of what they had been trained for decades to sell abroad as India's image.

Vasudhaiva Kutumbakam Vs Hindutva

At home, the Modi government attacked not just pluralism, liberalism and secularism but also the words themselves and those associating with those words. But if there was an image of India abroad that was an asset, it was that the Indian State and society were liberal and secular and similar, at least in terms of aspiration, to modern Western democracies. It was not possible for the IFS officer to defend what the Indian State was actually peddling— the hard Hindu majoritarianism of the BJP school. And so the diplomat indulged in fudge and lie.

Just before the CAA protests began, Jaishankar headed off the question of Hindu nationalism aimed at India's minorities by trying to pitch it as being benign: 'Here is the difference, nationalism has a certain connotation in Europe which is not necessarily positive, but I think in Asia, nationalism is seen very much as a sort of natural corollary to economic progress... Almost like you're independent, you progress, you are prosperous and nationalism comes with all of that.'[48] This is clearly untrue to anyone who has observed the BJP, and certainly to anyone living through its years in power. Hindu nationalism is negatively oriented against other Indians and seeks to constantly harm and humiliate them. There is little positive about it.

The contradiction is fundamental and irresoluble. Vasudhaiva kutumbakam is an empty phrase to spout when even the people inside the immediate family are being brutalised.

After the BJP's leaders fuelled violence in Delhi in February 2020, the president of Turkey, Recep Tayyip Erdoğan, said at a speech in Ankara: 'India right now has become a country where massacres are widespread. What massacres? Massacres of Muslims. By who? Hindus.'[49] This was not the sort of language that had been used openly about an Indian government in the past. A previous government would have engaged with both the leader and the content. To dismiss it, as Jaishankar and Modi did in this case,[50] shows how cavalierly the foreign office was run.

As the violence continued, Indonesia summoned India's ambassador over the issue after there were protests in Jakarta over the citizenship laws and subsequent clashes.[51]

On 2 March, Iran's foreign minister, Javed Zarif, tweeted: 'Iran condemns the wave of organised violence against Indian Muslims. For centuries, Iran

---

[48] 'India would be a southwestern power, says Jaishankar', 3 October 2019, *The Hindu*
[49] 'Erdogan denounces "massacres" committed against Muslims in India', 27 February 2020, AFP
[50] 'Desist from commenting on India's internal affairs: Delhi tells Turkey', 28 February 2020, *The New Indian Express*
[51] 'Following domestic concern, Indonesia summons Indian envoy over Delhi riots', 1 March 2020, *TheWire.in*

has been a friend of India. We urge Indian authorities to ensure the wellbeing of ALL Indians & not let senseless thuggery prevail. Path forward lies in peaceful dialogue and rule of law.'

India's response was to summon Iran's ambassador the following day and tell him that Zarif's comments were 'totally uncalled for and unacceptable' because these were 'matters internal to India'.[52]

Two days after that, Iran's leader, Ayatollah Khamenei, tweeted: 'The hearts of Muslims all over the world are grieving over the massacre of Muslims in India. The govt of India should confront extremist Hindus & their parties & stop the massacre of Muslims in order to prevent India's isolation from the world of Islam. #IndianMuslimslnDanger.'[53]

What did India gain in terms of stature or advancement of its foreign interests by pursuing Hindu majoritarianism? Jaishankar was asked that by the media and he replied: 'Maybe we're getting to know who our friends really are.'[54] Was that sufficient recompense for the damage done to the country by its own government?

The other thing to examine in terms of gain here was that Jaishankar had made much of outcomes. The test of his policy of no name was what it eventually achieved.

In his Ramnath Goenka lecture, Jaishankar listed four outcomes he would seek to achieve through the nameless policy:
1) Greater prosperity at home
2) Peace on the borders
3) Protection of Indians
4) Enhanced influence abroad

We must examine what ultimately happened. On point number four we have seen already the effects on influence abroad. India played a defensive game abroad and not a positive one because of Hindutva. This was reduced influence, if influence means the capacity to effect external change. Point number three, the protection of Indians through foreign policy, we will examine in the chapter on Kashmir ('Final Solution').

Let us look at numbers one and two.

---

[52] 'Iranian envoy summoned on minister's tweet on Delhi riot, demarche issued', 3 March 2020, *Hindustan Times*

[53] '"Indian govt should confront extremist Hindus": Iran's supreme leader criticises Delhi riots', 5 March 2020, *The Indian Express*

[54] 'India getting to know its real friends: S Jaishankar on flak from a section of international community', 7 March 2020, *Deccan Herald*

On the first, Jaishankar said that in the economic sphere India may have looked good in the period before Modi but only when benchmarked against its past: it did not seem to look so good when compared to China or South East Asia. The outcome would be to ensure the policy would bring India greater prosperity than before. Here, the state of the economy revealed itself through the government's own numbers of declining GDP growth and increasing unemployment. Not only did Modinomics undo the growth trajectory as we have seen, it deliberately sank India into recession and harmed its productivity.

The poverty of Jaishankar's policy showed itself in another place here. You could only take advantage of the world if you actually showed up and played the game. If you ran away from competition, it didn't matter at all what grand game-plan you had conceived.

During his speech at the Council on Foreign Relations in the United States, Jaishankar spoke about a trade deal called the Regional Comprehensive Economic Partnership, which Modi's economic analysts had urged him to sign.[55] On this Jaishankar said: 'I would say at the moment, the strongest prospect of further opening up (of the Indian market) appears to lie in the RCEP negotiations... That would be a step forward. After that, whom would we look to for a limited or full Free Trade Agreement... I think that remains an open question.'[56]

For Republic Day in 2018, Modi had invited all ten ASEAN leaders (Indonesia, Vietnam, Brunei, Laos, Cambodia, Singapore, Myanmar, Thailand, Philippines and Malaysia).[57] In November 2019, Modi decided India would not join the RCEP free trade agreement between ASEAN and China, Japan, Australia, New Zealand and South Korea. Modi backed out of the deal because of his fear that India was incapable of handling the competition and this decision turned India towards protectionism ('Atmanirbharta'). Jaishankar was trotted out to dissemble. He said: 'In the name of openness, we have allowed subsidised products and unfair production advantages from abroad to prevail. And all the while, this was justified by the mantra of an open and globalised economy.'[58] Apparently, the problem was that the world was

---

[55] 'Not signing RCEP could be one of Modi's biggest blunders, "atmanirbhar" an admission of defeat', 21 November 2020, *ThePrint.in*

[56] '5 key highlights of India's foreign policy that Jaishankar amplified in the US', 8 October 2019, *ThePrint.in*

[57] 'In a subtle message to China, Pak, Modi invites ASEAN nation heads for R-Day 2018', 14 November 2017, *The Week*

[58] 'A day after RCEP, Jaishankar slams trade pacts, globalisation', 16 November 2020, *The Hindu*

playing Jaishankar's nameless and outcomes-focussed game better than India, and therefore he would not play at all.

In a newspaper article justifying the retreat, Amit Shah wrote that 'the PM can go to any extent to safeguard the interests of farmers, small and medium enterprises, textile, dairy and manufacturing, medicine, steel and chemical industries'.[59] This protectionism was attacked by Arvind Panagariya, who saw it as inconsistent with what he assumed had been Modi's liberalising instinct.[60] It also showed the degree to which Modi's personal outreach was detached from actual foreign policy objectives and gains.

What was the point of having a policy of opportunistic engagement with the world when India complained about the world's opportunism and fled the field? It is difficult to tell.

On 27 May 2022, BJP spokeswoman Nupur Sharma spoke on television about the marriage and consummation of the Prophet Muhammad in disparaging terms. This went relatively unnoticed, amid the general vulgarity and abuse the party's leaders were by now used to spewing. The fact checker from Altnews.in, Mohammed Zubair, shared the clip and it led to global outrage.

For a week the BJP did not react or respond, assuming it would blow over. On 1 June, the BJP's Naveen Jindal also tweeted something against the Prophet. The matter did not, in fact, blow over. On 5 June, a Sunday, Qatar and Kuwait summoned their Indian ambassadors and protested. Saudi Arabia and Iran also registered their anger.

Qatar's foreign ministry said it expected a public apology from the Indian government. The grand mufti of Oman said the BJP's 'obscene rudeness' towards Islam was a form of 'war'. Egypt's Al-Azhar Mosque called the remarks as 'real terrorism that can plunge the entire world into severe crises and deadly wars'. Kuwait warned that if the comments went unpunished, India would see 'an increase of extremism and hatred'.[61]

Many people in these countries began an economic boycott of Indian products and social media. That same day, Sunday, first the BJP disassociated itself from the remarks, saying they were from 'fringe elements' (both were, in fact, official spokespersons speaking for the party). Nupur Sharma was suspended, and Jindal's membership was terminated. Sharma also apologized

---

[59] 'The PM can go to any extent to safeguard the interests of farmers, small and medium enterprises, textile, dairy and manufacturing, medicine, steel and chemical industries', 13 November 2019, UNI

[60] 'Arvind Panagariya: RCEP in our interest, no MNC will come if we sit outside', 13 November 2019, *The Indian Express*

[61] 'Muslim nations slam India over insulting remarks about Islam', 6 June 2022, Associated Press

for her comments. This was not the first time that the BJP discovered that there were international consequences to its local mischief. Unable to impose its will abroad, the BJP government spent its wrath on Mohammed Zubair. He was arrested on 27 June, days after the Union government was chastened, and a series of FIRs filed against him in BJP states. It took the Supreme Court to give him bail on 20 July, a young man being kept in jail for no reason but the anger of the Union government.[62]

Neighbourhood First?

Soon, the paradox of vasudhaiva kutumbakam abroad versus Hindutva at home also showed itself in the area that the BJP said the UPA had failed: friendly relations in the neighbourhood. Let's move to number two on Jaishankar's list of outcomes, peace on the borders. India's relations with its neighbours were bound to be affected by the Modi government's pursuit of discriminatory citizenship laws. The stated reason for legislating the CAA was that Afghanistan, Bangladesh and Pakistan were all persecuting their non-Muslim minorities. The two largest migrant groups in India, the Tamils in the south and the Tibetans in the north, were inexplicably left out from the law's protection. The law assumed that only Muslim states discriminated and only non-Muslim individuals were discriminated against in South Asia.

When Amit Shah used the word 'termites' alluding to people from Bangladesh who he said were in India illegally, the fallout was immediate.

All Indian projects in the country were slowed down after the re-election of Sheikh Hasina as prime minister in 2019, along with the granting (despite India's concerns) of an airport terminal to a Chinese firm,[63] and the thawing of relations with Pakistan. The Indian ambassador, who had been trying to meet Hasina, was not given an appointment for four months.[64]

In December 2019, when the CAA was passed, Amit Shah alleged Bangladesh was hostile to its minorities. The Bangladeshi foreign minister rejected this, inviting Shah to spend some time in Bangladesh to educate

---

[62] 'Mohammed Zubair: Supreme Court grants bail to Alt News cofounder, moves cases to Delhi', 20 Jul 2022, *Mint*

[63] 'Deal signed for constructing new terminal building at Sylhet airport', 19 April 2020, *The Financial Express*

[64] 'Sheikh Hasina did not meet Indian envoy despite requests: Dhaka daily', 25 July 2020, *The Hindu*

himself on the reality, and then cancelled a visit he was to make to India hours before he was due to arrive.[65]

The attitude of the Modi government and the media towards Bangladeshis has been consistently hostile and Islamophobic, and the narrative of termites entering to damage India has taken hold strongly in Indian society. A rights group in Bangladesh claimed 25 of their civilians had been shot by India's BSF between January and June 2020.[66]

On a critical river project, Bangladesh said it would go with China instead of India. A report said that 'alarm bells are ringing in Delhi at Beijing's potential involvement in the hydro-politics of India and Bangladesh. Foreign Secretary Harsh Shringla's sudden visit to Dhaka is being seen in this light. China has offered a $987.27-million loan to Bangladesh for a comprehensive management and restoration project on the Teesta, a river Bangladesh shares with India.'[67]

The Modi government's fast and loose ways in foreign policy most visibly hurt Nepal. It had no qualms in meddling directly in the constitutional process of Nepal. The demands India made included asking Nepal to change the way it saw citizenship, and proportional representation for a part of Nepal bordering India and with which India had close ties (the Madhesis).[68] These demands were accompanied by a blockade that prevented fuel and other essential supplies from reaching Nepal. This produced a long period of hardship for Nepalis and damaged the economy.

The country soon ran out of cooking gas, diesel and even medicines. The BBC reported a UNICEF warning that more than 30 lakh Nepali children under the age of five were at risk of death or disease due to the acute shortage of fuel, food, medicines and vaccines. But the blockade continued, with India denying it was up to any mischief and the Nepalis convinced that this was the case.

A report put the loss of the four-month blockade at around $2 billion, about a quarter of Nepal's national budget.[69]

---

[65] 'Third Bangladesh minister cancels visit to India amid CAA protests', 11 January 2020, *DNA*

[66] 'Indian border forces killed 25 Bangladeshis this year: Report', 8 July 2020, *Al Jazeera*

[67] 'Dhaka's Chinese chequers on Teesta put India on back foot', 31 August 2020, *Business Standard*

[68] 'Make seven changes to your constitution, India tells Nepal', 25 September 2015, *The Indian Express*

[69] 'Blockade by India resulted in losses totally Rs 202 billion', 21 June 2016, *Kathmandu Post*

India's relations with Nepal have progressively deteriorated under Modi. The two nations do not even talk about contentious issues any longer because the differences have widened them so much.

On 13 June 2020, Nepali police opened fire at the border, killing an Indian citizen and wounding three others.[70] The same day, India said it had 'noted' the passage of a bill by Nepal's parliament updating the nation's map to include three territories claimed by India. All 258 legislators present voted for the change. The next month, Nepal's prime minister said that the god Ram had been a Nepali and the 'real' Ayodhya was in Nepal. India continues to use the phrase 'special relationship' to describe its ties with Nepal, but Nepal has stopped invoking the term.[71]

Ties with Bhutan have not become better than before either; it dropped out of an agreement allowing Indian, Nepali, Bangladeshi and Bhutanese vehicles to ply across borders. A Bhutanese legislative panel said that 'Bhutanese truckers and passengers continue to face harassments such as requirements to pay illegal money, unauthorised levies and coerced donations, aggravated by interferences of illegal and quasi-legal authorities as well as involvement of middle men. This will not be addressed (by the agreement)'.[72]

Even where India meant well and tried to do well by its neighbours, incompetence would undo it. Having made much of its vaccine diplomacy, the Modi government could not deliver a second dose to the Bhutanese on time because of the ferocious second wave of Covid in India.[73] The Bhutan government said it would find the vaccines elsewhere.[74] Nepal also felt the pain of India's mismanagement on both the issue of vaccines[75] as well as foreign investment because a weak India could no longer keep its commitment and China moved in.[76]

The rhetoric was usually disjointed from the action required to bring about changes in policy. The BJP's 2019 manifesto said, 'To forward our

---

[70] 'Nepal Police kills 1 Indian, detains another after skirmish with villagers near India–Nepal border in Bihar', 13 June 2020, *India Today*

[71] 'End of the special relationship?', 11 June 2020, *Kathmandu Post*

[72] 'With Bhutan out, Modi's plan for South Asian motor vehicle movement is down to three countries', 27 April 2017, *TheWire.in*

[73] 'India's COVID chaos puts Bhutan's vaccine success at risk', 21 May 2021, *Nikkei Asia*

[74] 'India in greater need for Covid vaccines, will not exert pressure for supply of doses: Bhutan', 22 May 2021, *Mint*

[75] 'As India halts vaccine exports, Nepal faces its own Covid crisis', 12 May 2021, *BBC*

[76] 'Foreign investment pledges fall 12.7 per cent as India's commitment slumps', 11 April 2021, *Kathmandu Post*

"Neighbourhood First" policy, we will extensively leverage forums such as BIMSTEC,[77] to accelerate regional coordination and economic co-operation with countries in our neighbourhood. Act East Policy, cooperation with ASEAN and ensuring an open, inclusive, prosperous and secure Indo-Pacic will be pursued vigorously.'

BIMSTEC had been struggling to make much headway as five of its members—Nepal, India, Bhutan, Bangladesh and Sri Lanka—belong to SAARC, while Thailand and Myanmar are part of the ASEAN.[78] The report said that the body 'needs a new charter to make itself more relevant and so far it has been guided largely by the Bangkok Declaration of 1997' and that 'it is yet to agree on setting up various mechanisms'. What was the purpose of engaging these nations through grand ceremony when there was little follow-up on the substance? The purpose was the ceremony, which was the centerpiece of the engagement.

India ostensibly has a policy named 'Neighbourhood First' but its neighbours have lined up instead to participate in China's Belt and Road Initiative. Pakistan, Nepal, Bangladesh, Maldives, Sri Lanka, Iran and Afghanistan have engaged with the project.

Indian interests in Iran for years had included trying to build a commercial route to Afghanistan and Central Asia bypassing Pakistan. This plan was initiated under Singh and was sought to be continued by Modi. In mid-2020, Iran announced that it was going ahead on its own with the help of China and dropping India from the project.[79] The problem was at India's end. Donald Trump had imposed sanctions on Iran, making it difficult for companies to participate in the project despite a waiver, and Modi, notwithstanding his deep friendship with Trump, was unable to push the project through. Iran also cut out state-owned ONGC Videsh from the development of a gas field that ONGC had discovered.[80] Power abhors a vacuum, it is said, and China stepped in, furthering India's fears about 'encirclement' from China.[81]

The foreign policy objectives of Modi may be vague, but the damage has been concrete.

---

[77] The Bay of Bengal states: Bangladesh, Bhutan, India, Myanmar, Nepal, Sri Lanka and Thailand

[78] 'Fifth summit of BIMSTEC uncertain amid Covid-19 pandemic', 2 September 2020, *Kathmandu Post*

[79] 'Iran drops India from Chabahar rail project, cites funding delay', 14 July 2020, *The Hindu*

[80] 'India loses ONGC Videsh discovered Farzad-B gas field in Iran', 18 May 2021, PTI

[81] 'China, Iran sign 25-year "strategic pact", 27 March 2021, *The Hindu*

The Man Inside That Suit

The standout physical feature of Indian diplomacy in the Modi years is his willingness and enthusiasm at inserting himself into the action. This concept of an individual powering a nation's relations with the world was cultivated and encouraged. A report said that Modi 'engaged in an exceptionally busy and a highly personalised style of diplomacy in 2015 with an aim to recalibrate India's external engagements that saw boosting of ties with major powers like the US, China, France and Japan, and a thaw in relations with Pakistan after prolonged bitterness'.[82]

Diplomacy à la Modi is usually meetings, almost familial in their intimacy, with no real agenda from his side, other than publicity to engender a personal closeness. The most striking example of these were Modi's 'informal summits' (informal here meaning without agenda) with China's leader Xi Jinping.

Another assessment praising his personalised style said that 'remarkable progress was made in ties' with a few countries, including the United Arab Emirates, Japan, Bangladesh and Iran. The report quoted an unnamed person in government saying: 'Modi is willing to lead from the front and isn't risk-averse. The policy at the end of the day is driven by the political will and the vision of the leader.'[83]

The writer added: 'From Pakistan to the US, from African continent to the G20, the government tried to adopt an innovative approach to diplomacy in sync with India's interests in trade, defence as well as to address its terror-related concerns though the basic contours of foreign policy remained the same as during the previous UPA government.'

The prime minister stressed on individual relations with leaders, especially those of great powers. Through such relations he sought to modify or fortify the relationship to India's advantage.

His charm, presence and attractiveness would overwhelm what was holding up progress in diplomacy, or at least that was the theory. In practice, this was not easy to pull off. Modi's inexperience in dealing with equals of state, his disinterest in detail and nuance of the type that diplomacy require, his certitude and self-belief and desire to solve the difficult issues through brilliant strokes, and his lack of counsel, given that those around him have no independent authority or source of power, all of these are obstacles.

---

[82] 'Narendra Modi's personalised style of diplomacy marked foreign relations', 3 January 2016, PTI

[83] 'Four years of Modi govt: PM's personalised diplomacy boosts India's influence', 26 May 2018, *Hindustan Times*

What is charismatic and dazzling to one might be off-putting to another. The scholarly and detail-minded Barack Obama was fond of Manmohan Singh, of whom he said during the global financial crisis in 2010 that: 'I can tell you that here at G20, when the prime minister speaks, people listen.' Obama advertised his middle-class values and was proud to tell a photographer who shot him on the campaign trail with his feet up on a desk that his worn-out shoes had already been resoled once.[84]

On 25 January 2015, when Obama was visiting India, Modi appeared before him wearing a suit with his name—NARENDRA DAMODARDAS MODI—embroidered in gold and all-capitals all over his jacket and trousers. India's prime minister made a show of humility, pouring tea for the US president, but likely did not give thought as to how he would appear to Obama or the world in that outfit. How this fit into the personalised style of diplomacy and to what extent it helped can be assessed. Such narcissism will be noticed by the one sizing you up professionally. Others also have outcomes to achieve. Obama produced the first volume of his memoirs in office in 2020, but they only included his first term, before his visit to India under Modi. But that book will also come. Modi's narcissism is something that other—harder and colder—opponents would have picked up immediately—and exploited.

On 16 May 2015, Modi visited China and spoke at an event for Indian expatriates in Shanghai. He elicited shouts of 'Modi, Modi' and claimed that Indians could now, with his win, be able to look into the eyes of the world with respect.[85] He said it was the first time in China's history that its president had left Beijing to greet a leader, as Xi Jinping had done for him in Xian.

Hieun Tsang, the ancient Chinese traveller, had described Modi's village Vadnagar and stayed there, because there was a Buddhist school there. Modi had ordered an excavation to ascertain this.[86] When he won the election, Xi called him and had referred to this. Xi had studied, Modi said, that '*Modi cheez kya hai* (What sort of phenomenon I am)!' When Xi visited India, he told Modi that Tsang—on his return to China—had come to Xi's village in Xian. Xi took Modi there and showed him Tsang's book and his description of the village.

[84] 'Obama's got sole', 24 October 2008, *blackbookmag.com*
[85] 'PM Modi at the Indian Community Reception in Shanghai', 16 May 2016, Narendra Modi YouTube channel
[86] 'Buddhist monastery remains found in Gujarat', 20 June 2016, *The Hindu*

Two leaders having such closeness and brotherhood—in itself, this was a 'plus one' in diplomatic relations, Modi said. The meaning of this 'plus one' would elude many people, he added. Such naïveté would be amusing if the stakes had not been as high as they were and with an unsentimental opponent alert to the main chance.

Modi met Xi 18 times, but if the engagements were outcomes-focussed he was unable to discern what his counterpart wanted.[87] When, in April 2020, China's army began to aggressively occupy parts of Ladakh and block India from patrolling the area as it had traditionally done, the move was neither anticipated nor even understood. The Chinese refusal to back off and strike peace even after a bloody clash baffled the Modi government. Jaishankar said: 'We have very large number of Chinese forces and frankly, we are at a loss to know why.'[88] The army chief was interviewed only days before the crisis at the border and he said that he foresaw no problem.

Where the personalised and charismatic diplomacy ran into real national interests on the other side, it came apart. In May 2019, India was forced to stop buying oil from Iran after Trump disallowed a waiver. Trump's former national security advisor, John Bolton, wrote in his book, *The Room Where It Happened*, that Trump dismissed Modi's concerns, telling his team that 'he'll be okay', with the decision.[89]

What this meant was a denial to India of oil that had come with concessions such as free transport and insurance and 60 days of credit. India tried to explain that many of its refineries had been calibrated to process Irani crude and couldn't suddenly shift, and also that the stopping of supply from Iran would affect prices and inflation.[90] However, this went unheeded and Trump bent Modi to his will, possibly with the promise of a visit or joint press conference.

When the Trump administration put together a regional framework to end the war in Afghanistan and bring the Taliban back in, India was left out of the group that included Pakistan, China and Russia.[91] It was revealed later that this had happened at the instance of Russia, heeding Pakistan's advice

---

[87] '18 Modi–Xi meetings, several pacts: Killings breach consensus, dent diplomacy', 17 June 2020, *The Indian Express*

[88] 'For peace along border, one must adhere to agreements', 30 August 2020, *Hindustan Times*

[89] '"He'll be okay"—An unsympathetic Trump said about Modi after Iran oil sanctions', 28 July 2020, *ThePrint.in*

[90] 'India apprehensive Iran sanctions could boost oil prices, inflation', 2 May 2019, *Reuters*

[91] 'India elbowed out of Afghanistan peace talks', 15 July 2019, *The Times of India*

that India not be included.[92] Both Putin and Xi would have sized Modi up in their first couple of meetings. It would be interesting to see their notes on what they thought of India's leader.

The personalised style does not yield the dividend the charismatic leader thinks it does in the tough world of international relations. The assumption that issues decades-old between nations are merely awaiting the arrival of an individual to be resolved at an instant is not rational. But this is Modi's diplomatic style and his popularity in India validates it for those who work for him. Failure usually ends in bafflement and moving on from the problem rather than trying to solve it through a non-charismatic, non-individualistic, more rigorous manner. Modi has visited China nine times in office—four as chief minister and five times as prime minister—but has been unable to understand what it wants from India because his focus is on himself and not the other side.

His website still preens that when he went as chief minister, the 'ruling Communist Party of China accorded unprecedented importance and highest level of protocol to the Chief Minister going beyond the established norms. Special arrangements for reception, escort, banquets, visits, security and high level of meetings were made.'[93] Of course they would. They understood him.

Towards the end of 2019, the Modi government believed that its relationship with China was 'very stable' and 'very mature'.[94] They also fed this narrative to the pliant media, which, not knowing much other than the bombast, also concurred that Modi's magic touch could solve the tensions. Only two weeks before the slaughter at Ladakh, reports were confident that Modi would carry the day because of his special powers.[95] When the water began to boil, Modi fled the field and did not even pick up the phone himself to ask his friend Xi what was going on and why he was squeezing India at the border. Modi was comfortable looking away and pretending there was nothing to see.

The diplomacy, if one can call it that, swings from intense personal effort to a refusal to engage at all. Modi invited Pakistan's Nawaz Sharif, along with

[92] 'Russia kept India out, US brings Delhi to talks table for Afghan peace plan', 9 March 2021, *The Indian Express*

[93] 'Gujarat chief minister Mr. Narendra Modi's historic visit to the People's Republic of China', 13 November 2011, narendramodi.in

[94] 'A conversation with foreign minister Subrahmanyam Jaishankar of India', 25 September 2019, cfr.org

[95] 'Modi, Jaishankar know Beijing better than most, & that could help defuse tension with China', 27 May 2020, *ThePrint.in*

other SAARC leaders, to his first swearing-in ceremony. He met Sharif again a few months later in Kathmandu, rang him for Ramzan the next year, and met him again a few weeks after that. He also visited Pakistan for Sharif's granddaughter's wedding. The national security advisors of the two nations met in this period and India's foreign minister visited Pakistan and said they would speak on all issues. Attacks on India's security forces in Pathankot, Uri and Pulwama ended the Modi effort to make nice with Pakistan. After the Chinese aggression in Ladakh, without explanation, Modi reached out to Pakistan and agreed to a ceasefire.

For the first time since 1947, under Modi, India is conducting a foreign 'policy' detached from the reality in India. It does not play to India's strengths or its soft power. Its actions within repel nations familiar with and accustomed to a particular representation of what India, the civilisational entity, was. On the other hand, it has attracted no nations toward it because of this shift. There appears to be little or no external benefit to India being a Hindutva-minded State.

The truth is that the manifesto line that Modi would 'integrate our soft power avenues into our external interchange' is stood on its head.

India has lost soft power under Modi in the most important foreign capitals that mattered to it because it has chosen to be a hard majoritarian State cast in the image of Modi personally. India's soft power was because of its inclusive culture. Under Modi, even Bollywood has been brutalised[96] constantly by Hindutva[97] and its allies[98] in the media.[99]

The IFS was pusillanimous and, along with the rest of the bureaucracy and the armed forces, went along with whatever mad plan was active at the moment. While the Indian State's behaviour was coming under fire from the world, Jaishankar claimed that 'the fact that we are a liberal democracy, the fact that there is a governance model based on rule of law, the fact that there is social pluralism … were all very powerful factors'.[100]

This was untrue: the reality of the Modi years is that its diplomatic efforts have essentially been forced to be defensive.

---

[96] 'Hindi film industry under attack as never before', 26 September 2020, *Deccan Herald*

[97] 'From Sushant Singh to Aamir Khan: Hindutva groups are using social media mobs to attack Bollywood', 19 August 2020, *Scroll.in*

[98] 'Deepak Chaurasia calls Bollywood "Gangs of Nashapur", Aaj Tak's attack on Deepika Padukone', 23 September 2020, *ThePrint.in*

[99] 'Picture abhi baaki hai: In Bollywood, a plot twist under BJP?', 11 October 2020, *The Indian Express*

[100] 'The text of S. Jaishankar's US talk on how he sees India's relationship with the West', 4 October 2019, *ThePrint.in*

The contradiction—pretending to be secular while enthusiastically going after the minorities—has not been easy for Modi to resolve. India's diplomats have had to contort themselves on missions abroad to square their words and demands for India to be given a greater global say with the reality of what was happening to pluralism and liberal government under Modi.

On a visit to the US in late May 2021, Jaishankar had an interview with Trump's former national security advisor, Gen. H.R. McMaster. The general, who is familiar with India and has visited it, asked Jaishankar: 'I wanted to ask you about how you see political developments in your own country. You are not a partisan person. You have served with great distinction across many administrations. There is concern in the midst of the pandemic about some of these Hindutva policies that could be undermining the secular nature of Indian democracy … and are India's friends right to be concerned about some of these recent trends?'[101]

Jaishankar first corrected McMaster to say that he is actually partisan: 'Let me clarify something. I served multiple administrations when I was a civil servant. I am today an elected member of parliament. Do I have a political viewpoint and political interest? Of course I do. Hopefully I will be able to articulate the interest that I represent.' He then said he would give two replies, a 'straight political answer' and a 'slightly more nuanced societal answer'. His straight political answer was that in the past India had 'votebank politics', but no longer because democracy had deepened. This had happened through 'broader representation in politics and in leadership positions and in civil society of people, of people who are much more confident about their culture, about their language about their beliefs. These are people who are less from the English-speaking world, less connected to other global centres.' Jaishankar said there is nothing to be concerned about because there is no problem and that this set of people he is referring to are 'judged politically harshly and it is often used to create a certain narrative'.

His nuanced societal answer was that the BJP government did not discriminate; they gave public distribution scheme (PDS) rations to people and put money in people's jan dhan accounts without separating them by religion.

McMaster's question was framed around the word 'Hindutva' and its policies. What are they? They are the introduction by India of religion into citizenship. Of criminalising Muslim marriage and criminalising Muslim divorce, or criminalising the possession of beef, the forced ghettoisation of

---

[101] Battlegrounds w/H.R. McMaster | India: Opportunities and challenges for a strategic partnership, 26 May 2021, Hoover Institution YouTube channel

Muslims in Gujarat by law (for details on this law, the Disturbed Areas Act, see the chapter 'Laws and Disorder'), the use of shotguns on crowds only in one part of India—Kashmir—and the demonisation by the government of Muslims, including for spreading Covid. These are the things that India's friends are concerned about. Jaishankar replied to McMaster without using the word 'Hindutva' even once and without referring to the laws that India was getting pulled up for around the world. The reason he ran away from the debate, of course, is that there is no defence. Obfuscation and avoiding the issue was the only way to respond to the accusation, a correct one, that India was harming itself and its own people through Hindutva.

How could such hypocrisy attract any allies? It couldn't and it didn't.

The fairytale of taking a permanent seat on the United Nations Security Council, and the mad, unsuccessful pursuit of a place in the Nuclear Suppliers Group (NSG)—a body originally set up to deny India nuclear material—has continued through the Modi years.

Manmohan Singh had already negotiated a waiver with the NSG in 2008 to allow India to import nuclear and dual-use items; why was India now pursuing membership which gave no benefit other than prestige?[102] This was left unexplained but was, of course, understood: it gave Modi another global platform to strut about and spend time deciding what to wear and what to tell the world.

India had been campaigning for reform of the UN Security Council for four decades, but it would be Modi who would turn it around, went the idea. Every now and then, a breathless report in the media would hint at imminent greatness being bestowed on India because of Modi's brilliance.[103] How and why all permanent members of the Council would agree, in addition to two-thirds of the General Assembly, was not mentioned.

To what end did India need to be a permanent member of the UN Security Council? What would we do with the veto? The answer to that was not to be found in any particular reason other than what the manifesto says about 'rightful place'. What would India do as a permanent member that it could not do now, and what could it do to fix that lack of material power? Surely, the focus should have been on building that lack of capacity. But as with the NSG membership, it spoke to the aching desire to be on the stage rather than achieving anything particular.

---

[102] 'Gaps in the casting of India's foreign policy', 15 August 2020, *The Hindu*

[103] 'PM Modi bats for permanent UNSC seat, offers to make vaccine for world', 26 September 2020, *Mint*

China's expansion of influence in the last two decades has come on the back of its economic rise, not its veto on the Security Council. We have already seen what the Modi government had done on that important front.

A review of former ambassador T.P. Sreenivasan's work, *Modiplomacy: Through a Shakespearean Prism*, says that the author 'defines Shakespearean heroes as full of many great qualities but also with a few tragic flaws that caused their undoing. It was jealousy for Othello, ambition for Macbeth, vanity for King Lear and indecision for Hamlet. In Modi's case, the "streak of overconfidence" and "illusions of grandeur" are the tragic flaws'.[104]

Sreenivasan wrote of his choice of title that 'Narendra Modi is nothing if not theatrical.'

This is true. What made him popular for his party in politics and on the campaign—his theatrical persona—have made him a liability for India in diplomacy.

The weaknesses have been spotted by many in the profession. Brookings scholar W.P.S. Sidhu said India needed 'to articulate a strategic vision for its foreign policy. Presently, instead of an overarching Modi doctrine, there are a series of catchy but vacuous foreign policy initiatives, such as Neighbourhood First, Act East, Think West and SAGAR. Sadly, these parts still do not add up to the sum of India's foreign policy'.[105]

What India has instead is Modi's seat-of-the-pants style which was supplemented after the 2019 election by Jaishankar's vague theoretical framework, even though it was clear that the latter had nothing to do with the former beyond providing some form of intellectual cover.

Former foreign secretary Shyam Saran wrote that, under Modi, 'there is no overall national security strategy within which a coherent and effective foreign policy may be formulated and effectively executed'.[106]

Saran observed: 'It is clear that Mr Modi wants to be seen as an international leader with a close and personal relationship with the world's key leaders. Personal diplomacy can be a useful instrument for advancing national interest provided one is clear about what one wants to extract as a benefit and what one must resist in making concessions demanded by the other side. One must never sacrifice substance for the privilege of getting a seat at the high table or being accorded pomp and ceremony. Image must serve substance not the other way around. There also continues to be

---

[104] 'Book review of *Modiplomacy: Through a Shakespearean Prism* by T.P. Sreenivasan', 25 January 2020, *The Hindu*
[105] 'India's underpowered foreign policy', 9 May 2016, *Mint*
[106] 'Mr Modi's mixed record', 12 May 2016, *Business Standard*

more stress on events and not enough on process in the conduct of foreign relations. The commitments made in the first wave of visits, for example to neighbouring countries, remain largely unimplemented.'

Pratap Bhanu Mehta, who would lose his position as Ashoka University's vice-chancellor[107] as well as professor[108] because of his views, observed: 'These are days where strong propaganda obscures the most basic of common sense. To begin with a simple question. A hallmark of the strategic success of any government is whether it expands the options available that can help you achieve your core objectives. Have the options available to India expanded?'[109]

His answer was that, 'On any measure, hard power, diplomacy, alliances, political framing, and consistency of domestic resolve, we seem to have fewer not more options. The vigour of Modi's travels can barely disguise the fact that in terms of India's security objectives, he is looking very weak indeed. Any other prime minister would have been hauled over the coals if India had been backed into the corner it is now.'

Modi went where no Indian leader had gone before and inserted India into the electoral politics of the US. On the Howdy Modi and Namaste Trump rallies, *The Hindu*'s Suhasini Haidar observed: 'The conclusion for the government is that it cannot own only that part of the diaspora that supports its decisions, and must celebrate the fact that members of the Indian diaspora, from both sides of the political divide, are successful and influential... In California primaries, local "Hindu-American" groups protested against Democratic candidates like Ro Khanna for joining the Congressional Pakistan caucus and for criticising New Delhi's actions. (Mr. Khanna won the primary).'[110]

The adventurism ultimately produced little. Modi could not conclude even a trade deal with Trump before he left, despite all the joint rallies and claims of closeness.[111] Ultimately, to whatever end these rallies were organised, they did not help India.

[107] 'Pratap Bhanu Mehta resigns as Ashoka University VC, citing academic reasons', 20 July 2019, *TheWire.in*
[108] 'Will not withdraw resignation, Pratap Bhanu Mehta tells Ashoka University students', 21 March 2021, *The Hindu*
[109] 'India in a corner: Beneath the foreign policy bluster is a great floundering', 15 February 2018, *The Indian Express*
[110] 'The ambit and the limits of "diaspora diplomacy"', 14 May 2020, *The Hindu*
[111] 'No limited trade deal; US attempts to shift entire blame on India', 22 February 2020, *The Economic Times*

The supposedly energetic foreign policy, underpinned by no real depth of thinking and so shallow as to not even submit itself to nomenclature, has come to grief. What Modi accused the UPA government of in 2014, on South Asia and India's neighbours, could be said to be true of him. India's relations with Pakistan and China were never especially good and had not been for decades. Through pageantry, Modi created the illusion that they had improved with both, which turned out to be untrue on the ground at the first instance. With Nepal and Bangladesh, India had deliberately chosen to be abrasive for no particular reason. This was not acknowledged or spoken about by Modi. He moved on, having thus diminished the foreign service, once the jewel of the Indian State apparatus, to the next thing that caught his fancy.

The Modi years will leave behind an India that is reduced in its neighbourhood, defensive in posture globally and tattered in image. This will not surprise those who but glanced at the utterly incompetent and random way in which this ministry, so beloved of Jawaharlal Nehru, has been run.

5

THE DOVAL DOCTRINE

The Modi school of diplomacy as grand gesture without depth and effectiveness is complemented by a cuckoo national security strategy which is also based on spectacle.

On the face of it, national security is the most important aspect of government, according to the BJP—at least it was in 2019. In the election manifesto of that year, Amit Shah wrote: 'Friends, this election is not merely to elect a government, it is an election to ensure the country's national security.'

Both Modi manifestos carried the statements 'Nation First' and 'India First' which were apparently axiomatic. Did 'India' mean its people or its territory or something else? And what did 'first' mean? Ahead of what or whom and at the expense of what? All that was assumed to be understood by voters and left unexplained.

The first point of the 2019 manifesto was 'zero tolerance approach to terrorism'. It claimed, 'Modi has fundamentally altered the national security paradigm of India in the last five years.'

The confident tone continued: 'India is now in a position to adopt an independent stand on national security, to successfully strive to strengthen our armed forces and to lead the world in various spheres. In the field of space too, India has emerged as a global power.' (It was unclear how and when Indian became a global power in space, given that it had not even put a man into orbit unlike the USSR, US, Russia, China and the private firm, SpaceX.)

Shah added: 'Our security doctrine will be guided by our national security interest only. This is exemplified by the Surgical Strikes and the air strikes carried out recently. We will continue our policy of "Zero Tolerance" against terrorism and extremism and will continue to follow our policy of giving a free hand to our security forces in combating terrorism.'

The belief was that Modi's ordering of these two attacks in September 2016 and February 2019 had 'fundamentally altered the national security paradigm of India'.

To what extent was this true?

To understand the background to this we have to look at what is called the Doval Doctrine. This is not a written text and has never been articulated in a book. This is because India doesn't have an intellectual national security advisor of the Henry Kissinger school, but a man of action and the field. Ajit Doval did not waste his time on thesis and dissertation; he got down to it.

In a profile which lampooned him, A.G. Noorani wrote, 'Doval does not hesitate to roll up his sleeves and get into action. He went to Iraq on a rescue mission for Indians taken hostage by the Islamic State; organised the Indian Army's "hot pursuit" into Myanmar and then went over to smoothen ruffled feathers; phoned Pakistan's High Commissioner in New Delhi and instructed his counterpart in Islamabad to berate Pakistan for the firings on the LoC; supervised, astonishingly, the arrangements for crowd control at the funeral of Yakub Memon in Mumbai; questioned the Delhi Police on the Uber cab rape case; and much else. This is a real man of action, the kind of whom we have never seen before.'[1]

And all this was only in the first year and a half of the Modi government.

So what is the Doval Doctrine? It may not be out yet in print but it is available on video.

In February 2014, a few weeks before he became national security advisor, Doval spoke at the Sastra University in Thanjavur. During his speech, he made the following points:[2]

- Terrorism was a strategic threat to India because it was an international phenomenon; because Pakistan fed and promoted it; and because India has a large Muslim population.
- However, terrorism could not be fought because it was an idea, a word. Only terrorists could be fought (or 'degraded' in capacity), because only a tangible enemy could be defeated, not a word.
- India thus had to name its threat, in this case, Pakistan.

Having identified the enemy, he asked the question, 'How do you tackle Pakistan?' and then proceeded to explain.

The problem of India's national security strategy was Pakistan's ability for sub-conventional warfare (cross-border terrorism and militancy) and India's inability to escalate militarily in response because of the nuclear threat.

---

[1] 'The Doval Doctrine', 13 November 2015, *Frontline*
[2] Tenth Nani Palkhivala Memorial Lecture, 21 February 2014, YouTube

Doval said: 'I talked about their having the nuclear threshold, having the strategic weapons systems, missiles, strategic partnership with China. How do we tackle this?'

It was simple. He said: 'You know we engage an enemy in three modes. One is a defence mode. Chowkidars and chaprasis. That if somebody comes here we will prevent him (from entering). One is defensive-offence. To defend ourselves we will go to the place from where the offence is coming. (The) third is the offensive mode where you go outright. Nuclear threshold is a difficulty in the offensive mode, but not in the defensive-offence.'

At the moment, he said, meaning under Manmohan Singh, 'we work only in the defensive mode'.

What he was recommending was that India attack Pakistan in various ways short of conventional war. In his words: '… working on the vulnerability of Pakistan. It can be economy, internal security, it can be political. International isolation. I am not going into details. But … you change the engagement from defensive mode.'

He implied that there was no option but to do this since the offensive mode was closed because there was no control of escalation leading up to the nuclear threshold. Similarly, for him, the defensive mode was useless.

'You throw hundred stones on me, I stop ninety but ten still hurt me. I can never win. Either I lose or there is a stalemate. You start war at your time, throw the stone with what you want, you talk when you want, you have peace when you want.

'If you have defensive-offence we will see where the balance of the equilibrium is. Pakistan's vulnerability is many, many times higher than that of India. Once they know that India has shifted its gear from defensive to defensive-offence they will find that it is unaffordable for them. You can do one Mumbai, you may lose Balochistan. There is no nuclear war involved. There is no engagement of troops. If you know the tricks we know the tricks better than you.

'Our only difficulty has been we have been in the defensive mode. If we had been in defensive-offence mode we could have reduced the casualties we have suffered.'

This was the Doval Doctrine. It posited India's strategic threat as terrorism from Pakistan, and its response was to do unto the enemy what was being done to you. Sastra University tweeted out this speech and Subramanian Swamy, the maverick in the BJP, tweeted in reply that 'defence strategy cannot be announced as in a fast food counter'.

It should not be surprising then that—given this quality of intellectual engagement with its reduction, focus on imaginary enemies inside and obliviousness to geopolitics—India's national security has deteriorated in the Modi years. The primary problem lies, once again, in the lack of application of thought. Modi does not want to, and perhaps cannot, take ownership of national security because it is a serious intellectual exercise. He was presented with a thesis from Doval, which said that Pakistan, specifically cross-border terrorism, was the primary national security threat. He embraced it. Addressing his first Combined Commanders' Conference, Modi reinforced this perception to the Indian military. He de-emphasised threats from other States ('full scale wars may be rare') and stressed that terrorism was India's primary national security threat, saying that 'the threats may be known, but the enemy may be invisible'.[3] India's prime minister believes and insists that terrorism is not just the primary threat to India but to the world. He said it at a BRICS summit,[4] on a visit to Africa,[5] to the Maldives,[6] at the United Nations,[7] and while addressing the United States Congress, to whom he stated, 'Globally, terrorism remains the biggest threat.'[8]

But this idea that terrorism is the primary threat has proved itself to be untrue during the Modi years itself, when Xi played his card and the national security strategy was upended.

Terrorism in Jammu and Kashmir is a political problem and not a military one. But that is unacceptable to Modi's closed way of thinking, which sees 'terrorism' and 'separatism' in a particular light, and views only force as a solution.

Pakistan and terrorism has remained the focus of the defence establishment, which was used as a political tool in the mindless spectacle of the 'surgical strike' and the Balakot attack.

Previous Union governments, lacking a majority in the entire period after the Kashmir insurgency began in 1990, indulged the army by going along with its fantastic ideas of a 'two-front war'. This was finessed recently

---

[3] 'PM's address at the Combined Commanders Conference', 17 October 2014, pmindia.gov.in

[4] '"Terrorism biggest threat to humanity": PM Modi at informal BRICS leaders' meeting in Osaka', 25 May 2020, *Hindustan Times*

[5] 'Terror gravest threat to world, says PM Modi in Mozambique', 7 July 2016, PTI

[6] 'State sponsorship of terrorism biggest threat world facing today: Modi', 8 June 2019, PTI

[7] 'In UN speech, Narendra Modi calls for global action against terrorism; asks "are we hobbled by our politics"', 28 September 2014, *The Financial Express*

[8] 'Modi addresses US Congress: Full text of PM's speech', 8 June 2016, *Hindustan Times*

as 'hybrid war', and even 'two-and-a-half-front war'. Meaning that the army would be organised to handle both Pakistan and China along with a raging insurgency which it would also be responsible for tackling, as it is still doing. This was a plan that had fructified due to political inertia.

Lacking a majority and vulnerable to accusations, especially from the BJP, that they were being soft, governments resisted engaging Pakistan meaningfully. They also resisted engaging Kashmiris for the same reason, and after the arrival of Modi, the engagement there was purely on hostile and adversarial terms. Modi had the space and the political capital to settle Kashmir and make peace with Pakistan. This would have allowed the military establishment to focus India's national security on China, which is and will remain into the future, to anyone who is not wearing blinkers, India's primary strategic threat.

Modi was not able to do this and did not attempt to. He lacks the intellectual heft and his prejudice hampers his imagination. The inability to think in depth carried into his dramatic 2019 action on Kashmir, gutting Article 370 and taking away its statehood. An action aimed solely at his domestic constituency, and meant to bolster his image as a man of firm action, Modi could not bring himself to consider what his Kashmir move meant for national security. Because of it, China no longer recognised Ladakh—any part of it—as Indian territory and insisted that the position after Modi's action was that of 1948, as it stood in the United Nations (UN), with Kashmir's accession under question. Kashmir itself was fully under the rule of the Indian gun. This was seen as Modi 'settling' an old issue, though it is hard to see how. It had, in fact, been deliberately and mindlessly unsettled.

Let us examine the four questions that have been thrown up by the Doval doctrine and manifesto which guided Modi's actions:

1) Was terrorism from Pakistan a strategic threat to India?

2) If yes, has the Doval Doctrine of defensive-offence made a difference?

3) What had been the effectiveness of what Amit Shah calls 'zero tolerance' against terrorism and extremism?

4) Has Modi altered the national security paradigm of India?

Let us take the first question, on whether terrorism from Pakistan is a strategic threat. To answer that we must ask what strategic threat means and if it is something that is long term and planned and hinders India's progress in a meaningful way. The data will tell us something here.

Militancy began in Kashmir in the late 1980s. The South Asia Terrorism Portal maintains data on violence across the region. In 1989, a total of 92 people were killed in Kashmir. The next year, violence exploded and took

1,177 lives, of whom 862 were civilians, 132 security forces personnel and 183 militants.[9]

The number increased by a few hundred in 1991 and 1992 and, in 1993, 2,567 people were killed. Of these, the number of civilians (1,023) and security forces personnel (216) remained about the same, but the number of militants killed shot up to 1,328. This remained the case for the next few years, though there was also a gradual increase in the number of deaths in the security forces, which reached 441 in the year 2000 when almost 3,000 people were killed in Kashmir. This was staggering levels of violence because the population of Kashmir without Jammu is only that of an Indian metropolis (about 5 million, smaller than Bengaluru).

Fatalities peaked in Kashmir in 2001, when a total of 4,011 people were killed. Of these, 628 were in security forces, 1,024 civilians and 2,345 militants. The next year, the number dipped for the first time by 1,000 to end at 3,098 dead, and the year after that further to 2,507. What explains the dip in fatalities after what was a long-term escalation?

The two events of significance are the 11 September attacks in the US, following which Pakistan became a partner in the 'war on terror', and the attack on the Indian parliament three months later in December 2001, in which nine Indians and five attackers died.

After the second event, India mobilised for war on the Pakistan front and pressurised Pakistan to act against those sending terrorists over. On 13 January 2002, Pakistan's president, Pervez Musharraf, banned Lashkar-e-Taiba (LeT) and Jaish-e-Muhammad (JeM), the two most active and lethal groups in Pakistan. Vajpayee demobilised the army after the ban. India has long said since that the ban was a fraud and that Pakistan was not serious about clamping down on terror. It is certainly true that the Pakistan Army and its wings have nurtured these groups and used them over time. It is difficult to say, given the opacity with which the Pakistan military establishment functions, whether this has changed. We can however look at the data.

From 4,000 fatalities in 2001, 3,000 in 2002 and 2,000 in 2003, the number fell again in 2004 to 1,788 and to 1,125 the next year. In 2007, the number fell to under 1,000 (744 killed) for the first time since 1990. It fell further to 548 in 2008, then 373 in 2009, then 181 in 2011. It did not go above 200 till Manmohan Singh left office in 2014.

This is one set of data that tells us how effective Pakistan's actions against

---

[9] Datasheet—Jammu & Kashmir, satp.org

terrorism really have been. If India believes that Pakistan is responsible for the rise in fatalities, it stands to reason that credit must be given for the fall.

The second set of data is what happened in Pakistan in the same period. Though Pakistan had seen extreme levels of violence in Karachi in the 1980s and 1990s, this was violence that was not sectarian but political (between, for instance, the migrants from India, the so-called Muhajirs, and the Pashtuns). In 2000, 2001 and 2002, while Kashmir was burning, Pakistan fatalities from terrorism were 166, then 295 and then 257.[10] In 2003, the year after Musharraf banned the JeM and the LeT, an assassination attempt was made on him twice in December. In the first, a bomb was set off as his convoy crossed a bridge, and on Christmas Day 2003, two suicide bombers tried to ram their cars into his convoy. Sixteen people were killed but Musharraf escaped.

The next year, fatalities rose sharply to 925, of whom 208 were security forces personnel and 302 militants. In 2006, they reached 1,466. In 2007, another attempt was made on Musharraf's life when his plane was attacked as it was taking off. A total of 3,594 people died that year. This doubled to 6,683 in 2008. In 2009, the most violent year in the history of Pakistan, 11,317 people were killed, including 1,012 security forces personnel and 7,884 militants. In India, in the same period, 373 people were killed in Kashmir as we have seen.

In 2010, the Pakistan Army began to smother the violence and fatalities fell to 7,342 and then again to 6,050 the following year. In 2013 and 2014, deaths were at 5,000, falling to 3,685 in 2015 and then 1,797 and 1,269 in 2016 and 2017. Since 2019, numbers have been below 400, returning, like India, to the relatively peaceful phase of decades ago.

The obvious question is why did terrorism, which was not a major threat to Pakistan in 2002, suddenly shoot up after that year? The logical answer is that the action of the State in trying to suppress it, control it or end it produced a vicious blowback.

It is difficult not to conclude that in trying to stop the damage it had inflicted on India all these years, Pakistan was paying the price in blood. Over 64,000 people were killed in Pakistan in these two decades, of whom over 33,000 were militants, many from the groups India had wanted banned.

We looked at where the fatalities were in Kashmir when Manmohan Singh left, before returning to what happened there in the Modi era. Let us also look at Islamist violence in India outside of Kashmir. Here the numbers

---

[10] Datasheet—Pakistan, satp.org

are low if we remove the Mumbai attack of 2008. In most years, the number is in single digits. Often there is not even any attribution to Islamists when violence occurs (such as in Malegaon in 2008 when blasts were set off allegedly by BJP MP Pragya Thakur, or in Hyderabad, first in a mosque in 2007 and then again in 2013), so it is difficult to say with certainty what the real numbers are. But the data is clear that fatalities were insignificant. There had been some bombings in the Gujarati areas of Mumbai—Ghatkopar, Zaveri Bazar, Mulund—immediately after the riots in Gujarat in 2002, but these were apparently internal acts and were not attributed to Pakistan.

Outside of Kashmir, there is no real threat of terrorism, especially of the Islamist sort.

Let us return to Kashmir and look at the data during the Modi years. The declining trend of violence saw 121 dead (84 of them militants) in 2012. Each of the last three years of the UPA saw fatalities at under 200. In 2016, they rose to 267, then to 357 in 2017, then 452 in 2018. In 2019, the year in which Article 370 was gutted, the number was 283 and in 2020 it was 321.

Two things are striking. First, that the long-term trend of declining violence in Kashmir began to be reversed by Modi's policies in Kashmir. The number of security forces personnel being killed went from 18 in 2012 to 88 in 2016, then 83 in 2017 and 95 in 2018, the years which saw Kashmiri civilians take to the streets to try and drive the security forces from their cities.

The 'zero tolerance' approach was not showing results in terms of numbers. India has pursued a policy of humiliating Kashmiris along with brutalising them. When an army officer tied a civilian to a vehicle's bonnet and paraded the individual around Kashmir for hours, the perpetrator was given a medal instead of a court martial.[11]

The army also used 12-gauge shotguns for firing birdshot out of unrifled barrels on Kashmir's citizens. This weapon (referred to by the less menacing name 'pellet gun') has killed people, blinded hundreds, including babies nowhere near the crowds, and even wounded the security forces firing them.[12] The weapon is not used for crowd control anywhere else in India or in the world.

Kashmir has no new economy—no Uber, Ola, Dunzo, Swiggy—because internet is either patchy or totally blocked. Its economy resembles the Indian

---

[11] 'Human shield row: Army major who "tied" Kashmiri man to jeep honoured', 26 May 2017, *Hindustan Times*

[12] 'Losing sight in Kashmir: The impact of pellet-firing shotguns', 13 September 2017, Amnesty International India

economy of decades ago. The denial of internet makes no sense from a security point of view because, as we have seen, Kashmir was most violent and with the most fatalities in a period two decades ago, when there was no mobile telephony in Kashmir, leave alone mobile internet.

It is only in 2021, after India ended a 17-month internet and mobile blockade[13] that violence began to taper off.[14] The carrot was more effective than the stick, but this is not understood by India under Modi.

There is no correlation between the internet and militant violence, and its denial is purely an Indian device to harass and humiliate Kashmiris.

That brings us to the other striking thing about the violence in Kashmir in the Modi era, and it is the composition of those killed. They were Kashmiris, like the 21-year-old Burhan Wani, who was demonised in India but remains a hero to his people. The LoC has been fenced to the point where it is not possible for exfiltration to happen with any degree of ease, and Kashmiris cannot go across and get themselves trained in any meaningful way. What has happened in Kashmir because of this is that raw recruits, willing to kill and die for their cause, face the Indian security forces and get slaughtered within days of becoming active.

If we consider again the questions we were examining, question one: Was terrorism from Pakistan a strategic threat? The answer is no. The data is clear here. Outside Kashmir, it is absent; inside Kashmir it is not a factor any longer.

Question two, had the Doval Doctrine of defensive-offence made a difference to it? No. The violence in the Modi era has been internal and not external for the most part or perhaps even entirely. Even if we were to assume that all the violence in Kashmir was the doing of Pakistan, as Doval suggests, his theory of defensive-offence has failed. The 2016 'surgical strike' was followed by an increase in both the incidents of violence (163 in 2017 and 206 in 2018 versus 112 in 2016) as well as an increase in fatalities (357 in 2017 and 452 in 2018 and then 321 in 2020 versus 267 in 2016).

On the other hand, a ceasefire with Pakistan following the restoration of the internet reduced violence even according to the army itself.[15]

Modi also had no moral problem with what Doval (whom he would make national security advisor weeks after that doctrine was made public)

---

[13] '17 months on, 4G internet services restored in Jammu and Kashmir', 6 February 2021, *Hindustan Times*

[14] 'Signs of normalcy in J&K, onus on Pak: Army chief MM Naravane', 4 June 2021, *The Indian Express*

[15] '"First step on long road": Army chief's assessment of 3-month-long LoC ceasefire', 29 May 2021, *Hindustan Times*

was suggesting be done in Balochistan. That India follow a course of action that Pakistan had, purely as a kind of tit for tat ignoring that it a) was inherently wrong; b) had cost Pakistan thousands of its own citizens' lives because the State had relinquished its monopoly over violence to 'non-state actors'; and c) had attracted the attention of international bodies like the Financial Action Task Force looking at Pakistan and the funding of terror. Is that what India wanted for itself? The answer would not come from Modi or Doval because they likely hadn't given it a thought just as they hadn't given a thought to the causes of militancy in Kashmir. Phrases like 'zero tolerance' are not the product of subtlety of thinking. They are facile and naive reactions to a complex problem.

In 2016, India clandestinely sent across a team of soldiers to strike at a terrorist launchpad (a temporary shelter) rather than hit Pakistan Army posts directly. No details of what happened and what was the damage to the other side were released then or later by the Modi government.

After the attack, it informed Pakistan immediately that it had ended the operation: 'The operations were basically focused to ensure that these terrorists do not succeed in their design of infiltration and carrying out destruction and endangering the lives of citizens of our country.

'During these counter terrorist operations, significant casualties have been caused to the terrorists and those who are trying to support them. The operations aimed at neutralising the terrorists have since ceased. We do not have any plans for continuation of further operations.'[16]

This signalled that India had no capability or capacity or political will for escalation. If the strike had genuinely been surgical (i.e., it had cut off some aspect of Pakistani capacity), the response from the other side would have been immediate.

The attack was not a surgical strike. It did not degrade enemy capacity. It was a political strike. Its objective was optics in India. This was the view even of those who led the attack.

Lt. Gen. D.S. Hooda, who was the general officer commanding-in-chief of the Indian Army's Northern Command during the surgical strikes said that there was an 'attempt to keep a purely military operation in the political domain by selective leaks of videos, photographs... Did the overhype help? I say, completely no. If you start having political resonance in military operations, it is not good.'[17]

[16] 'Transcript of joint briefing by MEA and MOD', 29 September 2016, mea.gov.in
[17] 'Surgical strike overhype did not help, says General who oversaw operations', 8 December 2018, *The Indian Express*

Asked if the strikes were purely tactical in nature with short-term goals and of no strategic value to deter the Pakistan Army from backing future terror attacks, Hooda said: 'When we were planning it, there was no thought in our mind that Pakistan will stop doing Uri-like incidents. At least in the Northern Command, there was simplicity of purpose.' Meaning that, other than signalling, there was no military or strategic end to the action.

Having taken this action once, Modi and India would be under pressure each time there is a terror incident, whether local or exported, to act militarily against Pakistan. How this would unfold on the escalation matrix and how India would manage to ensure that the conflict remained conventional and sub-nuclear was not a matter of concern. The joyous celebrations on news channels were the objective rather than anything of substance in military terms or deterrence.

On 14 February 2019, a convoy of the paramilitary Central Reserve Police Force (which operates in Jammu and Kashmir under the Union home ministry) was attacked by a suicide bomber in Pulwama and 40 personnel were killed. The bomber was identified as a 20-year-old local youth[18] and Pakistan condemned the attack.[19] But a precedent had been set by announcing the 2016 retaliation. On 26 February, the government said that India had carried out an air-strike in Balakot, a village in the province of Khyber-Pakhtunkhwa. This was, once again, not against the Pakistan Army but infrastructure belonging to the JeM. Here also, no details were released officially about what happened or what the damage was.[20] The Modi government said that 'a very large number of JeM terrorists, trainers, senior commanders and groups of jihadis who were being trained for fidayeen action were eliminated' and that 'this facility at Balakot was headed by the brother-in-law of Masood Azhar'. It was left to the Godi media to make up stories.[21]

This time Pakistan did not allow the violation of its airspace to go unpunished and scrambled its fighters, shooting down an Indian jet and capturing its pilot. India was not prepared for retaliation and shot down its

[18] 'Pulwama bomber was radicalised after cops forced him to rub nose on ground, beat him up, say parents', 17 February 2019, News18

[19] 'Islamabad condemns Pulwama attack, rejects charge that Pakistan is involved', 15 February 2019, PTI

[20] 'Statement by foreign secretary on 26 February 2019 on the strike on JeM training camp at Balakot', 26 February 2019, mea.gov.in

[21] 'Doctored video was ANI's source on Pak "accepting" Balakot deaths, Indian media runs with story', 11 January 2021, TheWire.in

own helicopter in panic, killing six Indian Air Force personnel.[22] The Indian military did not reveal this blunder till the 2019 general election was over.[23]

What was the net effect of the Balakot action? India had struck at night; Pakistan sent its fighters across in the day. India hesitated to call this an 'act of war' and chose not to react.[24] It claimed a Pakistani F16 had been downed by India but this turned out to be false.[25] It seemed the prime minister and the army were not prepared for escalation and had not accounted for Pakistan's actions. Pakistan's countermove, and India's losses of a plane, a captured pilot and six dead soldiers, meant that Balakot did not in fact change the paradigm and did not lay down any red lines. India signalled that it would cross the border by air if it faced any terror attack, and Pakistan signalled that it would cross right back in retaliation.

Modi showed little or no appreciation of what operating under a nuclear threshold meant in undertaking these military performances. His language was reckless and alarming.[26] He lowered the threshold for war through his actions of 2016 and 2019. And he jeopardised national security by introducing Pakistan loosely and frequently into the domestic political debate.

That concern about escalation played on India's establishment is clear. India did not retaliate when its plane was downed and its pilot captured. The grand strategy was that some action, any action was sufficient if it could be publicly announced, because it was aimed not at Pakistan but at the audience in India.

It is hard to conceive what will follow the next time there is an attack in Kashmir or elsewhere that is pinned on Pakistan.

Here it should be added that India had been opaque in both what it had done and what it had achieved through the two actions referred to. In the past, both sides have sent teams across the border to kill each other's soldiers in vengeance.[27] This was acknowledged but not claimed, because

---

[22] 'Budgam Mi-17 crash: IAF chief admits big mistake, says our own missile hit chopper', 4 October 2019, *India Today*

[23] 'The Daily Fix: Why were details of IAF shooting down its own chopper released only after elections?', 22 May 2019, *Scroll.in*

[24] 'India–Pak standoff: All signs suggest that New Delhi wants to de-escalate', 28 February 2019, *TheWire.in*

[25] 'Did India Shoot Down a Pakistani Jet? U.S. Count Says No.', 4 April 2019, *Foreign Policy*

[26] 'Have we kept our nuclear bomb for Diwali, asks Narendra Modi', 21 April 2019, *The Hindu*

[27] '4 times Indian commandos crossed the LoC for surgical strikes: All you need to know', 9 October 2016, *India Today*

claiming served no purpose beyond escalation. What India achieved through the claiming of these two actions, other than publicity for Modi, is not apparent. The number of casualties or damage to capacity was not known. Years after the incidents, it is still unclear what happened. India's former spy chief Vikram Sood, who headed the Research and Analysis Wing, has said the term 'surgical' was inappropriate because it communicated[28] severance of capacity, which had not happened in this instance.

Twenty-two soldiers died in the Uri and Baramulla attacks on army camps by four militants (this prompted the 'surgical strikes' in September 2016), but Indians were not told what the casualties inflicted in the retaliation were. Forty CRPF jawans were killed by a single suicide bomber (in Pulwama), but Indians did not know and were not told what the casualties were of the response in Balakot.

Despite the noise about the episodes, India did not claim to even have crossed into Pakistan physically, leading to speculation that the first episode might have involved artillery or rocket fire from the Indian side, and the second was an airborne attack by aircraft that targeted Pakistan from inside or just outside Indian territory.

Observed in action during the Modi years, there is nothing to show that the Doval Doctrine is effective or even that it made any sense given the situation India found itself in.

Question three to consider was what had been the effectiveness of 'zero tolerance' against terrorism and extremism? The answer was that it showed no effectiveness against terrorism or violence or fatalities. Instead, its effect had been to ensure that more Kashmiris joined battle against India. Pakistan no longer is a factor and doesn't need to do anything to aggravate violence in Kashmir: it is Modi's 'zero tolerance' that is doing the job now. The most lethal attack of Modi's era, the bombing of the convoy in Pulwama, was carried out by an unlikely candidate,[29] 20-year-old Adil Ahmad Dar, who left a video message asking his fellow Kashmiri men to not fall in love but instead to fight and die.[30]

In his Sastra University lecture, Doval defined terrorism as a function of joblessness. He said, 'If the other side spends Rs 1,200 crore on terror and

---

[28] 'Have proof of surgical strikes along LoC, but will not release it: Centre', 6 October 2016, *Hindustan Times*

[29] 'Adil Ahmad Dar: Diehard Dhoni fan turned Pulwama suicide bomber', 17 February 2019, *The New Indian Express*

[30] 'Profile of Pulwama suicide bomber: "Don't fall in love"', 16 February 2019, *The Economic Times*

you are willing to spend Rs 1,800 crore, the terrorists will be on our side. At least they won't do (sic).' And that his plan was '… to smother terrorists, deny them weapons, funds and manpower. They're mercenaries. What are they fighting for. It's only because they don't have a job. Counterfeit. Deny them recruitment. Work among Muslim youth. Use Muslim organisation (sic).' If it did all this, Doval said, India 'will have no problem of terrorism 10 years after we do this'.

Here we have two things to consider. First, this idea that 'terrorism', in Kashmir especially, is the product of joblessness is quite innocent of reality. People do not line up to be killed at the age of 21 because someone is paying their phone and coffee bills. The second is that this is not the approach taken in Kashmir, best described by the BJP's own phrase 'zero tolerance'. No internet, no bail, no democracy, no free media, no protests and ritual humiliation daily on the street and through the Indian media. Zero tolerance.

Raghu Raman, former head of the counter-terror group, the National Intelligence Grid, has written that India was locked in a status quo in Kashmir because of flaws in its counter-insurgency (COIN) strategy. COIN recognised that the insurgent could blend into the local population, and any attempt to engage him would risk collateral damage. The strategy then hinged on sourcing information. 'If the information is precise—which is rare—and the troops can move undetected—rarer still—then the troops occasionally score a tactical victory.' But absent intelligence and a hostile local population, the army's cordon and search approach were extremely unpopular and only served to 'exacerbate the problem and aid the enemy rather than attrite him. The strategic picture remains the same, with new players taking the place of fallen terrorists despite over 700 of them being killed in the last three years'.[31]

He said that the strategy reflected a bias towards militarising what was a complex political, social, commercial, cultural and psychological issue. 'There are obvious examples of this strategic meandering,' he wrote, adding that '27 years into the insurgency and we still haven't focused on training troops in local languages, dialects and culture in any meaningful fashion'. (In 2015, the Indian Army floated a tender inviting bids to construct a training village inside the Officers' Training Academy in Gaya. This simulated village was to have a mosque and mannequins dressed in pherans, burkhas, pathani suits and skull caps.)[32]

'Zero tolerance' is hard enforcement of what Raman is saying we should actually be staying away from.

---

[31] 'India needs to reboot its counter-insurgency doctrine', 15 July 2019, *Hindustan Times*
[32] 'How the Modi Government Has Used—and Dropped—the "Terrorism" Bogey', 9 October 2020, *TheWire.in*

Question four, the last one, was whether Modi had, as his manifesto claimed, 'altered the national security paradigm' of India. Paradigm is a fancy word for model. So what is being claimed here is that there is now a new model for national security. What is that model? Defensive-offence. When India thinks Pakistan has done something, India will do something to it. The numbers show that this is not actually needed and violence has come down on its own and will remain down unless India continues its actions on Kashmiris.

The Doval Doctrine is high decibel, low impact action. Another 'surgical strike' was carried out against Naga militants.[33] This was sold as the precursor to a settlement with them, which could not be fully concluded,[34] even though India conceded 'shared sovereignty' under a 'new relationship'.[35]

Modi was attracted to the simplicity of Doval's formulation of the problem, his marking of Muslims as being the threat and the drama ensuing from this course of action—'surgical strike!', 'Balakot!'. Its actual potency and effectiveness was besides the point and unnecessary detail. A defence analyst told me 'the reason for Modi–Doval's focus on terrorism is because of their ideological prejudice against Muslims; and raising the level of terrorism to strategic threat acts as a dog whistle towards Indian Muslims'. And that 'The fall-out of this has been weakening of our conventional defence. With terrorism cast as the primary military threat and elevation of Rawat as army chief because of his counter-terrorism expertise, the military only focussed on that. It is because of this that it has been unable to foresee the extent of Chinese aggression.'

The presumption that Pakistan is the enemy and terrorism is the strategic threat has meant India's defence forces have been as focussed, if not more, on counter-insurgency as they have been on war. During the China crisis of 2020–21, both the chief of defence staff Rawat[36] and the army chief M.M. Naravane,[37] who were in charge of military affairs, were counter-insurgency experts.

---

[33] 'Myanmar operation: 70 commandos finish task in 40 minutes', 10 June 2015, PTI

[34] 'Centre extends ceasefire agreement with 3 Naga insurgent groups by a year', 13 April 2021, *India Today*

[35] 'NSCN-IM releases details of 2015 Naga framework agreement', 11 August 2020, *The Hindu*

[36] 'Counter-insurgency ops expert Gen Rawat is India's first CDS', 30 December 2019, IANS

[37] 'India names counter-insurgency expert Lt Gen. Naravane as next army chief', 16 December 2019, *Defence Capital*

The manifestos of both 2014 and 2019 reflected no awareness of the strategic threat from China. The 2014 manifesto, under the heading 'External security—its boundary, beauty and bounty', spoke only of shortage of staff, pensions, war memorials, cross-border terrorism, illegal immigration and universities. There was no reference to any threat or even potential threat on the north-eastern front.

The 2019 document headlined 'Nation First' had 14 subheads: on making rifles in India, increasing pensions, better arming the police, stopping infiltration and enforcing the NRC, coastal and border security, gutting Article 370 in Kashmir and combatting left-wing extremism. Again, neither a reference to nor seemingly even any awareness of the Chinese threat, which was remarkable given what had transpired in Doklam only months before the manifesto was published.

In June 2017, Chinese troops began extending an existing road on the Doklam plateau at the junction where India, Bhutan and China meet. The Bhutanese protested and Indian troops moved in 150 metres to stop the construction. The area is strategically important because it is quite close to the only road that connects mainland India with its Northeast states.

The Chinese protested the Indian intervention and India issued a statement which said China's actions were 'a direct violation of the 1988 and 1998 agreements between Bhutan and China' and that Indian forces were obliged to act 'in keeping with their tradition of maintaining close consultation on matters of interest' with Bhutan.[38]

It turned out that the intervention was decided and executed at the local level. The general on the spot was given a 'free hand' by Delhi to do as he thought fit.[39] The general calculated that more forces would be needed to be brought in and did so. China responded by also bringing in more forces and ratcheting up its rhetoric. In July, Modi sought out Xi at the G7 summit in Germany and spoke about de-escalation. Both sides agreed to a 'simultaneous withdrawal'. The crisis appeared to have ended soon thereafter and construction halted with India claiming a win.

What happened instead was that, while Indian forces unilaterally went back 150 metres to their original position, the Chinese began to consolidate the positions behind where they were.

This appeared to have undone the 1993 peace and tranquility agreement between India and China. Article 2 of this agreement reads: 'Each side will

[38] 'Recent developments in Doklam area', 30 June 2017, mea.gov.in
[39] 'General who diffused Doklam impasse praises Modi govt for giving a "free hand"', 15 September 2018, PTI

keep its military forces in the areas along the line of actual control to a minimum level compatible with the friendly and good neighbourly relations between the two countries.'[40]

What this minimum level was, was determined mututally and carried out in stages. This did not happen because of intrusions, all one-sided, from the Chinese. The first four months of 2020, according to official data, saw 170 Chinese transgressions, including 130 in Ladakh. There were only 110 such transgressions in Ladakh during the same period in 2019. In all of 2019, there were 663 separate intrusions, up from 404 in 2018.[41] The Chinese were escalating, but why? This, the Modi government did not appear to know. It was apparent that Xi was up to something. Surely they were doing this to some end, and that end could only be to consolidate their hold over more Indian parts of the Line of Actual Control (LAC).

China's army engaged in what is called salami-slicing, gradually either encroaching into spaces India claimed or preventing India from patrolling areas that both claimed, effectively giving China 'control' over that part of the LAC.

This was because the agreement left the border between the two open: 'The two sides agree that references to the line of actual control in this Agreement do not prejudice their respective positions on the boundary question.' Essentially, whatever could be held on to was the line. For this reason, China refused to accept the line as fixed on the map, despite entreaties from Modi to Xi during the latter's visit to India in 2014.

Modi said that, in his meeting with Xi, he had sorted the problem out: 'I raised our serious concern over repeated incidents along the border. We agreed that peace and tranquility in the border region constitutes an essential foundation for mutual trust and confidence and for realising the full potential of our relationship. This is an important understanding, which should be strictly observed.'[42]

Noting that previous border-related agreements and confidence-building measures had worked well, Modi had suggested that 'clarification of the LAC would greatly contribute to our efforts to maintain peace and tranquility'. He said he had requested Xi to 'resume the stalled process of clarifying the LAC … we should also seek an early settlement of the boundary question'.

[40] 'Agreement on the maintenance of peace and tranquility along the Line of Actual Control in the India–China border areas', 7 September 1993, peacemaker.un.org
[41] 'Chinese intrusions at 3 places in Ladakh, army chief takes stock', 24 May 2020, *The Indian Express*
[42] 'As Modi raises border issue, Xi agrees with a Chinese yes', 18 September 2014, *India Today*

But even during Xi's visit to India, the Chinese encroached at Chumar and Demchok.[43]

Chinese transgressions went from 296 in 2016 to 404 in 2018 to 663 in 2019.[44]

Instead of reduction, the LAC was now looking at an increase in the aftermath of Doklam. The People's Liberation Army brought in 200,000 troops into the Tibet Autonomous Region,[45] and had built the capacity to deploy large numbers of these quickly to the LAC with India, both in the sector where Doklam was and farther to the west, in Ladakh. In effect, the Chinese had used the Doklam escalation as an excuse to get out of the two agreements limiting its troops.

It appears, the editor of *Force* magazine Pravin Sawhney has speculated, that the Doklam situation was likely created to provoke India to react, which it did. The media was handed talking points[46] and told[47] to declare[48] victory.[49] The Doklam geography favoured India and it was unlikely that the

---

[43] 'Big surge in Chinese transgressions, most of them in Ladakh', 22 May 2020, *The Indian Express*

[44] A 29 November 1996 Confidence-Building Measures Agreement had also specified what sort of equipment would now be reduced or limited in the area: 'The major categories of armaments to be reduced, or limited are as follows: combat tanks, infantry combat vehicles, guns (including howitzers) with 75 mm or bigger calibre, mortars with 120 mm or bigger calibre, surface-to-surface missiles, surface-to-air missiles and any other weapon system mutually agreed upon.'

Further, the agreement required the two sides to exchange data on the size of the force they had deployed and mandated ceilings. Both sides would avoid holding large-scale military exercises 'involving more than one Division (approximately 15,000 troops) in close proximity of the line of actual control'. And that if such exercises were to be conducted even involving more than one Brigade Group (approximately 5,000 troops) it shall give the other side 'prior notification with regard to type, level, planned duration and area of exercise as well as the number and type of units or formations participating in the exercise' along with 'the date of completion of the exercise and deinduction of troops... within five days of completion or deinduction'.

[45] 'The long game: what India is getting wrong about China's intentions in Ladakh', 4 October 2020, *TheWire.in*

[46] 'End of Doklam crisis, big diplomatic victory for India', 29 August 2017, *The Quint*

[47] 'India's greatest diplomatic victory in decades, know why China pulled back from Doklam', 29 August 2019, *India TV*

[48] 'Doklam standoff comes to an end, India's greatest diplomatic victory in years', 29 August 2019, *Aaj Tak*

[49] 'Doklam standoff resolution: India's greatest diplomatic victory in decades', 29 August 2019, *Business Standard*

Chinese would want to offer battle there. But the Chinese had been up to mischief in that area for some time. Why? Some thinking about what they were up to before India called up more troops was required, but this did not happen and India took the bait.

From 2017, the force levels were not the same as before, they were higher, but the threat from the Chinese was not spoken of by the government nor was it perhaps even internalised. This was no longer just management of the border as had been the case after the agreements of 1993 and 1996 but something more serious. However, as mentioned earlier, there was no reference to China in the manifesto that came after Doklam or any indication from the government that the situation had changed.

In 2019, months after his sweeping second victory, Modi gutted Article 370 and changed the status of Jammu and Kashmir from a state to two union territories—one comprising Jammu and Kashmir and the other Ladakh. On 6 August, the day after the deed was done, home minister Amit Shah said in the Lok Sabha that India would take back Pakistan Occupied Kashmir and Aksai Chin (the part of Ladakh that China has claimed and held since the 1962 war). He clarified next what he meant when he spoke of Jammu and Kashmir.

'I am aggressive because don't you consider the Pakistan-occupied part of Jammu and Kashmir, as part of India?' Shah asked.

'*Iske liye jaan de denge. Aap* aggressive *hone ki baat karte hain? Hum iske liye jaan de denge*' (I am ready to give my life for this. You are talking about getting aggressive? I am ready to give my life for this), Shah screamed in the House, egged on by the Treasury benches.

Then he referred to Aksai Chin. 'Mr Speaker, I want to put this on record that whenever I say state of Jammu and Kashmir in the House, then both PoK and Aksai Chin are part of it,' Shah said. 'The boundaries of Jammu and Kashmir decided in our Constitution, and also in the Constitution of Jammu and Kashmir, include PoK and Aksai Chin,' he added.[50]

Modi had dismantled Kashmir's constitutional status in secrecy. It is not known if he had asked for a paper on how this legal change would be received in strategic terms externally or if, given that it would, he had given it due consideration. Jammu and Kashmir was subject to United Nations Security Council Resolution 47, which had been introduced by China in 1948. It required India to hold a plebiscite in the state after first Pakistani

[50] 'When Shah thundered on Aksai Chin: "*Iske liye jaan de denge*"', 18 June 2020, *The Telegraph*

and then Indian troop withdrawal from the state.[51] This was a resolution that was redundant, but it was still operational. The final settlement of Jammu and Kashmir was also subject to the Simla Agreement, which bound India by treaty to negotiating it bilaterally with Pakistan. How would Modi's 370 move affect these? This was not made clear in parliament. When Congress leader Adhir Ranjan Chowdhury asked specifically, Shah's response was that bombastic statement above.

Further, it is unclear whether Modi had thought through or even sought information about what the implications of the legal change would be on China, and how Xi would react, especially after the brave words from Amit Shah. It is remarkable how little material there is even in the triumphal Modi-leaning media, in rapture about Kashmir being put in its place, regarding what this meant for India's relations with China.

Only ten days before the change in status, *India Today* interviewed the army chief Bipin Rawat, who was at the border. He was asked about the build-up of Chinese infrastructure on the LAC. Rawat said: 'With China we have got very good mechanisms in place to ensure peace and tranquility. And specially so after the Wuhan spirit. Under the Wuhan spirit everything has been sorted out.'[52] Rawat said also that what the Chinese were doing in terms of ramping up infrastructure was understandable because 'Tibet was a neglected region'.

But on 6 August, the same day that Shah spoke in parliament, China expressed 'serious concern' that India had 'unilaterally' changed the status of Jammu and Kashmir. China also rejected the status of Ladakh as a union territory. A separate statement on Ladakh said: 'China always opposes India's inclusion of Chinese territory in the western section of the China–India boundary under its administrative jurisdiction' and that 'this position is firm and consistent and has never changed. The recent unilateral revision of domestic laws by the Indian side continues to undermine China's territorial sovereignty, which is unacceptable and will not have any effect'. Further, the statement asked India 'to be cautious in its words and actions on the boundary issue, strictly abide by the relevant agreements reached between the two sides and avoid any move that further complicates the boundary issue'.

India's foreign ministry spokesperson, when asked about this, underplayed the Chinese concern. He stated that this was India's internal matter and

[51] 'Resolution 47 (1948) / [adopted by the Security Council at its 286th meeting], of 21 April 1948, un.org
[52] 'Army Chief General Bipin Rawat speaks exclusively to *India Today*', 27 July 2019, India Today Social, YouTube

pointed to the peace and tranquility agreement, saying that China was obliged to maintain it. But India's worry and lack of preparedness showed when Jaishankar had to fly to China to placate it.[53] He said to China's foreign minister, Wang Yi, that, despite Shah's words, 'Delhi was not making any additional territorial claims with regard to China.'

Two days later, China's permanent representative in the UN said the change in Article 370 'challenged China's sovereign interests and violated bilateral agreements on maintaining peace and stability in the border area'.[54] The Chinese diplomat added: 'And, we wish to emphasize that such unilateral practice by India is not valid in relation to China and will not change China's exercise of sovereignty and effective administrative jurisdiction over the territory.'

This was reported in India only a week after it was said, though, of course, the Modi government knew immediately.

On 19 September 2019, Gen. Rawat was interviewed. The following sequence was reported:

'Asked if he foresees the possibility of China escalating things at the LAC to a larger extent, like a war, he said no.

'"The Chinese have got a vision and a plan. I don't think they are going to come in and do anything at this moment. These pricks (making Ladakh a separate union territory) will not make them waver from their plan. They know when they have to do something. These small skirmishes will happen," the Army chief said.'[55]

There was little that prepared Indians for what was to come next. The Chinese, in fact, did not leave much time for speculation and acted swiftly. In the words of Sawhney, Modi changed the status of Ladakh on paper; Xi changed it on the ground.

The background to what follows was that, after the 1962 war, the Chinese had unilaterally withdrawn 20 kms from their 1959 claim line in Ladakh. In the years following this, India had set up some infrastructure in this space. Now, China was insisting that India dismantle this infrastructure and go back to behind China's original claim line. Xi wanted the status quo ante of 1962 (the 1959 claim line) restored.

[53] 'China tells India it is highly concerned about situation in Kashmir', 12 August 2019, *South China Morning Post*

[54] 'China raked up status of Aksai Chin at UNSC closed session', 20 August 2019, *The Economic Times*

[55] 'Pakistan knows we'll retaliate, they should remain in fear: Indian army chief Bipin Rawat', 19 September 2019, *ThePrint.in*

From April 2020 onwards the Chinese had diverted troops sent to the Tibetan plateau for training towards the Indian border and consolidated their positions without Indians having been told by the Modi government that this had happened. India had sighted hundreds of Chinese heavy military vehicles, moving northward from areas opposite Demchok.[56] Either the government had ignored this intelligence or had thought nothing of it.

On 5 May 2020, Indian troops in the area north of a lake called Pangong Tso were violently stopped from carrying out their usual patrols. These originated from a feature known as Finger 4 towards Finger 8, a few kilometres away. The space in the middle was a sort of no-man's land claimed by both nations and patrolled, with prior understanding, by both sides without arms. The skirmish of 5 May involved about 250 men indulging in stone-throwing and attacks by the Chinese with clubs and maces with nailed and barbed-wire heads. China's blocking of India's patrolling effectively gave it control over the entire space. The same day, China also blocked Indian patrols for the first time in the Galwan Valley, according to reports in the Indian media that were published in June. (The government did not conduct a single media briefing from the military through the entire crisis.)

On 7 May, India's foreign secretary called China's ambassador and presumably asked why things were deteriorating, because India did not appear to know. The next day, Doval was reported to have called Chinese politburo member Yang Jiechi to ask why Indian patrols were being blocked.

A day after that, on 9 May, another skirmish was provoked by the Chinese further to the east, at the Sikkim border. These two clashes were revealed on 10 May to the media by 'sources' in the Indian government, which said the 'matter had been resolved'. On 14 May, Gen. Naravane said incidents along the LAC were 'not part of a bigger plan' by China and these multiple incidents were 'not interconnected'. A day later, Naravane again dismissed China's aggressive tactics on the ground: 'Daily, we are meeting at 10 different places which is absolutely business as normal. It is only at one or two places where this has happened. And this does happen from time to time. It also happens when there is a change of commanders on ground.'[57]

On 19 May, China said that its actions were taken as 'necessary countermeasures' against India. On 22 May, Gen. Naravane made an unpublicised visit to Leh for a security review, following troop build-up from both sides.

---

[56] 'First intel on PLA came mid-April, long before Pangong clash', 15 July 2020, *The Indian Express*

[57] 'Nepal a proxy protester, warns army chief, hinting at China', 15 May 2019, *NDTV*

On 26 May, it was reported in the media that satellite imagery showed the Chinese having intruded 4 kms into India in Ladakh. It also showed the Chinese rapidly developing an airbase less than 200 kms from Pangong Tso. That day, Modi met with Doval, Gen. Rawat and the three service chiefs. Reports suggested that the government had decided to take a 'tough stand' against the Chinese.[58]

At a media briefing, external affairs ministry spokesperson Anurag Srivastava said, 'Any suggestion that Indian troops had undertaken activity across the Line of Actual Control in the Western Sector or the Sikkim sector is not accurate' and that 'Indian troops are fully familiar with the alignment of the Line of Actual Control in the India–China border areas and abide by it scrupulously. All Indian activities are entirely on the Indian side of the LAC.' Meaning, as has been noted before, all the intrusions were one-sided and from the Chinese.

On 30 May, defence minister Rajnath Singh said that the Chinese had been engaged in talks at the diplomatic and military level, and that the Modi government would 'not allow India's dignity to be hurt'. On 6 June, a general from the Indian Army travelled to meet a general from the People's Liberation Army to discuss de-escalation. Three days later, it was claimed that 'limited military disengagement' had started.[59]

On 10 June, and again on 12 June, generals from both sides met at a patrolling point in Galwan to discuss de-escalation. Reports said the Chinese had by now mobilised another 8,000 troops, tanks, artillery, fighter bombers, rocket batteries and air defence radars.[60] On 13 June, Gen. Naravane said 'the entire situation has been under control', that talks had been 'very fruitful' and would 'settle all differences' and that the two sides were 'disengaging'.[61]

Two days later, on 15 June, the two sides clashed in a barbaric duel without modern weaponry, using clubs, maces and shields to butcher each other. The following day, the Indian Army released a series of statements which did not immediately lead the nation to understand the gravity of what had happened. The first statement was only 49 words: 'During the de-escalation process underway in the Galwan Valley, a violent face-off

---

[58] 'PM Modi's strategy on China after meeting Ajit Doval, armed forces chiefs', 28 May 2020, *Bloomberg*

[59] 'LAC row: India, China agree to ease standoff', 9 June 2020, *The Hindu*

[60] 'A timeline: India–China's deadliest border clash since 1975 explained', 17 June 2020, *Hindustan Times*

[61] 'Indian, Chinese armies disengaging in phased manner: Army chief on eastern Ladakh row', 13 June 2020, *The Hindu BusinessLine*

took place yesterday night with casualties. The loss of lives on the Indian side includes an officer and two soldiers. Senior military officials of the two sides are currently meeting at the venue to defuse the situation.' Fifty Indian soldiers had been captured. This was not mentioned and they were returned the next day.[62]

Note the words 'de-escalation' and 'defuse'. This statement was amended a few hours later to make it 52 words: 'During the de-escalation process underway in the Galwan Valley, a violent face-off took place yesterday night with casualties on both sides. The loss of lives on the Indian side includes an officer and two soldiers. Senior military officials of the two sides are currently meeting at the venue to defuse the situation.'

The three additional words are 'on both sides'. Later on the same day, the army released a third statement: 'Indian and Chinese troops have disengaged at the Galwan area where they had earlier clashed on the night of 15/16 June 2020. 17 Indian troops who were critically injured in the line of duty at the stand off location and exposed to sub-zero temperatures in the high altitude terrain have succumbed to their injuries, taking the total that were killed in action to 20. Indian Army is firmly committed to protect the territorial integrity and sovereignty of the nation.'

Note again the opening words—'troops have disengaged', signalling de-escalation from the Indian side. These were the first combat fatalities on that border with China for more than 40 years, but the Modi government's focus was not on retaliation but trying to move on by looking the other way.

At this point, and even later on, it was not revealed by the Indian government that the Chinese had captured and were still holding another 10 Indian soldiers. These men were released on 18 June, without acknowledgement from the Indian side.[63]

India gave no details about the clash at any briefing, about how and why it had happened, and did not even acknowledge the deaths in a way it had done before (the prime minister did not go to receive the coffins as he did of those who had been bombed in Kashmir). Modi did not refer to China by name during the entire period of the crisis. When confronted by Opposition members and asked to come clean at an all-party meeting on 19 June, Modi said, '*Na koi wahan hamari seema mein ghus aaya hai, na hi koi ghusa hua hai, na hi hamari koi post kisi dusre ke kabze mein hai*' (No one has intruded and

---

[62] 'How 10 Indian Army men were kept in Chinese custody for 3 days: An inside story from Galwan', 25 June 2020, *India Today*

[63] '10 Indian soldiers return from Chinese custody after matter raised in talks', 20 June 2020, *The Indian Express*

nor is anyone intruding, nor has any post been captured by someone). The remarks were broadcast live on television.

This was immediately seized upon by the Chinese as evidence that it was the Indian Army that was to blame for the clash.[64] The official statement in English used tense to make it appear that Modi was only speaking about the present: 'Neither is anyone inside our territory nor is any of our post captured: PM.'[65]

Modi also indicated again that India's political establishment had devolved border strategy on China to the military. He said: 'The army has been given the freedom to take necessary steps and India has also conveyed its position clearly to China through diplomatic means.'

Former prime minister Manmohan Singh then issued a statement that Modi 'must always be mindful of the implications of his words and declarations on our nation's security as also strategic and territorial interests'. And that the prime minister 'cannot allow them to use his words as a vindication of their position and must ensure that all organs of the government work together to tackle this crisis and prevent it from escalating further'.[66]

The day after the all-party meeting and with a furore in parts of the media about why India was hiding the facts of the intrusion and the clash, the PMO issued another statement, this time saying that 'attempts are being made in some quarters to give a mischievous interpretation to remarks by the Prime Minister at the All-Party Meeting yesterday'.

Offering no explanation on what the factual position on the intrusion was, the statement said: 'At a time when our brave soldiers are defending our borders, it is unfortunate that an unnecessary controversy is being created to lower their morale.'

On 25 June, Modi's official YouTube channels edited the video to remove the line denying intrusion in an attempt to move on from the controversy.[67]

On 26 June, the wire agency PTI interviewed India's ambassador in Beijing, Vikram Misri, and flashed the headline: 'India hopes China will realise its responsibility in de-escalation and disengaging by moving back to its side of LAC: Indian envoy to China'. The words 'back to its side of the

---

[64] 'Chinese media lauds Modi's speech', 21 June 2020, *The Hindu*

[65] 'PM holds all party meeting to discuss situation in India–China border areas', 19 June 2020, pmindia.gov.in

[66] 'Ladakh face-off: Manmohan Singh asks PM Modi to be mindful of implications of his statements on national security', 22 June 2020, *The Hindu*

[67] 'Narendra Modi didn't watch his words on Chinese intrusion so PMO "censors" official video', 25 June 2020, *TheWire.in*

LAC' clearly meant that China had been on India's side. Another flash from the same interview read: 'China has to stop the practice of transgressing and trying to erect structures on the Indian side of the LAC: Indian envoy to China'. Again, it was clear that it was the Indian side which had been transgressed. Though neither the ambassador nor PTI nor the Ministry of External Affairs denied the accuracy of the words, the final interview published later did not carry these sentences.

The next day, officials at Prasar Bharti told reporters that the public broadcaster—which runs Doordarshan and All India Radio—was sending a 'strong letter' to PTI ahead of its next board meeting expressing 'deep displeasure on anti-national reporting by PTI'.[68]

In his 15 August speech in 2020, Modi did not name China but said instead that 'from LOC to LAC' the army had responded. By now, multiple reports had emerged that showed Chinese acquisition of Indian territory across Ladakh. At the end of August, it was reported that another 900 square kms in the Depsang Plains had gone.[69] This report was neither refuted nor addressed by the government.

The following month, the same journalist, Vijaita Singh of the *Hindu*, reported that 10 patrolling points in eastern Ladakh had been blocked for the Indians.[70] This effectively handed the territory to the Chinese, who continued to patrol and hold the lands behind the points. This was revealed to her by a source in the government and was not refuted either. The government's primary interest appeared to lie in continuing to ignore the fact that land had been lost on Modi's watch. The land had gone weeks before. The next day, another newspaper confirmed this was the case.[71] And the following day, yet another.[72]

On 10 September, Jaishankar met Wang Yi in Moscow and the two released a statement, the salient points of which were:

1) No reference at all to the LAC. The statement mentioned instead 'border areas'. In the absence of delimitation, this vague definition gave advantage to the side which was militarily more powerful: China.

---

[68] 'Irked by China interviews, govt gets Prasar Bharati to turn heat on "anti-national" PTI', 27 June 2020, *TheWire.in*

[69] 'China controls 1,000 sq km of area in Ladakh', 31 August 2020, *The Hindu*

[70] 'LAC standoff | 10 patrolling points in eastern Ladakh blocked by Chinese People's Liberation Army, says senior official', 18 September 2020, *The Hindu*

[71] 'Ladakh standoff: Indian Army unable to patrol 5 posts due to PLA presence', 19 September 2020, *The New Indian Express*

[72] 'Month before standoff, China blocked 5 patrol points in Depsang', 20 September 2021, *The Indian Express*

2) That 'both sides should continue their dialogue, quickly disengage, maintain proper distance and ease tensions'. However, there was no reference to the restoration of the status quo ante of April 2020. If India did raise the issue at all, it was dismissed. In essence this meant that if and when disengagement happened, China would hold on to what it had occupied.[73] (Disengagment did not in fact come after this statement.)

3) Both sides would 'avoid any action that could escalate matters'. China had no cause to escalate because it had secured what it had wanted. It was up to Modi to escalate to get China to move back. He gave up that option here.

Former soldier and analyst Sushant Singh explained what the problem was: '(Modi) can't accept Beijing's aggression in the region without denting his own nationalist strongman credentials, but he can't stand up to China militarily without making enormous investments in his military—investments that are impossible in the midst of an economic crisis.'[74]

Modi could ask for external help, but that would not be easy given that India had been brutalising its minorities and pursuing policies which, Singh wrote, 'have reduced India's attractiveness as a liberal, secular democracy'.

Singh noted that 'Modi is quick to inveigh against Pakistan, but he has been very careful in his choice of words about China, rarely discussing in public Beijing's aggressive moves on the border. Modi likes to pose as a Hindu nationalist strongman and a bold leader, but he realises that India is in no position to risk a military conflict with China. In a joint press statement issued on September 22 after the recent meeting of senior military commanders, the two sides agreed to "stop sending more troops to the frontline" and "avoid taking any actions that may complicate the situation". But by agreeing to "refrain from unilaterally changing the situation on the ground", Modi's government conceded that it was not willing to force the Chinese to withdraw from recently grabbed territory or to stop the PLA from building new watchtowers and other outposts along the border. India intends to avoid a military escalation, which in all likelihood means that it will accept the new Chinese-established status quo on the border.'

China's actions meant that Modi would have to bin the Doval Doctrine and turn the military's gaze to the other side. Analyst Ajai Shukla reported that, 'without fanfare', India was shifting focus away from Pakistan towards China.[75]

---

[73] 'China is fortifying defences across Ladakh border, not prepping to disengage', 19 November 2020, *Hindustan Times*

[74] 'Modi's Himalayan dilemma', 6 October 2020, *Foreign Affairs*

[75] 'Army's pivot to the north', 7 January 2021, *Business Standard*

Of India's 14 army corps, only four and a half had faced China, Shukla wrote, but more than twice that number was ranged against Pakistan. The army was now transforming Mathura-based 1 Corps to a mountain strike force, and was changing its patterns of training to conform to their new role.

Before Galwan, of the army's 38 divisions, 12 faced China, while 25 divisions were deployed on the India-Pakistan border with one division in reserve. After the reassignment, 16 divisions would face China. A total of 200,000 Indian troops were now on the China border, fully stretching the army and reducing India's military options.[76]

Why this was done 'without fanfare' was not clear, but we can speculate. It would require explanations about why this was not done earlier. And that would raise questions about why the threat had not only not been foreseen but had also been dismissed citing the 'Wuhan spirit'. Thus was buried the useless Doval Doctrine and the ending of the idea that terrorism was the primary national security threat, and the government reached out to Pakistan.[77]

In February 2021, India and China disengaged from Pangong Tso. India would go further back, to Finger 3. China would remain at Finger 8, and neither side would patrol the middle.[78] India would vacate the Kailash Range, a position it had taken unchallenged in August 2020 and which analysts felt should not have been vacated since it was India's only tactical advantage.[79]

China would not discuss the other area where it had intruded: Depsang. Former general H.S. Panag said the Chinese refused to discuss the disengagement in Depsang and south of Demchok due to the terrain configuration. He concluded that 'there is no scope whatsoever for India to gain any tactical advantage. Thus, the acceptance of the 1959 Claim Line is a fait accompli'.[80]

One year after negotiations for disengagement had begun, the armies remained mobilised with no progress on a return to the pre-Galwan status quo ante.[81]

---

[76] 'India Shifts 50,000 Troops to China Border in Historic Move', 28 June 2021, *Bloomberg*

[77] 'Armies of India, Pakistan agree to ceasefire along LoC from Feb 24. midnight', 25 February 2021, *Hindustan Times*

[78] 'India, China complete disengagement at Pangong Tso', 19 February 2021, *The Hindu*

[79] 'If India loses grip on Kailash Range, PLA will make sure we never get it back', 12 November 2020, *ThePrint.in*

[80] 'LAC disengagement done. India, China can now return to old love-hate routine', 18 March 2021, *ThePrint.in*

[81] 'China–India clashes: No change a year after Ladakh stand-off', 1 June 2021, *BBC*

As late as February 2021, the government claimed through the media that no land in Ladakh had been lost[82] and it had always claimed that patrolling in Depsang had not stopped[83] and that whatever area had been inaccessible was a legacy issue from Manmohan Singh's time.

In April 2021, on the website of a foundation associated with Doval, a retired general revealed the truth: 'In management of the LAC, patrolling to and domination of area of responsibility, including the PPs (patrolling points), are sacred and compulsive tasks for commanders and troops' and a 'minimum of eight to ten patrols per year from 2013-2019, would have roughed in the most difficult of terrain and weather conditions for five to six days of patrolling of PPs 10-13'.

And finally, 'to now state that we were not able to reach our Limit of Patrolling (LOP) since 2013 as PLA was blocking our movement, is pure heresy, and challenging integrity and honour of devoted Indo-Tibetan Border Police (ITBP)/Army soldiers, units formations and commanders up-the-chain'.[84] There it was. India had lost access to land in Ladakh under Modi, but it would not be spoken about. India would just have to accept that it had no access to the patrolling space that it had earlier. And it would also have to now manage two active borders with deployment in the most difficult terrain in the world.

From bombast the Modi regime turned to what can only be described as pusillanimity. Even brave words were too dangerous. In October 2020, Doval went to a religious function and said this: 'We will fight where you want us to fight, that is also not mandatory. We fight where we feel the threat is coming. We have never done it for selfish reasons. We will fight a war on our land and others' land too but not for our selfish reasons but for the highest good of others.'[85]

This was of course the Doval Doctrine, and it was interpreted in the media as signalling intent towards China.[86] But the government immediately put out a clarification through *ANI* that Doval 'was speaking purely about

[82] 'India hasn't ceded territory, Depsang issue will be taken up in next round—defence ministry', 12 February 2021, *ThePrint.in*

[83] 'No power can stop Indian forces from patrolling Ladakh areas, asserts Rajnath Singh', 18 September 2020, *Hindustan Times*

[84] 'Eastern Ladakh: NTR—"trust but verify" information!', 26 April 2021, vifindia.org

[85] 'हम युद्ध तो करेंगे लेकिन…' देखें जंग पर क्या है NSA अजीत डोभाल की राय', 26 October 2020, *Aaj Tak*

[86] 'Ajit Doval warns China, says "We will fight for greater good, not for self"', 25 October 2020, *The Economic Times*

a civilisational and spiritual context and not referring to any country or specific situation'.[87] What was the need for the clarification? It was to avoid provoking the Chinese and to avoid internal pressure on resisting the Chinese incursion.

Meanwhile, Modi and Doval continued to have the army commanders meet with their Chinese counterparts, who insisted that the first acceptable step towards disengagement could only be an exchange of maps detailing where each side now stood on the LAC. Naturally, the Indian commanders were not authorised to cede the land on paper that had already been ceded on the ground. This would be an endorsement of Chinese intrusion. And also because it would reveal that what the prime minister had said about there being no intrusion was untrue.

India's most visible push-back against China was to ban some mobile phone apps, most notably one popular with poor Indians, TikTok. This was projected in some parts of the media, especially *Republic TV*, as some sort of strategic attack which would leave China reeling.[88] On the ground, too, the media was left to defend Modi, coming up with fantasy stories of Chinese fatalities as being sufficient recompense for the death of India's soldiers.[89] After promoting a boycott of Chinese goods, the government went back to normalcy in months. India's goods imports from China in 2020–21 were more than they had been in 2016–17.[90]

When satellite imagery in January 2021 showed permanent Chinese intrusion of up to 5 kms inside India's border in Arunachal Pradesh, the Ministry of External Affairs said India 'takes necessary measures to safeguard its sovereignty and territorial integrity'[91] but did not mention what it was doing about this intrusion.

What were the proximate causes for China's aggressive posture in Ladakh? The national security establishment and the government neither offered an explanation nor did they feel the need to. The Chinese did not explain their actions other than to blame India. The changing of Ladakh's status

---

[87] 'NSA Ajit Doval's speech not about China or any specific situation, govt officials clarify', 26 October 2020, *Hindustan Times*

[88] 'TV Newsance Episode 95: Arnab Goswami on TikTok ban', 4 July 2020, *NewsLaundry.com*

[89] 'India Today Group, *Times Now* air old images of PLA cemetery as graves of Chinese killed in Galwan', 1 September 2020, *AltNews.in*

[90] 'India, China and the quest for Atmanirbharta', 11 March 2021, *vivekkaul.com*

[91] 'Taking necessary measures to safeguard sovereignty: Govt on reports of Chinese village in Arunachal', 18 January 2021, *The Tribune*

was certainly likely to be one. There was also some speculation that it was intended to put pressure on India to not interfere with the China–Pakistan Economic Corridor (a $50 billion infrastructure project linking China to the Arabian Sea).[92]

We are left with the facts to see if the dots can be joined. Jaishankar's no-name opportunistic foreign policy was combined with a jettisoning of 'strategic autonomy' and Modi offering India up to Trump as a tool against China. This appears to have been done not as some overarching strategic exercise but a reactive one, as events show.

A February 2018 paper declassified by the United States in January 2021[93] gives us details. The US national security challenge, the paper says, is 'to maintain US strategic primacy … while preventing China from establishing new, illiberal spheres of influence'. It lays out the case of how China's rise will change the region and challenge US influence globally, and concludes that 'a strong India, in cooperation with likeminded countries, would act as a counterbalance to China'.

To this end, the 'desired end state' the US sought, was to be 'India's preferred partner on security issues', and 'the two cooperate to preserve maritime security and counter China's influence'. As part of this, the Americans would also have as an objective the creation of a quadrilateral ('Quad') framework that would pull in the navies of India, Japan, Australia and the US as the 'principal hubs' ranged against Chinese influence. Over a couple of pages, the US lays out the plan of how it will make India a 'Major Defense Partner' and how 'a strong Indian military (would) effectively collaborate with the United States'.

The document lays out also what is intended to be done with China: prevent it from 'harming US competitiveness' and 'prevent China's acquisition of military and strategic capabilities'.

Why was India signing up for this? It is not clear.[94] With no discussion in parliament, with no interviews to the media and no press conferences,

---

[92] 'Analysis | China's Belt and Road Initiative fuels Ladakh standoff', 4 June 2020, *The Hindu*

[93] 'US strategic framework for the Indo-Pacific', trumpwhitehouse.archives.gov

[94] It was not even clear what the Americans actually wanted. In April, the Americans said their warship USS John Paul Jones 'had carried out a Freedom of Navigation operation west of Lakshadweep Islands, inside India's exclusive economic zone, without requesting India's prior consent, consistent with international law'. Why needle your ally? Nobody knew. New Delhi's response was: 'We have conveyed our concerns through diplomatic channels.' See 'US warship stirs the waters "without Indian consent", Delhi conveys concern', 10 April 2021, *The Indian Express*

with no reference to this in his manifestos, Modi began drifting India into a strategic partnership and military alliance with the US. In February 2020, during Donald Trump's visit to India and days before the Ladakh crisis began, Modi committed India to this agreement essentially ranged against China.[95]

On 27 October 2020, during the visit of US defence secretary, Mike Pompeo, India signed the Basic Exchange and Cooperation Agreement (BECA). It would help India access American intelligence to improve the accuracy of the Indian Army's missiles and armed drones. This portended air force-to-air force cooperation.

The second agreement signed was the Logistics Exchange Memorandum of Agreement (LEMOA). It allows the two nations' militaries to replenish from each other's bases, and access supplies, spare parts and services from each other's land facilities, air bases and ports, which could then be reimbursed. LEMOA is for India–US navy-to-navy cooperation.

Signing the BECA pact in Delhi, Pompeo attacked China directly: 'I am glad to say that the United States and India are taking steps to strengthen cooperation against all manner of threats and not just those posed by the Chinese Communist Party.' Secretary of State Mike Esper said: 'We stand shoulder to shoulder, in support of a free and open Indo Pacific for all, particularly in light of increasing aggression and destabilising activities by China.'

Rajnath Singh and Jaishankar, who were standing next to Pompeo and Esper, did not name China. Rajnath Singh's prepared remarks (which were later changed) had reference to this line, which was later deleted: 'Excellencies, in the area of defense we are challenged by reckless aggression on our northern borders.' Exhibiting the usual incompetence, this change was not given to the Indian translator in English, who read out the original text and the Americans released it.[96]

When the paper on America's strategy had been declassified, China said that 'its content only serves to expose the malign intention of the United States to use its Indo-Pacific strategy to suppress and contain China and undermine regional peace and stability'. And that 'the US side is obsessed with ganging up, forming small cliques and resorting to despicable means such as wedge-driving, which fully exposed its true face as a trouble-maker

---

[95] 'India, US agree to expedite work on BECA, strengthen defence ties', 26 February 2020, *The Times of India*

[96] 'Rajnath skipped China mention, no one told interpreter, US', 31 October 2020, *The Indian Express*

undermining regional peace, stability, solidarity and cooperation'. India did not react to the release of the document.

The third pact, signed earlier, was the Communications Compatibility and Security Agreement (COMCASA). It allows India access to encrypted communications equipment and systems so that Indian and US military commanders, and the aircraft and ships of the two countries, can communicate through secure networks. BECA, LEMOA and COMCASA completed a troika of 'foundational pacts' for deep military cooperation between the two countries.

COMCASA was signed in September 2018, five months after Modi travelled to Wuhan to meet Xi. The Wuhan spirit that Gen. Rawat spoke of referred to the agreement between Modi and Xi, signed on 28 April 2018, that India and China would not be rivals but would cooperate with each other. They would 'push forward bilateral trade and investment'. The rest of the statement is anodyne, in keeping with Modi's fondness for informal summits with no particular agenda, but the spirit Rawat referred to is that of cooperation and not rivalry.

The problem, obvious to anyone, was that, whether he fully understood it or not, Modi was hunting with the hounds and running with the hares. At the same time as he was holding hands with Xi, he was also winking at Trump's Indo-Pacific strategy. China's response was to activate the Ladakh border so that India's military focus and resources would remain on land and not the sea.

Former national security advisory M.K. Narayanan, writing the same day as casualties in Ladakh were revealed, cautioned Modi against what he was doing, saying: 'This is not the time for India to be seen as the front end of a belligerent coalition seeking to put China in its place.'[97]

He revealed something that Modi is unlikely to have known and perhaps was not told: 'Almost all India–China border agreements are premised on the presumed neutrality of both countries.' Narayanan wrote that 'as the Special Representative for Border Talks with China (2005 to 2010), this sentiment was an ever present reality during all border discussions. The document, "Agreement between the Government of the Republic of India and the Government of the People's Republic of China on the Political Parameters and Guiding Principles for the Settlement of the India–China Boundary Question" (2005), one of the very few documents relating to the China–India border, reflects this reality.'

---

[97] 'Remaining non-aligned is good advice', 16 June 2020, *The Hindu*

Essentially, India's actions under Modi were to undo the agreements of 1993 and later, giving China space and options. And there does not seem to be any understanding from Modi about the sanctity of treaties, even informal, that he is signing India up for.

On 18 April 2020, India had introduced a law which would allow Chinese FDI into India only with government approval. The revised FDI policy read that 'an entity of a country, which shares land border with India or where the beneficial owner of an investment into India is situated in or is a citizen of any such country, can invest only under the Government route'. Pakistan and Bangladesh were already subjected to prior approval, and so this law was clearly specifically aimed at China, and the reason cited, unofficially of course, was that it was meant to curb opportunistic takeovers during the Covid pandemic.

Where this left the 'push forward bilateral investment' bit is difficult to say. But it was in keeping with the scattershot and cavalier manner with which such things are run. China's response was both harder and more subtle. It put malware in India's electricity grid and instigated a blackout in Mumbai through a cyber-attack.[98] The government acknowledged the attack but said 'no data had been lost' and that the 'threat had been averted because of timely action by various agencies'.[99]

The refusal or inability to take ownership of national security has also affected capability, because expenditure on modernisation has been spent on the wrong strategic aims. When the thinking at the top is awry or missing and the foundation is shaky, spending is aimless.

Ownership means ensuring that territorial integrity is secure through the right strategy. This has not happened under Modi and it is fair to see it as failure, because the claim was that Modi would keep India strong and secure. The emphasis, ultimately, only remained on the management of perceptions.

There was no ownership even of response once the threat had bared itself. As Modi said on 15 August 2020, and as his ministers often say, they have given the army 'a free hand' to respond to China's aggression. This freedom to the military was really abdication of responsibility from the elected government, which should have owned national security, its higher strategy and the consequences of action.[100] Even retired generals felt that giving a

[98] 'China appears to warn India: push too hard and the lights could go out', 28 February 2021, *New York Times*

[99] 'Chinese malware attack: Centre denies report even as Maha minister confirms it; China calls claim "fabrication"', 1 March 2021, *News18.com*

[100] 'Don't give military a free-hand against China and wash your hands off diplomacy', 24 June 2020, *ThePrint.in*

'free hand' to the armed forces 'when one was dealing with a nuclear power cannot be acceptable from a national security perspective'.[101]

Analyst Sushant Singh has pointed out that while India's generals and diplomats have reached out, unsuccessfully, to their Chinese counterparts several times to resolve the situation, Modi has not once telephoned Xi. After 18 meetings, Modi has done what sulking children do and refused to speak to his erstwhile friend and try to solve the problem at his level and understand what Xi's issues and motivations were.

This is likely to save face and it is aimed again at a constituency which sees his abdication as strength ('Modi firmly refused to talk').

India's national security has slid by default under a negligent Modi away from the Doval Doctrine towards China and a two-front problem.

After the Chinese disengagement at Pangong Tso and the Kailash Range was complete, India engaged with Pakistan, perhaps under Chinese influence. The surprising and rare joint statement said that India and Pakistan 'agreed to address each other's core issues and concerns which have propensity to disturb peace and lead to violence' and also that both sides would follow 'strict observance of all agreements, understandings and cease firing along the Line of Control and all other sectors'.[102]

India had gone from the Doval Doctrine, 'bomb for bullet' and Balakot to a focus on China and peace with Pakistan all in a matter of months.

Why?

There was no explanation, of course. It just happened. This move for peace on the Pakistan front puzzled and angered those hawks who had thought that the earlier theatrics—surgical strike and Balakot—had constituted something meaningful.[103]

Under Modi, India's other front became hostile. Even with the Pangong Tso disengagement, the lack of trust required India to send large numbers of untrained, unequipped soldiers to take on the Chinese who were in habitats that were built after Doklam. India's jawans will pay the price for years for the signal incompetence of Modi at the one thing that his supporters thought he was good at: national security.

India under Modi was compelled by China to change its military strategy.

---

[101] 'Narendra Modi's "free hand" to armed forces is misleading and problematic', 19 February 2019, *ThePrint.in*

[102] 'For first time in 18 years, India, Pakistan agree to "strictly" observe LoC ceasefire', 25 February 2021, *TheWire.in*

[103] 'India–Pak DGMOs announce ceasefire: What about Balakot "policy"?', 26 February 2021, *The Quint*

General Rawat accepted in June 2021 that China was now India's primary threat: 'When you have a larger neighbour, which has got a better force, better technology, you obviously prepare for a larger neighbour.'[104] This was of course obvious, but had not been to Doval or Modi. The Lowy Institute, which downgraded India's status in 2020 from a major power, observed that after Ladakh 'this new strategic reality imposes unequal costs on India and China. India is likely to defer much-needed military modernisation and maritime expansion into the Indian Ocean—which would impair its ability to compete strategically with China.'[105] Only a handful of journalists and analysts, Sushant Singh, Pravin Sahwney and Ajai Shukla among them, recognised what had happened. The rest of the media moved on from the story once the new normal in Ladakh had been enforced by China.

In 2021, China passed a law 'to strengthen border defence, support economic and social development as well as opening-up in border areas, improve public services and infrastructure in such areas, encourage and support people's life and work there, and promote coordination between border defence and social, economic development in border areas'. In effect, reports said, this suggested a push to settle civilians in the border areas. The law also said it was up to the Chinese to unilaterally determine where their borders were. The law came into effect on 1 January 2022.[106]

In April 2023, China 'renamed' places in Arunachal Pradesh, in an attempt to claim sovereignty over the area.[107]

What this means for India in the long run is unclear because the government refuses to discuss the border situation. Asked in an interview what was happening in Ladakh, Jaishankar said: 'Look, they [China] are a bigger economy. What am I going to do? As a smaller economy, I am going to go pick up a fight with bigger economy? It is not a question of being reactive, it is a question of having common sense.' Thus has India's national security policy been run under Modi: a combination of bluster and pusillanimity.[108]

---

104 'Exclusive: For India, China a bigger security threat than Pakistan, Chief of Defence Staff General Bipin Rawat tells WION', 11 June 2021, WION

105 'The crisis after the crisis: How Ladakh will shape India's competition with China', 6 May 2021, lowyinstitute.org

106 'Explained: China's new land border law and Indian concerns', 27 October 2021, *Indian Express*

107 'China renames 11 places in Arunachal Pradesh, calls it "southern Tibet"', 4 April 2023, *India Today*

108 '"Is Jaishankar suffering from Stockholm syndrome?" Congress attacks Foreign Minister on China issue', 22 February 2023, ThePrint.in

In January 2021, a think-tank put out a paper by a retired general. He wrote that the changes introduced in the military gave an opportunity for the pioneering incumbent (Rawat) to display his strategic and military acumen.

Unfortunately, the report concluded that the CDS was 'yet to articulate a defence strategy'. This sort of thing may have been too much to expect from a national security establishment led by Modi and Doval.

Yet another bureaucratic boondoggle was the creation in 2018 of the Defence Planning Committee. This was to be chaired by Doval and include the foreign secretary, defence secretary, chief of defence staff, three service chiefs and secretaries of the Ministry of Finance.

It had the enormous tasks of looking after 'national defence and security priorities, foreign policy imperatives, operational directives and associated requirements, relevant strategic and security-related doctrines, defence acquisition and infrastructure development plans, national security strategy, strategic defence review and doctrines, international defence engagement strategy', and so on.[109]

It met once, on 3 May 2018, and does not appear to have met after that.

Former general Prakash Menon has noted that, for several decades, India's political guidance to the military had been oriented towards Pakistan as the immediate threat.[110] But now that the Chinese threat was at the doorstep, this would have to change. The political objectives expected to be achieved by the military resided in a document called the 'Raksha Mantri's Directive'. That directive 'continues to lack parentage for the lack of a coherent National Security Strategy. The Defence Planning Committee, headed by the NSA, was assigned this task two years ago. Nothing has emerged so far.'

This is what happens to complex enterprises that are run from the top but with no interest in detail. The national security strategy of an aspiring great power has come apart in a short time under Modi. There is no ownership of the intellectual aspects of the work, little application, little enthusiasm for the hard but boring tasks and too much focus and emphasis on meaningless and marginal spectacle. The doctrine of the national security advisor was bound to come to grief, and it has.

---

[109] 'Creation of Defence Planning Committee: A step towards credible defence preparedness', 19 April 2018, idsa.in

[110] 'Defence allocation: Shrinking budget, rising threats', 9 February 2021, *Deccan Herald*

6

BAD MUSLIM

Part 1: Modi's Gift

India (and the subcontinent generally) has always had a history of spontaneous street violence. Rule of law is flexible here. It is not effective; certainly it is not guaranteed. The State lacks the means to prevent such violence and also lacks the competence, even if it has the desire, which often it doesn't, to prosecute offenders.

Such violence appears to be acceptable: the bystander often participates in the violence and mobs are quick to form in India. Those who do not join in often observe and record the event rather than step in. Thus both the aspects of prevention and deterrence are poor. Lynchings of those accused of theft, trespass and other misdemeanours are not uncommon.

However, 'beef lynching' as a category of violence has been introduced to India after 2014. Journalists know this because they are familiar with the sort of crimes that make the front pages. Three years into Modi's first term, a research report found that 97 per cent of all cow-related violence in India came after he was elected.[1] The report was from 2017 but already it showed that 84 per cent of those killed were Muslims. In 30 per cent of the attacks, the police registered cases against the victims. The data also showed that half the attacks were based on rumours.

National and state crime data do not distinguish general violence from cow-related attacks and lynchings. For this reason, it is not easy to collect such data from the State (unlike categories of violence like murder, sexual assault and so on, which are specifically classified by the government). There is no category called lynching in India's penal code and the police is under

---

[1] '84% dead in cow-related violence since 2010 are muslim; 97% attacks after 2014', 28 June 2017, *IndiaSpend.com*

no obligation to record it and report it to the media as being such. What is manifestly a lynching could as well be noted as murder or assault and pass unnoticed.

This is similar to 'rioting', a vague term which the police can use at its discretion. An act of mob brutality can be 'rioting' or just another form of violence depending on which sections the offence is registered under.[2] A state with many incidents of rioting can report that it has actually not seen much rioting at all because the offences are registered under other sections. For example, if a vigilante group engaged in rioting and it leads to a death, the case would be counted as one of murder and not of rioting. Even so, offences promoting enmity between groups more than doubled over 2016. From 478 cases in 2016, the numbers rose to 958 in 2017 and 1,114 in 2018.[3]

A second factor makes it difficult to tabulate the actual number of these hate crimes. It is the nature of the media to demote stories that become commonplace because they are no longer 'news'. When the lynching and assault of Muslims for their faith and culture first begins to happen, it is a national and perhaps even an international story. In time, other stories come to the front page and the assault and lynching incidents begin to recede into the back pages. They are no longer prominent and no longer noticed. Violence and hatred against Muslims became normalised under Modi. One interesting data point is that Google searches from India for the word 'Muslim' overtook searches for 'Hindu' in 2017 and remained higher. Searches for 'Hindu' were five times higher before Modi.

A third factor is that the State is sensitive to this data and does not want it published.

Media proprietors are alert to the Union government's sensitivities for the business reasons we have seen in the chapter on the media. And the tracking of hate crimes is something that particularly concerns the Modi government. Editors who pursued projects compiling data on this were replaced and the project dismantled as the evidence shows. This happened at the *Hindustan Times*[4] and with *India Spend*.[5]

---

[2] 'Data: Significant decrease in the registered cases of "rioting" in 2019', 9 October 2020, factly.in

[3] 'Telling Numbers: In riot cases, signature of economy', 20 January 2020, *The Indian Express*

[4] '*Hindustan Times* takes down Hate Tracker project from website after change in leadership', 26 October 2017, *scroll.in*

[5] 'FactChecker shuts down Hate Crime Watch, Samar Halarnkar's stint with India Spend ends', 12 September 2019, *NewsLaundry.com*

We will look at what triggered the spate of violence, why it began and analyse the pattern. First let us look at the incidents to familiarise ourselves with what has been inflicted on Indians. This is the data compiled by the journalists of *Article-14.com*, who have worked on the issue over the years.

2015

30 May, Nagaur, Rajasthan

Sixty-year-old Abdul Ghaffar Qureshi was killed, after being lynched following rumours that Muslims had killed more than 200 cows for a feast.[6]

Pictures of the carcasses had been circulating on social media. Young men in the thousands gathered in the fields of Kumhari village where the carcasses were lying. A municipal contractor had rented the field to dispose of cattle carcasses as a routine exercise. Tension, however, spread and Qureshi was beaten with iron rods and killed in the marketplace, although some of his Hindu neighbours tried to protect him.

2 August, Dadri, Uttar Pradesh

Three men, Nazin, Arif and Anaf, were killed, lynched by a mob after being accused of being cattle thieves.[7] An FIR was filed against the dead men. Police said it would 'likely' file an FIR against the killers.

28 September, Dadri, Uttar Pradesh

Mohammad Akhlaq, 52, was killed after being lynched by a mob that broke into his house and accused him of cow slaughter.[8] Akhlaq's son, Danish, was also assaulted but survived. This was the famous case that brought beef lynching to national attention. Five years after the murder, the government began a 'fast track court' trial.[9]

6 October, Udupi, Karnataka

Cattle trader Ibrahim Padubidri was attacked by Bajrang Dal activists with metal rods and chains over a rumour about a stolen cow.[10] Ibrahim had

---

[6] 'Accused in lynching of man in Rajasthan still remain free', 1 November 2015, *The Hindu*

[7] '3 suspected cattle thieves beaten to death in Dadri, truck set ablaze', 3 August 2015, *The Indian Express*

[8] 'Indian man lynched over beef rumours', 30 September 2015, *BBC*

[9] 'Fast-track court begins trial five years after Akhlaq's murder', 26 March 2021, *Hindustan Times*

[10] 'Bajrang Dal attacks cattle trader in Karnataka', 9 October 2015, *Hindustan Times*

purchased three cows and two calves from farmers, whom the Bajrang Dal members berated for selling to a Muslim despite being Hindu themselves. The police arrested the Bajrang Dal members, but the farmers were forced by the Bajrang Dal to file a case of theft against Ibrahim. He was arrested and taken to a hospital.

8 October, Srinagar, Kashmir

Independent legislator Engineer Rashid, who had served beef kebabs and patties on the lawns of the state legislators' hostel to oppose restrictions on cow slaughter, was beaten, kicked and punched by BJP MLAs inside the Jammu and Kashmir Assembly.[11] He was assaulted by the VHP over the same issue again the following month[12] and then yet again in February 2016.[13]

9 October, Mainpuri, Uttar Pradesh

Police had to resort to firing to control a mob that went on a rampage, burning vehicles and shops, after rumours spread that two men, Rafeeq and Habib, had been spotted slaughtering a cow.[14]

The mob also physically assaulted the butchers. Later, it was found that the cow had actually died the previous day and the butchers had a licence to remove the skin and were just doing their job.

11 October, Udhampur, Jammu

Zahid Rasool Bhat, the 16-year-old conductor of a truck, was murdered, burnt alive by a mob on the Jammu-Srinagar Highway.[15] The truck was standing near the Shiv Nagar area because traffic had been stopped in view of the day-long strike called by various Hindu outfits after three carcasses of cows were found. Bhat suffered severe burn injuries and died five days later.

14 October, Sirmaur, Himachal Pradesh

A Muslim youth, 22-year-old Noman, was bludgeoned to death by a mob

---

[11] 'Ink attack on Jammu and Kashmir MLA Rashid Engineer over beef party', 20 October 2015, *The Indian Express*

[12] 'VHP activists attack J-K MLA engineer Rashid', 25 November 2015, *Hindustan Times*

[13] 'Independent MLA Engineer Rashid "attacked" in J-K', 20 February 2016, PTI

[14] 'UP: Cow slaughter rumours spark arson in Mainpuri's Karhal', 10 October 2015, *Hindustan Times*

[15] '16-year-old victim of Udhampur truck attack dies in Delhi', 19 October 2015, *India Today*

after being accused of 'smuggling' cattle.[16] Four of his companions, Nishu (37), Salman (20), Gulzar (22) and Gulfaam (24), were assaulted. The police arrested the victims and jailed them. They said they could not locate the killers.

2 November, Imphal, Manipur

A government madrassa headmaster Mohammed Hasmat Ali, 55, was murdered, after being lynched by a mob that accused him of stealing a calf.[17]

3 December, Palwal, Haryana

A man was assaulted for carrying camel meat from Mewat to Uttar Pradesh's Aligarh via Palwal.[18] The violence continued for five hours and the injured included five policemen. The mob insisted that the meat was beef.

9 December, Ambala, Haryana

Khush Noor, 25 years old, was murdered after a cow vigilante team opened fire on a group of migrant workers going to Uttar Pradesh.[19] Another man, Ehsaan, was wounded. Police said there was no evidence of cow 'smuggling'. The murder happened three days after Haryana Chief Minister M.L. Khattar said all cases against cow vigilantes would be withdrawn.

2016

13 January, Harda, Madhya Pradesh

A cow vigilante group assaulted a Muslim couple on a train, accusing them of carrying beef. The meat, which was buffalo, was found to belong to another passenger.[20] The police filed a complaint against the couple's relatives, who resisted the vigilante group.

---

[16] '"Cow smuggler" lynched in Himachal, police yet to make arrest', 16 October 2015, *Hindustan Times*

[17] 'Headmaster lynched for "stealing cow"; shutdown call in Manipur', 4 November 2015, *Hindustan Times*

[18] 'Dadri like incident reported again, this time in Palwal', 3 December 2015, *The Hindu*

[19] '"Cow vigilante" team shoots dead migrant in Karnal', 9 December 2015, *Hindustan Times*

[20] 'Muslim couple on train beaten in MP over beef suspicion', 15 January 2016, *The Indian Express*

14 March, Chittorgarh, Rajasthan

Local students manhandled their Kashmiri fellow students, saying they had beef in the hostel of the private Mewar University. The police arrested four Kashmiri students. The lab report said the meat was not beef.[21]

18 March, Latehar, Jharkhand

Two Muslim cattle herders, one of whom, Imtiyaz Khan, was a 13-year-old boy, were lynched and their bodies hanged by a cow vigilante group. Five of the group were arrested.[22]

27 March, Kurukshetra, Haryana

Mustain Abbas was murdered after being lynched by four men for buying a bull to plough his fields.[23] No arrests were made. After the family moved the high court, it ordered the immediate transfer of the Kurukshetra district magistrate, superintendent of police, deputy superintendent of police and station house officer of the Shahbad police station. The Supreme Court stayed the decision.

6 May, Gurugram, Haryana

Twenty-year-old Waseem was assaulted by cow vigilantes who were carrying guns. The vigilantes posed for photographs with their victim. An FIR was filed against Waseem while his assaulters went free.[24]

2 June, Karnal, Haryana

A Muslim man was shot dead by cow vigilantes.[25]

2 June, Pratapgarh, Rajasthan

A mob of vigilantes assaulted a Muslim youth and posed for pictures with his naked body with their feet on his head after he fell unconscious.[26]

---

[21] 'In the name of the cow: Murder, flogging, humiliation of Muslims, Dalits', 5 August 2016, *The Indian Express*

[22] 'Five held after two Muslim cowherds hanged to death in India', 19 March 2016, *Reuters*

[23] 'Killed allegedly by "cow protectors", justice eludes the family of Mustain Abbas', 8 July 2016, *TheWire.in*

[24] 'In the name of the cow: Murder, flogging, humiliation of Muslims, Dalits', 5 August 2016, *The Indian Express*

[25] 'Suspected cattle smuggler killed in shootout in Haryana', 3 June 2016, *NDTV*

[26] 'Cow lynching timeline: Steady increase under BJP with a spike in 2017', 17 October 2017, TheCitizen.in

10 June, Faridabad, Haryana

Two men, Rizwan and Muktihar, were forced by vigilantes to eat cow faeces by a mob that accused them of possessing beef.[27]

11 July, Una, Gujarat

Seven Dalits were assaulted by vigilantes for stripping a bovine carcass.[28] Four of them were kidnapped and taken from their village to Una town and then stripped, humiliated and assaulted with metal rods as onlookers recorded with their phones.

26 July, Mandsaur, Madhya Pradesh

Two women were assaulted for half an hour by a mob that the police was unable to control.[29] They were accused of carrying beef, but a veterinary test showed the meat was from a buffalo.

30 July, Muzaffarnagar, Uttar Pradesh

A cattle trader, Zeeshan, was assaulted and his house vandalised by a vigilante mob.[30] The mob was not charged. Zeeshan and his nephews were in jail for nine months.

9 August, Panipat, Haryana

Two days after Prime Minister Modi made a speech asking for gaurakshak groups to be restrained, two men who were transporting cows were beaten by a mob and their vehicles set on fire in a Panipat village.[31] The victims, Imrani Ali and Asheef Ali, residents of Uttar Pradesh's Tanda village, were then arrested following a case registered against them at Panipat's Model Town police station.

---

[27] 'Two "beef transporters" forced to eat cow dung by gau rakshaks', 29 June 2016, *The Indian Express*

[28] 'Dalit family stripped, beaten as "gau raksha" vigilantism continues', 13 July 2016, *TheWire.in*

[29] 'Mob beats Muslim women in MP over beef rumour, Oppn corners govt in House', 27 July 2016, *Hindustan Times*

[30] 'Muzaffarnagar: Mob attacks Muslim family over cow slaughter, two days on no police case filed yet', 2 August 2016, *The Indian Express*

[31] '2 cow "traders" beaten up in Panipat', 9 August 2016, *The Times of India*

23 August, Surat, Gujarat

Tempo driver Ilyas Shaikh was assaulted by 10 cow vigilantes after skin and bones were found in his tempo.[32] Shaikh told police that he had signed a contract with Surat Municipal Corporation to transport dead animal skin and bones from the waste disposal site at Khajod to Chhota Udepur. He was carrying the necessary papers, which were shown to the police.

24 August, Mewat, Haryana

A 20-year-old woman and her 14-year-old cousin were raped by vigilantes inside their home.[33] Their uncle and aunt were battered to death the same night. The survivors said: 'They asked if we eat beef. We said that we don't, but they said that was why we were being punished.' The police arrested four men, Sandeep, Karamjeet, Amarjeet and Rahul, one of whom was said to be a gaurakshak.

9 September, Rangareddy, Telangana

Cow vigilantes attacked two Muslim youths who were accused of ferrying cattle that they had purchased.[34] The police said members of a group named the Jai Shri Ram Ganesh Association and another named Siddi Vinayaka Hills Youth Association were responsible. The police said it had 'rescued' the animals.

10 September, Madikeri, Karnataka

P.A. Basheer, 36 years old, was assaulted by around 20 cow vigilantes while he was returning with two oxen from Koggodu village, 12 kms away from his village.[35] Basheer had purchased the oxen for Rs 17,500.

13 September, Ahmedabad, Gujarat

Mohammad Ayyub was murdered by a lynch mob accusing him of 'illegally transporting' cattle.[36] His associate, Sameer Sheikh, was also assaulted during

---

[32] 'Surat: "Gau rakshaks" beat up man ferrying cattle hide', 23 August 2016, *The Indian Express*

[33] 'We were gangraped for "eating beef", says Mewat woman', 11 September 2016, *India Today*

[34] '4 cow vigilantes held for attack on cattle truck in Hyderabad', 9 September 2016, *Deccan Chronicle*

[35] 'Cow vigilantes assault farmer', 13 September 2016, *The Hindu*

[36] 'Beaten up by suspected gau rakshaks in Gujarat, 29-year-old dies', 17 September 2016, *NDTV*

the lynching. The vigilantes registered an FIR against the dead man. A murder case was filed against 'unknown people'.

15 September, Delhi

Despite permission from the police to avoid confusion over the sacrifice of buffaloes on Eid-al-Adha, two Muslim men were assaulted by vigilantes a day after Eid.[37] The men were on their way to dump the remains of animals, sacrificed in their madrasa in outer Delhi.

16 September, Bengaluru, Karnataka

Three men, Nazir Ahmed, owner of a farmhouse in Bannerghatta, and his two sons, Mohammed Masi and Fateh, were wrongly detained by the police on charges of slaughtering a cow.[38] Half a dozen men barged into the farmhouse and harassed them. Outside the station, more than 20 vigilantes, who had lodged a complaint with the police, gathered to protest. The mob assaulted Fateh, who was trying to record a video of his family being harassed. It was later found that two oxen and not cows had been legally slaughtered.

17 November, Dakshina Kannada, Karnataka

A Bajrang Dal mob, accompanied by the police, barged into 42-year-old Mohammad Shakir's house and forcibly took away a calf he was rearing.[39] The police did not file an FIR, saying nobody had complained, though they were present when the calf was taken away.

2017

9 January, Kathua, Jammu

A mob of 500 vigilantes opened fire on tribal Muslims, accusing them of slaughtering a cow. Five were wounded, including a minor girl.[40]

[37] 'Cow vigilantes strip, thrash two Muslim men for dumping buffalo carcass after Bakr-Eid sacrifice', 16 September 2016, *India Today*

[38] 'Family harassed for "cow slaughter"', 16 September 2016, *The Hindu*

[39] 'Bajrang Dal activists accused of threatening hotel owner', 17 November 2016, *The Hindu*

[40] 'Mob attack in Kathua creates a sense of insecurity among Muslims of Jammu', 20 January 2017, *TwoCircles.net*, https://twocircles.net/2017jan20/403146.html

18 March, Jaipur, Rajasthan

A mob of more than 100 vigilantes lay seige to hotel Hayat Rabbani in Jaipur over allegations that it served beef. Cries of 'Bharat Mata ki Jai' and 'Narendra Modi Zindabad' were heard.[41]

22 March, Amroha, Uttar Pradesh

A man, Nasir, was murdered after being lynched by a mob that accused him of cattle theft.[42]

1 April, Alwar, Rajasthan

Cattle trader Pehlu Khan was murdered, and four others, including two of his sons, were assaulted in a lynching that was filmed by bystanders and widely broadcast on television.[43]

Though the video evidence was clear, all accused were soon out on bail.[44]

19 April, Ernakulam, Kerala

A house was attacked by over a dozen BJP and RSS workers after they accused an individual of slaughtering a cow on the eve of Easter.[45]

20 April, Reasi, Jammu

A mob of 200 vigilantes assaulted three nomadic Bakerwal families on the suspicion that they were cattle 'smugglers'.[46] Reports said the attackers were VHP and Bajrang Dal activists, but the police said the affiliation of the arrested with any organisation was to be ascertained.

24 April, Delhi

Three men, Rizwan, Kamil and Ashu, were assaulted by a dozen vigilantes for transporting 14 buffaloes. Delhi Police said the three men were transporting

---

[41] 'When a mob of "gau rakshaks" laid siege to a Jaipur hotel over beef rumours', 21 March 2017, *Hindustan Times*

[42] 'Villagers lynch cow thief in Amroha', 22 March 2017, *Hindustan Times*

[43] 'Man transporting cows beaten to death in Rajasthan', 5 April 2017, PTI

[44] 'Pehlu Khan lynching case: All held in the case are out on bail', 29 September 2017, *The Indian Express*

[45] 'Kerala: 14 BJP-RSS men booked for attack over cow slaughter', 19 April 2017, *The Indian Express*

[46] 'Mob attacks nomadic family over suspicions of cattle smuggling in Jammu's Reasi', 22 April 2017, *Hindustan Times*. '8-year-old among 5 hurt as Jammu nomad family attacked by VHP', 23 April 2017, *The Indian Express*

the animals for legal slaughter, but arrested them anyway under the Prevention of Cruelty to Animals Act.[47]

1 May, Nagaon, Assam

Two men, Abu Hanifa, 23, and Riazuddin Ali, 24, were beaten to death by a vigilante mob that accused them of stealing two cattle.[48]

26 May, Washim, Maharashtra

Two meat traders were assaulted by a group of cow vigilantes. A video of the assault, recorded by the attackers, showed the men demanding that the Muslims say 'Jai Shri Ram'.[49]

6 June, Dhanbad, Jharkhand

Ainul Ansari, 35, was assaulted by about 20 men for taking meat to an Iftar party.[50]

20 June, Etah, Uttar Pradesh

Two men, Asif and Rehan, were tied to a tree and assaulted by a mob of 50 vigilantes who also paraded them, accusing them of stealing buffaloes.[51]

26 June, Giridih, Jharkhand

A Muslim dairy trader was assaulted and his house set on fire by a mob of 1,000 people after a cow was found dead near his house.[52]

28 June, Ramgarh, Uttar Pradesh

Alimuddin Asgar Ali Ansari, 40, was murdered, after being lynched by a mob of more than 100, instigated by a Bajrang Dal man who accused him of having beef on his person.[53]

---

[47] 'Kalkaji "gau rakshak" attack: Delhi Police arrest "PFA member"', 24 April 2017, *The Indian Express*

[48] 'Two "cattle thieves" lynched in Assam', 1 May 2017, *The Indian Express*

[49] 'Maharashtra: Cow vigilantes attack two youths for allegedly possessing beef in Washim district', 30 May 2017, *India Today*

[50] 'Jharkhand: Muslim man attacked by irate mob for taking "beef" to Iftar party', 16 July 2017, *Hindustan Times*

[51] 'Cow vigilantes strip, tie and beat up "cattle smugglers" in Etah', 20 June 2017, *News18.com*

[52] 'In Jharkhand, man beaten up, his house set on fire after dead cow found outside', 28 June 2017, *The Indian Express*

[53] 'Gau rakshaks followed Jharkhand trader for hours before lynching him | A blow by blow account by police', 7 July 2017, *Hindustan Times*

12 July, Nagpur, Maharashtra

Ismail Shah, 36, was assaulted by a mob that accused him of carrying beef. Shah kept telling them it was mutton and not beef, but the men continued to assault him.[54]

18 July, Dhanbad, Jharkhand

A man undergoing treatment for mental illness was tied to a tree and assaulted after being accused of stealing cattle. According to police, Mohammad Afroz was in his mid-twenties. When he saw some cows grazing, he started herding three of them, triggering the fury of villagers.[55]

3 August, Bhojpur, Bihar

Three Muslim men were assaulted by vigilantes for transporting meat. The victims were arrested after they were beaten up.[56]

17 August, Champaran, Bihar

Six Muslim men were assaulted after being accused of slaughtering a calf. When Qudus Kureishi, the husband of the village head, tried to intervene, he was beaten by the mob as well. A case was filed against the men who were attacked for animal cruelty and 'hurting religious sentiments'.[57]

19 August, Garhwa, Jharkhand

An Adivasi man, Ramesh Minj, was murdered after vigilantes lynched a group of Oraon tribals who were accused of cattle slaughter.[58]

25 August, Bulandshahar, Uttar Pradesh

A vigilante mob of about 100 men assaulted several Muslims and vandalised their houses and two mosques after a cow's carcass was spotted in the village pond.[59]

---

[54] 'Cow vigilantes beat up Muslim man in Nagpur for "carrying beef", 4 arrested', 13 July 2017, *Hindustan Times*

[55] 'Mentally unwell man beaten up in Jharkhand over suspected cow theft bid', 21 July 2017, *The Indian Express*

[56] 'Cow vigilantes assault three Muslim men in Bihar on suspicion of carrying beef', 3 August 2017, *Hindustan Times*

[57] 'Six thrashed in Bihar on suspicion of slaughtering cow: Police', 18 August 2017, *Hindustan Times*

[58] 'An Adivasi woman in Jharkhand is taking on the "Gau Rakshaks" who killed her husband', 26 August 2018, *TheWire.in*

[59] '10 held after clashes over cow carcass in Bulandshahr village', 27 August 2017, *The Indian Express*

26 August, Rajouri, Jammu

A man, Lal Hussain, was assaulted when he was on his way to hand over a cow he had purchased to the person he had in turn sold it to. Kuldeep Raj and others attacked him, thinking he was 'smuggling' the animal.[60]

27 August, Jalpaiguri, West Bengal

Two men, Hafizul Sheikh and Anwar Hussain, were murdered, lynched by a mob that accused them of cattle theft.[61]

2 September, Faridabad, Haryana

Six Rohingya Muslim refugees in a slum were assaulted after 40 families pooled in money to buy two buffalo calves for Eid sacrifice. Locals first accused the refugees of having stolen the animals. On being shown proof of purchase, the mob offered to buy back the calves. The same evening, two men came to the slum cluster and ordered the Muslims not to sacrifice the animals. Anticipating danger, the refugee families promised to return the animals. But around two dozen men, some of them on motorcycles, reached the settlement, abducted four men and assaulted them with lathis. Two women were sexually assaulted and had their clothes torn off.[62]

2 September, Giridih, Jharkhand

Two Muslims, including a woman, were injured when a mob attacked a family and set fire to their house for having allegedly slaughtered a bovine animal for Eid.[63]

2 September, Araria, Bihar

A Bajrang Dal mob seized several pieces of meat from the huts of their Muslim neighbours at Eid. When the police arrived, the mob demanded that the Muslims be handed over to them for 'punishment'.[64]

---

[60] 'Villager assaulted over rumours of cattle smuggling', 27 August 2017, *The Tribune*

[61] 'Two lynched over suspicion of cow theft in West Bengal's Jalpaiguri district', 27 August 2017, *The Hindu*

[62] 'Ballabgarh again: Rohingyas beaten up over buffalo sacrifice, no arrests yet', 2 September 2017, *Hindustan Times*

[63] 'Jharkhand "bovine" slaughter: Mob attacks family, sets house on fire', 3 September 2017, *The Indian Express*

[64] 'Post alliance, communal row in Bihar points to slow rise of BJP's Hindutva', 5 September 2017, *Hindustan Times*

4 September, Bhojpur, Bihar

A mob said to be from the Bajrang Dal and BJP threatened to set on fire the homes of two Muslim men after accusing them of cow slaughter. The police arrested the two Muslim men.[65]

13 October, Faridabad, Haryana

Five Muslim men were assaulted by cow vigilantes on suspicion of transporting beef. After the meat turned out to be that of a buffalo's, police booked a case against the attackers.[66]

10 November, Alwar, Rajasthan

A dairy farmer, Umar Khan, 35, was murdered by cow vigilantes and his body tossed on to the railway tracks. Eight men were arrested and charged.[67]

23 December, Alwar, Rajasthan

Zakir Khan, 46, sustained brain injuries and fractures after being assaulted by a mob that accused him of 'smuggling' cows.[68]

2018

16 January, Meerut, Uttar Pradesh

Two Muslim men who bought cows were assaulted by vigilantes. Those who had sold the animals were also harassed. Following this, the local Muslim councillor (Abdul Gaffar Khan) handed over his own cow to the local police station in protest.[69]

5 March, Gandhinagar, Gujarat

A Muslim man, 32-year-old Farnaz Saiyed, was killed and his mother, Roshanbiwi Syed, was wounded when they were out grazing their cattle. Roshanbiwi's fingers were chopped off while Farnaz was hit on the head.[70]

---

[65] 'Communal tension grips Bihar village over beef', 3 September 2017, IANS

[66] 'Cow-vigilantes thrash five men in Faridabad, booked after meat found to be buffalo's', 14 October 2017, *The Indian Express*

[67] 'After Pehlu Khan, Umar Mohammed, transporting pet cows, shot dead in Alwar', 13 November 2017, *TheWire.in*

[68] 'Rajasthan: Cow smuggler thrashed by villagers in Alwar, suffers severe injuries', 24 December 2017, *India Today*

[69] 'Muslim councillor from Meerut hands over cow to Police, says "it is a dangerous animal"', 16 January 2018, *TwoCircles.net*

[70] 'Muslim youth dies, five of seven "Bajrang Dal members" arrested', 13 March 2018, *The Indian Express*

7 March, Dakshina Kannada, Karnataka

Two Muslim men—Noorul Amin, 40, and Ghufran Pothe, 35—were assaulted by vigilantes for transporting two buffaloes and a bullock.[71]

17 April, Koderma, Jharkhand

A Muslim man was assaulted by a mob that accused him of serving bovine meat at his son's wedding reception. The mob also vandalised his house and those of his neighbours, several vehicles and the property of a nearby mosque.[72]

18 May, Satna, Madhya Pradesh

A Muslim man was killed and another wounded grievously after vigilantes accused them of carrying beef. Riyaz, 45 years old, was murdered, while 35-year-old Shakil sustained major injuries.[73]

30 May, Udupi, Karnataka

A 61-year-old cattle trader, Hussain Baba, was allegedly murdered by Bajrang Dal activists who stopped his vehicle and killed him.[74]

13 June, Godda, Jharkhand

Two Muslim men—Sirabuddin Ansari (35) and Murtaza Ansari (30)—were murdered by a mob, after being accused of stealing 13 buffaloes.[75]

18 June, Hapur, Uttar Pradesh

A Muslim man, Qasim, 45, was killed and another, Sameuddin, wounded grievously after a mob accused them of cow slaughter. The assault was recorded and uploaded on social media.[76]

---

[71] 'Duo assaulted in Honnavar', 9 March 2018, *The Hindu*

[72] 'Jharkhand: Man assaulted for serving "banned meat", section 144 imposed', 18 April 2018, PTI

[73] 'Muslim killed over suspicion of cow slaughter in Madhya Pradesh', 20 May 2018, *Hindustan Times*

[74] 'Death of cattle trader: Police, kin give two versions', 31 May 2018, *The Hindu*

[75] 'Jharkhand: Two Muslim men lynched on suspicion of cattle theft', 14 June 2018, PTI

[76] 'UP: Hapur lynching linked to cows, claim victim's kin; police deny, say road rage', 20 June 2018, *The Indian Express*

19 June, Ramgarh, Uttar Pradesh

Touhid Ansari, 45, was found killed after some meat fell off his motorcycle. His family said that Ansari's body bore severe bruises and acid burns.[77]

20 July, Alwar, Rajasthan

A Muslim man in his thirties, Rakbar Khan, was bludgeoned to death by a mob that accused him of stealing two cows.[78] The Vishwa Hindu Parishad individual who led the lynching was only arrested three years later.[79]

21 August, Gandhinagar, Gujarat

Fifty-year-old Fakir Mohammed Syed was assaulted by three vigilantes for transporting his cattle. The police booked Syed for 'ferrying livestock without permission' under the Prevention of Cruelty to Animals Act, while his assailants were booked for assault and criminal intimidation.[80]

22 August, Rohtak, Haryana

A mob vandalised the house of a Muslim man and also vandalised the village mosque after a calf was killed in an accident.[81]

26 August, Moradabad, Uttar Pradesh

A van carrying animal remains from Bakri Eid celebrations was set ablaze and its driver, Wasim Ahmad, was assaulted.[82]

29 August, Darrang, Assam

A Muslim man, Zakir Hussain, was battered to death by a mob with lathis, after being accused of cow theft. Onlookers recorded the lynching on their phones, while police who tried to intervene were also roughed up by the mob.[83]

---

[77] 'Ramgarh man carries "beef", found dead three hours later', 21 June 2018, *The Times of India*

[78] 'Alwar lynching: Police took three hours to take victim to health centre 4 km away, even stopped for tea', 20 August 2018, *The Indian Express*

[79] 'Rakbar Khan Lynching: Alwar VHP Leader, Who Claimed to Help Police, Arrested', 21 June 2021, *TheWire.in*

[80] 'Gujarat: Gau rakshaks beat up man ferrying buffaloes', 23 August 2018, *The Times of India*

[81] 'Muslim man's house, village namaz ghar vandalised in Rohtak on suspicion of cow slaughter', 23 August 2018, *Hindustan Times*

[82] 'Moradabad: Truck with animal remains set ablaze, driver assaulted', 28 August 2018, *The Indian Express*

[83] 'Mob attacks man for cow "theft" in Assam', 2 October 2018, *The Times of India*

29 August, Bareilly, Uttar Pradesh

A 20-year-old Muslim youth, Shahrukh, was accused of stealing a buffalo and was killed by a mob of 50.[84]

18 November, Ahmedabad, Gujarat

Zaheer Qureshi, the assistant of a truck driver, was stabbed in the chest by vigilantes, for transporting buffaloes 'without the mandatory papers and permission'. The truck driver, Mustufa Sipai, was arrested, though the assailants were missing.[85]

2019

19 January, Rohtak, Haryana

Naushad Muhammad, 24, was assaulted and spent the night of 19 January illegally chained to the bedpost in the local police station, on suspicion of 'cow smuggling'. He had been denied medical treatment.

A case was later registered against Muhammad, who had been transporting buffaloes. The main attacker, against whom a police report was filed, said he was not worried since he acted in the name of 'gaumata'.[86]

31 January, Hassan, Karnataka

A 70-year-old Muslim woman was assaulted by eight men, and her makeshift canteen vandalised and set on fire, after being accused of selling beef. The woman, Khamrunissa, had been selling food at the APMC market in Sakleshpur in Hassan district for 40 years. The local Bajrang Dal unit claimed responsibility for the attack in a Facebook post.[87]

7 April, Biswanath, Assam

Shaukat Ali, 68 years old, was assaulted, beaten bloody by a mob and force-fed pork, for selling cooked beef—which is not a crime in the state. Ali had

---

[84] 'UP: Shahrukh Khan lynched by mob on suspicion of cattle theft in Bareilly', 30 August 2018, *Mirror Now*

[85] 'Gujarat: "Gau rakshaks" stab truck conductor for "illegally" ferrying buffaloes; 2 FIRs lodged', 19 November 2018, *The Indian Express*

[86] 'Man attacked by mob in Haryana; after rescue, cops keep him chained', 24 January 2019, *NDTV*

[87] 'Forum seeks action against possibility of communal violence', 14 February 2019, http://www.coastaldigest.com/forum-seeks-action-against-possibility-communal-violence?page=11http://www.coastaldigest.com/forum-seeks-action-against-possibility-communal-violence?page=11

been operating his restaurant for 35 years, but was taken to a police lock-up the night after the attack.[88]

10 April, Gumla, Jharkhand

A Christian Adivasi man was killed and three others were wounded by a Hindu mob for carving up a dead ox. The victims were beaten for four hours with rods, stabbed with daggers, forced to drink urine when thirsting for water, and left lying on the road outside a police station for three hours after midnight.[89]

22 May, Seoni, Madhya Pradesh

Three Muslims, including a woman, were assaulted by a mob of vigilantes after being accused of 'carrying beef'. A video of the attack, recorded by the attackers for Facebook, showed five men kicking and beating the three with lathis. The attackers then forced one of the male victims to beat the woman with a rubber slipper, insisting he shout 'Jai Shri Ram' as he did so.[90]

1 June, Bareilly, Uttar Pradesh

Four Muslim labourers were assaulted while they were having their lunch. They were accused of eating beef. The police were puzzled: 'This sort of an incident has never happened before—Hindus and Muslims have lived in harmony for years here. It is a random and unplanned attack that happened within minutes.'[91]

11 July, Nagapattinam, Tamil Nadu

Mohamed Fisan, 24, was allegedly assaulted by four men from the Hindu Makkal Katchi after he posted photos of himself eating beef (not a crime in Tamil Nadu) on Facebook.[92]

---

[88] 'Assam: Mob thrashes 68-year-old Muslim man for selling beef, forces him to eat pork', 9 April 2019, *India Today*

[89] 'Jharkhand: Lynched Adivasi man was dragged for 1 km, mob chanted Hindu slogans', 18 April 2019, *TheWire.in*

[90] 'Three Muslims beaten by gau rakshaks, then arrested in MP's Seoni over beef rumour', 26 May 2019, *TheWire.in*

[91] 'उत्तर प्रदेश: बरेली में धार्मिक स्थल के पास मांस खाने के शक में 4 मजदूरों की पिटाई', 1 June 2019, *NDTV*

[92] 'Man in Tamil Nadu attacked for eating beef, four men arrested', 12 July 2019, *The News Minute*

22 September, Khunti, Jharkhand

A Christian tribal was lynched by a mob, and two others were seriously wounded after being accused of carving out a cow's carcass. The police made no arrests because there was 'no clarity on the sequence of events', according to the DIG.[93]

23 September, Bhiwadi, Rajasthan

A Muslim man, Munfed Khan, was assaulted by a mob accusing him of illegally transporting cattle. They broke his bones and he sustained several fractures before the police intervened.[94]

This is the sequence of beef lynchings, a category of violence that the data shows was introduced to India after Modi took office. And once lynchings began, there was little or no effort from the State to end the violence against India's minorities, predominantly Muslims.

The question is: why did beef lynching as a category of violence not exist in India before Modi? And what has caused it to erupt in his term? The answer to that may be found in a parallel in Pakistan's blasphemy law.

In all of undivided India, and then in independent Pakistan in the 60 years from 1927 to 1986, only seven cases of blasphemy were registered. Pakistan's National Commission for Justice and Peace says that, in the 35 years after 1986, 1,540 cases of blasphemy were registered.[95]

So what changed in 1986? Did people suddenly begin blaspheming more? Of course not. In 1986, Pakistan introduced a change in the law for blasphemy. It was now punishable by death. This happened under Gen. Muhammad Zia-ul-Haq, when Islamism was being forced on the population. So the atmosphere there was akin to the charged one here in India today, in terms of religious majoritarianism.

Of the 1,540 Pakistani accused, 505 were Ahmadi, 776 were Muslim, 229 were Christian and 30 were Hindu. Non-Muslims, who were only 4 per cent of Pakistan's population (Ahmadis or Ahmadiyyas have been constitutionally apostatised and are considered non-Muslims in Pakistan), accounted for 50 per cent of those accused of blasphemy.

---

[93] 'Tribal lynched, 2 injured over "cow slaughter" in Jharkhand', 23 September 2019, *Hindustan Times*
[94] 'Man beaten up by mob on suspicion of cow smuggling in Rajasthan's Alwar', 23 September 2019, *India Today*
[95] 'What are Pakistan's blasphemy laws?', 8 May 2019, *BBC*

The same story has repeated itself in India through the cow slaughter laws. Knowing that the State is incapable of controlling violence, knowing that the passions stirred will produce extreme violence, including killings, against Muslims, such laws are still pushed by the government.

The law has been weaponised by certain interest groups to brutalise Muslims. The law banning beef is an instrument, and it is not the only one. Indeed, the issue is not by itself as important as the persecution of Muslims that it produces. The persecution and the attendant torture is the real outcome that is sought. This is easily proven. The promotion of animal husbandry, which is the claimed reason for the ban on cattle slaughter, is not the reason for the violence over beef. It is religious passion and hatred that is the driver. The very idea that this violence is happening because people are concerned about animal husbandry is lunacy. And the laws themselves reveal this with clarity.

Buffaloes, which produce more milk and more valuable, fattier milk than cows, are not protected by the slaughter laws even in Gujarat.

There is no relationship between milk production and cow slaughter. The world's largest producer of cow milk, the US with 97 million tons a year, also slaughters the most cows, over 32 million each year.[96]

The legislations and speeches on cattle and beef are written to provoke. They are catalysts deliberately stirred up to produce the violence needed for polarisation, which in turn is beneficial in electoral policies and appeases the Hindutva constituencies. The Constitution's instruction to the State was to legislate the prohibition of cattle slaughter. It says nothing about beef.

Through his 2014 campaign, Modi pushed for more laws against beef and cow slaughter. On 2 April, in Nawada in Bihar, he said:

'I am coming from Dwarka which has a direct connection to the Yaduvanshis (referring to Bihar's Yadav caste). And because of this connection, I feel at home here. I am therefore shocked that the same Yadavs who worship Shri Krishna, who keep cows as livestock, who serve the cow, it is their leaders who are in bed with the same people who proudly massacre animals.

'We've heard of the Green Revolution, we've heard of the White Revolution but today's Delhi sarkar wants neither; they've taken up cudgels for a Pink Revolution. Do you know what that is? When you slaughter an animal, then the colour of its meat is pink. This is what they call a Pink

---

[96] 'Artifice for the holy cow', *Our Hindu Rashtra*, Aakar Patel, 2020, Westland Publications

Revolution. Across the countryside, our animals are getting slaughtered. Our livestock is getting stolen from our villages and taken to Bangladesh. Across India too, there are massive slaughterhouses in operation. And that's not all. The Delhi sarkar will not give subsidies to farmers or to Yadavs keeping cows but will give out subsidies to people who slaughter cows, who slaughter animals, who are destroying our rivers of milk, as long as they set up slaughterhouses.'[97]

On 3 March 2015, Maharashtra under the BJP responded to Modi and passed its law which criminalised the possession of beef.[98] Those found with it would be sentenced to five years in jail. This law includes this section:

'9B. Burden of proof on accused. In any trial … the burden of proving that the slaughter, transport, export outside the State, sale, purchase or possession of flesh of cow, bull or bullock was not in contravention of the provisions of this Act shall be on the accused.'[99]

Meaning that you are guilty unless you can prove yourself innocent. If you are found with a bloody knife next to a corpse, you are presumed innocent. It is the State that has to demonstrate that you committed murder. But if you are found with or found near meat and accused of possessing beef, you are presumed guilty. This is an invitation to violence.

Two weeks later, on 17 March 2015, Haryana under the BJP passed its law criminalising possession of beef. The law has this section: 'No person shall directly or indirectly sell, keep, store, transport or offer for sale or cause to be sold beef or beef products.'[100] Burden of proof was reversed here also. Punishment is up to five years.

On 30 March 2015, Rajnath Singh said: 'How can we accept the fact that cow slaughter is allowed in this country? We will use all our might to ban it.'[101]

On 30 May 2015, the lynchings began.

Days after the assault on Dalits in Una on 11 July 2016 (more details on the incident and its aftermath are in the chapter 'The Devil's Workshop'), Modi made a theatrical speech asking gaurakshak mobs to attack him instead of Dalits.[102] It is difficult to understand what he meant. Was he serious about

[97] 'How Narendra Modi helped spread anti-beef hysteria', 6 October 2015, *Scroll.in*
[98] 'Indian state bans possession and sale of beef', 3 March 2015, *The New York Times*
[99] Maharashtra Animal Preservation (Amendment) Act, 2015, cjp.org.in
[100] 'The Haryana Gauvansh Sanrakshan and Gausamvardhan Act, 2015', PRS Legislative Research
[101] 'Modi govt says to push for cow slaughter ban in India', 30 March 2015, *Reuters*
[102] 'Shoot me, not my Dalit brothers: PM Modi', 7 August 2016, *Business Standard*

sacrificing himself? If so, why did he believe the mobs would want to attack him instead of those who were their targets—Muslims and Dalits—because of hate? Was Modi giving up his SPG security to facilitate this offer of his to martyr himself? Of course not. His words carried no meaning.

An event that took place after one of the cases listed above showed how comfortable the BJP government is with the lynchings.

Not only did a Union minister meet the lynch mob, he went ahead and garlanded them.[103] These were men convicted of murdering 40-year-old Alimuddin Ansari on 28 June 2017. Jayant Sinha did this at an event organised by the BJP to felicitate the convicts. Felicitate them for what achievement? This was left unsaid and did not need to be said: it was for lynching a Muslim.

As noted earlier, the media moves on from the violence, demoting the story over time because of its lack of 'newsworthiness'. We will therefore never have a proper record of this category of violence. Have a look at these headlines from 2020, both of which relate to Muslims being assaulted violently:

- 'Truck driver transporting meat beaten up by several men in Gurugram; FIR lodged'[104]
- 'Two buffalo traders from Ghasera beaten up, police deny link to earlier "beef" attack'[105]

The lynching of three Muslim men in Tripura in June 2021 was reported as a reaction to cattle theft.[106] The lynching of a Muslim man in Rajouri was also passed off in similar fashion and barely reported in the mainstream media.[107]

Also, the State will continue to go after the victims of assault so long as they are Muslims. On 8 January 2021, Abid Ali, who was transporting a dozen head of cattle, was brutalised by a Hindu mob in Sringeri, Karnataka.[108] The police charged Abid Ali under the state's new cow law, which allows them

---

[103] 'Union Minister Jayant Sinha met eight people convicted in the Ramgarh lynching case in Jharkhand', 6 July 2018, *India Today*

[104] 31 July 2020, *Hindustan Times*

[105] 12 August 2020, *Hindustan Times*

[106] '3 lynched in Tripura on suspicion of cattle theft: Police', 20 June 2021, PTI

[107] 'Cow Vigilantes Lynch Muslim Youth in J&K's Rajouri District', 22 June 2021, Clarion India

[108] 'First case registered under anti-cow slaughter ordinance', 14 January 2021, *The Hindu*

to make arrests without a warrant, permits them or 'competent authorities', such as veterinarians, to seize cattle and enter premises merely on suspicion, and provides immunity to vigilantes if they act in 'good faith'.

The animal husbandry minister said that cases against vigilantes previously booked for violence would now be withdrawn.[109]

In one instance, it was reported that 'three policemen allegedly allowed cow vigilantes to lynch a cattle trader in Karnataka and then dumped the body on a roadside to cover the murder up'.[110] (While watching a television news report on a lynching in Haryana, the author noticed that a senior IPS officer, who was commenting on the murder of a man accused of smuggling cattle, spoke instead about how upset she was by the condition in which the animals were being transported.)

Cow vigilantism has not ended in India; it may not even have decreased as we can see from reports of May and June 2021 in Nuh,[111] Moradabad,[112] Mewat,[113] Jhabua,[114] Jammu[115] and Hyderabad.[116] What has happened is that it has simply gone off the radar and ceased to become a big enough issue. The media has begun to shrug at it and demoted it to the inside pages. Television has no 'debates' on this issue or reports it any longer. Vigilantes appear to act with more impunity and often cannot be arrested because of police complicity and fear of mob violence as these instances show.[117]

---

[109] 'Karnataka minister says cases against "cow vigilantes" will be withdrawn', 20 January 2021, *The Times of India*

[110] 'Cow trader lynched, cops held', 6 June 2018, *The Telegraph*

[111] 'What power do gau rakshaks have to raid homes, asks HC', 5 May 2021, *The Times of India*

[112] 'Muslim Man In UP Assaulted By Cow Vigilantes, Cops File Case Against Him', 24 May 2021, *NDTV*

[113] 'Cow vigilantes shoot "smuggler" dead', 5 June 2021, *Hindustan Times*

[114] '"Cow vigilantes" lynch MP man transporting cattle in Rajasthan', 15 June 2021, *The Indian Express*

[115] 'J&K man "returning home with buffalo" lynched, locals blame cow vigilantes', 23 June 2021, *The Indian Express*

[116] 'Cow vigilantes harassing cattle traders: Owaisi to Telangana DGP', 29 June 2021, *Siasat*

[117] 'Cattle trader in Karnataka killed by cow vigilantes, suspects on the run', 2 April 2023, *India Today*; 'Mewat lynching: Slain Muslim man booked for cow slaughter, Police refuses to file FIR against Bajrang Dal', 3 April 2023, Maktoob Medi; 'Junaid-Nasir murder case: Mahapanchayat warns against Monu Manesar's arrest; "cops" chased away', 21 February 2023, *Economic Times*

Having desensitised society to such violence and normalised it, the BJP moves on to the next thing, 'love jihad', or whatever issue it is that the party deliberately stokes from the top. Once the pattern of violence is formatted, it spreads spontaneously in copycat attacks. For example, the *Article-14.com* hate tracker recorded half a dozen incidents in June and July of 2019 of Muslim individuals in Jharkhand, West Bengal, Maharashtra, Uttar Pradesh and Assam being accosted by groups of Hindus and forced to say 'Jai Shri Ram'.

Those keeping data on their hate-trackers will not find it easy to locate these stories from secondary sources like the mainstream media because they will not be reported under 'lynching'. The stories will also fall off the headlines through a normalisation of language. For example, the word 'smuggling' is used quite casually, with the presumption of guilt, when it is clear that smuggling, meaning the illegal export of something outside the country, is not what is happening here. So why is it used instead of the word 'transporting'? Its use makes it easier to condone the violence.

In 2017, the punishment for cow slaughter in Gujarat was made life imprisonment, and the burden of proof is of course reversed. Remember that cow slaughter bans are meant to help the agriculture economy and improve animal husbandry—meaning the ban punishes an economic crime—but no white collar crime attracts life imprisonment in India. After Modi, the BJP has become unhinged in its desire to persecute Muslims on this issue. After the lynching of a Muslim man, Asif Khan, in Haryana on 16 May 2021, a gathering was held in support of his killers on 30 May. The man who called the meeting said: 'Muslim brothers? What brothers? These bastards are butchers.' He was made the BJP's spokesman for Haryana a few days later.[118] In 2020, more than half the arrests under the anti-terror National Security Act (a law that allows preventive detention, meaning jail without a crime having been committed) in Uttar Pradesh were for cow slaughter cases.[119] Court proceedings showed how the cases were filed in bad[120] faith,[121] but that will surprise only those innocents who were unaware of what the

---

[118] 'Karni Sena Chief Suraj Pal Amu Named Haryana BJP Spokesperson', 12 June 2021, *The Quint*

[119] 'In Uttar Pradesh, more than half of NSA arrests this year were for cow slaughter', 11 September 2020, *The Indian Express*

[120] '94 out of 120 orders quashed: Allahabad High Court calls out abuse of NSA in Uttar Pradesh', 7 April 2021, *The Indian Express*

[121] 'Express investigation: Citing lack of due process & glaring gaps in FIRs, Allahabad HC struck down 20 of 20 orders', 7 April 2021, *The Indian Express*

BJP wanted to achieve: the continual harassment[122] by the State of India's Muslims.

Part 2: A Capital Pogrom

In December 2019, the Modi government faced its first real resistance from Muslims, who were being threatened with a loss of citizenship, disenfranchisement and incarceration. This was the sequence that was vowed by Amit Shah during the campaign for the 2019 election. On 23 April 2019, he said: 'Understand the chronology, first we will bring Citizenship Amendment Bill and after that we will bring National Register of Citizens and the NRC will not only be for Bengal but for the entire country.'[123] It had already been implemented in Assam, where Muslims were being made to line up to prove their citizenship. The people making the decisions were government employees on two-year contracts, who were only given extensions if they marked the maximum number of people as 'foreigner'.[124] Those who could not prove their citizenship were jailed—entire families with men separate from women, without crime or trial and little hope of getting out. (See 'The Devil's Workshop' for a fuller discussion on the NRC and the Shaheen Bagh protest) If they managed to come out after a few years, they were faced with a loss of their citizenship, meaning that their papers—licences, bank accounts, passports, property—were now useless.

This exercise was now being threatened on Muslims around India. If they did not act to protect themselves, the same fate awaited them. Bravely, they chose to resist. Within hours of parliament passing the CAA in December 2019, the first step in Amit Shah's chronology, the protests began in Delhi.

The defiance of protestors, especially Muslim women, who mobilised against the citizenship laws was new for the BJP, which was unused to resistance. The party's response was to unleash violence against the protestors.

On 15 December 2019, four days after CAA was passed, Delhi Police encroached on the campus of the Jamia Milia Islamia in New Delhi, whose students were protesting. The police brutalised and sexually assaulted the student protesters.[125] Individuals, including faculty members, filed multiple

[122] '94% acquittal rate under Haryana's cow slaughter law in Muslim-dominated Nuh', 5 February 2023, *The Hindu*

[123] 'Understanding the chronology: A few fundamental truths about the CAA, NRC, NPR and all the threads that bind the three together', 28 December 2019, *firstpost.com*

[124] Affidavit filed by the government of Assam in Mamoni Rajkumari Vs State of Assam, http://ghconline.gov.in/Judgment/WPC44762017.pdf

[125] '15 women, 30 men sexually assaulted by Delhi Police at February CAA clash in Jamia, report says', 11 August 2020, *ThePrint.in*

complaints but no FIR was registered, though video evidence clearly showed gratuitous violence by the Delhi Police, which reports to Amit Shah.[126]

In August 2020, the police objected to public interest litigations seeking a fact-finding committee into their actions.

On 5 January 2020, a masked mob, armed with rods and hammers, laid siege to the Jawaharlal Nehru University for more than two hours, injuring over two dozen students and teachers. Students and faculty filed 40 complaints but, again, not a single FIR was registered. Instead, FIRs were filed against the students who were protesting against the violence.

On 27 January, Amit Shah asked the audience at an election rally to 'press the EVM button with such anger that the current is felt at Shaheen Bagh'.[127] That same day, Union minister of state for finance, Anurag Thakur, encouraged a crowd to chant *'Desh ke ghaddaron ko, goli maaron saalon ko'* (Shoot the traitors of the nation).[128]

On 30 January, the anniversary of Mahatma Gandhi's assassination and shortly after Thakur's speech, a man fired a pistol at a group of anti-CAA protesters, injuring a student before walking away while waving the firearm and shouting *'Yeh lo aazaadi'* (Here, take your freedom). The video footage of the attack showed police officers standing on the sidelines, not taking any action against the man.

On 22 February, a group of women began a peaceful sit-in at the Jaffrabad Metro Station in northeast Delhi to protest against the citizenship laws.

On 23 February, the BJP held a rally in nearby Maujpur, in which party leader Kapil Mishra made an aggressive speech and gave the police (who were present) a 'three-day ultimatum' to remove the protestors. If they didn't, Mishra said, his people would act.[129] The mob began pelting stones the same day.

On 24 February, Maujpur saw violence and that night a market operated by Muslim traders was set ablaze. A peaceful sit-in by Muslim women in Kardampuri that had been on for a month was tear-gassed by police.

---

[126] 'Camera nails official denial: Police did enter Jamia library, beat students', 27 February 2020, *The Indian Express*

[127] 'Press the EVM button with such anger that the poll result is felt at Shaheen Bagh: Amit Shah', 27 January 2020, PTI

[128] 'Minister Anurag Thakur chants desh ke gaddaron ko, poll rally crowd completes goli maaro…', 28 January 2020, *The Indian Express*

[129] 'Remove CAA protesters within 3 days or we won't listen to you: Kapil Mishra warns Delhi Police', 23 February 2020, *The Indian Express*

On 25 February, the rioting spread to a half-dozen adjoining neighbourhoods. By now, the situation was out of the control of the State, whether by design or not, and mobs ruled the streets, beating up even journalists. The Delhi Police had apparently been given 'shoot at sight' orders, but the violence continued unabated. Masked rioters desecrated and vandalised a mosque in one of the neighbourhoods, Ashok Nagar, and a mazar in Chand Bagh. In all, over half a dozen mosques and some dargahs were attacked and burnt. President Trump was only a few kilometres away, being entertained at a banquet, while there was mayhem on the streets. The same night, a new police commissioner was given charge of Delhi.

On 26 February, the Supreme Court rebuked the police for its 'inaction' and failure to stop the rioting. The Union government acted and sent national security advisor Doval to the neighbourhoods. Delhi High Court asked the police to 'take a conscious decision' regarding the filing of FIRs against Kapil Mishra, Union minister Anurag Thakur and others for incitement to violence. The FIRs were not filed, the Delhi Police claiming that the time was 'not conducive'[130] and the judge, S. Muralidhar, was transferred from Delhi High Court to the Punjab and Haryana High Court the same night.[131]

On 27 February, US lawmakers Bernie Sanders and Elizabeth Warren condemned the violence and rebuked Trump for not raising the issue despite being in India.[132] The police began booking anti-CAA protestors for the violence, including rights activists with no connection to the rioting. One of them was a pregnant woman.[133] United Nations high commissioner for human rights Michelle Bachelet said she was 'concerned by reports of police inaction in the face of attacks against Muslims'.[134]

By 28 February, the official toll of those killed had reached over 50.

An Amnesty International India investigation into the pogrom found that the police did not respond to the multiple calls that were made to

---

[130] 'Delhi violence: Time not suited for hate speech FIRs, police tell HC; Centre gets 4 weeks to reply', 27 February 2020, *Scroll.in*

[131] 'Justice Muralidhar's transfer timing raises eyebrows', 28 February 2020, *The Economic Times*

[132] 'Delhi violence: Trump's reaction a "failure of leadership", says Bernie Sanders', 27 February 2020, *Scroll.in*

[133] 'Safoora Zargar: Bail for pregnant India student blamed for Delhi riots', 23 June 2020, https://www.bbc.com/news/world-asia-india-53149967

[134] 'High Commissioner updates the Human Rights Council on human rights concerns, and progress, across the world', 27 February 2020, ohchr.org

100—the emergency helpline number—leaving those under attack to fend for themselves over the period of six days of violence in Delhi.[135]

According to a news report filed by *NDTV* on 29 February, Delhi Police received more than 13,000 calls for help during the period of violence.

On 11 March, Amit Shah gave a clean chit to the Delhi Police in the Lok Sabha saying: 'I must say that Delhi police did a commendable job.'[136]

A compilation of court orders by *Live Law* showed the way in which Delhi Police (directly under Shah) had behaved. It was high on malice and low on competence.

In one case, an individual, Faizan Khan, was arrested under UAPA for selling a SIM card without due verification. After nearly three months in custody, Delhi High Court granted him bail (despite the law's stringent bail conditions), after raising serious doubts about the police case. Shah's Delhi Police was unwilling to let it go and appealed. The Supreme Court confirmed the bail and dismissed the special leave petition against the earlier order.

In several cases, the police could produce no witnesses other than their own staff. In the case of one man, Firoz Khan, the Delhi High Court refused to accept the statement of a police constable who claimed to have personally witnessed the burning down of a shop during the riots. The court noted that an informant had given a statement that, though he had contacted the police control room when his shop was being attacked, there was no immediate response. 'Even on first blush, it is not understood as to why the complainant would say that he failed to reach the police by telephone, if Constable Vikas was already present there,' the court observed.[137]

While granting bail to a man, Irshad Ahmed, the court said that the eyewitnesses 'seemed to be planted'. These eyewitnesses were police constables who claimed that they were at the spot of the crime and could identify the accused, but had waited three days to lodge their FIR.

In another case, the court noted that two police constables, who claimed to be witnesses to a crime allegedly committed by a man named Qasim, waited for a week before implicating him.

In another case, the police again pretended to be eyewitnesses but implicated someone only a week after. There was no CCTV footage or photographs given as proof, but the man, Mohammad Rehan, spent six

---

[135] 'Police's failure to prevent the riots', Page 6, Investigative Briefing, Amnesty International India

[136] Ibid., p. 2

[137] 'Delhi riots: Damning observations in court orders raise questions over Delhi police probe', 28 November 2020, *LiveLaw.in*

months in jail. In yet another, the Delhi police named a victim as a suspect in his own murder.[138]

The police falsely accused people of 'instigation', including arrested student leader Devangana Kalita. In her case, the judge said: 'I have gone through the inner case diary produced in a sealed cover along with pen drive and found that though her presence is seen in peaceful agitation, which is fundamental right guaranteed under Article 19 of the Constitution of India, (the police) however, failed to produce any material that she in her speech instigated women of particular community or gave hate speech.'[139]

The court noted that there was no evidence that the 'No CAA No NPR No NRC' agitation, which had been on for months in the presence of print and electronic media, had led to any acts of violence. This order was also challenged by Shah's police. 'She is not going to run away,' the Supreme Court remarked while dismissing the special leave petition submitted by the Delhi Police against Kalita's bail.

In its order granting bail to anti-CAA activist and member of United Against Hate, Khalid Saifi, the Karkardooma Sessions Court said: 'In my humble opinion, chargesheeting the applicant in this case on the basis of such an insignificant material is total non-application of mind by the police which goes to the extent of vindictiveness.' This observation by additional sessions judge Vinod Yadav was in response to the oral evidence relied on by the Delhi Police to allege that Saifi was part of a conspiracy behind the Delhi riots. The witness had told the police that he had seen Saifi dropping Tahir Hussain (a legislator accused in the murder of Intelligence Bureau officer Ankit Sharma) outside a building on 27 February, and then had seen Saifi and activist Umar Khalid entering the building.

'I fail to understand from the aforesaid statement how a lofty claim of conspiracy can be inferred,' the judge said. The same court granted bail to another accused, Anwar Hussain, after noting that video footage produced by the police did not relate to the date of the alleged crime.

Delhi Police arrested the Muslim complainant himself in a case of arson and vandalism at a mosque that was targeted during the riots. Hearing the matter, Vinod Yadav called the arrest absurd.[140] In another case, a 23-year-

---

[138] 'How to chargesheet a dead man in his own murder case', 14 June 2021, *Millennium Post*

[139] 'Delhi riots: HC grants bail to Pinjra Tod member Devangana Kalita, says police failed to prove charges', 1 September 2020, *The New Indian Express*

[140] 'Delhi riots: Complainant in mosque vandalism is held, court says absurd', 18 March 2021, *The Indian Express*

old Muslim man died immediately after being detained by police during the riots. The police told the Delhi High Court that CCTV cameras at the police station, which would have revealed the cause of his death, 'were not working between February 24 and March 4 due to technical reasons'.[141]

In other examples of how the police acted incompetently and with malice, they closed cases where there was evidence because the complainant was Muslim. A court ordered the registration of an FIR in which a man, Saleem, complained that his neighbours, Subhash and Ashok Tyagi, opened fire on him on 24 February. Video recordings of this were submitted but the police closed the inquiry and instead arrested the complainant saying he had made a 'false complaint to save himself'.[142] On hearing the matter, magistrate Fahad Uddin asked for the FIR to be registered.

The courts also asked the police to stop maliciously releasing material on those accused. In the case of Devangana Kalita, the court said: 'Selective disclosure of information calculated to sway the public opinion to believe that an accused is guilty of the alleged offence; to use electronic or other media to run a campaign to besmirch the reputation or credibility of the person concerned; and to make questionable claims of solving cases and apprehending the guilty while the investigations are at a nascent stage, would clearly be impermissible.'

This was important for the presumption of innocence, the court said.

In July 2020, it was reported that Delhi Police had instructed its officers on 8 July to be mindful of 'Hindu resentment' following the arrests of 'some Hindu youth'.[143]

In several cases where the police said there was a 'larger conspiracy', there was no evidence to back up the claim. But it used the vague definition to jail several prominent activists like Safoora Zargar, Umar Khalid, Gulfisha Fatima, Natasha Narwal and Asif Tanha. The police used this pretence to book them under UAPA and deny them bail, ensuring those that the courts did not free would stay imprisoned for years.[144] The police were under no

---

[141] 'Northeast Delhi riots: Man died hrs after release from station, police tell HC CCTVs weren't working', 23 March 2021, *The Indian Express*

[142] 'Court orders FIR and probe into a riots complaint which Delhi Police had shelved', 30 November 2020, *The Indian Express*

[143] 'Resentment in Hindus on arrests, take care: Special CP to probe teams', 16 July 2020, *The Indian Express*

[144] Zargar was given bail because of her pregnancy, and Delhi High Court in a liberal and well reasoned judgment gave bail to Narwal, Kalita and Asif Tanha in June 2021, a judgment whose wider implications the Supreme Court unfortunately stayed.

obligation and no pressure to prove a conspiracy existed and the courts did not press them either, giving the police four extensions to show their case.[145] Going through its 17,000-page chargesheet, scholar and activist Yogendra Yadav remarked that Amit Shah had shifted from saying that the riots were spontaneous to now blaming the anti-CAA protestors for them. Shah had concluded, Yadav wrote, that 'the main victims of the Delhi riots were its real perpetrators'.[146]

An analysis of 40 FIRs by the People's Union for Democratic Rights uncovered evidence of bias against Muslims and the dilution of charges against Hindus. 'It is imperative, for the sake of justice that all FIRs pertaining to the riots be opened to public scrutiny,' the activists said.[147] The data showed that, despite a higher number of cases filed against Hindus, the police had charged more Muslims. There were 410 FIRs filed by Muslims and 190 filed by Hindus. But the police had arrested 582 Muslims and 571 Hindus.

After revelations of how maliciously the Delhi Police (functioning under the command of Amit Shah, it must again be stressed) had acted, nine retired IPS officers, including Julio Ribeiro, wrote a letter to the Delhi Police commissioner saying: 'Basing investigations on "disclosures" without concrete evidence violates all principles of fair investigation. While implicating leaders and activists, who expressed their views against CAA, all those who instigated violence and are associated with the ruling party have been let off the hook. Such investigation will only make people lose faith in democracy, justice, fairness and the Constitution.'[148] A day later, eight more retired IPS officers wrote to add their voice to those of the nine.[149]

Delhi's police commissioner, S.N. Shrivastava, said the allegations were a 'false narrative'.[150]

---

[145] 'Police get more time to prove "CAA Conspiracy" in Delhi riots', 18 August 2020, *Article-14.com*

[146] 'Delhi Police's riots charge sheet is a parody scripted to prove the boss is always right', 23 September 2020, *ThePrint.in*

[147] 'In Delhi violence investigation, a disturbing pattern: Victims end up being prosecuted by police', 23 May 2020, *Scroll.in*

[148] 'Nine former police officers call Delhi riots investigation "Flawed", 14 September 2020, *TheWire.in*

[149] 'Delhi violence: Eight more retired IPS officers join Julio Ribeiro in questioning "flawed probe"', 14 September 2020, *Scroll.in*

[150] 'Delhi Police chief responds to ex-IPS officer's letter, says "false narrative of bias" against force', 15 September 2020, *Scroll.in*

But the allegations of police malice and bias were accurate and demonstrably true, both through the observations we have seen of the courts, and backed up by independent investigations, including that of *Scroll*, which published its investigation. It said the police had deliberately gone after over 70 anti-CAA protestors, who were abused, threatened and coerced into giving false statements.[151] They were mostly Muslim, of course.

Part 3: Covid a la Tablighi

In March 2020, the evangelical Muslim organisation, Tablighi Jamaat, held a meeting in Delhi from the 10th to 13th. This was scheduled before the onset of Covid-19 and they were congregating at a time when the Modi government was itself dismissive of the threat of the pandemic.[152] It was held before India issued guidelines on public gatherings.

But as the cases in India began to rise towards the end of March, the government determined that it would scapegoat the Muslims and enlisted the media to do this, spreading the conspiracy of 'Corona Jihad'.

The Union made much of evacuating the area where the congregation was being held (Modi sent Doval to 'reason' with the organisers, who had been asking for safe evacuation for days). The novelty of the virus and the first deaths reported from it coincided with the Tablighi Jamaat gathering and open season was declared on it.

Delhi chief minister Arvind Kejriwal called the gathering at the centre 'an irresponsible act',[153] though this was not borne out by the facts.

'The main reason for increased number of cases is that members of the Tablighi Jamaat have travelled across the country,' said Lav Agarwal, joint secretary of the health ministry at a press conference.[154]

Also on 1 April, the BJP's IT cell head Amit Malviya tweeted that the Tablighi gathering was akin to an 'Islamic insurrection'.[155] Kapil Mishra accused the group of 'terrorism'.[156] On 4 April, Maharashtra Navnirman Sena (MNS) chief Raj Thackeray suggested that the group's members be

---

[151] 'Special report: A silent crackdown sweeps through Delhi in the guise of probing riots conspiracy', 8 October 2020, *Scroll.in*

[152] 'Covid-19 is not health emergency, no need to panic: Health Ministry', 13 March 2020, *The Hindu*

[153] 'Gathering at Nizamuddin a highly irresponsible act, says Kejriwal', 31 March 2020, *The Hindu*

[154] 'Centre blames Tablighi Jamaat for sudden spike in cases', 1 April 2020, *The Week*

[155] https://twitter.com/amitmalviya/status/1245083081305776128?lang=en

[156] https://twitter.com/kapilmishra_ind/status/1246049847720853511?lang=en

shot: 'The meeting of Tablighis had taken place at Markaz in Delhi. Such people be killed by firing bullets at them. Why give them treatment? A separate section be created and their treatment be stopped.'[157] In Uttar Pradesh, the group's members were jailed and booked under the anti-terror National Security Act.[158]

On 5 April, Lav Agarwal said: 'The doubling rate in India is 4.1 days, had the congregation at Nizamuddin not happened and additional cases not come, this would have been about 7.14 days.'[159] As later events proved, this was nonsense, but it was par for the course for this government. The Godi media did its job: 'India won't put up with Tablighi insolence' was the Arnab Goswami debate on 7 April.

On 18 April, Agarwal made another claim, stating that the group was the dominant single cause of the pandemic.[160] Thus the poisonous lie was spread and its effect began to take place in the citizenry as fast as Covid itself.[161]

Hindi daily *Amar Ujala* reported that members of the Tablighi Jamaat quarantined in a facility in the western Uttar Pradesh town of Saharanpur had 'demanded' non-vegetarian food and were defecating in the open inside the hospital. The Saharanpur police tweeted that no such thing had happened and the story was taken down.[162]

During the months of active persecution, the group's members, including foreigners, were jailed and charged with attempted murder and the provisions of Section 269 ('whoever wilfully or negligently does any act which is likely to spread the infection of any disease dangerous to life').[163]

The theories being promoted were that they were deliberately spreading the virus around India by getting themselves infected, spitting on fruit,

---

[157] 'Tablighi Jamaat members should be killed by firing bullets: MNS chief Raj Thackeray', 4 April 2020, PTI

[158] 'UP govt invokes NSA against Tablighi quarantined for "misbehaving" with Ghaziabad medical staff', 3 April 2020, *The Indian Express*

[159] 'Cases doubling in 4.1 days; without Jamaat, it would've been in 7.4 days', 5 April 2020, *The Economic Times*

[160] 'Tablighi Jamaat responsible for 30% total coronavirus cases in India: Health ministry', *ABPLive*

[161] 'Coronavirus: Yogi Adityanath's tough move against quarantined Islamic sect members', 3 April 2020, *NDTV*

[162] 'Police refute *Amar Ujala* report about Tablighi Jamaat members misbehaving with medical staff', 5 April 2020, *NewsLaundry.com*

[163] 'Tablighi Jamaat assembly caused spread of Covid among many persons: Home ministry in Rajya Sabha', 21 September 2020, *The Times of India*

refusing to wear masks, running around naked in their wards, harassing nurses and so on. None of this was true.

The world noticed India's malice against Muslims and it was reported: 'It was already dangerous to be Muslim in India. Then came the Coronavirus'[164]; 'Coronavirus: Islamophobia concerns after India mosque outbreak';[165]; 'In India, Coronavirus fans religious hatred'[166].

Without being convicted and even without any evidence, Jamaat members were 'blacklisted' from receiving visas in the future. In June, the Modi government amended the policy for visa applications to India to introduce a Tabligh-specific clause:[167]

'Restriction on engaging in Tabligh activities—Foreign nationals granted any type of visa and OCI cardholders shall not be permitted to engage themselves in Tabligh work. There will be no restriction in visiting religious places and attending normal religious activities like attending religious discourses. However, preaching religious ideologies, making speeches in religious places, distribution of audio or visual display/ pamphlets pertaining to religious ideologies, spreading conversion etc. will not be allowed.'

This was the first time in India that a particular religious group had been mentioned in the list of visa guidelines. This was purely to fuel the fire that was already raging in the media, blaming the group for the deliberate spread of Covid in India and absolving the government from its responsibility, especially for the fallout of the 2020 lockdown.

The impact of the persecution and the concocted narrative was felt across India. Wedding-singer Mohammed Dilshad killed himself after returning from quarantine because he was harassed by neighbours in his Himachal Pradesh village. In Punjab, some 80 Muslim men, women and children were chased out of their village, and Muslim milkmen from the same area were denied entry into neighbouring Himachal Pradesh.[168]

On 11 April, nine Kashmiri Muslim labourers were attacked by four men with cricket bats in Mandi, Himachal Pradesh. The bones of the labourers were broken. The village's sarpanch, Ranjana Devi, said that the blaming of Muslims was all over TV, WhatsApp forwards and Facebook.[169] In Gujarat,

---

[164] 3 April 2020, *Time*

[165] 3 April 2020, *BBC*

[166] 12 April 2020, *The New York Times*

[167] 'Tablighi activity a specific visa violation, says Ministry of Home Affairs', 4 June 2020, *The Hindu*

[168] 'How India's government set off a spiral of Islamophobia', 20 April 2020, *Article-14.com*

[169] '"Minds Have Been Poisoned": HP Villagers On Attack on J&K Workers', 17 April 2020, *The Quint*

a hospital segregated patients by religion.[170] The same day, the United States Commission on International Religious Freedom tweeted expressing concern about the 'ongoing stigmatisation of Muslims in India'.

A Muslim security guard had an FIR filed against him for 'giving' his employer Covid. The police said the guard's mobile phone records 'had placed him in the Nizamuddin area', near the Tablighi Jamaat gathering. The guard turned out to be Covid negative.[171]

It was only after it became generally accepted that the virus was an unstoppable global phenomenon which had spread through multiple ways that the 'Tablighi conspiracy' story faded.

On 19 May, the foreign members of the Jamaat moved court to be released from institutional quarantine, where they had been held for over a month and a half, despite repeatedly testing negative for Covid. The Delhi government told the court that none of the visitors had been 'detained', they were merely 'asked to join the investigation'. But the passports of over 700 Jamaat members had been seized and they were not in fact free.

On 6 July, before the chief metropolitan magistrate at Delhi's Saket court, 44 Tablighi Jamaat members refused to pay a fine of between Rs 4,000 to Rs 10,000 in exchange for closing of cases and bravely chose trial.

By December, eight months after 11 states had filed 20 FIRs against more than 2,500 Tablighi Jamaat members, nobody was convicted. And courts fiercely criticised the actions of the government. Judges called the cases 'malicious', 'a virtual persecution', 'abuse of process', 'abuse of power', and said the Tablighi Jamaat members were 'scapegoats of a political government' who had acted against the group though having 'not an iota of evidence'.

Yet an enormous amount of State resource and time had been expended in pursuing the conspiracy theory. *Article-14.com*'s report, 'Criminalised by govt, cleared by courts: The Tablighi story', (18 December 2020) described a litigation in Delhi of 150 hearings, 955 bail applications, 5 writs, 44 discharge applications, 26 quashing petitions, 80 revision petitions and 15 hearings before the Supreme Court and then a trial in a Delhi court over nine months.

All charges were thrown out with the unambiguous observations referred to above.

---

[170] 'Ahmedabad hospital splits Covid wards on faith, says govt decision', 17 April 2020, *The Indian Express*

[171] 'Delhi man dies of Covid-19, guard blamed for infection tests negative', 17 April 2020, *NDTV*

On 16 December, a Delhi court in Saket acquitted all the 36 foreign nationals that claimed trial by observing that it's 'reasonably possible' that 'none of them was present at Markaz during the relevant period and they had been picked up from different places so as to maliciously prosecute them'. The court also said that there's 'no iota of evidence on record to suggest that the order promulgated under section 144 of IPC was brought to the notice of persons staying in Markaz'.

On 2 December, the Allahabad High Court ordered that a charge of attempt to murder to be dropped. It said such a charge reflected an 'abuse of power under the law'.

On 19 October, a metropolitan magistrate in Andheri acquitted 28 foreign nationals of all charges by holding that the prosecution did not produce even 'an iota of evidence to indicate the visitors had violated government orders'.

On 21 September, the Nagpur Bench of the Bombay High Court quashed an FIR against eight foreign nationals by holding that the 'investigating agency acted without jurisdiction while registering the FIR for allegedly breaching Covid-19 advisories'. The court also noted that 'allowing the prosecution to continue would be nothing but an abuse of process of the court'.

On 21 August, the Aurangabad Bench of the Bombay High Court called it a 'virtual persecution' of the foreign nationals. While quashing the FIR against 29 foreign nationals, the court said these visitors were possibly made 'a scapegoat of the pandemic by a political government'.

The bench said that the government seemed to have forgotten our culture of Atithi Devo Bhava (the guest is akin to god): 'The circumstances of the present matter create a question as to whether we are really acting as per our great tradition and culture. During the situation created by Covid-19 pandemic, we need to show more tolerance and we need to be more sensitive towards our guests particularly like the petitioners before us,' the bench said, adding, 'but instead of helping them we lodged them in jails.'

On 15 June, while discharging 31 foreign visitors, the Madurai Bench of the Madras High Court said 'there is absolutely nothing on record to indicate that they had contributed to the spread of the novel coronavirus'.

On 16 December, *The New York Times* published an investigation of what had led to India's becoming the second-most infected nation in the world. It was headlined: 'The virus trains: How lockdown chaos spread Covid-19 across India', and it opened with the paragraph: 'Prime Minister Narendra Modi's coronavirus restrictions sent migrant workers fleeing. To get them home, the government offered special trains. But the trains would spread the virus across the country.' In May 2020, after suffocating millions of migrant workers in their urban hovels without any food, money or work, the government began to run trains. Desperate to go back to their villages, the migrants piled into them, carrying the virus with them. This investigation, attributing the spread to not the Tablighi Jamaat but to something quite different, did not receive the same coverage in India.

Part 4: India Criminalises Love

Anti-miscegenation laws are those that regulate marriage and interbreeding. Essentially, the State determines whom you cannot marry. These laws have existed in several nations in the past. The US had them till 1967, preventing whites and blacks from marrying and forcing racial segregation.

South Africa had them till 1985, segregating white from 'coloured', Asians and, of course, the native Africans themselves.

Germany had its Nuremberg Laws, which included restrictions on marrying Jews. In *The Quint*, Vakasha Sachdev wrote about the effect of the Nuremberg Laws: 'Mixed couples grew weary of the "condemnation and harassment they faced on a near daily basis" from the rest of their community … Smaller happenings, such as harassing couples until they stopped going to __ together, occurred regularly. Some confrontations turned violent as __ men and their __ girlfriends were assaulted in the street and paraded around town, announcing their crime of having social and sexual relations with someone of a different __. The communal disapproval began even before the __ Laws were enacted; due to their passage, many mixed couples simply decided that it was better to split when their relationship became a burden and source of danger.'[172]

Sachdev blanked out the words regarding religion and location, knowing an Indian reader would assume that the paragraph was about 'love jihad' laws. In fact, it is a description of Germany's Nuremberg Laws. And it is what the victims of 'love jihad' in India also go through.

What is love jihad?

Nobody knows or has seen it, including the Union government.[173] And yet it has been introduced into law and has resulted in the sending of

---

172 '"Love jihad": A homage to Nuremberg & anti-miscegenation laws', 22 November 2020, *The Quint*
173 'Love jihad not defined in laws, no case reported: Government', 4 February 2020, *The Times of India*

Muslims to jail. Love jihad is a classic conspiracy theory that began from the random observations of a Kerala judge in 2009[174] and became an obsession under the Modi government. And predictably, India's judiciary has played a negative role and ruled against individual freedom on the matter of anti-miscegenation laws. On 21 November 2017, a judge in fact directed that Uttarakhand legislate against inter-faith marriage: 'In order to curb this tendency, the state government is expected to legislate the Freedom of Religion Act on the analogy of Madhya Pradesh Freedom of Religion Act as well as Himachal Pradesh Freedom of Religion without hurting the religious sentiments of citizens.'[175]

The judge accepted he was overstepping his brief: 'We are well aware that it is not the role of the court to give suggestions to the state government to legislate but due to fast changing social milieu, this suggestion is being made.'

The state responded and, in March 2018, the BJP government tabled a bill that mimicked the laws of the other states as the judge had wanted. Changes of faith after marriage would render the marriage void. The Bill stipulated that 'any marriage, which was solemnised for the sole purpose of conversion by the man of one religion with the woman of another religion, may be declared null and void by the family court'. How the State would determine that the conversion was the 'sole purpose' of the marriage was not specified and did not need to be. Essentially, all marriages that involved conversion would be struck down.

On 7 November 2020, Uttar Pradesh passed an ordinance restricting inter-faith marriage, the Vidhi Virudh Dharma Samparivartan Pratishedh Adhyadesh (in English, Prohibition of Unlawful Conversion of Religion Ordinance). It repeated from the laws in Uttarakhand and elsewhere the paragraph on making inter-faith marriages void, and the requirement that applications for conversion be made 60 days in advance and post-conversion notices be put on display. The law reversed burden of proof on the members of the family the woman was marrying into.

It read: 'The burden of proof as to whether a religious conversion was not effected through … marriage, lies on the person who has caused the conversion.' Even if a woman said she was changing her faith willingly, it was up to the husband to prove his innocence in the matter. (The full list

---

[174] 'Kerala HC asks govt to frame laws to stop "love jihad"', 10 December 2009, *The Economic Times*

[175] 'Uttarakhand High Court asks state to make law to curb conversions', *The Indian Express*

of anti-miscegenation laws legislated after 2014 is in the chapter 'Laws and Disorder')

Uttar Pradesh governor Anandi Patel admitted that 'there are not many complaints' about love jihad. However, she claimed that the government had conducted a 'survey that shows how many girls married, how many faced problems, how many girls came back, how many girls lodged complaints. Even parents come forward seeking arrests, alleging that the boy changed his name. When such incidents are increasingly reported during a survey, in such a situation such a Bill is brought and is pursued.'[176] This survey was not made public or discussed before the law was brought into effect. A probe by the government only weeks before had found the opposite of what the love jihad conspiracy theory had claimed.[177]

The effect of the law was that Uttar Pradesh used it retrospectively to try and annul Hindu-Muslim marriages solemnised before its passing.[178] Two women converting to Hinduism from Islam to marry Hindus and a man converting to Islam from Hinduism to marry a Muslim were not given protection by Allahabad High Court, which cited this law and held their marriage illegal because they hadn't given sixty days of notice before converting.[179]

Among the FIRs filed on the night of 28 November (the day the ordinance came into effect) was one in Bareilly on the basis of which a Muslim man was arrested. The complainant had filed a case against the same man in 2019, accusing him of kidnapping his daughter. The woman denied knowing the accused and the case was dismissed by the magistrate. Now, with the woman married elsewhere, the father had filed a case under the love jihad clause and had the man jailed.

FIRs were being filed and people were arrested before investigation. In Bareilly, three Muslim men in their twenties had charges dropped against them and the FIR expunged after the complaint was found to be fake.[180]

---

[176] 'Anandiben Patel interview: "Anti-conversion law not passed just like that…survey showed need"', 7 January 2021, *The Indian Express*

[177] 'SIT in Kanpur does not find conspiracy in "love jihad" cases', 24 November 2020, *The Hindu*

[178] 'The UP govt has effectively banned interfaith marriage', 15 December 2020, *Article-14.com*

[179] '"Marriage illegal:" Allahabad High Court cites non-compliance with UP anti-conversion law to refuse protection to 3 interfaith couples', 30 June 2021, Bar and Bench

[180] 'UP: "Love jihad" case against 3 Muslim men dropped within 24 hours after "charges turn out to be false"', 3 January 2021, *The Times of India*

India's laws allow inter-faith marriages only under the Special Marriage Act (SMA), making it difficult for couples to keep their faith when marrying someone of another. Under the provisions of the SMA, couples must give 30-day notice, a copy of which is to be displayed in 'some conspicuous place' in the office of the marriage officer, usually a district magistrate. This has allowed Hindutva groups to intervene and prevent unions. The police also misuse the notices by visiting the homes of inter-faith couples and interviewing their parents, though adults wanting to marry do not require parental consent.

In one case, a Muslim man and his brother were arrested in Uttar Pradesh's Moradabad after he and a 22-year-old Hindu woman tried to get their marriage registered. A Bajrang Dal mob surrounded the family inside the police station, threatening them. The woman told journalists, 'I am an adult, I am 22 years old. I got married of my own free will on 24 July. This is the fifth month that we have been married.'[181] But this was not enough to stop the arrests of her husband and his brother. The woman was sent to a shelter home and suffered a miscarriage as a result of the torture inflicted on her there.[182]

Another FIR under the ordinance was registered in Sitapur, leading to the arrests of seven individuals of a Muslim family. Other than the provisions of the ordinance, police also charged them with criminal conspiracy and wrongful confinement, though the woman they had allegedly kidnapped was not with them. More cases were also registered in Moradabad, Muzaffarnagar and Mau.

In one case, the adult woman gave a statement to a magistrate that she had married of free will in a court and not converted, but that didn't stop the harassment. Several people from the woman's village, the neighbouring Jamalpur, gathered outside the house of the man and chased his family members. Despite her testimony, a case under the 'love jihad' ordinance was filed by the police.[183]

Along with the courts, the police have also shown enthusiasm in stepping in and acting as vigilantes. In December 2020, police stopped the wedding in Lucknow of a Hindu woman to a Muslim man being solemnised under

---

[181] '"Law for those like you": UP Hindu woman heckled, Muslim husband arrested', 6 December 2020, *NDTV*

[182] 'UP "Love jihad" arrest: Private lab confirms miscarriage of 22-year-old woman', 20 December 2020, *The Wire*

[183] 'Firozabad: Woman denies "love jihad" charge, mob chases man's family members', 8 January, *The Indian Express*

Hindu rituals. The families of the couple were present and said they had consented to the union, but the police stopped it anyway after receiving a 'complaint' from a group calling itself Rashtriya Yuva Vahini.[184]

In Kushinagar, a couple, both Muslims, aged 39 and 28, were jailed after a phone call to the police.[185] The man was assaulted in custody and released the next day after the police blamed 'miscreants for spreading rumours of love jihad'.

The Uttar Pradesh Police under the BJP has also gone after Muslims purely for social contact. In one case, an 18-year-old Muslim boy was arrested in December 2020 for meeting his former classmate over pizza. He was kept in jail for six months and not released till July though his companion stood up for her friend and protested that he had done nothing wrong.[186]

Parents also use rape laws to try and harass inter-faith couples. In Salamat Ansari vs State of Uttar Pradesh, Allahabad High Court Justice Pankaj Naqvi recorded an order undoing the charges in such a case, noting:

'We do not see Priyanka Kharwar and Salamat as Hindu and Muslim, rather as two grown-up individuals who out of their own free will and choice are living together peacefully and happily over a year. The Courts and the Constitutional Courts in particular are enjoined to uphold the life and liberty of an individual guaranteed under Article 21 of the Constitution of India.'

The Karnataka High Court also passed a similar judgement after an NGO abducted a woman at the behest of her parents to prevent her from marrying a Muslim man: 'It is well settled that a right of any major individual to marry the person of his/her choice is a fundamental right enshrined in the Constitution of India and the said liberty relating to the personal relationships of two individuals cannot be encroached by anybody irrespective of caste or religion,' a bench of Justices S. Sujata and Sachin Shankar Magadum said.[187]

Despite their manifest unconstitutionality, the Supreme Court has refused to stay the love jihad laws, asking petitioners to move high courts

---

[184] 'Lucknow: Families give consent but cops stop interfaith wedding, cite anti-conversion ordinance', 4 December 2020, *The Indian Express*

[185] '"Love jihad" rumour: Wedding stopped in UP, Muslim couple kept overnight at police station', 11 December 2020, *The Indian Express*

[186] 'UP Muslim teen meets Dalit girl for "pizza outing", lands in jail under anti-conversion law', 23 December 2020, *ThePrint.in*

[187] 'Marrying a person of choice is a fundamental right, says Karnataka High Court', 2 December 2020, *Scroll.in*

instead. On being told by the petitioners that the laws impose a reverse burden of proof and intimation to police for marriage and that there were daily reports of people being picked up by force, Chief Justice Sharad Arvind Bobde said, 'You are asking for relief which we cannot entertain…'[188]

The Uttar Pradesh government wanted to persecute Muslims even after admitting to the judiciary that it had no case against them. One such instance was revealed when the government said on affidavit that 'the Investigating officer has found that it is not a case of UP Prohibition of Unlawful Conversion of Religion Ordinance 2020 and the Act UP Ordinance No. 21 of 2020' and 'there is no evidence found that the accused Nadeem is having an illicit relation with Parul, nor has any evidence come forward that he tried to change the religion of Parul'. And yet the state was proceeding with filing charges against Nadeem, now for 'criminal intimidation and provocation causing breach of peace'.

Love jihad is a conspiracy being peddled in and being pushed by BJP states. The laws have all come after the Modi government took office, in Uttarakhand in 2018, Uttar Pradesh and Madhya Pradesh in 2020 and Gujarat in 2021.[189] The BJP states of Haryana,[190] Assam,[191] and Karnataka,[192] have also promised to legislate laws similar to Uttar Pradesh's. In 2023, a body calling itself the Hindu Sakal Samaj held rallies across Maharashtra demanding a law against 'Love Jihad'. The BJP minister for women and child welfare Mangal Prabhat Lodha told the Maharashtra Assembly that there were 1 lakh cases of Hindu girls marrying Muslim boys under duress in the state.[193]

When Samajwadi Party MLA Riaz Shaikh wrote to the Women and Child Welfare Commission, which Lodha chairs and under which a committee had been constituted to probe love jihad cases, he received a reply that the number of 'love jihad' cases in the state was 'none'.[194]

---

[188] '"Love Jihad": SC refuses to stay UP ordinance on religious conversion, inter-faith marriages', 6 January 2021, *The Tribune*

[189] 'Gujarat Assembly passes "love jihad" law', 1 April 2021, *The Hindu*

[190] 'Haryana forms three-member committee to frame law on "love jihad"', 26 November 2020, *Scroll.in*

[191] 'Assam to enact laws mandating disclosure of religion, income before marriage', 1 December 2020, *TheWire.in*

[192] 'Karnataka will have law against "love jihad", officials asked to look into UP ordinance: Home minister', 4 December 2020, PTI

[193] 'Maharashtra minister Mangalprabhat Lodha's 1 lakh "love jihad" cases claim sparks furore in House', 11 March 2023, *Times of India*

[194] 'BJP lies exposed as minister claims one lakh love jihad cases, his office puts number at zero', 22 March 2023, *National Herald*

The state has set up a committee that would approach couples in inter-faith marriages, empowering it to 'review inter-caste and inter-faith marriages in the state, whether registered, performed in religious places or by elopement'.[195]

In Assam, momentum on the matter had been picking up for months before. A popular television serial, *Begum Jaan*, was 'banned' (taken off air) for two months by the police after complaints from groups called Hindu Jagran Manch and Hindu Janajagruti Samiti.[196] The 'ban' came after a committee set up by the police and headed by the police chief decided it should go off air.

The serial, which had begun in July 2020, was about a Hindu woman who is caught in a difficult situation and is helped by a Muslim man. The lead actor of the serial, Preety Kongona, told reporters, 'There is no communal angle in the serial. In fact, it depicts humanity above faith.' She received threats of acid attack and rape, and filed a complaint. Two weeks after the 'ban', the Gauhati High Court undid it after the government accepted that the committee which banned the serial was illegal. The madness continues, however. Assam has proposed a law under which all couples intending to marry will need to inform the government about their income, family details, education, source of income, profession and permanent address along with religion in a prescribed form one month before their wedding or face jail.[197]

Love jihad follows the pattern and format of beef lynchings and the cow slaughter laws. The State, top-down, deliberately stokes sentiment and introduces the legal mechanism through which Muslims can be harassed. Society takes the cue and acts. Polarisation ensues, which is beneficial and necessary for majoritarian politics because it makes voter choice easy. India is damaged permanently but that is acceptable to those doing it. It is only collateral damage, if the damage is thought about at all, which it usually isn't.

The repeated findings of no conspiracy, the acceptance by the Union that no such thing as love jihad exists, the widespread harassment of Muslims particularly and inter-faith couples in general, and the observations of the high courts have not had an effect either in the media reporting or the furtherance of the conspiracy theory. The laws are here to stay in India along

[195] 'Maharashtra forms committee to track inter-caste, inter-faith marriages', 14 December 2022, *Frontline*
[196] 'Assam TV serial banned after protests alleging it promoted "love jihad"', 29 August 2020, *The Week*
[197] 'Amid "Love Jihad" row, Assam's new law will ask couples to declare religion, income', 1 December 2020, *Outlook*

with the brutalisation of those against whom love jihad is used by the BJP and its associates as an instrument of torture.

Part 5: Bulldozing Muslims

On 14 June 2022, three former Supreme Court justices, three former high court judges and a few lawyers wrote a letter to the Supreme Court. They said the Uttar Pradesh administration was 'making a mockery of the constitution' by demolishing the homes of Muslims protesting against remarks made by a BJP leader against Prophet Muhammad. In Allahabad, the house of Javed Ahmad, owned by his wife, was demolished on 12 June, two days after the protests.[198] A day before that, demolitions were carried out through bulldozers sent to the homes of two other protestors in Saharanpur.[199] The families said there was no notice given before the bulldozers arrived.

UP chief minister Adityanath had announced that his administration would use demolition as a means to show 'strictness' against those he called mafia.[200]

This was what the retired judges were referring to, calling this action an 'unacceptable subversion of rule of law'. A few weeks before that, the BJP conducted demolitions in Delhi's Jahangirpuri, where also there had been communal violence. Even after the residents of the area showed the authorities that they had won a stay from the Supreme Court, the demolitions continued.[201] In Madhya Pradesh at the same time, bulldozers razed the homes of people protesting against provocative slogans raised near a mosque during Ram Navami, which led to violence and a riot. Less than 24 hours later, the BJP government razed 16 residences and 29 shops.[202] Again, no notice had been given, and the State was acting out of vengeance and anger rather than applying rule of law. The month before that, the homes of men accused of rape were demolished in MP's Shahdol and Sheopur.[203]

---

[198] 'Prayagraj Violence Accused's House Razed, Lawyers Go To High Court', 12 June 2022, NDTV

[199] 'After Violence Over Prophet Remark Row, Bulldozers Out In Two UP Cities', 11 June 2022, NDTV

[200] 'Bulldozer on mafia will continue, vows CM Yogi day after protests rock UP over Prophet remarks', 11 June 2022, *Hindustan Times*

[201] 'Bulldozers roll, raze in Jahangirpuri in the face of Supreme Court order', 21 April 2022, *Indian Express*

[202] '"All Gone to Dust": MP Govt Razes 16 Houses, 29 Shops After Ram Navami Violence', 12 April 2022, The Quint

[203] '"Bulldozer running . . .".: MP chief minister warns miscreants of house demolition', 23 March 2022, *Hindustan Times*

In November 2020, the MP government destroyed more than two dozen Muslim-owned shops a week after clashes between locals and the police over an arrest.[204] That month, after a Congress MLA led a protest, parts of his school and college were demolished.[205]

The manner in which the Muslims were treated was markedly different from other Indians who had been accused of illegal construction, and on a much bigger scale.[206] Though the actions were without due process, a trial or conviction, and patently illegal on the face of it, often the media echoed the voice[207] of the BJP,[208] regularly.[209]

Though it was the UP chief minister Adityanath—termed 'Bulldozer Baba'—who was most closely associated with extra judicial demolitions, his counterpart in MP, Shivraj Singh Chouhan—'Bulldozer Mama'—also unleashed the State's power against Muslims regularly. In 2017, the police officer tasked with overseeing demolitions said, 'It does not matter who owns the house. If these repeat offenders live here and operate from these spaces, we have to find ways to stop it. Now the families know clearly what happens if they support a criminal.'

There was no law under which this was being done, as was demonstrated time[210] and again[211] by the few[212] in the media who were concerned.[213]

---

[204] 'Bhopal: A week after attack on cops, shops razed at Irani Dera', 29 November 2020, *Times of India*

[205] 'Govt demolishes parts of college building owned by Arif Masood in Bhopal', 6 November 2020, *Times of India*

[206] 'As bulldozers target the poor again, let's also remember Delhi's "Republic of Sainik Farms"', 22 April 2022, ThePrint

[207] 'House, illegal shops of goons razed in Indore', 10 December 2020, *Times of India*

[208] 'Goons' properties razed in Aishbagh, Gautam Nagar', 30 March 2022, *Times of India*

[209] 'Madhya Pradesh: Historysheeter's house razed in Dhar', 17 January 2022, *Times of India*

[210] 'Rule of law is the first casualty of the bulldozer', 23 June 2022, Bar and Bench

[211] 'Bulldozer justice is illegal, immoral and unjustifiable', 14 June 2022, *New Indian Express*

[212] 'Totally illegal, says ex-CJ of Allahabad High Court; bulldozer cases in limbo', 13 June 2022, *Indian Express*

[213] 'Bulldozing justice: Arbitrarily razing houses to punish alleged crimes has no legal basis', 13 April 2022, Scroll

Any excuse was good enough to flatten homes,[214] including, of course, in Gujarat[215] and also in Karnataka.[216]

Even homes that had been paid for by the Union government's Pradhan Mantri Aawas Yojana scheme were called illegal and broken.[217] Places, including old educational institutions, were not spared.[218]

The Indore police demolished 150 houses across the city in that month.[219] The BJP tore down the homes even of those who rented property to those it accused of criminal activity[220] or of relatives of those it despised, as happened in Kanpur.[221]

Over the Modi years and particularly in the second term, the infection spread. The justice system could not hold the State to account, or make it follow the law. What began in the states where the BJP was confident spread to others, including Kashmir, where even former chief ministers were reduced to begging the administration to issue notices before sending in the bulldozers.[222] Opposition leaders in Delhi were unable to stop the assault on their constituents, and were often locked up when the bulldozers were sent out.[223]

In one village in Assam, Bengali-speaking Muslims were unable to even collect their belongings and lost their standing crops. In this particular instance in Mohghuli, 200 bureaucrats, 600 policemen and CRPF personnel

[214] 'Three homes razed after conflict over Garba Pandal, five more Muslim families served eviction notices: MP', 10 October 2022, SabrangIndia.net

[215] 'Gujarat: Govt Removing Muslim Properties Weeks After Ram Navami Violence', 26 April 2022, Maktoob Media

[216] '"Revenge for protesting hijab ban": SDPI leader's hotel demolished by Karnataka authorities', 27 March 2022, Maktoob Media

[217] '"Our Home Wasn't Built in a Day but Got Razed in 1": MP's "Bulldozer Raj" Victim', 19 July 2022, TheQuint.com

[218] 'Bulldozer terror: Kanpur administration demolish 50 year old Madrasa Islamia', 8 May 2022, IndiaTomorrow.net

[219] 'In a Controversial Campaign, Police in Indore Go After Criminals and Also Their Families', 23 October 2017, The Wire

[220] 'Bulldozer Terror: UP Government Brings Down House Rented Out To Atiq Ahmad's Wife', 3 March 2023, IndiaTomorrow.net

[221] 'Prophet Row: Bulldozers Raze Buildings of Violence Accused in Kanpur, Saharanpur', 11 June 2022, TheQuint.com

[222] 'Make bulldozer last resort; give people chance to prove their claim; issue notices before demolition: Omar to J&K Admin', 6 February 2023, Kashmir Bulletin

[223] 'Protests prove futile as bulldozers demolish 3 buildings in Delhi's Madanpur Khadar', 12 May 2022, NewsLaundry.com

came along with 43 excavators and 25 tractors[224] in January 2023. Another 2500 Muslims lost their homes the following month.[225] The overwhelming force regularly deployed against the marginalized meant that their resistance was soon gone.[226]

Every so often the courts would try and intervene, usually after the event,[227] but illegal action by the State was so widespread that it came to be normalized.[228]

Only the brave people of Shaheen Bagh were able to push back and stop the State's oppression.[229]

---

[224] 'Bulldozers being used to evict Bengali-speaking Muslims in Assam, 299 households put in the dark', 11 January 2023, *Muslim Mirror*

[225] 'Assam: Mass evictions continue as approximately 2500 Bengali-speaking Muslim families get displaced; pleas go unheard', 17 February 2023, SabrangIndia.in

[226] 'Why eviction drives in Assam are no longer facing resistance', 30 December 2022, Scroll

[227] '"You've Made It a Spectacle": Patna HC Slams Police for "Illegal" Demolition of House', 4 December 2022, TheWire.in

[228] 'No Illegal Bulldozing, Supreme Court Warns Yogi Government', 16 June 2022, NDTV

[229] 'Bulldozer reaches Shaheen Bagh, but retreats in face of protests', 10 May 2022, *Times of India*

7

GOOD GOVERNANCE

Part 1: Swachh Bharat, Aswasth Bharat

The Total Sanitation Campaign was introduced in 1999 by the Vajpayee government to accelerate sanitation coverage, by helping the poor build toilets throughout India and especially in villages.[1]

In 2012, under Manmohan Singh, the campaign was renamed as Nirmal Bharat Abhiyan. It was bonded to the MNREGA scheme for rural employment and 2022 was set as the date for an open defecation-free (ODF) India.

The scheme was simple to execute: it gave a subsidy to those who constructed a toilet, and it managed to increase rural sanitation coverage by 6 per cent in the two years between 2012 and 2014.[2] Under MNREGA, sanitation-related works were included, allowing a beneficiary to earn up to Rs 5,400 while constructing their own toilet. The government would add another Rs 5,500, bringing the total to Rs 10,900 as subsidy. The National Sample Survey Organisation survey in 2013 said that 40.6 per cent of rural households had access to a toilet.[3]

On 24 September 2014, the campaign was renamed a second time, with the Modi government calling it Swachh Bharat Mission. Swachh, like Nirmal, also means clean, so it is unclear what the renaming was intended to achieve.[4]

---

[1] 'India's total sanitation campaign', 25 August 2017, Centre for Public Impact

[2] 'India@70: The short-lived Nirmal Bharat Abhiyan in 2012 increased toilet building subsidy without much success', 11 August 2017, *NDTV*

[3] 'Majority of rural households without toilet facility: NSSO', 25 December 2013, *Business Standard*

[4] 'Restructuring of the Nirmal Bharat Abhiyan into Swachh Bharat Mission', 24 September 2014, Press Information Bureau

The subsidy was raised to Rs 12,000, of which the Union would pay Rs 9,000 and the state Rs 3,000. Provision would be made to add the sum to the government scheme subsidising housing (which was then called Indira Awas Yojana and was later renamed Pradhan Mantri Awas Yojana—the prime minister's housing scheme).

Modi discontinued the work-related link to NREGA—building your own toilet no longer qualified you to get that part of the subsidy. He also circled 2 October 2019, the 150th birth anniversary of Gandhi, as the date by which to achieve Swachh Bharat.

The strategy 'will focus on behaviour change, triggering of the population with regard to toilet construction, and their use. Triggering of communities for behaviour change and usage of toilets shall be given top priority to ensure increased demand, which will lead to use of assets created', said the press statement and the government would encourage corporates to contribute from their CSR fund towards this cause.

The Swachh Bharat scheme was launched on 2 October 2014, with a speech by Modi standing in front of a backdrop with two giant images, his own and Gandhi's. He spoke about a clean India and the role of the individual in this, asking people to upload images of garbage and then of them cleaning it up. He invited nine individuals to do this—including Salman Khan, Priyanka Chopra and Sachin Tendulkar—and asked them to invite nine others in turn, creating a chain of people uploading videos of them sweeping public areas and streets. He said the World Health Organisation estimated that Indians lost on average Rs 6,500 per citizen from illness caused by a lack of cleanliness ('gandagi'). Well-off ('sukhi') families lived in clean spaces and so it was the poor who paid the price disproportionately for this, in his estimate between Rs 12,000 and Rs 15,000 per head.

He made a reference to toilets once, in the 24th minute of his 30-minute speech, saying that women and girls were inconvenienced by the lack of toilets in villages and in schools.

The focus of the speech was on the aesthetic aspects—on littering and not on sanitation. At the end of the speech, he read out a rambling and poorly drafted oath, called the Swachhta Pledge, which he made the crowd take. It was also focussed on littering and made no reference to sanitation or toilets. It read:

'Mahatma Gandhi dreamt of an India which was not only free but also clean and developed. Mahatma Gandhi secured freedom for Mother India. Now it is our duty to serve Mother India by keeping the country neat and clean.

'I take this pledge that I will remain committed towards cleanliness and devote time for this.

'I will devote 100 hours per year, that is two hours per week, to voluntarily work for cleanliness.

'I will neither litter nor let others litter.

'I will initiate the quest for cleanliness with myself, my family, my locality, my village and my workplace.

'I believe that the countries of the world that appear clean are so because their citizens don't indulge in littering nor do they allow it to happen.

'With this firm belief, I will propagate the message of Swachh Bharat Mission in villages and towns.

'I will encourage 100 other persons to take this pledge which I am taking today.

'I will endeavour to make them devote their 100 hours for cleanliness.

'I am confident that every step I take towards cleanliness will help in making my country clean.'[5]

Promoting the event and mission on his website, Modi once again underplayed the toilet aspect, giving it only a single line, saying that he had 'simultaneously addressed the health problems that roughly half of the Indians families have to deal with due to lack of proper toilets in their homes'. The photographs he posted were of him with a broom cleaning public spaces. This is what he also encouraged others to do.

The problem that the Total Sanitation/Nirmal Bharat missions were aimed at addressing was not littering and garbage. It was sanitation, and there was not an aesthetic reason for this. India leads the world in the number of children who are stunted and wasted (suffering from impaired growth and development because of malnutrition and repeated infection). One cause of this is poor sanitation. This was the primary focus of the campaigns in the past, and it was also the focus of Swachh Bharat, but that was lost in the messaging, which focussed instead on garbage, perhaps because this appealed to his base, the urban middle class.

The campaign was well funded and added 10 crore toilets, increasing coverage of households by 61 per cent. As unemployment rose, the link to MNREGA was reintroduced through the labour component of building a toilet again, paid through the employment scheme.[6]

In December 2018, Swachh Bharat Urban had declared 4,123 cities

5 Swachhta Pledge, darpg.gov.in
6 'Demand for work under MNREGA has sharply increased', 7 July 2020, PTI

and towns ODF. Just five states—Maharashtra, Uttar Pradesh, Gujarat, Madhya Pradesh and Tamil Nadu—accounted for 53 per cent of all toilets constructed in India.[7] Maharashtra alone accounted for one-fourth of all public toilets. In July 2019, the government said that the problem stood solved in large measure.[8]

On 2 October 2019, on cue, all the villages of India were declared 100 per cent ODF. But a survey released the following month by the National Statistical Office (NSO)—'Drinking water, sanitation, hygiene and housing conditions in India'—found that 28.7 per cent of village households had no access to a toilet. Another 3.5 per cent of households had access but didn't use it. Sanitation coverage had increased by 6 per cent in the two years before the launch of Swachh Bharat. In the five years of the scheme, it increased coverage by 12 per cent.

Several states declared 100 per cent ODF in March 2018 were found by the survey conducted six months later to not have achieved this. The NSO said that in Gujarat 75.8 per cent, in Maharashtra 78 per cent and in Rajasthan 65.8 per cent of rural households had access to any type of toilet—whether personal, communal or paid—though all three states had been declared ODF by the government. Madhya Pradesh had been declared ODF with only 71 per cent of households having access of similar nature, while in rural Tamil Nadu, access was 62.8 per cent.[9]

A survey done first in 2014 and then in 2018 by the IZA Institute of Labour Economics found that the number of people who had access to some type of toilet but still defecated in the open was constant between 2014 and 2018 at 23 per cent. The study found that at least 43 per cent of rural people in the states they surveyed—Bihar, Madhya Pradesh, Rajasthan, Uttar Pradesh—continued to defecate in the open.[10]

One of the issues faced was toilets that were constructed had no running water, rendering them unusable. This was caused by a mismatch of resources. In 2016–17, Swachh Bharat received about Rs 14,000 crore but rural water infrastructure received only Rs 6,000 crore. The Ministry of Water Resources estimated that a household required a total of 40 litres of water a day, of

[7] 'Four years on, how swachh is Bharat?', 17 May 2019, *TheWire.in*

[8] 'Many states became open defecation free, achieved 100% toilet coverage since Swachh Bharat Mission launch: Economic Survey', 4 July 2019, PTI

[9] 'Is rural India open defecation-free like Swachh Bharat data concludes?', 2 January 2020, *The Hindu*

[10] 'Changes in open defecation in rural north India: 2014–2018', http://ftp.iza.org/dp12065.pdf

which 15 to 20 litres was for sanitation.[11] But even a well-supplied rural household received only between 8 and 10 litres of water a day, and that was used up for cooking, drinking and washing, with sanitation being the last priority. And many villages had no access to piped water at all.[12]

The problem was not unknown to the government. A survey from 2016 by the National Sample Survey Organisation ('Swachh Survekshan') showed that only 42.5 per cent of village households had water for their toilets. The others only had access enough for cooking and drinking. But this did not stop states from making the claim that they had resolved the problem.

The Union government told the Lok Sabha in February 2018 that 11 states had been declared ODF under the Swachh Bharat Mission. A year after Gujarat government declared that the state had achieved ODF status, the Comptroller and Auditor General (CAG) of India dismissed the claim, saying 'it does not appear to be correct'. The CAG report quoted a survey conducted in 120 gram panchayats in eight districts, which found that, in fact, about 30 per cent of Gujarat's households had no access to toilets, either individual or public.[13]

Even with all these issues, some of which are to be expected, it must be accepted that Swachh Bharat carried forward and vastly expanded what Total Sanitation and Nirmal Bharat had begun. The question is what it achieved with regard to the problem all three were intended to tackle, and that is the illness arising from poor sanitation that Modi had spoken about.

Let us first look at the situation prior to Modi's Swachh Bharat Mission. A study by the Water and Sanitation Program showed the cost of poor sanitation to India to be 6.4 per cent of GDP, or Rs 2,180 per Indian.[14] It said that 'diseases such as diarrhoea have conventionally been called "water-borne" diseases but many communicable diseases are overwhelmingly explained by inadequate sanitation (that is having faecal matter origin) rather than water that acts as a medium to spread diseases'.

Another study published in 2016 by a group including Water Aid and Oxford Economics[15] showed that India's losses due to sanitation were $106 billion, or about Rs 5,700 per Indian. Half of the world's total losses from poor sanitation, about $222 billion, were because of India.

---

[11] It is unclear how this number was arrived at. A toilet cistern holds about seven litres.

[12] '3 crore toilets but not enough water. Why the Swachh Bharat Abhiyan needs a dedicated water policy', 30 May 2017, *NDTV*

[13] 'CAG report picks holes in Gujarat's open defecation-free claim', 21 September 2018, *The Indian Express*

[14] 'Inadequate sanitation costs India Rs. 2.4 trillion (US$53.8 billion)', wsp.org

[15] 'The true cost of poor sanitation', Indian Environment Portal

Three of the top seven causes of death and disease in India—malnutrition, dietary risks and water sanitation and hygiene—were directly linked to the sanitation campaign.[16] Better implementation would deter diarrhoea, malnutrition, cholera, worm infestations and hepatitis. *Hindustan Times* quoted Sujatha Rao, former secretary of the Ministry of Health and Family Welfare as saying: 'Apart from lowering diarrhoeal deaths, estimated at 8 lakh a year, Swachh Bharat will, if implemented well improve the nutrition status of children and their overall immunity against infectious disease for life.' Indeed, the government's website—swachhbharatmission.gov.in—itself advertises its mission on its homepage as being 'committed to building a Swachh and Swasth Bharat'.

Unfortunately, the campaign made no dent in this primary aspect. Under Modi, the problem in fact became more pronounced. The government's National Family Health Survey of 2019–20 revealed some awful numbers.

On four key metrics which represent the nutritional status of children, states recorded a significant fall in 2019–20 compared to the levels in 2015–16.[17] In states like Gujarat, Maharashtra and West Bengal, the share of anaemic and wasted (low weight for height) children was significantly higher than the levels recorded 15 years earlier in 2005–06. This indicated a reversal of progress that had been hard to win. Even in states such as Kerala, which continued to lead in these indicators, the levels recorded in 2019–20 were poorer than the 2015–16 figures.

The survey put out data for 22 states and Union territories and an analysis of 10 major states was conducted. Anaemia among children was higher in all the 10 states in 2019–20 compared to 2015–16. In Gujarat, Himachal, Maharashtra and West Bengal, a higher percentage of children were anaemic in 2019–20 than were in 2005–06.

The percentage of wasted (low weight for height) children was higher in half of the 10 states. In Assam, Gujarat, Karnataka, Maharashtra and West Bengal, a higher percentage of children were wasted in 2019–20 compared to 2005–06.

In 7 of the 10 States analysed, a higher percentage of children were underweight (low weight for age) in 2019–20 compared to 2015–16.

Stunting (low height for age) was higher in 6 out of the 10 states compared to 2015–16.

---

[16] 'How Swachh Bharat can enhance nutrition, immunity of children', 25 September 2018, *Hindustan Times*

[17] 'Progress on child nutrition derailed as wasting and stunting increases in several states', 17 December 2020, *The Hindu*

The study also found that incidents of diarrhoea had increased in half the states, including Andhra Pradesh, Bihar, Gujarat, Maharashtra, Karnataka and West Bengal. In Bihar, it was up from 10.4 per cent in 2015–16 to 13.7 per cent in 2019–20.[18] There was some good news in states like Bihar, Jharkhand, Madhya Pradesh and Uttar Pradesh, which have high levels of malnutrition, but a reversal in so many states was something that had happened for the first time.

In 2021, the programme was renamed Swachh Bharat 2.0, to continue till 2026 with a focus now on cities. The initial campaign launched with no focus on its true objective had delivered on 2 October 2019 the reversal of that objective. Government spending showed no reflection of this reality.

The year 2021 produced one of the most regressive budgets the country has seen from the perspective of social welfare. The mid-day meal scheme, on which crores of children depend for their one good meal of the day, found its budget cut from Rs 13,400 crore in FY 2020–21 to Rs 11,500 crore in 2021–22. This was lower in nominal terms than what it had been seven years earlier. Adjusting for inflation, it was 38 per cent lower. The Integrated Child Development Scheme (ICDS), meant to provide food, education, primary healthcare, immunisation services, health check-ups and referral services to children under six and their mothers, was also lower in nominal terms, at Rs 16,888 crore in FY 2021–22 versus Rs 18,691 crore in 2014–15. The programme, which runs rural anganwadis or crèches, is meant to improve the nutritional and health status of children 'to lay the foundation for proper psychological, physical and social development of the child', to 'reduce the incidence of mortality, morbidity, malnutrition and school dropout' and 'to enhance the capability of the mother to look after the normal health and nutritional needs of the child through proper nutrition and health education'.

Inflation adjusted, the ICDS figure was 36 per cent lower for 2021–22 than it had been the year Modi took over.

Poshan Abhiyan, the flagship programme to improve nutritional outcomes by 2022, was also hurt. The government had released only 46 per cent of the annual outlay by 31 October 2020, and, in 2021, the budget was cut by 27 per cent.

The Drinking Water and Sanitation department saw its budget officially rise from Rs 21,000 crore to Rs 60,030 crore, but of that, Rs 50,000 crore was for the 'Central road and infrastructure fund', suggesting a fudge to avoid embarrassing questions. The numbers seemed deliberately made hard to compare with previous spends. ICDS was clubbed with Poshan Abhiyan,

---

[18] 'Diarrhoea in children under 5 more prevalent in rural India: NFHS-5', 21 January 2021, *Down to Earth*

the Scheme for Adolescent Girls and the National Creche Scheme, and the whole thing was called Saksham. Its budget for 2021–22 was less than the previous year's budget for ICDS alone.

The Pradhan Mantri Matru Vandana Yojana, the Union's maternity benefit programme, was clubbed with the Beti Bachao Beti Padhao scheme for girls' education, the Mahila Shakti Kendra and other general gender budgeting and the whole thing was called Samarthya. It received Rs 2,522 crore in 2021–22, less than the Rs 2,858 crore allocated in the last budget.

The allocation for Ayushman Bharat (dubbed 'Modicare' by Amit Shah when it was launched) was the same for 2021–22, Rs 6,400 crore, as it was for the year before. The usefulness of this scheme and of focussing on insurance rather than building infrastructure may be seen in the fact that of its 11 crore population only 19 people in Bihar received Covid-19 treatment under 'Modicare' and of Uttar Pradesh's 20 crore only 875.[19] There was no provision for minimum wage and health insurance for Anganwadi and Accredited Social Health Activist (ASHA) workers, the individuals whom Modi had called 'Covid warriors'. (More about the struggle of ASHA workers in the chapter 'The Devil's Workshop'.)

Part 2: Smart Cities

A programme launched in 1985 that subsidised housing for the poor was renamed by the Modi government in 2016.[20] (A detailed comparison of the performance of the UPA and the NDA on this scheme and others has been drawn up by journalist Ravi Nair.)[21] This social welfare programme had Rs 15,184 crore allocated to it by the previous UPA government in 2013–14.[22] It ran parallel with the Pradhan Mantri Awas Yojana (PMAY) (Urban)— previously the Rajiv Awaas Yojana—and was intended, Modi said at its launch, to provide homes for all by 2022.

This would be done in four ways:

1.   Rehabilitation of slums by building houses through private participation for eligible slum dwellers on the land the slums were standing on

[19] 'Under Ayushman Bharat, huge disparities among states where Covid patients availed scheme', 16 June 2021, *India Today*

[20] 'Modi govt changes Indira Awaas Yojana's name; it's now Pradhan Mantri Gramin Awaas Yojana', 25 April 2016, *Zee News*

[21] 'Has the Modi government really improved upon the UPA's existing schemes?', 28 October 2017, *TheWire.in*

[22] 'Rural sector gets major boost in Budget 2013-14', 18 March 2013, Press Information Bureau

2. Affordable housing for the poor through Union assistance of Rs 1.5 lakh for housing projects run by the states

3. Direct Union assistance for house construction or house enhancement by the poor

4. Loans at lower rates of interest for middle-income sections for construction or renovation of existing homes

The PMAY Urban project first set a target of constructing two crore homes by 2022. This was halved to a crore.[23]

Of the four verticals, more than half (55 per cent) came under the third category, which required presenting proof of ownership of land and the means to bear the full cost of construction after government subsidy. Maximum houses had been sanctioned in Uttar Pradesh (17 per cent) followed by Madhya Pradesh, Tamil Nadu and Andhra Pradesh (12 per cent each).

A further 33 per cent of the total came from the second category, which was dependent on the price at which the units were put on sale. Four states—Andhra Pradesh, Maharashtra, Gujarat and Karnataka—made up 60 per cent of such units.

The other two categories, the first for slum rehabilitation and the fourth for loans to middle-income sections, were only 12 per cent of the total. In the former, Maharashtra alone accounted for half the houses sanctioned.

Overall, the scheme had over Rs 1 lakh crore sanctioned for it in the first four years, of which only a third was released. Of this one-third, only 62 per cent was then utilised, i.e., only a fifth of the sanctioned sum was actually spent. This was a continuation of the struggle that previous governments have also had with the same project, under a different name, a report by *The Wire* showed.[24]

The ratios remained more or less the same over the years. In 2021, the sanctioned money had gone up to Rs 1.72 lakh crore while what was released was Rs 76,000 crore. Houses built/repaired were said to be 38 lakh.[25]

Many of the problems in implementation were structural. In dense cities like Mumbai and Delhi, the limited nature of government assistance meant that this could only be used to build homes far away from the places where employment was available.

---

[23] 'How the PM's affordable housing scheme went from promising to dysfunctional', 14 May 2019, *TheWire.in*

[24] Ibid

[25] 'Budget 2021: PM Awas Yojna—here's the progress so far', 1 February 2021, *Business Today*

This issue of not being able to crack the core governance problem afflicted another of Modi's schemes, the Smart Cities mission. It was set up with a concept note that said the aim was to make cities that would offer 'decent living options to every resident', which would provide a 'very high quality of life comparable with any developed European city', according to the urban ministry's concept note on Smart Cities.[26] All this would happen by 2020. These Smart Cities were required, Arun Jaitley told parliament in 2014, to service the middle class that Modi's economic policies would expand.[27]

The following year, the target was made more modest and, instead of emulating a European city, it was stated that the Smart City of India would provide citizens with adequate water supply, assured electricity supply, sanitation, public transport, affordable housing for the poor, safety of women, health and education.

This was, of course, not different from what cities were focussed on in any case. The problem was one of hard governance and not logo and nomenclature alone. This may be why the Modi government's interest in this waned almost immediately.

It was reported in 2021 that the 'Smart Cities project had failed to take off, with half of its funds unspent'.[28] The project 'should have been on its winning lap come 2020', the report said, but instead, the reality was that by 2019, of the total Rs 48,000 crore 'approved' between 2015–19, only half was actually allocated. Of this half, only three-fourth was then actually released, and of what was released a mere 36 per cent was then utilised. While Rs 48,000 crore had been 'approved', only Rs 6,160 crore was spent.

The Parliamentary Standing Committee on Urban Development said it was 'perplexed about the actual progress made so far under the Mission at ground level' and it also 'observed numerous instances of one agency undoing the work of another'. Out of the 35 states and Union territories, 26 had utilised less than 20 per cent of the funds released.[29]

The usual problems associated with India also came to light. The standing committee said it was 'surprised to find that in spite of available mechanisms, the complaints about poor work under the Mission are still pouring in before the Committee'. It recommended that 'all those cases questioning the claim

[26] 'India's "smart" cities plan risks leaving millions behind', 16 December 2016, AFP

[27] 'Achche din coming for neo-middle class' Smart Cities', 12 March 2014, *The Hindu BusinessLine*

[28] 'Budget 2021 is a chance to revitalise the Smart Cities mission', 30 January 2021, *The Week*

[29] 'Without an overhaul, smart cities won't fulfil urban needs', 16 May 2019, *TheWire.in*

of work done under Smart Cities emanating from local MPs be probed expeditiously and the guilty be brought to book'.

The Wire's piece referred to above and written by Shaguna Kanwar pointed out some primary flaws with the Smart Cities mission. It emphasised high-end infrastructure and technology-driven surveillance, but did not address amenities—water, schools, public hospitals, housing. With its area-based development, it was focussed on spending most of the money on small patches of city centres that were already developed.

In Bangalore, the Smart Cities allocation was used on developing Church Street—which was already developed more than most of the rest of the city—and elite neighbourhoods like Infantry Road, Kamaraj Road, Tata Lane, Wood Street, Castle Street, Dickenson Road, Kensington Road, St John's Road, Residency Road, Kasturba Road, Bowring Hospital Road, Millers Road, Lavelle Road, McGrath Road, Convent Road, Queen's Road, Hayes Road, Raja Ram Mohan Roy Road and Race Course Road.[30]

In Delhi, it was the area under the New Delhi Municipal Corporation, also already the most developed part of the National Capital Region. The mission was aimed at a particular section, the upper class, which comprised a very small part of the population and not any neo-middle class, which Modi's economic policies in any case didn't produce.

The elitism showed elsewhere, for instance in the public bicycle sharing project implemented by many cities, including Pune, Delhi, Bhopal and Coimbatore. The instructions for hiring a bicycle on the company's website were only in English and it only accepted online payment, The Wire report said, with the concern that Smart Cities was pushing the urban poor further to the margins.

'Allocations' in 2019 remained the same as that of 2018. And, in the 2021 Budget, the phrase 'Smart Cities' was not used at all. The former deputy mayor of Shimla, Tikender Singh Panwar, explained why: 'These smart cities were supposed to be the lighthouses for other cities in the country. The Budget is completely silent over it owing to the fact that it has become one of the biggest embarrassments to the Modi government.'[31]

---

[30] 'Commercial Street to turn "smart" by December 1', 21 November 2020, The New Indian Express, and '20 Bengaluru roads to get smart look', 7 May 2019, Deccan Herald
[31] 'Budget 2021: Where are the smart cities and urban employment guarantee, FM and PM?', 2 February 2021, Newsclick.in

Part 3: Governance by Nomenclature

When Congressman Shashi Tharoor complained in a tweet in 2017 that the BJP had merely changed the names of 23 Congress schemes, and said that Modi's was a 'name-changing' government and not a 'game-changing one', his claim was put to the test. It was found that he was right about 19.[32]

It turned out that the Pradhan Mantri Jan Dhan Yojana was the UPA's Basic Savings Bank Deposit Account; Beti Bachao, Beti Padhao Yojana was the same as the National Girl Child Day programme; Deen Dayal Upadhyay Gram Jyoti Yojana was the Rajiv Grameen Vidyutikaran Yojana; Atal Mission for Rejuvenation and Urban Transformation was the Jawaharlal Nehru National Urban Renewal Mission renamed; the BJP's neem-coated urea was the same as Congress's neem-coated urea; the Soil Health Card scheme was the National Project on Management of Soil Health and Fertility; the Atal Pension Yojana was the Swavalamban Yojana; and even Make in India was the National Manufacturing Policy (NMP) under a new name.

And it was not mere renaming; the entire policy framework in many cases was also a copy-paste job, as a comparison of the Department for Promotion of Industry and Internal Trade's press note 2 (2011) and the Make in India website page on national manufacturing showed.

The UPA's NMP scheme spoke of 'enhancing the share of manufacturing in GDP to 25 per cent within a decade and creating 100 million jobs'. Make in India seeks 'an increase in the share of manufacturing in the country's GDP to 25 per cent' and to 'create 100 million additional jobs by 2022 in manufacturing'.

The NMP says it will 'increase manufacturing sector growth to 12–14 per cent over the medium term'. Make in India says it will 'increase in manufacturing sector growth to 12–14 per cent over the medium term'.

The NMP says the policy needs 'creation of appropriate skill sets among the rural migrant and urban poor to make growth inclusive'. Make in India says it needs 'creation of appropriate skill sets among rural migrants and the urban poor for inclusive growth'.

The NMP policy says it will 'increase domestic value addition and technological depth in manufacturing'. Make in India says it will 'increase domestic value addition and technological depth'.

In fact, the Make in India website not only reflected the Congress scheme but a broken download link also unsuccessfully directed readers to a 2011 document of the older policy.

---

[32] 'Shashi Tharoor says BJP renamed 23 Congress schemes. He's right about 19', 24 June 2017, FactChecker.in

Elsewhere, Digital India was the same as the earlier National eGovernance Plan; Skill India the same as the National Skill Development Programme; Mission Indradhanush was the Universal Immunisation Programme; and PAHAL the earlier Direct Benefits Transfer for LPG. BharatNet was the National Optic Fibre Network approved on 25 October 2011, aiming to provide broadband connectivity to all panchayats.

When the Rajiv Awaas Yojana was renamed the Sardar Patel National Urban Housing Mission, it came with a claim from the minister of Housing and Urban Poverty Alleviation, Venkaiah Naidu, that housing for all would come by 2022. A parliamentary committee, headed by Biju Janata Dal member Pinaki Mishra, asked the government how merely changing the name could accelerate implementation. This went largely unreported.

The reality is that the UPA's schemes had anodyne and unmemorable names even though they may have had the same aims. Modi's schemes have catchier names because he spends so much effort personally polishing coinage.[33] Not as much effort on implementation though: Make in India's target was shifted from 2022 to 2025 as manufacturing collapsed in India, and instead of going from 16 per cent in 2014 to 25 per cent in 2022 in fact dropped to 13 per cent in 2021. Make in India has a nice logo though.

Tharoor's good-natured acceptance that such things represented continuity (Manmohan Singh did not say a thing about the renaming) sat in contrast with the BJP's contempt for the very schemes they appropriated. Particular hostility was reserved for the UPA's Unique Identity scheme, Aadhaar. During the 2014 election campaign, *The Times of India* ran a headline on 12 March 2014: 'Aadhaar a "fraud", will review it if voted to power: BJP'.

The party alleged that Aadhaar was a criminal programme and that it would have the CBI investigate it. 'This is a dangerous programme to regularise the stay of illegal immigrants in the country. Is Bharat Mata so open to illegal immigrants? The Aadhaar is also in contravention of Supreme Court directives,' Meenakshi Lekhi said in Bangalore while campaigning against the Congressman and Aadhaar architect Nandan Nilekani. 'The entire biometric data of people enrolled has been stored outside the country,' she added. Nilekani's opponent, Ananth Kumar (who would eventually win), said: 'Aadhaar is the biggest fraud on the country.'

---

[33] A friend observed that Modi's schemes targeted at the wealthy had English names— Digital India, Skill India, Start-up India, Make in India—signalling aspiration. However the schemes for the poor were in Hindi—Ujjwala Yojana, Swachh Bharat Abhiyan, Beti Padhao Beti Bachao, Jan Dhan, Garib Kalyan, PM Kisan, Mudra Yojana—reflecting the branding priority.

The next month, Ananth Kumar said the BJP would scrap Aadhaar.[34] Modi himself weighed in against Aadhaar, saying that the money spent on it was wasted, that the NREGA was meant to line the pockets of the Congress and that the Right to Information Act (RTI) was useless.[35]

As it turned out, the BJP under Modi would not only embrace Aadhaar, it would also force it upon all Indians, willing or unwilling, as the NDA expanded India's social welfare schemes, many of which they had inherited. One of the schemes Modi showcased as his best also had its roots in a social welfare initiative of the UPA. This was the Pradhan Mantri Ujjwala Yojana under which any adult woman from a Below Poverty Line family could apply for a deposit-free LPG gas connection, if no other connection existed in the household. She needed to submit her address, Jan Dhan bank account number and Aadhaar number. After the first free cylinder, she could get subsidised refills.

While there resulted a substantial increase in the number of customers with LPG connections due to the scheme, data showed no significant growth in the consumption of LPG cylinders. The number of LPG customers grew from 9.4 per cent of the population in 2014–15 to 16.2 per cent in 2016–17. However, the same data revealed that the annual growth in LPG consumption decreased from 10.5 per cent to 9.8 per cent over the same period. In 2018–19, it rose only 6.9 per cent. In November 2018, it actually declined year-on-year for the first time in over five years.[36] In 2020, it rose 4.3 per cent over 2019.

The reason why usage could not be sustained, was the scheme's pricing structure. The BPL family received a stove and the first cylinder as a loan. This would be recovered in instalments against subsidies for subsequent cylinders, the cost of which the family would have to bear. This kept gas more expensive than kerosene or firewood. As early as 2018, a study found that that 85 per cent of the scheme's beneficiaries in Rajasthan, Uttar Pradesh, Bihar and Madhya Pradesh were still using traditional wood chulhas for cooking.[37] The price of a 14.2 kg domestic LPG cylinder went up 40 per cent in four months from Rs 594 a cylinder on 1 November 2020 to

---

[34] 'NDA will scrap Aadhaar if it gets mandate', 13 April 2014, *The Hindu*

[35] 'In Karnataka, Narendra Modi targets UPA's Aadhaar, RTI; In Kerala, slams Antony', 9 April 2014, *The Indian Express*

[36] 'India's LPG consumption drops for the first time in 5 years', 13 December 2018, *The Economic Times*

[37] 'India's poor were struggling to refill LPG cylinders. Now with record price hike, many have given up', 9 March 2021, *Scroll.in*

Rs 819 a cylinder on 1 March 2021.[38] In this period, the Union's LPG subsidy budget collapsed from Rs 39,000 crore in 2020–21 to Rs 14,000 crore for 2021–22.[39]

The success of the initial sign-up was because of efficient targeting. Ujjwala data was used to deliver other direct benefit transfer schemes.

The key here was the identification of BPL families and this came through the data from the Socio Economic Caste Census (SECC), which was conducted by the UPA in 2011 and without which identification would not be possible.[40]

'Before the availability of SECC data,' the Modi government itself acknowledged, 'Below Poverty Line list prepared in 2002, by States/UTs was being used for identifying beneficiaries of development programmes and schemes including Pradhan Mantri Awaas Yojana-Gramin and National Social Assistance Programme.' However, it added: 'The 2002 BPL list attracted claims of biases.'[41] The Modi government planned to 'update' the data from 2011 with new parameters, but was unable to do so because of the hostility it created against government surveyors with the citizenship laws. It was reported that the new parameters would exclude some existing families.[42]

A few months after taking office, Modi said in the Lok Sabha that NREGA would be continued only because it would show how poorly Manmohan Singh's government had performed: 'My political instincts tell me that MNREGA should not be discontinued,' he said, mocking the Opposition benches, 'because it is a living memorial to your failures. After so many years in power, all you were able to deliver is for a poor man to dig ditches a few days a month.'[43]

Modi would instead let the scheme die naturally as his government would create better jobs and NREGA would not be required.

After the government had taken office, Nitin Gadkari indicated that

[38] 'High price of LPG cylinders forcing the poor to return to firewood', 17 March 2021, *Business Standard*

[39] 'Why Covid is a reality check for Modi's flagship welfare schemes', 12 May 2021, *The Indian Express*

[40] 'Over 25 lakh LPG connections released under PM Ujjwala Yojana', 3 August 2016, Press Information Bureau

[41] 'Cabinet approves revision of cost of Socio Economic and Caste Census 2011', 26 July 2017, Press Information Bureau

[42] 'Socio Economic Caste Census-2021 to define eligibility of rural household for benefits under government schemes', 17 March 2020, *The Economic Times*

[43] 'Modi says MNREGA will continue as a living monument to Congress failure', 27 February 2015, *Scroll.in*

NREGA would be limited to less than a third of India's districts and that wages would be lowered and delayed for beneficiaries to make the scheme unattractive.[44] Again, the assumption was that job creation under Modi would make the scheme redundant.

By December 2014, except for five states, all others had received significantly lower funds from the Union in 2014, compared to 2013.

As India's economy began to weaken under Modi and unemployment rose, he began to invest more and more in the scheme he had called a failure. In 2014–15, NREGA got Rs 32,000 crore; in 2015–16, Rs 37,000 crore; in 2016–17, 48,000 crore; in 2017–18, Rs 55,000 crore; in 2018–19, Rs 61,000 crore; in 2019–20, Rs 71,000 crore and in 2020–21, Rs 111,000 crore. The memorial under Modi was almost three times the size it had been under Manmohan Singh.

Campaigning for the 2019 elections, Modi claimed that he was the chowkidar (security guard) who was protecting the nation against the loot of public funds. This had resulted in savings of Rs 90,000 crore, he said. 'Who will protect the rights of the poor? We have stopped the loot of Rs 90,000 crore. This money used to go into the pockets of people who used to purchase big cars and fly in aeroplanes. But now these things have stopped, so their anger against Modi is natural. Now they want to take revenge against me. But with your blessings, their efforts will not be successful.'[45]

He was referring to the direct benefits transfer programme which was, as we have noted, thought up, put together and begun under the previous government. Modi had merely extended it after resisting its implementation in the first instance. However, the question was whether it had been implemented competently under him and whether the idea of money saved specifically because of his governance was true. The facts showed that it was not.

For instance, Rs 1,364 crore was sent to ineligible individuals under the PM-Kisan scheme.[46] This was money sent during the same election campaign under a scheme launched the month after Modi made his chowkidar speech. The government's own data showed that it had sent money to the wrong people. On the other hand, of those who were meant to get the money, 11.2

[44] 'Internal NREGA note blames Nitin Gadkari, then does a rewrite', 9 January 2015, *The Indian Express*

[45] 'Conspiracy to oust me as I stopped the siphoning of Rs 90,000 crore through bogus documents: PM', 15 January 2019, *The Indian Express*

[46] 'RTI reveals: Government of India paid out more than Rs 1360 crore to undeserving persons under PM Kisan Yojana', 11 January 2021, Commonwealth Human Rights Initiative

lakh did not. After the blunder, tens of thousands of individuals were sent letters by the government asking that they return the money with the threat of legal action. The problem lay in governance. Bureaucrats had been given targets for putting money into the accounts of a certain number of farmers. In their hurry to meet the target, the names of ineligible individuals were included in the list of beneficiaries.[47]

On 23 May 2012, attacking the Manmohan Singh government at the Centre, Modi had tweeted: 'A massive hike in petrol prices is a prime example of the failure of Congress-led UPA. This will put a burden of hundreds of crores (of rupees) on Gujarat'. A common joke on the supposed unaffordability of petrol under the UPA was spread by Modi's supporters, including the actors Akshay Kumar and Amitabh Bachchan: that they had asked the petrol pump attendant to only sell them a few drops to spray on their car so that they could set it alight, because it was unaffordable to run.

In May 2012, the price of crude was $100 a barrel and the price of petrol Rs 65. In May 2020, crude was $30 a barrel but the price of petrol much higher. This has been true for most of the Modi years, where international crude prices have stayed soft, but domestic fuel prices have soared.

The ridiculousness of fuel prices under Modi invited a jibe from the BJP's stormy petrel, Subramanian Swamy, who tweeted that petrol was cheaper in Sita's Nepal and Ravan's Lanka than it was in Ram's India. This was in February 2021, when petrol was over Rs 92 in Mumbai, while it was Rs 68 in Nepal, Rs 60 in Sri Lanka and Rs 51 in Pakistan (all calculated in Indian rupees). Taxes on fuel were about 60 per cent of the price of petrol and diesel, making India the nation with the highest fuel taxes in the world.[48] Indians paid more tax for petrol and diesel than Italians, the French, Germans, Britons, Spaniards, Japanese, Canadians and Americans. This list is revealing: it is the wealthy nations where fuel is expensive because indirect taxes, such as those on petrol and diesel, affect all users, poor and rich alike. Poor nations do not have high taxes on fuel for this reason. However, under Modi, the economic decline has affected government revenue, and he has kept the squeeze on consumers to recover money squandered elsewhere.

Having budgeted to get Rs 1.3 lakh crore from the cess on petrol and diesel, the Union instead got Rs 2.3 lakh crore.[49] That was an additional Rs

---

[47] 'PM Kisan scheme: Ineligible farmers avail funds, govt to recover', 20 December 2020, *The Quint*

[48] 'India now has the highest fuel taxes in the world', 7 May 2020, *The Economic Times*

[49] 'Government mopped up 80% more from fuel cess than expected', 4 February 2021, *The Economic Times*

740 per Indian. From being 13 per cent of all government revenue in 2014, tax on fuel brought in as much as 33 per cent of all revenue by 2021.[50] This also undid the idea of deregulation, carried out in 2010 so that fuel prices would rise and fall with the price of crude. They no longer fell. When crude rose, the cost was passed to the consumer, when it fell, the government took in more. The price of fuel had been deregulated because the consumer was protected by the government each time the price of crude rose and the state-run oil companies took a hit. The opposite has happened under Modi: now the government is protected and the logic of deregulation is undone. The amount of money raised as tax on fuel went up 300 per cent between 2015 and 2021.[51]

Wherever the government was under pressure, it added a cess to fund that particular problem. When the farmers' agitation troubled it, the Agriculture Infrastructure and Development Cess was added to fuel to fund measures to assuage the protestors. This would be Rs 2.5 per litre on petrol and Rs 4 on diesel.[52]

Petrol and diesel prices were briefly frozen in the Modi era only to avoid criticism during elections. There was a 19-day freeze before the Karnataka polls of May 2018, followed by 16 consecutive days of price increase after 14 May 2018. Before the Gujarat elections in December 2017, the Union froze fuel prices for 14 days. Prices were frozen between 16 January 2017 and 1 April 2017, when polls were held in five states—Punjab, Goa, Uttarakhand, Uttar Pradesh and Manipur. June 2020 saw 21 consecutive days of hikes in petrol and diesel prices.[53] Prices were frozen for 18 days in April 2021 before the West Bengal election, after which petrol went past Rs 100 for the first time.[54]

There was no explanation or apology from Modi for why it was that Indians—including autorickshaw and Uber drivers and truckers—were paying through their nose for fuel to fund his government's incompetence.

---

[50] 'Story of Budget 2021, in 9 charts', 1 February 2021, *Mint*

[51] 'Central govt's tax collection on petrol, diesel jumps 300% in six years', 22 March 2021, *Business Standard*

[52] 'Nirmala Sitharaman imposes new agri cess on petrol, diesel for FY22', 1 February 2021, *The Times of India*

[53] '21-day consecutive hike in fuel prices halts: Petrol selling at Rs 80.38/litre, diesel at Rs 80.40/litre in Delhi', 28 June 2020, *The Economic Times*

[54] 'Petrol, diesel prices rise again, reach record highs', 14 May 2021, PTI

Part 4: Electrifying

While fuel was not spoken of, electricity came with a great deal of bombast.

'28th April 2018 will be remembered as a historic day in the development journey of India. Yesterday, we fulfilled a commitment due to which the lives of several Indians will be transformed forever! I am delighted that every single village of India now has access to electricity,' Modi tweeted on 29 April of that year.

This came 11 months after his government promised to 'electrify' all villages by May 2017.[55] This produced ecstatic coverage, such as 'Modi's village electrification is among world's biggest successes this year, says this report' (13 November 2018, *Financial Express*). The story reported that 'since 2000, more than 900 million people have gained access to electricity in developing countries in Asia continent with 91 per cent of the region getting electrified by 2017 compared with 67 per cent in 2000. Of this, about 61 per cent of this progress has happened in India only'.

The problem with calling this Modi's village electrification was that it was not true for a couple of reasons. Firstly, while average villages thus electrified were 6,000 per year under Modi, they had been 10,000 per year under Manmohan Singh in his second term, and over 12,000 a year in his first.[56] When the Modi government announced its new rural electrification scheme, only 18,452 villages lacked power supply.[57]

Secondly, the definition of 'village electrification' in India is quite narrow and, according to the revised version issued in February 2004 under Vajpayee, a village is considered electrified when the necessary infrastructure, such as a power transformer, is made available in the inhabited locality and the Dalit hamlets (where they exist), ensuring that electricity can reach public places, and to at least 10 per cent of the total number of households in the village/hamlet. This is a very different thing from what the phrase '100 per cent electrification' suggests, even if we were to leave aside the problem of episodic availability of power that large parts of India still suffer from, especially in villages.

According to a study by the Council on Energy, Environment and Water,

---

[55] 'All villages in the country to be electrified by May 2017, says Piyush Goel', 8 October 2016, PTI

[56] 'Environmental polices delinked from Aam Aadmi', Shouvik Chakraborty, *A Quantum Leap in the Wrong Direction?*, Rohit Azad, Shouvik Chakraborty, Srinivasan Ramani, Dipa Sinha (eds), Orient BlackSwan, 2019

[57] 'Modi announces 100% electrification—but that doesn't mean everyone has power', 29 April 2018, *TheWire.in*

63 per cent of Odisha households experienced two or more days of 24-hour blackouts in a month, and 31 per cent experienced three or more days of low voltage supply.[58] If we use the measure of households instead of villages, then it may not be accurate to see 28 April 2018 as historic. In Uttar Pradesh, Jharkhand and Assam, fewer than 60 per cent of households had electricity then, four years after the BJP came to power on the promise of 'electricity for all'. In 12 out of 29 states, fewer than 80 per cent of the households were electrified.

On 4 November 2016, the Paris Agreement on climate change came into force. Nations would limit their emissions to try and ensure that global warming was limited to no more than two degrees Celsius. Ten months later, in September 2017, Nitin Gadkari shocked the automobile industry and the world when he announced that India would move to 100 per cent electric cars by 2030.

'I am going to do this, whether you like it or not. And I am not going to ask you. I will bulldoze it,' he said at a conference of the Society of Indian Automobile Manufacturers.[59] He added: '*Petrol, diesel gaadi banane walon ka band bajaana hai* (We are going to take to task the manufacturers of petrol and diesel cars). For pollution, for imports. My ideas are crystal clear… The government has a crystal-clear policy to reduce imports and curb pollution,' he said.

This came out of the blue because there had been no government investment or plan to electrify the grid to make such a transition possible. The US, Europe and China have tens of thousands of public charging stations to service battery-powered cars, including direct current fast-charging networks which can add hundreds of kilometres of range in a few minutes. India had done no work on this front but was asking manufacturers to completely retool their factories, throw away the systems supporting the internal combustion engine and begin investing in lithium ion cells and electric powertrains.

Gadkari's bluster came at a time, 2017, when the economy was tracing a false arc. Consumption had already begun to collapse by then because of demonetisation, but the shift from the unorganised to the organised sector hid this and the trend appeared to be positive.

We have seen what happened to the automobile sector soon thereafter, in the chapter 'Modinomics'. When Gadkari made that speech in September 2017, it was after automobile sales had grown 9 per cent between April and

---

[58] Ibid
[59] 'Switch to clean vehicles or get bulldozed: Nitin Gadkari tells automakers', 7 September 2017, PTI

August, with sales of cars growing by 8 per cent, two wheelers by 10 per cent and even commercial vehicles at 1.6 per cent.

Two years later, speaking to the same set of people, a deflated Gadkari sang quite a different tune: 'We are as worried with the slowdown in this industry. The economic growth of this industry is important as it is a huge employment generator. The finance ministry is trying to find solutions to help growth,' he said. 'I would like to clarify that the government does not intend to ban petrol and diesel vehicles. We aren't going to do anything like that.'[60] His words came after 300 dealerships had been shuttered, and 15,000 jobs in manufacturing and 2 lakh jobs in sales and servicing had been lost.[61]

Things that were difficult to do and required hard governance were first taken up and then abandoned. This was true even when the project was as hallowed as the Namami Gange, taken up in June 2014 immediately after the election victory. It was given an outlay of Rs 20,000 crore 'to accomplish the twin objectives of effective abatement of pollution, conservation and rejuvenation of National River Ganga'.

The Ganga required not so much cleaning—because it flowed continually into the sea—as ensuring that further pollutants did not enter it. This was a granular problem that had to do with hundreds of places where effluent was being discharged into the river. Once it was learned that cleaning up required substantial effort, enthusiasm for the project waned.

In February 2017, the National Green Tribunal observed that 'not a single drop of river Ganga has been cleaned so far', and that government efforts were 'only wasting public money'.[62]

The next year, the 86-year-old environmentalist G.D. Agarwal, who had been on a fast unto death for 111 days, died, having given up even water. A professor at the Indian Institute of Technology in Kanpur who had served on the Central Pollution Control Board, Agarwal had been demanding a law to protect the Ganga. A day before he died, Gadkari (who was Union minister for Water Resources, River Development and Ganga Rejuvenation) said almost all of Agarwal's demands had been met.

Allocations to Namami Gange fell from Rs 2,500 crore in 2016–17 to Rs 2,300 crore in 2017–18 and then to Rs 687 crore in 2018–19. In 2019–

---

[60] 'Slowdown blues: Nitin Gadkari does a U-turn, says no ban on petrol, diesel cars', 5 September 2019, *Business Today*

[61] 'Slowdown blues: 15,000 workers lost jobs in auto manufacturing firms in 3 months, says SIAM', 4 August 2019, *Business Today*

[62] 'Public money wasted, not a drop of Ganga cleaned: National Green Tribunal', 6 February 2017, PTI

20, about Rs 375 crore was spent. That year, the project was folded into a larger one now called Jal Shakti. When the lockdown in March 2020 led to the temporary shutting down of polluting units, the Modi government claimed that the Ganga had been cleaned.

Part 5: Coercive Federalism

One of the most significant, long-lasting and damaging aspects to Modi's governance is his sacrificing of Union–state relations at the altar of his recklessness.

On 15 August 2017, Modi said in his Red Fort speech: 'Since I have myself been a chief minister for long, I know that states are important for the growth of a country. I understand the importance of chief ministers and state governments. And that is why we focused on cooperative federalism and now competitive cooperative federalism. And now we are taking all decision together.'[63] Modi would go on to use the phrase 'cooperative federalism' often.

As chief minister, he had made much of state autonomy and federalism—rejecting GST, resisting the Planning Commission, asking for more authority and taunting the Union government. But the record shows that, as prime minister, he defaults to the RSS position which sees the Union alone as India and the very existence of states as a nuisance.

The states had signed on to GST on the assurance that their interests would not only be secured but guaranteed in writing by the Union government. Having given up to the Union, as we have noted, their right over most forms of taxation on the assumption that their revenues were assured, they found themselves facing not merely a non-cooperative but actively hostile Delhi under Modi.

As the economy began to soften and revenues fell short, the Union delayed paying the compensation it had promised to the states. In late 2019, the finance ministers of Punjab, Delhi, Kerala, West Bengal and Rajasthan issued a joint statement on the delay, after they had been forced into overdraft: 'The current delay has shaken the confidence of the states who have so far supported GST in a spirit of rare bonhomie,' the statement said.[64]

There was no accountability or explanation at first for this default from

---

[63] 'Narendra Modi's idea of competitive cooperative federalism brilliant: Narayana Murthy', 15 August 2017, PTI
[64] 'Punjab, five other states urge Centre to release GST dues', 20 November 2019, *The Tribune*

the Union. Much before Covid and the lockdown, it was clear that Modi's finances were in trouble, as dues began to be released in tranches.[65] Punjab's finance minister threatened to move the Supreme Court against the Union's reneging of its commitments, as did Kerala's finance minister.

On 29 August, the Union said it foresaw a shortfall in GST collections of Rs 3 lakh crore. The compensation cess—levied on a small group of luxury goods like cars and tobacco—would yield Rs 65,000 crore, leaving a gap of Rs 2.35 lakh crore.

The Union arbitrarily attributed a sum of Rs 1.38 lakh crore to Covid-related causes and disclaimed its responsibility to fork out the sum since it was not covered by the GST legislation.

The Union offered two choices to the states: borrow a sum of Rs 97,000 crore from the RBI, or raise the entire sum of Rs 2.35 lakh crore as loans on market rates.

The reason given for refusal to pay states their share was the invocation of force majeure—'act of God' or the doing of a higher power—for what was purely an act of the Modi government. India's 2020–21 economic disaster was entirely avoidable; Bangladesh and Pakistan did not go through recession. It was the predictable product of an arbitrary lockdown.

Instead of assuming responsibility for his actions as leader of the nation, Modi instead told chief ministers to fend for themselves. The Union as the sovereign should have raised or printed money to fill the hole it had created. But states were instead 'given permission' to borrow money from the market. This was not the reneging of a commercial deal between two acquaintances. This was the betrayal of Bharat as a union of states, as per Article 1 of the Constitution. It was done casually and, in fact, Modi had so little interest in the issue that even waving the chief ministers away was left to his minister, Nirmala Sitharaman.

At the meeting she held with the states, she put the choices before them, following which there was chaos when a bureaucrat, finance secretary Ajay Bhushan Pandey, declared: 'The meeting is closed. The department of economic affairs has assured that it would help the states to borrow. The meeting is closed.'[66]

This meant that the states would have no choice but to accept the first option, which was to borrow a sum of Rs 97,000 crore on their account.

The Opposition-led states immediately demanded a vote and said the

[65] 'Facing attack on GST compensation delay, govt releases funds worth Rs 35,000', 16 December 2019, *The Financial Express*

[66] 'Centre bows to states on GST', 6 October 2020, *The Telegraph*

outcome would then be binding on all. At this, Sitharaman backed down and scheduled another meeting to resolve their differences.

The resistance from states, including some allies, forced the Union to then say it would borrow and make good about half the shortfall.[67] How the future would be managed, given that the problem would continue for years due to the economic wreckage and the invocation of force majeure, was left for later.

The deferring of compensation due for the quarter ending June 2023 was already coming up for discussion in February 2021.[68] The states were left in anxiety, unable to predict what would come next from Modi.

The 2020 lockdown itself had been coercively imposed on them by invoking the Disaster Management Act, which gave the Union the ability to exercise direct executive authority over the heads of the states. Modi sent teams to monitor and lecture states on what they should be doing, and made sure they understood that they had to come to heel. Partial 'unlocks' were offered to those states that would meet what the Union saw as good behaviour.

After three decades of coalitions and governments led by parties in a minority, India had become accustomed, wrongly, to the notion that cooperative federalism was baked into the polity. Modi provided a cold and harsh reminder that it was not. Power resided overwhelmingly with the Union government and in the hands of a man willing to exercise it freely and recklessly—this would be made manifestly clear to the chief ministers. With this power came no desire to assume responsibility. When the Supreme Court pointed out that the Disaster Management Act obliged the government to pay victims of the disaster, Modi said he had no money.[69]

The abolition of the Planning Commission by Modi had severed the political link that was present between the Union and the states. The Planning Commission was concerned with the development of states. Its replacement, the NITI Aayog operates as Modi's personal think-tank; there is no accountability and therefore it is free to do whatever takes its or, more precisely, Modi's fancy. It has sprung to the defence of Modi's most eccentric initiatives and provided some convoluted justifications for them. It has busied itself with producing clickbait lists—aspirational districts, innovation

---

[67] 'GST compensation: Centre to borrow Rs 1.1 lakh crore to meet shortfall', 15 October 2020, *Business Today*

[68] 'More run-ins likely over FY22 GST compensation', 10 February 2021, *Mint*

[69] 'Supreme Court pulls up government on COVID-19 ex gratia', 30 June 2021, *The Hindu*

index—and engaged in other meaningless and ultimately pointless exercises. Every so often it makes asinine statements.[70] NITI has no real relationship with the states, unlike the Planning Commission, with which they had, whether positively or negatively, as with chief minister Modi, robust engagement.

In 2015, the government accepted the recommendations made by the 14th Finance Commission set up by Manmohan Singh that states would get a 42 per cent share of Union-collected taxes, up from 32 per cent. This was celebrated as a great act of federalism. Modi wrote a letter to chief ministers: 'This naturally leaves far less money with the Central government. However, we have taken the recommendations of the 14th Finance Commission in a positive spirit, as they strengthen your hand in designing and implementing schemes according to your priorities and needs.'

What followed is instructive.

In the first year of the award, the actual share the states got fell from the promised 42 per cent to 34 per cent. By 2020, it fell further to 30 per cent,[71] below even the original 32 per cent, leave aside the aspired for 42 per cent.

Why was this?

Because the Union was consistently increasing its share of taxes through endless cesses and surcharges, from which states received no share because they were raised for specific Central causes: Swachh Bharat cess, Infrastructure cess, Health and Education cess, Agri Infra cess and so on. Money taken by the Union as cess, cutting out the states, quadrupled between 2014 and 2020.[72] The proportion of cess and surcharge collected as the Union's gross tax revenue doubled under Modi, leading to complaints from Opposition-led states.[73]

Having tossed aside what had been recommended and seemingly accepted previously, the 15th Finance Commission was given a mandate that was openly contemptuous of the states—it had phrases such as 'control or the lack of it in incurring expenditure on populist measures', referring to how states functioned. And it was clear that there was to be a reneging on Modi's previous acceptance of giving states a fairer share: the commission was asked

---

[70] 'Cards, ATMs, POS will be redundant by 2020 in India: Niti Aayog', 7 January 2017, PTI

[71] 'States likely to face crisis as govt pegs tax share at 30%', 2 February 2021, *Hindustan Times*

[72] 'Budget 2019: Cess a bit in excess, and other tax trends', 1 July 2019, *Bloomberg Quint*

[73] 'Centre imposing cess, surcharges to deny states: Amit Mitra', 6 February 2021, *The Economic Times*

to assess 'the impact on the fiscal situation of the Union Government of substantially enhanced tax devolution to States following recommendations of the 14th Finance Commission'.

Even with regard to internal security and law enforcement, the relationship that the Union has with the states has never been as strained as it has become under Modi.

The Union's misuse of agencies, especially the Enforcement Directorate and the Central Bureau of Investigation, against the Opposition and activists has become intolerable.

It has led Andhra Pradesh, Punjab, West Bengal, Rajasthan, Jharkhand, Maharashtra, Kerala, Chhattisgarh and Mizoram to withdraw their general consent for the CBI probing cases in their state.[74] The CBI manual says: 'The Central government can authorise CBI to investigate such a crime in a state but only with the consent of the concerned state government.'

This will affect internal security, but there is no point in blaming the states: it is manifest that Modi is misusing the authority in naked fashion. Former home secretary G.K. Pillai said the CBI 'has lost its credibility. The onus is on the Centre to take the states along and enhance their confidence in such central agency'.[75]

States worked out other ways in which to counter Modi's encroachment. They rebelled against the Union's appropriation of a subject squarely within their domain, agriculture, through the farm laws. Three states—Punjab, Rajasthan and Chhattisgarh—passed their own laws to neutralise the effect of the Union's legislation.

The most egregious assault on federalism through harsh governance came when farmers in Punjab protested and instituted a 'rail roko'. This is a common protest technique in the subcontinent, used widely including by the BJP itself when in the Opposition in Haryana,[76] Telangana,[77] Bihar,[78] and West Bengal.[79]

The Union's response to the protestors was to impose a blockade on

[74] 'Punjab becomes ninth state to revoke general consent for CBI probe', 9 November 2020, *News18*

[75] 'How rising Centre–state friction is chipping away at Modi's "cooperative federalism" mantra', 19 November 2020, *The Print.in*

[76] 'BJP-HJC to launch "rail roko" stir in Haryana', 20 March 2012, *Hindustan Times*

[77] 'Rail roko cripples train services in Telangana', 1 March 2011, PTI

[78] 'BJP's rail roko disrupts train services in Bihar', 28 February 2014, *The Hindu*

[79] 'BJP's Lok Sabha candidate Arjun Singh leads rail roko at Jagaddal station', 25 March 2019, UNI

Punjab in October 2020. The Union suspended trains when the farmer unions announced their agitation on 24 September and began to lie on railway tracks at 33 places in Punjab. But they lifted their dharna and cleared the tracks in all but three places by 22 October. They also said they would allow the passage of goods trains on all tracks.

The Railways restored goods train traffic for a couple of days before suspending them again on 24 October. The Union claimed this was because their trains had been stopped on 22 October, a charge denied by the farmers, who said activists from the largest farmers' union (BKU-Ugrahan) were squatting on only two private lines leading to the L&T Thermal Plant in Rajpura and Vedanta Thermal Plant at Talwandi Sabo. This was a symbolic protest against corporates and did not affect railway traffic on the main lines. Even this dharna was lifted, but that did not move Modi to resume rail services. The protestors said, with justification, that what was being done was to teach Punjab a lesson using the dharna as an excuse.

The rest of India may not have paid attention to what happened after this, just as most did not know what the Modi government had done to Nepal during the blockade of 2015. Within days, Punjab began to suffer.

On 6 November 2020, chief minister Captain Amarinder Singh said that 'the decision is obstructing movement of essential supplies not just in Punjab, which has run out of coal and power, storage for foodgrains and fertiliser, but also to other states, including the armed forces in Ladakh and Kashmir'.[80] By then, the state-owned thermal power plants at Bathinda, Ropar, Goindwal and Lehra Mohabbat had stopped producing electricity. The privately-owned stations Nabha Power in Rajpura and Talwandi Sabo in Mansa also shut. There were power cuts across the state. Punjab's government spent Rs 15 crore a day purchasing power from other sources to try and make up. The lifting of paddy and picked cotton was affected and the crop lay in the open in the absence of bags, which had been offloaded from trains and were therefore stuck.

Fertilisers that were to be used in the current season did not arrive. Of the expected 2.5 lakh tons of diammonium phosphate, only 56,000 tons came while the farmers were sowing wheat. Of the 10 lakh tons of urea, only 66,000 tons came.

The hosiery industry, reeling from the lockdown and trying to recover, was hit again. Its 2.3 lakh units employing 16 lakh workers struggled for

---

[80] 'Punjab struggles for essentials amid suspension of goods trains', 6 November 2020, *The Indian Express*

raw material, causing a loss of Rs 8,500 crore. Seasonal sales to places like Kashmir were lost, and festive season business was also wiped out, including for Diwali, which was on 14 November.

The steel industry suffered as well, with large plants shutting down in Ludhiana.

Meanwhile, the Union government ministers were calling Punjab's farmers naxals, leading Amarinder Singh to write to the BJP president, warning that what was being done had 'dangerous consequences not just for the state but the entire nation'.[81]

The Modi government lifted its rail blockade on 24 November, two months after it had begun. The farmers began their march to Delhi and Haryana, under the BJP, sealed its borders with Punjab. On 26 November, a mass general strike was called against the government, which was reported to be the largest in history.[82]

By 27 November, the farmers were at Singhu on the border of Delhi, and the response from the Modi government was again to blockade, this time digging trenches into highways and, later, also using spikes. The hostility to the protestors was not disguised and they were called Khalistanis and terrorists (more on this in the chapter 'The Devil's Wokshop'). There was no restraint from the government and no thought to the damage done to federalism when so attacking the protestors, the bulk of whom came from Punjab. The Modi government kept them on the road for months through the Delhi winter, taunting them from parliament as professional agitators ('andolanjeevi') and parasites ('parjeevi'). He claimed they were being instigated by external forces, coining the phrase 'Foreign Destructive Ideology'.[83]

There was absolutely no concession: it was 'my way' for Modi and the highway for the states and their farmers.

Modi thought nothing of putting his personal interest and that of his government above federalism and national unity. When the second wave of Covid crashed into India, and it became apparent that the vaccine plan— more accurately the lack of it—had failed, Modi dumped the problem on states (more on this in the chapter 'Mahabharat'). Having blundered in not

[81] '"Naxal-Backer In Photos Of Farmers": Nitin Gadkari Questions Protest', 15 December 2020, https://www.ndtv.com/india-news/farmers-protest-nitin-gadkari-raises-questions-says-person-backing-naxals-in-farm-protest-photos-2338815

[82] 'At least 25 crore workers participated in general strike; some states saw complete shutdown: Trade unions', 26 November 2020, *Deccan Herald*

[83] 'I am seeing a new jamaat, all andolanjivis are parasites: PM Modi', 9 February 2021, *The Times of India*

ordering enough vaccines or ensuring supply in advance, he shunted the problem and asked states to procure them instead. After a dressing down from the Supreme Court[84] and facing a rebellion from the states,[85] Modi was forced to reverse the Union's abdication of responsibility. It was only when there was external force and pushback in his later years as his loss of control became apparent that some of his damage on this front came to be healed.

---

[84] '"Arbitrary, irrational": SC on Centre's vaccination policy for 18–44 age group', 2 June 2021, *The Economic Times*

[85] 'Get vaccines, make them free for all: 12 parties, 4 Oppn CMs write to PM Modi', 13 May 2021, *The Indian Express*

8

THEIR LORDSHIPS

On 12 January 2018, four judges of the Supreme Court called a press conference to say that the justice system was being damaged by the Chief Justice of the Supreme Court, Dipak Misra. Their principal grouse appeared to be that 'sensitive' cases were being given by the Chief Justice to particular judges.[1]

A letter had also been sent to Misra by the four men, which outlined their case against him. They wrote that certain judicial orders had 'adversely affected' the functioning of the justice delivery system and the independence of the high courts besides impacting the administrative functioning of the Chief Justice of India's office. They said the Supreme Court was a century younger than the high courts of Calcutta, Bombay and Madras, and that its traditions, which had 'roots in Anglo-Saxon jurisprudence and practice', had been taken from these three courts.

One of these principles was that the Chief Justice was 'master of the roster'—meaning that he would decide which case would be sent to the court of which judge. However, the corollary was that he was only first among equals as a judge and had no arbitrary power to send cases to benches where they did not belong. The four judges wrote that 'any departure from the above two rules would not only lead to unpleasant and undesirable consequences of creating doubt in the body politic about the integrity of the institution. Not to talk about the chaos that would result from such departure.'

However, they said, the court under Chief Justice Misra had departed from tradition:

'We are sorry to say that of late the twin rules mentioned above have not been strictly adhered to. There have been instances where cases having

---

[1] 'India's top judges issue unprecedented warning over integrity of supreme court', 12 January 2018, *The Guardian*

far-reaching consequences for the nation and the institution had been assigned by the Chief Justice of this court selectively to the benches "of their preference" without any rationable basis for such assignment. This must be guarded against at all costs.'[2]

The four judges were Justices J. Chelameswar, Ranjan Gogoi, Madan Lokur and Kurian Joseph. They told the media that they had attempted and failed to persuade the Chief Justice to change his course and that they had no choice now but to address the nation directly given the gravity of their concerns.

The Chief Justice's power to assign cases is important because the judges of India's Supreme Court do not sit together as do the justices of the US's Supreme Court. In India, cases are heard in smaller benches—usually two judges and sometimes three. Allocation and assignment of cases thus becomes crucial.

Justice Chelameswar had previously heard a petition seeking an inquiry into corruption by Chief Justice Dipak Misra. He allocated it to a bench consisting of the senior-most judges of the Supreme Court, on the understanding that since the Chief Justice was himself involved, he could not allocate the matter on the administrative side.

Chief Justice Misra hurriedly assembled another five-judge bench headed by himself and including Justice Arun Mishra. This bench decided that the power to allocate cases resided with the chief justice alone, meaning he was claiming the arbitrary power that the four judges had warned him against appropriating.

It appeared that the immediate provocation was the decision by the Chief Justice to give the Justice Loya case to Justice Arun Mishra (about whom we shall hear more later in this chapter). PTI's report of the press conference included this paragraph: 'Asked what these issues were, he [Chelameshwar] said they included the "allocation of cases by CJI". The remarks assume significance as the Supreme Court today took up for consideration the issue of alleged mysterious death of special CBI judge B.H. Loya, who was hearing the sensitive Sohrabuddin Sheikh encounter case.'[3]

The four judges, having made a show of defiance, then went back to their regular duties. The press conference was the first indication Indians got that the Supreme Court, a hallowed institution, was no different from the rest of the polity, according to the judges themselves.

---

[2] 'The chief justice is only the first amongst the equals—nothing more or nothing less', 12 January 2018, *Scroll.in*

[3] 'Supreme Court crisis: All not okay, democracy at stake, say four senior-most judges', 18 January 2018, PTI

Justice B.H. Loya, who was then 48, died of an apparent heart attack in Nagpur, where he was visiting for a wedding. *The Caravan* published an investigative report in mid-2017, which indicated that some of the circumstances surrounding the death were dodgy. Even when other media houses, notably *The Indian Express*, revisited the case to show that the death was natural, some problems remained. For instance, the purported ECG test on Justice Loya was dated 30 November, the day before he was taken to hospital. And his family had received calls that he had died before the time of his official death. Justice Loya's phone was returned to his family only a couple of days after his death, and the data on it appeared to have been deleted.

The Caravan published a series of investigative pieces on the issue throughout the second half of 2017, including one in which the judge's family said he had been offered a bribe.[4] Justice Loya was one of three judges to hear the case, which was related to the murder of a suspect and his wife by the Gujarat Police. Amit Shah was one of the accused in the case.

According to a February 2015 report accessed for a story published in the newsmagazine *Outlook* in November 2017,[5] the first judge was transferred out of the case wrongly: 'During the CBI court's hearings that Utpat (the judge) presided over for this one year, or even after, court records suggest Amit Shah had never turned up even once—including on the final day of discharge. Shah's counsel apparently made oral submissions for exempting him from personal appearance on grounds ranging from him being "a diabetic and hence unable to move" to the more blase: "he is busy in Delhi".'

The *Outlook* report continued: 'On 6 June 2014, Utpat had made his displeasure known to Shah's counsel and, while allowing exemption for that day, ordered Shah's presence on June 20. But he didn't show up again. According to media reports, Utpat told Shah's counsel, "Every time you are seeking exemption without giving any reason."' Utpat, the story noted, 'fixed the next hearing for 26 June. But on 25th, he was transferred to Pune.'

This was in violation of a September 2012 Supreme Court order that the Sohrabuddin trial 'should be conducted from beginning to end by the same officer'.

After Utpat's transfer, the case was given to Justice Loya, who heard it from July to November, when he died. A third judge, Justice M.B. Gosavi, heard Amit Shah's discharge petition from 15 to 17 December and delivered a 75-page order on 30 December 2014, dropping the charges against Shah.

---

[4] 'Chief Justice Mohit Shah offered Rs 100 crore to my brother for a favourable judgment in the Sohrabuddin case: Late Judge Loya's sister', 21 November 2017

[5] 'The Amit Shah files', 16 February 2015, *Outlook*

On 19 April 2018, a bench headed by Chief Justice Dipak Misra rejected a probe into Justice Loya's death despite the problems thrown up by *The Caravan*'s reporting. The court said the death was from 'natural causes'. Justice Arun Mishra had earlier recused himself from the case.

The Omnipresent Justice Arun Mishra

On 22 February 2020, at an event where Modi was present, Justice Arun Mishra said: 'India is a responsible and most friendly member of the international community under the stewardship of internationally acclaimed visionary Prime Minister Shri Narendra Modi. We thank the versatile genius who thinks globally and acts locally—Shri Narendra Modi—for his inspiring speech which will act as a catalyst in initiating the deliberations and setting the agenda for the conference.'[6]

Justice Mishra's praise was in violation of the universally accepted Bangalore Principles of Judicial Conduct, which state that: 'A judge shall not only be free from inappropriate connections with, and influence by, the executive and legislative branches of government, but must also appear to a reasonable observer to be free therefrom.

'The behaviour and conduct of a judge must reaffirm the people's faith in the integrity of the judiciary. Justice must not merely be done but must also be seen to be done.'[7]

Justice Mishra was condemned by the Bar Association, which said, 'The Supreme Court Bar Association (SCBA) believes that any such statement reflects poorly on the independence of the judiciary and so calls upon the Honourable Judges not to make any statements in future nor show any proximity or closeness to the Executive, including Higher Functionaries.'[8]

Justice Mishra was made a judge of the Supreme Court on 7 July 2014, just after Modi was elected. There were many justices in the Supreme Court other than him. His influence came purely from the number of 'sensitive' cases he was allotted by the Chief Justice.[9]

On 13 October 2015, a bench of which Justice Mishra was a member,

[6] 'Modi a versatile genius who thinks globally and acts locally: Justice Arun Mishra', 22 February 2020, *The Hindu*

[7] www.un.org/ruleoflaw/files/Bangalore_principles.pdf

[8] 'SC Bar Association condemns Justice Mishra's open praise of PM', 26 February 2020, *The Hindu*

[9] 'Eight out of the eleven Constitution bench judgments of the Supreme Court in 2020 were delivered by benches headed by Justice Arun Mishra', 28 December 2020, BarandBench.com

dismissed a plea by former Indian Police Service officer Sanjiv Bhatt, an antagonist of Modi, who had been jailed, seeking a fair, credible and independent probe into the two FIRs lodged against him by the Gujarat state government. The court also rejected Bhatt's plea to make Amit Shah, who was home minister in Gujarat, a respondent to the case.[10]

Bhatt said he was present at a meeting on 27 February 2002 at Modi's home, when Modi had authorised reprisal attacks on Muslims following the Godhra train fire in which 57 Hindus were killed. Bhatt also submitted a series of emails between Tushar Mehta, who was then additional advocate general of Gujarat, and some of the accused in the riots, alleging that Mehta shared confidential information and legal documents with the accused against whom the state was conducting cases. The bench dismissed all of this. The judgement said Bhatt's claims were not credible because he had been in touch with Modi's political rivals and activists. Bhatt remained in jail, Mehta was made solicitor general of India by Modi.

On 11 January 2017, a bench headed by Justice Mishra dismissed a probe into a diary seized from the Aditya Birla group during an income tax raid, which appeared to show bribes paid to public servants. One entry said Rs 25 crore had been paid to Modi. The bench said such a probe could not be ordered only on the basis of documents.

On 8 May 2017, a bench headed by Justice Mishra said Lalu Yadav could be convicted in the fodder scam again, though some of the elements in the second offence were the same as in his first conviction. This did not amount to double jeopardy—barred under the Constitution—the bench found. Lalu, a foe of Modi's, remained in jail for another four years till he got bail in April 2021.

On 1 December 2017, a bench comprising of Justice Mishra dismissed a petition seeking a probe against Chief Justice Dipak Misra in a case where he was accused of corruption, and an FIR could not be filed by the petitioner because of SC guidelines.[11] The bench imposed costs of Rs 25 lakh on the petitioner, Campaign for Judicial Accountability and Reforms (convened by Prashant Bhushan), for filing a 'petition [that] is not only wholly frivolous, but contemptuous, unwarranted, aim[ed] at scandalising

[10] See, 'How Justice Arun Mishra rose to become the most influential judge in the Supreme Court', 1 September to 5 September 2020, a five-part series in *The Wire* by V. Venkatesan, and 'Justice Arun Mishra's controversial tenure leaves questions on public confidence in judiciary', 2 September 2020, LiveLaw.in
[11] 'The curious saga of how the chief justice of India handled two medical college cases', 2 February 2018, *TheWire.in*

the highest judicial system of the country, without any reasonable basis and filed in an irresponsible manner...'[12]

On 2 July 2018, Justice Mishra authored a judgment that dismissed a PIL questioning the appointments of K.V. Chowdary and T.M. Bhasin as chief vigilance commissioner and vigilance commissioner respectively on the contention that they failed to fulfil the criteria of 'institutional integrity'. Chowdary, as the head of the Central Board of Direct Taxes and advisor of the special investigation team on black money, had gone slow on the investigation into the Sahara–Birla papers and black money trails. The bench's judgement took no note of the facts, and observed: 'We are nowadays in the scenario that such complaints cannot be taken on face value. Even against very honest persons, allegations can be made. Those days have gone when filing of the complaints was taken as serious aspersions on integrity.'

On 20 April 2019, Justice Mishra appeared on a bench with Chief Justice Gogoi in a case where the latter himself was party (details of this below), being accused of sexual harassment. Chief Justice referred to the woman as a criminal.[13] The court's order did not refer to the CJI's name, though he was apparently heading the bench. The bench also entertained reckless allegations that the woman's accusation against the Chief Justice was a plot to destabilise the judiciary.

On 5 July 2019, a bench headed by Justice Mishra overturned a Gujarat High Court verdict which acquitted 12 men in the murder of former home minister and Modi rival Haren Pandya. The finding that the CBI investigation was 'botched up' was reversed. He also endorsed the CBI's finding that the murder was part of an 'international conspiracy' executed to 'spread terror amongst Hindus' to avenge the anti-Muslim Gujarat riots of 2002. The judgement came under severe criticism after it was reported that inconsistencies and improbabilities were ignored in the testimony of the sole eyewitness, which was relied on to reverse the acquittal.[14] It has been noted that Justice Mishra always ruled in favour of the government when it was an appellant.[15]

[12] 'Justice Arun Mishra & the Supreme Court's rule of whim', 5 September 2020, *Article-14.com*

[13] https://www.indiatoday.in/india/story/cji-led-supreme-court-bench-hold-unusual-hearing-on-matter-of-great-public-importance-1506092-2019-04-20

[14] See Prem Shankar Jha's analysis: 'The shadow of Haren Pandya's case lies long over Justice Arun Mishra', 30 August 2020, *TheWire.in*

[15] 'As judge, Arun Mishra was almost predictable when the state was before him', 3 September 2020, *TheWire.in*

On 14 August 2019, a bench headed by Justice Mishra declined to act on behalf of Kashmiris suffering under curfew and a total communications blockade that cut off landline and mobile phones and made even medical services inaccessible.[16] The bench said that 'no one is aware of the ground realities in Kashmir', and therefore it would not be proper to intervene. He made a show of support by adding 'we are with you (Kashmiris) on the issue of liberty with the people', while accepting the government position that normalcy would come in a few days.

On 16 August 2019, senior advocate Dushyant Dave wrote a letter to the Supreme Court's judges,[17] in which he repeated the accusation made by the four rebel judges: that cases dear to Modi were being given to a bench headed by Justice Mishra out of turn.

Dave said that Chief Justice Gogoi had surprised the legal fraternity by putting himself and Justice Mishra on the vacation benches for the summer of 2019 (when only a few judges work and senior judges are usually off), and then taking up and deciding cases of import.

Cases concerning the Adani group were taken up by Mishra without a regular bench ordering their hearing by a vacation bench, and without there being any urgency in the case.

One such case was heard and disposed of on 22 May. The next day, Justice Mishra took up another Adani case, which had last been heard in February 2017. Justice Mishra finished it off the next day. The benefit to Adani from these two cases, wrote Dave, would 'run into thousands of crores'.

Dave said that out-of-turn allotment to Justice Mishra and then quick judgements in Adani's favour had also happened on 29 January 2019 and 29 May 2018. Justice Mishra and Chief Justice Gogoi did not respond to this accusation or initiate any action. None of the other judges said anything. An investigation by journalists Abir Dasgupta and Paranjoy Guha Thakurta into seven Adani cases showed that Justice Mishra had always ruled in favour of Adani.[18]

On 27 August 2019, *The Wire*'s petition to quash the criminal defamation suit filed against it by Jay Shah, son of Amit Shah, for a story it had published on his business dealings, should have been heard by either Justice D.Y. Chandrachud or Justice A.M. Khanwilkar, who had been part of earlier hearings. Instead, it was listed before a bench comprising of Justice Mishra.

---

[16] 'Won't intervene in Kashmir for now: SC', 14 August 2019, *The Times of India*

[17] 'Why were Adani's cases listed and heard by Justice Arun Mishra in a tearing hurry?', 16 August 2019, *TheWire.in*

[18] 'Have Justice Arun Mishra's judgments helped Adani group', 7 August 2020, *NewsClick.in*

The publication withdrew its petition and said it would defend itself in trial court.

On 6 July 2020, a bench headed by Justice Mishra reversed a Delhi High Court order asking the National Investigation Agency (NIA) to produce its records on why activist Gautam Navlakha (charged under the draconian UAPA) was being sent from Delhi to Mumbai with 'inexplicable, frantic hurry'. Instead of following the high court order, the NIA—headed by Y.C. Modi, the man who had investigated the Haren Pandya case—went to the Supreme Court. The bench also expunged the remarks made against the NIA. Navlakha, an author, remained in jail.

On 10 August 2020, a petition filed by N. Ram, Arun Shourie and Prashant Bhushan challenging the constitutional validity of the Contempt of Courts Act was deleted from the cause list of Justices D.Y. Chandrachud and K.M. Joseph and listed instead before a bench comprising of Justice Mishra, who was already judging (and would go on to convict) Bhushan in another case of contempt. The three men withdrew their petition.

On 10 May 2019, just before the election results were declared, Justice Mishra's younger brother, Vishal, was made a judge of Madhya Pradesh High Court before he completed 45 years of age, the usual minimum age for such judicial appointments.[19] The high court collegium recommended him in September 2018 and the Supreme Court collegium of which Justice Arun Mishra was part cleared his name despite this apparent obstacle. The high court had recommended five names. The Supreme Court approved two, including Justice Vishal Mishra.

The resolution adopted by the Supreme Court collegium, comprising the then Chief Justice of India, Ranjan Gogoi, and Justices S.A. Bobde and N.V. Ramana, said: 'As far as age factor of Vishal Mishra is concerned, the collegium is fully satisfied with the justification given by the high court collegium while recommending his name.' (This justification was not actually revealed.)

Justice Arun Mishra was not part of the selection committee but, as No. 4 in the Supreme Court's hierarchy of judges at the time, he was part of the five-member collegium which recommends names for Supreme Court judges.

Born on 17 July 1974, Justice Vishal Mishra will retire in 2036. If elevated to the Supreme Court, he will retire in 2039. His young age means

---

[19] '#MoP: Age criterion for elevation to High Courts from Bar? Collegium says 45 to 55', 26 March 2017, BarandBench.com

he is likely to not only become chief justice of India if elevated, but will have a long tenure in that position.

Justice Vishal Mishra, in a Facebook post on 12 October 2013, said the Nehru–Gandhis were Muslims and this was why the 'Gandhi family hates Hindus'.[20] He later deleted this post.

After his retirement, Justice Mishra did not leave his official bungalow for eight months.[21] In June 2021, he got his sinecure, a three-year term as the chairman of the National Human Rights Commission (NHRC). He was the first non-chief justice appointed to the position after a change Modi made in the rules in 2019.[22]

The Saga of Chief Justice Ranjan Gogoi

On 19 April 2019, all the judges of the Supreme Court received an affidavit from a court employee. The 35-year-old woman, who had been an assistant to Chief Justice Gogoi from October 2016 to October 2018, had been fired by him, she says, after she rebuffed his sexual advances.

At the same time, incredibly her husband and his brother, employees of Delhi Police, had also been suspended by the body, which is headed by Amit Shah. Another brother-in-law of hers, who had been appointed a court attendant through Chief Justice Gogoi's discretionary quota on 10 October 2018, was also dismissed without reason.

The woman was then arrested in March 2019, three months after her dismissal, and jailed.

The woman had been employed for some time with another judge, and was sent to assist the CJI in October 2016, having received appraisal reports rated 'good' and 'very good' for the years 2014–15 and 2015–16 respectively. Chief Justice Gogoi reportedly asked her to prepare case briefs, not usually a responsibility given to a junior court assistant, which she was. She said she acted as his assistant, from noting his instructions to allegedly preparing a 'Hindi film song list' for him.[23]

[20] 'How Justice Arun Mishra rose to become the most influential judge in the Supreme Court', 1 September 2020, TheWire.in
[21] 'Ex-SC judge Arun Mishra still to vacate bungalow', 27 April 2021, The Times of India
[22] 'Justice Arun Mishra is new NHRC chief: First non-CJI to hold post; ex-SC judge had called Modi "versatile genius"', 2 June 2021, firstpost.com
[23] All the material here and in the following pages pertaining to this incident is taken from the reports '"CJI Ranjan Gogoi sexually harassed me": Former Supreme Court employee, SC Secretary General's office denies allegations', 20 April 2019, The Leaflet, and 'Former Supreme Court employee alleges sexual harassment by Chief Justice Gogoi', 22 April 2019, TheWire.in

Chief Justice Gogoi reportedly invited her to attend the launch of a book by Nobel Prize-winner Kailash Satyarthi in June 2018, where the CJI was to speak. The woman expressed her reluctance as her LLB final semester exam was the same day, but Gogoi insisted: '…he told me that there would be a lot of important people, that I should get out of my comfort zone of the court and be a bit more social… On his insistence, I could not refuse and so me and my husband attended the event after finishing giving my exam,' she wrote in her affidavit.

Chief Justice Gogoi allegedly would call and text her multiple times during the day for work, during non-court hours and even late in the evening, when she was at home. In August 2018, he reportedly wanted to appoint her to the office in his residence. The excuse was that he would have more work on taking over as Chief Justice in October. He met her immediate boss at the library section, B.A. Rao, to inform him about her imminent transfer. She began working at the CJI's residence from 11 August 2018. Chief Justice Gogoi allegedly asked her to wish him 'Good Morning' over WhatsApp every morning, and send him a text once she reached home every evening. He would allegedly call her on WhatsApp to discuss matters unrelated to work. 'Several times,' she said, 'he would call me into his office room, make me show him my phone and make me delete the WhatsApp messages between us.'

The woman was invited to attend Chief Justice Gogoi's swearing-in ceremony on 3 October 2018. He allegedly told her she was only the third person he had invited, after his wife and mother. Both she and her husband attended the event. Her brother-in-law, who is disabled, was given the appointment letter on 9 October. The CJI allegedly told the woman he had authorised the appointment despite the man not clearing a medical test.

After this, the woman said, Chief Justice Gogoi behaved inappropriately with her. She wrote:

'Though I usually wear a uniform of black and white clothing, on that day since it was the first day of Navratri, I had worn an orange kurta and dupatta. The CJI referring to my clothes, told me, "You are looking pretty good today." The CJI asked me to come and stand next to him, he got up from his chair. The CJI then asked me, "What can you do for me?", I kept repeating that I was very grateful and that everybody in my family was very happy. The CJI then slid his hand from the back of my head, along my back to my hipline, till my lower back. I immediately froze and my body stiffened. I think the CJI sensed this, and so he immediately pulled both my cheeks, like one would do to a child. He told me that he is like this with his daughter too.'

The next day, the CJI allegedly again brought up the topic of her brother-in-law's appointment and fondled her. He kept asking her to write down what she would do for him, what she would not disclose and so on, and then make her show him what she had written: 'I was so scared and shocked that I wrote whatever he dictated.' That evening, she said she received calls from the Supreme Court administration department asking if things were fine between her and her husband. Her neighbours said the police colony she was living in received a call from the police station near the Supreme Court asking the same thing. The colony's president, a policeman himself, told reporters that he had received the call; he said he had told the caller that the couple were not fighting.

The woman then reportedly phoned the CJI to say she did not want to work in his office any longer. She said she was told by another of Gogoi's assistants not to disturb the Chief Justice at night. After this, she was transferred three times in a month—on 22 October 2018 to the Centre for Research and Planning, then to the Administration Material Section, and finally to the court's library on 22 November. On 19 November, she was told a disciplinary inquiry was being initiated against her.

Three charges were listed. She was accused of showing reluctance and 'questioning the decision' of where she was seated. She was also accused of trying to 'bring influence' from 'unacceptable quarters' to exert pressure on her supervisors who moved her around. Thirdly, she was told that she had 'unauthorisedly absented herself from duty' on 17 November and had showed 'insubordination, indiscipline and lack of devotion to duty'.

Her request for a defence assistant in the inquiry was refused. On 21 December, she was dismissed from service by registrar Deepak Jain after the inquiry committee conducted ex parte (without her presence) proceedings and found her 'guilty' on all three charges. A week after she was dismissed, her husband and his brother—both constables with the Delhi Police—were suspended from service. The reason was not specified. The husband called the Chief Justice assistant to apologise, but his calls were reportedly ignored.

On 9 January, an order from a deputy commissioner of police stated that the husband and his brother were suspended because they had 'links with local gamblers' and that he had 'allowed satta (gambling) activities of one person against whom a criminal case had already been registered'. After being suspended, the two men were also transferred and an inquiry opened against them.

On the night of 11 January 2019, the head of the police station near the

Supreme Court took the couple to the Chief Justice. He was unavailable, but the CJI's wife allegedly told the woman: 'In the presence of the SHO and Mr. Deepak Jain, Mrs. Gogoi told me "*naak ragad ke jao*" (rub your nose on the ground).'

A copy of a surreptitiously recorded video showing a conversation between SHO Naresh Solanki, the woman and her husband was with *The Wire*. The video showed Solanki trying to convince her to meet the CJI for a compromise and seek forgiveness.

The other brother-in-law, whom Chief Justice Gogoi had appointed, was also now dismissed. His termination letter did not give any reason. On 8 March 2019, when she was in Rajasthan at her in-laws' house, a Delhi Police party arrived to arrest her. The FIR against her said she had taken Rs 50,000 to get someone a job in the Supreme Court. Her husband and her sister-in-law were also detained by the police. She was allegedly mocked by the police chief at the station, who asked her why only she had been summoned and had gone to the Chief Justice's room at home.

On 12 March, the woman received bail, but the case was moved to the Crime Branch which opposed the bail, saying the woman was threatening the complainant. Police refused to say why there was no case against the complainant (who admitted to having paid a bribe). The case was with the Crime Branch, which did not act against the alleged bribe-giver, a 31-year-old man who was also the complainant. After her arrest, the woman wrote to the judges asking for justice.

When *The Wire* wrote to the Chief Justice seeking his response to the woman's allegations, it received an email from a court official at 3.37 a.m. on Saturday, 20 April 2019. It read: 'The allegations regarding 11 October 2018, as well as other allegations as can be discerned from your emails, are completely and absolutely false and scurrilous and are totally denied.'

The woman was 'dismissed from service as per procedure', the mail said, though it did not explain why ex parte inquiry proceedings were conducted against her. The brother-in-law was terminated as his 'performance and conduct' were unsatisfactory.

'It appears that these false allegations are being made as a pressure tactic to somehow come out of the various proceedings which have been initiated in law, against her and her family, for their own wrong doings. It is also very possible that there are mischievous forces behind all this, with an intention to malign the institution,' the email said.

Initially, only four publications reported the affidavit and what it contained—*Scroll.in*,[24] *The Caravan*,[25] *TheLeaflet.in*[26] and *TheWire.in*. Observe the names. None of India's newspapers touched this story. The Godi media manifests itself through acts of omission as well as commission. The mainstream media was terrified and chose to stay away. The same day, Saturday, the Supreme Court listed a 'MATTER OF GREAT PUBLIC IMPORTANCE TOUCHING UPON THE INDEPENDENCE OF JUDICIARY'. There was no case here, only an allegation, and it was unclear what the bench was sitting in judgement over.[27]

The court passed a sort of order: 'Having considered the matter, we refrain from passing any judicial order at this moment leaving it to the wisdom of the media to show restraint, act responsibly as is expected from them and accordingly decide what should or should not be published as wild and scandalous allegations undermine and irreparably damage reputation and negate independence of judiciary. We would therefore at this juncture leave it to the media to take off such material which is undesirable.'[28]

The Supreme Court Bar Association president Dushyant Dave said, 'The chief justice had done great disservice to himself and the Supreme Court in presiding over a bench to hear a non-existent matter and to scotch the allegations, against himself, even if false. What is more sad is that the learned attorney general and solicitor general did not advise him correctly and joined in this rather unfortunate turn of events.'[29]

On 6 May 2019, the Supreme Court announced that an inquiry panel that had examined the allegations of sexual harassment found no substance in them. The findings were not made public. The complainant had withdrawn from the process on 30 April, giving the following reasons:

'1. I have not been allowed to have the presence of my lawyer/support

---

[24] 'Chief Justice of India sexually harassed me, says former SC staffer in affidavit to 22 judges', 20 April 2020, *Scroll.in*

[25] 'Supreme charge: "I have been victimised for resisting and refusing the unwanted sexual advances of the CJI Ranjan Gogoi": Former Supreme Court employee', 20 April 2020, *The Caravan*

[26] '"CJI Ranjan Gogoi sexually harassed me": Former Supreme Court employee, SC Secretary General's office denies allegations', 20 April 2020, *TheLeaflet.in*

[27] 'Supreme Court—Daily Orders In Re: Matter Of Great Public … vs Unknown on 20 April, 2019', https://indiankanoon.org/doc/66031978/

[28] 'The bizarre order in the sexual harassment allegations against CJI Ranjan Gogoi', 20 April 2020, *BarandBench.com*

[29] 'Chief Justice says sexual harassment charge part of "bigger plot" to "deactivate" him', 20 April 2020, *TheWire.in*

person despite my impaired hearing, nervousness and fear. 2. There being no video or audio recording of the Committee proceedings. 3. I have not been supplied even a copy of my statement as recorded on 26th and 29th April 2019. I was not informed about the procedure this committee is following.'

She said there was no external person on the committee despite it being mandatory in cases of sexual harassment, according to the Sexual Harassment of Women at Workplace (Prevention, Prohibition and Redressal) Act 2013. The judges who were on the panel examining the issue were all reporting to Chief Justice Gogoi, the man accused. There could be no fair hearing in these circumstances. She was told by the judges on the first day, 'We are not here as a sexual harassment committee, it is not a departmental proceeding and it is not even an in-house proceeding. We are here just to work on your complaint.' It was very informal, she said, and they told her, 'We can assure you no harm will come to you in your future.' Justice Bobde, who would later become chief justice, allegedly said to her: 'You know, you will get your job back.'[30]

On 17 November 2019, Chief Justice Gogoi retired. He had only eight days earlier delivered the Babri judgement. On 14 November, Chief Justice Gogoi refused to order a probe into a case the Modi government did not want pursued.[31]

On 22 January 2020, the woman was reinstated by the Supreme Court without explanation.[32] If indeed the accusations against the CJI were false, why had she been brought back? It was not said. It was revealed that the case against her had also been withdrawn after the complainant refused to show up.[33]

On 30 October 2019, two weeks before he was to retire, Gauhati High Court 'resolved' to give permanent post-retirement benefits to Chief Justice Gogoi, including a private secretary, two peons, a car and driver, and an officer to coordinate. On 17 March 2020, the government announced it was sending him to the Rajya Sabha. Dushyant Dave said: 'This is totally disgusting,

---

[30] '"I've lost everything. Financially, mentally, everything," says ex-SC staffer in CJI case', 9 May 2019, *Scroll.in*

[31] 'Supreme Court dismisses Rafale review petition seeking criminal probe in fighter jet deal', 14 November 2019, *India Today*

[32] 'SC reinstates woman employee who levelled charges at ex-CJI', 22 January 2020, *The Indian Express*

[33] 'Delhi Police set to close cheating case against former SC employee', 8 September 2019, *The Indian Express*

a clear reward in quid pro quo. The semblance of independence of the judiciary is totally destroyed.'[34]

Former Justice A.P. Shah said, 'The message it sends to the judiciary as a whole is that if you give judgments that are favourable to the executive, you will be rewarded. If you don't do so, you will be treated adversely or you might be transferred or not considered for elevation.'[35]

On 15 January 2021, the former CJI was given discretionary work.[36] He was appointed sole arbitrator in a case referred to the Mumbai Centre for International Arbitration (MCIA). On 23 January 2021, it was reported that he has been given Z+ security, 'covered by a special VIP force' under the control of Amit Shah.[37] On accepting the Rajya Sabha nomination from Modi, former Chief Justice Gogoi said: 'My presence in parliament will be an opportunity to project the views of the judiciary before the legislature and vice versa.' This turned out not to be true: one year after he came to parliament he had not participated in a single debate.[38]

Nobody in government and nobody in the Supreme Court, including all its judges, did a thing in this tawdry matter. The media, as we have noted, was afraid to take it up. The matter was allowed to slide as if nothing had happened. From being an accused to appearing as judge in his own cause, to an inquiry which wasn't really an inquiry, which found for the accused but reinstated the complainant, the dropping of charges, the arbitrary and vengeful arrests and suspension of family members, the complicity of the Delhi Police in this, the nomination to the Rajya Sabha, the cases settled in the government's favour before that—all of this was normal in Modi's India.

The Rafale Reprieve

In March 2015, Modi undid a previous deal under the Manmohan Singh government to purchase 126 Rafale fighter jets. Under Modi's deal (which he struck himself), India would instead buy 36 jets and Anil Ambani's Reliance Aerostructure Limited, and not the State-owned Hindustan Aeronautics Ltd,

---

[34] 'In unprecedented move, Modi government sends former CJI Ranjan Gogoi to Rajya Sabha', 17 March 2020, *TheWire.in*

[35] '"Death knell for power separation": Retired judge on Ranjan Gogoi's new role', 17 March 2020, *NDTV*

[36] 'Supreme Court refers two cases to Mumbai Centre for International Arbitration; Ranjan Gogoi J appointed sole arbitrator in one dispute', 15 January 2021, BarandBench.com

[37] 'Ex-CJI Gogoi gets "Z+" VIP security cover', 23 January 2021, The *Indian Express*

[38] 'Sealed cover MP: The silence of parliamentarian Ranjan Gogoi', 20 March 2021, *TheWire.in*

was selected as the Indian Offset Partner. France would not offer a sovereign guarantee to India on the deal, and its leader, Francois Hollande, said Ambani had been inserted into the deal by Modi.[39] The new deal was challenged in court by litigants who alleged that it was filled with irregularities on the decision-making process, including the price difference between the first and second deals and the selection of Ambani's firm as an offset partner.

On 14 December 2018, the Supreme Court under Chief Justice Gogoi delivered its judgement and held that the deal did not suffer from any apparent irregularities. It dismissed the prayer for ordering the CBI to file an FIR and conduct an investigation into the deal. It said that the court had a limited degree of judicial scrutiny over defence contracts. And in any case, 'the pricing details have, however, been shared with the Comptroller and Auditor General, and the report of the CAG has been examined by the Public Accounts Committee'. This was factually incorrect—it had not happened.

This judgement was challenged by lawyer Prashant Bhushan and former BJP ministers Yashwant Sinha and Arun Shourie. They said the judgement had 'errors apparent on the face of the record'. For instance, it did not deal with the primary prayer of the petitioners, that of a filing of an FIR in the case. This challenge was also dismissed by a bench, again under the CJI. The court admitted it had made a factual error regarding its observation about the CAG but felt that it had not been misled by the Modi government. (More on Rafale in the chapter 'Transparency'.)

On Kashmir, an Abdication

On 5 August 2019, the Modi government 'de-operationalised' the special constitutional provisions of Jammu and Kashmir, removed its status as a state and broke it up (see the 'Final Solution' chapter for more details). Political leaders, civil society figures and even businessmen were picked up and jailed arbitrarily in the wake of this move. They were locked up under the Public Safety Act, which the Supreme Court itself had in the past called a 'lawless law' because it allows people to be held without a crime or trial. More than 600 habeas corpus petitions were filed by Kashmiris, but fewer than 1 per cent were decided by the Jammu and Kashmir High Court.[40] Habeas corpus petitions require the State to produce prisoners before courts to determine whether

---

[39] 'Indian govt suggested Reliance as partner in Rafale deal, Hollande tells French website', 22 September 2018, *TheWire.in*

[40] 'A year when courts failed to hear petitions and left jailed Kashmiris at the mercy of the government', 2 August 2020, *Scroll.in*

or not the detention is lawful. They are required to be heard with urgency. And yet the Supreme Court did not decide on the Kashmiri habeas corpus petitions, including those from former chief minister Mehbooba Mufti (whose matter kept being deferred by a bench headed by Justice Arun Mishra), till the end.

Kashmiris were also denied the internet, in an act of collective punishment. The Supreme Court gave the Modi government a pass on this matter too. Bizarrely, the same court also later said the internet was a 'fundamental right'.[41] It asked the government to allow internet access to Kashmiris, but had no problem with its order being repeatedly flouted and the 'fundamental right' of India's citizens being deliberately violated by the State.

The court did not take up the challenge to the constitutionality of the Article 370 move with any sense of urgency, giving it no priority and not hearing it regularly. An RTI revealed that, as of February 2021, there were 54 pending habeas corpus petitions in the Supreme Court, of which one was 16 years old.[42] The habeas is one of the most important checks on State power and, by ignoring these petitions, several Indians have been permitted to be detained without charge or trial for indeterminate periods.

A Free Hand on PM CARES

The court also did not intervene in the matter of the PM CARES fund. The prime minister has no obligation to transfer the money to the National Disaster Response Fund, which is subject to an audit by the CAG. The PM CARES account would not be similarly audited and the court dismissed petitions that Modi be compelled to do so.[43]

It dismissed another plea the following month that said the fund violated the Disaster Management Act. A few months later, the problems with allowing Modi to do as he pleased with the money came to light through reports which showed inconsistencies in the basic set-up of the fund and the total opacity under which it functioned.[44]

---

[41] 'Access to internet is a fundamental right, rules Supreme Court', 10 January 2020, *The Hindu Businessline*

[42] '58 Habeas Corpus petitions pending before Supreme Court, oldest is from 2005: RTI response', 22 February 2021, *BarandBench.com*

[43] 'Funds from PM-CARES needn't be transferred, Supreme Court rejects request', 18 August 2020, *NDTV*

[44] 'PM-CARES "controlled by government" but RTI doesn't apply: new flip-flop', 25 December 2020, *NDTV*

Forcing Aadhaar Down India's Throat

In the case of linking Aadhaar with SIM cards, which was opposed by several groups as a violation of fundamental rights on several grounds, the Supreme Court dithered for six years, allowing the Modi government to pretend it was voluntary while it used that time to ensure that ultimately it was, in fact, mandatory. This is how the sequence of events unfolded:[45]

In 2015, the court issued an order saying Aadhaar could not be made mandatory till it ruled on the fundamental rights challenge.

In 2016, the Aadhaar Act was passed, but it focused on subsidies and welfare and did not cover phone connections.

In February 2017, the court ordered the government to verify and register every SIM card in the country, but it did not require this to be done by linking them with Aadhaar.

Despite this, the Modi government spread the message that the Supreme Court had made linking Aadhaar to your SIM card mandatory, a false claim.[46]

The confusion was deliberate and has resulted in authorities insisting on Aadhaar for various services, including for the Covid vaccine.[47] The State in India has a powerful tool for mass surveillance, possessing the biometric details of individuals, including retinal scans, with no checks or safeguards in place.[48] And it has tormented India's poor, denying them their entitlements while the judiciary continues to pretend it is still 'not mandatory'.[49]

Locking Down the Poor

The Supreme Court's neglect of protecting citizens' fundamental rights showed in the manner in which migrants who had hit the road during the 2020 lockdown were treated. The court accepted the demonstrable lie of the government, that there was 'no migrant person walking on the road', a statement by solicitor general Tushar Mehta on 31 March 2020, while every

---

[45] 'At the very end of SC's Aadhaar hearings, government admits it has been dishonest all along', 26 April 2018, *Scroll.in*

[46] Ibid

[47] 'For Covid-19 vaccine Aadhaar is mandatory even if registration on CoWin done with other ID. Sort of', 21 May 2021, *India Today*

[48] 'Aadhaar is mass surveillance system, will lead to civil death for Indians: Edward Snowden', 20 August 2018, *India Today*

[49] 'Denial of ration due to non-linking of Aadhaar: Supreme Court seeks response from govt', 18 March 2021, *The Financial Express*

day there were reports showing that there were hundreds of thousands on the road with their children.

The court said on that day that 'the migration of large number of labourers working in the cities was triggered by panic created by fake news that the lockdown would continue for more than three months. Such panic driven migration has caused untold suffering to those who believed and acted on such news. In fact, some have lost their lives in the process'. The Chief Justice, S.A. Bobde, said of the migrants that 'if they are being provided meals, then why do they need money for meals?'[50]

And then when it was pressed for relief, the court said it was impossible for it to do anything in this matter. It accepted the Modi government's claim that it had given transportation to migrants, but they had declined it and were choosing to walk instead.[51]

On 26 May, it said that 'the newspaper reports and the media reports have been continuously showing the unfortunate and miserable conditions of the migrant labourers walking on-foot and cycles from long distances'.[52] But it did nothing. The lockdown took 989 lives, probably more.[53]

The court's other failure towards workers was on the issue of their wages. After ordering the lockdown, the government instructed all employers to pay their workers wages, on the due date and without any deduction, for the period that they had been under closure. In May, this order was withdrawn after 54 days, which was the length of time for which salaries would now have to be paid. This was challenged in the Supreme Court. The court decided against the workers by subterfuge. First, it stayed any coercive action against employers for not paying wages. Then it delayed hearing the case, and then on 12 June it gave the absurd direction that workers and their employers should 'negotiate' with each other to figure this out among themselves. After this, it did not hear the case further.

The Jurisprudence of the Sealed Cover

Along with the preference of one judge to handle 'sensitive' cases, the other innovation the Supreme Court has introduced in the Modi years is the

---

[50] 'My lord, migrant labourers need more than just food, just like we all do', 9 April 2020, *ThePrint.in*

[51] 'Can't monitor or stop migrant workers walking on roads, says Supreme Court', 15 May 2020, PTI

[52] 'Supreme Court takes note of migrant workers' problems, asks govts to respond on steps taken', 26 May 2020, *TheWire.in*

[53] 'India's manufactured amnesia over its Covid-19 lockdown deaths', 23 March 2021, *Article-14.com*

jurisprudence of the sealed cover. Essentially, this is submission by the State of evidence and material it is obliged to give the court but does not want in the public domain. The court wants to play its role but is mindful of what the Modi government wants. The sealed cover is a compromise, eliminating transparency from the judicial process.

On 19 January 2018, the Supreme Court asked the Modi government to give 'in a sealed cover' the names and details of those who had defaulted on loans of over Rs 500 crore. The Modi government had not wanted the names revealed to the public, saying it would affect the 'economic interest' of the country.[54]

On 16 August 2018, Justice Gogoi (who was then not yet chief justice) asked the officer leading Assam's NRC to hand over 'in a sealed cover' a list of the people excluded from citizenship.[55] The draft had left out over 41 lakh people, including a former chief minister. Justice Gogoi, Assamese himself, said that the exclusions did not matter. He would also push the state to jail those excluded. He refused to recuse himself from the case.

On 10 October 2018, Chief Justice Gogoi asked for information on the Rafale fighter jet deal's pricing to be given to the court 'in a sealed cover'.[56] This was in response to four public interest litigations alleging corruption given the difference in pricing between the first deal, signed by the UPA for 126 jets, and the one struck personally by Modi for 36.

On 16 November 2018, the Central Vigilance Commission (CVC) submitted, as it had been ordered to, 'in a sealed cover', details of a case involving a CBI director the Modi government wanted pushed out.[57] Chief Justice Gogoi observed, 'The report is very complimentary, not so complimentary and very uncomplimentary towards CBI Director Alok Verma. CVC has said in its report that some charges need further probe.' With this opacity, a man who was said to be on the verge of filing an FIR in the Rafale case was shunted out.

On 12 April 2019, Chief Justice Gogoi asked political parties to submit the details of their donations received through electoral bonds 'in a sealed cover'.[58]

---

[54] 'Over Rs 500 cr defaults: SC gets loan defaulters' names, in a sealed cover', 18 April 2018, *The Indian Express*

[55] 'Supreme Court asks NRC coordinator to submit detailed report on those excluded from draft list', 16 August 2018, *Scroll.in*

[56] 'Rafale deal: SC asks Centre to submit in a sealed cover details of decision-making process', 10 October 2018, *The Hindu*

[57] 'CBI director Alok Verma should be given CVC report in a sealed cover: SC', 16 November 2018, *The Hindu*

[58] 'Give info to ECI on each donor, each electoral bond in sealed covers: SC orders political parties', 12 April 2019, *The Hindu*

The court was hearing an application from the Association of Democratic Reforms, which said that the anonymity of the electoral bonds scheme, introduced by Modi, would lead to corruption and influence by corporates on India's democracy because of the lack of transparency in who was giving money to which party. To this, the Modi government said that this was not the concern of citizens.[59] When he was hearing the case, the CJI said the electoral bonds matter was 'a weighty issue which would require an in-depth hearing'. After he was made a Rajya Sabha MP by the Modi government, he said, 'Electoral bond issue, I do not remember, frankly.'[60]

On 15 April 2019, Chief Justice Gogoi asked the Election Commission (EC) to watch a hagiography of Modi (called *PM Narendra Modi*, with Vivek Oberoi playing Modi) and submit its report 'in a sealed cover' on whether the film violated the norms of the general election that was taking place.[61] Even on such a banal matter, the Supreme Court was wary of offending Modi.

On 21 August 2019, it was reported that the findings on the 'conspiracy' to undermine the judiciary through the sexual harassment allegation against Chief Justice Gogoi would be submitted 'in a sealed cover'.[62]

Justice Patnaik submitted a detailed 40-page report on his investigation into allegations of a 'larger conspiracy hatched by a powerful lobby of fixers, disgruntled apex court employees and corporate figures to compromise the functioning of the highest judiciary'. The court refused to make this report public.[63]

While sitting in judgement on the case along with the accused CJI, Justice Mishra had said: 'The day has come to tell the rich and mighty that they cannot run the SC. They are playing with fire', and also, 'What's going on in this country? People in this country should know the truth' behind what he said was the 'wider conspiracy'.

But when the report was submitted, it was in fact not taken in for hearing, Justice Patnaik said, '…because the court was busy with the Ayodhya issue.

[59] 'It is not a voter's concern where political parties' money comes from, attorney general tells SC', 11 April 2019, *TheWire.in*

[60] 'Don't remember electoral bonds case, says Rajya Sabha MP & former CJI Ranjan Gogoi', 22 March 2020, *ThePrint.in*

[61] 'Biopic on PM Modi: SC directs EC to watch full movie, submit decision in sealed cover', 15 April 2019, PTI

[62] 'Justice Patnaik completes probe into larger conspiracy against CJI Ranjan Gogoi, report likely in September', 21 August 2019, *India Today*

[63] 'Supreme Court refuses to disclose Justice Patnaik's probe report on "larger conspiracy" against judiciary under RTI', 18 March 2021, LiveLaw.in

It will be taken up for hearing in open court shortly.' It was not and there was no pressure on the court to make it public.

Anything Modi had an interest in or would reflect on the government was kept hidden from the public. The Supreme Court appointed a committee to examine the three farm laws Modi passed first through fiat and then legislation in 2020—their findings came in a 'sealed cover'.[64] Why was material that was mere opinion to be kept secret was not explained, but it did not need to be. When the shortselling firm Hindenburg's allegations of fraud against the Adani group crashed the group's stock prices, the Supreme Court, this time under Chief Justice D.Y. Chandrachud, asked for a committee to submit a report in a sealed cover.[65]

Sealed cover jurisprudence has led to not just a lack of transparency but also to errors, given that the other side cannot refute what the government is claiming.[66] Another mistake, discussed in a later chapter, was in the court's accepting of a government lie on the issue of corruption in the purchase of Rafale aircraft. Bizarrely, the Supreme Court said that it disapproved of the sealed cover practice that it had begun itself, saying that it was 'against fair trial'.[67] This observation came from a bench that did not include Justices Gogoi or Mishra.

Under Modi, the Supreme Court has become an executive court, as described by the lawyer Gautam Bhatia—an extension of the Modi administration rather than the guardian of the Constitution focussed on fundamental rights and civil liberties. It became a court that 'speaks the language of the executive, and has become indistinguishable from the executive'.[68]

In the case of the NRC, the court actually took over the process of taking away citizenship, the right that confers other rights.

Under Justice Gogoi, after the state coordinator of the NRC in Assam gave his report 'in a sealed cover', the court itself began to direct the

[64] 'Supreme Court-appointed panel submits report on farm laws in sealed cover', 31 March 2021, *India Today*

[65] 'Supreme Court forms expert panel to probe any regulatory failure on Adani issue', 2 March 2023, *The Hindu*

[66] 'In denying bail to Chidambaram, Delhi HC mixes up facts from 2017 money laundering case', 17 November 2019, *ThePrint.in*

[67] 'SC frowns on HC judge for "sealed cover jurisprudence"', 5 December 2019, *The Times of India*

[68] 'Mouse Under the Throne: The Judicial Legacy of Sharad A. Bobde', 24 April 2021, *TheWire.in*. Also see, 'A Constitutionalism without the Court', 1 August 2020, indconlawphil.wordpress.com

implementation of the NRC. On 17 December 2014, the court gave a timetable of completion, circling January 2016 for the first draft. The court also approved a new form of verification of citizenship called the 'Family Tree'.

Individuals would have to show not only their own documents but specific ones of their ancestors. In the words of Prateek Hajela, the NRC coordinator: 'People had to submit manually their family trees, which included their ancestors whose legacy data they would quote in their application. We would then match the digitized family tree record with the manual one in case of any discrepancy.'[69] Unsurprisingly, large numbers of people were left out in the draft NRC, putting them through severe trauma.

The draft NRC of July 2018 left out 40 lakh individuals, after which the court gave 60 days to process the objections of those excluded.

In implementing the NRC, the Supreme Court turned itself into part of the executive. Bhatia wrote that 'it had done so in secrecy, through a jurisprudence of "sealed covers" and "confidential reports", where even the government is not kept in the loop (let alone affected parties). Not only is the court—as a matter of expertise—not suited to doing this, but also, it deprives the individual of a vital, constitutional remedy. Where is the individual to go if she wants to challenge the contents of the reports filed in sealed cover? And which body can she approach to ask that the content of the "confidential reports"—that may ultimately subject her to deportation—be made public and subject to challenge? An exercise in which the court decides—in secret consultation with the State Coordinator—makes a mockery of both open justice, and judicial review. The executive court has set itself up as the first and final tribunal, without appeal or recourse.'[70]

The lack of transparency carried through in other matters concerning the highest levels of the judiciary. The chief minister of Andhra Pradesh alleged that the children of a judge who was in line to become the next chief justice of India had conspired to make a fortune on land. This had to do with the making of the new capital city of Amravati, whose exact location only a few who were privy to the plans knew. These individuals included the daughters of Justice N.V. Ramana, and were named in an FIR.[71] On 15 September 2020, the Andhra Pradesh High Court stayed the investigation into the case, and also told the media it was forbidden from reporting on the case. The following month, chief minister Jaganmohan Reddy wrote to the Chief Justice

---

[69] 'Assam: How NRC spurred applicants to trace family trees', 6 August 2018, *Mint*

[70] '"A little brief authority": Chief Justice Ranjan Gogoi and the rise of the executive court', 17 November 2019, indconlawphil.wordpress.com

[71] 'Andhra land scam FIR names daughters of Supreme Court judge', 25 November 2020, *TheWire.in*

of India, Bobde, alleging that Justice Ramana was interfering in the Andhra Pradesh High Court, including fixing the roster.[72] Members of the judiciary were discussing this in private, including one former chief justice of the high court whose WhatsApp conversation with another judge was tapped.[73] On 25 March 2021, Chief Justice Bobde dismissed Reddy's complaint and issued a two-line note: 'A complaint dated 6th October, 2020 sent by the Chief Minister of Andhra Pradesh to the Supreme Court was dealt with under the In-House procedure and the same, on due considerations, stands dismissed. It be noted that all matters dealt with under In-House Procedure being strictly confidential in nature, are not liable to made public.'[74] The same day, Chief Justice Bobde named Justice Ramana as the next chief justice.[75]

A Justice of Double Standards

As my previous work *Our Hindu Rashtra* has examined at length, the judiciary, particularly in the Modi era, often holds Hindu concerns in higher regard than the concerns of other faiths. In the 2 May 2018 judgement on the preservation of the Mahakaleshwar temple in Ujjain (in his home state of Madhya Pradesh), Justice Mishra wrote that the temple's lingam 'has so much importance for spiritual and other gains, there is a constitutional duty to protect it as envisaged in Article 25, Article 26 read with Article 49, at the same time there is a fundamental duty under Article 51A of the Constitution to promote harmony and the spirit of common brotherhood'.[76]

But the deterioration of the 'lingam'—caused by the daily pouring of thousands of litres of water and milk—had not created any communal tension or disturbed this spirit of common brotherhood. It was unclear what the role of the Supreme Court was in any of this, but just before leaving in 2020, Justice Mishra ordered the Union government to give Rs 41.3 lakh towards the maintenance of the lingam. He observed that 'unfortunately the performance of necessary rituals is the most neglected aspect in the temples, and new Poojaris do not understand them; the same should not be the state

---

[72] 'In explosive letter, Jagan alleges future CJI Justice Ramana is destabilizing his govt', 11 October 2020, *The News Minute*

[73] 'AP judge Eswaraiah admits voice in clip asking about Justice NV Ramana was his', 18 January 2021, *The News Minute*

[74] 'SC dismisses Andhra CM's complaint against next Chief Justice NV Ramana after in-house inquiry', 24 March 2021, *Scroll.in*

[75] 'CJI Bobde recommends name of Justice NV Ramana as his successor', 24 March 2021, PTI

[76] 'There must be no double standards in using public funds for religious places', 9 June 2018, *TheWire.in*

of affairs. There is no scope for commercialisation. The myriad religious rituals and ceremonies are to be performed regularly'. He also instructed the temple committee to use only the purest pooja material and directed it to improve its gaushala (cattle shed) so that unadulterated cow milk products could be prepared in the temple.

Justifying his order for the State to bear a religion's expenses, Justice Mishra wrote: 'There is a constitutional obligation to preserve the religious practices of all religions, culture and there is also a corresponding duty to act in that direction. Similarly, such acts which are necessary for the preservation of such historical monuments/deities. State is duty bound to spend the amount so that not only the archaeological, historical and ancient monuments are preserved but sanctum sanctorum, as well as the deity.'

In saying this, he ignored Article 27 of the Constitution which says: 'No person shall be compelled to pay any taxes, the proceeds of which are specifically appropriated in payment of expenses for the promotion or maintenance of any particular religion or religious denomination.'

In a 2017 judgement delivered by Chief Justice Dipak Misra, the Supreme Court specifically rejected this same argument Justice Arun Mishra was putting forth, on the matter of Muslim religious places deliberately defiled and destroyed by Hindu mobs. The court then overturned a Gujarat High Court judgement, which directed the state government to reimburse the cost of rebuilding the destroyed mosques and dargahs.[77] Justice Misra, in that judgement, accepted the BJP government's plea that such a payment by the state would violate Article 27. This gave us the bizarre situation of the Supreme Court, in the matter of a few months, delivering a judgement for Hindus that was the opposite of what it had ordered for Muslims.

Similar hypocrisy is to be found in the Supreme Court's judgements on Ayodhya and Sabarimala. In the first, the court reversed burden of proof on Muslims, who were asked to demonstrate the fact that they had been praying in and had been in possession of their mosque through the centuries, while the claim of the Hindus that they had been praying there was taken at face value.[78] The court also refused to hear the appeals on Ayodhya, closing the book on it forever. However, in the Sabarimala case, in which the court had first ordered that women of all ages should be allowed to access the temple from which they had been prohibited, it sent the case to a larger bench, in

---

[77] 'Supreme Court junks Gujarat High Court order asking state to rebuild mosques, shrines damaged in 2002 riots', 29 August 2017, *India Today*

[78] More details of some of these judgements are in the chapter 'Supreme Complicity', *Our Hindu Rashtra*, 2020, Westland Publications

violation of settled law. There was no new fact that had been presented or any error pointed out in the judgement which required the court to send the matter to a larger bench.

'The Majesty of the Law'

As chief justice, Bobde snapped at a young advocate, a student, who addressed the bench with the words 'your honour'. This offended the CJI who said: 'When you say Your Honour, you either have the Supreme Court of the United States or the Magistrate in mind.'[79] Apologising, the petitioner said he would use 'my lords'. To which Chief Justice Bobde responded: 'Whatever. But don't use incorrect terms.' He then refused to hear the matter further.

Bizarrely, Chief Justice Bobde himself had been on a bench that had said it was not necessary to call Supreme Court justices 'my lord', and that 'your honour' was fine: 'You call us sir, it is accepted. You call your honour, it is accepted. You call lordship, it is accepted.'[80]

But this had been said in January 2014, before the Modi years had infected India's judiciary and its Supreme Court.

The list of quids and of pro quos is long and it is embarrassing. The Supreme Court tried to skewer the activism of high courts when they determined, correctly, that the government was incompetent during the second Covid wave. As the government came under pressure and faced withering criticism from the high courts, the Supreme Court under Chief Justice Bobde stepped in suo moto. This was seen as the taking away of the cases from the high courts into safer and more obliging hands. But it came under such heavy and open fire that the CJI retreated, tail tucked.[81]

It was only when thousands of citizens were dying every day, not from disease but from lack of oxygen and medicine and hospital care that a bungling government had not cared to put in place, that the justice system decided it would hold the Modi government to account. But this was too little too late and the record will show that the Modi years have been one of the most shameful periods in the history of the Indian judiciary.

---

[79] 'CJI Bobde takes exception to "your honour": Don't use incorrect terms', 24 February 2021, *The Indian Express*

[80] 'Calling judges lord, lordship, your honour not mandatory: Supreme Court', 6 January 2014, PTI

[81] 'We never intended to transfer Covid-crisis cases from high courts: SC', 23 April 2021, *Business Standard*

9

FINAL SOLUTION

This chapter looks at three aspects of Modi's gambit in Kashmir. The first examines the background to the dismemberment of the Jammu and Kashmir state and its bifurcation into two Union territories. Some of the historical material on this is analysed. Then we look at the actions taken leading up to the hollowing out of Article 370 and what their impact on Kashmiris was. Lastly, we consider the implications of Modi's actions and what has changed since it was taken.

The problem in Kashmir was that it required more autonomy, not less. The state had acceded to India conditionally in 1947. The condition was autonomy. India's parliament would have the authority to make laws which concerned defence, external affairs (visas, treaties, citizenship), communications (post, telegraph, wireless, railways, aircraft) and elections to parliament. All else would remain the domain of the Kashmir legislature unless it decided of its free will to do otherwise. This is why India accepted the United Nations Security Council solution, which was never implemented for various reasons, for a plebiscite—because it had been written and signed and agreed to.

Jammu and Kashmir's instrument of accession to India, signed by Maharaja Hari Singh, was given to and signed by Viceroy Mountbatten (who continued as head of State till June 1948). Mountbatten's reply was:

> My dear Maharaja Sahib,
>
> Your Highness' letter dated 26 October has been delivered to me by Mr. V.P. Menon. In the special circumstances mentioned by your Highness my Government have decided to accept the accession of Kashmir State to the Dominion of India. Consistently with their policy that in the case of any State where the issue of accession has been the subject of dispute, the question if accession should be

decided in accordance with the wishes of the people of the State, it is my Government's wish that as soon as law and order have been restored in Kashmir and her soil cleared of the invader the question of the State's accession should be settled by a reference to the people.

Meanwhile in response to your Highness' appeal for military aid action has been taken today to send troops of the Indian Army to Kashmir to help your own forces to defend your territory and to protect the lives, property and honour of your people.

My Government and I note with satisfaction that your Highness has decided to invite Sheikh Abdullah to form an interim Government to work with your Prime Minister.

With kind regards, I remain,

Yours sincerely,

October 27, 1947.

Mountbatten of Burma.[1]

Note the specific reference to the will of the people.

In a letter to Kashmir's prime minister, Sheikh Abdullah, dated 17 May 1949, Prime Minister Jawaharlal Nehru, with the concurrence of Vallabhbhai Patel, wrote: 'It has been settled policy of Government of India, which on many occasions has been stated both by Sardar Patel and me, that the Constitution of Jammu and Kashmir is a matter for determination by the people of the state represented in a Constituent Assembly convened for the purpose.'[2]

The fact that this was dishonoured by Nehru and his successors does not mean that the promise itself vanished.

This then was the background to the erstwhile state of Jammu and Kashmir in August 2019, when the Modi government acted to 'de-operationalise' Article 370. This was hardly new: other governments had also 'de-operationalised' Article 370 to make the instrument of accession completely irrelevant.

Indeed, they had even used its provisions to 'integrate' Kashmir.

On 27 November 1963, Nehru said in the Lok Sabha that 'Article 370 has eroded'. India used Article 370 at least 45 times to extend provisions of the Indian Constitution to Jammu and Kashmir. This is, the legal scholar

---

[1] Mountbatten's conditional acceptance of accession. Text of Lord Mountbatten's letter dated 27 October 1947 to signify his acceptance of the Instrument of Accession signed by the Kashmir Maharaja, https://www.mtholyoke.edu/acad/intrel/kasmount.htm

[2] 'Article 370, federalism and the basic structure of the constitution', 27 September 2019, *The India Forum*

Faizan Mustafa has said, the way through which 'by mere Presidential Orders, India has almost nullified the effect of J&K's special status'.[3] Post Kashmir's accession in October 1947, by 1954, more or less the entire Constitution was extended to Kashmir. Out of the 97 entries in the Union List, 94 are applicable to Jammu and Kashmir, as well as 26 out of the 47 items of the Concurrent List. 260 of 395 articles have been extended to the state, besides 7 of the 12 Schedules.[4]

Over the decades, India eroded the conditionality, hollowing out the meaning of Article 370, which repeated what the instrument of accession said, and was solemnly agreed to, namely that 'the power of Parliament to make laws for the said State (Jammu and Kashmir) shall be limited to those matters in the Union List and the Concurrent List which, in consultation with the Government of the State, are declared by the President to correspond to matters specified in the Instrument of Accession governing the accession of the State to the Dominion of India as the matters with respect to which the Dominion Legislature may make laws for that State'.

By 1989, Kashmir already bore no resemblance to the state that had acceded conditionally and for which Article 370 was added to the Constitution. Kashmir not only had absolutely no autonomy, it was also under military rule from that time on. Even in periods when a chief minister was elected, the power to arrest and kill with immunity was something the armed forces, controlled directly by Delhi's Ministry of Defence and Ministry of Home Affairs, exercised. The idea that Kashmir was autonomous in any way at all, leave alone in the sense promised by the instrument of accession, was ridiculous. And yet, it was felt by the BJP and Modi in particular that Article 370 was offensive. The reason was that it apparently treated Kashmir as being separate from India.

The 'one India one constitution' argument, put forward as the reason for the constitutional mischief in Kashmir, is a spurious one.[5] The special provisions for Kashmir were not unique to it. The constitutional differentiation of states based on laws was not because of Article 370. As it stands, we have the following:

- In Nagaland, Article 371A of the Constitution was introduced to protect Naga culture. Parliament cannot legislate on Naga religion or social practices without the approval of the Nagaland Legislative Assembly. No act of parliament applies to the state of Nagaland in

---

[3] Ibid

[4] 'Explained: What are Articles 370 and 35A?', 6 August 2019, *The Indian Express*

[5] 'We are now one India, one constitution, says PM Modi', 15 August 2019, *Mint*

matters relating to religious or social practices, Naga customary law and procedure, administration of civil or criminal justice involving decisions according to Naga customary law, and ownership and transfer of land and its resources.

- Article 371B in Assam has a special provision for a committee in the legislative assembly consisting of members elected from the tribal areas of Assam.
- Article 371C in Manipur has a similar special provision regarding a committee elected from its 'hill areas'. The governor must submit an annual report to the president regarding the administration of these hill areas.
- Article 371D and E for Andhra Pradesh give the state space to safeguard people's rights in matters of employment and education. The state government may organise civil posts or direct recruitment to posts in local cadre as required.
- Article 371F for Sikkim gives seats to different sections of the population in the assembly.
- Article 371G for Mizoram repeats the laws for Nagaland and specifies that an act of parliament would not apply to Mizoram in matters relating to religious or social practices of Mizo, Mizo customary law and procedure, administration of civil or criminal justice involving decisions according to Mizo customary law, ownership and transfer of land and its resources.
- Article 371H for Arunachal Pradesh, again like Nagaland, says that the governor (who reports to the Union) will have special responsibility for law and order.
- Article 371J grants special status to six backward districts of the Hyderabad–Karnataka region in Karnataka state (so named because they were part of the Nizam of Hyderabad's kingdom before 1947). The special provision requires that a separate development board be established for these regions, and also ensures local reservation in education and government jobs.
- Under Article 371, Maharashtra and Gujarat's governors are given special responsibilities to set up development boards in regions such as Vidarbha, Marathwada and Kutch, similar to Hyderabad–Karnataka.

Moreover, the issue of outsiders being unable to purchase land in Kashmir, which was stated as one of the reasons to do away with Article 370, applies also to Himachal Pradesh.

If the contention was that Kashmir was making India a place that had, like China, 'one country two systems', it was wrong. In fact, it could be argued that it was not Article 370 that produced the different treatment of Kashmir but the bigotry and the injustice of the Union over several decades when it came to dealing with that state. The ostensible reason for dismembering Article 370 was that the state's citizenry was receiving some sort of special treatment, but this was not only bogus, it was the opposite of what was the case.

In no other state have the armed forces been given absolute power to kill, rape, torture and kidnap with not just impunity, but immunity. Parliament was told on 1 January 2018 that in none of the chargesheets that the Jammu and Kashmir Police had filed against individuals of the armed forces involving the crimes named above, had a trial in a civil court been approved.[6]

The only other state where AFSPA, the law which gives immunity, was being misused to this extent was Manipur. Here, the Supreme Court stepped in and held the government to account for its fake encounters by the military.[7] No such action was taken in Kashmir, which was truly different for the reason that it was a Muslim majority state. No other state in India has to deal with the pellet gun, the chosen method for crowd control by the armed forces on protesting crowds in Kashmir. This 'non-lethal' weapon has blinded hundreds and killed many.[8]

The reasons cited for 'de-operationalising' Article 370 also revealed a lack of thinking through of the wider and strategic implications.

What Modi did in addition to 'de-operationalising' Article 370 was to dismember the state and hive Ladakh off as a Union territory separate from Jammu and Kashmir, which also jointly became a Union territory. To what end? He did so without considering the national security implications, and the immediate result of changing the status of Ladakh we have seen in the Chinese actions at the LAC.

There was no real reason to undo Article 370, except for the fact that the RSS and the BJP from the beginning had always wanted India to appropriate Kashmir without any reference to its citizens. In their view, it was the land that constituted the nation and not the people.

The 1951 manifesto of the Bharatiya Jana Sangh (the earlier avatar of the

---

[6] Rajya Sabha, unstarred question No 1463, 1 January 2018, humanrightsinitiative.org

[7] 'Supreme Court slams claim that Manipur fake encounter probe will "demoralise" army', 13 November 2018, *TheWire.in*

[8] 'Faces in the darkness: The victims of "non-lethal" weapons in Kashmir', 6 September 2018, *Time*

BJP) reads: 'Since Kashmir is an integral part of India and having regard to developments at UNO the reference made to the latter should be withdrawn and there should be no further question of plebiscite. To end the state of uncertainty about Kashmir's future it should be integrated with Bharat like other acceding states and not given any special position.'

The 1954 manifesto came after the death of Syama Prasad Mookerjee, whom the RSS had earlier picked to head the Jana Sangh, in Kashmir. The party said it would 'bring the state entirely within the framework of the Constitution of Bharatvarsh so that there be no constitutional difference between it and any other state'.

In 1957, the manifesto has a subject headlined 'Liberation of Pak-held Kashmir', which says that 'the proposal to divide that state along the ceasefire line is cowardly and anti-national'. The first reference to the repeal of Article 370 is made here and features in subsequent manifestoes in 1958 and 1962. In 1967, there is no reference to Article 370 but a commitment to the 'integration' of Kashmir.

In 1977, the Bharatiya Jana Sangh folded itself into the umbrella Opposition, the Janata Party. The manifestos of the Janata Party carried no mention of Kashmir or Article 370, including the one for 1980 when the Jana Sangh was still a constituent of the Janata Party.

The demand returned in 1984. By this time, the Jana Sangh had split from the Janata Party and, under Atal Bihari Vajpayee, formed the BJP. Under the subject of 'National unity and positive secularism', the party said it would 'delete the temporary Article 370 of the Constitution'.

The 2019 manifesto claimed that, under Modi, the party had 'in the last five years, made all necessary efforts to ensure peace in Jammu and Kashmir through decisive actions and firm policy'. The facts did not bear this out. Fatalities in Kashmir, which had been falling since 2001 (when 4,011 people were killed), had come down under Vajpayee and Manmohan Singh to less than 200 by 2014. As mentioned earlier (in the chapter 'The Doval Doctrine'), the decline in violence in Kashmir was principally because Pakistan, under President Pervez Musharraf, ended official support to two terrorist groups in 2002 after an attack on the Indian parliament. Following this, violence began to escalate in Pakistan, while it began to progressively taper off in Kashmir. This trend reversed under Modi. From 189 deaths in 2014, the number went to 267 in 2016 and 357 in 2017. In 2018, there were 452 deaths. In 2019, the number was 283 and in 2020, the year after the Article 370 move, it rose to 321. Covid and the restoration of the internet appeared to have eased the violence in 2021.

But having claimed that the BJP had made Kashmir more peaceful, the manifesto went on to say that it would 'reiterate its position since the time of the Jana Sangh to the abrogation of Article 370'. It also committed to 'make all the efforts to ensure the safe return of Kashmiri Pandits'.

As the first step towards abrogation, on 21 November 2018, the Kashmir Assembly was dissolved. Some subterfuge was required. The BJP first walked out of the ruling coalition with Mehbooba Mufti's People's Democratic Party (PDP). This left the government in a minority.

Mufti, however, was able to secure the support of the Congress. She and the others sensed that the BJP was not acting in good faith. At 8.16 p.m. on 21 November, she tweeted that she had faxed the Congress letter of support, showing she had a majority in the assembly, to the governor Satya Pal Malik who was in Jammu. She wrote: 'Have been trying to send this letter to Rajbhavan. Strangely, the fax is not received. Tried to contact HE Governor on phone. Not available. Hope you see it @jandkgovernor'.

At 9.12 p.m., the news agency ANI tweeted out a letter from the governor that the legislative assembly stood dissolved.[9]

Governor Malik would later say that his fax machine was not working, and that the tweet from Mufti had not been seen and, in any case, there was horse-trading going on in the state and therefore the assembly had to be dissolved. Kashmir remained under governor's rule till it was dismembered as a state and Article 370 was 'de-operationalised' on 5 August 2019.

This was accompanied by a crackdown that had no place in a democracy. Hours before the move, Modi moved thousands of more troops into what was already one of the most militarised places on earth.[10]

Kashmir had never been accepted by the outside world as a democratic space, given the problems of rigged and infrequent elections and violence that have been the primary narrative for decades. But this time, the Indian State made no effort to disguise what it was doing.

All the major political figures of the state were locked up without trial or charge. Those jailed had to sign a bond that they would not make any comment(s) or issue statement(s) or make public speech(s) or hold or participate in public assembly(s) related to recent events in the state of Jammu and Kashmir' for one year. They had to deposit Rs 10,000, and if

---

[9] 'J&K drama: Governor's fax not working, Mehbooba stakes claim via tweet', 21 November 2018, *The Indian Express*

[10] 'Kashmir: Why Centre is sending additional 38000 troops to J&K', 2 August 2019, *India Today*

they 'breached' this 'bond', they would have to pay Rs 40,000.[11] Many of them refused to sign and chose to remain in custody.[12]

Over 1,000 people were jailed though there was no data made public on who they were and how many. They included those who had previously held high office. At least 70 political leaders, including three former chief ministers—Mehbooba Mufti, Farooq Abdullah and Omar Abdullah (the latter two having also served in the Union cabinet in Delhi)—were locked up on 5 August 2019.[13] The next day, Amit Shah made his speech in parliament and announced that Kashmir had lost its 'autonomy'. He said this was done for the triumph of democracy but omitted to mention that the state's democratically elected leaders were jailed. Bizarrely, the ability of one leader to get Kashmiris to come out and vote despite boycott calls from separatists was used as the reason to lock him up.[14]

The change in status was done through what can only be described as sleight of hand. Article 370 permitted the president of India to make modifications in articles applicable to Jammu and Kashmir. This power was used to introduce a clause that changed the meaning of Article 370. The 'Constituent Assembly of Jammu and Kashmir' would now mean legislative assembly, and the 'Government of State' would now mean the governor acting on the advice of the Union council of ministers. And under president's rule, the power of the state's legislature was transferred to parliament, controlled by the BJP. Parliament acting on behalf of the Kashmir Assembly acting on behalf of the original Kashmir Constituent Assembly recommended that Article 370 be hollowed out. The article was not deleted, merely made useless. In short, an executive move had undone the Constitution, and those who may have had the real authority to make such a recommendation were now in jail.

Those locked up included members from the PDP, Jammu & Kashmir National Conference, Jammu & Kashmir People's Movement, Indian National Congress, Awami Ittehad Party, Dogra Swabhiman Sangathan and the Jammu & Kashmir National Panthers Party. No BJP figure from the state was detained. Others—we were not told how many—including businessmen

[11] 'In Kashmir, bonds prohibit detainees from holding meetings or speaking about Article 370', 21 October 2019, *Scroll.in*

[12] 'J&K leaders refuse to sign release bonds', 26 November 2019, *The Hindu*

[13] 'Situation update and analysis: Jammu and Kashmir after one year of abrogation of Article 370', Amnesty International India

[14] 'J&K leader's ability to convince people to vote during boycotts cited as reason for PSA charge', 8 February 2020, *TheWire.in*

and civil society activists were also jailed, several of them sent out of Kashmir to prisons across India.[15]

The Modi government used laws of preventive detention, meaning commission of a crime was not necessary for the State to jail people. The laws included the Public Safety Act (a Kashmir-only law which the Modi government chose to retain though it made much of not wanting separate status and laws in the state), which allowed for 'detention', without trial or charge, for up to two years.

Many may not be aware that such laws, which those gathered at Jallianwala Bagh were protesting, not only remain in India, but the powers of the State to jail people without crime have actually expanded. India has laws which allow the police to make an arrest without a warrant or a magistrate's orders (CRPC 151) and without a crime having been committed.

Preventive detention laws violate human rights and circumvent fair trial safeguards of criminal proceedings. They lack even the poorly deployed procedures, rules of evidence and burden and standard of proof in the Indian criminal justice system. It was unacceptable for the government to circumvent these safeguards and detain people it did not intend to prosecute. This was a blatant abuse of laws by the Government of India, undermining accountability, transparency and respect for human rights, Amnesty India said in a briefing on the situation in Kashmir after August 2019.[16] The role of the Supreme Court in allowing this to happen has already been discussed.

After August 2019, the Indian State declared open season on Kashmiris. Executive magistrates (meaning bureaucrats) unlawfully issued verbal orders of detention under CRPC 151 and 107, without keeping any records. A subsequent Amnesty India briefing in February 2020 said at least 1,249 Kashmiris, including children, had been held in preventive detention, often on 'verbal' orders.

The laxity in process, lack of accountability of the State and the abdication by the judiciary all showed when the Modi government said in the Supreme Court that senior leader Saifuddin Soz was not detained, though media visiting him found that he was, in fact, under house arrest.[17]

The crackdown was also extended to journalists. A group always under

---

[15] 'The Kashmiris detained more than 700km away from home', 19 September 2019, *BBC*

[16] 'Situation update and analysis: Jammu and Kashmir after one year of abrogation of Article 370', August 2020, Amnesty.org

[17] '"I am not a free man": Saifuddin Soz claims he is under house arrest', 30 July 2020, *The Hindu*

pressure and lacking even the minimal space to be able to report on the State found itself now facing further pressure to stay silent. (I had personal experience of this in June 2019, at a press event Amnesty was holding to release a report on the Public Safety Act. The police came to our hotel in Srinagar to stop us. They even had a problem with my speaking to individual reporters.[18])

After the Article 370 move, every second journalist was summoned by the police or questioned on the phone or intimidated in another way, the Amnesty briefing reported. A month before the August lockdown, Fayaz Ahmad Kaloo, editor of *Greater Kashmir* and the president of the Kashmir Editors Guild, was summoned to Delhi and questioned by the NIA for six days between 1 and 6 July 2019. Earlier, the government stopped advertising in two of the largest newspapers of the region, *Greater Kashmir* and *Kashmir Reader*. This is significant because, in the absence of the internet and a modern economy, the Kashmiri media has become helplessly dependent on the government to survive—the same government which victimises and brutalises their readerships.

Journalists were also detained without reason. On 14 August 2019, Irfan Amin Malik, a journalist with *Greater Kashmir*, was detained. He was not informed of the reasons for his arrest and was released later the same day. Peerzada Ashiq, the Srinagar correspondent for *The Hindu*, was summoned on 1 September 2019 by the police, and asked to reveal the sources for his story on unlawful detentions in Jammu and Kashmir after the abrogation of Article 370. He was again summoned on 19 April 2020 in relation to social media posts about one of his reports. On 20 May 2020, the Srinagar Police summoned Fahad Shah, editor of *The Kashmir Walla*—a multimedia news and views platform—for covering the encounter between militants and security forces in the Nawakadal neighbourhood of downtown Srinagar. The police claimed that the stories 'maligned the police'. Fahad was allowed to leave the police station after five hours of questioning. He was summoned again on 9 July 2020 and questioned on the same matter.

In December 2019, Azaan Javaid, a journalist with *The Print*, was physically assaulted while attempting to cover a student protest at Srinagar's Islamia College of Science. On 10 February 2020, the Kashmir Press Club issued a statement saying that security agencies were threatening and intimidating journalists working in the Valley.[19]

---

[18] 'Amnesty not allowed to release Kashmir report', 12 June 2019, *The Hindu*
[19] 'Situation update and analysis: Jammu and Kashmir after one year of abrogation of Article 370', Amnesty International India

On 2 June 2020, the Modi government announced 'New Media Policy 2020', a policy specific to Kashmir. Again, note that the pretence behind all this was the ostensible integration of Kashmir and the abolition of laws that distinguished it from the rest of India. Yet, here was another Kashmir-only policy. Over 50 pages long, it gave the government unbridled powers to determine what was 'fake', 'unethical' or 'anti-national' news. On the basis of this, it could take legal and other punitive action against journalists and media organisations. Media watchdogs abroad noted the use of ambiguous and undefined terms such as 'fake', 'unethical', 'anti-national' and 'anti-social', which opened the doors for misuse because they offered the bureaucrat judging the news no guiding standards or principles.[20] It was entirely at the discretion of the government.

The press in Jammu remained silent on the matter, while the media in Kashmir voiced their strong opposition to the policy. Speaking to Amnesty India, journalist Zafar Choudhary said, 'The Press in Jammu mainly reflect the dominant political sentiment of the regional majority. The political culture of Jammu is mostly constructed on reactions to Kashmir with no major agency of its own. So, when a difficult law, rule or policy comes in, the journalists think it is directed against Kashmir and must be in national interest. As a result, no journalist/media house in Jammu has spoken against the media policy.'

On 10 January 2020, hearing a case related to the restoration of internet in Kashmir, the Supreme Court determined that access to the internet was a fundamental right of Indians.[21] This was the way several papers reported the story even the following day: 'Access to internet is a fundamental right, says Supreme Court'[22] and 'SC recognises internet users' right, also formalises their accountability'.[23]

Globally, and especially in the West, access to the internet is a right inextricably linked to freedom of expression. The Supreme Court of India had now aligned itself to the rest of the civilised world.

But had it? No. Another report on the same hearing was headlined 'SC has no views on "if access to internet" is a fundamental right' (*The Hindu*, 10 January 2020). This report, by Krishnadas Venugopal, quoted the 130-page

---

[20] 'RSF appalled by Orwellian press policy in Indian-held Kashmir', 19 June 2020, rsf.org
[21] 'Right to access internet a fundamental right, can't be curbed arbitrarily: SC on J&K restrictions', 10 January 2020, *The Indian Express*
[22] 11 January 2020, *Hindustan Times*
[23] 13 January 2020, *The Times of India*

judgement and noted that the court merely directed the Modi government to 'forthwith review' its orders suspending internet services in Jammu and Kashmir. The court said: 'None of the counsels have argued for declaring the right to access the internet as a fundamental right and therefore we are not expressing any view on the same.'

The total blockade of Kashmiris from using the internet continued. It was left for the Modi government to tell the court what the law was at the next hearing. The Kashmir administration, run directly by the Union, said: 'The right to access the internet is not a fundamental right and thus the type and breadth of access for exercising the right to freedom of speech and expression under Article 19(1)(a) and/or to carry on any trade or business under Article 19(1)(g) of the Constitution of India through the medium of internet can be curtailed.'[24]

The justification given for this collective punishment of Kashmiris was that 'post August 2019 constitutional developments, Pakistan handlers, either directly or indirectly, have increased activity on social media intending to and aiming at disturbance of peace in the region, inciting violence and abetting terror activities'.

Solicitor general Tushar Mehta argued in court: 'Unfortunately, internet jihad is a successful one. It is a global phenomenon. The jihadi leaders can engage through the internet to spread hatred and illegal activities.' The bench asked if internet access could be permitted with some restrictions. 'Increase in internet speed,' the Union submitted, 'will lead to swift uploading and posting of provocative videos and other heavy data files.'[25]

'The only solution is that either you have internet or you don't have the internet,' Mehta said.[26]

It should be noted here that the peak of violence in Kashmir, with over 4,000 killed in 2001, happened when there was no internet and not even any mobile telephony in Kashmir.[27] There is no linkage between the levels of violence and access to the internet, according to the data. But this was not the way that the government or the court saw it.

Since the 2019 constitutional change, internet access has been disrupted in Jammu and Kashmir by at least 90 government-imposed internet shutdowns—the highest in the world. The world noticed.

---

[24] 'Access to internet not a fundamental right, Jammu and Kashmir administration tells Supreme Court', 30 April 2020, *Hindustan Times*

[25] 'Access to internet not a fundamental right: J-K', 30 April 2020, *Hindustan Times*

[26] 'His master's voice: Tushar Mehta holds court', 1 October 2020, *The Caravan*

[27] 'Vajpayee launches mobile phone services for J&K', 4 August 2003, *The Economic Times*

It was reported[28] that the shutdown (17 months in all, including seven months when even 2G mobile telephony was suspended) was the longest ever imposed in a democracy, according to Access Now, the international advocacy group that tracks internet suspensions.

I asked a former colleague from Srinagar what it was like to use 2G, and the person replied: '2G internet has a top speed of 350 kbps. Opening emails on the phone takes lot of time. A document or media file that takes one minute to open or download on 4G (on mobile phone) usually takes 15 to 20 minutes on 2G, sometimes even more. Uploading a 5MB document or file takes around half an hour.

'2G internet on laptops and desktops is more problematic. Opening of email home pages is difficult. Logging into an email account usually takes 5 to 10 minutes. One can't access most sites.'

Mind you, even this patchy connectivity was often unavailable. Amnesty India documented a total of 67 government-enforced internet shutdowns between 14 January 2020 and 4 August 2020. Despite the 'restoration' of the internet in Kashmir, arbitrary suspension of internet services remains the norm. Any incident, and any whim from the administration, results in the sending back of Kashmiris to a pre-modern era.

The petitioner in the case that was heard on 10 January 2020 was Anuradha Bhasin, editor and publisher of the newspaper *Kashmir Times*. She had told the court she could not publish the newspaper due to communications restrictions imposed by the Government of India.

She petitioned the Supreme Court for the removal of restrictions imposed on the access of internet, mobile and landline phones, and for other appropriate relief (the inability of media to publish without communications is another reason why the court had to judge the matter from the free speech angle). The court did not respond as it should have and the restrictions continued. This produced in Kashmir, inside India, a one-country, two-systems style government.

The UN has previously noted, in its two special reports on Kashmir in 2018 and 2019, that several Kashmiri journalists and human rights defenders reported that social media platforms Twitter and Facebook had suspended their accounts or removed their posts for Kashmir-related content.

Other than the media's right to publish and the individual citizen's rights to freedom of expression and to access information, India's attack on the internet in Kashmir had implications elsewhere.

---

28 'India's internet shutdown in Kashmir is the longest ever in a democracy', 16 December 2019, *The Washington Post*

During the first year of the Covid-19 pandemic, Kashmiris had no access to telemedicine and online education. Hospitals had no access to the internet and doctors had no proper means to research or find out what was happening and what to do at a time when information was vital and constantly changing.

On 11 April 2020, the Private Schools Association of Jammu and Kashmir moved the Supreme Court asking for 4G services in what was now a Union territory. The petition contended that the lack of proper internet connectivity violated the fundamental right to education of children. Kashmiri children were the only section of India's population who were being denied an education because of the deliberate policy of the State (again 'one country, two systems'). The court did not act here either and did not give the children access to learning.

Video classes and other online educational content was impossible in Kashmir. This not only impacted the children's education, but also disadvantaged students from Kashmir preparing for competitive exams.

Access to justice, which had been shifted online by the courts, was also impacted because of the internet ban in Kashmir. The guidelines from the Supreme Court on the functioning of the judiciary during Covid-19 came with a grand pronouncement: 'Technology has facilitated advances in speed, accessibility and connectivity which enable the dispensation of justice to take place in diverse settings and situations without compromising the core legal principles of adjudication.'

The high court of Jammu and Kashmir began holding virtual hearings from 23 March 2020. But pandemic-related travel restrictions, combined with no internet, meant that petitioners had no access to justice—even by the poor standards prevailing in Kashmir. Those held in detention without charge or trial did not have a functional way in which they could engage the judicial system. Habeas corpus petitions fell from the hundreds filed each year (371 in 2019 and averaging over 500 each year for several years in the Modi era) to virtually none in 2020—though more people had been locked up randomly following the constitutional change.

Access to justice was curbed in other ways. The Jammu and Kashmir State Human Rights Commission was among the seven different commissions abolished after the Jammu and Kashmir Reorganisation Act repealed many of the state's laws.[29] The justification was that it would now be the NHRC sitting in Delhi that would look at the grievances of Kashmiris. This was

---

[29] 'Government shuts down J&K Human Rights Commission, Information Commission', 24 October 2019, *TheWire.in*

false. The NHRC (of which Justice Arun Mishra was made chairman) already had jurisdiction over Kashmir; what happened as a result of the action was that local access was taken away. The State Commission for Protection of Women and Child Rights was also disbanded.

The role of the judiciary in what has been done to Kashmiris under Modi is shameful. There has been a lot of handwringing from their lordships but no action. Indeed, the court has been guilty of violating its own judgements in trying to justify what it has allowed the Modi government to do.

On 11 May 2020, the court rejected a petition which alleged violations of the January judgement in Anuradha Bhasin vs Union of India.[30] In that judgement, the court had set down safeguards for the government to follow before shutting off the internet. The plea focussed on the violations of Kashmiris' rights to health, education, freedom of speech, freedom of trade and access to justice.

In its May judgement, while the court accepted that the government had violated the principles of the Bhasin judgement, it did nothing to get the State to enforce them.

In January, the court had said that the minimal requirement for an internet ban should be the listing of reasons for it and that 'orders (banning the internet) passed mechanically or in a cryptic manner cannot be said to be orders passed in accordance with law'. The petitioners said the permanent and repeated suspension of the internet in Kashmir disclosed no reason, and this was in contravention to the order. The court agreed. Also in contravention was the idea of proportionality. If the claim was that the internet ban served a purpose—curbing violence—it should be enforced only in those parts which had seen violence. Where there was no disturbance to public order, it made no sense to have a ban. The court again agreed, but did not lift the ban. Its judges made some noises about the situation in Kashmir being different from the rest of India and thus allowed another rule for that state.

Finally, the judges abdicated their principal task of deciding upon the constitutional validity of internet suspension, palming it off to a 'special committee'—composed of members of the executive.[31] Instead of the judges, it would be the Union home secretary, the Union communications secretary, and the chief secretary of Jammu and Kashmir, who would 'immediately' decide whether the internet ban should continue.

---

[30] 'SC refrains from restoring 4G services in J&K, sets up special committee', 11 May 2020, *TheWire.in*

[31] 'Supreme Court verdict on 4G in Jammu and Kashmir undermines the rule of law', 14 May 2020, *TheWire.in*

An analysis published in *The Wire* said that 'in a unique approach to rights adjudication, the court carved out an ad hoc exception to the norms of legality and proportionality enunciated in Bhasin—in extraordinary circumstances, the court seemed to imply, constitutional safeguards are suspended.'[32]

The charge of abdication, a serious one against the Supreme Court, was made elsewhere also.[33] It was noted in this report that the court, with no data presented and no real explanation, balanced 'the submissions of the Petitioners, (which) in normal circumstances, merit consideration' with the 'compelling circumstances of cross border terrorism in the Union Territory of Jammu and Kashmir, (which) at present, cannot be ignored'. Of course, this 'at present' notion is a fudge. It has been the Indian State's justification for denying Kashmiris their rights for three full decades.

It is the case that the judiciary does not feel it is empowered to interpret the Constitution and the validity of laws and has to make pleas instead to the Modi government.[34]

Despite this, with no recourse and no other options, the Kashmiris continued trying to get the Indian judiciary to take an interest in them.[35]

In January 2021, an association of 3,800 schools challenged yet another arbitrary ban, saying that their fundamental rights under Article 14, 19 and 21 of the Indian Constitution had been violated. The appeal said that doctors were unable to download the latest studies, protocols, manuals and advisories due to slow internet speed.[36] This received almost no coverage in India's media, which has little interest in such things as India's judiciary.

The Modi government's justifications for its actions on Kashmir were absurd. Amit Shah's speech in parliament said the existence of Article 370 produced violence, without citing the evidence for this claim.[37] The fact that violence measured in fatalities has not disappeared after the act was abrogated should have produced more scepticism about Shah's claim than it actually has

---

[32] Ibid

[33] 'Supreme court's order on Kashmir internet shutdown: Judicial abdication or judicial restraint?', 13 May 2020, *The Times of India*

[34] 'Supreme Court asks Centre if 4G internet can be restored in select areas of J&K', 7 August 2020, *The Hindu*

[35] 'Internet restrictions in Jammu & Kashmir challenged in Supreme Court for the third time after abrogation of Article 370', 23 January 2021, BarandBench.com

[36] Ibid

[37] 'Article 370 root cause of terrorism in Jammu and Kashmir: Amit Shah', 5 August 2019, *The Times of India*

in the media. To take Shah's statement to its logical conclusion, Kashmiris were rebelling against India because they were demanding a repeal of Article 370.

Shah blamed the lack of democracy in Kashmir on Article 370, which would have been news to Kashmiris. The Indian State has, since Independence, used every form of violence and coercion available to it to suppress, undo and violate the will of the Kashmiri people.

Shah said of concerns from the Opposition regarding the recklessness with which his government was proceeding that 'Nothing will happen... It won't be allowed to turn into another Kosovo'; Kashmir 'was heaven on earth and will remain so'.[38]

It was said that the special provision prevented the 'development' of Kashmir. To a large extent, the Indian State—especially in the Modi era— is responsible for Kashmir not being able to integrate with the modern economy. Kashmir has a large set of people with a mercantile ethic, as those who have encountered Kashmiris around the world know. India put its boot on their throats and then has looked around for the suspects. The Indian State has created and encouraged the active demonisation of Kashmiris as 'stone-pelters' and 'anti-nationals' and then pretended to be acting for their benefit.

Another reason cited for the action was that Article 370 was never meant to be permanent. This is deceit, because it was temporary only subject to the will of its population.

The most important element here is the one that the government did not raise. It is unlikely that Modi even considered it. The reality of his Article 370 move is that not only was it not a solution, it destroyed the keystone to any future solution. Without Article 370 in place, the basis for a legitimate solution no longer exists. India will continue to face the same restlessness in Kashmir that will keep the state militarised (there has been no reduction of forces there). But India has now no means of responding to any future questioning of the legality of its occupation of Kashmir.

Note that the United Nations Security Council Resolutions on Kashmir are dormant but are not dead. The UN continues to have a military presence in India, called the United Nations Military Observer Group in India and Pakistan. It has a liaison office on Purana Qila Road in Delhi, field stations in Poonch, Rajouri and Jammu, and a headquarters in Srinagar.

---

[38] 'Article 370 didn't allow democracy in J&K: Amit Shah's speech', 5 August 2019, *NDTV*

Its website, unmogip.unmissions.org, says: 'Given the disagreement between India and Pakistan about UNMOGIP's mandate and functions, the Secretary-General's position has been that UNMOGIP can only be terminated by a decision of the Security Council. In the absence of such a decision, UNMOGIP has been maintained with those same arrangements since then.

'To fulfill UNMOGIP mandate, military observers conduct field tasks (area recce, field trip, field visit and observation post) along the Line of Control. As part of the 1949 Karachi Agreement, UNMOGIP also conducts investigations into alleged ceasefire violation complaints, which the two parties can submit to the Mission. The findings of the investigations are shared with the Secretary-General and a summary of investigations with the two parties.'

Days after Modi's action, on 16 August 2019, the UN website carried a news item under the headline 'UN Security Council discusses Kashmir, China urges India and Pakistan to ease tensions'.[39]

Its opening paragraph read: 'The Security Council considered the volatile situation surrounding Kashmir on Friday, addressing the issue in a meeting focused solely on the dispute, within the UN body dedicated to resolving matters of international peace and security, for the first time since 1965.'

India ignored this, but it cannot change the facts and has little control over what other nations and organisations can do. The fact is that the UN had taken up an issue that it had not addressed in over five decades. The item contains another troubling paragraph. 'The position of the United Nations on this region is governed by the Charter... and applicable Security Council resolutions,' says the statement. 'The Secretary-General also recalls the 1972 Agreement on bilateral relations between India and Pakistan also known as the Simla Agreement, which states that the final status of Jammu and Kashmir is to be settled by peaceful means, in accordance with the UN Charter.'

The UN has said that it backs the Simla Agreement. What does that agreement say? Signed on 2 July 1972 after Pakistan's defeat in the Bangladesh war, its operative part reads that India and Pakistan have agreed 'to settle their differences by peaceful means through bilateral negotiations'. And that neither side shall unilaterally alter the situation.

The text reads: 'In Jammu and Kashmir, the line of control resulting

---

[39] 'UN Security Council discusses Kashmir, China urges India and Pakistan to ease tensions', https://news.un.org/en/story/2019/08/1044401

from the cease-fire of 17 December 1971 shall be respected by both sides without prejudice to the recognised position of either side. Neither side shall seek to alter it unilaterally, irrespective of mutual differences and legal interpretations. Both sides further undertake to refrain from the threat or the use of force in violation of this Line.'

The Congress leader in the Lok Sabha, Adhir Ranjan Chowdhury, pointed out that the Lahore Declaration signed on 21 February 1999 by Atal Bihari Vajpayee and Nawaz Sharif committed both nations 'to implementing the Simla Agreement in letter and spirit'. The declaration specifies that 'the resolution of all outstanding issues, including Jammu and Kashmir, is essential' for peace, and that the two nations 'shall intensify their efforts to resolve all issues, including the issue of Jammu and Kashmir'. How, given this, could the Modi government proceed to unilaterally change the status in Kashmir?

It is this intervention from Chowdhury that, as noted earlier, provoked Shah to let go of reason and take instead to emotion, saying what he did about being willing to give up his life to take back Pakistan Occupied Kashmir from Pakistan and Aksai Chin from China (see the chapter 'The Doval Doctrine'). The Indian media vilified Chowdhury for pointing out the truth.[40] But the Congressman was right, though unable to push his point further given the unhinged and illiterate manner in which both the BJP and the media saw the issue.

What was the 'de-operationalising' of Article 370 if not a unilateral altering of the situation? What was the demotion of Jammu and Kashmir from state to Union territory and the splitting off of Ladakh into another Union territory if not a unilateral altering of the situation?

India was in apparent violation not only of the Security Council resolutions in which it had committed itself to a plebiscite to settle the issue but also in clear violation of the Simla Agreement and the Lahore Declaration, signed by a BJP prime minister. For this reason, the issue would not stop being taken up in places where India did not want it to be.

A report from the following month said that Kashmir had been discussed in the General Assembly.[41] India gave its boilerplate response but Indians should ask: what did we get in exchange for creating trouble for ourselves?

Is Kashmir more democratic now? No, it has no democracy and no elected assembly today. Is it more peaceful? No. Is it more prosperous? No,

---

[40] 'Adhir Ranjan embarrasses Congress, says Article 370 not an internal issue, Amit Shah hits back', 6 August 2019, *India Today*
[41] 'China raises Kashmir issue at UN, India says it is "internal matter"', 28 September 2019, PTI

and given the seemingly permanent control on communications and absence of freedom of assembly, it has been given few means to be prosperous. Have the Kashmiri Pandits returned? No, and why would they want to return to a bucolic place with either patchy or no internet? The Pandits are an urban and middle-class community spread out across India's cities. Why would they want to go to a place that offers them less economic progress than where they migrated to? This is not even considered, much less asked when there are noises made about their return to the Valley.

India's external posture on Kashmir also became narrower and more parochial. An opinion piece justifying Kashmir's dismemberment by India's ambassador to the US, Harsh Shringla, made seven references to Imran Khan and 10 references to terrorism.[42]

Across the Atlantic, Jaishankar was trotted out to write about Pakistan and cross-border terrorism.[43] He claimed that now 'there is a new reality in the making in Jammu and Kashmir. It is driven by economic development, social progress and gender justice. Its future is based on freedom from intimidation and fear of terrorists. Those who identify with these goals will surely welcome the change.' Time has shown this not to be true.

Having written these op-eds, unsurprisingly, not much by way of justification came from the Ministry of External Affairs in the months after, as news of the mass arrests and internet shutdowns dominated the discourse.

The outside world has not accepted India's reasons for its actions and has not concluded that the issue is settled. The foreign media's view of what India has done in Kashmir is uniformly negative.

One report said that 'draconian laws such as the Public Safety Act, the Unlawful Activities (Prevention) Act, and tight internet curbs have resulted in real curbs on the most basic democratic rights such as freedom of expression and freedom of assembly'.[44] It pointed out that in the first six months of 2020, the civil society group JKCCS had already documented 107 cordon-and-search operations resulting in 229 killings, in addition to 55 territory-wide internet shutdowns, and the destruction of 48 properties on the pretext that militants might be hiding inside.

The publication most consulted by political and business leaders around the world—*The Economist*—has been scathing. It has run reports with headlines like 'In its struggle to subdue Kashmir, India is stripping it of

[42] 'India is building a more prosperous Kashmir', 19 September 2019, *The New York Times*
[43] 'Changing the status of Jammu and Kashmir will benefit all of India', 24 September 2019, *The Financial Times*
[44] 'India's Article 370 experiment in Kashmir has failed', 3 August 2020, *Nikkei Asia*

liberties' (17 August 2019); 'The courts' refusal to curb repression in Kashmir' (5 October 2019); 'India is still trampling on civil liberties in Kashmir' (10 September 2020); and 'India's government puts nationalism before education in Kashmir' (20 March 2021).

The New Yorker reported that Modi's 'Hindu-nationalist government has cast two hundred million Muslims as internal enemies'.[45] *Harper's* reported that Kashmir's doctor to patient ratio was 1 to 3,060, while its troops to civilians ratio was 1 to 7.[46] It is hollow to talk about 'development' when the world confronts you with such numbers.

What was achieved other than the humiliation (or at least what the BJP thinks is the humiliation) of Kashmiris? The rest of India may not have been aware of what was in the offing but that was not true inside the state. Kashmiris worried that India was conspiring to harm them and they were right. Former chief minister Omar Abdullah, in an interview to *The Indian Express* on 29 July 2020, said that one of his colleagues had specifically told him what the intentions of Modi were: *'Nahin inko sab kuch karna hai. Ye 370, 35A hatayenge, ye UT bhi banayenge aur ye riyasat ko todenge bhi.'* (They want it all, they will remove 370, 35A, they will also make Kashmir a Union territory and they will break up the state).

What was being presented as an act to strengthen democracy was really the completion of a hostile takeover.

A scan of who is actually administering Kashmir in 2021[47] shows that almost all the major departments are being controlled by non-Kashmiris:

Home and revenue: Shaleen Kabra; finance: Arun Kumar Mehta; general administration and industries and commerce: Manoj Kumar Dwivedi; law, justice and parliamentary affairs: Achal Sethi; agriculture and cooperatives: Navin Kumar Choudhary; transport: Hirdesh Kumar; public works: Shailender Kumar; estates: M. Raju; science and technology and social welfare: Bipul Pathak; information and public relations: Rohit Kansal; labour and employment: Saurabh Bhagat; housing and urban development: Dheeraj Gupta; food, civil supplies, consumer affairs, information technology: Simrandeep Singh; hospitality and protocol: Indu Kanwal Chib; education: Bishwajit Kumar Singh; forests, environment and ecology: Sarita Chauhan.

The Kashmiris have been given tribal affairs: Rehana Batul; floriculture, gardens and parks: Sheikh Fayaz Ahmad; health and medical education: Atal

---

[45] 'Blood and soil in Narendra Modi's India', 2 December 2019, *The New Yorker*

[46] 'Valley of unrest: India's unending occupation of Kashmir', July 2020, *Harper's*

[47] https://www.jk.gov.in/jammukashmir/?q=departments

Dulloo; stationery and supplies: Abdul Majid Bhat; rural development: Qazi Sarwar; civil aviation: Rukhsana Ghani; culture: Sarmad Hafeez; fisheries: Bashir Ahmad Bhat and horticulture: Ajaz Ahmad Bhat.

When I checked in July 2021, the website for the tourism department—http://www.jktourism.org—was a dud, as was the one for the irrigation department—http://jkpheirrigation.nic.in—and the website for the department of power development. The link that the official government website provides for the department for planning, development and monitoring—https://jandkplanning.com—is actually a website promoting tourism in Denmark.

Amusingly, the link to the election department—https://ceojammukashmir.nic.in—was not only a dud but the browser produced the warning: 'This website may be impersonating ceojammukashmir.nic.in to steal your personal or financial information. You should go back to the previous page.'

Of course, this takeover by outsiders was not commented on or reported or even noticed except by a very few in the media.[48] When a Kashmiri man, part of a civil society delegation, said he had no expectations from non-local officers, he was jailed on the orders of the Krittika Jyotsna, deputy commissioner of Ganderbal, who was angered by the comment.[49]

In his first press conference after Kashmir lost its statehood, governor Satya Pal Malik said that 50,000 government posts would be filled in the next few months.[50] And yet, as of March 2021, the Modi administration had not recruited a single person, the Ministry of Home Affairs told parliament.[51] Till April 2023, only 185 people from outside the former state had purchased any land there (a key promise Modi had made, which would apparently align Kashmir to the rest of India and unite the nation).

But immediately after the move to change the status of Kashmir, the Modi government began to parcel out land in the state to the Indian Army. A report said that 727 hectares of designated forest land was diverted between 18 September and 21 October 2019.[52]

[48] 'Kashmir gets a new bureaucracy: Fewer locals, more officers from outside', 24 January 2021, *Scroll.in*

[49] 'J&K: Man jailed for saying he "can't have expectations from non-local officers"', 14 June 2021, *TheWire.in*

[50] 'Governor Satya Pal Malik promises 50,000 government jobs in J&K', 29 August 2019, *The Hindu*

[51] 'No outsider bought land in J&K: Government', 17 March 2021, *The Hindu*

[52] 'Under President's rule, J&K has given up 243 hectares of forest land for army and paramilitary use', 16 December 2019, *Scroll.in*

This was done by merely notifying parts of the state as 'strategic areas' for the armed forces.[53] These 'strategic areas' were those where the Indian armed forces could carry out unhindered constructions and other related activities aligned with their 'security needs', as the vaguely worded official statement put it. The administration also withdrew a 1971 circular, which required the armed forces to get a no-objection certificate from the home department for acquisition or requisition of land in favour of the Indian armed forces, making it possible for the army to acquire any land without bureaucratic clearance.

In 2018, Mehbooba Mufti said that over 200 sq. kms. of land in Kashmir was already in the unauthorised and illegal control of the army, which had built houses, schools and public buildings. This was unrelated to the lands that the armed forces were already occupying officially in military camps, arms depots, border fencing and landmines.[54] The Article 370 gambit appears much less noble in the light of the facts and what has come to be.

Of course, this is not a new thing. The Indian State has misbehaved with Kashmiris since Independence and defrauded them of what had been promised. From Nehru to Manmohan Singh, this did not change in substance, as we have seen.

But Modi made the Indian State behave in a way that is unconscionable, and this went unnoticed because of the hyper-nationalistic discourse on Kashmir. And because the Indian courts were complicit. And because of the fact that the wretched Kashmiris had, even less than other Indians, no access to freedom of speech and expression and peaceful assembly. They lived lives that were different from those lived by other Indians, no matter which strata of society they belonged to. Even if they had the money, they could not access the sort of economy and employment and education that other Indians could. They were denied these privileges because of who they were.

This was accentuated and not diminished by the changes made through 'de-operationalising' Article 370 on 5 August 2019.[55] India operates a State that, like the People's Republic of China in Hong Kong, has different rules based on which part of the country one is in. Kashmir is treated like an

---

[53] 'Army, CRPF, BSF will no longer require NOC for land acquisition in Jammu and Kashmir', 28 July 2020, *India Today*

[54] 'The inheritance of loss progression: A journal from Kashmir, a year after losing autonomy', 5 August 2020, *The Caravan*

[55] 'Government brings Resolution to repeal Article 370 of the Constitution; Shri Amit Shah introduces Jammu and Kashmir (Reorganisation) Bill, 2019', 5 August 2019, Press Information Bureau

occupied territory where the Constitution is suspended permanently and citizenship is more like subjecthood. The future of Kashmir and India will have to accommodate this primary problem. It has been hidden from our view because Kashmiris literally have no freedom of expression and no forum to express their opinion with. They have no space for public demonstrations, even of the limited sort that Indians elsewhere enjoy—they would be immediately shot.

What has been the result of the flashy Article 370 move given all that we now know? That needs to be examined now that the euphoria and the triumphalism is behind us.

Kashmir to the RSS and the BJP and, ultimately, to Modi was a problem understood through reduction. The main issue, to their mind, was 'Pakistan sponsored terrorism'. This was encouraged by separatism. This, in turn, was kept alive by Article 370. If the lines of that provision—a clause in the Constitution—were to be erased, separatism and militancy would disappear. The issue of separatism and Kashmiri disaffection was not that India had not upheld its side of the bargain, but that Kashmiris had no right to feel disaffection because India owned their lands.

Such reduction was not mere innocence, it was rank stupidity.

10

TRANSPARENCY

In both 2014 and 2019, the Modi manifestos made much of reducing the opacity that surrounds the functioning of government in India.

In 2014: 'Open Government and Accountable Administration: Administrative reforms will be a priority for the BJP. Hence, we propose to implement them through an appropriate body under the PMO. The objective will be to bring in transparency in Government's decision-making process. Government systems and processes would be relooked to make them citizen friendly, corruption free and accountable.'

In 2019, the claim was made that before Modi arrived, 'it was a phase when the hope of seeing a corruption-free and transparent government realised seemed impossible. Nobody was ready to believe that multi-dimensional developmental goals could be achieved without resorting to corruption. However, the government led by Prime Minister Shri Narendra Modi turned this belief into a reality by successfully running the government in a transparent manner. We have succeeded in conveying this message to the people at large that governance is possible without corruption.

'In last five years, our government has done incredible work in establishing a transparent system of governance, furthering economic development and increasing people's participation in the country's progress.

'This government has made historic efforts made (sic) towards empowerment of the ordinary Indian, establishment of a strong and transparent system of governance.

'Under the leadership of PM Modi, every effort has been made to re-establish probity in public life, introduce transparency in policy-making and in the management of national assets as well as to bring offenders to book.'

Having understood the claim, let us examine the record.

The Prime Minister Cares Very Much

On 28 March 2020, as the effect of the suddenly declared lockdown was visible in the migrants' crisis, Modi tweeted: 'People from all walks of life expressed their desire to donate to India's war against Covid-19. Respecting that spirit, the Prime Minister's Citizen Assistance and Relief in Emergency Situations Fund (PM CARES) has been constituted. This will go a long way in creating a healthier India.'

And: 'It is my appeal to my fellow Indians, Kindly contribute to the PM CARES Fund. This Fund will also cater to similar distressing situations, if they occur in the times ahead. This link has all important details about the fund.'

The link led to a press release which said that the fund was being set up 'with the primary objective of dealing with any kind of emergency or distress situation, like posed by the COVID-19 pandemic, and to provide relief to the affected'. It would be a public charitable trust, with the prime minister as chairman, and members would include the defence minister, home minister and finance minister.

Questions about the fund began immediately, particularly about opacity. The Prime Minister's National Relief Fund already existed, which was managed from the PMO and gave the prime minister discretion in how to spend the money. It had thousands of crores in its corpus. Why then the need for another fund?

An RTI was filed the following day by activists seeking the trust deed of PM CARES. This was not replied to within the stipulated 30 days. Later, it was announced that the PM CARES fund was a private trust exempt from public scrutiny. It was not a 'public authority', meaning it wasn't part of the government.[1]

However, it dodged requirements that other private entities had to follow. For instance, it was given permission to take foreign money despite not having been active for three years, a condition imposed on other private trusts.

It also brushed aside the legal requirement that none of its trustees have a criminal case pending against them. Per his own admission, one of the trustees, Amit Shah, had acknowledged pending prosecutions against him.

PM CARES was also apparently exempt from the transparency provisions of the Foreign Contributions Act, not having filed its quarterly reports in the prescribed form as all other FCRA entities are required to do after a change

---

[1] 'PM CARES is not a public authority under RTI Act: PMO', 30 May 2020, *The Hindu*

in the law in 2015, effected by Modi himself. This requirement is for the fund to reveal, within 15 days of each quarter ending, the details of donors, amounts and dates of receipt.

Because the fund was declared by the Supreme Court as not part of the government, this implies that the fund was in violation of FCRA,[2] which was a crime.

The whole thing appeared to have been put together in haste and on a whim without thinking through the legal framework. In May 2020, the Companies Act was amended with retrospective effect to make PM CARES eligible for receiving the corporate donations it had already taken.[3]

This was under the rule that 'contribution to any fund set up by the Central Government for socio-economic development and relief qualifies as CSR expenditure'. However this would also bring the fund into the purview of RTI, which the government continued to resist.[4]

The retrospective amendment had repercussions: it apparently meant that corporate social responsibility (CSR) activity would no longer be dependent on whether the fund had been set up by the Union government or not. P. Chidambaram asked, 'If the Fund is a private established fund, why are donations to the Fund counted against CSR? Will donations to other privately-established funds be also counted against CSR?'[5] He further asked, 'Was the Fund set up by the Central government as concluded by the Ministry of Corporate Affairs? If not, who set up the Fund and in what capacity? If the Fund was not set up by the central government, why are the PM and three Ministers serving as Trustees? Who appointed them as Trustees?'

RTI information regarding the setting up of the PM CARES fund from the Cabinet Secretariat, the Union law ministry, and the Union labour and employment ministry produced a response from the Cabinet Secretariat that there was 'no agenda item in any Cabinet meeting' related to the PM CARES fund. It was strange, activist Anjali Bharadwaj noted, that the decision to set up a body in which the PM was the chair and three ministers were trustees

---

[2] We have discussed this law, which has been used to strangle NGOs and civil society, in chapters 'Good Governance' and 'The Devil's Workshop'.

[3] 'Modi govt amends Companies Act, makes PM CARES eligible to receive CSR funds', 27 May 2020, *India Today*

[4] 'Ministry of Corporate Affairs' document shows PM-CARES fund should fall under RTI', 22 August 2020, *TheWire.in*

[5] 'Why count corporate donations to PM Cares under CSR if fund privately established: P Chidambaram', 21 August 2020, *The Financial Express*

did not go through the Cabinet and had not been approved by the Cabinet Secretariat.

In July 2020, the BJP prevented parliamentary scrutiny of PM CARES. The Public Accounts Committee was stopped from taking up the matter after BJP MPs did not allow it to do so.[6]

Overwhelmed by questions about the lack of transparency, the PMO refused to respond to further RTI queries pleading a lack of manpower.[7]

In December 2020, the government claimed PM CARES was in fact a body 'owned by, controlled by and established by the government of India', but it still was exempt from the RTI law.[8]

This contradicted the deed under which the fund was established on 27 March, which said it was not owned or controlled by the government: 'The trust is neither intended to be or is in fact owned, controlled or substantially financed by any government or any instrumentality of the government. There is no control of either the central government or any state governments, either direct or indirect, in the functioning of the trust in any manner whatsoever.'[9]

Earlier in the year, the fund's website was updated to note that SARC & Associates would audit the fund. That is, PM CARES would not be audited by the government machinery but an external auditor. The excuse was that the National Relief Fund wasn't audited by CAG either. SARC & Associates is headed by an individual named Sunil Kumar Gupta. He had previously appeared on news channels to 'educate the youth' about various 'nation building' initiatives of the Modi government such as Make in India, Skill India, Start-Up India, Stand-Up India, Mudra Yojana and Credit Guarantee Fund. He had also authored a book on Modi's Make in India scheme.[10]

Gupta was also the statutory auditor of Oil and Natural Gas Corporation Limited, Indian Overseas Bank and the state-owned SBI General Insurance Company. And he was concurrent auditor of the RBI. He also served as

[6] 'BJP blocks parliament panel review of PM CARES fund, Coronavirus response', 11 July 2020, *NDTV*

[7] 'PMO blocks RTI requests on PM-CARES again, says responding will "divert resources"', 18 August 2020, *TheWire.in*

[8] 'PM-CARES "controlled by government" but RTI doesn't apply: new flip-flop', 25 December 2020, *NDTV*

[9] '"PM Cares" 16-page trust deed says there's no government control over working of the trust', 16 December 2020, *The Economic Times*

[10] 'PM CARES fund now has "independent auditor" but remains beset by lack of transparency', 19 June 2020, *TheWire.in*

'advisor' to government entities including the Northern Railway, Delhi Development Authority, Ministry of Petroleum and Natural Gas, New Okhla Industrial Development Authority (NOIDA) and the Greater Noida Industrial Development Authority. He was a member of an NGO named the Rashtriya Antyodaya Sangh, linked to the RSS. Having such a person audit an already secretive and non-transparent entity raised questions that the government was unwilling to answer.

Modi was accused of coercing government employees into contributing to PM CARES. A government circular on 17 April 2020 said that unless individuals had 'objection to recover', a day's wages would be deducted from their salaries and sent to PM CARES. This was corrected later with another circular which said the deduction wouldn't be by default if there was no objection but would happen if the individual was 'willing to contribute'.

The armed forces sent Rs 203 crore from their salaries and public sector banks gave Rs 204 crore. Teachers and other employees of central educational institutions gave Rs 21 crore. A total of 38 government firms, including ONGC, Indian Oil and NTPC, gave Rs 2,100 crore. Public-sector units (PSUs) were not allowed to donate to the Prime Minister's National Relief Fund, but were lining up to give to PM CARES. Trinamool MP Mohua Moitra described the PSU contributions as 'courtiers of the emperor giving gifts to the emperor out of public money'.

Another problem with the circular was that it offered the government employee no choice as to which fund they would like to contribute to in the fight against Covid-19. They couldn't send the money to the National Relief Fund or to any other charitable organisation except PM CARES.[11]

PM CARES cornered the lion's share of CSR funding in India as well, as corporates naturally rushed to shower money on it over the NGOs that were competing for the same funds. (A law passed by Manmohan Singh requires companies to give 2 per cent of their profit towards CSR activity.) PM CARES received more than a third of the Rs 15,000 crore of total CSR money.[12]

It was revealed that Chinese firms that were banned by the government in the aftermath of the Ladakh crisis had contributed to PM CARES. TikTok gave Rs 30 crore, Huawei Rs 7 crore, Xiaomi Rs 15 crore and PayTM, with a 38 per cent Chinese stake, gave Rs 100 crore.[13] This was particularly striking

[11] 'The PM-CARES fund: flip-flops on an unnecessary issue?', 2 May 2020, *NewsClick.in*

[12] 'PM CARES received at least $1.27 bn in donations—enough to fund over 21.5 mn COVID-19 tests', 20 May 2020, *IndiaSpend.com*

[13] 'PM CARES: Cong questions Huawei, TikTok donations, seeks PM Modi's reply', 29 June 2020, *The Indian Express*

because the BJP had vociferously attacked the Congress after it was revealed
in 2020 that the Rajiv Gandhi Foundation had received donations from the
Chinese in 2005.

Other problems plagued the fund, also associated with its proclivity for
opacity. The PM CARES website said that it had allocated Rs 2,000 crore for
the supply of 50,000 'Make in India' ventilators. It turned out that contracts
were being given to firms that had no experience in making these medical
devices.[14]

A Gujarat firm that claimed to have developed ventilators in 10 days was
given a contract for 5,000 ventilators. These turned out to be dud machines,
forcing hospitals to put out an SOS for real ventilators.[15] This firm was
linked to the individual who had gifted Modi the famous suit with his name
in pinstripes.

RTIs from activist Anjali Bharadwaj showed there was inconsistency in
what was being paid to the suppliers, with ventilators being procured from
some firms at Rs 1.66 lakh and from others at Rs 8.62 lakh.[16]

Crores of rupees were given in advance to firms whose products, when
delivered, weren't good enough to be used.[17] One of these 'ventilators' even
caused a blaze in a Baroda hospital.[18] During the second wave of Covid, the
PM CARES ventilators were desperately required but were found[19] to be
unusable.[20]

In its second year as well, PM CARES continued to trouble those who
understood what it was doing to the polity. In January 2021, 100 retired
civil servants, including a former Research and Analysis Wing chief, wrote
to Modi. 'We have been keenly following the ongoing debate about the
Citizen Assistance and Relief in Emergency Situations, or "PM-CARES"—a
fund created for the benefit of people affected by the Covid pandemic.

---

[14] 'Company with no ventilator model got Rs 373 cr PM CARES order to make 10,000
ventilators', 23 September 2020, *Huffingtonpost.in*

[15] 'Behind Ahmedabad's ventilator controversy, a backstory of connections to top BJP
leaders', 21 May 2020, *TheWire.in*

[16] 'PM Cares ventilators: RTI reveals huge gap in pricing, 2 firms have no technical
clearances', 25 August 2020, *India Today*

[17] 'Gujarat ventilators fail clinical trial', 23 August 2020, *Ahmedabad Mirror*

[18] 'Fire in Gujarat hospital: PM Cares fame ventilator explodes; 39 patients have narrow
escape', 10 September 2020, *International Business Times*

[19] 'At least 592 PM Cares ventilators not used in Rajasthan: "571 complaints made to
BEL"', 26 May 2021, *The Indian Express*

[20] '"PM Cares" ventilators: 113 of 150 supplied in Marathwada "defective", Bombay HC
asks Centre to explain', 25 May 2021, *The Indian Express*

Both the purpose for which it has been created as well as the way it has been administered have left a number of questions unanswered,' they said in the letter.[21]

'It is essential that the position and stature of the Prime Minister is kept intact by ensuring total transparency in all dealings the Prime Minister is associated with,' they wrote.

There was no response.

The Sale of India's Democracy

In its 2014 manifesto, the BJP had one paragraph on electoral reforms. It read:

'BJP is committed to initiate electoral reforms to eliminate criminals. The BJP will seek, through consultation with other parties, to evolve a method of holding Assembly and Lok Sabha elections simultaneously. Apart from reducing election expenses for both political parties and Government, this will ensure certain stability for State Governments. We will also look at revising expenditure limits realistically.'

There is nothing about anonymous electoral bonds.

The electoral bonds scheme was announced by the Modi government through the Budget in 2017. The bonds would be a way for political parties to receive money through anonymous donors. The donor would have to reveal their identity to the bank while making the bond purchase, but the identity would not be revealed on the bond itself. Political parties could accept the money without being required to reveal who gave it. Voters would therefore not know who was funding and influencing political parties.

The change would allow foreign companies and even shell companies to donate to India's parties without having to inform anyone of the contribution or having their name revealed. It also undid that part of the Companies Act under which corporates had to disclose details of their political donations in their annual statement of accounts. Now they were no longer required to do so. The corporates had previously also been limited to donating a maximum of 7.5 per cent of their average three-year net profit to political parties. No longer, because they could now just go through the electoral bond route as the cap had been lifted legally.

The process to fund a party anonymously was made easy. Bonds would be available in multiples of Rs 1 crore, Rs 1 lakh and smaller sums at State

21 '100 former civil servants raise questions on transparency in PM CARES fund', 16 January 2021, PTI

Bank of India branches in 29 cities, including New Delhi, Gandhinagar, Chandigarh, Bengaluru, Bhopal, Mumbai, Jaipur, Lucknow, Chennai, Kolkata and Guwahati. A donor could purchase them through their bank account and hand them over to the party or individual of their choice, who could then encash them. They would be valid for 15 days. Bonds would be made available for purchase for the first 10 days of each quarter (in January, April, July and October). They would be available for an additional 30 days in years that had a Lok Sabha election.

This then was the scheme. Four days before the Budget of 2017, a bureaucrat spotted it in finance minister Arun Jaitley's speech, and noted that the assent of the RBI was required for such a large shift.[22] This was because the introduction of bonds required changes to the RBI Act, something that apparently the government did not know.

The officer drafted a proposed amendment to align the Act with the change and sent the file up the ranks for the finance minister to see. The same day, 28 January 2017, a Saturday, the RBI was sent a five-line email seeking its comments. The reply came on Monday, 30 January. The RBI said it was a bad idea because it went against the RBI's authority as the sole issuer of bearer instruments, meaning cash. These bonds, because they were anonymous, could become currency and undermine the faith in India's cash. On this point, the RBI was unambiguous: amending the law to facilitate this 'would seriously undermine a core principle of central banking legislation and doing so would set a bad precedent'.

The second objection the RBI had was that 'even the intended purpose of the transparency might not be achievable as the original buyer of the instrument (the bond) need not be the actual contributor to the party'. If person A purchased the bond and then sold it, at face value or more, to any entity, including a foreign government, that entity could gift it to a party. The nameless bond was as good as cash. 'The bonds are bearer bonds and transferable by delivery,' the RBI said, 'hence, who finally and actually contributes the bond to the political party will not be known.'

This would affect the money laundering law as well, the RBI said. The last point it made was that what was being proposed through the electoral bond scheme—the transfer of money from bank accounts of entities to political parties—could be done through a cheque, bank transfer or demand draft. 'There is no special need for, or advantage by, the creation of an Electoral Bearer Bond, that too by disturbing an established international practice.'

---

[22] 'Electoral bonds: Seeking secretive funds, Modi govt overruled RBI', 17 November 2019, *Huffingtonpost.in*

The man charged with steering the thing through the bureaucracy was Hasmukh Adhia, an IAS officer from Gujarat with a PhD in yoga. (He had earlier chaperoned the GST bill, and after he retired, Adhia was made chairman of Bank of Baroda and chancellor of the Central University of Gujarat). He dismissed the RBI's objections on two grounds.

Firstly, he said, 'It appears to me that the RBI has not understood the proposed mechanism of having pre-paid instruments for the purpose of keeping the identity of the donor secret, while ensuring the donation is made only out of fully tax paid money of a person.' By this he meant that because the original purchaser had to acquire the bonds through their official account, it made the donation clean. This was not a response to the RBI's specific objections. Adhia said that the 15-day time limit for redemption would mitigate against the RBI's other fears, without explaining how.

Secondly, he said, 'Also this advice has come quite late at a time when the Finance Bill is already printed.' It had actually come within hours of being sent for. It was hardly the RBI's fault that the advice had not been sought earlier. This was clearly deceit, but Adhia concluded that 'we may, therefore, go ahead with our proposal'. His colleague economic affairs secretary Tapan Ray, concurred with Adhia the same day, and on Wednesday, 1 February, Jaitley announced the scheme which became law with the passage of the Budget.

Asked by journalist Nitin Sethi of the *Huffington Post* (which carried a six-part investigation into electoral bonds, based on documents procured by RTI activist Commodore Lokesh Batra) why the government had ignored the RBI's objections, the finance ministry said it had taken the decision 'in good faith and in the larger public interest'.

At the stage when the law was passed, the details were not yet made public. This came in June 2017, when Tapan Ray revealed how the bonds would work in practice: 'The information regarding purchaser and payee shall be kept secret by the issuer bank. These details would also be beyond the purview of RTI.' (Ray was made chairman of Central Bank of India after he retired in 2018, and in 2019 he was also made CEO and managing director of Gujarat International Finance Tec City.)

The next body to say that the electoral bonds scheme was dangerous was the EC of India. In an affidavit to the Supreme Court, it said that to exclude the reporting of donations received by political parties through electoral bonds would have 'serious repercussions on the transparency aspect of political funding of political parties'.[23]

---

[23] 'Election Commission expresses reservations on donations via electoral bonds', 20 November 2019, *Business Standard*

Even earlier, the body had been alarmed by the changes to come.[24]

The chief election commissioner, Sunil Arora, wrote to the government asking it to reintroduce the cap of 7.5 per cent of net profit on corporate donations to political parties. The EC expressed its apprehension that the abolition of this provision 'would lead to increased use of black money for political funding through shell companies'. Like the RBI, the EC was unambiguous: 'The commission is of the view that the earlier provisions ensured that only profit making companies with a proven track record provide donations to political parties and accordingly, it is recommended that this provision may be reintroduced.'

It also sought a change in the law requiring companies to declare their party-wise contributions in the interest of transparency.

The RBI was anxious because another warning from them, through a letter on 26 May 2017, had also been ignored by the Modi government. The EC had called the electoral bonds mechanism of anonymity 'a retrograde step as far as transparency of donations is concerned and this proviso needs to be withdrawn'. This referred to another change in law made by Modi in the Representation of the People Act, exempting parties from revealing how much money they had received through electoral bonds. The EC reiterated the concern raised by the RBI: that the bonds would make it impossible to ascertain whether the political party has taken donations in violation of the law which prevented contributions from foreign entities. The EC remained opposed to the law even after it was enacted and continued to resist though the Supreme Court gave the Modi government a pass.[25]

In the winter session of Parliament in 2018, Rajya Sabha member Mohammad Nadimul Haque asked the Modi government: had the EC of India raised concerns about electoral bonds? The government lied. It had not received 'any concerns from Election Commission on the issue of Electoral Bearer Bonds', it claimed.[26] When this lie was caught, the government dissembled—apparently, the EC letter had been sent to the Ministry of Law and not to the Ministry of Finance and so this could not be counted as a concern.

---

[24] 'EC had flagged concerns over electoral bonds to Modi govt after Lok Sabha elections too', 28 November 2019, *ThePrint.in*

[25] 'EC likely to oppose electoral bonds in Supreme Court, once again', 27 January 2020, *ThePrint.in*

[26] 'Electoral bonds: Confidential EC meeting exposes Modi govt's lies to Parliament', 19 November 2019, ADR, https://adrindia.org/content/electoral-bonds-confidential-ec-meeting-exposes-modi-govts-lies-parliament

The bonds also gave the government a handle on who was giving money to their rivals. This came to light after *The Quint* bought two bonds for Rs 1,000 each and had them tested.[27] The lab report found a hidden serial number 'visible on the right top corner of the original document showing fluorescence when examined under Ultra Violet Light'. It turned out that the bank was obliged to share these numbers with the ED and CBI, both notorious for being misused by the government (the Supreme Court had called the CBI a 'caged parrot' once), if they asked for them. The donor would have anonymity from public scrutiny but not from the BJP. This secret numbering of bonds opened a route to the government to go after those who had donated to the Opposition, further disincentivising corporates from funding any party other than the one in power.

Even within this framework, the Modi government ordered the violation of the bonds scheme rules the year they were introduced. The idea of a fixed window of time during which bonds could be purchased was jettisoned in 2018 to facilitate the receipt of money for state elections in Karnataka, Chhattisgarh, Madhya Pradesh, Mizoram, Rajasthan and Telangana.

The BJP received 95 per cent of the money from bonds in the first sales of 2018.[28] This is not surprising. Corporates donate to parties for a reason. Money comes to the party in power, because the party in power can facilitate the change the corporate requires. The Modi government made it easier for corporates and foreign entities to intervene in Indian politics and government policy. By May 2019, more than Rs 6,200 crore worth of electoral bonds had been sold and secretly donated to political parties.[29] Of the Rs 6,210 crore of bonds that were sold till December 2020, Rs 5,702 crore was in 5,702 bond denominations of Rs 1 crore each. Another Rs 491 crore came in 4,911 bond denominations of Rs 10 lakh each.

Only 47 bonds of Rs 1,000 each, which presumably ordinary citizens were using to fund the parties of their choice, were sold, and only 70 bonds of Rs 10,000 each. This meant that almost the entire sum was coming to political parties from large entities of unknown provenance.

RTI activists who asked the State Bank of India to reveal the names of those who had purchased the Rs 1 crore bonds were told that this was a

[27] 'Secret policing? The Quint finds hidden numbers on electoral bonds', 12 April 2018, *The Quint*
[28] 'Electoral bonds: Ruling BJP bags 95% of funds', 29 November 2018, *The Economic Times*
[29] 'Electoral bonds worth Rs 6,210 crore sold since 2018, Rs 1.85 crore of taxpayers' money spent: RTI', 7 December 2020, *Scroll.in*

private matter which could not be revealed.[30] The Information Commission, now firmly under the grasp of the government, concurred: 'There appears to be no larger public interest overriding the right of privacy of the donors and donees concerned.'[31]

It was not in the interest of voters to know who was funding political parties in Modi's India. To put the money coming in through the bonds into perspective, consider that in 2014, the BJP had received only Rs 171 crore in donations from unknown sources.[32] In 2017–18, before the bonds scheme was enforced, the BJP got Rs 437 crore. This was 93 per cent of all political donations in the country.[33] It was not market share that was the issue for the BJP; it was the overall size of the market, which was limited by not having a mechanism for corporates and other entities to make large, anonymous donations. Over Rs 3,600 crore in electoral bonds was purchased in March and April 2019 alone, just before the Lok Sabha election, and most of it, as we have noted earlier, was given to the BJP.

This is why the electoral bonds scheme was an absolute triumph for Modi, though it permanently compromised the transparency and integrity of the political and electoral funding of India's democracy.

Sleight of Hand

Electoral bonds were legislated into the polity through a dodgy manner which the Modi government has used to undermine federalism and parliament. This is the use of the Money Bill. This is a prospective law or amendment that may only be introduced in Lok Sabha and needs to be passed there with a simple majority. Following this, it may be sent to the Rajya Sabha for its recommendations, which the Lok Sabha may reject if it chooses to. If such recommendations are not given within 14 days, it will deemed to be passed by parliament. In essence, the Rajya Sabha has no say on a law if it is pushed as a Money Bill.

The content of a bill determines whether it is a Money Bill or not. A bill is said to be a Money Bill if it only contains provisions related to taxation,

---

[30] 'Electoral bonds: SBI refuses yet again to divulge information on Rs 1 crore donors', 11 January 2020, *TheWire.in*

[31] 'Electoral bonds: CIC says revealing names of donors not in public interest, violates RTI', 23 December 2020, *The Indian Express*

[32] 'BJP top recipient of donations to political parties in fiscal 2015', 8 December 2015, *Mint*

[33] 'Election Commission data reveals 93 percent of donations in 2017–18 went to BJP', 17 January 2019, *The Caravan*

borrowing of money by the government, and expenditure from or receipt to the Consolidated Fund of India. Bills that only contain provisions that are incidental to these matters would also be regarded as a Money Bill. Note the two times the word 'only' has been used.

But who decides whether or not a piece of legislation is a Money Bill? At his discretion, the Speaker. In the Westminster tradition, the Speaker is a hallowed figure who, once elected, becomes an independent member respected and obeyed by all parties. In India, the Speaker is a lackey who has no autonomy and toes the party line (this is why, in Indian elections with close results and the prospect of horse-trading, parties mount a fearsome battle to control the Speaker's chair).

The Modi government knew that the electoral bonds issue would run into serious trouble with the Opposition, given that it was meant to foundationally erode India's democracy. In the Lok Sabha, where the numbers were overwhelmingly in Modi's favour, this did not matter. In the Rajya Sabha, the Opposition was strong. To ensure that the funding of elections through bonds would happen, the change was disguised as a Money Bill.

The bonds scheme required amendments in the Foreign Contribution Regulation Act, 2010, Representation of the People Act, 1951, Income Tax Act, 1961 and the Companies Act, 2013. The change in the Companies Act would get rid of that provision which limited corporates from donating a maximum of 7.5 per cent of their net profit and the provision that forced companies to reveal which party they had funded. The changes to these were passed off as being related to taxation, though that was not true.

For the bureaucrats, this was dangerous territory and they were wary. Under Jaitley, the corporate affairs ministry held a meeting on 8 March 2017 to discuss some matters unrelated to electoral bonds, such as the role of independent directors in companies. A week after the meeting, a file noting made on 16 March revealed that the amendment relating to the bond had also been discussed and decided 'among other things'. The file did not say who made the proposal but said that it had been raised in 'informal discussions'.

Nitin Sethi of the *Huffington Post*, who reported this, pointed out that the Supreme Court, in an October 2013 judgement, had ruled such informal decisions were illegal: 'We are of the view that the civil servants cannot function on the basis of verbal or oral instructions, orders, suggestions, proposals, etc. and they must also be protected against wrongful and arbitrary pressure exerted by the administrative superiors, political executive, business and other vested interests.'[34]

But this was the way in which India's pressured bureaucrats succumbed to what the Modi government wanted so badly. The same day, 16 March 2017, the corporate affairs ministry asked the law ministry: 'Whether the proposed changes in section 182 of the Companies Act may be made through official amendment in the Finance Bill, 2017.'

The law ministry also replied the same day, through a note prepared by their legal advisor. It said that what was being proposed 'in the light of the above factual and Constitutional position… may not be considered as money bill'.

But having said this, they let it pass with the hope that 'in order to avoid considering this practice as a precedent it is advisable to adopt the extant regular legislative practice and procedure in future'. These revelations came from the material dug up by RTI activist Saurav Das. When he asked the PMO to reveal the material it had on the electoral bonds issue—file notings, correspondence, minutes of meetings and so on, he was told by the PMO: 'The request of the applicant is sweeping, roving and generic in nature. It does not highlight any specific information the applicant intends to seek from this office.' He was also given the standard deflection also used in the PM CARES matter: 'The supply of information in this form would divert resources of the public authority disproportionately.'[35]

The decision by the Modi government to violate parliamentary tradition, transparency and, in all probability, the law was taken much earlier.[36] The Budget for 2015 had other laws inserted into it that were passed off as Money Bills. In March the next year, the Aadhaar (Targeted Delivery of Financial and Other Subsidies, Benefits and Services) Bill, 2016, was passed as a Money Bill. P.D.T. Acharya, the former secretary general of the 15th and 16th Lok Sabha, a position held by someone who assists and guides the Speaker in their constitutional duties, analysed the legislation.

He wrote that Aadhaar did not deal with imposition, abolition, alteration of tax, did not deal with the regulation of borrowing or giving a guarantee by the government and did not deal with the Consolidated Fund of India.[37] It dealt with a unique identity number, regulated the enrolment process

[34] 'Law ministry said Modi govt's route to pass electoral bonds was illegal but signed off anyway', 27 January 2020, *Huffingtonpost.in*

[32] 'RTI reveals electoral bond scheme passed after only "informal discussion" among officials', 28 January 2020, *TheWire.In*

[36] 'Government's Money Bill strategy makes Opposition wary', 6 August 2015, *The Hindu*

[37] 'Show me the money', 12 March 2016, *The Indian Express*

to collect demographic and biometric information, and created a statutory authority for regulating and supervising the process. It did not meet any of the requirements for it to be called a Money Bill, and yet it was.

Acharya wrote that the Constitution reposed faith in the fairness and objectivity of the Speaker. His decision needed to conform to constitutional provisions, else it was not a decision under the Constitution. And yet it was taken. This was duplicity through nomenclature.

As we have noted, the Supreme Court judgement that validated Aadhaar also sanctified its passing as a Money Bill. When it first took up the matter, the court, then under Chief Justice J.S. Khehar, said, 'If the Speaker says blue is green, then we will ask the speaker to say it's blue. We can't let it go as green.' However, the judgement, under Chief Justice Dipak Misra, decided it could let blue go as green. The bench passed the order 4:1. The dissenting judge, Justice D.Y. Chandrachud, said that 'the passing of the Aadhaar Act as money bill is a fraud on the constitution'.[38]

The 2017 Budget had passed with 40 non-financial amendments snuck into the Finance Bill. Other than electoral bonds and Aadhaar, it included one in which the Modi government appropriated power over the appointments, tenure, removal and reappointment of chairpersons and members of 26 different tribunals. These included the National Green Tribunal, the Income Tax Appellate Tribunal, the National Company Law Appellate Tribunal and the Industrial Disputes Tribunal, which performed roles that were originally undertaken by the higher judiciary. This was altered by the change, basically attacking the separation of powers.

The tribunals are judicial bodies, each governed by a separate statute, with separate rules for selection and removal of members, salaries and service conditions. The Finance Act gave the government absolute power to govern their operations. The Supreme Court, likely because this was intrusion into their own domain, stepped in and struck down this part of the Finance Act. It did not address the other aspects of the spurious legislation.[39]

The cavalier use of the Money Bill by Modi was attacked—in the expected courteous manner—by his predecessor: 'In the recent past, we have seen instances of misuse of the Money Bill provision by the Executive, leading to bypassing the Rajya Sabha on crucial legislations of importance, without any deliberation. Those in Treasury benches must ensure that such instances are

[38] '"Aadhaar Act is unconstitutional": The fiery dissent of Justice D.Y. Chandrachud', 26 September 2018, TheWire.in
[39] 'Supreme Court refers passage of Finance Act 2017 as money bill to a larger bench', 23 November 2019, Scroll.in

avoided. It dilutes the stature and importance of our institutions, including the Rajya Sabha,' Manmohan Singh said in parliament, adding that the body 'has a central role to provide checks and balances to a majority government in the Lok Sabha, along with its other key role is to represent the interest of the states in our federal Union.'[40]

The government did not respond.

In fact, the government disallowed the Rajya Sabha from voting on a most important legislation—the farm bills.[41]

On 20 September 2020, ordinances that had cleared the Lok Sabha were pushed through the Rajya Sabha on a 'voice vote' and not a division vote, meaning an actual vote where ayes and noes are counted. The excuse given was that the individual in control, deputy chairman Harivansh Narayan Singh, was distracted by the disorder in the House and did not notice that a division vote had been demanded. Rajya Sabha television stopped its live broadcast while this was happening and the microphones of the MPs were switched off. (The BJP took the cue and followed the same pattern elsewhere. In the Karnataka Legislative Council, where it lacked a majority, the BJP passed its anti-cow slaughter bill through a voice vote, ignoring the demand for a division vote.)[42]

The two laws given birth in this manner were the Farmers' Produce Trade and Commerce (Promotion and Facilitation) Act, 2020 and the Farmers' (Empowerment and Protection) Agreement of Price Assurance and Farm Services Act, 2020. The first law removed the monopoly of government-run agriculture markets, or mandis, and allowed the sale of produce outside these. It also forbade the taxing of these new spaces. This meant that, over time, the mandis, which are taxed, would become redundant. This would damage the interests of farmers in those states where the mandis were efficiently run and procurement happened to the satisfaction of farmers.

The second law made contract farming possible. However, the law said that aggrieved farmers could not move court in case the buyer defaulted—they could only approach the State bureaucracy for resolution. A third law undid the banning of hoarding of essential commodities, allowing corporations to stock up as much grain as they wanted. The Modi government said it had the farmers' interests in mind when it wrote up these legislations (the intent,

[40] 'Manmohan Singh raps Modi govt for misuse of "money bill" provisions', 18 November 2019, *Business Standard*
[41] 'Video of farm bill vote shreds government version, deputy chairman reacts', 28 September 2020, *NDTV*
[42] 'Anti-cow slaughter bill passed in Karnataka', 8 February 2021, *The Hindu*

it was said, was to double the incomes of farmers, which had stagnated over years). But if that was the case it was unexplained why the laws had provisions which seemed to deliberately go against the interest of the farmers.

Other than the manner in which they were passed, the laws also appeared to violate the Constitution under which agriculture is a state subject. It is for the states to legislate laws on the subject and not the Union. Here, the excuse given was that these laws really regulated trade and not agriculture itself. The bills were signed by the president a week later and became law, triggering a protest that became a mass movement (more about this in the chapter 'The Devil's Workshop').

The government had not allowed scrutiny of the bills by agreeing to send them to a committee. In fact, this passing of laws without any real understanding of what they contained through any rigorous process has accelerated through the Modi era. In the 14th Lok Sabha (2004–09), 60 per cent of the bills were referred to committees for scrutiny. In the next Lok Sabha (2009–14), this number was 71 per cent. In the first Modi government, this fell to 25 per cent. It wilfully undid the parliamentary convention of referring bills to department-related parliamentary standing committees for scrutiny and examination right after his first victory.

The number of laws that were scrutinised before being passed collapsed after Modi's second victory. The Opposition noticed, and 17 MPs from the Congress, Samajwadi Party, Bahujan Samaj Party, Telugu Desam Party and the Communist Party of India (Marxist) wrote to the government expressing their concern at the 'hurried passing' of bills without scrutiny.[43] They wrote that public consultation—in which groups and individuals engaged with particular subjects are invited by legislators to put forward their views on prospective legislations—had also stopped. 'Public consultation is a long established practice where parliamentary committees scrutinise bills, deliberate, engage and work towards improving the content and quality of the legislation,' they wrote.

This had no effect on Modi, and in 2020, not a single bill was sent to a committee for scrutiny. Between March and August that year, the government promulgated 11 ordinances, including one that amended the Income Tax Act and allowed 100 per cent tax exemption to donations made to the PM CARES fund. Ordinances are meant to be passed only when parliament is not in session and the government is required to take

---

[43] 'Rajya Sabha: Opposition MPs complain to Venkaiah Naidu about "hurried passage" of bills', 26 July 2019, *Scroll.in*

immediate action. No ordinance is allowed to be in force for more than six months without parliamentary approval. Here was legislation by ordinance that was voted into law without any scrutiny.

Even where there had been committees, the government prevented them from working.[44] Government MPs were 'using the rule book to stonewall scrutiny on issues that may raise uncomfortable questions for the government'. The committee on home affairs actually met to discuss Kashmir after the state had already been bifurcated.[45] After the pandemic, standing committees were disallowed from meeting even virtually, with the excuse that this might violate confidentiality.[46]

While the Opposition MPs complained, parliament took up and dispatched contentious laws on triple talaq and the RTI (both passed after a walkout from the Opposition), and the amendment to UAPA which allows the government to designate individuals as 'terrorists'. Similarly, the farm bills, the bill that skewered Kashmir's special status and the one amending citizenship were not referred to any of the committees of parliament for in-depth deliberation on a non-partisan basis. All would produce trouble later.

PRS Legislative Research's Chakshu Roy wrote why the abandonment of legislative scrutiny was a problem:

'In a nutshell, all laws do not receive the same amount of parliamentary attention. A few undergo rigorous scrutiny by Parliamentary Committees. Others are passed with just a simple debate on the floor of the House. When the treasury and Opposition agree, even the most far-reaching laws are passed by Parliament with alacrity. When there is disagreement on politically contentious Bills such as the two Bills related to agriculture, then the swift passage results in unruly scenes in Parliament. The outweighing factor is the government's urgency in enacting a particular legislation. When the government is in a hurry, even Bills amending the Constitution can be passed in two to three days.

'When Parliamentary Committees do not scrutinise Bills, it increases the chances of the country being saddled with half-baked laws.'[47]

---

[44] 'House panels, NDA members wave rule book to skirt debate', 22 November 2019, *The Indian Express*

[45] 'In Modi era, the role of parliamentary standing committees is getting diminished', 16 September 2020, *Scroll.in*

[46] 'A year later, same stand: no virtual meetings of House panels', 14 May 2021, *The Hindu*

[47] 'Modi govt's hasty passage of farm bills shows there is no sanctity to law-making in India', 22 September 2020, *ThePrint.in*

Modi reversed a tradition of consultation that even the British had followed as India's masters. When a law on forcible indigo cultivation began to be framed, and the Champaran Agrarian Bill was introduced in the Bihar–Odisha Legislative Assembly, many members demanded that it be referred to the select committee of the House for scrutiny and examination. The British government conceded and Gandhi was requested to examine the bill.[48]

When the Modi government decided to defang the RTI Act by exercising control over its officers, the Union did not even ask the Central Information Commission (CIC) for comments before amending the law. Asked by an RTI activist if it had been consulted, the CIC replied: 'No comments were sought and provided by CIC.'[49]

This was in violation of a policy requiring all draft rules to be placed in the public domain as well as sections of the RTI law obligating the government to publish facts affecting the public. In fact, on 27 July 2019, when asked to put this in public, the government had said in the Rajya Sabha through minister of state in the PMO Jitendra Singh: 'It is between the government and the officers, not the public. That is our response.' The RTI amendment also went through with no external input or scrutiny.[50]

The Modi government's attack on transparency continued in his treatment of the Whistle Blowers Protection Act. This law had received the assent of President Pranab Mukherjee on 9 May 2014, one week before Modi won the election.

It set safeguards ensuring that no public servant was harassed for making a disclosure. It said the burden of proof to show that the individual was not being victimised would lie on the State. It also protected witnesses and the identity of the complainant.

The law offered statutory protection to individuals who exposed corruption, and was required in a nation where such people are especially vulnerable. Data collected by the National Campaign for People's Right to Information and other groups revealed that 80 RTI applicants had been killed since 2014 and many hundreds assaulted around the country for seeking information from public authorities.[51]

[48] 'Even the British had Gandhi scrutinise the Champaran Agrarian Bill before it became law', 22 September 2020, *TheCitizen.in*

[49] 'Centre changed RTI law and rules on salaries, tenures without consulting CIC', 29 November 2019, *TheWire.in*

[50] 'Parliament approves RTI amendment; RS negates demand for select committee', 25 July 2019, *The Economic Times*

[51] '80 RTI activists killed since 2014, yet Modi govt "refuses" to implement whistleblowers act', 12 December 2019, *Counterview.net*

In 2018 alone, 18 people were killed for whistle-blowing, a letter to Modi from the activist groups in February 2019 said. 'These people could have been afforded protection had the government implemented the law,' a letter from RTI activists to Modi in May 2019, the fifth anniversary of the passage of the law, said.[52]

The Modi government not only did not implement the law, delaying this by refusing to frame its rules, rendering it redundant, but also chose to amend it. The 2015 amendment, which did not go through because of resistance from activists, diluted the provisions to the extent of making the law useless. The Modi government's amendments proposed the removal of the clause which safeguarded whistleblowers from prosecution under the Official Secrets Act for disclosing information as part of their complaint.

Offences under the Official Secrets Act were made punishable by 14 years, and this sort of harsh punishment would deter whistleblowers and defeat the purpose of the law: to encourage people to come forward and report wrongdoing, the activists' letter to Modi said.

The amendment also prevented the dissemination of any information which would 'prejudicially affect the sovereignty, integrity, security, strategic, scientific or economic interests of the State', which was over-broad and meaningless, giving the State too much discretion. And lastly, it also said that whistleblowers could not reveal information related to the 'competitive position of a third party' and other material of 'commercial confidence', unless it had previously been obtained through RTI. This again defeated the purpose of whistleblowing.

Facing resistance in diluting the Act, the Modi government chose instead to put it into cold storage, allowing the active brutalisation of those brave individuals who take on the State and the corrupt through their RTI activism.

Rafale Scandal: Modi 'Haggles' But Pays More

The story of Rafale is about how Modi made India pay 40 per cent more per aircraft than was agreed in a deal struck under Manmohan Singh, and how an agreement to make 108 of the planes in India was changed to make them all in France.

There are plenty of side stories as well: about how the deal was taken away from the experienced and profit-making public-sector Hindustan Aeronautics Ltd (HAL) and given to a broke Anil Ambani; how the French

---

[52] 'Five years after passing law to protect whistleblowers, govt yet to operationalise it', 22 February 2019, *TheWire.in*

president said this was at the instance of Modi; how Ambani's Reliance Entertainment signed a deal to jointly produce a film for this president's actress-partner two days before Modi struck his new Rafale deal.[53]

There was the usual complicity and tawdriness. The Supreme Court was lied to by the government and yet absolved it of any wrongdoing; a CBI chief was sacked in a midnight coup just before he was going to open an investigation into the Rafale scandal; the court itself, in its judgement, used factual errors to support Modi's case—and all this happened at the same time when the Chief Justice of the Supreme Court was being accused of sexual harassment.

The story ended with India having, even in February 2021, during the stand-off with China, only 11 Rafales. The previous deal would have given it 18 in flyaway condition, so the idea that 36 were needed urgently made no sense. And even after the Supreme Court dismissed a PIL to register an FIR and have the case investigated, the questions remained.

There are so many aspects to this story that it is best understood through a timeline.

The first part of it relates to the period before Modi became prime minister.

On 28 August 2007, the Ministry of Defence issued a Request for Proposal to manufacturers for procurement of 126 medium multi-role combat aircraft. This is a versatile sort of fighter able to conduct diverse operations, including air support for ground troops, unlike the Sukhoi which is classified as an air-superiority fighter.

The air force needed 10 squadrons of this type to take its 35 squadrons to the required 45, with 18 fighters in each squadron, meaning about 800 in all.

On 27 April 2011, the Indian Air Force (IAF) ruled out four of the six competing fighters: Boeing's F/A-18E/F Super Hornet; Lockheed Martin's F-16IN Super Viper; Saab's Gripen NG; and the Russian MiG-35. These were adjudged not to have met the IAF's performance requirements.

In May 2011, the IAF shortlisted two planes: Dassault's Rafale and the Eurofighter Typhoon. Their commercial bids were compared on a 'life cycle basis' to select the lower bidder.

On 31 January 2012, Dassault Aviation's Rafale aircraft was determined to have the lowest bid on a 'life cycle basis', and was selected. *The New York Times* reported that 'the contract with India would be Dassault's first export sale for the Rafale, which has been in service with the French military for

---

48 'Rafale talks were on when Reliance Entertainment helped produce film for François Hollande's partner', 31 August 2018, *The Indian Express*

more than a decade' and quoted an expert as saying that the French had been desperate: 'It would be a wonderful contract to win,' said Alexandra Ashbourne, an aerospace and defence industry consultant in London, because 'until now, Rafale has sort of (sic) an embarrassment for Dassault, kind of a white elephant.'[54]

On 15 May 2012, Francois Hollande became president of France.

On 13 March 2014, an agreement was signed between HAL and Dassault Aviation, under which HAL was responsible for 70 per cent and Dassault 30 per cent of the work, for 108 aircraft. The other 18 would be delivered to India in 'flyaway' (meaning fully manufactured) condition. This agreement transferred technology to HAL, which had previously worked on such arrangements to manufacture MiGs and Sukhoi fighter jets in Bangalore, Nasik and Koraput, Odisha.

On 16 May 2014, the NDA won the election and Modi became prime minister.

On 1 July 2014, French foreign minister Laurent Fabius came to India to meet Modi. At this time, the deal was still for 126 aircraft. A month before the meeting, Dassault Aviation chief executive Eric Trappier said that the company was hopeful of closing the deal by the end of 2014.

On 8 August 2014, defence minister Arun Jaitley told parliament that the 18 flyaway Rafales were expected to be delivered in three to four years from the signing of the contract, and the remaining 108 aircraft would be delivered in the next seven years (by 2021).

On 2 December 2014, French defence minister Jean-Yves Le Drian came to India and met Manohar Parrikar, who was now defence minister. They met to 'expedite contracts for 126 Rafale fighter jets' and also to iron out a guarantee clause, but reports now said that 'some differences have cropped up over transfer of technology'.[55]

On 1 January 2015, the Rafale deal suddenly ran into trouble. Parrikar told the media that there were 'complications' in the negotiations, without specifying what they were. He said the French were 'reluctant to meet their commitments', but again these commitments were not specified. Parrikar hinted that if HAL made additional Sukhoi fighters in Nasik, the Rafale might not be needed at all.[56]

---

[54] 'Dassault chosen to bid on $10 billion Indian military contract', 31 January 2012, *The New York Times*

[55] 'French defence minister Jean-Yves Le Drian meets Manohar Parrikar to push ahead with Rafale fighter jet deal', 2 December 2014, *The Economic Times*

[56] 'Rafale in storm clouds, Parrikar says IAF can make do with Sukhoi-30s', 1 January 2015, *Business Standard*

On 7 February 2015, Modi appeared to distance himself from the deal with Dassault. In response to a report saying he would be flying in a Rafale at the Aero India show from 18 to 22 February, his office put out a statement: 'With reference to a news item in a section of the media that "At Aero India, PM may fly in a Rafale", it is clarified that there is no plan for the Prime Minister Shri Narendra Modi to fly in any fighter jet. The news item is incorrect, misconceived and is not based on facts.'[57]

On 16 February 2015, a report quoted a Ministry of Defence source saying that the Rafale proposal was 'effectively dead'. This was blamed on the previous deal where an 'inexperienced MoD, working off incomplete and sketchy details provided by Dassault, had incorrectly adjudged the Rafale cheaper' because it had no experience in working with 'life cycle costing'. Having re-examined the deal and 'after three years of obtaining clear figures from the French, we find India would be paying significantly more than had been initially calculated'.[58] Once again, details were not given, nor was the official on the record.

On 10 March 2015, Dassault contradicted events unfolding in India. In a report, the company spoke about 'the continuation of exclusive negotiations with the Indian authorities and Indian industrial partners to finalise the contract for the sale / licensing of 126 Rafale'. The following day, Eric Trappier was quoted saying there had been progress in the contracts: 'Now, there will be a shared warranty as each partner will be responsible for its own work, and HAL will provide warranties for its own work.'[59]

On 8 April 2015, briefing the media on Modi's upcoming visit to France, foreign secretary Jaishankar was asked if progress on Rafale was expected and whether Modi was taking Parrikar with him. He ducked the Parrikar question and said Modi would not bring up Rafale: 'My understanding is that there are discussions under way between the French company, our Ministry of Defence, the HAL which is involved in this. These are ongoing discussions. These are very technical, detailed discussions. We do not mix up leadership level visits with deep details of ongoing defence contracts. That is on a different track. A leadership visit usually looks at big picture issues even in the security field.'[60]

---

[57] 'No plan for PM Narendra Modi to fly in any fighter jet', 7 February 2015, *India Infoline*

[58] 'Rafale proposal "effectively dead" as Dassault bid not cheapest', 16 February 2015, *Business Standard*

[59] 'Fact check: BJP's claim on why HAL was dropped from Rafale deal just doesn't fly', 20 September 2018, *TheWire.in*

[60] 'Transcript of media briefing by foreign secretary on Prime Minister's forthcoming visits to France, Germany and Canada', 8 April 2015, mea.gov.in

On 10 April 2015, Modi not only took up the issue in the absence of Parrikar, he concluded a new deal for the acquisition of 36 flyaway Rafales. This would give the RAF two squadrons instead of the 10 they required. The procurement rulebook, which mandated a process for acquisition, was tossed aside. Modi said at a press conference that 'our civil servants will discuss (terms and conditions) in more detail and continue the negotiations'. The French were quoted saying that this was a separate deal which came about because of India's 'urgent requirements'. Apparently, the original 126 plane deal was still on.[61]

On 11 April 2015, Parrikar said in Delhi that he was 'very happy that the Prime Minister has taken the initiative to purchase 36 aircrafts in "flyaway" and probably more in "Make in India" whether in Rafale or other mechanism'.[62]

On 14 April 2015, Parrikar said in an interview that 'I feel that some more Rafale jets maybe required but need to figure out how we acquire them … but how many will hinge on the cost factor.' On 1 June, he said India was not in fact buying more but only the 36.[63]

On 24 January 2016, Anil Ambani's Reliance invested 1.48 million Euro (then about Rs 12 crore) in a film produced by Hollande's partner, the actress Julie Gayet.[64]

On 26 January 2016, India and France signed the MoU for the 36 planes, leaving the issue of pricing still unresolved

On 19 March 2016, it was reported that negotiations had broken down, over the issue of a sovereign guarantee, which India was seeking.[65]

On 23 September 2016, a deal was struck for a price that would be 40 per cent higher per plane than the deal for the 126 aircraft.[66] The French would not give India a sovereign guarantee but would give instead a 'letter of comfort'.

On 3 October 2016, a year and a half after it had been signed, the MOU with Reliance was made public and Dassault announced it was forming a

---

[61] 'India orders 36 French-made Rafale fighter jets—PM Modi', 10 April 2015, *Reuters*

[62] 'Parrikar expresses delight over PM Modi's decision to purchase Rafale aircraft from France', 11 April 2015, ANI

[63] 'Parrikar says India will buy 36 Rafale jets from France instead of 126', 1 June 2015, *Hindustan Times*

[64] 'Rafale row: Reliance Entertainment confirms it paid 1.4 million euros for film by Hollande's partner through partner', 27 September 2018, *The Indian Express*

[65] 'Paris acknowledges India may not purchase Rafale', 19 March 2016, *Business Standard*

[66] 'India and France sign Rafale fighter jet deal', 23 September 2016, *BBC*

joint venture—Dassault Reliance Aerospace—with Anil Ambani holding 51 per cent in the company.[67]

On 18 November 2016, the government told parliament that the cost of each Rafale would be Rs 670 crore.[68]

On 31 December 2016, Dassault Aviation's annual report revealed that the actual price paid for each of the 36 aircraft was about Rs 1,600 crore, more than twice what the government of India had said it was.[69]

On 13 March 2017, Parrikar resigned as defence minister and returned to Goa as chief minister.

On 14 May 2017, Hollande's term as French president ended.

On 13 March 2018, a PIL was filed in the Supreme Court by Congressman Tehseen Poonawalla, which asked the government to disclose the transaction cost, and also asked why the cabinet's approval was not sought as part of the Defence Procurement Procedure before signing the procurement deal with France on 23 September 2016.

On 20 September 2018, T. Suvarna Raju, who had stepped down as HAL chief a few days earlier, said the organisation could have built the Rafales in India and should have been given the contract.[70]

On 22 September 2018, Hollande was quoted in an interview as saying that it was the Modi government that had insisted on Dassault partnering with Anil Ambani for Rafale. He said in an interview: 'The Indian government proposed this service group, and Dassault negotiated with Ambani. We did not have the choice, we took the interlocutor who was given to us.' When *India Today TV* spoke to the French journalists concerned, they were told that Hollande said the 'Indian government imposed Reliance on us'. The Congress alleged corruption and Rahul Gandhi coined the phrase 'chowkidar chor hai'.[71]

The next day, 23 September, Hollande confirmed what he had said, and added that the name of Reliance appeared as part of a 'new formula' by the Modi government after it came to power.[72]

---

[67] 'Dassault Aviation, Reliance Group form joint venture in India', 3 October 2016, *Defence News*

[68] 'Each Rafale to cost Rs 670 cr: Govt', 12 March 2018, *Hindustan Times*

[69] 'Government says Rafale cost secret, but had disclosed it in 2016', 7 February 2018, *The Times of India*

[70] 'HAL could have built Rafale jets in India, says former boss', 20 September 2018, *Hindustan Times*

[71] 'Ex-French prez Hollande's big Rafale shocker: Indian government wanted Reliance', 22 September 2018, *India Today*

[72] 'No, French ex-President Hollande did not deny his Rafale remarks to AFP: Here's what he said', 23 September 2018, *Scroll.in*

On 10 October 2018, the Supreme Court asked the government to file, in a 'sealed cover', details of the Rafale agreement. On 24 October, former Union ministers Yashwant Sinha and Arun Shourie and lawyer Prashant Bhushan moved the Supreme Court, seeking the registration of an FIR in the Rafale deal.

On 23 October 2018, at 2 a.m. in the morning, Modi divested CBI chief Alok Verma of his powers, apparently after he showed interest in filing an FIR on the Rafale matter. Delhi chief minister Arvind Kejriwal tweeted two days later: 'Is there a co-relation betn Rafale deal and removal of Alok Verma? Was Alok Verma about to start investigations into Rafale, which cud become problem for Modi ji?'

On 1 November 2018, it was revealed that Dassault had invested 40 million euro in another Anil Ambani firm (Reliance Airport Developers), which in 2016 had no revenues and, in 2017, revenues of Rs 6 lakh. This translated to a profit of Rs 284 crore for Anil Ambani's Reliance Infrastructure.[73]

On 10 November 2018, it was revealed that the government's claim that it was not paying a higher price but getting more extras turned out to be false. The India-specific enhancements, including helmet-mounted sights, radar warning receivers, radio altimeters, Doppler radars and cold starts, had been mentioned in the earlier tender as well.[74] In effect, Modi's negotiations resulted in HAL losing out on work and India paying 40 per cent more, or more than Rs 500 crore extra per plane.[75]

On 12 November 2018, the Union gave the pricing details in a 'sealed cover'. It told the court that HAL required '2.7 times higher man-hours compared to the French side for the manufacture of Rafale in India' and therefore could not be made the offset partner, and Dassault had been free to pick its partner.[76]

On 14 December 2018, the Supreme Court dismissed all petitions asking the CBI to file an FIR in the deal. The bench, headed by Chief Justice of India Ranjan Gogoi, was 'satisfied that there is no occasion to doubt the process'.

---

[73] 'Exclusive: Post-Rafale, Dassault investment in inactive Anil Ambani company gave Reliance Rs 284 crore profit', 1 November 2018, *TheWire.in*

[74] 'Most "extras" in 36-Rafale contract were also specified in earlier tender', 10 November 2018, *Business Standard*

[75] 'IAF's 36 Rafale aircraft cost 40% more than Dassault's earlier offer', 10 November 2018, *Business Standard*

[76] 'Rafale deal: HAL failed as offset partner due to unresolved issues with Dassault', 12 November 2018, PTI

November and December 2018 was also the same period in which the court and the home ministry acted against the woman who, as we have seen earlier, had accused Gogoi of sexual harassment. A week after she was dismissed, her husband and her brother-in-law—both Delhi Police constables—were suspended from service. The reason was not specified at the time.

The Supreme Court judgement absolved Modi on the basis of the government submission that 'pricing details have, however, been shared with the Comptroller and Auditor General, and the report of the CAG has been examined by the Public Accounts Committee'. The chairman of the PAC, Congressman Mallikarjun Kharge, said the same evening that this was a lie and it had not been examined by the body.[77]

On 15 December 2018, the government filed an affidavit to say that the 'error' appeared 'perhaps on account of misinterpretation of a couple of sentences in a note handed over to this Hon'ble Court in a sealed cover'.[78]

On 15 November 2018, Sudhanshu Mohanty, former financial advisor (defence services) and former controller general of defence accounts (defence services), in whose tenure the 36-plane deal was negotiated, said in an interview that the initial price of 5.2 billion euros was increased arbitrarily by India to 8.2 billion euros. This lower price by the negotiating team was 'overruled by the ministry'. He said that 'the Defence Acquisition Council headed by the defence minister and consisting of all top MoD honchos didn't recommend the case, and instead left it to the Cabinet Committee on Security to take a call. Why? This needs to be looked into. For, not in my fallible memory of defence capital acquisition can I recall such a thing— because it is strange, even queer.'[79]

On 2 January 2019, Sinha, Shourie and Bhushan moved court seeking a review of the 14 December judgement.

The same day, the Congress said that Parrikar was blackmailing Modi. The party produced audio recordings of a conversation between a Goa minister and a journalist. The minister says Parrikar has boasted about how 'each and every document of Rafale is with me'. Apparently, this was because he wanted to use it as leverage and remain chief minister despite being incapacitated by illness. Parrikar did not respond to the story.[80]

[77] 'Government did not share price of Rafale jet with parliament but revealed it to CAG, says Supreme Court', 15 December 2018, *CNBC*
[78] 'Centre says CAG–Rafale error in SC verdict is a grammatical "misinterpretation"', 15 December 2018, *TheWire.in*
[79] 'Letter of comfort gives little comfort, no guarantee future govt will honour it: Sudhanshu Mohanty', 15 November 2018, *The Economic Times*
[80] 'Parrikar is blackmailing PM: Rahul', 2 January 2019, *The Telegraph*

On 10 January 2019, the Supreme Court reinstated CBI chief Alok Verma. The next day, the Modi government transferred him out of the CBI and into the fire services.

On 8 February 2019, it was reported that the Ministry of Defence had in 2015 objected to Modi's conducting 'parallel negotiations' with Dassault. This had 'weakened the negotiating position of MoD and Indian negotiating team' and 'undermines our negotiating position seriously', the note said.[81]

On 17 March 2019, Parrikar died of cancer.

On 14 November 2019, the Supreme Court dismissed the review pleas and said there was no need for an FIR. In its judgements, it had confused Anil Ambani's firm with one owned by Mukesh Ambani, accepting the lie by the defence ministry which submitted to court that Dassault already had an MoU with Reliance when the UPA was in power.[82]

Gogoi retired three days later on 17 November, and was immediately appointed to the Rajya Sabha. Thus ended the saga of the Rafale deal.

The questions, though, remained.

Why was the requirement for 126 planes changed to 36, especially if only 11 would be delivered six years later? Why was there no record of the claim that, in March 2015, it was decided to end the 126-plane contract, especially when the French seemed unaware of this? Why did Modi sacrifice Make in India and State-owned HAL, if the only issue was man-hours? Surely the 'good governance' mantra could have improved the rate of production in a firm that was controlled by the Ministry of Defence? Why was the price 40 per cent higher when the equipment and accessories were the same? How and why did Ambani manage to insert himself into the deal? In April 2021 it was revealed by an investigation in France that Rafale had paid an Indian middleman Sushen Gupta over Rs 8 crore as a 'gift'. Why? This was not revealed.[83]

Following this, in July 2021, the French government appointed a judge to probe the Rafale deal and accusations of 'corruption', 'influence peddling', 'money laundering' and 'favouritism'.[84] All of this was brushed aside in India, and in time was forgotten in the media and disappeared from the public domain.

---

[81] 'Defence ministry protested against PMO undermining Rafale negotiations', 8 February 2019, *The Hindu*

[82] 'Which Ambani was it and why that matters', 22 September 2019, *The Telegraph*

[83] 'Rafale deal: Dassault paid 1 million euros to Indian middleman as "gift", claims report', 5 April 2021, *Scroll.in*

[84] 'Un nouveau cadeau de Dassault découvert Rafale Papers: la justice ouvre une enquête', 2 July 2021, mediapart.fr

The Ending of Transparency

'The CAG is the supreme audit institution of India and is expected to promote financial accountability and transparency in the affairs of the audited entities,' the CAG of India said in its 2019–20 performance report. But Modi's stranglehold on institutions has showed in the decay at the government's internal watchdog; CAG has stopped functioning effectively. The total number of CAG reports relating to Union government ministries and departments came down from 55 in 2015 to 14 in 2020, a fall of 75 per cent.[85] The fall was sequential going from 55 to 42, 45, 23, 21 and 14. Defence audit reports went from 7 in 2017 to zero in 2020. This was the same body that had done much to undo the Manmohan Singh government's reputation through its several strong reports, including on the 2G auction, coal block auction and the Commonwealth Games.

The CAG of India is Girish Murmu, a Gujarat officer so loyal to Modi that, in the past, he has been caught on tape intimidating senior officials from testifying against his boss.[86]

Former DGP of Gujarat R.B. Sreekumar, who headed the State Intelligence Bureau from 9 April 2002 to 17 September 2002, in an affidavit to the Nanavati Commission probing the Godhra riots, said Murmu 'tutored, intimidated, forced and pressured' him to depose in favour of Modi. Murmu was then principal secretary to Modi.

Sreekumar named another bureaucrat who was also present at the meeting and said he was told not to give his deposition in such a way that, 'more names would be opened up, leading to their summoning for cross-examination. I was also threatened that if I gave a statement contrary to the government's interests, I will be declared a hostile witness and dealt with suitably later. I told them that I would depose before the Commission as per the statutory requirements and will not suppress truth, because that would be an act of perjury'.

Murmu had been 'authorised and entrusted with the task of tutoring and briefing government officials deposing before the Nanavati Commission by the highest authorities of the government and Home Department' and that 'such a posture by Shri Murmu is possible only if he has the specific support and clearance from the higher authorities in the government, i.e. the Hon'ble

---

[85] 'CAGed? Top audit body's reports on Centre's money management down by 75 per cent', 7 March 2021, *The New Indian Express*

[86] 'GC Murmu—principal secretary to Narendra Modi—coaching witnesses to subvert truth', 25 October 2013, *TruthOfGujarat.com*

Home Minister / the Hon'ble Chief Minister'.[87]

Modi made him governor of Kashmir and then the CAG.

The government's website, pmindia.gov.in, has a section on transparency which reads: 'Prime Minister Narendra Modi firmly believes that transparency and accountability are the two cornerstones of any pro-people government. Transparency and accountability not only connect the people closer to the government but also make them equal and integral part of the decision making process.'

It is hard to reconcile these words with the actual actions of Modi and his government on vital issues where opacity was preferred and promoted. This entire section, headlined 'Quest for transparency' on the PM's site, has only 184 words and reads as if they were strung together by someone with little intellectual capacity: 'Rules and policies were not framed in AC Chambers but among the people,' it says. 'Draft policies were put online for people to give their feedback and suggestions' is apparently an instance of transparency.

It states that Modi's 'strong resolve to transparency backed by the manner in which he put this commitment to practice indicates an era of open, transparent and people-centric government for the people of India'.

No, it doesn't. The Modi years have been as opaque, and in many ways even more so, as those of any government before him.

---

[87] 'The controversial record of a Modi aide who may head the Enforcement Directorate', 10 October 2015, *TheWire.in*

11

MAHABHARAT

Three things were required from the Indian government in the battle against the coronavirus pandemic, which the prime minister had likened to the Mahabharat. Firstly, to take the threat seriously, emphasise responsible behaviour and ensure that no large gatherings were permitted. Secondly, to use the initial period, when there weren't too many cases, to prepare and strengthen the healthcare system in anticipation of the coming waves. Thirdly, to fully vaccinate as many Indians as quickly as possible, the only real defence against the virus.

Let us examine the record on each in turn. On the first, the Modi government did not take the threat seriously. It assessed firstly that India's economy would not be affected by the pandemic.[1] In a triumphant speech to the Davos World Economic Forum in January 2021, Modi himself declared India's victory over the pandemic.

In his address, he first dismissed what unnamed others had apparently predicted: 'I remember what many reputed experts and top institutions in the world said in February, March, April last year. It was predicted that India would be the most affected country from Corona all over the world. It was said that there would be a tsunami of Corona infections in India, somebody said 700–800 million Indians would get infected while others said 2 million Indians would die.'[2]

Then he laid out how disaster had been averted: 'India did not allow itself to be demoralised. Rather, India moved ahead with a proactive approach with public participation. We worked on strengthening the Covid-specific

---

[1] 'Coronvirus won't have adverse impact on Indian economy: Anurag Thakur', 18 March 2020, *Business Standard*

[2] 'English rendering of PM's address at the World Economic Forum's Davos Dialogue', Prime Minister's Office, pib.gov.in

health infrastructure, trained our human resources to tackle the pandemic and used technology massively for testing and tracking of the cases.'

India had done this, he said, while also going from being reliant to 'Atmanirbhar': 'In the initial period of Corona, we were importing masks, PPE kits and test kits. Today, we are not only taking care of our domestic needs, but also serving the citizens of other countries by exporting these items. And today it is India which has also launched the world's largest Corona vaccination programme.'

All of this had produced success, he concluded: 'Today India is among those countries which have succeeded in saving the lives of the maximum number of its citizens and … the number of people infected with Corona today is rapidly decreasing.'

Modi located his success in the global space: 'It would not be advisable to judge India's success with that of another country. In a country which is home to 18 per cent of the world population, that country has saved humanity from a big disaster by containing Corona effectively.' Lastly, having saved humanity, Modi would also come to the rescue of the rest of the world: 'India is saving the lives of citizens of many countries by sending Covid vaccines and helping set up vaccination infrastructure there.'

Modi made the Davos speech on 28 January. It was apparently his mic drop moment. In all of February, he had one single engagement related to Covid, and even this was unrelated to India: he spoke to leaders of 10 neighbouring nations. In all of March, again, he had but one engagement related to Covid: a gathering of the country's chief ministers.[3] This was despite the government having received a warning on the second wave having begun and to expect a peak in May.[4] In April, as it became apparent that something was very wrong, the number of his engagements suddenly rose to 21, an act of reaction.

The slackness ran through the whole administration. The Covid taskforce Modi set up did not meet in February or March.[5] Modi had himself chaired its meeting in May 2020 when it was formed,[6] but now appeared to have lost interest or thought it was not important or necessary.

---

3 'PM Modi held 21 meetings over second wave of Covid', 20 April 2021, Hindustan Times

4 'Told Modi govt in March second Covid wave afoot, expect peak in mid-May: Expert panel chief', 30 April 2021, *ThePrint.in*

5 'India's COVID-19 taskforce did not meet in February, March despite surge, say members', 22 April 2021, *The Caravan*

6 'PM chairs task force meeting on COVID-19', 5 May 2020, *The Hindu BusinessLine*

On 21 February, the BJP adopted a resolution which read: 'It can be said with pride that India not only defeated Covid under the able, sensitive, committed and visionary leadership of Prime Minister Shri Narendra Modi, but also infused in all its citizens the confidence to build an "Atmanirbhar Bharat". The party unequivocally hails its leadership for introducing India to the world as a proud and victorious nation in the fight against Covid.'[7]

It is not easy to understand why the government said India had defeated the pandemic except if one assumes that Modi meant it and believed it. He was himself not wearing a mask when he got vaccinated with his first dose on 1 March. He appeared without a mask at a handicraft fair on 17 December, and when a stall owner offered him one, Modi refused it.[8] The casualness was infectious and by February 2021 many states had dismantled health infrastructure they had set up during the first wave.[9]

On 10 March, the BJP replaced its chief minister in Uttarakhand because he wanted to restrict the Kumbh Mela coming up the following month to a purely ceremonial and symbolic one, i.e., without physical attendance by the masses. This was vetoed and he was replaced overnight.[10] He would later say that he had worried about the Kumbh becoming a super-spreader event.[11] The Kumbh Mela takes place every 12 years and should ordinarily have happened in 2022. However, astrologers convinced the BJP government that April 2021 was more auspicious.

On 21 March, front-page advertisements with Modi's photograph were released in newspapers across India, inviting people to the Kumbh Mela. Perhaps this was to communicate the confidence that the government felt that it had overcome the pandemic. Not only had a religious festival involving millions in close proximity for a month been allowed, it had actually been advanced by the government, and the individual attempting to mitigate against the damage of the pandemic was removed.

The confidence that Covid was not a serious threat perhaps came from

---

[7] 'Resolution passed in BJP national office bearers meeting at NDMC Convention Centre, New Delhi', 21 February 2021, BJP.org

[8] 'Video of Indian PM Narendra Modi refusing a mask goes viral', 18 December 2020, *The Independent*

[9] 'State after state shut down special Covid centres just before second wave', 26 April 2021, *The Indian Express*

[10] 'BJP fired ex-Uttarakhand chief minister T.S. Rawat for restricting Kumbh gatherings', 8 May 2021, *The Caravan*

[11] 'Always feared Kumbh could act as super-spreader, my worst fears have come true, says former Uttarakhand CM Trivendra Rawat', 20 June 2021, *The Times of India*

India's relatively low number of positive cases (a figure of uncertain value given that testing levels in India were lower than in most democracies) and relatively low official fatality rate. Some experts in the government body were also misled by national sero surveys (indicating what part of the population had already been exposed to Covid-19) with samples taken from a few areas to conclude that, because real infections were perhaps 30 times the official number, a sort of herd immunity had been arrived at.[12]

India compared itself to Italy, the US, Brazil and the UK, and concluded to its satisfaction that it had done a better job than the world. A more appropriate and more honest comparison would have been with the rest of South Asia, which has similar infrastructure, or with China, the only nation comparable for size. Here, the numbers were against India, the leader in both per million cases and fatalities in South Asia and so far behind China as to beggar belief. China had actually contained the spread of the virus by April 2020, almost immediately after the outbreak in Wuhan had been contained.[13]

Many had peddled the belief that Indians had some special immunity because of the unhygienic conditions they were surrounded by, and perhaps Modi believed that as well. Meanwhile, his cabinet actively promoted quackery through the entire pandemic. In May 2020, Modi's minister for heavy industry and parliamentary affairs promoted a brand of papad saying it would 'be very helpful in fighting Coronavirus by developing antibodies'.[14]

On 19 February 2021, the Union health minister himself appeared at an event to launch a cure (which it wasn't) for Covid formulated by the yoga teacher turned billionaire businessman Ramdev that was 'certified by the World Health Organisation' (which it wasn't). Dr Harsh Vardhan was joined on this stage by another cabinet minister, Nitin Gadkari, who also held out the magic potion, legitimising it for crores of Indians as a cure.[15]

Modi himself promoted measures to 'combat' coronavirus which were featured by the government ministries and included yoga and meditation, cooking with haldi, jeera, dhaniya and lahsun, eating chyawanprash and drinking herbal tea. The government said these would boost immunity

---

[12] 'There may not be a second peak of COVID-19 in India: Experts', 19 December 2020, PTI

[13] 'China's successful control of COVID-19', 1 November 2020, The Lancet

[14] 'Minister Arjun Ram Meghwal claims papad helps fight COVID-19, here's how netizens reacted', 24 July 2020, The Indian Express

[15] 'IMA "shocked" over Patanjali's claim on Coronil; demands explanation from Harsh Vardhan', 22 February 2021, The Hindu

against the virus.[16] The Ayush ministry said it had developed a 'poly-herbal drug' called Ayush-64, which was apparently useful—though it did not explain how—for those who had Covid-19 but were 'asymptomatic', meaning feeling no effects.

In March 2021, the Union government's science ministry funded research to see if chanting the Gayatri Mantra could treat Covid.[17]

Even in May 2021, when there were over 4,000 deaths daily and hospitals were overwhelmed with patients dying because of a lack of equipment, medicine or treatment, the BJP's leaders were promoting cow urine as a cure for the coronavirus.[18] A BJP minister in Madhya Pradesh performed a 'yagna treatment', which would head off the third wave of Covid.[19]

In India, this absence of seriousness from the government generally and the prime minister and the cabinet specifically produced a dangerous neglect that the virus exposed ruthlessly. In this Mahabharat, India's delinquent general marched his side into an ambush where Covid had been waiting. It took a savage toll on Indians, slaughtering them in the thousands daily.

On the first day of April 2021, the daily death toll was 400. After 15 days, it tripled to 1,200, and then tripled again to 3,600 by 28 April, showing the world what a virus able to spread exponentially can do. And yet the government not only continued to believe the country was over the pandemic, it was actively and gratuitously encouraging the spread of the virus.

The first order of business in tackling a pandemic is to take it seriously. It is fair to conclude that Modi did not. Politics and appeasing religious sentiment came first. In February 2021, the EC announced an eight-phase election cycle in Bengal, which would carry on till the beginning of May. The ruling party in Bengal, Mamata Banerjee's Trinamool Congress, vehemently opposed this saying it was designed to help the BJP, because it could concentrate its effort and have the prime minister personally campaign across more constituencies.

Modi began holding rallies in Bengal on 7 February, beginning with

[16] 'Ministry of AYUSH: Ayurveda's immunity boosting measures for self care during COVID 19 crisis', mohfw.gov.in

[17] 'Science ministry funds trial on effect of Gayatri Mantra in treating COVID-19', 19 March 2021, *The Hindu*

[18] 'BJP MP Pragya Thakur says cow urine saves people from Covid-19', 17 May 2021, *Hindustan Times*

[19] 'Holy smoke, cow urine, yagna chikitsa: BJP leaders and their unscientific claims on Covid cure', 19 May 2021, *The Indian Express*

one in Haldia. At this point, new cases were rising by 11,000 daily. In the first week of March, a government group of experts on genomic sequencing warned of a second wave.[20] It is not known if their paper was read by Modi. At the same time, another expert spoke directly to Modi's primary Covid advisor and warned him of the lethality of the Delta variant. It is not known whether Modi knew of this either.[21] On 7 March, Modi held a rally in Kolkata, for which his party set a target of 10 lakh attendees. At this point, India's daily new cases were at 18,000. The same day, Harsh Vardhan said India had reached the endgame on the Covid front and the country had emerged as an example to the world.[22]

On 11 March, the first 'Shahi Snan' or royal bath at Kumbh in Haridwar saw 32 lakh people participate. Daily cases were now rising by 21,000. On 20 March, Modi held two rallies in Kharagpur and Harsh Vardhan praised the size of the gatherings. Cases were going up by 43,000 a day. There was evidence that the Kumbh gathering was a super-spreader event.[23] The next day, the government released full-page advertisements in newspapers across India, in which Modi invited more people to come to the Kumbh. Daily cases were now at 47,000.

On 30 March, Harsh Vardhan assured citizens that the situation in India was under control.[24] Cases rose by 53,000 that day.

The National Taskforce on Covid did not meet in either February or March, and by 1 April cases were rising by 81,000 daily with 400 official deaths. On 12 April, the second Shahi Snan took place at the Kumbh. The daily rise in cases had by now doubled to 160,000 with 800 deaths. At the same time, officials were fudging tests at the Kumbh to show things were normal.[25]

---

[20] 'Scientists say India government ignored warnings amid coronavirus surge', 3 May 2021, *Reuters*

[21] 'Health experts say India missed early alarm, let deadly coronavirus variant spread', 15 June 2021, *Reuters*

[22] 'We are in the endgame of COVID-19 pandemic in India: Vardhan', 7 March 2021, *The New Indian Express*

[23] 'Covid-19 pandemic in Haridwar: Tell-tale signs of Kumbh as super spreader', 13 June 2021, India Spend

[24] 'Covid-19 situation under control in India: Health minister Harsh Vardhan', 30 March 2021, *Mint*

[25] 'Private labs entrusted with Covid tests simply collected Aadhaar and mobile numbers to produce fake test results during Maha Kumbh to meet targets; Uttarakhand govt orders probe', 12 June 2021, *The Times of India*

The fudge was done by a firm linked to the BJP.[26] On 15 April, the National Taskforce met for the first time in three months (the last meeting was on 11 January). Cases were now at 216,000 and deaths over 1,100. On 17 April, Modi held what he said was his largest-ever rally in Asansol, with lakhs of people in the audience. Daily cases that day were 260,000 with 1,500 deaths.

Till this time, Modi appeared to be oblivious to the power of exponential growth as it was unfolding in real time. In fact, the government was warned specifically and severally about an impending second wave.[27] It was only after he returned that evening from Bengal and perhaps internalised the commentary on television of the devastation in Delhi's hospitals that Modi shifted his stance. The next day, 18 April, Modi cancelled further activity at the Kumbh. The damage it had caused was sought to be concealed.[28] Daily cases were now at 275,000. It was only four days after that, on 22 April, that Modi cancelled his rallies in Malda, Murshidabad, Birbhum and Kolkata. He said the rallies would be 'virtual' (in reality, only the speaker was virtual and appeared on a screen; the crowd still gathered). By now, cases were at 332,000 with 2,200 deaths daily. The same day that Modi cancelled his rallies, the obliging EC banned rallies for all parties.

In guiding India through this second wave, Modi flew by the seat of his pants. Structurally, there was nothing other than his office running the Covid strategy. The Union cabinet did not decide or discuss a single issue related to the pandemic as the second wave surged through March and April 2021. It met five times, but only to clear things like the second phase of Bangalore's metro project and some memoranda of understanding with foreign nations.[29] On 11 May, it met to approve things like a ropeway project in Uttarakhand. Ministers did not appear to know what Modi's vaccination strategy was, or if indeed he had any. On 18 May, Nitin Gadkari asked for more firms to be issued the licence to make the vaccine.[30] This was reported the next day, and it was pointed out that this was exactly what Manmohan Singh

---

[26] 'Fake COVID tests at Kumbh: New CM gave job to "unfit" company with BJP ties', 23 June 2021, *TheWire.in*

[27] 'Told Modi govt in March second Covid wave afoot, expect peak in mid-May: Expert panel chief', 30 April 2021, *ThePrint.in*

[28] 'No record of 65 deaths at Haridwar Covid facility', 16 May 2021, *The Times of India*

[29] 'COVID-19: No role for cabinet in pandemic control, PMO calls the shots', 16 May 2021, *The New Indian Express*

[30] 'Nitin Gadkari: More firms should get licences for vaccines', 19 May 2021, *The Indian Express*

had suggested to Modi a month before (a suggestion that was met with an insolent reply from Harsh Vardhan). Gadkari then said he had been unaware that the government 'was already facilitating vaccine manufacturing by 12 different plants/companies'.[31]

Twice in 2020, in April and in November, the government had been warned that an oxygen shortage was looming.[32] The minutes of one meeting said in clear terms: 'In the coming days India could face a shortage of oxygen supplies. To address this, CII will coordinate with Indian Gas Association and mitigate the lack of oxygen supply.'

This meeting was 'headed by NITI Aayog CEO Amitabh Kant and attended by India's Principal Scientific Adviser K. Vijay Raghavan; Secretary, Department for Promotion of Industry and Internal Trade; NDMA member Kamal Kishore; and over half a dozen officials from various wings of the Government including the Prime Minister's Office; Ministry of Home Affairs; Ministry of External Affairs; Cabinet Secretariat; Central Board of Indirect Taxes and Customs; and NITI Aayog. A dozen industry representatives, including CII Director General Chandrajit Banerjee, participated in the meeting'.

Asked what follow-up action was taken after this warning about oxygen shortage was given by the group, *The Indian Express* was told: 'It was decided that, henceforth, the DPIIT (the Department for Promotion of Industry and Internal Trade, headed by Piyush Goyal) will look into the issue of Oxygen Supply.' Goyal made much of his 'Oxygen Express' trains—in reality tanker trucks carrying oxygen being ferried on trains—but did not reveal that it was his incompetence that now required all the ferrying.

While Modi did not himself take the pandemic seriously, he also insisted on managing it personally. If there was any strategy at all in tackling the pandemic, it came directly from Modi's office; there was 'no role for the cabinet in pandemic control, PMO calls the shots', as an *Indian Express* headline put it. This was in keeping with the way in which he has run the government all this time.

The *BBC* filed more than 240 RTIs to learn that Modi had ordered the national lockdown of 2020 without consulting any government departments or ministries. Neither health, finance nor disaster management knew that the nation was going into an extended shutdown and they were not asked about

---

[31] 'After urging firms to make vaccines: Gadkari says was unaware govt started efforts to boost production', 20 May 2021, *The Indian Express*

[32] 'April, November last year: Officials, House panel flagged oxygen need, shortage', 23 April 2021, *The Indian Express*

what the effects would be on migrants, on the poor and on the economy.[33] Nobody was apparently asked how effective this strategy could be and what it was intended to achieve.

This time around, Modi and his office publicised his 'high-level' meetings with bureaucrats, and he even held meetings with India's district magistrates, but the anodyne press releases put out carried no reference to outcomes or dates by when to achieve them.[34] The holding of these meetings alone was deemed sufficient by way of intervention. This was abdication of duty and the results showed immediately given the nature of the viral outbreak.

A wave that began at the end of February was not only allowed to gather momentum, it was goaded on. Through four weeks of March, through three weeks of April, India held gigantic gatherings directly organised by the BJP or approved and encouraged by it. The consequences were felt by the country's healthcare system, which was always fragile and unavailable to the poor at the best of times. Here, the second aspect to tackling a pandemic, the anticipation of the effects of a sudden wave and the preparation of a war-chest of medical equipment, came into play.

In the eight weeks between 1 March and 30 April, India's daily cases grew 40 times from 11,000 to more than 400,000. No healthcare system in the world can handle an explosion of patients of this sort. The only way to protect the population is to stockpile things that may not be immediately required today but are produced and procured and set aside in anticipation of a wave's peak. India did not do that. In April 2020, the government decided it would procure 50,000 'Make in India' ventilators, but ultimately only procured 35,000 of them after it determined that the pandemic had been seen off. Corporates like Maruti said they had made ventilators, but the government did not ultimately procure them.[35]

The government first took eight months to invite bids for oxygen generation plants worth just Rs 200 crore. And then wasted more time so that, six months later, in mid-April 2021, as the second wave raged through the Indian population, it had put up only 33 of the 162 plants planned.[36] India was producing 9,000 tons of oxygen daily in April 2021. The daily

[33] 'India Covid-19: PM Modi "did not consult" before lockdown', 29 March 2021, BBC
[34] 'Innovate, adopt best practices to tackle Covid: PM Modi to district magistrates', 19 May 2021, The Economic Times
[35] 'Ventilator shortage: "Make in India" devices not picked up by govt', 22 April 2021, Business Standard
[36] 'India is running out of oxygen, Covid-19 patients are dying—because the government wasted time', 18 April 2021, Scroll.in

requirement of just four states—Delhi (970 tons), Karnataka (1,790 tons), Gujarat (1,500 tons) and Maharashtra (1,700 tons)—was two-thirds of the national total in that month. The BJP would later blame Delhi for inflating its need for oxygen, but didn't explain why, if this was so, people had died by the thousand without oxgyen. There was not enough production to handle peaks of the sort the second wave brought. India exported 9,000 tons of oxygen in the 10 months between April 2020 and January 2021, which was twice what it had exported in the year before that.[37] The breezy confidence that oxygen would not be needed turned out to be misplaced. Modi's sabotaging of foreign funding of India's NGOs (see the chapter 'The Devil's Workshop' for more details on the FCRA law) meant that it was difficult, if not impossible, for them to help Indians though the outside world was sending aid. Vital aid sat around at the airport for days as the government figured out what to do with the mess it had made.[38]

The *BBC* quoted Jennifer Liang, co-founder of The Ant, an NGO that has been working in the Northeast for 20 years, as saying that the FCRA legislation was costing lives. It 'had stopped her organisation from distributing oxygen concentrators from foreign donors and supplying them to the government, because they were unable to open a new bank account in Delhi' as the law required them to.[39]

The other problem regarding lack of preparation was insufficient transport capacity. Liquid medical oxygen is transported in specialised containers that can handle its supercooled cryogenic form. When the second wave hit, India had a total of 1,224 tankers able to ferry liquid oxygen, with a total capacity of 16,700 tons.[40] Each tanker had a capacity of 15 tons and a turnaround time—i.e., being filled, transported, unloaded and then returning to be filled again—of about six days. This was inevitable because some states, like Delhi, did not produce any oxygen. And so the total amount that could be delivered on average daily was not the production capacity of 9,000 tons but 2,700 tons—less than half of what just Delhi, Gujarat, Karnataka and Maharashtra alone required. The result could only be a gross shortfall of what was needed across the country. And when that happened, Indians began to die from a

---

[37] 'Despite COVID-19 crisis at home, India doubled oxygen exports in FY21', 21 April 2021, *Business Today*

[38] 'Where are the 300 tonnes of emergency Covid-19 supplies that have landed in Delhi in last five days?', 3 May 2021, *Scroll.in*

[39] 'India Covid: How law stops NGOs distributing essential aid', 13 May 2021, *BBC*

[40] 'Oxygen crisis: More than supply, lack of tankers and plant location key challenges', 28 April 2021, *The Indian Express*

lack of oxygen. The first deaths from a lack of oxygen had actually come during the first wave. In May 2020, it was already known that a surging wave caused deaths because normally functioning hospitals could rapidly run short of oxygen, a problem that had killed several patients in Mumbai that month.[41]

Aditi Priya, a research associate at Krea University, compiled the instances of oxygen deaths in the second wave that were reported in the media. The Modi government itself produced no document on the shortage or what it had wrought. The numbers were frightening:

On 6 April in Madhya Pradesh four deaths.[42] On 12 April in Maharashtra seven deaths.[43] On 13 April in Maharashtra five deaths,[44] in Chhattisgarh one death.[45]

On 15 April in Maharashtra 15 deaths,[46] in Madhya Pradesh 17[47] deaths.[48] On 14 April in Maharashtra one death.[49] On 17 April in Madhya Pradesh one death,[50] in Bihar one death,[51] in Tamil Nadu six deaths.[52] On 18 April in Madhya Pradesh 13[53] deaths.[54] On 19 April in Tamil Nadu

[41] 'Low oxygen pressure kills 12 in 2 weeks at Jogeshwari hospital', 30 May 2020, *Mumbai Mirror*

[42] 'Four deaths due to lack of oxygen', 8 April 2021, mpbreakingnews.com

[43] '7 Deaths in Maharashtra hospital spark anger, oxygen shortage blamed', 13 April 2021, *NDTV*

[44] '5 patients die at Kandri CCC for want of oxygen, proper care', 14 April 2021, *The Times of India*

[45] 'अस्पताल में ऑक्सीजन नही, डॉक्टरो ने बेटी से कहा जुगाड़ करो, किसी तरह लाई तो लगाया नही, चंद घंटे मे पति की मौत', 14 April 2021, *Rajasthan Patrika*

[46] 'Gondia Corona | गोंदियात 15 रुग्णांचा ऑक्सिजनअभावी मृत्यू ; पालकमंत्री नवाब मलिक म्हणतात...', 17 April 2021, *ABP Marathi*

[47] 'MP मे कोरोना का कहर: रीवा जिला न्यायालय के जज की मौत, ऑक्सीजन कमी से गई जान!', 15 April 2021, *News18*

[48] '11 died due to lack of oxygen in Khandwa, Collector reaches hospital', 16 April 2021, *Rajasthan Patrika*

[49] 'Malegaon death brings to fore acute medical oxygen shortage in town', 16 April 2021, *The Times of India*

[50] 'Neemuch: Uproar over deaths of two at kids' Covid centre', 19 April 2021, *Rajasthan Patrika*

[51] 'कोरोना से संक्रमति शकिक्षक की इलाज के दौरान मौत', 17 April 2021, *Dainik Jagran*

[52] 'Oxygen disaster in Tamil Nadu again; Six people, including a pregnant woman, died', 17 April 2021, realnewindia.com

[53] 'कांग्रेस ने लगाए आरोप, ऑक्सीजन की कमी से हो रही मौतें, जांच की मांग', 22 April 2021, *Nai Dunia*

[54] 'MP hospital tells a story: 6 Covid patients die in a night as oxygen runs out', 19 April 2021, *The Indian Express*

five deaths,[55] in Rajasthan two deaths,[56] in Madhya Pradesh 10 deaths,[57] in Odisha two deaths.[58] On 21 April in Maharashtra 24 deaths[59], in Uttar Prades six[60] deaths,[61] in Bihar two[62] deaths,[63] in Uttar Pradesh another four deaths.[64] On 23 April in Delhi 25 deaths,[65] in Gujarat eight[66] deaths,[67] in Madhya Pradesh seven[68] deaths,[69] in Delhi 25 deaths,[70] in Punjab six deaths,[71] in Uttar Pradesh one death,[72] in Bihar three deaths.[73]

[55] 'Oxygen shortage in Vellore hospital led to deaths allege relatives, officials deny', 19 April 2021, *The News Minute*

[56] 'कोटा: अस्पताल में अचानक रुकी ऑक्सीजन सप्लाई, दो मरीजों ने आधी रात तड़पकर तोड़ा दम', 21 April 2021, *Amar Ujala*

[57] 'ऑक्सीजन खत्म होने से 10 कोरोना मरीजों की मौत; एक महिला ने भाई, पति और चाचा को एकसाथ खोया', 19 April 2021, *Dainik Bhaskar*

[58] 'Odisha's Nuapada a snapshot of how COVID-19 is affecting rural India', 26 April 2021, *Down to Earth*

[59] 'Families mourn Covid patients' deaths due to oxygen leak in Maharashtra', 22 April 2021, *NDTV*

[60] 'Grappling with oxygen shortage, two UP hospitals ask kin to shift patients', 22 April 2021, *The Indian Express*

[61] 'Five Covid-19 patients die at UP hospital, family members allege oxygen shortage', 22 April 2021, *The Indian Express*

[62] 'बिहार स्टेट बार काउंसिल के सदस्य की ऑक्सीजन नही मिलने से मौत, कोरोना संक्रमित होने के बाद पीएमसीएच में थे भर्ती', 21 April 2021, *Hindustan*

[63] 'Bihar: लखीसराय में कोरोना संक्रमित किसान की सदर अस्पताल में मौत, परजिनों का आरोप—ऑक्सीजन के अभाव में चली गई जान', 22 April 2021, *Hindustan*

[64] 'इटावा: कोविड अस्पताल में ऑक्सीजन खत्म, चार की मौत, प्रशासन का दावा—कमी नही', 22 April 2021, *Amar Ujala*

[65] 'Waiting for oxygen: 25 Ganga Ram patients die as O_2 dwindles in Delhi hospitals, Kejriwal pleads for help', 23 April 2021, PTI

[66] 'Gujarat: Rajkot hospitals complain of acute shortage of oxygen', 23 April 2021, PTI

[67] 'Gujarat records 13,105 new Covid cases; hospitals short of oxygen', 23 April 2021, *The Indian Express*

[68] 'MP में अस्पताल की बड़ी लापरवाही:जबलपुर के गैलेक्सी हॉस्पिटल में ऑक्सीजन की कमी से 5 कोरोना पेशेंट्स की मौत; मरीजों को तड़पता छोड़कर भाग गए डॉक्टर', 23 April 2021, *Dainik Bhaskar*

[69] 'Gwalior reports two deaths amid massive oxygen crunch as acute shortage continues in MP', 24 April 2021, *News18*

[70] '25 patients die due to oxygen shortage: Jaipur Golden Hospital to Delhi HC', 24 April 2021, *India Today*

[71] 'Oxygen shortage | Six patients die at private hospital in Punjab's Amritsar', 24 April 2021, *The Hindu*

[72] 'मैनपुरी: बरेली के अस्पताल में ऑक्सीजन न मिलने से पूर्व सैनिक की मौत, बेटी ने लगाए गंभीर आरोप', 25 April 2021, *Amar Ujala*

[73] 'कोरोना से प्रोफेसर व लोजपा नेता समेत चार संक्रमितों की मौत, 161 नए पॉजिटिव', 22 April 2021, *Dainik Jagran*

On 24 April in Madhya Pradesh four deaths,[74] in Uttar Pradesh one death.[75]

On 25 April in Gurgaon ten[76] deaths,[77] in Uttar Pradesh four deaths,[78] in Madhya Pradesh four deaths,[79] in Bihar seven[80] deaths.[81]

On 26 April in Maharashtra four deaths,[82] in Madhya Pradesh five deaths,[83] in Andhra Pradesh three deaths,[84] in Uttar Pradesh[85] seven[86] deaths,[87] in Gujarat eight deaths,[88] in Kashmir one death.[89]

On 27 April in Haryana five deaths,[90] in Uttar Pradesh five deaths,[91] in

[74] 'MP: 4 Covid patients die in Chhatarpur District hospital due to lack of oxygen supply', 25 April 2021, *ABP News*

[75] 'Meerut: Inspector dies due to lack of oxygen; family accuses hospital of negligence', 25 April 2021, *ABP News*

[76] 'Two more deaths in Gurugram as hospitals grapple with low oxygen supply', 26 April 2021, *Hindustan Times*

[77] '8 Covid-19 patients die in Haryana hospitals due to oxygen shortage, probe ordered', 26 April 2021, *India Today*

[78] 'बरेली में ऑक्सीजन की कमी से चार मरीजों की मौत के बाद बवाल, तीमारदारों ने अस्पतालों में की तोड़फोड़', 25 April 2021, *Hindustan*

[79] 'नहीं थम रही ऑक्सीजन की कमी से मौतें:तेजनकर में ऑक्सीजन की कमी एक दिन में 4 मरीजों की मौत; बेटा बोला—ऑक्सीजन नहीं मिलने से गई जान', 24 April 2021, *Dainik Bhaskar*

[80] 'Patna's 2 big Covid facilities left with 2-day oxygen stock', 28 April 2021, *The Indian Express*

[81] 'Patna: Three Covid-19 patients dies at NMCH due oxygen shortage', 25 April 2021, *ETV Bharat*

[82] '4 Covid patients die at Thane hospital; kin allege oxygen shortage', 27 April 2021, *Hindustan Times*

[83] 'Kin of 2 Covid patients allege death due to oxygen outage, hospital denies charge', 27 April 2021, *News18*

[84] 'Three COVID-19 patients die as oxygen level drops in Vizianagaram hospital', 26 April 2021, *The Hindu*

[85] 'सांसो पर संकट: आगरे के अस्पतालों में ऑक्सीजन की कमी से पांच मरीजों की मौत', 26 April 2021, *Amar Ujala*

[86] 'कोरोना से एक की मौत, कोतवाली की पुलिस सहित 137 संक्रमति मिले', 26 April 2021, *Dainik Jagran*

[87] 'फरीजाबाद: सरकारी मेडिकल कॉलेज में ऑक्सीजन खत्म होने से मरीज की मौत, कई गंभीर', 26 April 2021, *Amar Ujala*

[88] 'વડનગરની સવિલિ હોસપટિલમાં ઓક્સજિન પ્લાન્ટ ફૈઇલ થતા કોરોનાના 8 દર્દીઓના મોત', 27 April 2021, *Gujarat Samachar*

[89] 'India COVID crisis: "The hospital ran out of oxygen and mum died"', 4 May 2021, *Al Jazeera*

[90] '5 COVID patients dead, oxygen shortage blamed', 27 April 2021, *The Hindu*

[91] 'ऑक्सीजन की कमी से पांच मरीजों की मौत', 27 April 2021, *Amar Ujala*

Andhra Pradesh two deaths,[92] in Madhya Pradesh two deaths,[93] in Gujarat one death.[94]

On 28 April in Rajasthan 10 deaths,[95] in Uttar Pradesh eight[96] deaths,[97] in Bihar seven deaths,[98] in UP another three deaths,[99] and in Rajasthan another four deaths.[100]

On 29 April in Uttar Pradesh six deaths,[101] on 30 April in Tamil Nadu two deaths,[102] in Jharkhand 16 deaths,[103] in Delhi seven deaths,[104] in Bihar one death,[105] in Uttar Pradesh three[106] deaths.[107]

On 1 May in Delhi 12 deaths,[108] in Andhra Pradesh 16 deaths,[109] in Karnataka four deaths,[110] in Madhya Pradesh four deaths,[111] in Jammu four

[92] 'Covid, asthma patients die in Kadapa hospital, probe ordered', 28 April 2021, *The New Indian Express*

[93] 'अस्पताल में अचानक खत्म हुई ऑक्सीजन! डॉक्टर ने की 2 की मौत की पुष्टि', 27 April 2021, *Punjab Kesari*

[94] 'Gujarat: Patient dies as oxygen supply 'snapped' by hospital staff', 28 April 2021, *The Times of India*

[95] 'Rajasthan: जयपुर, बीकानेर व कोटा में ऑक्सीजन की कमी से 10 मरीजो की मौत', 28 April 2021, *Dainik Jagran*

[96] 'Agra: 8 Covid patients die due to lack of oxygen days after UP govt's claim of no shortages', 28 April 2021, *India Today*

[97] 'छह लोगों की मौत, 12 स्वास्थ्य कर्मी सहित 99 संक्रमित', 28 April 2021, *Amar Ujala*

[98] 'कोरोना से प्रोफेसर व शक्षिक समेत सात की मौत', 28 April 2021, *Dainik Jagran*

[99] 'Coronavirus | Meerut hospitals say patients died due to shortage of oxygen', 28 April 2021, *The Hindu*

[100] 'अस्पताल में बिना पानी की मछली के जैसे तड़प रहे थे मरीज, अपनों को ऐसे देख बेहोश हो गए परजिन', 28 April 2021, *Rajasthan Patrika*

[101] 'Uttar Pradesh: Lack of oxygen killed patients, allege kin; govt rebuts charge', 30 April 2021, *The Indian Express*

[102] 'Kin allege oxygen shortage led to death of two COVID-19 patients', 30 April 2021, *The Hindu*

[103] 'सदर अस्पताल में 16 मरे, रात को पहले बजिली कटी, फिर ऑक्सीजन का प्रेशर घटा', 1 May 2021, *Dainik Jagran*

[104] '7 COVID patients die due to oxygen crisis in Gurugram hospital', 1 May 2021, IANS

[105] 'बेकाबू हुआ कोरोना:ऑक्सीजन की कमी से वृद्ध की मौत, बोले डॉक्टर-वाहन नही है, कटि देते है ले जाएं शव', 30 April 2021, *Dainik Bhaskar*

[106] 'नही थम रहा ऑक्सीजन की कमी से मौत का सलिसिला, फर्रुखाबाद मे मचा रहा कोहराम', 30 April 2021, *Hindustan*

[107] '"Yogi has left us to die": Oxygen crisis devastates Meerut', 4 May 2021, *News Laundry*

[108] 'Oxygen shortage: 12 lives lost in Delhi's Batra hospital', 1 May 2021, *The Hindu*

[109] '"Oxygen shortage" in two Andhra Pradesh hospitals kill 16 Covid patients', 2 May 2021, *The Times of India*

[110] '4 Covid patients die in Kalaburagi due to oxygen shortage', 2 May 2021, *Bangalore Mirror*

[111] '"Oxygen Stopped": Families allege 4 deaths, official denies charge', 3 May 2021, *NDTV*

deaths,[112] in Maharashtra one death.[113] On 2 May in Jammu four deaths,[114] on 3 May in Karnataka 24 deaths,[115] in Uttar Pradesh eight[116] deaths,[117] in Andhra Pradesh eight deaths.[118]

On 4 May in Karnataka[119] 14[120] deaths,[121] in Uttarakhand five deaths,[122] in Tamil Nadu 13 deaths,[123] in Andhra Pradesh 10[124] deaths.[125]

On 5 May in Tamil Nadu four deaths,[126] in Andhra Pradesh eight[127] deaths.[128] On 6 May in Jharkhand five deaths.[129]

[112] 'Jammu: Shortage in oxygen supply at Batra hospital kills 4', 1 May 2021, *APB News*

[113] 'कोल्हापुरात ऑक्सिजनअभावी माजी सैनिकाचा मृत्यु, नातेवाईकांचा आरोप', 3 May 2021, *Saamana*

[114] 'J&K: Four COVID deaths at ASCOMS hospital allegedly due to oxygen shortage, govt to probe the matter', 3 May, *Times Now*

[115] '24 Covid-19 patients dead after Chamarajanagar hospitals run out of oxygen', 3 May 2021, *Deccan Herald*

[116] 'जिला महिला अस्पताल में आक्सीजन की कमी, CMS बोले—नही हो रही ठीक से सप्लाई', 3 May 2021, *Navbharat Times*

[117] 'Probe into death of 5 due to disruption of oxygen supply in Uttar Pradesh', 3 May 2021, *The Hindu*

[118] 'Eight die in Hindupur government hospital in Andhra, kin allege oxygen shortage', 3 May 2021, *The New Indian Express*

[119] 'Bengaluru hospital runs out of medical oxygen, two patients die', 4 May 2021, *The News Minute*

[120] 'Oxygen crisis deepens in Karnataka: 7 die in Kalaburagi and Belagavi govt hospitals', 5 May 2021, *The News Minute*

[121] 'Karnataka: 5 COVID-19 patients die in Hubballi hospital, kin allege oxygen shortage', 5 May 2021, *India TV*

[122] '5 die in Roorkee hospital amid oxygen shortage, probe ordered', 5 May 2021, *ANI*

[123] '13 patients die at Chengalpattu GH after oxygen supply is allegedly disrupted', 5 May 2021, *The News Minute*

[124] 'Vijayawada: Six Covid patients die in district hospital, oxygen scarcity blamed', 5 May 2021, *Hans India*

[125] 'Andhra hospital runs out of oxygen, 4 Covid patients die, security tightened at facility', 5 May 2021, *India Today*

[126] 'Row over death of four Covid negative patients at Tirupathur GH', 7 May 2021, *The New Indian Express*

[127] 'Oxygen shortage leads to death of six covid patients at Nellore GGH', 5 May 2021, ap7am.com

[128] 'Two die as hospital runs out of oxygen in Vijayawada', 5 May 2021, *The Hindu*

[129] 'सदर अस्पताल में ऑक्सीजन आपूर्ति बाधित, पांच की मौत', 6 May 2021, *Amar Ujala*

On 9 May in Telangana 15[130] deaths,[131] in Bihar three deaths.[132] On 10 May in Andhra Pradesh 11 deaths,[133] on 9 May in Delhi one death,[134] on 11 May in Calcutta one death,[135] in Madhya Pradesh one death.[136]

On 12 May in Maharashtra ten deaths,[137] in Tamil Nadu 13 deaths,[138] in Uttar Pradesh one death.[139] Between 11 and 15 May in Goa 83 deaths.[140] On 13 May in Karnataka one death,[141] on 14 May in Rajasthan 3 deaths,[142] in Bihar one death.[143] On 18 May in Odisha one death,[144] in Tamil Nadu five deaths.[145] On 19 May in Bihar one death.[146]

These were only the cases that found media coverage and were traced. In the face of the calamity, the Modi government froze. In the seven months from March to September 2020, Modi made 82 public appearances—physical as well as virtual. In the next four months, he made 111 such appearances. From February to 25 April 2021, he clocked 92 public appearances. From 25

[130] 'Eight deaths at TIMS due to alleged oxygen shortage', 11 May 2021, *The Hindu*

[131] '7 Covid patients reported dead due to oxygen crisis at Telangana's King Koti Hospital', 10 May 2021, *Deccan Chronicle*

[132] 'मोतिहारी मे ऑक्सीजन की कमी से तीन मरे, नाराज स्वजनो ने हंगामा और तोडफ़ोड़ की', 9 May 2021, *Dainik Jagran*

[133] '11 patients die in Andhra Pradesh hospital after oxygen tanker delayed', 11 May 2021, *The Indian Express*

[134] 'YouTuber's FB post: "Could have lived if I'd got treatment"', 10 May 2021, *The Indian Express*

[135] 'Patient dies, hospital denies oxygen dearth in Kolkata', 12 May 2021, *The Times of India*

[136] 'ऑक्सीजन नही मिलने से हुई मौत, मानवाधिकार आयोग मे शिकायत', 11 May 2021, *Dainik Bhaskar*

[137] '10 patients die due to lack of oxygen in Nalasopara hospitals', 10 May 2021, *MumbaiLive.com*

[138] 'Oxygen crisis: 13 die at Nellai government hospital due to lack of critical supply', 13 May 2021, *ABP News*

[139] 'Family loses both parents to Covid-19 in 24 hours in UP's Juggaur village', 12 May 2021, *India Today*

[140] 'After 83 deaths, Health minister says oxygen supply streamlining at Goa's biggest Covid hospital', 16 May 2021, *NDTV*

[141] 'Woman dies, oxygen shortage alleged', 13 May 2021, *Deccan Herald*

[142] '3 Covid patients die due to disruption in oxygen supply at Jaipur's RUHS hospital', 15 May, *nyoooz.com*

[143] 'औरंगाबाद मे ऑक्सीजन की कमी से मरीज की मौत, मृतक के परजिनो का फूटा गुस्सा', 14 May 2021, *firstbihar.com*

[144] 'आइजीएच मे ऑक्सीजन की कमी से मरीज की मौत पर हंगामा', 20 May 2021, *Dainik Jagran*

[145] 'Tamil Nadu oxygen crisis sees private hospitals say no to Covid patients', 18 May 2021, *NDTV*

[146] 'आरोप: बेटे ने कहा ऑक्सीजन की कमी से हुई मेरी मां की मौत', 20 May 2021, *Hindustan*

April, after he called off the Kumbh and his Bengal rallies, Modi disappeared. He made no public appearance for *20* days.[147] The prime minister of India fled the field when his people needed the government most.[148]

Through all of April and much of May, upper class Indians flooded Twitter with calls for help to find hospital beds, oxygen cylinders, drugs like Remdesivir and ventilators.[149] The Union did not think to set up a helpline to guide those who needed this help.

Into this space strode the youth Congress leader B.V. Srinivas (@srinivasiyc) who, with a team of volunteers, began to help people reaching out for aid on Twitter. He was so effective in the absence of the State and any government presence that even the embassies of New Zealand and the Philippines contacted him for help when staffers fell ill with Covid.[150] Focussed on the government's image, Jaishankar tweeted: 'This was an unsolicited supply as they had no Covid cases. Clearly for cheap publicity by you know who. Giving away cylinders like this when there are people in desperate need of oxygen is simply appalling.'

The New Zealand embassy staffer who had received oxygen from Srinivas on 2 May died 18 days later.[151]

Most people died unable to access a hospital or afford an oxygen concentrator or even a cylinder, and they died without publicity. An oxygen cylinder that lasted a couple of hours cost Rs 8,000, and by May 2021 was being sold for more than Rs 60,000.[152] How many families would even attempt to get one, have the ability to find one or have the resources to keep procuring replacements? For this reason we will not know what the oxygen shortage toll was.

[147] 'PM Narendra Modi's public presence during two Covid-19 pandemic waves', 26 May 2021, *Business Standard*

[148] This tendency to disappear when needed has been noted before. It would repeat itself through the Modi years when misgovernance was obvious or when the problem was difficult. See 'Why is PM Modi still silent on Manipur, asks Congress', 7 June 2023, *India Today*

[149] 'Indians turn to social media for help as Covid crisis overwhelms the health-care system', 24 May 2021, *CNBC*

[150] 'Winning praise for Covid relief work, IYC chief Srinivas says: "Helping everyone in need, don't want to do politics on this"', 5 May 2021, *The Indian Express*

[151] 'Staffer, for whom New Zealand mission had sought oxygen, passes away', 20 May 2021, *The Indian Express*

[152] 'Antivirals, oxygen biggest draw in Delhi's Covid black market', 6 May 2021, *Hindustan Times*

What counted as a Covid death was itself vague. Many people died at home, unable to access healthcare. The vast majority were untested. Even the majority of those who had tested positive and died were unlikely to be counted as a Covid fatality because local instructions were to underplay the virus as the cause. Guidelines from the Indian Council on Medical Research (ICMR) and the World Health Organisation (WHO) on what to count as a Covid death were regularly flouted[153] across the country from 2020 itself.[154]

India's state governments kept their official numbers low to avoid the appearance of failure. The Union hamstrung itself by accepting the fake numbers and making no effort to proactively try to ascertain a true national count. The lower official count made the problem falsely appear smaller than it was and made resolution difficult. It also came at severe cost to India's credibility on Covid numbers, which was already quite low. Along with their reporting[155] on the shocking scenes[156] across India, the country came under a hammering[157] from the foreign media on the numbers as well.[158]

With the government reluctant or wary about revealing the reality, it was left to the local media to try and arrive at the actual toll of the second wave.

On 14 May, the newspaper *Divya Bhaskar* reported that, in the 71 days between 1 March and 10 May 2021, Gujarat had issued 1.23 lakh death certificates, of which only 4,218 were registered as Covid deaths. But in the same period in the previous year, 58,000 death certificates were issued. A sudden doubling of deaths did not make sense unless a majority of the additional 65,000 were also Covid-related. An analysis of the newspaper's numbers compared to previous years found that the death toll in Gujarat was around 10 times the official one.[159]

Gujarat's numbers were daily collated from local newspapers and tweeted out by the PTI journalist Deepak Patel, bringing global attention to the work being done by Gujarati reporters.[160]

---

[153] 'India is undercounting its COVID-19 deaths. This is how', 4 August 2020, *TheWire.in*
[154] 'Tamil Nadu flouting norms while counting deaths, experts wary of under-reporting', 25 June 2020, *The Times of India*
[155] 'India's official COVID-19 numbers are shocking. The true count is likely far worse', 3 May 2021, *Los Angeles Times*
[156] 'Why India's Covid problem could be bigger than we think', 17 September 2020, *BBC*
[157] 'India is counting thousands of daily COVID deaths. How many is it missing?', 30 April 2021, *NPR*
[158] 'As Covid-19 devastates India, deaths go undercounted', 24 April 2021, *The New York Times*
[159] 'The scale of Gujarat's mortality crisis', 25 May 2021, *The Hindu*
[160] 'India's Covid crisis: The newsroom counting the uncounted deaths', 11 May 2021, *BBC*

On 6 May 2021, the *Sandesh* newspaper reported that 17,822 bodies had been cremated or buried with Covid-19 protocols in seven major cities of Gujarat (Ahmedabad, Gandhinagar, Baroda, Surat, Jamnagar, Bhavnagar and Rajkot) in the previous 30 days. The Gujarat government had acknowledged only 1,745 Covid deaths in the same period. This meant that the fudging of numbers in that period was 1:10. A study published in August showed that the undercount was higher and that the death toll in the state was 2.8 lakh till April 2021.[161]

A similar analysis for Chennai showed the real numbers for the city to be four times higher than the official toll.[162] In Kolkata, the analysis showed that 'excess deaths' in April and May of 2021 were 6.8 times the official Covid toll. Twice as many people had died in this period (17,587) than had in the same period between 2015 and 2019 (average of 9,353).[163] In Rajkot, the number of those dead in April and May (13,471) was six times the number of those dead in that period (2,250) in 2019.[164]

In Bhopal, against the official toll of 104 in April 2021, the number of bodies cremated or buried with Covid protocols was 2,557.[165] In Haryana, the difference between those cremated with protocols against the official toll was three times.[166] In Rajasthan, against an official toll of 3,918 over 50 days in April and May 2021, the number of those who had died in just a fraction of the villages was 14,482.[167] In Kanpur, against the official toll of 196 in 12 days between 17 and 29 April 2021, the number of those cremated merely in two crematoria was 1,044.[168] As many deaths were recorded in a single hospital in Ahmedabad in a month as had been claimed for the entire state of Gujarat in that period.[169] After Gujarat, media elsewhere began to compile

[161] 'Gujarat: Data from death registers suggests COVID toll undercounted by 27 times', 17 August 2021, *TheWire.in*

[162] 'Interpreting deaths in Chennai', 26 May 2021, *The Hindu*

[163] 'Kolkata's COVID-19 deaths in 2021 could be 4 times higher', 29 May 2021, *The Hindu*

[164] http://epapergujaratsamachar.com/nd/gsnews2.php?pageid=GUJARAT_RAJ_20210528_2

[165] 'Bhopal deaths: Government says 104, crematoriums 2,557', 3 May 2021, *The Tribune*

[166] 'हरियाणा के 22 जिलों से कोरोना की मौतों का सच:अप्रैल में कोविड प्रोटोकॉल से 3814 संस्कार हुए, सरकारी रिकॉर्ड में कोरोना से 1225 मौतें ही दर्ज', 4 May 2021, *Dainik Bhaskar*

[167] 'भास्कर ग्राउंड रिपोर्ट:राजस्थान सरकार ने 50 दिनों में जिन 25 जिलों में 3,918 कोरोना मौतें बताईं, उनके सिर्फ 512 गांव-ब्लॉक से उठीं 14,482 अर्थियां', 25 May 2021, *Dainik Bhaskar*

[168] 'UP में छिपाया जा रहा कोरोना से मौतों का डेटा? कानपुर,वाराणसी का सच', 24 May 2021, *The Quint Hindi*

[169] 'झूठ का पर्दाफाश:गुजरात सरकार का दावा—एक महीने में प्रदेश में कोरोना से 3,578 मौतें; जबकि हकीकत में अहमदाबाद के सिविल हॉस्पिटल में ही इस दौरान 3,416 मौतें हुईं', 7 June 2021, *Dainik Bhaskar*

'excess deaths' in early 2021 compared to previous years. Tamil Nadu had over 60,000 more dead,[170] the city of Hyderabad alone had 10 times as many dead, over 32,000, as the tally for the entire state,[171] Kerala had 15,000 excess deaths,[172] according to one study and over 2.5 lakh according to another.[173] Andhra Pradesh reported over 100,000 excess deaths and Tamil Nadu 129,000, Madhya Pradesh over 130,000.[174] Bihar had 75,000 extra deaths,[175] Karnataka had 95,000 extra deaths and Delhi 30,000. Just the four cities of Jaipur, Jodhpur, Bikaner, and Udaipur recorded 15,000 more dead in the second wave.[176] In the less governed spaces of India, with poor documentation and record-keeping, the anecdotal evidence showed that the carnage was similar. A public health survey in Jharkhand showed a death rate over 40 per cent higher than before.[177] The death rate in 24 Uttar Pradesh districts was 43 times the official toll and, remarkably, this was before April 2021.[178] In Assam, 28,000 more deaths were recorded in the first wave of 2020, meaning in in the first wave itself the dead were 30 times the official toll.[179] Just four states accounted for many more dead than the Covid toll for the whole of the country.[180] Bangalore had 19,000 excess deaths and the only place to record a decrease in deaths was Thiruvananthapuram in Kerala.[181] It

---

[170] 'Excess deaths in Tamil Nadu over four times official COVID-19 tally', 16 June 2021, *The Hindu*

[171] 'Excess deaths in Hyderabad are 10 times the official COVID-19 toll for Telangana', 13 June 2021, *The Hindu*

[172] 'Excess deaths' in Kerala 1.6 times official COVID-19 toll', 25 June 2021, *The Hindu*

[173] 'Bihar recorded 251k excess deaths since Covid-19 pandemic: Data', 21 August 2021, *Hindustan Times*

[174] 'Andhra Pradesh saw 400% increase in deaths in May, Tamil Nadu saw more modest excess mortality', 13 June 2021, *TheWire.in*

[175] 'Bihar Saw Nearly 75,000 Unaccounted Deaths Amid 2nd Covid Wave, Data Shows', 19 June 2021, *NDTV*

[176] 'Excess deaths challenge India's official Covid toll', 23 June 2021, *India Today*

[177] 'Jharkhand door-to-door survey: April-May deaths up 43% from 2 years ago', 14 June 2021, *The Indian Express*

[178] 'Death count in 24 UP districts 43 times more than official Covid-19 toll', 21 June 2021, *Article-14.com*

[179] 'Assam saw 28,000 more deaths than normal in months when first wave of Covid-19 struck', 17 June 2021, *Scroll.in*

[180] 'The challenge of saying how many excess deaths could be due to Covid-19', 26 June 2021, India Spend

[181] 'Coronavirus | Thiruvananthapuram bucks excess deaths trend', 24 June 2021, *The Hindu*

took the judiciary to get the states to correct some of their absurd figures and Bihar had to change its toll overnight because of a court's intervention.[182]

This could also explain another thing. India's annual mortality means that, on an average, around 27,000 people die daily. When the official Covid death toll was around 3,000 to 4,000 daily, the crematoria were totally overwhelmed; they ran out of wood for funerals and electric furnaces broke down. The visuals of mass funerals were reported globally, including striking images by the brilliant Reuters photographer Danish Siddiqui, who was then murdered by the Taliban while on assignment in Afghanistan on 16 July 2021. The government responded by walling up cremotaria and shooing away photographers. But the stories had already been reported.[183]

A 15 per cent rise in fatalities would not produce such a breakdown. However, if the numbers were around twice or more than twice the normal consistently for many days, then it would. This meant that the daily toll of the pandemic for several weeks was likely at least around 27,000 dead, meaning a toll in the second wave of 10 lakh or more dead.

Thousands of the poor in northern India were left half-interred in river banks without cremation.[184] The horror of this sight produced verse by a Gujarati poet who wrote of the Ganga as the 'shav vahini' or bearer of corpses, under a naked emperor.[185] Days after this poem was published, visuals of dogs pulling out and eating partially buried corpses emerged.[186] The dead were bearing witness to the State's incompetence in a way that the poor were not able to.

An analysis by *The New York Times* showed that, by 24 May 2021, India's actual toll—at that point officially a little over 3 lakh—was closer to 16 lakh.[187] In July, two research papers showed that the toll may have been

---

[182] 'Bihar's Covid-19 death toll shoots up 73% after recount ordered by high court', 9 June 2021, *Hindustan Times*

[183] Note that all this work was done by and can only be done by newspaper reporters. The point made in the chapter on the Godi media, about scrutiny of the government ending with the death of newspapers, needs to be emphasised.

[184] 'UP में गंगा किनारे के 27 जिलों से ग्राउंड रिपोर्ट:1140 कमी में 2 हजार से ज़्यादा शव; कानपुर, उन्नाव, गाजीपुर और बलिया में हालात सबसे ज़्यादा खराब', 15 May 2021, *Dainik Bhaskar*

[185] 'पारुल खक्कर की कविता से गुजरात की बेहसी के बीच उम्मीद दिखती है...', 23 May 2021, *The Wire Hindi*

[186] 'Watch: Dreadful and disturbing sight of dogs digging riverbed graves to devour bodies in Prayagraj', 20 May 2021, *National Herald*

[187] 'Just how big could India's true Covid toll be?', 25 May 2021, *The New York Times*

more than twice that. One put the figure at between 31 and 34 lakh dead.[188] Another said the dead may have been as many as 49 lakh.[189]

The third thing that Modi had to do to protect Indians and India in the pandemic, was to ensure that as many people as possible were vaccinated as soon as possible. Here the record reveals that he failed as fully as he did in the previous two responsibilities.

On 7 August 2020, the Serum Institute of India (SII), the country's largest vaccine manufacturer, signed an agreement with the global vaccine alliance GAVI and the Gates Foundation to supply 10 crore doses of vaccine to 92 poor countries, including India, by the first half of 2021. The total number of vaccines SII would produce in 2021 of Covishield would be 100 crore (1 billion) doses. This would be distributed among the 92 nations, including India, with a total population of 4 billion. The alliance said that: 'A founding principle of COVAX (Covid Vaccine Global Access) is that access will be equitable. That doesn't just mean ensuring that all countries get fair access to COVID-19 vaccines, it also means having an allocation mechanism, driven by the World Health Organisation (WHO), to guide how vaccines are distributed within countries and territories.'[190] The GAVI alliance would also sell the vaccine produced to rich nations, and use that money given upfront to ramp up production. The key point here is that, in 2020, Modi knew, or should have known, that the maximum possible doses of Covishield India could get in 2021 from the 100 crore doses covering 50 crore people would have to be its equitable share. This would at most be enough to cover 10 per cent or 15 per cent of India's population. GAVI planned with SII to mass produce another vaccine, Novavax, with a target for another billion doses in 2021.[191] Novavax could not come to the market before June, and so this did not happen. But even with Novavax, the number of vaccines India would have had by the end of 2021 would have only been enough to cover a third or less of the population. The only way to vaccinate India quickly would be to ramp up production by investment. This was not done by Modi.

By 30 September 2020, SII had been given $300 million (a little more than Rs 2,500 crore) by GAVI to set up the infrastructure to deliver these

---

[188] 'Excess mortality in India from June 2020 to June 2021 during the COVID pandemic: death registration, health facility deaths, and survey data', medrxiv.org

[189] 'India's excess deaths could be up to 49 lakh, says estimate', 21 July 2021, *Reuters*

[190] 'The Gavi COVAX AMC explained', gavi.org

[191] 'Novavax announces COVID-19 manufacturing agreement with Serum Institute of India', 15 September 2020, ir.novavax.com

doses. The same week, SII's owner, Adar Poonawalla, tweeted to Modi: 'Quick question; will the government of India have 80,000 crores available, over the next one year? Because that's what @MoHFW_INDIA needs, to buy and distribute the vaccine to everyone in India. This is the next concerning challenge we need to tackle. @PMOIndia'.

He then added: 'I ask this question, because we need to plan and guide, vaccine manufacturers both in India and overseas to service the needs of our country in terms of procurement and distribution.' We have seen how the vaccine numbers broke; it was a fact that if India wanted to vaccinate its population in 2021, it would need to procure the vaccines from somewhere.

In response, however, the government said through its health secretary that it had 'constituted a National Expert Group on Vaccine Administration which has held five meetings so far' in which they had 'mulled over the process of vaccine distribution and the amount required for it' and that the 'amount is available with the government'.[192] Apparently, things were under control.

In his Independence Day address on 15 August 2020, Modi had said that, 'three vaccines are in different stages of testing. When scientists give the go-ahead, we are ready with a plan for production. How the vaccine will reach every Indian in the least amount of time—we have a roadmap ready for that'.[193]

The following month, Modi told the United Nations General Assembly that India would deliver vaccines to the world: 'As the largest manufacturer of vaccines in the world, I want to assure the world that India's vaccine production and delivery capacity will be put to help pull out all of humanity from this calamity. India would also help other nations with cold chain and storage facilities.'[194] This bombast sent the Godi media into raptures and it began to portray Modi, no doubt with the approval and likely the instructions from the PMO, as the world's 'Vaccine Guru'.[195]

Modi assured the world that he would take care of the problem on 26 September 2020, by when it was clear that India's first wave was ebbing, and the fatality rates were probably lower than had been feared.

[192] 'Don't agree with Adar Poonawalla's Rs 80,000 crore calculation for COVID vaccine, says govt', 20 September 2020, *Business Today*

[193] '3 Covid vaccines at trials, plan for distribution ready: PM at Red Fort', 15 August 2020, *NDTV*

[194] 'PM Modi delivers virtual speech at United Nations General Assembly', 26 September 2020, *The Hindu*

[195] 'Bharat Ki Baat LIVE: वैक्सीन "गुरु"', 9 December 2020, *ABP News*

Satisfied that he had seen the pandemic off, Modi did not act on vaccines till it became apparent he was wrong. Till February 2021, India had ordered only 11 crore doses while it required 200 crore doses for the eligible population or 270 crore doses for all Indians including those under 14, assuming there was no wastage. Compare India's 11 crore to the numbers ordered and paid for by Canada (33 crore), the US (120 crore), UK (45 crore), Brazil (23 crore), African Union (67 crore), Indonesia (19 crore) and the European Union (180 crore).[196] India ordered fewer doses than even Australia (12 crore), which has a population smaller than India's National Capital Region.

India said it had 'approved' the paying of Rs 3,000 crore in funding to SII (and another Rs 1,500 crore to Bharat Biotech, the maker of the indigenous Covaxin) only on 19 April 2021. This was not a payment; it was only the setting aside of money for shipments India would buy. And even this was more than seven months after SII received its funding from the Gates Foundation. In comparison, the US had set up a programme to facilitate the manufacturing and distribution of vaccines in April 2020 with initial funding of Rs 75,000 crores.[197] By the end of 2020, this would go up to a total of $12.4 billion or Rs 90,000 crores.

Around the world, governments invested in private companies to share risks with them, and later bought back vaccines from them. The US tied up with Moderna, Germany with BioNTech and CureVac, and the UK with Oxford-AstraZeneca (which eventually created what India knows as Covishield). This was taking the threat seriously and allocating resources to the principal defence mechanism against the pandemic: vaccination.

Modi on the other hand appeared to take the vaccine strategy lightly. Though it gave some assistance through the ICMR, the government did not fund vaccine development or production, including for the indigenous Bharat Biotech's Covaxin.[198] Meanwhile, as the second wave began, Modi was making statements on the essentiality of vaccines that were casual and reflective of government laxity.[199]

---

[196] 'India's Covid crisis hits Covax vaccine-sharing scheme', 17 May 2021, *BBC*

[197] 'Trump's "Operation Warp Speed" aims to rush Coronavirus vaccine', 29 April 2020, *Bloomberg*

[198] 'No financial aid given to SII & Bharat Biotech: Govt in SC', 11 May 2011, *The Times of India*

[199] '"We defeated Covid without vaccines": PM Modi tells CMs on way forward', 8 April 2021, *Hindustan Times*

Till 16 April, India was exporting vaccines to other nations. Whether this was a commercial deal the importing nation had with the manufacturer in India (SII) or part of the consignment that the Gates Foundation had paid for in advance or part of the Vaccine Maitri scheme under which India was providing free vaccines to other nations—all consignments were sent off with publicity from Jaishankar's Ministry of External Affairs as an act of saving the world. The Government of India effectively commandeered the stock and controlled the dispatch even of the supplies they had nothing to do with. By mid-April, India had sent out more than 6.6 crore doses. This included about 2 crore doses to GAVI,[200] 3.5 crore sold by SII to nations through commercial contracts and 1 crore doses given as grants by the Indian government to neighbouring and other poor countries (Pakistan, though a part of GAVI, got none). All of these were packaged as Modi's doing. When Canada was given 50 lakh doses, which it had paid for, the BJP's supporters in Canada put up billboards thanking Modi for them.[201]

The government put out a statement in which Canada's prime minister Justin Trudeau said that 'if the world managed to conquer COVID-19, it would be significantly because of India's tremendous pharmaceutical capacity, and Prime Minister Modi's leadership in sharing this capacity with the world.' The statement said that the 'Prime Minister thanked PM Trudeau for his sentiments.'[202]

Modi took the role of global saviour seriously, and the Indian envoy to the UN made the extraordinary boast that, at the end of March, India had vaccinated more foreigners than it had its own citizens.[203] On 26 March 2021, Harsh Vardhan said India had become a global leader and was on the way to becoming a Vishwaguru. Hours before that, *The New York Times* reported that India had actually stopped all exports because it had realised only now that it was in trouble at home.[204]

---

[200] GAVI, officially Gavi, is a public–private global health partnership with the goal of increasing access to immunisation in poor countries.

[201] 'Giant billboards in Canada thank Indian PM Modi for providing Covid-19 vaccines', 11 March 2021, *Hindustan Times*

[202] 'PM receives a telephone call from H.E. Justin Trudeau, Prime Minister of Canada', 10 February 2021, Press Information Bureau

[203] 'We have supplied more vaccines globally than having vaccinated our own people: India tells United Nations', 27 March 2021, PTI

[204] 'India cuts back on vaccine exports as infections surge at home', 25 March 2021, *The New York Times*

Soon after, Adar Poonawalla fled to London because of threats from India's 'most powerful' people.[205]

The government 'never realised that the wave would hit this badly and assumed that these two firms (SII and Bharat Biotech) would take care of the requirement', K. Sujatha Rao, a former secretary of health and family welfare, said.[206] The government also assumed that its strategy of vaccination by age groups and state by state was fine and that government investment in speeding up the process was not required.

As the second wave ravaged north India, it finally dawned on Modi that vaccination was the only way out and that India did not have enough stock and, exports of vaccine were banned. In true Modi fashion, the move was disguised so as to not harm his image. While no vaccines were allowed to be exported, the government claimed there was no ban.[207]

The ban hurt poorer nations,[208] and by the end of May, two months after India claimed exports had not been blocked, the world was analysing what went wrong. *The Wall Street Journal* summed it up: 'Most of the world's poorest nations were left highly dependent on a single vaccine, produced by a single manufacturer in a single country. In a cruel twist, that supplier—the Serum Institute of India—ended up engulfed by the world's worst Covid-19 outbreak.'

Because of this, GAVI, which had already paid upfront for the vaccines, did not get its deliveries. In a letter to 92 developing nations (including India), GAVI's head wrote, 'Dear Participant, we regret to inform you that, given the heightened Covid-19 crisis in India, Covax no longer expects deliveries … to resume in May.'[209] When asked whether the strategy to depend on India was flawed, he said: 'We hear a lot of criticism, and the truth is, we've tried to do something that we think is the right thing. Hindsight's 20:20. Should we have not invested in India? Well, that was the fastest way to get there.'

Not only was it not the fastest way, it turned out to have sabotaged the global fight because of the mess India was in by April.

---

[205] 'Serum's Adar Poonawalla moves to London, cites threatening phone calls from powerful people', 2 May 2021, *Business Today*

[206] 'Centre abdicating duty towards vaccine drive: K. Sujatha Rao', 22 April 2021, *TheWire.in*

[207] 'India has not imposed any export ban on Covid-19 vaccines: MEA', 2 April 2021, *The Hindu*

[208] 'Africa scrambles as India vaccine export ban bites region', 4 May 2021, *Deutsche Welle*

[209] 'Why a grand plan to vaccinate the world against Covid unraveled', 26 May 2021, *The Wall Street Journal*

SII was due to ship 14 crore doses by the end of May but was stopped by the government after it had sent fewer than 2 crore. Far from being Vaccine Guru and saving the world, India under Modi was disrupting what others had planned for, paid for and organised. 'Not only did India fail to place firm orders with the two companies well in advance, but also it did not provide the companies (SII and Bharat Biotech) any funding till a month ago to expand the manufacturing capacities,' R. Prasad wrote in *The Hindu* on 23 May 2021. 'What it has done instead is to appropriate for its use the vaccine doses which were already paid for by other entities and were meant for other countries.'[210]

On 19 April 2021, Modi announced what was called a 'liberalised and accelerated phase-3 strategy of Covid vaccination from 1 May', meaning 11 days later. This strategy was, in essence, the Union washing its hands of the vaccination issue, having messed it up thus far. From 1 May, it would be the responsibility of states to purchase vaccines and administer them to their citizens. The Union would take half the vaccine production in India and distribute it based on certain criteria. Vaccine manufacturers would be free to sell the remaining 50 per cent to state governments and the open market.

The Union had said on 1 February 2021 that it had set aside Rs 35,000 crore for vaccines in the budget.[211] This would have taken care of 166 crore doses of Covishield. Now suddenly and without explanation this was being abandoned two months later. It turned out that this money had not been allocated at all.[212]

With not enough vaccine production and no infrastructure to produce them faster, Modi's 'strategy' included the farcical decision to let everyone over 18 be vaccinated when even those over 45 were struggling to find a slot. The existing policy for vaccines—for polio, tuberculosis, diphtheria, measles, Japanese encephalitis and so on—was that the Union government would provide them to state governments. The vaccines for these were also available in the private sector, but here the Union was asking 29 states to each negotiate with private companies in India and abroad.

Even in this moment of abdication, the press release could not resist self-aggrandisement and noted that the 'Government has been working hard

---

[210] 'Serum's supply to COVAX hit by India's poor planning'
[211] 'Budget 2021: Rs 35,000 crore for Covid-19 vaccines, committed to further support, says Nirmala Sitharaman', 1 February 2021, *India Today*
[212] 'The reality of Modi govt's vaccine funding: Rs 35,000 cr for states, zero for Centre', 10 May 2021, *ThePrint.in*

from over a year to ensure that maximum numbers of Indians are able to get the vaccine in the shortest possible of time: PM'.[213]

This 'liberalised and accelerated phase-3 strategy' was no real strategy, of course. The states were asked to procure vaccines from non-existent capacity in India. They were asked to import from a market abroad which had been overbooked for months.

Approval had not been given by the Modi government to vaccines produced abroad. In February, after waiting for approval that did not come, Pfizer withdrew its application for use of its vaccine in India. India had insisted on local trials for the vaccine which was being used across the world, including in the US and Europe. Phase three trial data (where 500 or 1,500 samples are tested to assess adverse reactions in individuals who have India's genetic pool) was waived for the locally made Covaxin but insisted upon for Pfizer.[214] In April, without an explanation for why, this position was reversed by India.[215]

After the new policy was announced, 13 states desperately floated global tenders, bidding against each other. But this was too late in the day and companies said they would not deal with states but only with the Union, and in any case they couldn't give India any vaccines because their order books were full.[216]

Modi had made 'India one of the only countries where life-saving vaccines are not only being sold, but sold at varying rates on the open market'. His policy had resulted in states 'struggling to procure vaccines on their own', and with 'multiple buyers competing in desperation, vaccine makers ... calling the shots in a seller's market'.[217]

The first lot of vaccines had been procured from the PM CARES fund for Rs 210 each (from SII). Now the manufacturer was asking for Rs 350 from the states.[218] Why was there a difference? This was not explained. The

---

[213] 'Government of India announces a liberalised and accelerated phase 3 strategy of Covid-19 vaccination from 1st May', 19 April 2021, Press Information Bureau

[214] 'Pfizer drops India vaccine application after regulator seeks local trial', 5 February 2021, *Reuters*

[215] 'India fast tracks emergency approvals for foreign-produced Covid vaccines', 13 April 2021, *Business Standard*

[216] 'Centre steps in after foreign Covid-19 vaccine makers say no to state govts', 25 May 2021, *Business Standard*

[217] 'Modi never bought enough COVID-19 vaccines for India. Now the whole world is paying', 28 May 2021, *Time*

[218] 'Covid: Covishield price for states reduced by 25% to Rs 300 per dose', 28 April 2021, PTI

private sector would be sold the vaccine at Rs 600 per dose and was free to charge what it wanted—which meant, of course, that it would vaccinate the rich.[219] Obviously, the supply would go to where the money was, and it did.[220]

The abdication by the Union, the absence of stock and preparation and the addition of yet another app (Co-WIN) on which citizens were to register to get a slot, meant that the rate of vaccinations collapsed. From an average of 30 lakh doses a day in April, it halved to an average of 16 lakh doses in May.[221]

Why an app only available in English and only usable on smartphones was thought to be a good idea as the instrument for universal vaccination in a poor and low literacy nation is hard to say. One reason could have been that the Union wanted to control certification (which, of course, featured Modi's photo).

In the US, vaccinations were walk-in and the certificate written out by hand. In India, hundreds of millions began a game of one-time passwords and captchas and frustration at not receiving a slot. Of course, the primary problem was a shortage of vaccines. This showed immediately.

In April, India could vaccinate 40 lakh individuals on only two days. Numbers fell even during a four-day 'Tika Utsav' or vaccination festival that Modi announced that month.[222] Only 3 per cent of the Indian population was fully vaccinated at the end of May, four and a half months after vaccinations had begun, behind not just developed countries but also the global average (5 per cent). When this was pointed out, the Union said it was looking around for 'idle capacity' which it could now utilise.[223]

In April, Manmohan Singh wrote to Modi with suggestions on how to deal with the pandemic.[224] He made five points:

---

[219] 'Rs 700-Rs 1,500: Amid lack of clarity, what private hospitals are charging', 11 May 2021, *The Indian Express*

[220] 'India's Covid vaccine rollout favours the wealthy and tech-savvy', 26 May 2021, *Financial Times*

[221] 'India's daily average Covid vaccinations dipped by nearly 50% between April and May', 21 May 2021, *ThePrint.in*

[222] 'Intriguing story of India's slackening vaccination numbers despite Modi's "Tika Utsav" push', 18 April 2021, *ThePrint.in*

[223] '"Finding newer, idle capacities to enhance COVID vaccine production capacity": FM Sitharaman', 6 June 2021, *Business Today*

[224] 'Ex-PM Manmohan suggests 5 points to tackle Covid-19 crisis in letter to Modi', 18 April 2021, *Mint*

1) That the government reveal how many firm orders for doses had been placed on different vaccine producers and accepted for delivery over the next six months.

2) That the government should indicate how this expected supply will be distributed across states based on a transparent formula. The Union government could retain 10 per cent for distribution based on emergency needs, but other than that, states should have a clear signal of likely availability so that they can plan their roll out.

3) States should be given some flexibility to define categories of frontline workers who can be vaccinated even if they are below 45 years of age. For example, states may want to designate school teachers; bus, three-wheeler and taxi drivers; municipal and panchayat staff and possibly lawyers who have to attend courts as frontline workers. They can then be vaccinated even if they are below 45.

4) The government must proactively support vaccine producers to expand their manufacturing facilities quickly by providing funds and other concessions. And it should invoke compulsory licensing provisions in the law, so that a number of companies are able to produce the vaccines under a licence. This had happened before with drugs dealing with AIDS.

5) That any vaccine cleared for use by credible authorities, such as the European Medical Agency or the USFDA, should be allowed to be imported without insisting on domestic bridging trials.

Modi did not respond himself but asked Harsh Vardhan to send the reply, which the minister tweeted out with the message: 'History shall be kinder to you Dr Manmohan Singh ji if your offer of "constructive cooperation" and valuable advice was followed by your Congress leaders as well in such extraordinary times! Here's my reply to your letter to Hon'ble PM Sh @narendramodi ji'. He added a thumbs up emoji at the end of this tweet and then also tweeted: 'In all humility, a word of advice to you as well, Dr Manmohan Singh ji! A learned man of your stature could do well to surround himself with better advisors. All suggestions given by you have been implemented a week prior to your letter. PS: There's value in staying updated!'

The text of the letter continued in similar manner. Instead of responding to the points raised, it focussed on personalised criticism and crude language.

Not only would Modi refuse to admit the possibility that he may have failed Indians on Covid, he would not even acknowledge what his predecessor was suggesting to remedy the situation. The bombast was, of course, empty. Modi was forced to do as Manmohan Singh had suggested because that was the only sensible path. On 7 June, Modi made a speech announcing that the Union would now buy the vaccines, and on 8 June, the Union stated that it was placing orders for another 44 crore doses with SII and Bharat Biotech to be delivered till the end of 2021. Too late and too little for the lakhs and possibly millions who died because of hubris and incompetence of the Indian government. India felt and the whole world saw the trauma and damage of those weeks when India revealed itself to be helpless at saving its citizens, while the government chose to look away and the prime minister was absconding.

It is why the dirge by Parul Khakhar became popular. Here is its text, translated by Salil Tripathi:

Ganges, the Carrier of Corpses

Don't worry, be happy, in one voice speak the corpses
O King, in your Ram-Rajya, we see bodies flow in the Ganges
O King, the woods are ashes,
No spots remain at crematoria,
O King, there are no carers,
Nor any pall-bearers,
No mourners left
And we are bereft
With our wordless dirges of dysphoria
Libitina enters every home where she dances and then prances,
O King, in your Ram-Rajya, our bodies flow in the Ganges
O King, the melting chimney quivers, the virus has us shaken
O King, our bangles shatter, our heaving chest lies broken
The city burns as he fiddles, Billa-Ranga thrust their lances,
O King, in your Ram-Rajya, I see bodies flow in the Ganges
O King, your attire sparkles as you shine and glow and blaze
O King, this entire city has at last seen your real face
Show your guts, no ifs and buts,
Come out and shout and say it loud,
"The naked King is lame and weak"
Show me you are no longer meek,
Flames rise high and reach the sky, the furious city rages;
O King, in your Ram-Rajya, do you see bodies flow in the Ganges?.

12

LAWS AND DISORDER

The Modi years have been marked by regressive legislation across a range of subjects. The laws have conflated vengeance with justice and the obsession with Muslims has continued to take legal form in laws attacking freedom of religion and freedom of occupation. India's deviously named 'freedom of religion' laws had thus far targeted Christians, whose right to propagate had been guaranteed by the Constituent Assembly after much debate, but was taken away soon after Independence. The Muslims were brought into the picture after Modi through the so-called 'love jihad' laws.

The desire for absolute control has watered down one of India's best legislations, the RTI Act, and has also introduced the Kashmirisation of India through a law authorising the State to take away mobile telephony arbitrarily. The State has appropriated for itself more authority and claimed more rights at the expense of those of citizens, and to the detriment of individual liberty and access to justice. The laws have had a fallout on society and we will look at that in the second half of this chapter.

These are the legislations that the period has spawned.

The Karnataka Education Act (1983) Order of 2022

In 2022, Karnataka banned Muslim women and girls from covering their heads in schools and colleges that had uniforms. Even in colleges which did not have a prescribed uniform, the covering of heads by Muslims was prohibited because 'clothes which disturb equality, integrity and public law and order should not be worn'.[1] Sikhs were excluded from the order and by the courts.[2]

---

[1] 'Hijab row: Karnataka govt bars clothes that 'disturb equality, public order', 6 February 2022, TheNewsMinute.com

[2] '"Sikhism ingrained in India, can't compare with Islamic practices", says SC on Karnataka hijab row', 8 September 2022, *Deccan Herald*

Mobs arrived at schools to harass Muslim females coming in, and the courts consistently sided with the State against individual liberty, including for adult women, on what they should wear and whether they had the right to keep their head covered.

Juvenile Justice (Care and Protection of Children) Act, 2015

The idea that children accused of rape should be tried as adults came in the wake of the Nirbhaya incident in Delhi, one of whose accused was a minor. This incident produced a strong sentiment of vengeance in the media that seeped into the polity. On coming to power, the BJP government asked for a change in the law.[3]

The law says that if accused of 'heinous offences'—those where the maximum punishment is seven years or more under the Indian Penal Code—children over 16 should be tried as adults.

The process requires a Board to 'conduct a preliminary assessment with regard to his mental and physical capacity to commit such offence, ability to understand the consequences of the offence and the circumstances in which he allegedly committed the offence'. To divine this, it can take the assistance of 'experienced psychologists or psycho-social workers or other experts'.

The Board itself will consist of a judge and two 'social workers' (defined as anyone who is 'actively involved in health, education, or welfare activities pertaining to children for at least seven years or a practicing professional with a degree in child psychology, psychiatry, sociology or law').

If this Board determines that the child should face trial as an adult, the case is sent to a children's court, which will try the child as one, 'considering the special needs of the child, the tenets of fair trial and maintaining a child friendly atmosphere'. Convicted children are to be sent to 'a place of safety' till they reach the age of 21, at which point they will be sent to an adult jail. In 2021, a parliamentary standing committee on home affairs recommended that the juvenile delinquency age be reduced from 18 to 16, and all accused above 16 be tried as adults for cases registered under the Protection of Children from Sexual Offences (POCSO) Act.[4]

Right to Information (Amendment) Act, 2019

The amendment gives the Union the powers to set the salaries and service conditions of information commissioners at Union as well as state levels. The

---

[3] 'Treat rape-accused minors on par with adults: Maneka Gandhi', 14 July 2014, PTI

[4] 'Decoding the proposed changes in the POCSO Act', 23 March 2021, *Hindustan Times*

original Act set the terms of the Union chief information commissioner and information commissioners at five years (or until the age of 65, whichever was earlier). The amendment states that the appointment will now be 'for such term as may be prescribed by the Central Government', which gives the Union influence over the individuals it is appointing.[5] In 2021, even the new CBI director was appointed in this fashion.[6]

The amendment also gives the Union authority to arbitrarily fix salaries, allowances and other terms of service of the chief information commissioner and the information commissioners. The change says this money 'shall be such as may be prescribed by the Central Government'.

The Unlawful Activities (Prevention) Amendment Act, 2019

Before the amendment, UAPA only allowed organisations to be categorised as 'terrorist'. The State can now categorise any individual as a 'terrorist', if it suspects that the individual is involved in terrorism. Once the person is so categorised, their name will be added to the list, 'Terrorist Organsiations *and Individuals*' (italics mine), specified in Schedule 4 of the Act.[7]

These individuals need not even have any affiliation with any of the 36 terrorist organisations referred to in the First Schedule of the Act to be classified as terrorists.

The law defines a 'terrorist act' as one which causes 'injuries to any person, damage to any property, an attempt to overawe any public functionary by means of criminal force and any act to compel the government or any person to do or abstain from doing any act etc'. It also includes any act that is 'likely to threaten' or 'likely to strike terror in people', giving absolute power to the government to brand any citizen or activist a terrorist without these acts actually being committed. In 2023, the Supreme Court further tightened the law and gave the government authority to jail anyone it considered a 'member' of a banned organisation under UAPA. As lawyer Abhinav Sekhri noted in his review of the judgment, 'We are not dealing with neat lists of shareholders, but a hazy group of people where membership would depend upon perceptions and beliefs' and that 'proving membership did not need

---

[5] 'Explained: What has changed in RTI Act? Why are Opposition parties protesting?', 22 July 2019, *The Indian Express*

[6] 'Text of Centre's notification appointing new director ensures CBI remains a "caged parrot"', 2 June 2021, *TheWire.in*

[7] 'A tough law is required to uproot terrorism from India and our government would always support that: Shri Amit Shah', 2 August 2019, Press Information Bureau

much more than a confession and recoveries of inconvenient literature (even the Communist Manifesto might do)'.[8]

Maharashtra Animal Preservation (Amendment) Act, 2015

Under this law, anyone found in possession of beef can be jailed for up to five years.[9] It also bans the slaughter of bulls, bullocks and calves, in addition to the existing ban on cow slaughter.

The Haryana Gauvansh Sanrakshan and Gausamvardhan Act, 2015

Possession of beef is punishable by up to five years in jail. Sale of cows for slaughter to another state is punishable by seven years in jail. Cow slaughter will attract jail time of up to 10 years. The burden of proof is on the accused.[10]

The Gujarat Animal Preservation (Amendment) Act, 2017

This law extended the punishment for cow slaughter from seven years to life.[11] It allows permanent forfeiture of vehicles transporting animals except under prescribed conditions. It also increased the fine from Rs 1 lakh to Rs 5 lakh. Minister of state for home, Pradipsinh Jadeja, said the logic was to equal cow slaughter with murder.[12]

The Karnataka Prevention of Slaughter and Preservation of Cattle Act, 2020

---

[8] 'The Arup Bhuyan Review', 25 March 2023, theproofofguilt.blogspot.com

[9] 'Beef banned in Maharashtra after President Mukherjee passes Maharashtra Animal Preservation (Amendment) Bill 1995', 3 March 2015, *India Today*

[10] '10-yr jail, 1 lakh fine: What Haryana's tough cow protection law says', 19 October 2015, *The Indian Express*

[11] 'Gujarat: Bill proposing life term for cow slaughter gets governor's nod', 13 April 2017, PTI

[12] In 2019, a Muslim man was accused of stealing a calf and serving its meat at his daughter's wedding. He was tried and convicted not for theft but for cow slaughter. The prosecution had no evidence and couldn't prove that beef had been served at the wedding. However 'in such a scenario', sessions court judge Hemantkumar Dave noted, 'It is incumbent upon the accused to prove that the meat found in the biryani was not obtained by slaughtering the said calf.' The man was jailed for 10 years. The sentence was suspended by an embarrassed Gujarat High Court with the judge using 'judicial discretion' and the man was ordered to be freed. The government said it would appeal. 'Gujarat man gets 10 year jail term for cow slaughter', 7 July 2019, *The Indian Express*

It repealed the 1964 law, which allowed the slaughter of bullocks, and makes cow slaughter punishable by up to seven years. Purchase, sale, disposal or transport of cattle outside the state except in the prescribed manner is punishable by five years in jail. Fines of up to Rs 10 lakh can also be imposed.

Uttar Pradesh Recovery of Damage to Public and Private Property Act, 2020

Enacted after the Uttar Pradesh Police shot dead 21 protestors and killed two others during the protests against CAA, this law gives the state government the power to set up tribunals to decide damages to any public or private property due to riots, hartals, bandhs, protests or public processions.

The tribunal will issue notices for the appearance of the accused. Even if the party does not appear, the tribunal can hear the matter and order attachment of their properties. All orders passed by the tribunals will be final and cannot be appealed before any court.[13]

Uttarakhand Freedom of Religion Act, 2018

This is one of several state laws introduced and legislated by the BJP after the conspiracy theory of 'love jihad' began to be circulated.

It has a clause which reads that 'any marriage which was done for the sole purpose of conversion by the man of one religion with the woman of another religion either by converting himself before or after marriage or by converting the woman before or after marriage may be declared null and void'.

Any relative of the person changing their faith can file a complaint with the police.[14]

The law says that 'if any person comes back to his ancestral religion' then this shall not be deemed conversion, without defining what 'ancestral religion' means. Its meaning is that conversions to Hinduism will not be counted as conversion.

The district magistrate will then conduct an inquiry through the police 'with regard to real intention, purpose and cause of that proposed religion conversion'.

The burden of proof to show that the conversion was not fraudulent, through undue influence, coercion or by marriage, is on the person being

---

[13] 'Allahabad High Court terms U.P.'s recovery of damages ordinance arbitrary', 19 March 2020, *The Hindu*

[14] 'Interfaith couple booked for religious conversion in violation of Uttarakhand law', 31 December 2020, PTI

converted and the person 'facilitating' the conversion. If the State feels there was facilitation in the conversion then the burden of proof is also reversed on that individual, meaning the husband, wife and the family, or the priest.

Those who change their faith without applying to the government 'in the prescribed proforma' and without the consent of the government after the police inquiry face a year in jail.

Himachal Pradesh Freedom of Religion Act, 2019

This law came after the BJP chief minister, Jai Ram Thakur, said that in the past 13 years, 'not even a single case was filed under the 2006 Act'. And that this lack of cases being filed showed that a stronger act against religious freedom was required.[15]

On 31 August 2012, the high court had struck down that part of the 2006 law which required a person wanting to change their faith to give 30 days' notice to the government. That was brought back by Thakur in this law, which now requires 30 days' notice to be given by individuals wishing to change their faith, along with 30 days' notice also to be given by the priest officiating at the ceremony (if any). After this, the district magistrate will hold an inquiry to see if the change of faith can be allowed. If the state determines that these conditions have not been met, the conversion is 'illegal and void'. Individuals who change their faith without permission face a year in jail. Punishment for propagation (a fundamental right under Article 25) is up to seven years in jail.

Uttar Pradesh Vidhi Viruddh Dharma Samparivartan Pratishedh Adhyadesh, 2020 (Prohibition of Unlawful Conversion of Religion Ordinance)

Popularly known as the 'love jihad' law, though it was copied from other BJP states, this prohibits conversion except with government permission and 60 days' notice. Conversions for marriage are illegal. The burden of proof is on the family the woman is marrying into. Punishment is up to five years in jail. FIRs can be filed by any blood relative or relative by marriage or adoption against anyone for unlawful conversion of either person in the marriage.[16]

---

[15] 'Himachal's new anti-conversion law has an old provision quashed by high court', 19 September 2019, *The Indian Express*

[16] 'यूपी: धर्म परिवर्तन अध्यादेश लागू होते ही बरेली में दर्ज हो गई एफ़आईआर, क्या है पूरा मामला', 30 November 2020, *BBC*

The Madhya Pradesh Freedom of Religion Act, 2021

It replaces the Religious Freedom Act of 1968. It punishes conversion through marriage with 10 years in jail. It also nullifies such marriages. Children born in these nullified marriages can claim the right to their father's property. Conversions can only happen with government permission and 60 days' notice. FIRs can be filed by parents and siblings of either person in the marriage. Any other person who is related by blood, marriage, adoption, guardianship or custodianship can file a written complaint with court permission.[17]

After this, the BJP governments in Haryana[18] and Karnataka[19] said they will bring in similar legislation, and then they did, though there is no evidence there is a problem. It is, of course, to create a problem that the laws are being written.

Gujarat Freedom of Religion (Amendment) Act, 2021

This penalises 'forcible or fraudulent religious conversion by marriage' or 'love jihad'. It replaces the Freedom of Religion Act of 2003, and punishes individuals with up to 10 years in jail and a Rs 5 lakh fine. The law seeks to curb the 'emerging trend in which women are lured to marriage for the purpose of religious conversion'.

Gujarat's minister of state for home said that 'there is international finance being channelised to lure Hindu girls into marriage and then their conversion'.[20]

The Karnataka Protection of Right to Freedom of Religion Act, 2022

Coming into effect on 17 May 2022, and aimed at criminalising interfaith marriage like the rest, the Karnataka law requires people wanting to convert to give 30 days' notice to the district magistrate or additional district magistrate. This bureaucrat will then put the application up on a notice board in his office and in the office of the tehsildar, calling for objections. If anyone objects an inquiry will be conducted by through officials of the revenue

---

[17] 'Anti-"love jihad" law comes into effect in MP', 9 January 2021, *The New Indian Express*
[18] 'Haryana's proposed "love jihad" law: RTI shows 3 accused found innocent in only 4 similar cases', 4 March 2021, *The Indian Express*
[19] 'Anti-love jihad law in next assembly session', 17 February 2021, *The Hindu*
[20] 'Gujarat Assembly passes "love jihad" law', 1 April 2021, *The Hindu*

or social welfare department. These government servants will examine the 'genuine intention, purpose and cause of the proposed conversion'.

If the bureaucrat concludes based on this inquiry that the law has been broken, he will instruct the police to initiate criminal action. If you change your faith without asking for government permission, the conversion is annulled, and there is jail of a minimum of one year and maximum of three years. (How the bureaucrat's annulment would work at the level of faith was unclear. As one pastor told me, 'Suppose I stopped believing in Christ today. That would be a conversion. I am supposed to take permission from the State for this change, but I have already stopped believing.')[21] After it won the Assembly elections in May 2023, the Congress said it would undo this law.[22]

The Haryana Prevention of Unlawful Conversion of Religious Act, 2022

An additional innovation in this law, which came into effect on 20 December 2022, was to introduce punishment for those who 'abet or conspire conversion through any means including social media'. This attracts up to five years in jail.

Those wanting to change their faith must submit a declaration to the district magistrate stating their 'intention to convert out of free will and without an force, coercion, undue influence or allurement'. The application is put on display and objections invited. The bureaucrat has three months to approve or deny permission to convert and six months to give his reasons for doing as he did.

Like the Madhya Pradesh law, it can undo marriages, including those with children. Converting back to your parents' or grandparents' religion is not considered conversion.[23]

Temporary Suspension of Telecom Services (Public Emergency or Public Safety) Rules, 2017

This gives the Union and state governments the power to suspend, for any reason, mobile and internet services.

Authority is given to the secretary of the Ministry of Home Affairs in Delhi or the secretary of state governments in charge of home affairs.

Failing these two, authority is also given to any officer of the rank of joint secretary or above. The reasons for suspension will be reviewed by a

---

[21] 'The Karnataka Protection of Right to Freedom of Religion Act, 2022', dpal.karnataka. gov.in

[22] 'Karnataka to scrap anti-conversion law, reverse textbook changes', 16 June 2023, *The Hindu*

[23] 'The Haryana Prevention of Unlawful Conversion of Religious Act, 2022', indiacode.nic.in

committee within 24 hours, but there is no time limit on how long the suspension can last. The law was used in Haryana and Uttar Pradesh during the farmers' protest outside Delhi in 2020–21. In Kashmir, the suspension has lasted for months, as we have seen.

The Gujarat Prohibition of Transfer of Immovable Property and Provision for Protection of Tenants from Eviction from Premises in Disturbed Areas Act, 2019 Amendment

A law that kept Muslims segregated and ghettoised was tightened in 2019. The law—known as Ashant Dharo (Disturbed Areas Act)—required people to reveal their religion while selling and purchasing property. In areas that were declared 'disturbed' by the state, Hindus could not sell to Muslims and vice versa without government permission. Over the years, and especially after Modi became chief minister, more and more neighbourhoods in all major Gujarat cities have been included under the Act, even those where there has never been rioting. This has effectively ghettoised Muslims.

The amendment that was cleared in 2019 gives the collector authority to determine if the sale of a property would lead to the likelihood of 'polarisation' or 'improper clustering' of people from a particular religion. It also gives the government further power to review the decision of the collector, even if the buyer and seller make no appeal.

Property sales could trigger the creation of a special investigation team, with the collector, municipal commissioner and police commissioner as members. The amendment enables the state government to form a committee to advise it on the adding of new areas to the Disturbed Areas Act.

The amendment enlarged the scope of property transfer and included leasing. In effect, even foreigners can lease and buy property in those parts of Gujarat's cities where Indian Muslims cannot.

Transgender Persons (Protection of Rights) Act, 2019

The law requires India's transgender individuals to submit to certification process under a section called 'Recognition of identity of transgender persons'. Instead of the right to self-identify and the freedom to determine their sexuality, they have to make an application to the district magistrate for a certificate of identity.[24] Those who undergo surgery to change their sex/sexual characteristics must submit a certificate from a medical officer.

---

[24] 'The Transgender Persons Bill explained', 30 November 2019, *The Hindu*

A trans person would require this certificate of identity to access a variety of social-welfare programmes that exist or might be offered, including those relating to food, healthcare, educational opportunities and insurance.

Activists have other problems with the law.[25]

One of their main contentions is that, as per this law, sexual assault against a transgender person will attract a maximum term of two years in jail, against a minimum of seven years for sexual assault against cisgender women. Another objection is that, if young trans people want to leave home because of pressure to conform to the gender they were assigned at birth, they can no longer join the trans community. They have to go instead to a court, which will send them to a 'rehabilitation centre'.

The law also ignored a key demand of the community that they be given public-sector reservations in the way that those differently abled have been. They reject this being clubbed with their caste identity.

The 2019 law came after an earlier bill—the Transgender Persons (Protection of Rights) Bill, 2016—which was also opposed. It defined the transgender individual as a 'person who is neither wholly female nor wholly male'.

It included the proposal for 'screening committees' to determine who was transgender and who was not. It also criminalised begging, a source of income for a large number of transgender Indians.

Industrial Relations Code, 2020

The Lok Sabha cleared this law, which introduces more conditions restricting the rights of workers to strike, and more freedom for employers to fire workers.

It requires industrial employees to give a 60-day notice for a strike, and it also forbids strikes during the pendency of labour proceedings before a tribunal and a further 60 days after the conclusion of such proceedings, making strikes impossible. The law it replaced said employees in a public utility service (water, electricity, natural gas, telephone) could go on strike by giving between two weeks and six weeks of notice. The new code will apply for all industrial establishments.

---

[25] 'Why new bill meant to benefit transgender people is termed regressive', 22 August 2019, *IndiaSpend.com*

It has also relaxed the rules relating to layoffs and retrenchment in industrial establishments having 300 workers, up from 100 workers in the past. Such firms can retrench employees without government permission.[26]

The Aadhaar and Other Laws (Amendment) Act, 2019

The Modi government has revived the commercial use of Aadhaar, struck down as unconstitutional by the Supreme Court in September 2018.[27] The amendment reopens the door for exploitation by private entities and businesses built on data aggregation. It allows authentication by private firms and continues the confusion over Aadhaar being voluntary or mandatory.

The use of Aadhaar for authentication or offline verification on a voluntary basis is only specified in the new subsections being added to the Aadhaar Act. The specific provisions amending the Telegraph Act (which applies to telecom companies) and the Prevention of Money Laundering Act (which applies for banks) do not make Aadhaar voluntary. Instead, they say that the relevant entity 'shall identify' clients (meaning fulfil the Know Your Customer process) using Aadhaar, passport or other any other form of identification notified by the Union government. The option of a passport is really a false choice, as writer Vakasha Sachdev has pointed out,[28] since only 5 per cent of Indians have passports. This means Aadhaar will effectively be the only acceptable form of identification for large sections of the population when they try to get mobile numbers or open bank accounts, which would violate the Supreme Court's judgement.

Provisions of the law have been amended to allow a service provider to use Aadhaar to verify the identity of an individual, but do not provide a mechanism for the individual to assert receipt of a service. This can be used against individuals who cannot identify themselves, and individuals have no protection against their identity being misused when a service is delivered in their name to someone else.

[26] 'The Hindu Explains | What does the new Industrial Relations Code say, and how does it affect the right to strike?', 27 September 2020, *The Hindu*

[27] 'Why Modi government is amending the Aadhaar Act and what it means for you', 2 January 2019, *TheWire.in*

[28] 'Modi government's Aadhaar Amendment Bill violates SC judgment', 22 November 2019, *The Quint*

The Muslim Women (Protection) of Rights on Marriage Act, 2019

This law criminalises the utterance of the word 'talaq' three times in one sitting. The divorce emanating from this utterance had already been held illegal by an earlier Supreme Court judgement. In essence, this Act criminalises the saying of this word three times together by Muslim men even though the marriage remains intact. The law does not change the Muslim personal law of divorce, and the utterance of talaq in three different sittings (separated by menstrual periods and no intercourse) remains valid. The law also takes away the magistrate's discretion for giving bail in case of arrest, requiring a judge to first listen to the view of the wife before freeing the husband. The punishment for saying the word 'talaq' for Muslim men is three years in jail, the same as IPC 154 (rioting with a deadly weapon). Muslim men are the only section in India for whom divorce, a 'private wrong' for all other communities, is a crime against the State.[29]

The Citizenship (Amendment) Act, 2019

Muslim refugees from Afghanistan, Bangladesh and Pakistan were excluded from this law, which gave automatic citizenship to non-Muslims (Hindus, Christians, Parsis, Jains, Sikhs and Buddhists) who came to India before 31 December 2014. There were existing routes that could have delivered this; a new law was not needed. It was written purely to exclude and to humiliate India's Muslims and tell them that they were not wanted. And of course it was one part of the pincer, along with the NRC, on making millions stateless.

The law did not address the two largest communities of refugees in south India (Tamils from Sri Lanka) and north India (Tibetans). The law assumed that the only persecution in South Asia happens in Muslim states and against non-Muslim individuals. It did not address the groups persecuted for their political beliefs (such as in Burma and China) or their sexuality. It did not address those Muslims who were religiously persecuted, such as the Ahmadis and Shias of Pakistan.[30] Though the law was passed in late 2019, it has still not been implemented in 2021. The framing of its rules was delayed, after severe condemnation and intervention from foreign nations and institutions and the widespread protests in India.

---

[29] 'Why criminalising triple talaq is unnecessary overkill', 15 December 2017, *TheWire.in*
[30] 'Citizenship law fails three tests of classification: Faizan Mustafa, VC, NALSAR University of Law', 15 December 2019, *The Economic Times*

The Government of National Capital Territory of Delhi (Amendment) Act, 2021

After being defeated twice in the Delhi elections, the BJP took over the National Capital Region in devious fashion. This law demoted the elected assembly and gave its powers to the unelected lieutenant governor, currently a former IAS man named Anil Baijal. Like many of Modi's initiatives, this is a law introduced merely to influence the current position. The amendment says that the term 'government' in any law made by the legislative assembly will imply the lieutenant governor and not the assembly itself.

It prohibits the legislative assembly from making any rule to enable itself or its committees to consider the matters of day-to-day administration of Delhi. It also prohibits the elected assembly from conducting any inquiry in relation to administrative decisions. All extant rules allowing this have been made void. The amendment says all executive action by the government must be taken in the name of the lieutenant governor, and that his opinion will have to be obtained on matters specified by him before any action taken by the council of ministers.

The Gujarat Control of Terrorism and Organised Crime Act, 2015

Approved by the president in 2019, this law was blocked by the UPA under Manmohan Singh when Modi was chief minister. It was written up by the Modi government first in 2003 and was returned first by former president A.P.J. Abdul Kalam, who in 2004 objected to a section which admitted telephonic interception as evidence and asked Modi to remove the clause.

This continued over the years, with Modi refusing to make the changes and the Union refusing to let the bill become law.

The law has an over-broad definition for what is organised crime and terrorist acts. It clubs extortion, land grabbing, contract killing, economic offences, cyber crimes, prostitution and demanding ransom with using bombs, dynamite, firearms, lethal weapons, chemicals, poison, the destruction of public property and disruption of essential supplies.

It also has an open definition of what is organised crime and says that violence or intimidation or coercion 'by an individual, singly or jointly' or as a syndicate constitutes organised crime.[31]

An 'organised crime syndicate' is defined as a group of two or more people.

---

[31] 'First case under Gujarat Control of Terrorism and Organised Crime Act lodged', 15 January 2020, *India Today*

The law makes a confession before a police officer admissible in a court. This provision has been problematic in India because of the conditions under which such confessions are extorted by a police force that has no real accountability.

As home minister, P. Chidambaram opposed this clause. Another clause that he objected to gave the state extraordinary power over the conditions of bail.

Bail is to be denied if the public prosecutor opposes it. It can only be given if the judge is satisfied that the accused is innocent. Meaning that the burden of proof is reversed. If the accused cannot convince the judge by producing conclusive proof of innocence, he remains in jail pending trial. Chidambaram said that the court should have the power to grant bail even if the public prosecutor opposes it.

Modi did not want to make the changes and said that 'the amendments suggested by the Centre amount to taking away the teeth and nails of the Gujarat Control of Organised Crime Act'.[32] And also that 'when it comes to dealing with terrorists, we must draw a clear line between those who are on their side and those who are on the side of society'.[33]

When the law was passed again in the state assembly, ignoring all the objections, a group of Muslim activists sent a letter to then president Pranab Mukherjee signed in their blood.[34] The group included the activist Prof. J.S. Bandukwala, and the note read: 'Preventive detention laws from MISA to TADA to POTA have been widely misused in Gujarat. Victims have been predominantly Muslims and deprived segments. This happened even during Congress rule. One shudders at what will befall us when the powers at the state and Centre rests with forces that are so alienated from Muslims.'

Bihar Special Armed Police Act, 2021

This law gives the Bihar Special Armed Police the power to arrest people without a warrant. The Special Armed Police can arrest any person if he or she, in their opinion, poses a risk of 'causing disturbance'. Arrests can be made on suspicion. Any protest can be broken up by this Special Armed Police if they think it will disrupt a government function. It gives the police the power to search premises without a warrant from a magistrate. The bill

[32] 'Narendra Modi rejects amendments to GUJCOCA', 20 June 2009, NDTV
[33] 'Modi slams Centre over Gujarat anti-terror bill', 17 August 2009, PTI
[34] 'Activists want President to strike down GujCTOC Bill', 6 October 2015, The Times of India

gives them immunity and forbids courts from taking cognisance of any complaint against police personnel except with sanction of the government.

Environment Impact Assessment Notification, 2020

Proposed by the Ministry of Environment, Forest and Climate Change, this seeks to replace the existing notifications going back to 2006 under the Environment (Protection) Act, 1986.

It exempts 40 different types of projects, such as clay and sand extraction, digging wells or foundations of buildings, solar thermal power plants and effluent treatment plants, from having to secure environmental clearance.[35]

The notification exempts projects with 'strategic considerations as determined by the Central Government' from the stricter purview of Environmental Impact Assessment and from public hearings. No information relating to such projects shall be placed in the public domain.

It exempts from public consultation projects including those relating to production of halogens, chemical fertilisers, acids manufacturing, biomedical waste treatment facilities, building construction and area development, elevated roads and flyovers, highways or expressways, offshore and onshore oil, gas and shale exploration, hydroelectric projects up to 25 MW, irrigation projects between 2,000 and 10,000 hectares, small and medium mineral beneficiation units, small foundries involving furnace units, some categories of re-rolling mills, small and medium cement plants, small clinker grinding units, acids other than phosphoric or ammonia, sulphuric acid, micro, small and medium enterprises in dye and dye intermediates, bulk drugs, synthetic rubbers, medium-sized paint units, all inland waterway projects, and expansion or widening of highways between 25 kms and 100 kms.

The draft allows for post-facto approval for projects, meaning that the clearances for projects can be awarded even if they have started construction or have been running without securing environmental clearances. This also means that any environmental damage caused by the project is likely to be waived off as the violations get legitimised.

The notice period for public hearing has been cut from 30 days to 20, making it more difficult to study draft environmental assessment impact reports, particularly when they are not made widely available or provided in the local language and especially because they are full of jargon.

---

[35] 'Explained: Reading the draft Environment Impact Assessment norms, and finding the red flags', 10 August 2020, *The Indian Express*

It excludes reporting by the public of violations and non-compliance. Instead, the government will only take cognisance of reports from the violator-promoter themselves or a government authority. Such violating projects can then still be approved with conditions, including remediation of ecological damage, which, again, will be assessed and reported by the violators themselves.

The Information Technology (Intermediary Guidelines and Digital Media Ethics Code) Rules, 2021

This oversight mechanism was created without a law and aims to function for the internet as the Ministry of Information and Broadcasting does for TV regulation.[36] Through it, the government gives itself the power to censor and regulate all content on the internet and even on messaging services.

It requires messaging services, such as WhatsApp, Signal and Telegram, to enable the identification of the creator of a piece of content (for example, a cartoon criticising the prime minister). This requirement of traceability would break end-to-end encryption, which makes these messaging services secure. Also, the originator of a message has no control over who forwards the content, or how many times it is forwarded, or in which fora. Erotic content exchanged by a couple or group of friends could land up in a place where it would be seen differently.

The rules say there will be an 'oversight mechanism by the Central government' (censorship) of video content that is published on all web-based platforms. The government can block content and also get platforms to publish scroll apologies. Major platforms took the cue and put out a joint 'self-regulation toolkit' that portends self-censorship to align content with what the government wants and, more importantly, not publish or broadcast what it does not want. Presumably, they were encouraged by the fact that the Modi government called their executives in and threatened to jail them.[37]

The Information Technology Act, 2000 did not extend to news media, and so the guidelines did not have the legal authority to regulate news media. This change was pushed through by adding powers far beyond those in that parent legislation. The rules give the government the right to regulate content put out by a 'publisher of news and current affairs content', which is open-

---

[36] 'Deep dive: How the intermediaries rules are anti-democratic and unconstitutional', internetfreedom.in

[37] 'India threatens jail for Facebook, WhatsApp and Twitter employees', 5 March 2021, *The Wall Street Journal*

ended and vague and arbitrary. The rules exempt e-newspapers, meaning that established publishing houses (i.e., those which receive money from the government through the Directorate of Advertising and Visual Publicity) would be privileged over independent media houses like *TheWire.in*, *Scroll.in* and *NewsClick.in*.

On 6 April 2023, the government passed the rules, allowing it to identity what it thought was any fake or false or misleading content online related to the government. This would be done by a 'fact check unit' set up by the government which would send takedown orders to social media platforms. This determination that news was false or misleading would be solely at the government's discretion. The rules would give the government authority to force social media firms to take down such content or face action.

The Internet Freedom Foundation said, 'Assigning any unit of the government such arbitrary, overbroad powers to determine the authenticity of online content bypasses the principles of natural justice, thus making it an unconstitutional exercise. The notification of these amended rules cement the chilling effect on the fundamental right to speech and expression, particularly on news publishers, journalists, activists.'[38]

The Editors Guild of India said it was 'deeply disturbed' and that there was not even a mention of 'what will be the governing mechanism for such a fact-checking unit', what the judicial oversight, if any, was, or the right to appeal. 'All of this is against principles of natural justice and akin to censorship,' it added.

The pushing of all these laws and the narrative of the government of fighting internal 'enemies' has encouraged individuals in the State to often make up policy that supersedes written law.

Uttarakhand's director general of police (DGP) said his force would scrutinise social media behaviour of those putting 'anti-national' posts and may not clear the verification of such individuals for a passport.[39]

'Till now, in case a person was putting anti-national posts or fake news on social media, the police used to counsel him and ask him not to repeat it in future. A case was registered only if it was a very serious case,' DGP Ashok Kumar was quoted as saying. 'From now onwards, the police will scrutinise the accused's social media behaviour to check if he is habitually putting such

---

[38] The Internet Freedom Foundation's statement on the notification of the IT Amendment Rules, 2023, 6 April 2023, internetfreedom.in

[39] '"Anti-national" posts on social media? Uttarakhand police won't verify passport', 2 February 2021, *Hindustan Times*

anti-national posts. If it is found so, then the police would mention it in his/her police verification and may not clear in his application for passport or arms license.' He was speaking at the state police officers' conference held at the police headquarters in Dehradun.

The Bihar Police has warned that it will make it difficult for individuals in protest demonstrations to get passports, government jobs, financial grants by the state and bank loans. A note issued by the state's DGP said: 'All this will be duly mentioned in the Police Verification Report. Such people should be ready for grave consequences.'[40]

This came days after the Bihar Police, in another circular, said that social media posts against the government, ministers, MPs, legislators and state officials would now be treated as cyber crime and invite penal action. The IT Act has provision for imprisonment up to seven years and fine or both for those booked for cyber crimes.

Illustrating the Damage

The volume of news stories in the Indian media means that things are often lost. And stories are forgotten or they are seen as being merely isolated episodes. If viewed together, they may produce some context of what has happened to Indian society since 2014.

1) The Modi era has seen India's Muslims being told by the judiciary that their religion is provocation. Three men of the Hindu Rashtra Sena who murdered a 28-year-old Muslim man were given bail by Bombay High Court with the following observation: 'The fault of the deceased was only that he belonged to another religion. I consider this factor in favour of the applicants/accused. Moreover, the applicants/accused do not have any criminal record and it appears that in the name of the religion, they were provoked and have committed the murder.'[41]

2) Muslims who have visited temples in an act of harmony have instead been arrested for spreading communal hatred. Four young men, two Muslims and two Hindus, belonging to Khudai Khidmatgar, a Delhi-based organisation promoting communal harmony, were booked in Uttar Pradesh after they prayed together at a temple in Mathura.[42] The men, Faisal

[40] 'Bihar government won't hire protestors', 4 February 2021, *The Hindu*

[41] 'Bail in Muslim youth's murder: Bombay HC cites his religion as provocation', 17 January 2017, *The Indian Express*

[42] 'Four booked for "defiling" Mathura temple, 1 held', 3 November 2020, *The Indian Express*

Khan, Chand Mohammed, Alok Ratan and Nilesh Gupta, were booked for promoting enmity between different groups on grounds of religion, defiling a place of worship and public mischief.

3) A Gujarati Muslim stand-up artist was jailed in Indore on 2 January 2021 on the complaint of the son of a BJP MLA. The police stated that the man, Munawar Faruqui, had not said anything offensive, but they felt that he may have gone on to do so had they not arrested him.

At his bail hearing in Madhya Pradesh High Court, Justice Rohit Arya said: 'But why you take undue advantage of other's religious sentiments and emotions. What is wrong with your mindset? How can you do this for the purpose of business?'

Faruqui's lawyer argued that he had committed no offence, but the judge refused bail anyway, based on allegedly derogatory social media posts made more than a year earlier. Justice Arya said, 'Such people must not be spared. I will reserve the order on merits.'[43] He told the police: *Inka achche se khayal rakhna taki aage se dhyan rahe. Yahan ke baad jab yeh UP jayega to pata nahin kya hoga,* (Take good care of him so that he behaves in future. From here he's being arrested by the UP police. Who knows what they will do). It took the Supreme Court to give Faruqui bail on 5 February, after he had spent a month in jail for no crime.

4) In January 2021, the Union government-run Agricultural and Processed Food Products Export Development Authority under the Ministry of Commerce and Industry removed the word 'halal' (denoting the Muslim ritual manner of slaughter) from its Red Meat Manual.

'The word "Halal" has been removed from the new manual since it was causing confusion. Whether it is meat or any other product, it basically depends on the requirement of the importing country and the buyer,' the government said.[44] The Vishwa Hindu Parishad welcomed the move.

Within days, the BJP-ruled South Delhi Municipal Corporation made it mandatory for all shops and restaurants serving meat to specify whether they serve 'halal' or 'jhatka' (slaughter without ritual) meat. This would essentially make it easier to segregate restaurants for Muslims and non-Muslims.[45] Two months later, the municipal corporation of Gurugram ordered all shops

---

[43] '"Such people must not be spared": MP HC reserves order on Munawar Faruqui bail plea', 25 January 2021, *TheWire.in*

[44] 'APEDA removes word "Halal" from meat export manual', 5 January 2021, PTI

[45] 'Traders, eatery owners question Delhi civic body's order to tag all meat "Halal" or "jhatka"', 22 January 2021, *TheWire.in*

selling meat to shut on every Tuesday.[46] This was because BJP legislators said Hindus held Tuesday to be auspicious and the sale of meat on that day to be offensive.[47] The licence fee for running these shops was doubled to Rs 10,000.

5) In January 2021, two men were detained and questioned for eight hours and three women for at least three hours by the Delhi Police—all because they were heard saying 'Pakistan Zindabad' as part of a cycling game near Khan Market metro station late Saturday night.

Their ordeal, which started at 1 a.m. on Sunday, ended only by noon with the police admitting that 'Pakistan Zindabad' was said in a 'lighter vein', and no case was made out.[48]

Outlook reported the incident in its diary: 'This charade could be the dumbest—a group of youngsters and chaperoning adults racing each other on rent-and-ride e-bicycles near Khan Market in Delhi's India Gate area before Republic Day. There's no curb on riding bicycles, but when the group decided to spice things up, giving each participant a name based on nations, such as Pakistan, the direction changed unbeknownst to them. When the young fellow, aka Pakistan, raced ahead, and "Pakistan Zindabad" rang out in collective applause, the game got serious. The six people spent several hours at a police station before they could convince they shouted the suffixed bywords for anti-nationalism "in a lighter vein". They were let off, but the probe continues.'

6) A woman who held up a placard saying 'Free Kashmir' was charged with sedition in Mysuru.[49]

Nalini Balakumar was part of a student protest on 8 January 2020 against the mob attack at Delhi's Jawaharlal Nehru University earlier that month. The protest was organised by the Dalit Student Organisation and Mysore University Research Students Association in the University of Mysore. After local media published photographs and videos of Balakumar with the placard, a police case was filed against her and the organiser of the

[46] 'All meat stores in city to remain closed on Tuesdays', 19 March 2021, *The Times of India*
[47] 'Gurugram to close meat shops on Tuesdays to respect "Hindu sentiments"', 24 March 2021, *TheFederal.com*
[48] 'Pakistan Zindabad: 11-hour police ordeal for family, friends over a game', 27 January 2021, *The Indian Express*
[49] 'Court grants bail to Mysuru woman who held "Free Kashmir" poster at CAA protest', 28 January 2020, *Scroll.in*

protests. Balakumar said she was trying to highlight the internet shutdown imposed in Kashmir.

7) A 19-year-old woman was arrested in Bangalore and jailed for over 100 days for no crime after she said 'Hindustan Zindabad, Pakistan Zindabad' at a protest event.[50]

Amulya Leona had written Facebook posts which said 'zindabad' to all the countries: India, Pakistan, Bangladesh, Sri Lanka, Afghanistan. She wrote: 'We as kids are taught that we should respect our motherland and as a kid I would like to say that a people make the country and that the people of the respective countries should be respected.' She was charged with sedition, a law that reads 'whoever, by words, either spoken or written, or by signs, or by visible representation, or otherwise, brings or attempts to bring into hatred or contempt, or excites or attempts to excite disaffection towards the Government shall be punished with imprisonment for life. The expression "disaffection" includes disloyalty and all feelings of enmity'.

8) On 5 October 2020, Siddique Kappan, a journalist from Kerala, was arrested on his way to Hathras, where a young Dalit woman had died after being gangraped by upper-caste men. He was charged by the Uttar Pradesh government under UAPA. The state said that he was acting 'under the garb of journalism with a very determined design to create caste divide and disturb law and order situation'.

Kappan was allowed to speak to his lawyer 43 days after his arrest. He was not given by the Supreme Court the relief that it gave Arnab Goswami, in which matter the court made much of personal liberty. Told that this was also a case of habeas corpus like Arnab's, Chief Justice Bobde said 'every case is different'.[51] Kappan spent 28 months in jail before being released on bail on 2 February 2023.

9) On 2 February 2021, it was reported that 96 per cent of the sedition cases filed against 405 Indians for criticising politicians and governments over the last decade were registered after 2014, with 149 accused of making 'critical' and/or 'derogatory' remarks against Modi, and 144 against Uttar Pradesh chief minister Yogi Adityanath.[52]

Of the five states with the highest number of sedition cases, a majority were registered during the BJP's time in power in four of them—Bihar,

---

[50] 'Bengaluru: Anti-CAA activist Amulya Leona Noronha given bail on condition of silence', 14 June 2020, *Deccan Herald*

[51] '"Every case is different," says CJI on bail pleas of Arnab Goswami and Kerala journalist Kappan', 2 December 2020, *Scroll.in*

[52] 'Our new database reveals rise in sedition cases in the Modi era', *Article-14.com*

Uttar Pradesh, Karnataka and Jharkhand. The fifth was Tamil Nadu under Jayalalithaa, who had filed mass sedition cases against citizens opposed to a nuclear power plant.

10) A student of Aligarh Muslim University in Uttar Pradesh was externed (banished) from Aligarh in January 2021. The Aligarh police report seeking to banish Arif Tyagi said he was 'reckless and frightful, and is a threat to the public'.[53]

The man was charged in several cases for his protests inside the campus, related to several issues, including the presence of a portrait of Pakistan founder Mohammad Ali Jinnah and against the CAA and the NRC.

11) In February 2021, former Test cricketer Wasim Jaffer resigned as coach of Uttarakhand, accusing officials of pushing undeserving players. The state unit's secretary, Mahim Verma, said he had received feedback from the team that Jaffer had 'communalised' the dressing room atmosphere and 'favoured' Muslim players.[54]

Jaffer had played 20 years for Mumbai and another five for Vidarbha, retiring in 2020. He played 31 Tests for India, won eight Ranji Trophy titles for Mumbai, and then moved to Vidarbha and won two more with them. He was the most prolific run-scorer in the history of first-class cricket in India, having scored more runs than any other batsman in the Ranji Trophy, the Duleep Trophy and the Irani Cup.

On 10 February, Jaffer tweeted:

'1. I recommended Jay Bista for captaincy not Iqbal but CAU officials favoured Iqbal.

2. I did not invite Maulavis

3. I resigned cos bias of selectors-secretary for non-deserving players

4. Team used to say a chant of Sikh community, I suggested we can say "Go Uttarakhand" #Facts'

He received no support from players Virat Kohli, Sachin Tendulkar and other grandees who otherwise tweet frequently in favour of the government.

12) Between 2017 and 2018, there were 50 cases of people arrested for posts or forwards on social media. *Mint* compiled some of the cases that it had come across, most of which involved Muslims.[55]

[53] 'AMU student externed from Aligarh under Goondas Act', 30 January 2021, *The Indian Express*
[54] 'Communal angle sad, says Wasim Jaffer after quitting as Uttarakhand coach', 11 February 2021, *The Indian Express*
[55] 'Prisoners of memes, social media victims', 5 December 2017, *Mint*

- Mohammad Shaqib, 18, of Saharanpur in Uttar Pradesh, shared a forward of a dark-skinned woman being touched by a man whose face was morphed to resemble that of Modi's. The text read that this was what had happened on the issue of black money (of which Modi had promised to give Rs 15 lakh to each Indian). On 18 November 2018, only days after he had acquired his first phone, police from Haryana arrested him for this forward and he spent eight days in the 'bachcha jail' (juvenile home). He was charged under Section 67 (publishing or transmitting obscene material in electronic form), 67 A of the IT Act (transmission or publishing of sexually explicit material), and Section 292A (putting into circulation a grossly indecent or scurrilous picture). A year after his arrest, there had been four hearings, and each court appearance involved a change of six buses from Saharanpur to Tohana, 210 kms away, and an expense of Rs 550 per person. His father, a labourer, decided not to give his son a smartphone again and not to let Shaqib step out of Saharanpur—even if that meant keeping his only son unemployed.

- In another case, Aleem Ahmad, 16, of Meerut, wrote a Facebook post expressing his anger at the demolition of the Babri Masjid and made reference to Atal Bihari Vajpayee, who had just passed away. Three days later, at 3 a.m., some 15 policemen came to his house. Aleem was away, and his father was taken 'for questioning' and told that he might lose his government job. On 20 August 2017, Aleem surrendered and spent 39 days in the bachcha jail. He was booked under Section 153 A (promoting enmity between different groups), 153 B (assertions prejudicial to national integration), 295 (deliberate and malicious acts intended to outrage religious feelings) of the IPC, and Section 67 of the IT Act (punishment for publishing or transmitting obscene material in electronic form).

Posts by Muslims on Vajpayee after his death resulted in arrests and several FIRs, including against one individual who had not named Vajpayee and others who had 'liked' the posts. Naushad Khan, 24, of Varanasi was in jail for three months for a post on Vajpayee.

- S. Thirumurugan, 19, of Virudhunagar in Tamil Nadu spent time in jail for his replies to a post that criticised a movie, *Mersal*, which referenced the botched roll-out of GST. The scenes had offended the local BJP and it asked for them to be deleted.[56] A local BJP leader posted a message criticising the movie and Thirumurugan replied to the post with some references to Modi, calling him names. He was arrested the next day, jailed and booked

---

[56] 'BJP objects to "incorrect references" on GST in Vijay's *Mersal*', 19 October 2019, *The Hindu*

under Section 67 of the IT Act and Section 505 (public mischief) of the IPC. His case was pending before a court and his parents had taken away his phone. He was not given it back even a year later and was barred from using social media.

• Zakir Ali Tyagi, 19, of Muzaffarnagar, posted a comment referring to '28 criminal cases against Yogi Adityanath, out of which 22 are serious offences'. This was made in reference to a speech made by Adityanath about ending goonda raj in Uttar Pradesh. Zakir was jailed for 42 days and disabled his Facebook account. He was charged with sedition and Section 420, besides the IT Act. Police also charged him under a law, Section 6yA on electronic communication, that had been scrapped years ago by the Supreme Court.

• Rahat Khan, 23, of Greater Noida, shared a photo of a Yogi Adityanath lookalike and was arrested from his shop. He was booked under Section 153A (promoting enmity between different groups) of the IPC and, illegally, also booked under the defunct Section 66A (punishment for sending offensive messages through communication services) of the IT Act, 2000. He spent 42 days in jail after his bail was rejected twice. His shop was shut and he lost his customers. His family had to borrow money to pay for his bail. He didn't know what he had been charged under and hadn't been given a copy of the FIR against him.

13) In March 2021, a 12-year-old Muslim boy was brutally beaten for going to a temple to drink water. A man, said to be Shringi Nandan Yadav, was seen in a video holding the boy by his shoulders and arms, and telling an accomplice, *'Donon ka chehra aana chahiye'* (both our faces should be seen). A male voice behind the camera agrees.

Then Yadav asks the boy, 'What is your name? What is your father's name?' making it apparent that the boy is a Muslim. Asked what he was doing in the temple, the boy said, 'came to drink water'.

Then the violence begins. The man hits the boy multiple times on his head and twists his right arm. When the boy falls on the ground, he is stamped on and repeatedly kicked. The boy is seen helplessly trying to shield himself. Police arrested Yadav after the public outrage.[57]

14) Four Christian women from Kerala were forced off a train in Jhansi and 'interrogated' by men from the Akhil Bharatiya Vidyarthi Parishad (ABVP, the student organisation affiliated to the RSS) and the Railway Police on 19 March 2021. The women, two nuns and two postulants (nuns in

---

[57] 'Muslim boy beaten for entering temple to drink water, man arrested: Cops', 14 March 2021, *NDTV*

training) from the Sacred Heart Congregation, were heckled by the mob and detained for five hours. The nuns were accused of 'forcible conversion' of the postulants and the women were compelled to remove their habits and robes and wear other clothes instead. They had to produce papers to show that they were all Christians. A VHP member who instigated the episode said: 'We did no wrong. It is our duty to inform the police. If we suspect terrorists, or that there is a bomb, who would we inform, if not the police.'[58]

15) A 23-year-old man who was illegally detained by the Delhi Police died. The man, Faizan, was seen in a video lying wounded on the ground as policemen goaded him to sing *Vande Mataram* during the Delhi pogrom. One year later, the police told Delhi High Court that they were still trying to ascertain the identity of their personnel seen in the video. They also told the court that Faizan and others detained at Jyoti Nagar police station were there of their own wish. Faizan's family said he was targeted and assaulted by the police and denied medical care because of which he died.[59]

16) A 24-year-old Muslim man working as a cook in Meerut was accused of spreading the coronavirus by applying saliva on rotis. The man, Naushad, was assaulted by a group called the Hindu Jagran Manch and then jailed after being charged under the NSA. He spent three months in jail till the Union home ministry recommended that the NSA charges against him be dropped. His employer said Naushad was a good worker but could not be hired again because of the controversy.[60]

These are not entirely disconnected events and episodes. They represent what has been done to a society by demonisation and consistent focus on 'othering' non-Hindus through laws, language and politics. State and society take cues from the top and, as these stories show, hate against minorities has been normalised under Modi. Such societal change is not easy to undo; once the infection has set in, it festers and damages the nation and its people, as we have seen elsewhere in our neighbourhood.

---

[58] 'Nuns forced off train; Shah promises action after protest by Kerala CM', 25 March 2021, *The Indian Express*

[59] 'Death of man made to sing national anthem: Year later, police tell court still trying to ascertain identity of cops in video', 2 February 2021, *The Indian Express*

[60] 'Uttar Pradesh: Cleared of NSA, catering staff "can't be hired back"', 13 June 2021, *The Indian Express*

13

THE DEVIL'S WORKSHOP

The Union government from 2014 began systematic harassment and persecution of civil society. This harmed civil society but it also hurt India. NGOs provide the third largest workforce in the United States and more than 10 per cent of all Americans work in an NGO.[1] In 24 American states out of 50, NGOs actually employ more workers than all the branches of manufacturing combined. It is similar in the United Kingdom. In Europe, 13 per cent of all jobs are in the NGO sector.[2]

To put this figure in perspective, consider that less than 10 per cent of all jobs in India are in the formal sector. Surely this was then a sector to be boosted and not obstructed, but obstruct is what Modi did. Through his years, the attack on civil society continued as the first two parts of this chapter will show. The third chronicles the heroic and sustained resistance from marginalised communites: Dalits, Muslims, Adivasis and farmers, which forced the government ultimately to retreat on vital issues.

Part 1: Repression

On 21 February 2016, Modi declared war on India's civil society. At a rally in Bhubaneshwar, he said he was 'a victim of a conspiracy by NGOs'. This conspiracy was aimed at 'finishing' him and removing his government.[3]

As evidence for this, he said: 'You would have seen that morning to night, I am being attacked. Some people keep at it.'

---

[1] 'Nonprofits account for 12.3 million jobs, 10.2 percent of private sector employment, in 2016', US Bureau of Labor Statistics, bls.gov

[2] 'The future evolution of civil society in the European Union by 2030', European Economic and Social Committee, europa.eu

[3] 'PM Narendra Modi says he is victim of NGOs' conspiracy', *The Economic Times*

Civil society was 'also upset because I told a few NGOs to give us an account of the foreign funds that they spend here. They ganged up and said "beat Modi, beat Modi, he's asking us for an account of our expenditure",' he said, adding: 'They conspire from morning to night on "how do we finish Modi, how do we remove his government, how do we embarrass Modi?" But, my friends, you have voted me to rid the country of these diseases.'

The antagonism towards civil society was not new. As chief minister, Modi had said in a speech: 'Another conspiracy—a vicious cycle is set up. Funds are obtained from abroad; an NGO is set up; a few articles are commissioned; a PR firm is recruited and, slowly, with the help of the media, an image is created. And then awards are procured from foreign countries to enhance this image. Such a vicious cycle, a network of finance-activity-award is set up and, once they have secured an award, no one in Hindustan dares raise a finger, no matter how many the failings of the awardee.'[4]

Modi's attack on NGOs manifested in different forms of coercive action and through use of criminal law, most notably through changes in the FCRA. The FCRA appeared in 1976 during the paranoid period of India's Emergency as a piece of legislation aimed at preventing external interference in India's electoral process and democracy. It prohibited the receiving of foreign money by political parties and their candidates, journalists and newspaper publishers, judges, bureaucrats and members of parliament.

In time, economic liberalisation meant that many of these categories were allowed to receive foreign money and the Indian government actively promoted the bringing in of such money. That was what came to be known as FDI, which was welcomed and whose numbers Indian governments were proud of.

For instance, the media, both print and television and certainly online, which came to be the most consumed form of media, could not only receive foreign investment, it was dominated by it. The largest media companies in India were Facebook and Google, which were entirely foreign-owned and managed. Newspapers could receive equity investments from foreign firms as also could news channels.

Even political parties managed to get themselves off the hook on FCRA. In January 2013, a public interest litigation was filed in Delhi High Court claiming that the BJP and the Congress had received donations from the same foreign company, Vedanta/Sterlite, which were in violation of the

---

[4] 'IB's NGO-scare report to Modi plagiarises from old Modi speech', 13 June 2014, *The Indian Express*

FCRA Act. On 28 March 2014, the court held that the BJP and Congress were guilty of FCRA violation and, in May, asked the Modi government and the EC to act against the two parties. In July and August, the Congress and BJP moved petitions in the Supreme Court against the high court decision.[5]

By October 2015, the Modi government had figured a way out. A change in the law would define any company registered in India, regardless of who owned it, as an Indian company.[6] In essence, 'foreign' was redefined as 'Indian', which was a fraud on the Indian people, but because both major parties were complicit in the fraud, it passed without resistance.

In December 2015, it was reported that the Modi government was making amendments that would get both the parties off.[7] This change happened in the Budget of 2016, when the definition of foreign source was changed, legitimising the donation received by the political parties. Characteristically, this change was written in fairly slipshod fashion and the Modi government had amended the wrong version of the law. And so another amendment was passed in 2018 to again try and get the parties off. This finally happened in March 2018, through the amendment of a law that had previously already been repealed, an entirely farcical operation.

With this change, and later with the electoral bonds scheme, the BJP and other parties were free to accept unlimited and even anonymous contributions from foreign sources. What remained regulated in the law were non-government organisations (NGOs). And these were relentlessly squeezed and defunded through FCRA amendments under Modi.

Along with the farm bills in 2020, Modi passed a law which would tighten the provisions under which NGOs could receive foreign money.[8]

The changes were, in the main, five: first, that the 23,000-odd NGOs which had an FCRA licence to receive foreign money could receive funds only in a single branch of the State Bank of India—the one at Sansad Marg in New Delhi. Only 1,488 NGOs were registered in Delhi, and so the rest would have to come to the city to open an account. The branch would report to the home ministry the details of the remittance, the sources and manner in which it was received. Over 46 per cent of the NGOs had received no foreign

[5] 'The chronology of subterfuge on amending the FCRA', 27 April 2018, TheWire.in

[6] 'FCRA changes may cause coffers of political parties like BJP and Congress to swell', 25 October 2015, The Economic Times

[7] 'Government's FCRA tweak plan to benefit BJP, Congress', 21 December 2015, The Economic Times

[8] 'Choking NGO sector with the FCRA amendment', 4 October 2020, The New Indian Express

money in 2018–19 though they had an FCRA licence, and another 41 per cent had received less than Rs 1 crore.

The second change was that the NGO could spend only 20 per cent of the money it received on 'administrative expenses'. Salaries, travel expenses, the cost of hiring individuals, consumables like electricity and water charges, telephone charges, postal and courier charges, repairs to the office, stationery and printing charges, transport, the cost of accounting for and administering funds, running and maintenance of vehicles, cost of writing and filing reports, legal and professional charges and rent were all classified as administrative expenses. No more than 20 per cent of their foreign funding could be spent on these things (keep in mind that such restrictions are not applicable to any other sector in India). This would affect those organisations whose work concerned research and advocacy and other things that required hiring professionals such as lawyers and academics, and were unrelated to pure brick-and-mortar activity, such as building hospitals and schools.

Third, the law now prevented an NGO from redistribution of funds it had received to other NGOs even if they were FCRA-compliant. This would hit the sector because NGOs do not compete with one another as the rest of the private sector does; they operate as networks. This change would damage their alliances and capacity to work with one another. Larger NGOs could no longer work with smaller ones, especially those organisations working on the ground that had no means of or expertise in raising money themselves. A study by Ashoka University[9] showed that half of the 4,107 NGOs that received money in this fashion in 2018–19 got Rs 7.6 lakh or less. They would no longer get even this.

Fourth, the law required NGOs registering or renewing their FCRA licence to mandatorily give the Aadhaar numbers of all office-bearers, directors and other key functionaries. It also gave the government the authority, at its discretion, to suspend FCRA for as long as it wanted.

The fifth change was that 'public servants' were now forbidden from being a part of FCRA organisations. This appeared to be a change in the law aimed at a specific individual whom the Modi government had previously targeted. This was the Supreme Court advocate Indira Jaising, who had represented Mohammad Afzal Guru and Yakub Memon, both of whom were hanged, the first in 2013 for the parliament attack of 2001 and the second in 2015 for the Mumbai bomb blasts of 1993.

---

[9] 'Estimating philanthropic capital in India', 2019, Centre for Social Impact and Philanthropy, Ashoka University

On 1 June 2016, the Modi government had suspended the FCRA licence of Lawyers Collective, the organisation managed by Jaising, on the grounds that Jaising, who in 2009 had been the additional solicitor general of India, had violated FCRA norms. To this, Jaising had responded that she was not a 'government servant' but a 'public servant'.[10]

These were the changes through which Modi attacked the NGO sector. His government invited foreign investment in arms and ammunition and bombs and guns,[11] and in alcohol and tobacco, and petroleum and drugs.[12] But it restricted investment in health, education, civil and human rights.

In September 2019, an amendment to the FCRA rules required office bearers, key functionaries and members of NGOs to certify on affidavit to the government that they were not 'engaged/likely to engage in the propagation of seditious or violent acts',[13] that they had not been 'prosecuted or convicted' for 'conversion' from one faith to another or for creating 'communal tension and disharmony'.[14]

In the Budget of 2020, the Modi government slipped in an amendment which would make NGOs permanently beholden to the government. This came through a change in the Income Tax Act and required NGOs to re-register themselves under the act by the end of August that year. After that, they would receive fresh registration that was valid for five years. Their charitable status for tax purposes would be subject to bureaucratic discretion. This implied that donations to them, eligible for income tax deductions, would become fully taxable at the government's discretion.[15] NGOs which had registrations going back decades were made to line up again and seek fresh permission to operate. FCRA registrations, like this one, would also have to be renewed every five years.

The endless tinkering with the law to try and screw over NGOs produced some internal problems also, in this instance of what to do with the assets

---

[10] 'Leading NGOs believe FCRA changes will "Kill" voluntary sector', 22 September 2020, *TheWire.in*

[11] 'FinMin nod for 74% FDI in Defence sector under automatic route', 9 December 2020, *The Hindu Businessline*

[12] 'FDI in drugs & pharma sector rose to Rs 2,065 cr in April-Sept FY20: Govt', 7 February 2020, PTI

[13] 'Conversion, sedition in focus as government tightens FCRA norms', 17 September 2019, *The Times of India*

[14] 'Government tightens religious conversion rule for NGOs in foreign funding tweaks', 17 September 2019, *Hindustan Times*

[15] 'Having to reapply for IT registration, NGOs say Finance Bill MHA-inspired', 3 February 2020, *Outlook*

of thousands of NGOs which would be affected and made defunct. On 5 November 2018, Amit Shah's Ministry of Home Affairs passed a notification authorising a bureaucrat to take over the assets of an NGO whose FCRA registration was cancelled. This bureaucrat—the additional chief secretary or principal secretary (home) of the state in which the entity was operating— would take over the assets but could not dispose them. They would have to continue the NGO's charitable work till such time as the entity could get its registration restored. If the NGO had a presence in more than one state, the bureaucrat only had authority over the state where he was located. If the NGO had funds from both foreign and domestic sources, he could not administer the domestic but only the foreign. To say this was absurd is not necessary, but this is what was delivered after promises of minimum government.

Civil society is defined as charities, development NGOs, community groups, women's organisations, faith-based organisations, professional associations, trade unions, social movements, coalitions and advocacy groups. In India, which has a relatively small but vibrant civil society, this also includes individuals such as human rights lawyers, activists, academics, journalists and the liberal intelligentsia. During the Modi era, they have faced constant attacks aimed at making their functioning difficult if not impossible.

My organisation Amnesty International India had cases regularly filed against it in Bangalore. The ABVP filed a sedition case against us in 2016.[16] This was over an event in which the mothers of those who had been killed in Kashmir by security forces but received neither justice nor acknowledgment from the government were telling their stories. Their sons had been murdered in what the police had accepted were fake encounters, but no action had been taken. The event was an attempt to bring these stories to the rest of India.

The case was frivolous and was thrown out by the court more than two years later.[17] But this came at great expense both to the government—it had to send the video material from the event for forensics testing and spent, according to what I was told by the police, over Rs 1 crore on the entire matter, other than considerable human resources—and to Amnesty India. We were hit in terms of our ability to raise money because of the particularly nasty media coverage. Of course, harassment was the primary reason for the case being filed.

---

[16] 'Sedition case filed against Amnesty International', 15 August 2016, *The Hindu*
[17] 'Court closes sedition case against Amnesty India', 11 January 2019, *The Hindu*

After accusations that we were violating FCRA in some way (though Amnesty India did not even have an FCRA registration), we were 'raided' by the ED in October 2018.[18] I was in the office when it happened and was interrogated from around 1.30 in the afternoon to 11 at night. The officers who came were unprofessional and annoyed that we should be working on such issues as Kashmir and justice for the 1984 riots, being a private company (which is how Amnesty India had been registered). And they were indignant that a 'foreign' body should 'interfere' in India: neither I nor any of the office bearers, directors or any other individuals at Amnesty India were foreigners.

When I asked at one point if our accounts were to be frozen, I was told by one of the officers that 'goats are not informed if their throats are to be cut'.

The accounts were, in fact, frozen, but through a writ in the high court, we got them unfrozen in a couple of months. The ED action was vulnerable because it was illegal and did not follow due process, and the court agreed. The next year we were 'raided' by the CBI.[19] I spent a couple of days with the CBI at that point, going through much the same thing as I had with the ED, being asked the same things and being accused of the same things. A further two days were spent with officers of the Ministry of Home Affairs, who came to the office to check our documentation, asked the same things and left, and were never heard from again, presumably because it was all in order but more likely because the baton for harassment had been passed on to the CBI.

Through the period when I was with Amnesty India, our doors were knocked on by some or the other part of the government wanting to see if it could tie us down or prevent our operating in some way. The Ministry of Corporate Affairs sent three notices for inspection, again of the same documents. This is not the way in which the rest of the private sector is treated.[20]

Greenpeace India, which had been working on the issue of coal mining, was also subjected to a raid by the ED and had to go through the same

---

[18] '"Rights groups being treated like criminal enterprises": Amnesty on raids', 26 October 2018, *NDTV*

[19] 'CBI raids Amnesty India offices in Bengaluru and New Delhi', 16 November 2019, *The Economic Times*

[20] My term at Amnesty India ended in November 2019. In October 2020, the organisation was forced to suspend its operations and lay off all staff after the ED again froze the accounts, this time accusing it of money laundering. I returned to the organisation and hope to revive it soon.

process to get their accounts unfrozen. Lawyers Collective had a five-day 'inspection' from the MHA and were also raided by the CBI. The Centre for Justice and Peace, led by the redoubtable Teesta Setalvad who had worked on justice for the victims and survivors of the Gujarat pogrom, was also raided by the CBI on 14 July 2015. Others targeted have been the Navsarjan Trust, working on caste issues; ANHAD, which works on secularism; and the Indian Social Action Forum (INSAF).

The judiciary has shown little interest in the abuse of authority by the government and has been content to look away while India's civil society has been brutalised by the State under Modi. The world has noticed. The United Nations Special Rapporteur on the Rights to Freedom of Peaceful Assembly and Association said that FCRA was 'not in conformity with international law, principles and standards'. The law was analysed and found to be defective and oppressive for its violation of freedom of association.[21]

After the attack on Jaising's Lawyers Collective, three UN human rights experts asked India to repeal FCRA, saying that its provisions were 'being used more and more to silence organisations involved in advocating civil, political, economic, social, environmental or cultural priorities, which may differ from those backed by the Government'.[22]

And this was before the 2020 amendments that made FCRA even more restrictive.

The downgrading of India's civic space on the Civicus monitor to first 'Obstructed' in 2014 and then to 'Repressed' in 2019 reflects a change that most in the sector have experienced first-hand. Civicus is a global alliance of civil society organisations and activists. The attack on civil liberties was also noted, as we have seen in the chapter 'Brand Vs Product', in the Economist Intelligence Unit's degrading of India's democracy, Freedom House's report, the World Justice Project's index and Reporters Sans Frontiers' index.

Modi's actions have wreaked havoc on the civic sector, as he desired. In the space of 35 days starting from 5 May 2015, the registration of 4,470 NGOs was cancelled on the grounds that they had delayed in submitting their tax returns.[23] The list included Panjab University, Gargi College and Lady Irwin College Delhi, the Vikram Sarabhai Foundation and the Supreme Court Bar Association.

---

[21] 'Analysis on international law, standards and principles applicable to the FCRA 2010, 2011', 20 April 2016, OHCHR.org

[22] 'UN rights experts urge India to repeal law restricting NGO's access to crucial foreign funding', 16 June 2016, OHCHR.org

[23] 'Government cancels registration of 4,470 NGOs in fresh crackdown', 9 June 2015, PTI

In April 2016, another 9,000 NGOs had their licences cancelled for 'FCRA violations'.[24]

In December 2019, parliament was told that since Modi had taken office, 14,500 NGOs had been barred from accessing foreign funding.[25] Funding fell 90 per cent from $2.2 billion in 2018 to $295 million in 2019 (though not all returns had been filed because of the pandemic).[26] A report by Ashoka University's Centre for Social Impact and Philanthropy found that incoming donations under FCRA's 'prior approval' route fell from Rs 326 crore in 2013 to Rs 49 crore in 2017.[27] The number of NGOs funded through this route fell from 233 in 2014 to 139 in 2017. Excluding faith-based organisations, the number had fallen from 207 in 2012 to 21 in 2017.

It is not known how many Indians were affected because of this, not only the employees of the NGOs but those people who they were working with and for.

A Civicus report said, 'India's vibrant associational life and its media are threatened by the actions of the government of Prime Minister Modi, which severely limit the social and economic contributions of civil society and leave victims of human rights violations exposed without recourse to justice. With millions of Indian CSOs (civil society organisations) working on a range of issues, it is time for the government to review its response to civil society and recognise the contributions civil society makes to Indian communities, human rights and democracy.'[28]

It added that the 'public vilification and demonisation of civil society organisations, human rights defenders and journalists only empowers state and non-state actors, including members of the private sector, vigilante groups and some sections of communities, to attack those who stand for human rights. This climate of demonisation comes from the top. If the Prime Minister and senior government officials, rather than attacking civil society publicly, condemned attacks from non-state actors, high levels of self-censorship would reduce and the environment in which civil society operates would greatly improve.'

[24] 'Home Ministry cancels registration of 9,000 foreign-funded NGOs', 28 April 2015, *Hindustan Times*
[25] '14,500 NGOs banned from receiving foreign funds: Govt', 5 December 2019, *The Indian Express*
[26] Ibid.
[27] 'Advocacy, Rights and Civil Society: The Opportunity for Philanthropy in India', Ashoka University
[28] 'India: Democracy threatened by growing attacks on civil society', 9 November 2017, Civicus.org

This was, of course, akin to asking the perpetrators to empathise with their victims and it did not happen. What has happened through all the Modi years is the stepping up of attacks on the sector and its individuals through the use of not just FCRA but also UAPA. Suspicion and conspiracy theories have been used by the State to discredit and demonise the groups it has sought to attack and shut down. In June 2014, the Intelligence Bureau submitted a report to Modi titled 'Impact of NGOs on Development'. It claimed foreign-funded NGOs had impacted GDP growth negatively by up to 3 percentage points. The report described Greenpeace's work as 'a threat to national economic security'.[29] In January 2015, the government offloaded Greenpeace's Priya Pillai from a flight.[30] She was to speak to British parliamentarians. A few months later, Greenpeace's FCRA licence was cancelled.[31]

Ford Foundation, which funded the Green Revolution in India and has operated here since 1952, found itself hounded by the Modi administration because it was supporting justice for the victims of the Gujarat pogrom. The Gujarat government accused the Ford Foundation of interfering with the judicial system, defaming the Indian military, and acting against the stated goal of promoting communal harmony. It accused the funding agency of encouraging Setalvad's NGOs to advocate 'a religion specific and Muslim supportive criminal code and also keep the 2002 riots incident alive'.[32]

The government has also accused the Ford Foundation of 'blatantly supporting one religion (Islam) with a strange argument that it helps secular democracy'.

The head of the organisation in India left and for a while it seemed like Ford Foundation would shut in India. Part of the problem was that the bureaucracy had no explicit instructions on this and divined their cues from what they thought Modi wanted done. Thus the bureaucrats who operated the machinery 'lean towards the most conservative course until given some clear, unambiguous direction'.[33]

Modi's crusade against India's civil society, as his language showed, was for personal reasons. There was no State imperative to persecute Indians

[29] 'IB report to PMO: Greenpeace is a threat to national economic security', 11 June 2014, *The Indian Express*

[30] 'Greenpeace campaigner Priya Pillai offloaded at airport', 11 January 2015, *The Hindu*

[31] 'Government cancels Greenpeace India's FCRA licence', 4 September 2015, *The Economic Times*

[32] The author's column 'Gujarat's attack on the Ford Foundation', 18 April 2015, *Mint*

[33] 'Revealed: How the Ford Foundation got the Modi government to back off from its expulsion move', 26 October 2016, *TheWire.in*

who were working on causes for India, and often those causes on which almost nobody else worked. When we examine the scale of what he did in his vindictiveness, the long-lasting and real harm done to the country begins to be clear.

When the second wave of the Covid pandemic hammered India, Modi turned to the same NGOs he had brutalised for help.[34] Ten NGOs the *BBC* spoke to for a report on its *Newsnight* show said they all had trouble distributing aid because of FCRA.[35] Indian hospitals and charitable trusts could not receive Covid relief material sent by donors abroad because, though the Modi government on 3 May 2021 permitted imports without GST for these items, it did not exempt them from FCRA law.

This jeopardised plans to donate oxygen plants and concentrators, especially for rural areas. In one hospital where two dozen people had already died for lack of oxygen, foreign donors could not donate an oxygen production plant because FCRA approval was holding up the process.[36] No entity could receive foreign aid, even as medicines or equipment, without FCRA registration. Moreover, the very stringent provisions of the law meant that the intended use of the foreign contribution had to also 'match the specified objective of the trust at the time of FCRA registration'.

In addition, remember that the 2020 amendment prohibits entities receiving aid in whatever form from regranting it to others.

The damage could not be undone and the direct harm to Indians from Modi's FCRA changes now became apparent to the world.[37]

Part 2: Demonisation

Koregaon Bhima is a village in Pune district, on the banks of the Bhima river. It was where, on 1 January 1818, the British defeated the remnants of the Maratha empire. The British side had many Dalit Mahar soldiers who overpowered a larger army led by the Brahmin Peshwa. On 31 December 2017, on the eve of the 200th anniversary of the battle, an evening programme was organised in Pune. The event was called the Elgar (or 'Yalgar', meaning battle cry) Parishad or Elgar Council. Those who spoke included an MLA from Gujarat, Jignesh Mevani, activists Radhika Vemula and Umar Khalid,

34 'PM wants NGOs, volunteers to help health sector', 1 May 2021, *The Indian Express*
35 'India Covid: How law stops NGOs distributing essential aid', 13 May 2021, *BBC*
36 'FCRA rules hit overseas COVID aid to hospitals, NGOs', 8 May 2021, *The Hindu*
37 'India's strict rules on foreign aid snarl Covid donations', 12 May 2021, *The New York Times*

and two judges who organised the event, B.G. Kolse-Patil, a former high court judge, and P.B. Sawant, a former Supreme Court judge. The organisers of this event included Sudhir Dhawale, of the Republican Panthers Caste Annihilation Movement, and Sagar Gorkhe, of the Kabir Kala Manch, a group of activist-artists involved in poetry and theatre, who draw inspiration from the mystic poet-saint Kabir.

The next day, 1 January, as they had done since 1927 when Ambedkar (who was from the Mahar community himself) visited the village to speak of the victory, hundreds of thousands of Dalits came to Koregaon Bhima to gather at the obelisk raised to mark the battle. But in 2017 there had been tension because of events in the neighbouring village of Vadhu Budruk. This had to do with conflicting claims about who had cremated Sambhaji, the son of Shivaji who was executed by Aurangzeb in 1689 near Koregaon Bhima. The Mahars claimed it was one of them, Gopal Govind, who had cremated the Maratha in defiance of Aurangzeb's orders. This offended the Marathas, who claimed that two of their own, a couple named Bapu Buva and Padmavati, had performed the rituals. Govind's tomb in Vadhu Budruk was in the same village square as Sambhaji's. On 28 December, a board was placed over Govind's tomb, proclaiming his role in the cremation of Sambhaji. The next day, Govind's tomb was desecrated—the board was removed and the umbrella structure over the tomb was damaged.[38] A complaint was filed by the Dalits under the Scheduled Castes/Scheduled Tribes Prevention of Atrocities Act against individuals in the village, including Hindutva leader Milind Ekbote.[39]

The Marathas filed a counter-complaint, saying that the Dalit mobilisation at Koregaon Bhima was aimed at violence. The Maharashtra government, then under the BJP, said it would repair the tomb. However, it did not act with urgency.[40]

The Koregaon Bhima panchayat asked its residents to boycott the Mahar event of 1 January and called for shops to remain shut. That morning, violence broke out between Dalits—who said they were attacked by a group carrying saffron flags—and the local Marathas—who said they had been attacked by the Dalits. One Maratha was killed.[41]

---

[38] 'Removal of Mahar samadhi board near Pune sparked clashes', 4 January 2018, *The Indian Express*

[39] 'Destruction of Dalit tomb may have caused Bhima Koregaon unrest', 4 January 2018, *The Quint*

[40] 'Reconstruction of Govind Gopal samadhi stuck', 8 September 2018, *Pune Mirror*

[41] 'From Pune to Paris: How a police investigation turned a Dalit meeting into a Maoist plot', 2 September 2018, *The Quint*

The violence spread to other towns in western Maharashtra and 300 Dalits, including some children, were held by the Mumbai Police. On 3 January, the police registered an FIR against Milind Ekbote and also Sambhaji Bhide, an 86-year-old RSS man known to Modi and about whom Modi had spoken warmly in 2014. The two men were accused of rioting, unlawful assembly and burning Ambedkarite flags. Bhide was never questioned by the police. Another complaint was filed the same day by an ABVP member, a student of Pune University. This named Mevani and Khalid for promoting enmity in their speeches at the Elgar Parishad. A complaint was also filed by a man from Pune, who said that the agenda of the Elgar Parishad event was 'to mislead the Dalit community, to convert them to Maoist thought ... and adopt the path of violence', and that 'through their publications, books and speeches, they want to increase enmity in society'. The man who filed the complaint, Tushar Damgude, was a disciple of Bhide, whom he referred to as 'Guruji' in a Facebook post with a picture of the two of them together. Damgude said he followed a 'simple' rule for his Hindutva: 'We should keep things which are helpful for Hindus; rest should be abandoned.'[42]

This complaint became the basis for the case under which activists were arrested around India. On 8 January, the police filed an FIR and named Dhawale of the Republican Panthers, Gorkhe of Kabir Kala Manch and four others. There was no link between those who sung, spoke and recited at the 31 December event in Pune and the violence of 1 January at Koregaon Bhima, which was entirely the product of local tensions. But under the BJP government of Maharashtra, the 8 January FIR would later be spun into a conspiracy theory about a plot to overthrow the government and an assassination attempt on Modi.

The first part of this conspiracy was written not by the police but by a Pune organisation called the Forum for Integrated National Security, led by RSS men including its secretary general, Seshadri Chari, who was on the BJP's National Executive Committee. A report by this body claimed that the Elgar Parishad distorted history by presenting the battle of 1818 as a fight against caste oppression.

The report said the 'root-cause of the riot is systematic and consistent distortion and falsification of Indian history. There have been three attempts of provocation for these riots as follows: Elgar Parishad at Shaniwarwada was the culmination of Prerana March ... started on Dec 23, through which

---

[42] 'Tushar Damgude, whose complaint sparked nationwide raids, is a Bhide disciple', 29 April 2018, *India Today*

people in Maharashtra were mobilised to end "New Peshwai", a word used to represent the current Government of BJP as casteist and Brahmanical'.[43]

This, the report said, was a Maoist strategy to lure people into joining 'mass organisations' concerned about such issues as caste, justice and equality. Such organisations would then help Maoists recruit for the final armed struggle against the State, the report, released on 9 March 2018, said.[44]

Another report by the same author was submitted to the Maharashtra chief minister in April. In May, the UAPA law was added to the Bhima Koregaon case. On 6 June, the Maharashtra police arrested five people: Dhawale of the Republican Panthers, lawyer and Dalit activist Surendra Gadling, scholar Mahesh Raut, who worked on Adivasi rights, assistant professor of English at Nagpur University Shoma Sen and Rona Wilson of JNU, who worked with the Committee to Release Political Prisoners. They were described by the police as the 'top brass of the urban Maoists'.[45]

Police told the court it found a letter in Wilson's house, which they said alluded to a plot to assassinate Modi. This letter, dated July 2017, said: 'Comrade Kisan and few other senior comrades have proposed concrete steps to end Modi-Raj. We are thinking along the line of another Rajiv Gandhi type incident. It sounds suicidal and there is a great chance that we might fail but we feel that the party PB (polit bureau)/CC (central committee) must deliberate over our proposal. Targeting his road shows could be an effective strategy. We collectively believe that survival of the party is the supreme to all the sacrifices.' This letter, which was addressed to 'Com Rona', was shown to the judge to seek the remand of the five arrested individuals. Material also showed that 'two rounds of funds' had been sent to 'Com Sudhir, Com Surendra and Com Shoma'. Another letter referred to 'Com Gautamji and Com Anand', and yet another letter, which the police said was from the lawyer Sudha Bharadwaj, who worked on Adivasi rights, said 'JNU and TISS (Tata Institute of Social Sciences) students have to be sent to the interiors'.

On the basis of this material, the police identified and arrested Bharadwaj, Gautam Navlakha, an author who also wrote for the *Economic and Political Weekly*, and Anand Teltumbde, an assistant professor at the Goa Institute of Management who was married to a granddaughter of Ambedkar. On 28 August 2018, the police also arrested Arun Ferreira, an activist lawyer from

---

[43] 'Report on Koregaon Bhima riot', Captain Smita Gaikwad, *finsindia.org*

[44] 'Bhima Koregaon case: A curiously prescient report puts focus on a Mumbai security think tank', 31 August 2018, *Scroll.in*

[45] 'PM Modi assassination plot revealed in Maoist letter: Pune cops to court', 8 June 2018, *NDTV*

Mumbai who was defending the accused in this case.[46] Vernon Gonsalves, a professor who taught business management and economics at Ruparel College, HR College of Commerce and Economics, and Akbar Peerbhoy of the College of Commerce and Economics were also arrested.

The same day, the police arrested Varavara Rao, an author and poet who had been a lecturer on Telugu literature and had translated the work of Kenyan writer Ngugi wa Thiong'o. He, along with Gonsalves and Ferreira, were brought to Pune where the public prosecutor told the sessions court that they had been part of an 'anti-fascist front' planning to overthrow the government. This suggested that the BJP government was fascist. One of the activities that was cited in the accusation had to do with a fact-finding team led by Ferreira to inquire into an incident on 21 April 2018 in Gadchiroli, Maharashtra, in which security forces had killed 40 villagers in an 'encounter'. The prosecutor said this was done to portray the State in a bad light and that the 'FFT', named in the various communications of the accused, was not an abbreviation for 'fact finding team' but likely something more 'sinister'.

'Possessing Naxalite materials is one aspect, but spreading thoughts of the Naxalites … that is the agenda of urban Naxals,' the prosecutor said. 'They are not innocent. They are intelligent persons. This is a top-level conspiracy to threaten the sovereignty and integrity of India.' For good measure, she threw in terrorism in Kashmir as well.[47]

The defence pointed out the fact that there was nothing linking them with the violence at Koregaon Bhima and there was no logic to the application of UAPA, the anti-terror provision under which the individuals had been booked. Ferreira, representing himself, said that the basis of the arrests was the letters taken from Wilson's computer and materials seized from all the rest, and so custodial interrogation was unnecessary. Most of them had not even been named in the FIR on the basis of which they were arrested, nor had they been present at the event for which the Bhima Koregaon case was filed. But bail is impossible to get under UAPA, and so they would remain in jail.

Many of them had experienced the misuse of the law before. Dhawale had been booked under UAPA in 2011 and jailed for 40 months before a

---

[46] 'Knock on Ferreira's door came at 6 am, arrest 9 hours later', 29 August 2018, *The Times of India*

[47] 'An "anti-fascist front" to overthrow government: Pune police claims about arrested activists', 30 August 2018, *Scroll.in*, https://scroll.in/article/892464/photo-shows-about-lynchings-seeking-arms-from-nepal-claims-against-activists-arrested-on-tuesday

sessions court released him.[48]

Ferreira was first arrested in 2007. He was acquitted in 2011 by the Chandrapur sessions court but immediately re-arrested. He managed to get bail later.[49]

On 19 August 2007, the Maharashtra Anti-Terror Squad arrested Gonsalves from his Mumbai flat. They alleged that he was a 'top-level' Naxalite who possessed explosives, that he was an ex-central committee member and former secretary of Maharashtra State Rajya Committee of the Maoists. He was charged in 20 cases under the UAPA. On 27 June 2013, Gonsalves was released from prison. He was acquitted in 17 cases, discharged in one, with one underway trial, and convicted in one case for which he had already spent time in jail.[50]

The poet Rao was first arrested in 1973 by the Andhra Pradesh government under the then Maintenance of Internal Security Act (MISA). He was again arrested under MISA in 1975 during the Emergency. Released after the 1977 elections, he was arrested on charges of conspiring to overthrow the government in 1985. Released, he was arrested again in 1986 on charges of attending a meeting in which a plot was hatched to kill a constable and an inspector of police. Rao was acquitted of this 17 years later, in 2003.

He was arrested again in 2005 under the Public Security Act and released the following year. He was arrested four times after 2014, and was never convicted in a single case.[51]

Born in Boston in 1961 to parents who were engaged in postdoctoral studies, Sudha Bharadwaj moved to India with her mother and later gave up her US citizenship. A mathematics graduate from IIT Kanpur, she became a lawyer at the age of 40.

Opposing her bail in July 2020, the NIA said that 'Bharadwaj along with other accused is also involved in training and laying booby traps and directional mines … in providing strategic inputs in furtherance of the objective of armed rebellion'.[52]

In 2019, the results of the Maharashtra state elections did not go the

---

[48] 'Sudhir Dhawale a Dalit activist, not a Naxal: Republican Panthers', 7 June 2018, *Hindustan Times*

[49] 'Knock on Ferreira's door came at 6am, arrest 9 hours later', 29 August 2018, *The Times of India*

[50] 'Who is Vernon Gonsalves?', indiacivilwatch.org

[51] 'Who is Varavara Rao (VV)?', indiacivilwatch.org

[52] 'The Sudha Bharadwaj the govt doesn't want you to know', 28 August 2020, *Article-14.com*

BJP's way. Rather than have the Shiv Sena–NCP–Congress government take control of the prosecution once they came to power, the Modi government, in February 2020, moved the case to the NIA, reporting to Amit Shah. The NIA is headed by Y.C. Modi, who had cleared Modi in the Gujarat riots as part of a Special Investigation Team, and also led the investigations into the Haren Pandya murder. This ensured that the Union could keep opposing bail, and that the accused would remain in prison without conviction, given UAPA's harsh bail provisions.

On 28 July 2020, the NIA arrested Hany Babu, a professor of linguistics at Delhi University. In September, three members of the Kabir Kala Manch, Sagar Gorkhe, Jyoti Jagtap and Ramesh Gaichor, were arrested. On 8 October 2020, Stan Swamy, an 83-year-old Jesuit and theologian who worked with Adivasis in Jharkhand, became the sixteenth person to be jailed in the case under UAPA.[53]

Meanwhile, those who had been named in the original FIR for instigating and participating in the violence—Ekbote and Bhide—were treated very differently. Ekbote disappeared after the violence, was arrested in March and bailed out in April 2018.[54] Bhide was never arrested. A petition was filed for his arrest in Bombay High Court in August 2018 but nothing came of it.

The same month, the Supreme Court dismissed in a majority opinion a petition filed by historian Romila Thapar, seeking an independent inquiry into the case. The dissent came from Justice Chandrachud, who wrote that there was a 'serious bone of contention in regard to the authenticity of the letter which, besides being undated, does not contain any details including the email header'. This letter was one purportedly from Sudha Bharadwaj of which Justice Chandrachud said 'the letter is an obvious fabrication made by a Marathi speaking person because in as many as seventeen places, it contains references to words scribed in Devanagari, using forms peculiar to Marathi', a language Bharadwaj did not speak.[55]

Three years after the case was registered, *Newslaundry* listed the human rights violations that had been perpetrated. They are summarised below.[56]

The Pune Police had twice sought a search warrant to seize material

---

[53] 'The NIA and Father Stan Swamy: Hunting down a Samaritan', 20 November 2020, *Frontline*

[54] 'Bhima-Koregaon violence: Prime accused Milind Ekbote gets bail', 19 April 2018, *The Hindu*

[55] 'Bhima-Koregaon case: NIA summons defence lawyers', 28 August 2020, *The Hindu*

[56] 'Bhima Koregaon case: Three years of legal and rights violations', 2 January 2021, *NewsLaundry.com*

from the accused, saying they would not cooperate with the investigation. The court denied the requests, saying the police couldn't assume that there would be no cooperation without sending them a notice to appear. The police raided the homes of Gadling (Nagpur), Wilson (Delhi) and Dhawale (Mumbai) without the warrant anyway.

During their raids, the police brought along their own witnesses, instead of asking residents of good public standing in the neighbourhood as they were required to do. The police also did not submit the list of materials confiscated to a local court. Gadling's niece's laptop was taken by the police, and from the office of Dhawale, used by activists around India as a place to stay when they were in Mumbai, the laptops of others were also seized. The IT Act says that the 'hash value', which uniquely identifies data, something like a fingerprint, has to be taken before hardware is sent for forensic analysis so that it is not tampered with. This was not done.

The equipment seized in April 2018 was sent to the Regional Forensic Lab in Pune from where the police obtained the files stored on them on 25 April. They were sifting through these files, the police alleged, when they found the letter detailing Modi's assassination. Despite learning about this alleged plot to kill Modi on 25 April, the Pune Police did not arrest Wilson and other activists until 6 June, over 40 days later. The police did not even call in Wilson, Gadling and Dhawale for questioning during this time.

Police records showed the raid at Wilson's house began at 6.05 a.m. and ended at 2.02 p.m., when all seized devices were sealed. The memory card of the camera the police used to videograph the raid was also sealed in an anti-static bag. But the forensic report said the memory card was last used at 5.22 p.m. It also said Wilson's computer was turned on that night at 11.16 p.m. and stayed on till 11.20 p.m.

Wherever the court refused or objected, the police broke the law. While bringing Gadling from Nagpur, the police didn't take him to the local court but to Amravati instead. When the magistrate there refused to give them a transit remand, they took him to Nagpur airport and flew Gadling to Pune without the remand.

They did the same with Shoma Sen, Swamy and Bharadwaj, who were arrested from Nagpur, Ranchi and Faridabad.

Having produced them in court on 7 June 2018, the police didn't let them have their own lawyers, choosing a lawyer for them instead. Gadling said he would represent himself but wasn't allowed to, since the police's lawyer had already filed papers in court.

The Pune Police arrested Teltumbde despite the Supreme Court having given him interim protection. A Pune sessions court said his arrest was illegal and ordered his immediate release. He was rearrested and jailed again on 14 April 2020.[57]

The accused individuals, two of whom were around 80 years old at the time (Stan Swamy and Varavara Rao), were put through a series of humiliations by the police. Stan Swamy, suffering from Parkinson's disease, was disallowed a glass with a sipper straw for weeks. Shoma Sen, suffering from arthritis, found it difficult to use the Indian commode in jail. Her daughter brought her a commode chair but was turned away.

Surendra Gadling asked to access books including the UAPA and IT Acts, some paper to take notes on and four books by Swami Vivekananda. The government opposed this vehemently, with the prosecutor even saying she was unsure whether Vivekananda's books were banned or not in India.[58] After the court allowed the books to be brought, prison authorities still did not allow them to be given to Gadling.

Gadling was disallowed a sweater despite a court order, being told that only thermal sweaters were allowed and not woollen ones. When his wife brought him a full-sleeved thermal sweater, this was disallowed saying that only half-sleeved ones were allowed.

Seventy-year-old Navlakha's spectacles were stolen on 27 November. He was virtually blind without his glasses. But he was not permitted to make a call to ask for a replacement for three days. His partner sent a pair to the jail but the jail authorities refused to accept it though they had been informed that the packet was coming.[59]

When Gadling's mother died, he applied to be allowed to attend the funeral. It was denied on the grounds that his application didn't have her death certificate without which the NIA would not accept that she was dead.[60] The family could not get the certificate because of the lockdown. When the certificate was produced, the NIA said the funeral had already been conducted so they saw no reason to let him out temporarily. When Gadling applied to go to the condolence meeting, this was turned down

---

[57] 'Elgar Parishad case: Anand Teltumbde, Gautam Navlakha surrender to NIA', 14 April 2020, *The Hindu*

[58] 'State of Maharashtra opposes request for cot, commode, books on Vivekananda by Bhima-Koregaon arrestees', 26 June 2018, *TheLeaflet.in*

[59] 'After Stan Swamy struggled for his sipper, jailed Gautam Navlakha can't get his spectacles', 7 December 2020, *Scroll.in*

[60] 'NIA raises objection over Surendra Gadling's interim bail after his mother's demise, says death certificate not filed', 5 September 2020, *Free Press Journal*

because he hadn't submitted a 'copy of the meeting' with his application.

When Sudhir Dhawale's brother died, the application was supported with documentary evidence, an announcement card for the post-funeral meeting and the death certificate. This application was rejected only on the grounds that bail could not be given because the offence was 'serious'.[61] Mahesh Raut's sister married while he was in jail as an undertrial. When Vernon Gonsalves's mother died in May 2021, he chose not to put his family through the rigmarole of attempting to get him bail.[62]

As mentioned earlier, the transfer of the case to the NIA happened after the change in the state government. The Union was satisfied with the Pune Police's investigation till November 2019. When the BJP was defeated in the Maharashtra elections, the case was taken away from the Pune Police. Uddhav Thackeray was sworn in on 28 November 2019. The Union told Maharashtra that it had given the case to the NIA on 24 January 2020.[63]

Though the Modi government made the most serious allegations against these individuals, including planning to assassinate the prime minister, waging war against India and colluding with Pakistan's Inter-Services Intelligence (as Navlakha was accused of doing),[64] it was lax in prosecuting them and did not begin trial. It preferred to keep the individuals as undertrials in jail, knowing bail was not possible for them.

After making their sensational claims about the purported assassination plot, the police filed a chargesheet of 5,000 pages in December 2018, of which fewer than 10 pages were devoted to this plot. This was mere repetition of what had been earlier released in the press conference—the alleged emails referring to a 'Rajiv Gandhi type incident'.[65] The rest was devoted to showing their connections to Communist ideology. However, the BJP continued to claim that the case was a 'conspiracy against Modi'.[66]

The world was not convinced, and the individuals' reputations and the absurdity of the charges ensured that the Bhima Koregaon accused won a

---

[61] 'Lawyers withstood pressures and defended activists in the Bhima Koregaon case', 1 January 2021, *TheLeaflet.in*

[62] Author's conversation with his son, 19 June 2021

[63] 'NIA takes over Bhima Koregaon probe', 25 January 2020, *Mint*

[64] 'Gautam Navlakha had links with Pakistan's ISI, says NIA in Bhima Koregaon chargesheet', 10 October 2020, *The Print*

[65] 'In a 5000-page charge sheet, little on plot to kill Prime Minister Narendra Modi', 6 December 2018, *Mumbai Mirror*

[66] 'Bhima Koregaon case was a conspiracy against Narendra Modi: Shahnawaz Husain', 25 January 2020, *ANI*

lot of empathy. On 29 May 2020, Marie Arena, the chair of the human rights subcommittee of the European parliament, wrote to Amit Shah over the arrests of activists Anand Teltumbde and Gautam Navlakha. She wrote, 'The European Parliament has noticed that various forms of legitimate peaceful protests against laws, policies and governmental actions, including the Citizenship Amendment Act, have been portrayed as terrorist activities.'

She also named activists Safoora Zargar, Gulfisha Fatima, Khalid Saifi, Meeran Haider, Shifa-Ur-Rehman, Dr Kafeel Khan, Asif Iqbal and Sharjeel Imam, all jailed purely for dissent. She said: 'It is particularly alarming to note that human rights defenders cannot conduct advocacy activities, notably in favour of India's poorest and most marginalised communities, without becoming subject to intimidation and harassment, but equally worrying is the fact that terrorism charges, including under the Unlawful Activities Prevention Act, are used to silence them. As pointed out by United Nations Special Procedures, this clearly represents a violation of international human rights standards.'[67]

An investigation by Amnesty International in June 2020 revealed that activists and lawyers connected to the Bhima Koregaon case had been targeted through spyware.[68] In February 2021, *The Washington Post* reported that the letters 'found' by the police on Rona Wilson's laptop had been planted.[69] Malware had been used to introduce them to the computer, an independent analysis had found. These letters, including the one on the Modi assassination, had been created using a newer version of Microsoft Word that did not exist on Wilson's computer, the report said. There was no evidence that the documents or the hidden folder were ever opened. In April 2021, a leading firm in digital forensics said it had 'irrefutable' proof that Wilson's computer was hacked. Files were planted on it on 11 January 2018, 11 days after the Bhima-Koregaon violence.[70] In July 2021, an investigation revealed that India and nations like Hungary, Saudi Arabia, Kazakhstan and Azerbaijan had hired an Israeli firm to hack into and spy on their citizens. The investigation was published by *The Wire* in India, *The Guardian*, *Le Monde*, *Süddeutsche Zeitung* and *The Washington Post*. The material they

---

[67] 'Europe flags rights concern', 31 May 2020, *The Telegraph*

[68] 'India: Human rights defenders targeted by a coordinated spyware operation', 15 June 2020, Amnesty.org

[69] 'They were accused of plotting to overthrow the Modi government. The evidence was planted, a new report says', 10 February 2021, *The Washington Post*

[70] 'In Bhima-Koregaon case, more damning signs of planted evidence', 21 April 2021, *Article-14.com*

published had been verified and authenticated by Amnesty International's tech division, which in turn had its analysis independently peer reviewed.[71]

Those marked for snooping were dozens of journalists including *The Wire*'s editors, Sushant Singh, the reporter quoted in this book, Union ministers Ashwini Vaishnaw and Prahlad Singh Patel, political strategist Prashant Kishor, Mamata Banerjee's nephew Abhishek Banerjee, former Vishwa Hindu Parishad leader Pravin Togadia, the personal secretaries to several politicians including former Rajasthan chief minister Vasundhara Raje, Arivnd Kejriwal, former prime minister Deve Gowda, his son and Karnataka Congress leaders, activist Umar Khalid, Rahul Gandhi and two of his aides, Ashok Lavasa who was the election commissioner, Bhima Koregaon accused Hany Babu, Rona Wilson, Vernon Gonsalves, Anand Teltumbde, Shoma Sen, Arun Ferreira, Sudha Bhardwaj and her lawyer Shalini Gera, Varavara Rao's daughter Pavana, Surendra Gadling's wife Minal and his lawyers, virologist Gagandeep Kang, the head of the Bill and Melinda Gates foundation in India Hari Menon, CBI chief Alok Verma and his deputy Rakesh Asthana, Anil Ambani, the Dalai Lama's aides, several leaders of the Hurriyat Conference including Mirwaiz Umar Farooq, the head of the Border Security Force, an officer in the Research and Analysis Wing, Prashant Ruia of Essar, Ajay Singh of SpiceJet and Naresh Goyal of Jet Airways, Supreme Court registrars NK Gandhi and TI Rajput, Justice Arun Mishra (whom we have met previously) and the Supreme Court employee who had accused Chief Justice Ranjan Gogoi of sexual harassment and her family.[72]

Amnesty said that the revelations 'blow apart any claims by NSO (the Israeli firm that offered the hacking service) that such attacks are rare and down to rogue use of their technology. While the company claims its spyware is only used for legitimate criminal and terror investigations, it's clear its technology facilitates systemic abuse. They paint a picture of legitimacy, while profiting from widespread human rights violations.'[73]

The costs paid by Indian taxpayers for this surveillance was a $500,000 installation fee, followed by $650,000 to spy on 10 iPhones or Android users. After 10 targets, further surveillance was an additional fee of $800,000 for 100 extra targets; $500,000 for 50 extra targets; or $150,000 for 20 extra targets. In addition, NSO also charged an annual system maintenance fee of

[71] 'Pegasus: Spyware sold to governments "targets activists"', 19 July 2021, *BBC*

[72] 'Pegasus project: 161 names revealed by *The Wire* on snoop list so far', 4 August 2021, *TheWire.in*

[73] 'Massive data leak reveals Israeli NSO Group's spyware used to target activists, journalists, and political leaders globally, 18 July 2021, Amnesty International

17 per cent of the total cost every year after the initial order. The charges were for an initial fixed period of time, with renewals costing extra.[74]

In response to the revelations the Modi government said 'there has been no unauthorised interception by government agencies. The allegations regarding government surveillance on specific people has no concrete basis or truth associated with it whatsoever'[75], but it refused to say it had not used Pegasus. Why the Indian government was targeting through 'authorised' surveillance the democratic opposition, the judiciary, journalists, activists, a victim of sexual harassment and her family, its own officers, its own ministers and businessmen was left unexplained.

Part 3: Resistance

The Tail of the Cow

On 11 July 2016, Dalit men who were skinning a cow's carcass were assaulted and humiliated for hours in the village of Una, near the Somnath temple. Videos taken by those who participated in and witnessed the assault were watched by millions over the next few days. The police stood by. This was during the beef lynching madness India was going through. The men had not killed the cow, merely skinned a dead one.

On 18 July, it was reported that seven Dalits attempted to immolate themselves in protest.[76] Another nine made the attempt the following day. One of the men, who had consumed poison, died.[77]

Dalit organisations then discovered a manner of protest that was effective: they brought the carcasses of the dead cows they worked with to their protests. The carcasses were dumped outside government offices and on top of government vehicles.

On 18 July, in Surendranagar in central Gujarat, 250 kms from Una, 15 trucks of cattle carcasses were brought and parked outside the collector's office. This was shocking for the population, which had not seen dead animals on this scale before, because the work of skinning and cleaning carcasses was always done in Dalit areas.

'She's your mother, you take care of her,' the Dalits said as they did this

---

[74] 'Cost of putting Pegasus in phones runs into crores', 21 July 2021, *Indian Express*

[75] 'Full text: Government's response on Pegasus project', 18 July 2021, *Times of India*

[76] 'Seven Dalits attempt suicide in Gujarat', 18 July 2016, *The Hindu*

[77] 'Protests all over Gujarat against attack on Dalit men who were skinning a cow, 16 attempt suicide', 19 July 2016, *Scroll.in*

across towns and cities in Gujarat.[78] Of course, no gaurakshak was around to clean up what he had all this time pretended to revere. The Surendranagar Collectorate said it was forced to bury 80 cow carcasses because there was nobody who could usefully strip them as Dalits did. 'The Dalit community, which usually skins the dead animals and then disposes of the carcass has been on a strike in the district for one week, so we told the municipal staff to dispose of the dead animals,' the collector, Udit Agarwal, said.[79]

This manner of protest was replicated and Dalit groups called on their community to act. They were led by those who had never protested before, including a Dalit businessman, Hirabhai Chawda, who traded in the by-products of dead cows. Till these carcass protests began, the mainstream media was uninterested in the Una story and the plight of Gujarat's Dalits. *Scroll* reported that, on the morning of 18 July, the day the carcasses were taken to the Surendranagar Collectorate, *The Times of India*'s main story was about the RBI governor Raghuram Rajan. The next day, the paper took up the assault on Dalits as its main story. A day later, the chief minister finally met the victims' families.

The turbulence produced new leaders including the 35-year-old activist and former journalist Jignesh Mevani. He likened the actions of those who had attempted suicide to the 2004 protest by Manipuri women against sexual assault by the Indian armed forces. The women had appeared naked outside Kangla Fort in Imphal—headquarters of the Assam Rifles—with banners that read 'Indian army, rape us'. 'Those women had to strip naked and say "Indian army rape us" in order for the nation to pay attention to their plight,' Mevani said. 'The suicide attempts are similar.'[80]

In August, Mevani mobilised thousands of people for a 400 km march from Ahmedabad to Una. He used the momentum to push material changes, primarily by picking up the issue of surplus land, which had been taken from feudal landowners by the law but not redistributed to Dalits as it should have been.

In 2006, 115 landless Dalit families of Saroda village near Ahmedabad were allotted 222 bigha (around 136 acres, or about 1.1 acres per family) of land under the Agriculture Land Ceiling Act. However, the possession

---

[78] '"Your mother, you take care of it": Meet the Dalits behind Gujarat's stirring cow carcass protests', 23 July 2016, *Scroll.in*

[79] 'After Una atrocity, Dalits protest and refuse to dispose of carcasses in Gujarat', 30 July 2016, *The Hindu*

[80] 'An assault on Dalits may have triggered the biggest lower-caste uprising in Gujarat in 30 years', 20 July 2016, *Scroll.in*

remained only on paper, and the land, which had been encroached upon by people from the dominant caste, did not actually change hands. The Dalits had made representations to the government to no effect.[81]

Mevani picked up the issue, which also impacted other Dalits in Gujarat, and affected the allotment of over 56,000 acres, forcefully. His slogan was '*Gai nu puchdu tamey rakho, amne amaari jameen aapo*' (Keep the cow's tail for yourself and give us our land).

On 8 August 2016, with protests mounting, Modi finally responded by saying Hindutva vigilantes should kill him rather than attack Dalits.[82] This response did not move the protestors and they continued their agitation.

In September 2016, a rail roko was announced when Modi was to visit Gujarat to celebrate his 66th birthday.[83] The agitation was planned at Maninagar, Modi's former constituency, and the threat goaded the state government into engaging with the group they had previously been contemptuous of. The home minister made an assurance that their demands on land would be met. On 20 September, the government began mapping the land at Saroda.

Two days later, on 22 September, the state government announced the setting up of 16 special courts across Gujarat for the speedy trial of cases under Scheduled Caste/Scheduled Tribe Prevention of Atrocities Act, to take up cases like Una.[84] Courts would be set up in 15 districts, with Ahmedabad getting two. Anand, Banaskantha, Bharuch, Bhavnagar, Gandhinagar, Jamnagar, Junagadh, Kutch, Mehsana, Patan, Rajkot, Surat, Surendranagar and Vadodara would get the rest. The notification said the courts were being established after consultation with the Chief Justice of Gujarat High Court. This had also been one of the long-standing demands of Dalits and it came only on the back of their protests after Una.

On 1 October, these courts began functioning. Five months later, on 25 March 2017, the first conviction came for a case that had been registered in 2013. Conviction rates under the SC/ST Act had been dropping before this. In 2012, a total of 1,026 cases were registered but saw only 65 convictions.

---

[81] 'What brought the Dalits' fight for land to the streets', 1 October 2016, *TheWire.in*

[82] '"Attack me, shoot me, not Dalits": PM Modi's message in Hyderabad', 8 August 2016, *NDTV*

[83] 'Dalits plan rail roko stir in Gujarat on Oct 1', 15 September 2016, *The New Indian Express*

[84] 'Una effect: Gujarat to set up 16 special courts to handle SC/ST atrocity cases', 22 September 2016, PTI

In 2015, of the 1,009 cases registered, a mere 11 convictions ensued.[85]

One of the reasons for the delay in disposal of cases was the high number of vacancies in judge positions. At the beginning of 2013, Gujarat had the highest number of vacancies (794) in all of India.[86]

It was the pressure resulting from the mobilisation after Una that brought about change for Dalits. In December 2017, only 17 months after the events of Una, Mevani was elected to the Gujarat Assembly, having become a nationally recognised figure.

ASHA Nirasha

The reality is that, unless mass mobilisation of a sustained sort happens, the State does not engage with Indians on protest. It does not matter that the cause is just and of a pressing nature. It doesn't matter even that it is something that is vital for the nation and its citizens. If it can be ignored because it is not seen as politically important, it will be.

Six lakh Accredited Social Health Activists (ASHA) went on a two-day strike across India in August 2020, demanding that they get the same protection from Covid that doctors were being given, health insurance and basic salaries. These were the frontline workers, the Covid warriors, according to Modi, who had been valourised in speech but not given PPE kits or sanitisers, masks and gloves.

These were workers employed under the Union health mission. They were paid no salary but received some basic compensation. They were given the following responsibilities:

- Create awareness and provide information on nutrition, sanitation and hygiene
- Counsel women on birth preparedness, safe delivery, breastfeeding, immunisation, contraception and prevention of common infections
- Work with the Village Health and Sanitation Committee of the gram panchayat to develop a comprehensive village health plan
- Escort/accompany pregnant women and children to the nearest health centre
- Provide primary medical care for minor ailments such as diarrhoea and fevers, first aid for injuries, and the short course for tuberculosis
- Supervise storage of essential provisions being made available to

---

[85] 'First conviction by Gujarat's special SC/ST atrocity courts offers ray of hope to many victims', 8 May 2017, *TheWire.in*

[86] 'An overview of fast-track courts', 31 December 2012, PRSIndia.org

every habitation, like oral rehydration therapy (ORS), iron folic acid tablet, chloroquine, disposable delivery kits and contraceptives like pills and condoms[87]

For this work, they received, depending on the state, between Rs 2,000 and Rs 4,500 a month, through funds from the Union and the state governments. If they completed some 'recurring' tasks, like updating the lists of children to be immunised, they received small incentives. ASHA workers were aged between 25 and 45 and were literate, having studied up to Class X.[88]

After the lockdowns and the spread of Covid-19, many ASHA workers were working 14 hours a day, documenting people's quarantine schedules and tracking their districts for influenza-like symptoms. And they would be required to vaccinate the rural Indian population.

In Delhi, they were paid Rs 4,000 a month and were asking for Rs 10,000. Their protest in Jantar Mantar—the 'designated area' where causes are sent to die—went unheard and, in fact, a hundred of the Covid warriors were booked for protesting without permission.[89] Women who had been force-marched to the frontline of the pandemic with no protection faced charges brought by the Delhi Police for 'violating social distancing norms' at their protest.

In Bihar, many of the 90,000 ASHA workers were on strike in August 2020.[90] Many of them had not been paid for four months. Some had contracted Covid on the job and many died.[91]

In Karnataka, ASHA workers had not been paid for a year. Many had not been paid the Rs 1,000 that the state government said it would give them for Covid-related work.[92] They had been on strike twice during the pandemic, in August and in September 2020, but were not able to even secure a meeting with the health minister.

In Gujarat, ASHA workers had not been receiving their dues for a year before Covid, a common occurrence in India given the state of finances.

[87] 'Guidelines on accredited social health activists', nhm.gov.in.

[88] 'Behind India's coronavirus vaccine plan is an army of poorly paid female health workers', 15 January 2021, *Quartz*

[89] 'FIR against 100 ASHA workers for Jantar Mantar protest', 11 August 2020, *Hindustan Times*

[90] 'Covid-19: 600k ASHA, anganwadi staff on 2-day strike over payments', 8 August 2020, *Hindustan Times*

[91] '162 doctors, 107 nurses, 44 ASHA workers died due to Covid in India till 22 January: Govt', 3 February 2021, PTI

[92] 'Nine months on, ASHA workers still unpaid, demands ignored', 8 December 2020, *The New Indian Express*

About 3,000 women in Gir, Somnath, Porbandar and Junagadh districts had been on strike for about 10 days leading up to Women's Day on 8 March.[93] They were told they would be given a 50 per cent hike in 2017 and withdrew a strike they had held then, only to later discover that the 'hike' had been accompanied by a withdrawal of their other benefits so there was no increase at all. They did not even make Rs 3,000 a month.

In Madhya Pradesh, ASHA workers went on strike even earlier, in 2018, and stayed on strike for over 10 days in October asking for a fixed salary and permanent employment.[94] The state paid ASHA workers between Rs 800 and Rs 1,000 per month and other 'incentives', such as Rs 250 for nine months' antenatal care resulting in an institutional delivery.

In Haryana, 20,000 ASHA workers struck work on 7 August 2020 and then again in October, demanding the unfulfilled implementation of the health department's assurance to them of 21 July 2018, which said they would be regularised in employment. They also sought incentives for services and risk allowances during the pandemic.[95]

In Rajasthan, they had struck work for days in September 2017, seeking more money than the Rs 1,850 they received from the state.[96] They struck work again at the end of 2020, dissatisfied with the renaming of their job title to ASHA Sahayogini and the merging of incentives resulting in a pay of Rs 2,700.[97] In January 2021, chief minister Ashok Gehlot wrote to Modi asking for more money for the state's 52,000 ASHA workers, saying that there had been no increase in the amount of incentives payable by the Union for their increased work.[98]

Even in Kerala, they were not prioritised to receive vaccines despite being 'frontline warriors'.[99]

In Punjab, ASHA workers were on hunger strike for the restoration of a Covid 'incentive' of Rs 2,500 that had been reduced in June 2020 to

---

[93] 'Gujarat: 3,000 ASHA workers on strike for over a week', 8 March 2019, *DNA*

[94] 'Har ghar se hamara nata hai, sarkar badalna aata hai', 12 October 2018, *NewsClick.in*

[95] 'ASHA workers stage protest against Haryana government in Karnal', 8 October 2018, *Hindustan Times*

[96] 'Anganwadi, ASHA workers sit on indefinite strike', 15 September 2017, *The Times of India*

[97] 'Panel to examine demands of ASHA Sahyoginis', 31 December 2020, *The Times of India*

[98] 'Ashok Gehlot asks PM Modi to increase incentive amount given to ASHA workers', 3 January 2021, *NDTV*

[99] 'ASHA workers protest against "non-registration" for vaccine', 7 February 2020, *The Hindu*

Rs 1,000. Most of them had no smartphones in which to record details of households surveys related to Covid. Of the 18,000 ASHA workers in Punjab, only around 3,000 had smartphones, the rest borrowed them from friends and relatives to input data. They were paid Rs 4 per family member whose details they recorded and who they would motivate to go for testing. ASHA workers got around 1,000 per month as incentives if the population they catered to was not below the poverty line. It was higher if the population was below the poverty line, but that came with significant other risks, such as dealing with patients who had tuberculosis.[100]

If the government tripled what the 11 lakh ASHA workers around India were paid and gave them Rs 12,000 a month, it would still be only a cost of around Rs 13,000 crore a year. Surely that was money well spent in a nation of generally poor health and especially to deal with a pandemic that was hurting it economically.

But the ASHA workers, despite their resolve, could not move Indians to give them justice. On 15 May 2021, unable to cope with the second wave of the pandemic, Modi asked for ASHA workers to be 'empowered with all necessary tools' so that they could carry out door-to-door testing in rural areas.[101] But he made no reference to paying them. Ten days later, they went on another strike, but once again their demands went unmet. Even the families of ASHA workers who died after contracting Covid on the job were not properly compensated.[102] By the time the second wave had begun to ebb, state governments including Delhi's began delaying paying even ASHA workers' meagre incentives for months, leaving them with no income at all.[103]

Their protests were supported by various national trade unions, such as INTUC, AITUC, HMS, CITU, AIUTUC, TUCC, SEWA, AICCTU, LPF and UTUC. But none of them appeared to have a large enough investment in this to be able to convert tens of thousands of willing agitators and what was obviously a massive problem into a large-scale, national and continuous protest.

For protest to work in India, it has to be sustained. If the State is not interested in the issue, or has a stake in the issue or is hostile to the

---

[100] 'Citing "nirasha" at govt attitude, ASHAs in Punjab stir up agitation', 19 August 2020, *The Indian Express*

[101] 'PM chairs a high level meeting on Covid and vaccination related situation', 15 May 2021, Press Information Bureau

[102] '"Made to run from pillar to post": Kin of deceased ASHA workers await compensation', 19 June 2021, *The News Minute*

[103] 'ASHA workers losing hope', 29 August 2021, *The Hindu*

protestors, the only way to draw its attention and hold it is through sustained defiance. The State, especially a government such as Modi's, understands the news cycle and can deflect, distract or ignore for long enough for the issue to die down due to a lack of enthusiasm, organisational ability or just stamina.

Written in Stone

In November 2015, the BJP government in Jharkhand approved a plan to expand the capital city of Ranchi.[104] This would involve acquiring 39,000 acres of fertile land and make thousands of Adivasis landless. RTI activism revealed that, in seven villages that had a total available land of 3,200 acres, the government would take 2,200 acres and the Central Industrial Security Force would take another 158 acres.[105]

The background to this was that some of Jharkhand's towns, such as Ranchi, Dhanbad and Bokaro, were not planned; they had just sprung up around mining. Nine out of 10 homes in Ranchi were built without clearance, the government told the Jharkhand High Court in 2011.[106]

The number of towns in Jharkhand grew from 13 in 1901 to 35 in 1951, and to 228 in 2011. The urban population of the state went from 2 per cent in 1901 to 24 per cent in 2011.[107]

The fifth schedule of the Indian Constitution provides for special administration of tribal areas specifically to prevent the alienation of Adivasis from their lands. No land in these areas can be transferred to non-Adivasis. In Jharkhand, this protection came from the Santhal Pargana Tenancy Act, governing the eastern part of the state, and the Chotanagpur Tenancy Act. Both laws were written by the British, the first after the Santhal rebellion of 1855 and the second in 1908 after the rebellion led by Birsa Munda. Munda died in 1900 at the age of 25, but the British conceded the protections to the Adivasis that he had been fighting for. After 1947, both laws remained, to restrict the sale and transfer of Adivasi land to non-Adivasis.

In 2016, the BJP passed amendments to the two laws.[108] A fifth of all

[104] 'Greater Ranchi master plan gets Cabinet approval', 25 November 2015, *The Times of India*
[105] 'Adivasis, the fifth schedule and urban development: A study of Greater Ranchi', October 2019, Vol 3(2), *Journal of the Sociological Society*
[106] 'Over 90% houses in Ranchi built without maps, court told', 14 April 2011, *Zee News*
[107] 'Jharkhand and homes without maps: Puny process of clearance at the heart of this mammoth developmental issue', 2 February 2021, *First Post*
[108] 'Jharkhand passes tenancy laws amid Opposition uproar in Assembly', 24 November 2016, *Hindustan Times*

land in the state had already been acquired for mining and dams, displacing 40 lakh Adivasis.

The party was then led by Jharkhand's first non-Adivasi chief minister, Raghubar Das. The changes in the laws, first through ordinance in May and then through the legislature in November, would enable the government to acquire land for non-agriculture use. At its discretion the government could acquire land for things 'like road, canal, railway, cable transmission, pipelines, and schools, colleges, universities, panchayat buildings, hospitals, anganwadis' as well as any other 'government purpose' notified in the gazette. The ordinances were opposed by Stan Swamy, whom we have met earlier in the chapter as one of those jailed in the Bhima Koregaon case. 'The extension of the listed use and intended purposes in sub-section 49(1)(C) are clearly for real estates, educational institutes and hospitals under private or PPP model,' Swamy pointed out.[109]

Jharkhand's chief minister, Das, had, at an investment roadshow in Mumbai, mentioned that the changes in law would make available 71,000 hectares (175,000 acres) to industry. At a Make in India event earlier in the year, Das had signed agreements with industrialists for investments of Rs 62,000 crore, with the Adani group alone accounting for Rs 50,000 crore.[110]

In August, the National Commission for Scheduled Tribes said the amendments violated two Central laws, including the Panchayat Extension to Scheduled Areas Act, which required the taking of consent from gram sabhas, the basic Adivasi governance unit, when land was transferred.

On 23 October, as it was clear that the ordinances would become law, the Adivasis rebelled and said they would not stand for the changes. Into a crowd of Munda tribals, the same community Birsa had come from, the police fired 11 rounds, killing an elder, Abhram Mundu.[111]

In January 2017, shoes were thrown at chief minister Das by tribals who were protesting against the laws.[112] In July, after the sustained opposition of the Adivasis, the governor of Jharkhand, Droupadi Murmu, a former BJP minister and a Santhal herself, returned the laws with questions, citing 192

---

[109] 'Amendments to century-old laws on tribal rights spark protests in Jharkhand', 24 November 2016, *Down to Earth*

[110] 'Jharkhand signs MoUs for Rs 62,000 crore', 18 February 2016, *Business Standard*

[111] 'In Jharkhand, Adivasis say changes to tenancy laws dilute their hard-won land rights', 17 February 2017, *Scroll.in*

[112] 'Shoes hurled at Jharkhand CM Raghubar Das', 1 January 2017, *The New Indian Express*

protest petitions she had received against them, and asking the government to explain how the changes would help the people.[113]

Tribal areas are part of the Constitution's fifth schedule, which gives special powers to the governor to safeguard their rights and ensure legislation is aligned with customary law, social and religious practices. However, the executive was usually able to avoid this provision and have its way, and Adivasi participation in decision-making remained limited.[114]

As this was happening, the Adivasis began to assert their rights more openly. They erected stone monoliths, called pathals, outside their villages, which:

- Declared their gram sabha as the sovereign authority.
- Banned 'outsiders' from their area.
- Asserted that Adivasis were the real inhabitants of this land by stating that 'jal, jungle, jameen (water, forest and land) is ours and no one can take them away from us'.
- Said that 'voter IDs and Aadhaar cards are anti-Adivasi documents'.
- Reproduced Article 13(3) which defines law as any 'custom or usage having in the territory of India the force of law'. This was taken to mean that existing Adivasi custom or law as defined by the village gram sabha (so far as it did not violate the Constitution) had the force of the Constitution.[115]
- Reproduced excerpts from the Panchayats (Extension to Scheduled Areas) Act, 1996, which gave them special rights over managing their affairs in accordance with custom and tradition, and to safeguard and preserve their cultural identity, community resources and the customary mode of dispute resolution.[116]
- Reproduced court judgements which supported what they were saying.

Some of these stone tablets stood 15 feet tall and 4 feet wide, painted in green with white lettering. As more Adivasi villages began to do this, the action took on the nature of a movement called 'Pathalgadi' (the erecting of pathals). Some villages had put them up a few years earlier, but most came

---

[113] 'Tribal Tenancy Act: Jharkhand CM on backfoot as Governor Droupadi Murmu returns bills seeking amendments', 10 July 2017, *India Today*

[114] 'Explained: What is the Pathalgadi movement, and what is JMM govt's stand on it?', 23 December 2020, *The Indian Express*

[115] 'Pathalgadi is nothing but constitutional messianism so why is the BJP afraid of it?', 16 May 2018, *TheWire.in*

[116] 'The Pathalgadi rebellion', 14 April 2018, *The Hindu*

up because of the recent laws. By September 2017, over 200 villages had erected them.[117]

On 17 August 2017, a police officer was seen as an intruder and not allowed to leave a village.[118] 'Why should we allow outsiders to enter into our villages?' they asked. 'When the peace is disturbed, the police come and brand us Naxals and beat us up for no reason.'[119]

In 2018, a former member of parliament's bodyguards were held by Pathalgadi supporters, who wanted their people to be released by the police in an exchange.

The Adivasis demanded that funds earmarked for tribal plans should be distributed to the gram sabhas; that the amendments to the land acquisition bills should be scrapped; and that all police and paramilitary camps should be withdrawn from the Scheduled Areas.

The BJP government responded by filing mass FIRs against the tribals, including for sedition. In just one district, Khunti, the administration booked 11,400 individuals, including more than 10,000 for sedition, between July 2017 and July 2018.[120] This was 2 per cent of the district population of Khunti, which was where Birsa Munda was from.

The Jharkhand Janadhikar Mahasabha, a network of social movements and organisations, sent a fact-finding team of activists, academics and lawyers to Khunti. They found that 'the state responded to Pathalgadi with severe repression and violence. Adivasis in some villages were severely beaten, houses were raided and ransacked. In Ghaghra village, a pregnant woman, Ashrita Munda, delivered a physically disabled baby, a couple of weeks after being beaten by the police during a raid'.

Their report said that 'the police has also forcefully set up camps in schools and community buildings without the consent of gram sabhas in many Adivasi villages'.[121]

The resistance from the Adivasis was one of the key issues the Opposition used in the 2019 state elections, in which the BJP was defeated. In December 2019, before voting, the Jharkhand Mukti Morcha said it would drop

---

[117] 'Indigenous India: Written in stone', 1 November 2018, *New Internationalist*

[118] 'Explained: What is the Pathalgadi movement, and what is JMM govt's stand on it?', 23 December 2020, *The Indian Express*

[119] 'The Pathalgadi rebellion', 14 April 2018, *The Hindu*

[120] '10,000 people charged with sedition in one Jharkhand district. What does democracy mean here?', 19 November 2019, *Scroll.in*

[121] 'Jharkhand: Rights body urges govt to withdraw cases against thousands of tribals', 11 October 2019, *TheWire.in*

the cases if it came to power. After its leader Hemant Soren became chief minister, he announced that all cases against the Pathalgadi movement in 2017 and 2018 had been dropped. In fact, the first decision of the new cabinet was to drop the cases of sedition.[122]

A year later, about two-thirds of the cases had been withdrawn.[123]

The Pathalgadi agitation, a sustained mass movement that many Indians outside Jharkhand did not know about, achieved a comprehensive citizenry victory over the State. Not only did they force it to rollback the offending laws, but they also defeated the party that wrote them, and got most of the cases against them withdrawn.

The Falcon's Garden

In January 2018, a team from the NHRC visited two detention camps in Assam, where those who could not prove their citizenship were being held.

The three-person team (senior superintendent of police Mahesh Bhardwaj, author and social activist Harsh Mander and the NHRC's assistant registrar Indrajeet Kumar) wrote a report. They found a situation of 'grave and extensive human distress and suffering'. The detainees were held in a corner of the two jails for several years, in a twilight zone of legality, without work and recreation, with no contact with their families, rare visits from their families, and with no prospect of release. In the women's camp, the women wailed continuously, as though in mourning, the team wrote.[124]

Men, women and children above six were each separated from members of their families. Many had not met their spouse for several years, several not even once since their detention, given that women and men were in different jails, and they were never given parole or permission to meet. Children who turned six were sent out to the care of relatives or the community, their future legal status uncertain.

The government made no distinction between these detention centres and jails. There was no legal regime governing the rights and entitlements of detainees, so though they were in jail, unlike convicts, they could not get parole or waged work. The NHRC took no action on the team's findings and

[122] 'Jharkhand: In first cabinet decision, Hemant govt drops Pathalgadi sedition cases', 29 December 2019, *The Indian Express*
[123] 'Jharkhand: Only 60% Pathalgadi cases withdrawn, one year after Soren government's promise', 11 December 2020, *Scroll.in*
[124] 'Report on NHRC mission to Assam's detention centres from 22 to 24 January, 2018', cjp.org.in

Mander quit.[125] The Assam NRC was released in 2019, and it left out about 19 lakh individuals. A year later, these 19 lakh people had still not received written confirmation of their exclusion, meaning that they could not file an appeal though they had been disenfranchised and could not vote.[126] All of them continued to live with thoughts of separation from family and the jail that the others who failed the NRC test had been sent to.

The first step was the making of this list that left people out. The second step of the NRC process involved submitting oneself before a Foreigners Tribunal. This was a kangaroo court which was run by individuals on two-year government contracts. Once an individual was accused of being a foreigner (and this accusation could be made anonymously by anyone), they would have to show the Foreigners' Tribunal documents to prove their ancestors had been in Assam before 24 March 1971. And they would then have to produce documents establishing their relationship with their ancestors.

The tribunal members' two-year contracts were extended by the BJP government only if they marked a higher number of people as 'foreigners', according to an affidavit the government itself submitted to Gauhati High Court.[127] Further, the tribunal's decision could not be appealed.[128]

This was the future that awaited the rest of India's Muslims if the BJP brought in the nationwide NRC. They were goaded and forced into protest by a State under Modi intent on penalising them through the citizenship law. Things came to a head at the end of 2019 when, high on his second victory, Modi executed a series of actions. The triple talaq law came into force on 1 August, and Kashmir was dismembered four days later on 5 August. On 31 August, the BJP government in Assam released its final NRC.[129] On 9 November, the Supreme Court passed its Babri Masjid judgement, which stipulated that the property the mosque had stood on would be handed over to a trust to build a Ram temple. On 11 December, the CAA was passed.

Amit Shah said that the law was to be read in conjunction with the NRC,

[125] 'Harsh Mander resigns as NHRC special monitor, citing inaction on report on Assam detention centres', 25 June 2018, *Scroll.in*

[126] 'A year after Assam's NRC released, citizenship of two million people remains under a cloud', 28 August 2020, *Scroll.in*

[127] 'Assam decides tribunal member's term on rate of declaring foreigners: Amnesty', 12 March 2020, *The Hindu*

[128] 'Those declared foreigners cannot file NRC appeal, says Assam govt', 16 September 2019, *Hindustan Times*

[129] 'Assam final NRC list released: 19,06,657 people excluded, 3.11 crore make it to citizenship list', 31 August 2019, *India Today*

which was coming down the pike. The CAA would identify and protect non-Muslims, after that the NRC would come for the Muslims.

There was no resistance from the polity on this, including from the Opposition. India's Muslims had been painted into a corner. If they did not stand up for their rights, they would be brutalised while the others looked on. They chose to make a stand in a spontaneous movement that defined Modi's second term, gave Indians hope and a model for peaceful resistance, drew the admiration of the world and, most importantly, finished off the idea of a nationwide NRC, making Amit Shah eat his words.

Shaheen Bagh—Shaheen is the Persian word for falcon—is a middle-class south Delhi locality in the vicinity of Jamia Millia Islamia, the university set up in 1925.

The Jamia Nagar area comprises localities like Batla House, Zakir Nagar and Ghaffar Manzil. Of these, Shaheen Bagh is the newest inhabitation.[130] Till 1990, it had no electricity or sewer lines. After the Babri Masjid was demolished in 1992, the population of the area grew exponentially as Muslims left the mixed neighbourhoods they were in and moved into the area.

On the night of 15 December 2019, angered by the police violence against the students of Jamia who were peacefully protesting the passage of the CAA, the residents of Shaheen Bagh sat out in the winter cold to announce their resistance. The road they occupied was a part of G.D. Birla Marg, which connects Delhi with Uttar Pradesh. This was a Muslim neighbourhood and it would not be easy for the police to storm the area and just boot them off the road. Also, the protest was led by and populated mostly by Shaheen Bagh's women, which further complicated the potential use of force.

The protest grew quickly in size and in significance and influence. It was simple enough to replicate as a model in other Indian cities. India's Muslims are forced to live in urban ghettos. They were therefore the majority in these neighbourhoods and felt safe in them. Muslim women, many who rarely left their home, could come down the road and occupy it to announce their protest and participation in the movement against the CAA and the NRC, which was coming—once again the Modi–Shah style showing itself—in devious fashion.

On 22 December, Modi said that the NRC had not been discussed by

---

[130] 'To better understand the Shaheen Bagh protest, we must understand the locality itself', 20 January 2020, *The Caravan*

his government and people had nothing to worry about. At a rally in Delhi, Modi said: 'I want to tell the 130 crore people of India that ever since my government came to power in 2014 ... from then until now ... there has been no discussion on NRC anywhere ... we only had to implement it in Assam to follow Supreme Court directives.'[131]

Modi's claim went against the public statements and threats made by Shah only days earlier. On 10 December, Shah had said in parliament that the NRC was coming. Shah's exact words were: '*Is desh mein NRC hokar rahega*'—there will definitely be an NRC in this nation—and '*maan ke chaliye NRC aane wala hai*' (you must assume that NRC is to come). At an election rally in Jharkhand on 3 December, he had even set a deadline for NRC's completion—2024, saying 'each and every infiltrator will be identified and expelled before the next election'.[132] India had no extradition treaty with Bangladesh or Pakistan. Assuming the National Population Register (discussed later in the chapter) and NRC would locate these 'termites' (as Shah referred to undocumented migrants in a speech on 11 April 2019 in Raiganj, West Bengal), the government had no means of sending them anywhere except to indefinite detention as it was already doing in Assam.

Modi had himself promised to bring the NRC in his 2019 manifesto, which read: 'There has been a huge change in the cultural and linguistic identity of some areas due to illegal immigration, resulting in an adverse impact on local people's livelihood and employment. We will expeditiously complete the National Register of Citizens process in these areas on priority. In the future, we will implement the NRC in a phased manner in other parts of the country.'

On 17 December, in an interview to *Aaj Tak,* Shah again repeated that the NRC was coming soon. Just five days later, Modi appeared to be walking back the NRC. However, two days after that, the government took the first step towards the NRC. The cabinet met to approve Rs 8,754 crore for the census to be conducted in 2021 and another Rs 3,941 crore for 'updation of the National Population Register'.[133]

At a press conference, the government underplayed the NPR move. It said that 'anyone', including non-citizens, would be counted in the NPR

[131] 'Did Narendra Modi backtrack on nationwide NRC?', 22 December 2019, *India Today*

[132] 'Why PM Modi chose to contradict Amit Shah's NRC vow', 23 December 2019, *India Today*

[133] 'National Population Register: Modi govt approves updation of NPR, allocates budget of Rs 3,941 crore', 24 December 2019, *The Financial Express*

for which 'no proof, no document, no biometric' was required because, according to the government, 'we trust the public'.[134]

The NPR exercise would begin in April 2020 and would conclude in September. The NPR, the government claimed, would not be used for the NRC.[135] Indeed, Shah specifically stated that the NPR had no relation at all to the NRC: *'Iska dur dur tak NRC se kuchh bhi sambandh nahin hai'* (It isn't even remotely connected to the NRC).[136]

In an interview to *ANI*, Shah continued the theme Modi had introduced: the NRC had 'not been discussed' and was not imminent. Of the exercise that had just been approved, Shah said: 'NPR is the database on which policy is made. NRC is a process in which people are asked to prove their citizenship. There is no connection between the two processes, nor can they be used in each other's survey. NPR data can never be used for NRC. Even the laws are different … I assure all the people, specially from the minorities, that NPR is not going to be used for NRC. It's a rumour.'[137]

It was not a rumour and the facts came out quite quickly. Twenty-two points of data would be collected in the NPR. The Modi government had added eight new ones. Details would be collected of an individual's Aadhaar, passport, driving licence, mobile number, voter identity card, mother tongue, and the date and birthplace of their parents.

These eight were not in the 2003 Citizenship Rules, which is the legal framework for the NPR, and had been specifically added by the Modi government to some end.[138] What was that end? When reporters pointed this out to Union minister Prakash Javadekar, he said he had 'not seen the form finalised by experts'.

Research into the laws and bylaws showed that this new headcount, the NPR, was not only linked to the NRC, it was its very foundation. The list generated by the NPR would be scanned by local officials going through it to mark, at their discretion, 'doubtful citizens'.[139] These individuals would then

---

[134] Ibid

[135] 'National Population Register won't be used for NRC, clarifies Javadekar', 24 December 2019, *The Indian Express*

[136] 'Alphabet soup simmers: CAA through, NRC hanging and now NPR from April', 25 December 2019, *The Indian Express*

[137] 'In U-turn, Home Minister Amit Shah says there is no link between NRC and NPR', 25 December 2019, *The News Minute*

[138] 'NPR rules do not allow Modi government to collect data on parent's birthplace and Aadhaar', 26 January 2020, *Scroll.in*

[139] 'CAA and NRC III: Who are 'doubtful' citizens NPR seeks to identify?', 24 December 2019, *Business Today*

have to line up and prove their citizenship. Once the list was drawn up and put on display, anyone could complain or name an individual or a family as being 'doubtful', even anonymously.

On 24 December, it was reported that the NPR was indeed the basis for NRC. Section 14A of the Citizenship Act empowered the government to compulsorily register every citizen of India and issue an identity card and to maintain a National Register of Indian Citizens. The citizenship register would be generated out of this NPR database.[140]

On the next day came news that the 2018–19 annual report of Shah's home ministry had itself said that 'the National Population Register is the first step towards the creation of the National Register of Indian Citizens'.

On 8 July 2014, minister of state for home Kiren Rijiju said: 'It has been decided that NPR should be completed and taken to its logical conclusion, which is creation of a National Register of Indian Citizens by verification of citizenship status of every usual resident in the NPR.'

On 26 November 2014, Rijiju told the Rajya Sabha: 'The NPR is the first step towards creation of National Register of Indian Citizens by verifying the citizenship status of every usual resident.' He made similar statements linking the NPR and the NRC in parliament on 15 July, 22 July and 23 July of 2014, on 13 May 2015 and 16 November 2016, when he said: 'The preparation of Population Register is a part of preparation of National Register of Indian Citizens under provisions of the Citizenship Act, 1955 read with the Citizenship Rules (2003).'

The other minister of state for home, Hari Chaudhary, repeated, on 21 April and 28 July 2015, Rijiju's statement that the NRC was the 'logical conclusion' of the NPR.

It was now clear that the Government of India was misleading, if not outrightly lying to citizens on this issue, and it was hard to believe even in what the prime minister was saying. The claim that 'no proof and no document' was required for the NPR and that is what made the exercise harmless was a fradulent one. If Muslims did not act now, the NRC would be upon them.

West Bengal, on 17 December, and Kerala, on 20 December, had already halted the collection of NPR data because of protests, which had begun even before the passage of the laws. In the Northeast, particularly in Assam, there was hostility towards the CAA. Many Assamese wanted the NRC, but they did not want the CAA. This was because they did not distinguish between

---

[140] Ibid

'outsiders', i.e., whether they were Muslims or Hindus. They wanted no exemptions to the NRC, which was essentially what the CAA was meant for: to filter out the non-Muslims, leaving only the Muslims to line up and prove their citizenship or be jailed and disenfranchised.

But it was Shaheen Bagh that made the protests a national movement and an international story—in September 2020, *Time* magazine named Bilkis Bano, one of the Shaheen Bagh 'nanis/dadis' (grannies) as one of the 100 most influential individuals in the world. The 82-year-old 'became the symbol of resistance in a nation where the voices of women and minorities were being systematically drowned out', the article on her said.[141]

The Shaheen Bagh model was that of a fixed protest site, continually occupied, showing unbroken resistance. It had a timetable of cultural activity, which made it easy for many to participate. There was music, performances, speeches and lectures through the day and late into the night. The women slept at the protest site. In the morning, a few of them occupied the site in turns. The women attracted solidarity. Fraternity shows itself most visibly, most meaningfully, in protest when those who are not directly concerned join hands and stand up for those who are.

If you felt strongly about the violations and the prejudice in the law and wanted to express solidarity, or even if you were merely curious, there was a place in your city or town you could go to and participate in the resistance. For those who attended and took part, one striking thing was that the movement lost no momentum with time. It could be said with accuracy that in fact the opposite happened. More cities, more students, more universities and more people continued to join in. This required the individuals at each protest site to very quickly learn new skills.

Though there were over 200 sites modelled on Shaheen Bagh across India and in all of its cities (several cities had more than one site), the original remained the focus. It was not only the most prominent but it also radiated defiance because of the road it had blocked. This was merely an irritant—there are alternative routes between Delhi and Uttar Pradesh—but Muslims defying the Modi government in the capital of India was intolerable.

When the sit-in began on 15 December, residents pitched tents on one side of the G.D. Birla Marg, blocking traffic leaving Delhi. The police shut off access to the other side as well, blocking traffic coming into Delhi from Noida. This stretch was used by protestors to display art installations, and also housed a library. Petitions were filed in Delhi High Court and

[141] 'The 100 most influential people of 2020', 22 September 2020, *Time*

the Supreme Court seeking the removal of the protest because of the road block. The government barricaded more roads around the area for no reason other than to amplify the problem.[142] The Delhi and Uttar Pradesh police barricaded entry points to two roads that could have acted as alternative routes. Asked why these alternative routes had been closed, Delhi Police said it was 'a security measure'. The Uttar Pradesh Police claimed they had placed barricades in response to Delhi Police's blockade.

Some of these were removed after the Supreme Court appointed 'interlocutors' (in a dodgy move that had nothing to do with the law) to try and get the protestors to move to a 'designated area'. Wisely, the women of Shaheen Bagh refused. They knew what happened to protests that were sent to the graveyard of Jantar Mantar and other designated areas. They knew also that the interest in them from the media, the government and now the Supreme Court, was in fact because of their current position. They did not move, even when attacked by individuals who opened fire on them.[143] They were inspirational in a way that no other group of urban protestors has been in India's history. Millions marched across India in protests that were linked to Shaheen Bagh. Their slogan was simple: *'Kaghaz nahin dikhayenge'* (We will not show you our papers). Once the masses showed themselves, the polity finally acted.

On 15 January 2020, Kerala challenged the constitutionality of the CAA in the Supreme Court. The following day, the Union removed the linking of PAN numbers in the NPR, in an effort to pretend that the exercise was benign. On 17 January, West Bengal refused to participate in an NPR meeting, and the same day the Union said that putting down parents' details on the NPR form was voluntary and could be done away with. On 28 January, Odisha said it would not include parents' details in the NPR form. On 25 February, the Bihar Assembly, which the BJP leads in an alliance, passed a resolution against the NRC. It was now clear that the NRC had been finished off by the brave protestors. The Covid pandemic gave Modi a way out and it was announced, through a bureaucrat, that the NPR was being postponed. The hostility of the citizenry to government officials entering neighbourhoods and recording details of individuals made it difficult to conduct the census as well—jeopardising one of the government's main sources of good data. For the first time in India since 1881, the decennial census was not conducted in 2021 and there was no indication of when it would be. This was entirely Modi's fault and we have the open threats from Shah to thank. In the absence

---

[142] 'The road that opened near Shaheen Bagh had been blocked by Delhi police, not protestors', 24 February 2020, *Scroll.in*

[143] 'Man opens fire in Delhi's Shaheen Bagh, taken into custody', 6 September 2020, *Hindustan Times*

of the vicious rhetoric that advertised what was in store for India's poor and its Muslims, the NPR exercise may well have been conducted quietly as a first step, leaving the nation in chaos. Shaheen Bagh and its sister protests across India stopped that.

On 24 March, with the pandemic restrictions, the Shaheen Bagh protest was vacated. But it had done the job, and more. The 'No CAA No NPR No NRC' movement produced a generation of talented mobilisers and organisers. Along with the invention of a workable and effective model of protest, this was the other contribution that the movement had made. Hundreds of young women and men, most of them in their twenties, were now activists with experience of how to manage a group of 200 or more people, how to raise money and get and distribute provisions, how to represent themselves before the media, how to spread the word and expand the protest, how to respond on social media and so on. They learned how to campaign.

These protestors were asking only for equality. They had no demand but that they not be harassed by a State intent on repeating the inhumanity of what was being done in Assam. They had no other ask. And yet they were demonised and continued to be demonised by the BJP and its media, merely for the fact that they were Muslims. The Delhi riots that were triggered against the protests were an impotent shriek from those who hated the idea that a group of Muslims led by women had won the most famous civil rights victory of independent India.

The Largest Protest in History

In the chapter 'Good Governance', we left the farmers' protest movement when it reached the outskirts of Delhi at the end of November 2020, having fought its way through water cannons, barricades and dug-up highways (the BJP chief minister of Haryana destroyed and damaged national property to stop the farmers from reaching Delhi, where they would be a nuisance for Modi).

Active demonisation of the protest movement had already begun while it was still limited to Punjab. At the end of November, when the farmers' march was finally stopped on the borders of Delhi, the rhetoric against them was ratcheted up. The BJP general secretary in Uttarakhand on 29 November 2020 called the protestors pro-Pakistan, pro-Khalistan and anti-national. Gujarat's deputy chief minister called the farmers anti-national elements, terrorists, Khalistanis, Communists and pro-China people having pizza and pakodi.[144] Madhya Pradesh chief minister Shivraj Chouhan wrote an

[144] 'Farmers' agitation hijacked by "anti-national" forces: BJP leader', 29 November 2020, PTI

article blaming the protests on vested interests.[145] Law and justice minister Ravishankar Prasad associated them with the mythical 'tukde-tukde' gang.[146]

The BJP vice president in Himachal Pradesh called the protests the work of anti-nationals and middlemen.[147] The same day, the party's spokesman in the state called the protestors miscreants who were the same people behind Shaheen Bagh. On 17 December, the BJP chief minister in Tripura, Biplab Deb, said Maoists were behind the protests,[148] while Uttar Pradesh chief minister Yogi Adityanath claimed Opposition parties were using farmers to fuel unrest in the country because they were unhappy about the construction of a Ram temple in Ayodhya. He also blamed communism and those who wanted to promote disorder and didn't want to see India prosper.[149] BJP national spokesman Sambit Patra called the farmers extremists in the garb of food-providers, another spokesman called them terrorists, and BJP IT cell head Amit Malviya called them anarchists and insurrectionists.[150]

On 17 January 2021, a BJP MP from Uttar Pradesh said the protests were backed by anti-national powers.[151]

A BJP MLA from Gujarat wrote to Amit Shah asking him to hang or shoot the protestors.[152] Even in March 2021, the slander of calling the thousands of protestors fake farmers and terrorists continued.[153]

The New York Times reported that this demonisation cleaved to a pattern from Modi's playbook: first the accusations of foreign infiltration, then police complaints against protest leaders, then the arrests of protesters and

[145] 'New farm laws will free the farmers, help increase their income', 18 December 2020, *The Indian Express*

[146] 'Tukde tukde gang taking advantage of farmer protests: Law minister', 13 December 2020, PTI

[147] 'Anti-national elements leading farmers' protest: Himachal BJP vice-president', 14 December 2020, *Hindustan Times*

[148] 'Top BJP leaders continue to claim that farmers are being "misled", defend laws', 18 December 2020, *TheWire.in*

[149] 'Opposition's Ram temple anger behind farmers' protest: Yogi Adityanath', 17 December 2020, *NDTV*

[150] '"Extremists" in garb of food providers, "insurrection" against government: BJP leaders', 27 January 2021, PTI

[151] 'Anti-national powers backing farmers protesting against farm laws, says BJP MP', 17 January 2021, PTI

[152] 'Farmers protest: BJP MLA demands hanging of leaders involved in January 26 violence, writes to Amit Shah', 27 January 2021, *DNA*

[153] 'These agitators are terrorists or Khalistanis, but not farmers: BJP MP Sakshi Maharaj', 15 March 2021, *The Times of India*

journalists, then the blocking of internet access in places where demonstrators gathered. All this was akin to India's actions in Kashmir, and against the protestors of Shaheen Bagh and elsewhere.[154]

Through this demonisation, the Samyukta Kisan Morcha or United Farmers Front, comprising about 40 unions, remained united. The government and the media made much of a couple of individuals from these groups withdrawing from the protests, but the grouping itself remained undivided. Thirty-two of the unions came from Punjab and, about half of all the protestors came from a single group, led by a former soldier named Joginder Singh from the village of Ugrahan in the district of Sangrur. This group, which mostly comprised small farmers from the southern Punjab region of Malwa, was stationed at Tikri. About 50,000 strong, it had a large component of women, which set it apart from the other major site, at Singhu, also about 50,000 strong and comprising farmers slightly better-off than the ones at Tikri.[155] The protestors remained on the highway in a parked convoy of tractors 20 kms long, and they spent their nights in the open-bed trailers known as trolleys.

The government and large sections of the media treated the individuals of the Morcha like some rustic rabble. Their demands were seen as and portrayed as being extreme, uncompromising and ignorant. They did not understand the laws Modi had passed, the BJP emphasised. Headlines like 'Protesting farmers haven't "properly understood" new farm laws, says NITI Aayog Member',[156] 'Farmers should understand farm laws, govt dedicated to helping farmers: Nitin Gadkari',[157] and 'Farmers don't understand farm laws, are being misled: Hema Malini'[158] were common.

Let us see if these statements hold true.

The Morcha did not change its demands, which had been given to the Modi government in the form of a charter. This document made eight demands of the Union:

1) Repeal the law that allowed tax-free trade of agricultural produce outside of regulated mandis (The Farmers Produce, Trade and Commerce Promotion and Facilitation Act)

---

[154] 'Modi's response to farmer protests in India stir fears of a pattern', 3 February 2021, *The New York Times*

[155] 'Tikri, Singhu are worlds apart', 13 December 2020, *The Tribune*

[156] 29 November 2020, PTI

[157] 15 December 2020, *Mint*

[158] 14 January 2021, *Hindustan Times*

- provide a guarantee for the Minimum Support Price (MSP)[159]
- continue the procurement through mandis
- ensure distribution of wheat and rice through the 5.2 lakh Fair Price Shops across India
- restrict multinational companies and Indian corporates from entering the agriculture sector

2) Repeal the law allowing contract farming—The Farmers (Empowerment and Protection) Agreement of Price Assurance and Farm Services Act

- implement the Swaminathan Report's recommendations and apply its formula for MSP
- prohibit multinational companies and Indian corporates from buying, leasing and contracting land owned by farmers or the state
- eliminate the interference of corporates in agricultural input and make these affordable

3) Repeal the law amending the Essential Commodities Act, decriminalising the hoarding of agricultural produce

4) Withdraw the amendments proposed in the Electricity Ordinance 2020, which would end power subsidies and replace them with a cash subsidy

5) Eliminate the taxes on fuel to align the price of petrol and diesel to international crude prices

6) Repeal the Straw Pollution Ordinance 2020, which criminalises the burning of stubble. This takes place between 15 October and 15 November to clear the residue of the rice crop on the land before seeding it with wheat. The burning is said to be one of the causes of Delhi's air pollution

7) Stop legislative encroachment into the domain of states—agriculture is a state subject and not a Central one—and decentralise powers

8) Unconditionally release those jailed in the Bhima Koregaon case and for the CAA protests

These were the eight demands on the charter which was handed to the government. The Swaminathan Report referred to in point number 2 had recommended[160] that:

---

[159] Minimum Support Price or MSP, first introduced in 1966, is the price at which the government purchases grain directly from the farmers to be distributed through the public distribution system or PDS. MSP ostensibly covers 23 different crops, including the grains bajra, wheat, maize, paddy, barley, ragi and jowar; the pulses tur, chana, masur, urad and moong; the oilseeds safflower, mustard, niger seed, soyabean, groundnut, sesame and sunflower; and the commercial crops raw jute, cotton, copra and sugarcane. But government intervention was, in reality, quite modest and limited to a handful of crops ('Quixsplained: What is MSP and how is it determined?', 7 October 2020, *The Indian Express*)

[160] 'Swaminathan Report: National Commission on Farmers', prsindia.org

- surplus and wasteland be distributed to landless farmers (50 per cent of rural households held only 3 per cent of land)
- the diversion of agricultural land and forests to the corporate sector be ended
- grazing rights and seasonal access to forests of tribals and pastoralists, and their access to common property resources be ensured
- National Land Use Advisory Service be established to link land-use decisions with ecological, meteorological and marketing factors on a location and season-specific basis
- a mechanism be set up to regulate the sale of agricultural land based on the quantum of land, nature of proposed use and category of buyer
- farmers be given an MSP at 50 per cent above the cost of production calculated by the Commission for Agricultural Costs and Prices and referred to as 'C2'. This C2 was calculated by adding expenses in cash or kind—seeds, fertilisers, pesticides, hired labour, fuel, irrigation—to the cost of unpaid family labour and to the cost of rent, interest and depreciation of fixed capital assets. Fifty per cent of this total cost was to be added to it to arrive at the MSP to be paid to farmers. Currently, the cost of rent of their land and interest on capital were not included in the MSP.

In 2004, prime minister Manmohan Singh asked M.S. Swaminathan, the man behind India's Green Revolution, to put together a series of reports and recommendations on agriculture and MSP and this is what he had come up with. Through this formula, Swaminathan sought to give India's farmers a dignified wage. Government surveys showed that the average Indian farmer's income was Rs 77,124 in a year, or Rs 6,427 per month. Their monthly expenditure was Rs 6,223.[161] These numbers give us an indication of how desperate the situation of agriculturists, the majority of India's population, is. Even in Punjab, where the farmer was said to be better off, the average monthly income of a farm household before expenses was only Rs 18,059.

The eight demands were not the product of ignorance, as the government had said. They were the result of understanding, in depth, issues that concerned the farmers and their families and their future. Indeed, the farmers had read the three main laws not just individually but also in conjunction to arrive at the Modi government's intent. This was, they concluded, to end the mandis, weaken the PDS system, load the legal framework against the farmer

---

[161] 'How much do Indian farmers actually earn?', 11 January 2021, *India Today*

by denying access to the justice system (the law said farmers could not move court against a corporate that reneged or defaulted), allow the private sector to engage farmers at an individual level, decriminalise hoarding of grain and create monopolies.

Trade would naturally shift away in time from the mandis, which were taxed and regulated, to the private marketplaces. The government saying it would not end the mandi system, as it did, would not change the trajectory that the farmers saw the laws taking. In places where the mandi system had been ended, private markets had worsened the position of the farmers. Bihar, under Nitish Kumar, shut down its entire state-run mandi system in 2006. This also put paid to the MSP in the state. Paddy sold for around Rs 950 per quintal (100 kilos) in Bihar, while the minimum support price was Rs 1,868.[162] The average monthly income for a farmer in Bihar was Rs 3,557.[163] By scrapping the mandi system and abdicating on governance, the state had harmed Bihar's farm households.

The Morcha read into the government's dissembling on the issue of MSP—Modi said he would guarantee 'in writing' that MSP would continue, but did not agree to making the guarantee legal—the atrophying and eventual ending of the MSP system everywhere. Their assessment that the individual small farmer, handicapped further by being forced to take disputes with the corporate to the collector rather than to court, would be disadvantaged and suffer is not the result of their ignorance but their experience of how the world works.

Their demands were the result of their analysis and this is why they did not shift position from the first round of talks, held on 1 December 2020, to the last one on 22 January 2021, at which point the government said it would meet the farmers only if they agreed to discuss its proposed suspension of the laws.

If the government felt that their concerns were based on ignorance, it would stand to reason that it was either the government itself that had not read its owns laws (Modi was likely to have been shown the laws through a few PowerPoint slides) and understood the implications. Or, this was the inescapable conclusion, it was lying.

The stoutness of the farmers' resistance and their refusal to compromise must be seen in this light. A government that was demonising them, that was

---

[162] 'Bihar scrapped APMC Act, mandi system 14 years ago; here's what it did to farmers', 7 December 2020, *Down to Earth*

[163] 'Rahul Gandhi attacks government over farm incomes', 11 December 2020, PTI

laughing away their concerns, was also claiming to be negotiating with them in good faith.

The farmer groups' leadership attended the protests together. The trade unions that bound them together and made mass mobilisation easier, their knowledge of their domain and understanding of the laws was matched with the brotherhood of the faith that the majority of them came from. It was the brotherhood of Sikhism that resulted in a negotiation that took place with all 32 of the Punjab bodies being represented at all of the meetings with Modi's ministers. They even refused the hospitality of the State and brought their own food with them.

After it made the initial show of defiance, the government began to soften and offered tweaks as a compromise. Private marketplaces would be taxed if the state government wanted; MSP 'would continue'; the laws on stubble and electricity would be taken back; access to the justice system would be given to farmers. The government even agreed to 'suspend' all the laws for 18 months—effectively killing them because the period after the suspension would be too close to the next Lok Sabha election of 2024. But there was a refusal to officially repeal the laws, to legally guarantee MSP and to accept the C2 formula. The first, repealing the laws, was not acceptable to Modi because, analysts concluded, it would damage his strongman image, erode the idea that he led a tough administration and produce further mass movements.[164]

If this was accurate, then Modi, having already put the laws away, continued with the charade that they were still alive and looked away as the farmers' protest continued and tens of thousands of people remained on the street for months, many of them dying.

And through all this the Morcha remained calmly firm on its position.

Much was made of the fact that most of the farmers were from Punjab and Haryana, insinuating that this was, in that sense, not a national but a regional movement. This was proved wrong by events in 2021, when the largest gatherings against the laws took place in Uttar Pradesh and there were protests around the country. But it is important to understand why Punjab dominated the opposition to the laws.

The Green Revolution, through which rice and wheat productivity climbed in India and made it self-sufficient in food grains, happened largely in Punjab and Haryana. More than 80 per cent of India's farmers are

---

[164] 'Modi's dilemma: Will farmer protests be his Thatcher or Anna Hazare moment?', 5 December 2020, *Business Standard*

subsistence agriculturists, meaning they eat what they grow and have little or no surplus. It was the farmer of Punjab and Haryana who had played a large part in the Green Revolution and it was their mandis which were well-organised, their surplus grain which was procured most efficiently by the government for the PDS. They had the most to lose here. The issue was not that MSP was unimportant because it was not paid out to farmers in other states; the issue was why it was not the system elsewhere. It was State failure. MSP was unimportant to many farmers outside Punjab and Haryana because they did not have the productivity or sufficient land to produce a surplus.

The farmers' reference to the continued distribution of food grains through the PDS (in point number 1) was re-emphasised by Joginder Singh Ugrahan in an interview.[165]

This concern was based on reality. As early as 2015, Modi had determined that India spent too much on food security.[166] He asked bureaucrats to prepare a plan that would limit access to subsidised food grains to 40 per cent of the population. This would be down from the 67 per cent mandated by the Food Security Act of 2013. A quarter of India's people who were receiving the food grains would be cut out. In that year, the government spent Rs 1.25 lakh crore on the consumer food subsidy. In 2017–18 it fell to Rs 1.05 lakh crore.[167] The slashing came through subterfuge. The Budget allocation in 2016–17 and 2018–19 was about Rs 1.4 lakh crore and Rs 1.6 lakh crore respectively, but money was not actually spent.

In 2019–20, the allocation (meaning the grand announcement) was Rs 1.92 lakh crore and the actual spend was Rs 1.15 lakh crore. Adjusted for inflation and with the population having risen, the cut Modi desired had been achieved and perhaps even exceeded. In time the desire to cut the food budget predictably ran into the problem of the economic crisis. The number of poor Indians dependent on subsidised food continued to rise through the Modi era and by the end of 2021 was 80 crore individuals (60 per cent of the population) getting five kilos of grain and a kilo of dal a month.[168]

There was every reason to believe, if one were a farmer, that not only was there a plan behind the farm laws that was aimed at the PDS and the MSP but that plan was in execution mode. This is why, through the demonisation

[165] 'Farmers protest: BKU Ekta Ugrahan ke president Joginder Singh Ugrahan ka interview', 12 December 2020, *Lallantop*

[166] 'Modi govt readies to cut flab out of UPA's flagship food security law', 2 February 2015, *Hindustan Times*

[167] 'Demand for grant analysis: Food and public distribution', prsindia.org

[168] 'The Pradhan Mantri Garib Kalyan Yojana/Package', india.gov.in

and the harassment, they did not flinch. They showed their quirkiness and their spirit by negotiating with Modi's ministers in innovative ways: for hours they would not speak but instead hold up placards in response to questions or proposals. 'Yes or No?' read one of them after they were convinced early on that the government was not negotiating in good faith but merely procrastinating with the intent of tiring them out and hoping to see the protests dissipate. The Morcha's leaders had predicted this and, as early as December, said that they had come prepared to stay till the summer and beyond. They rotated their presence: those who left for their villages after a few weeks were replaced by others who stayed for a few weeks in turn. The supply lines for food and essentials were robust and, given that they had their own means of transport—the trolley and the tractor, they were self-sufficient in a way few other Indian communities can be.

Aware of the reality of media in India, they also began a newspaper of their own, *Trolley Times*, circulated at the protest sites. They also opened social media accounts and began to broadcast live the events from the stages they had erected on the highway. They attracted support internationally. For one, their cause—the hardy peasant standing up to corporate greed—was popular and their protest both massive and striking. Celebrities jumped in and discovered how vicious the social media space in India is. Tweets from the singer Rihanna, climate activist Greta Thunberg and porn star Mia Khalifa became front page news and also, more ridiculously, earned them finger-wagging lectures from Jaishankar's foreign ministry[169] and pious and identical pushback responses from Indian celebrities like Sachin Tendulkar and Akshay Kumar in coordinated fashion.[170]

Most importantly, the Morcha received strong and sustained backing from parliamentarians in the UK and Canada (where there were more Sikhs—18—in the parliament of 338—than in India, which had only 13 Sikhs in the Lok Sabha). An intervention from Canadian leader Justin Trudeau came on 1 December 2020, when he expressed his concern at what was happening in India. The Modi government called this 'unacceptable interference' and summoned Canada's high commissioner to tell him that 'such actions, if continued, would have a seriously damaging impact on ties'.[171]

---

[169] 'MEA calls Rihanna, Greta Thunberg's remark on farmers' protest "inaccurate, irresponsible"', 3 February 2021, *Zee News*

[170] 'Rihanna versus Bollywood: Twitter influencers and the Indian farmers' protest'. 8 February 2021, University of Michigan, umich.edu

[171] 'India summons Canadian envoy over Trudeau's remark on farmers' right to protest', 4 December 2020, *TheWire.in*

The very next day, Trudeau again spoke out in support of the farmers' movement.[172]

Trudeau would, in fact, raise the matter directly with Modi on a telephone call the two had on 10 February.[173] The Indian briefing on the call did not refer to this. When the Canadians put it out, the Indian foreign ministry spokesman said Trudeau had actually 'commended efforts of government of India to choose path of dialogue'. Just as it had not calibrated the response that the citizenship laws would elicit abroad, the government did not anticipate the pushback here either.

Its attitude was contemptuous and mendacious. The media was told the farmers were merely intent on acting in truculent fashion and were not proposing anything. This was untrue. As early as 8 December 2020, the Morcha wrote up a draft law which entitled every farmer throughout India to a Guaranteed Remunerative MSP (GRMSP) by right, against the sale of any agricultural commodity.[174] In all agricultural markets in India, including the Agricultural Produce Market Committees (APMCs), the auction price for any agricultural commodity would begin at the GRMSP as the 'floor' price.

The Morcha's draft proposed that no trader, including one who entered into a contract farming agreement, could purchase an agricultural commodity below the GRMSP, and to do so would be to commit a cognisable offence. The GRMSP would be arrived at by a new body, the Central Farmers Agricultural Costs and Remunerative Price Guarantee Commission. GRMSP would be based on C2, adding 50 per cent as margin.

It was quite untrue that the farmers were merely intent on sabotage and had nothing constructive to offer, as the government and its supporters kept insisting.[175]

Modi had misread the issue. He had no understanding of the farmers' resolve and what a movement like this would bring in its wake. An early sign that this was not an ordinary protest was that unusual point number 8 of the Morcha's charter. The text reads: 'Unconditional release of arrested pro-democracy intellectuals and anti-CAA activists. Stop suppressing dissent.'

---

[172] 'Canada will always stand for the rights of peaceful protests and human rights anywhere in the world', 5 December 2020, *TheWire.in*

[173] 'Trudeau commended Modi govt's efforts with farmers': MEA responds to Canada raising protests', 12 February 2020, *TheWire.in*

[174] 'Farmers draw up draft law for govt, demand guaranteed MSP & to make purchase below that a crime', 8 December 2020, *ThePrint.in*

[175] 'Farmers don't know what they want, someone else behind protests: Hema Malini', 13 January 2021, *The Week*

Why would protestors on the subcontinent, where power is skewed disproportionately away from the citizenry and towards the State, insert demands that were unrelated to their movement? Why would they do this particularly with a government that prided itself in demonising those who said such things and those who stood in their support?

Because the Morcha believed in the things they were asking for. It may interest readers to know that all 32 of the Punjab groups signed on to the entire charter, including this demand, which was added to the charter in the very first internal meeting of the 32 farmer organisations held in Moga in the third week of September.[176] The farmers also raised their demand for the release of the activists in their meeting with the Union agriculture minister in November.

Through the protests, the farmers warmly accepted the support they got from abroad and were never defensive about it. When individuals backing them got into trouble, the Morcha's support of them was full-throated. One such individual was the young climate change activist Disha Ravi, who was arrested for sedition for sharing an internet 'toolkit'—a fancy word for guidebook—on peaceful protest. The action was spun as a global conspiracy against Modi and India, including by Modi himself.[177] But the Morcha did not feel the need to be defensive and stood by her and others. This encouraged political parties also to stand by Indians being abused with the usual slander in the usual sections of the mass media.

On 10 December, Human Rights Day, the Morcha's Tikri protest held an event, and on the stage were the photographs of Gautam Navlakha, Varavara Rao, Sudha Bharadwaj, Vernon Gonsalves, Arun Ferreira, Umar Khalid and others jailed in the Bhima Koregaon case and for the anti-CAA protests.

'What did people like Gautam Navlakha or Sudha Bharadwaj do? They showed how poor people in remote areas are living under extreme stress and how they were unfairly treated by the governments. There are others who show how people of Kashmir live in constant fear of the security forces. We believe that the Modi government put all of them in prison only to silence them. It is our responsibility, then, to speak up for the citizens,' Ugrahan said.[178]

---

[176] 'Jailed rights activists' release part of charter of demands, say unions', 11 December 2020, *The Tribune*

[177] 'India must save itself from "Foreign Destructive Ideology": PM Modi in Rajya Sabha', 8 February 2021, *The Indian Express*

[178] '"It's time we speak up for each other": Farmers' group supports political prisoners', 11 December 2020, *TheWire.in*

His BKU Ekta Ugrahan had launched protests in 2018, after the arrest of Navlakha. It had mass mobilisation programmes against the CAA, and Ugrahan himself attended the Shaheen Bagh sit-in.[179]

The timeline of events towards the end of 2020 and beginning of 2021 resembles what Hollywood calls a train wreck in slow motion. At some point the laws had actually already died but the farce was kept going because of ego. The farmers continued because, once demobilised, it was not easy to again deploy thousands on the ground. They had little faith in the polity's ability to stand up for them once their resistance on the street had dissipated.

On 16 December, the Supreme Court stepped in and spoke of brokering the deadlock through a panel it would put together.

On 30 December, the Union agreed to drop the amendments in the Electricity Ordinance (Point 4) and to exempt farmers from the stubble burning penalty (Point 6).

On 4 January, Reliance Industries said it had 'absolutely no plans' to enter contract farming.[180]

On 6 January the court observed there was 'no improvement' but the government spoke of 'healthy discussions'.

On 12 January, the Chief Justice said he was 'extremely disappointed' with the Modi government, that he didn't know 'why there is an insistence on implementation of the law', that he had given the Union 'a long rope' but it had 'failed' and 'not been effective'. The court said it would get a former Chief Justice to step in and solve the issue. It asked the Union to stay the laws. The Morcha responded by saying stays were temporary and what they sought was repeal.

On 13 January, the court 'stayed' the laws (a dubious action—it was uncertain what this meant because no legal ground was given). The media reported that the government was relieved as this gave it a way out without having officially surrendered to the Morcha.[181] The stay addressed Points 1, 2 and 3.

The court, also dubiously, set up a committee of four individuals, all of whom had publicly expressed support, including in published pieces, for the farm laws, to 'evaluate' the laws and give it a report in two months. One of the four immediately dropped out and said he wanted no part of the committee and was with the farmers now.

---

[179] 'Ugrahan wears his politics on his sleeve: "Called us Pak, now Naxals"', 13 December 2020, *The Indian Express*

[180] Media statement, 4 January 2021, RIL.com

[181] 'SC stays farm laws: Court ruling a way out for govt, minister calls on all to honour order', 13 January 2021, *The Indian Express*

On 20 January, the Union itself offered to put the laws on hold for 18 months. The farmers voted on this and it was reported by journalist Sandeep Singh that the farmers rejected the offer in a narrow majority decision. All accepted the vote and the Morcha remained unified.

On 26 January, the farmers held a tractor rally where the majority of tractors followed the route agreed with the police. However, a few went into Delhi and individuals hoisted the Khalsa flag at the Red Fort, though they left the Indian flag flying on the primary mast. The government expressed much shock and horror and likened the event to the insurrection at the US Capitol in Washington,[182] but except for the usual media support, it did not generate much negative sentiment against the farmers.

On 27 January, the police filed a series of FIRs and moved to evict the protest at Ghazipur, led by Uttar Pradesh farm leader Rakesh Tikait (whose father had led the previously largest farmer agitation, bringing hundreds of thousands of farmers to Delhi in 1988). The police also booked the academic and activist Yogendra Yadav, journalists Rajdeep Sardesai and Siddharth Varadarajan, the editor and owners of *The Caravan* magazine and Congressman Shashi Tharoor over their tweets on a farmer's death.[183] Till this time, Tikait had had a minor role in the Morcha which was dominated, as we have noted, by the Punjabis. When the police came to his protest site, Tikait broke down in public and said the BJP wanted to destroy the farmers and that he would die but would not give up and would not leave the protest. The Jats of Uttar Pradesh, till this time passive, rallied to him in emotion and huge gatherings called mahapanchayats were held across north India.[184] This led to the BJP assessing that its fortunes on dozens of seats across the cow belt were being affected and it put paid to the laws, removing any doubt that the laws were finished.

The protests would continue months into 2021, but Modi, having determined that he would not be able to enforce his laws, had moved on.[185] This then was the common thread through the years that he went after civil

---

[182] 'India equates Red Fort chaos with Capitol riots after US remarks', 5 February 2021, *Al Jazeera*

[183] 'FIR against Shashi Tharoor, journalists including Rajdeep Sardesai over tweets on farmer's death in Bengaluru', 30 January 2021, *Deccan Herald*

[184] 'Rakesh Tikait helped BJP win over Jats in 2014, his tears have now turned them against Modi', 4 February 2021, *ThePrint.in*

[185] In July 2021, the Modi government reversed position on the Essential Commodities Act and banned hoarding of pulses, undoing the farm laws. 'Stock limits on pulses: Govt order flies in face of farm law', 4 July 2021, *The Indian Express*

society. India's leader took pleasure in bullying those working hardest to uphold constitutional values and representing the poor, resorting to name-calling and planted evidence to target them. But he ran away from the fight each time civil society stood up to him. It was the Dalit, the Muslim woman, Adivasi and the Sikh farmer who made the BJP turn tail.

OUTRO

Narendra Modi had the political capital, the adoration of crores and no opposition. He could, if he had had the plan and wanted to, sell and push through transformational change. He had the will, but he had no plan.

He spent his capital on arbitrary and dramatic flourishes. He whiled away the time and opportunity he had earned through his popularity. He did little with it even if you were to ignore the damage. This goes back to the core idea of Hindutva and what it stands for and what it seeks.

Modi's handicap in running India once he had conquered it was that Hindutva's masters had left him no theory of State, no real ideology and neither advice nor direction on what to do and not do in government. Mobilising Hindus against India's minorities produced polarisation, which made voter choice easy and it brought the BJP to power. But what were they supposed to do once they got control of the government? That was not known because there was no doctrine.

V.D. Savarkar's book, *Hindutva*, merely defined Indian as Hindu. And because Muslim and Christian could never mean Hindu, India's religious minorities could never be Indian either. But this was only Savarkar's opinion. How was this exclusion to be effected in law when India became independent and Hindus took over the State? This Savarkar did not say because, written in the early 1920s, the work does not anticipate the end of the Raj and an independent India.

The individual referred to as the party's ideologue, Deendayal Upadhyaya, died in 1968 and left behind no book. Four speeches of his given in Bombay in 1965 have been published as the work *Integral Humanism*. The BJP calls it the party's 'basic philosophy', but it is such gibberish that nothing can be done with its words by a government.[1]

The specific instruction came in a different speech, this one in Pune,

---

[1] For a fuller analysis, see the chapter 'Hindutva's garbled mantras', *Our Hindu Rashtra*, 2020, Westland Publications

the same year as *Integral Humanism*. Upadhyaya said: 'Our quarrel is not with Mohammed, nor with Mullas and Maulavis. Our quarrel is with the way Muslims behave, coupling political ambition with religious zeal. This is why this war is not religious but political ... There is only one way to defeat Muslim bigotry, and it is to politically defeat them. That is the real solution of the Muslim problem. So long as they are not politically defeated, the rot will continue to grow. Only such a defeat will make them have second thoughts and the process of Hindu-Muslim cooperation will begin.'[2]

This was the task for Modi and we can say conclusively that in his terms, India's Muslims have been politically defeated and excluded from power and from influence as fully as possible. But the question remains: so what are Hindus to do after they have put India's Muslims in their place? These instructions Upadhyaya did not leave Modi.

The fact is that the RSS did not and does not think about this because it considers it unimportant. There is no text on Hindutva economics or on Hindutva strategic affairs.

There is nothing in the manifestos of the Jana Sangh that has consistency or anything discernible as an economic ideology or any ideas about how Hindutva would influence the State. The manifestos are a collection of rambling and inchoate pronouncements.

The Jana Sangh stood for mechanisation of agriculture and then immediately opposed it in 1954 (because the use of tractors would mean bullocks would get slaughtered). It wanted industry to calibrate its use of automation not based on efficiency but how many more individuals it could hire. It did not explain why a businessman should or would want to add cost rather than reduce it. In 1971 it said it wanted no automation in any industry except defence and aerospace.

In 1954, and again in 1971, it sought to cap the monthly incomes of all Indians at Rs 2,000 and wanted the State to appropriate everything earned above that sum.

It wanted residential bungalows to be limited to a size of 1,000 square yards.[3] In 1957, it spoke of 'revolutionary changes' it would bring without saying what these were, and in the very next manifesto dropped the reference without explanation. All this is, of course, because they were responding to Congress manifestos of the time and had nothing real to offer of their own. Nor did they think they needed to: with a national voteshare that till 1989

---

[2] 'Merchant of hate', 11 November 2016, *Frontline*
[3] 'Policies and Manifestoes, Bharatiya Jana Sangh 1952–1980', 2005, published by Bharatiya Janata Party

was in the single digits, the party knew it would not be in power, would not need to implement a policy and, therefore, was free to say whatever came to mind.

The Jana Sangh did not have any particular strategic view of the world and India's place in it besides saying that India should be friends with all who were friendly and tough on those who were not. India should seek a place in the Security Council but there was no reference to why or what India's role would be, or how its influence and strategic options would increase if it got this position. It offered no path for getting to the Security Council. Entitlement would apparently get India there.[4]

There was no continuity in the way the Jana Sangh thought about such things. Its 1957 manifesto opened with a grim warning of a threat emanating from a Pakistan–Portuguese alliance. The 1962 manifesto, coming after the 'police action' in Goa against Portuguese rule, made no reference to this alliance but opened with an admonition against Nehru for losing the war to China. The 1972 document made no reference to Indira's war in Bangladesh, which had been created out of Pakistan only weeks earlier. In the previous year's manifesto, Jana Sangh wanted to take India out of the Commonwealth, without saying why or to what end, and instead said it would align India to Southeast Asia, again without explaining how and to what end.

The Jana Sangh's idea of national security came through such demands as compulsory military training for youth, a two-year compulsory draft for all males, removal of licences for possessing muzzle-loading guns (an eighteenth-century weapon), expansion of the National Cadet Corps (NCC) and the manufacture of nuclear weapons.[5]

In 1954, the Jana Sangh said it would repeal the first amendment which imposed 'reasonable restrictions' on the freedom of speech, assembly and association. It stood for absolute individual freedom. It also opposed preventive detention, the principle on which UAPA and all anti-terror laws were founded. What the party once opposed as undemocratic it not only accepted but championed when it took power. The Jana Sangh/BJP did not think about any of these things at depth because they had no interest in much other than putting Muslims in their place.

Upadhyaya wanted the Constitution to be amended to abolish the states. He said the creation of linguistic and other states had produced 'Bihar

---

[4] 'PM Modi lashes out at UN over India's permanent seat, says "How long must we wait?"', 26 September 2020, *Republic*

[5] 'Policies and manifestoes', Bharatiya Jana Sangh, 1952–1980, Bharatiya Janata Party, 2005

Mata, Banga Mata, Punjab Mata, Kannada Mata, Tamil Mata'.[6] This was unacceptable to Upadhyaya, who wanted only one legislative body, the Centre in Delhi. What would connect it administratively to the village if there were no states? This he did not think about because someone else would figure out governance. His concern was the indivisibility of Bharat Mata.

RSS chief M.S. Golwalkar died in 1973, when the Jana Sangh was a minor party, having never won a state on its own and with only a single digit vote share nationally. He spent his life building a nationwide network of Hindu males who were influenced by pracharaks.

The pracharak's prachar was basic and reductive: India great, Hindus ancient, Muslims bad, Pakistan evil.[7]

Bharat Mata ki jai!

Even on the subject they obsessed over and were most passionate about, the followers of Hindutva can be accused of not applying much thought.

India had 20 crore Muslims. How were they going to be permanently suppressed? And to what end? Even if they were, then after that what? There was no consideration of that. It was a single-point agenda if there ever was one.

RSS pracharaks did their preaching to the converted. The RSS did not train one to solve difficult problems. RSS work does not require reading, absorption and analysis. A vertical structure with a top-down authoritarian hierarchy does not even require management skills beyond a point. The RSS connection to neighbourhood-level offices at a national scale produced one advantage and that was a capacity for quick and assured mobilisation before and during elections.

The Sangh's training was in 'organisation'. Of what? Of meetings and events of the cadre. Modi's training came at the shakha, whose importance Modi has described in his writing:

Shakha as life mantra[8]

In February 1946, Guruji Golwalkar was in Calcutta. Some eminent citizens invited him to tea. At the event, one of them, a doctor, said to Guruji: 'I agree with what the Sangh aims to achieve. I have a problem with the means. What's the point of all this physical stuff—playing kabaddi and the like? How can they ever assist in achieving those lofty goals?'

---

[6] 'Integral Humanism, Third Speech, 24 April 1965', bjpgujarat.org

[7] This reduction is also reflected in Modi's own speeches.

[8] Author's translation of Modi's work *Jyotipunj*—'Modi's biography of Golwalkar suggests RSS leader was vital influence', 9 July 2019, *Scroll.in*

> Guruji laughingly asked him: 'Doctor saheb! What's your master drug in allopathy?'
>
> The doctor replied: 'Penicillin.'
>
> Guruji asked: 'What is penicillin made from?'
>
> The doctor said: 'Everyone knows that it's made from foodstuff so rotten that nobody can stand its smell.'
>
> Guruji said [text in English in the original]: 'Does it mean that even the worst thing can yield the best results in the hands of experts?'
>
> Doctor saheb said: 'Yes.'
>
> Guruji said: 'And here we are the experts in the science of organisation.'
>
> Once, all the pracharaks had gathered in Sindi near Wardha. It was so arranged that all the senior pracharaks had to serve at mealtimes and the turn came of Pu Pandit Deendayal Upadhyaya. He was given charge of the basket of chapatis. As he approached Guruji, the basket fell out of his hand and he was flustered. Guruji laughed and said: 'Have you stopped attending the shakha?' He always believed that the shakha provided the energy and spirit for life's challenges.'

What science could there possibly have been to the regular playing of kabaddi, twirling of lathis, singing of songs and collective shouting of slogans? There was none.

Having never been to college (Modi's degree in 'entire political science' is from a correspondence course),[9] and with little interest in educating himself, Modi was further hamstrung. He was left to govern by instinct.

The rumoured unease the RSS was said to feel at Modi's manner of functioning was not expressible in any concrete words. This was because there was no real problem with his lack of substance, only one with his excessive style. The RSS, an unelected group led by a male appointed for life and with absolute authority to appoint his successor, could hardly accuse Modi of autocratic behaviour. An acquaintance met an RSS leader and asked whether Modi's overbearing style troubled them. The leader considered the question and replied: 'Would we rather be irrelevant under Congress or irrelevant under our own man?' This is why they let Modi be.

'Violence is the midwife of every old society pregnant with a new one,' wrote Hannah Arendt channeling Marx.[10] Hindutva could produce the violence, and it did so effectively under Advani and Modi, but it did not birth a new society. In power, it merely damaged the old one.

The Modi era has witnessed the destructive effect of vacuous charisma on

---

[9] 'Delhi University authenticates Modi's BA degree', 10 May 2016, *TheWire.in*

[10] *Between Past and Future*, 1968, Penguin Books

the entire polity. Consider the economy, judiciary, civil society, democracy, India's global image, neighbourhood relations, employment, free speech and civil liberties, communal harmony and federalism.

How many of these has Modi left stronger than he found them in 2014?

None. Through the Modi years, India's standing as an inclusive, diverse nation with an independent judiciary, rule of law and free media was degraded as the indices exposed. India's economic growth sputtered and it ceased to be the leader even on the subcontinent on this front. Consequently, it lost hard and soft power. India's foreign policy and national security were harmed because of the cavalier manner in the way they were run. Under Modinomics, India became poorer per capita than Bangladesh and suffered reversals in vital parameters like children's health. It became more polluted, more inward-looking and more regressive. It became less of a liberal democracy with guaranteed freedoms for its citizens than it ever was.

India has likely forever missed the opportunity to join the ranks of the developed countries, through the timing of its demographic growth coinciding with the failures of the Modi years. It will likely remain at the low end of the middle income trap. Fewer Indians were working and fewer looking for work under Modi than before him. What was meant to be a demographic dividend turned out to be a demographic disaster.

There has been no contrition, no acknowledgement and no accountability for the damage he has caused, even where it is most apparent—in the economy. Since there was no acceptance of failure, there was no analysis of failure and so there was no corrective. Modi had no vision for Indian society other than to reject inclusion and the constant manufacture of laws targeting minorities. These laws had no purpose other than harassment.

After damage was deliberately and gratuitously caused, he moved on. Repair was less important than pretending something hadn't happened. It secured the image; the damage was acceptable. Healing was never considered because the social damage caused was deliberate and produced out of gleeful malice.

India has not had such a figure as Modi. Messianic, full of self-belief and so adored for his charisma and charm. So full of himself. Offering wisdom endlessly and not liable for the consequences of his actions. Failure on the economy, on national security, across a range of social indicators and multiple indices is not his fault. It is the fault of India that it has not lived up to Modi's genius.

As prime minister, he has possessed an unusual mix of messianism and incompetence. Unusual in the sense that, while such individuals may be elected into office, they usually do not get a long crack at it once their flaws are exposed through data and fact. But Modi has survived and thrived through it all; his failures did not touch his image and certainly they did not touch his ego.

He belongs to the category Indians call Godman. His endless babbling is itself sufficient as achievement. Like Bal Thackeray, his core talent is that of a stand-up. He can entertain people for a set and then return with fresh material. Expecting actual delivery instead of mere entertainment is unfair. The material he produces is attractive in a low-intellect way, and appealing to those who like histrionics and strong emotion. Intellectually, it is barren.

Besides all the ethical problems Hindutva majoritarianism produces, the fact is that it is hollow. This is not a moral judgement. It has nothing to offer and has never claimed to offer anything, as its own texts show.

This is why Hindutva's most charismatic leader, trusted by hundreds of millions, given absolute power to take control of the State and no resistance from either the Opposition or the judiciary, has delivered the performance he has.

If the whole enterprise seems a confused hotchpotch, it is because that is what it is. To this, add a leader with a strong desire to do something great but no real idea of what, with little ability to grasp complexity and no patience for granularity.[11]

The mercantile mindset of the stereotyped Gujarati is marked by a sense of modesty, accountability, pragmatism and a low profile. The empty heroism and chest-thumping of Modi can be considered as alien to this ethos.

Modi constantly complains about being 'hated' by those who opposed his politics or see through him, and aches to be recognised. He named the world's largest stadium after himself. He was willing, as prime minister, to accept the 'Philip Kotler Presidential award'—a bauble not given to anyone before or since. This was in recognition, apparently, of his 'outstanding leadership for the nation'; 'selfless service towards India'; the 'extraordinary economic, social and technological changes in the country'; and, less convincingly, for the success of Make in India.[12] The adjectives reveal the laziness of thought,

---

[11] What bored him usually didn't get priority. In 2021, almost half (20 out of 45) of all universities did not have a vice chancellor because files with the shortlists were pending with the PMO. This left these institutions unable to take important academic decisions, recruit permanent teachers or implement key features of the National Education Policy. 'Twenty central universities left without a regular vice-chancellor', 31 May 2021, *The Telegraph*

[12] 'Prime minister Modi receives Philip Kotler award', 14 January 2019, PTI

if any, that went into the citation. Kotler, a retired professor of management, could not himself be bothered to show up to present the award, and another academic did the honours. An overwhelmed Modi immediately handed this person a Padma Bhushan.[13]

Through the pandemic's vicious second wave, with thousands dying every day and his lack of planning on vaccines exposed, he insisted on continuing with building the Central Vista, his project to himself.

Modi likes costume and pageantry, wearing combat fatigues when addressing the Indian Army, turbans when strutting about on Republic Day and that remarkable suit with his name embroidered on it. This was likely the only extent to which he actually prepared for such events. At the 2021 Combined Commanders' Conference, an event dealing with national security threats at the strategic levels, Modi puzzled the generals by asking non-commissioned officers—havildars, naiks and lance naiks—to sit in with the service chiefs while he 'gave strategic guidance'.[14] What was achieved was less important than how it all looked.

He owns the publicity that emanates from his power: it is a rare interaction the Indian has with her government—from vaccination certificate to gas cylinder delivery—which does not feature Modi's face. The failures are neither acknowledged nor owned.

He likes sending down actions that demonstrate his absolute power over India. Demonetisation and the nationwide lockdown showed his control over the nation and its people in the flesh.

It is easy to feel sorry for such a person, constantly under pressure to do something to satisfy his self-image as a reformer and a transformer, a messiah and a strongman though in reality fatuous and clownish. But pity is not necessary given all the chanting of 'Modi! Modi! Modi!'

Narendra Modi is seen as a nationalist who loves Bharat Mata and has devoted his life to it. From this perch, which is rarified and hallowed, he is exempt from wrongdoing and from criticism. His incompetence and his blunders, his capitulations and his wilful negligence are not only forgivable but can be overlooked entirely because he means well and has at least tried hard. The actions of his opponents are without redemption because they are the enemies of India—anti-nationals, the 'tukde tukde' gang. What passed before him was bad, dangerous and un-Indian. He is the supreme arbiter of national interest.

---

[13] 'US-based scholar who gave Modi leadership award is one of 16 Padma Bhushan awardees', 26 January 2020, *ThePrint.in*

[14] 'Why the military brass is scratching its head over Modi's Commanders' Conference speech', 11 March 2021, *ThePrint.in*

He has been defeated easily and overwhelmed in the first instance by the hard problems of India and Indians—the economy, unemployment, China. Where his agency as master of the State mattered, he was most effective in what Hindutva wanted: the constant torture of India's minorities, especially Muslims. He has been effective here, unfortunately, it is true.

On other things, he speaks. And speaks. It has been governance by utterance. He babbles on coining ever more slogans, catchphrases and acronyms.

In his second term, he has likened himself even more fully to a sage, long of beard and surrounded by exotic creatures of the forest. Like a holy man, he gives sermons, on radio, in rallies. He speaks in the abstract and in monologue. He avoids the reporters' questioning and interviews on specifics. His interest lies in offering wisdom. A compilation of all his banality would be a thing of wonder.

What will come after Modi?

The creed of Hindutva that shapes Modi's worldview says nothing original or new regarding modern government, if it says anything about this at all. It expresses a burning desire to make Bharat Mata great but articulates no pathway of leading her there.

Modi wanted to shake up the system but didn't know what to add to or remove from it. He was not conservative in the sense that he respected and continued with and built on the traditions of government. He was radical, intent on fundamental change. But his radicalism came without a central thesis and with no guiding text. It was introduction of chaos to no particular end. The result, unsurprisingly, was more chaos. His 'disruptions', a word beloved of the tech set but loaded with grave consequences for the weak and the poor, were unattached to any core ideology.

Disruption to what end? Disruption of whose lives? This was not important.

Modi's popularity does not come from his performance. The data and the record of his peformance across the spectrum of governance is clear. His popularity comes from his divisiveness and his hard majoritarianism. We should, therefore, expect from his successor a stronger dose of Hindutva. India has become less resistant to the poison, with its institutional capacity weakened, its media made rabid and society polarised and perpetually on edge. It has been yanked from its moorings by Modi. This has been his contribution to his country and its people. This is the price of the Modi years.

On the other hand, it is reassuring that his record in office is transparent and unambiguous. This is what his leadership is, this is what it has delivered and more of this is what can be expected.

It gives material to those who want to resist and push back against the direction India continues to be taken. It produces the obvious question—what exactly is Hindutva good for and why should India embrace it?

APPENDIX

These were *Times Now*'s primetime headline debates in May 2021:[1]

- 'Rishi Kapoor no more, Bollywood pays tribute to Indian cinema's heartthrob'
- 'National lockdown extended till May 17, will this be the final move?'
- 'Covid lockdown extended, lives saved but livelihood hurt?'
- 'Hudson's Michael Pilsbury speaks on China-US and Covid'
- 'Congress accuses NDA of exploiting migrants for train fares. Is Party faking fear?'
- 'Delhi government fumes over fuel. No help but only hardship?'
- 'Rahul Gandhi lauds pictures of "Azad"'. Sacrifice of braves insulted?'
- 'Why tax hike is a punishment'
- 'Handwara martyrs avenged. Dreaded terrorist killed but backers attack our braves?'
- 'Coronovirus dramatic spike in just 3 days. Should India brace for the long haul?'
- 'Aurangabad train tragedy crushes lives. Who let down India's "Builders"?'
- 'PoK on India weather map. Safest in PM Modi's hands?'
- 'India united to fight pandemic but Lutyens spreads "Communal virus?"'
- 'PM-CMs crucial meet to put lifeline back on track but why Opposition red flags?'
- 'PM Modi's motto to power self-reliance but Congress sees "No real relief"?'
- 'PM Modi to make India "Aatmanirbhar" but Congress handout culture?'
- 'Congress' Prithviraj Chavan proposal outrages Hindus?'
- 'Congress mocks "Aatmanirbhar Bharat". Is lifeline for poor a gimmick?'
- 'Congress sheds tears in Delhi but cheats in Rajasthan. Is there sympathy a sham?'
- 'NDA tries to bail out economy but fails to inspire investors?'
- 'Jammu and Kashmir big step to integration. Will "Ghar wapsi" upset Modi baiters?'
- 'After Congress truck sham, bus stunt fails, do they need to end "farzi wada"?'

---

[1] *Times Now* YouTube channel, https://www.youtube.com/c/TimesNow/playlists

- 'Why is Nepal copying Pakistan and China's playbook?'
- 'India's Covid recovery rate soars. What is story behind the scene?'
- 'Kalash, pillars and Shivling surface. Are Muslims misled by the Lobby?'
- 'Delhi riots conspirators tracked. Centre stands vindicated but Lobby silence?'
- 'Is Aghadi government lacking in action against Covid?'
- 'How Central Government "Locked" Down Coronavirus'
- 'Corona patients and train passengers abandoned. Is Sonia and Sena gang risking public lives?'
- 'Tirupati assets case over auction. Hindus' faith put under hammer?'
- 'Did Maulana Saad deliberately infect India?'
- 'Congress wants great power but no responsibility?'
- 'Jamaat Markaz to Mumbra, "Corona Gathering" gift for Eid?'
- 'China stresses on dialogue, after gunning "weak"'PM, Rahul and Lutyens left flushed?'
- 'After Congress-China chamchagiri, is Lobby inviting Beijing?'
- 'Donald Trump attacks "Leftist"'Twitter, time to tame pro-Lutyens Twitter?'
- 'What is India's verdict on the assessment of Modinomics?'
- 'America burns with hate but Lutyens sees parallels?'
- 'Kejriwal seals Delhi borders for a week. India unlocks but state blocks?'

Times Now's primetime headline debates in June 2021:

- 'Sena and Sonia linked to attack Hindus but militarises Islam (sic)?'
- 'Lobby sponsored Delhi riots. This was revenge against PM Modi?'
- 'Shaheen Bagh protestors exposed by police but set to re-emerge?'
- 'Tablighis get a free pass for "Dhaka". Centre suspects state complicity'
- 'India's road to China blocked by opposition. Why Congress going soft?'
- 'Why Delhi hospitals deny beds even after listed on Government app?'
- 'Ajay Pandit Bharti shot down by terrorists. Targeting the defenceless?'
- 'India mourns Ajay's killing but Congress clean-chits Islamists?'
- 'Indian Forces prove mettle. China begins de-escalation?'
- 'China talks of consensus. Did Rahul Gandhi score own goal?'
- 'Delhi riots crackdown truth. Will Lutyens take charge of sham?'
- 'Ramachandra Guha pits Gujarat against Bengal. Why citing only British intellectual?'
- 'Covid patients alarm. Dignity denied even in death?'
- 'JNU History Committee mocks Saraswati Civilisation webinar. Mighty opposed as myth?'
- 'Leading innovators take a stand. Will boycott call make China bow?'
- 'Will world make China pay for Covid cover-up?'
- 'Is Sushant Singh Rajput's death a murder and not suicide?'
- 'Indian staffers abducted for fake hit and run charge. Dialogue doves embolden Pak?'

- 'Pakistan's "sex terror' "on Kashmir woman exposed. Armed to unleash sexual horror?'
- 'India inflicts casualties on China's army. Is this just a warning for Dragon?'
- 'China's attack was pre-planned. Why did they lie about de-escalation?'
- 'Congress-China deal exposed. Why betray Indian forces?'
- 'All parties unite behind India but Sonia Gandhi won't slam China?'
- 'Congress disarmed our braves first and now supports "Tukde" ethos?'
- 'PM Modi's strong message over India-China LAC standoff decoded'
- 'Supreme Court allows Jagannath Yatra but critics slam Centre'
- 'Will pro-China Lobby apologise to Indian forces for their oversight?'
- 'Safoora Zargar granted bail after NDA's nod, Lutyens' duplicity exposed?'
- 'Congress admits 'China is superior' in 2013 but then doubts Indian army in 2020?'
- 'Galwan Valley to Gogra, China pullback on camera, undeniable proof from LAC'
- 'Congress-China nexus on file, Rs 1.3 crore donations to Rajiv Gandhi Foundation'
- 'Congress fund-gate explodes, put "parivaar" "over citizens?'
- 'Congress flagged for military espionage but were they friendly with the enemy?'
- 'Chinese pullback contested, are the questions justified?'
- 'Jeyaraj and son were abused and threatened by cops, CCTV footage exposes the truth'
- 'PM Modi lays out priorities, laser like focus on the poor?'
- 'India punishes China but opposition mocks, martyrs deserve better'
- 'China loses Rs 9000 crore 4G race, will opposition still doubt NDA?'

Times Now's primetime headline debates in July 2021:

- 'Pulitzer Lobby betrayed a 3-year-old child?'
- 'Priyanka Gandhi Vadra's princely perk but forgets PM ends concession?'
- 'Lobby forces 3-year-old toddler to relive trauma, 3-year-old's pain their political prop?'
- 'PM Modi's unprecedented visit to Leh Ladakh, hails Galwan gallantry'
- 'Rahul Gandhi refuses to travel to frontline but has time to meet Chinese envoy?'
- 'PM Modi punishes "expansionist "China, doubters put to shame?'
- 'China admits it was "pushed back"', will army doubters surrender?'
- 'China admits push back but Lobby continues to lie?'
- 'Congress chains workers to tracker collar, will watch where you sit and sleep?'
- 'Yes Bank and Choksi funded Rajiv Gandhi Foundation, "two"' many coincidences to ignore?'

- 'Vikas Dubey caught after 170 hour chase but was shielded for 29 years?'
- 'BJP wonder Wasim Bari killed by terrorists, but Lobby won't condemn?'
- 'Ujjain SP briefs media over Vikas Dubey's arrest'
- 'Detailed report of Vikas Dubey encounter, what went down at the site?'
- 'Farooq-AAP link exposed over Delhi riots, what will Lobby say now?'
- 'Talented Pilot mutinies on principle, Gandhis banking "Talent"' over "Taint'?'
- 'Kerala gold smuggling: Lens on conduit's neta link, call records EXPOSED'
- 'Sachin Pilot laid off for seeking due, Rahul Gandhi's glass ceiling in Congress?'
- 'BJP leader Mehrajuddin Malla kidnapped by a terrorist, released unharmed'
- 'Land meant for Congress headquarters but bagged by Gandhis, will NDA take action?'
- 'AMU student opposes Shaheen Bagh and receives a threat to wear hijab?'
- 'Is Congress still a party of aspirations?'
- 'Row over PM's Ayodhya visit, "Anti-Modi"' not Anti-Ram'?'
- 'Karnataka hit by Covid health crisis but medical infrastructure on a ventilator?'
- 'BJP hits back over "separatist"' lesson, new chapter in India's history?'
- 'NIA exposes Swapna's Islamist link, plan was to hurt nation?'
- 'AIMIM MP Imtiaz Jaleel resists "bhumi poojan"', why red-flag PM Modi's visit?'
- 'Delhi riots key witness intimidated, insidious "Islamist"' plot unravels'
- 'Sachin Pilot "victim »' not "villain", Congress attack falls flat?'
- 'Stars thrive on India's phrase, explosive dossier shows anti-India activity'
- 'How can India contain China? Should India and US become allies?'
- 'India acquires Rafale power, first batch on its way'
- 'Lord Ram to be honoured on August 5, will opposition stop blocking Bhumi Pujan?'
- 'Sushant Singh Rajput's B-town friend betrayed, did system suppress truth?'
- 'Roaring Rafales land in Ambala, Pakistan and China hear the thunder?'
- 'Sushant Singh Rajput probe: Are obvious leads strangely ignored?'
- 'Sushant Singh Rajput's death linked to big names, so CM Uddhav Thackeray blocks CBI?'

Now let us look at *Republic TV*. Its primetime debates and specials with Arnab Goswami in May 2021 were headlined:[2]

- 'Celebrating India's original rockstar Rishi Kapoor'
- 'Facts expose Palghar police coverup'
- 'Delhi riots masterminds face the law'
- 'Govt bust Congress' fake news on migrant rail fare'
- 'India salutes 8 Handwara bravehearts'
- 'PM Modi warns on "fake news, doctored videos"'

- 'Congress supporting fake theory on "Kashmir independence"'
- 'Hizbul terrorist nabbed by forces in Kashmir'
- 'Will opening liquor shops set us back in Covid war?'
- 'Forces annihilate Hizul Mujahideen chief Riyaz Naikoo'
- 'Indian army ready to crush Pak terror'
- 'India's focus back on Palghar investigation'
- 'Vizag gas leak: Man-made tragedy at the time of Covid'
- 'Chief of defence staff sends message to terrorist sympathisers'
- 'Coronavirus peak likely in June-July?'
- 'Congress and Lobby politicise Aurangabad tragedy'
- 'Time to contain Covid and rebuild India'
- '183 personalities expose fake narrative against India'
- 'PM Modi announces massive Aatmanirbhar package'
- 'PM Modi coins mantra: Be vocal about local'
- 'Govt injects hope into MSME and NBFC sectors'
- '"Go local India" blueprint starts emerging'
- 'Maj Gaurav Arya's warning spooks Pakistan'
- 'Rahul Gandhi aide to Nirav Modi's rescue?'
- 'Palghar lynching probe: Lawyer in case killed in road accident'
- 'Congress in trillion-dollar controversy'
- 'Are states blocking migrant movement?'
- 'Mystery over Congress' China strategy'
- 'Congress plays petty namecalling over 20 lakh crore package'
- 'India leads global fight to expose China'
- 'Migrants need trains, not lies and propagandaCongress dumps migrants'
- 'Proof demolishes Congress' '"1000 buses"' claim'
- 'Forces act on terror hitlist to make Kashmir terror free'
- 'India salutes Srinagar bravehearts, forces will avenge attack'
- 'Priyanka Gandhi's bus sham falls apart, Congress loses plot'
- 'Nepal provokes India with revised map stunt'
- 'Airlines and railways to resume operations, is India ready?'
- 'Cyclone Amphan ravages West Bengal and Odisha'
- 'US deports Al Qaeda terrorist to India'
- 'Pakistan plane crashes near Karachi airport'
- 'India and US unite to expose China'
- 'Congress' bus sham and bill truth exposed'
- 'Centre Vs Maharashtra Govt over Shramik trains'
- 'Lockdown rules don't apply for netas?'
- 'Rahul Gandhi exposes cracks in Maha Vikas Aghadi'
- 'Who is playing politics over plight of migrants?'
- 'Congress, Lobby launch joint attack on forces'
- 'Congress politicises national security, puts onus on Indian Govt'

- 'Maha Govt resorts to threats after expose on Covid mess'
- 'Embarrassment for Imran Khan, China softens stand on border'
- 'SC strikes down migrant politics, 'prophets of doom' exposed'
- 'Pakistan attempts to repeat Pulwama, forces thwart terror plot'
- 'More proof emerges on Pak role in terror, Cong questions forces'
- 'Is India ready for Lockdown 5.0?'

Republic TV's primetime headline debates in June 2021:

- 'Pak Spygate exposed: India catches ISI spies red-handed'
- 'Lobby wants US like "protests" "in India'
- 'Tahir Hussain met Umar Khalid to plot Delhi riots?'
- 'First cyclone to hit Mumbai in a century'
- 'Boycott China' campaign gains steam'
- 'Delhi riots conspiracy proof stares at Lobby'
- 'Forces annihilate Jaish terror at Pulwama; pelters unleash'
- 'India-US partnership corners China; Trump bars Chinese airlines'
- 'National outrage over elephant's death in Kerala'
- 'India's diplomatic strike to ring-fence China'
- 'India sees through Lobby's attempt to spread chaos'
- 'Biggest build-up to IndiaChina military commander level talks'
- 'Another attempt by Congress to demoralise forces'
- 'Mumbai to Delhi: Hospitals overburdened, citizens suffer'
- 'Terror mechanism obliterated by forces, sympathisers go in hiding'
- 'Rahul Gandhi's "psy-ops"' fail'
- 'Terrorists kill sarpanch in J&K, India unites for Ajay Bharti'
- 'Rahul Gandhi's pro-China remark angers veterans'
- 'Sleepless in Karachi: IAF spooks Pakistan'
- 'Lobby lionizes terrorists, stays silent on Kashmir sarpanch killing'
- 'Lobby goes on rant, attempts to divide India?'
- 'Demand for CBI probe in Palghar lynching case grows'
- 'Covid mess in Delhi and Maharashtra; unending apathy'
- 'Intolerance' bogey back, Congress abuses India before US diplomat'
- 'India unites for Ajay Pandita, Congress resorts to politics'
- 'Delhi Covid truth: State govt hammered over mismanagement'
- 'Save the sarpanches: Envoys of democracy targeted in Kashmir'
- 'IS abducts India HC officials in Pakistan, India issues warning'
- 'Kangana, Kapur open Pandora's Box, expose truth on 'super lobby'
- 'Violent Ladakh faceoff: India stands ground on Galwan'
- 'Congress questions forces over Ladakh standoff'
- 'Ladakh standoff: Nation salutes Galwan bravehearts'
- 'Unprecedented "boycott Chinese goods"' protests across India'
- 'National demand to make China pay'
- '"Unarmed" with facts, Congress insults army'

- 'Is there a "special relationship"' between Congress and China?'
- 'People's movement against China gets bigger'
- 'PM sends a powerful message to the nation on LAC'
- 'Cong traitor caught: 'Break India' forces reveal their agenda'
- 'India pulls out all stops against China, Cong demoralises forces'
- 'Lobby pushes China "psy-ops"' against India'
- 'Sonia-China' pact: demand to "disclose details" "grows"'
- 'Nation with forces: LAC disengagement plan takes shape'
- 'India puts Pakistan in its place with unprecedented diplomatic move'
- 'Congress gives clean chit to China on LAC standoff'
- 'Ultimate LAC proof reveal Ladakh facts'
- 'Probe Congress-China deal: a national demand'
- 'Congress' Rajiv Gandhi Foundation received "donations" "from China"'
- 'Congress insults army and martyrs: outrage across India'
- '45 years of Emergency, Congress yet to apologise'
- 'Sonia Trust Scam: Series of evidence stares at Congress'
- 'Right to report wins, massive victory for media rights'
- 'Mayawati slams Congress for LAC politics'
- 'Tuticorin clincher: India demands justice for Jayaraj and Bennix'
- '59 Chinese appls blocked in India, big setback for China'
- 'PM extends world's biggest scheme for poor, Congress mocks'

Republic TV's primetime headline debates in July 2021:

- 'Massive victory for journalists, judiciary upholds right to report'
- 'Pak terror sympathisers must be isolated'
- 'India begins isolating China economically'
- 'Karnataka medical apathy: Killed by Covid, denied dignity in death'
- 'Lobby echoes Pakistan's fake narrative on Sopore attack'
- 'Odisha shocker: Minor repeatedly raped by predator cop'
- 'India ensures China's global isolation'
- 'PM asserts power from terrains of Nimu'
- 'PM Modi's "expansionist"' jibe unsettles China'
- 'Prime Minister leads from the front'
- 'PM Modi's strong leadership pushes back China'
- 'Ladakh reality check: Galwan victory a slap in Lobby's face'
- 'Is Defence meeting not important for Rahul Gandhi?'
- 'China warned "expansionists"' feel the global heat'
- 'Arrest Vikas Dubey: Gangster's political links under scanner'
- 'Gold scandal rocks Kerala government'
- 'MHA orders probe into Sonia Trust scam'
- '357 days after defeat at ICJ, Pak blocks Jadhav review plea'
- 'Terrorists kill BJP neta, another attack jolts Kashmir'
- 'Multi-state hunt for Vikas Dubey ends after 172 hours'

- 'Pak backed terrorists kill Kashmir nationalists'
- 'Nepal decides to ban Indian news channels'
- 'Vikas Dubey encountered, 24 hours after dramatic arrest in Ujjain'
- 'Gold from UAE used for terror financing in India?'
- 'Powerful global military Quad taking shape against China'
- 'Rajasthan crisis: Sachin Pilot all set to quit Congress?'
- 'Mystery over West Bengal BJP MLA's death'
- 'Rape accused bishop runs out of excuses, can't escape law anymore'
- 'Sachin Pilot sacked: Congress forced out another talented neta?'
- 'Gold scandal hotline: Biggest clincher against Kerala govt'
- 'Where does India stand in global race for Coronavirus vaccine?'
- 'Kashmiris vs terror: Brave forces rescue BJP neta in 12 hours'
- 'Sachin Pilot delays announcement, what will be his next move?'
- 'Baloch army takes on Pakistan army'
- 'Kerala gold scandal: NIA begins probe, UAE attache flees India?'
- 'India exposes Pak lies on Kulbhushan Jadhav's consular access'
- 'West Bengal: Another political murder in last three days'
- 'Kerala gold scandal: international racket to push terror?'
- '"Gold for terror" becomes national headline'
- 'Rahul's diplomacy "'analysis'" backfires, EAM Jaishankar gives it back'
- '"Horsetrading"' charge becomes the focus in Rajasthan govt drama'
- 'Pawar draws Covid link to politicise PM Modi's Ayodhya visit'
- 'Sushant's death probe: Kangana's interview becomes turning point'
- 'Assam faces unprecedented calamity from Covid 19, floods, erosion'
- 'Covid: Oxford breakthrough gives massive hopes'
- 'As India wants Sushant truth, massive war breaks out in Bollywood'
- 'Supreme Court draws the line for anti-judiciary lobby'
- 'BJP VP puts focus on Bollywood-Pak link'
- 'Justice for Sushant: National anger against lobbies in Bollywood'
- 'Chorus grows to declare Assam floods as national disaster'
- 'Justice for Sushant: Demand grows for CBI investigation'
- 'Ayodhya polarisation: Communal twist to Ram mandir event?'
- 'Lobby Ayodhya setback: Anti-mandir brigade shown the door'
- 'Justice for Sushant: Demand for CBI probe grows'
- 'Speak up for Sushant: Inconsistencies in probe can't be overlooked'
- 'Shiv Sena's e-bhoomi pujan suggestion backfires'
- 'Congress on the verge of collapsing in Rajasthan?'
- 'Sushant death mystery: family rejects depression theory'
- 'Anti-mandir brigade attempts polarisation on bhoomi pujan'
- 'India for Sushant: Nation demands CBI investigation'
- 'Why is MVA govt adamant on Mumbai police to probe Sushant's case?'
- 'Sushant's death probe: financial angle becomes Number 1 focus'
- 'Sushant conspiracy: Evidence out, Bollywood lobby in hiding'

INDEX